Washington Quarters

—— THIRD EDITION ——

Q. David Bowers

Washington Quarters

THIRD EDITION

©2025 Whitman®
4001 Helton Dr., Florence, AL 35630
whitman.com

RED BOOK SERIES is a trademark of Whitman.

All rights reserved, including duplication of any kind and storage in electronic or visual retrieval systems. Permission is granted for writers to use a reasonable number of brief excerpts and quotations in printed reviews and articles, provided credit is given to the title of the work and the author. Written permission from the publisher is required for other uses of text, illustrations, and other content, including in books and electronic or other media.

Correspondence concerning this book may be directed to the publisher, Attn: *Washington Quarters*, at the address above.

ISBN: 978-07948-51323 / WW1764-0325 / Ebook ISBN: 978-07948-39116
Printed in the United States of America.

No part of this book may be reproduced or copied in any form without written permission from the publisher. Prices listed in this book may not be used in any form of computer database or program without written permission from the publisher.

The values shown here are not offers to sell or buy but are included only as general information. Descriptions of coins are based on the most accurate data available, but could contain beliefs that may change with further research or discoveries.

Advertisements within this book: Whitman does not endorse, warrant, or guarantee any of the products or services of its advertisers. All warranties, statements, and guarantees are the responsibility of the advertiser.

The Red Book Series™ builds on the historic *Guide Book of United States Coins* (popularly known as the *Red Book*). Each numbered volume takes a deeper look into a *Red Book* topic, with more history, more images, more data, and updated valuations from the *Greysheet* pricing team. Volume 7, *Washington Quarters*, is just one of nearly 30 volumes in the encyclopedic *Red Book* Series.

For a complete catalog of numismatic reference books, supplies, and storage products, visit Whitman online at www.Whitman.com.

If you enjoy United States coins, visit www.Greysheet.com for up-to-date news, pricing, and research.

Contents

Foreword *by John Feigenbaum* iv

Preface vi

How to Use This Book x

1. Setting the Scene in 1932 1

2. Early Quarter Dollars 9

3. The Life of George Washington 14

4. History of the Washington Quarter 24

5. Die Changes and Technicalities 40

6. The Minting of Washington Quarters 46

7. Secrets of Being a Smart Buyer 54

8. Washington Quarters, 1932–1998:
   History and Analysis by Date and Mintmark 67

9. State, D.C., and Territories Quarters, 1999–2009:
   History and Analysis by Date and Mintmark 132

10. America the Beautiful and Crossing the Delaware Quarters,
    2010–2021: History and Analysis by Date and Mintmark 262

11. American Women Quarters, 2022–2025:
    History and Analysis by Date and Mintmark 347

Notes 375

Credits and Acknowledgments 380

About the Author 381

Index 382

FOREWORD

In the summer of 1993, I was just 25 years old and four years removed from college. Despite my age, I was already in my third decade as a numismatist, having grown up following my dad to countless coin shows. All my life he was a collector, part-time dealer, and full-time dealer—as well as, for a time, an associate professor of marine biology. So Dad was passionate about coins, research, and education. I'm not sure if I could check any of those boxes at that time. My college degree in marketing management, with a computer science minor, did not exactly portend the life-long commitment to numismatics that lay ahead.

Regardless, I was looking for a way to make my own mark in the collecting community and Dad suggested I author a book. I recall that I was incredulous at the suggestion. How was I qualified to write a reference work on coins? What could I possibly offer that hundreds of other people didn't already know? True, I was fairly adept at layout and presentation of books for collectors, as he and I had already published several books under the DLRC Press imprint. Dad was the author, I was layout specialist.

We had published *The Complete Guide to Barber Quarters*, followed by similar works on dimes and half dollars. Envisioning a comprehensive series of reference books, we had also sought authors for Liberty Seated material (Brian Greer, Al Blythe), Buffalo nickels and Lincoln cents (David W. Lange), and others. Finding authors was extremely difficult as series experts are often not scholars or authors—they are, for lack of a better word, professional cherrypickers who use their expertise to seek out value in other dealers' inventories. Sharing this expertise is tantamount to giving away state secrets.

The 1935-D quarter, once a highly underrated issue, is now recognized as one of the key dates in the series.

However, Dad had a different belief. He managed to convince his potential authors that the credibility of authorship was more valuable than the giving away of such secrets. He also used his professorial experience to coach these series experts into newly minted authors. David Lange, for example, was just a collector working at Pacific Gas and Electric when Dad convinced him to write *The Complete Guide to Buffalo Nickels*. Lange would soon switch careers, and he eventually became the hobby's leading expert on die varieties at NGC.

In my case, Dad also convinced me that I knew far more than I realized. "What series do you feel is most under-appreciated and under-reported?" he asked me. That was quite easy. I had recently become enamored with Washington quarters—not because they were beautiful or highly sought in the market. Quite the contrary. In 1993, the market ignored this series with just a few exceptions. We all knew 1932-D and S-mint quarters were the key dates, and almost nothing else seemed to matter. Maybe the 1936-D.

I knew better. Dad and I attended shows all over the country, and I would cherrypick 1934-D's and 1950-D's and S's with previously undiscovered overdates, and otherwise high-grade examples of any dates. Few people realized how difficult it was to find a gem (MS-65 and up) Washington quarter, of any date. These coins were almost always stapled into cardboard 2x2 holders (mylars) and tucked away in dealers' three-ring binders, or else in unsearched Mint rolls.

My favorite date at the time was the 1935-D. Nobody knew how underrated it was! I liked the other early-mintmark coins as well. Discussing this with Dad, we both realized we were onto something. He pushed me to write and to become an expert in the process. What a novel concept—to learn as one writes!—but this is the university mindset, not the historic numismatic path to authorship.

The Complete Guide to Washington Quarters (1994) remains the only book I ever fully authored. (I did co-author a generalist book with Dad on Barber coinage.) Reading through it, I can feel my 25-year-old self's enthusiasm for collecting and seeking undiscovered value as both a hobbyist and a fledgling dealer. As CEO and publisher at Whitman, my career has come full circle, and I am honored to add my voice (and pricing!) to the 2024 edition of the reference work on a coin series that is very near and dear to me.

John Feigenbaum
Virginia Beach, VA
August 2024

John Feigenbaum has been a professional numismatist since 1979. His career path started as a partner in David Lawrence Rare Coins, and until 2015 he served as the company's president. In 2015, John formed (and he continues to manage) an investment group that acquired CDN Publishing. In 2024 the group acquired Whitman Publishing to form the holding company trading as Whitman Brands, combining the numismatic powerhouse publications of the *Red Book*, the *Blue Book*, the *Cherrypickers' Guides*, the 100 Greatest Series, and more, with the pricing and data strengths of the *Greysheet*, the *Greensheet*, and the *Banknote Book*. John has written for numerous trade publications and published *The Complete Guide to Washington Quarters* in 1991. In 2014, John received the PNG Abe Kosoff Founders Award for "his steadfast dedication to the entire numismatic community." In 2023 John also took over the role of executive director of the Professional Numismatists Guild (PNG).

PREFACE

About Washington quarters, minted from 1932 to date, everything is known. This is what I thought many years ago when I began keeping notes on the state-reverse quarters, adding these to my long-time files on earlier regular issues. I soon realized how much I did not know. There was a lot more to be learned about the past. As to the present, there has been a continuing flow of new information as the America the Beautiful issues continue to be released.

The 50 State Quarters Program®, as the U.S. Mint designated and registered it, unfolded year by year—a dynamic, wonderful, and unprecedented panorama of new designs available for face value by the general public. The quarters were released one at a time, five each year in the order of statehood. First out of the box was the 1999 Delaware quarter—a design that today many consider to be one of the best. Then in 2009 came a new series with the District of Columbia and the American territories, six different. One territory was forgotten. We will never know what a Palmyra Atoll quarter might have looked like!

From the outset I kept careful notes of everything I read, saw, and heard. The U.S. Mint website was and is a great source of *official* information. Excellently constructed, it has grown to include a tremendous amount of data. In addition, several past directors as well as the staff of the Mint have answered many questions and furnished insights. Tom Jurkowsky in particular enabled me to do much ground-breaking research.

Mint information is, however, *official*. For quite a few quarter designs, great controversy raged. Was the right design chosen? Was the sketch by the original artist altered too much by Mint staff when the models and dies were made? Is what was chosen what the people of the state wanted? Was the final design "pretty" or was it "ugly"?

Many of these questions have no single answer. I think the Maine, Rhode Island, and California quarters are appealing for their *scenic* aspects, I agree with just about everyone that the Delaware quarter with Caesar Rodney on horseback is compelling and dynamic. I could add more favorites to the list. In contrast, the Arkansas, Missouri, and Florida quarters seem to me to be a hodge-podge of items, with no unifying or "scenic" cohesion. As you review each of the state quarters, your opinions of aesthetic quality may be entirely different. After all, beauty is in the eye of the beholder.

The same can be said for the later quarters. The 2009 issue honoring the District of Columbia does not show the Capitol, White House, Washington Monument, or any other familiar icon. Instead it depicts a person—Duke Ellington—a famous musician who was born there but spent most of his illustrious career elsewhere.

To find more than the *official* information required a lot of delving into source material—correspondence with committee members of the various states, off-the-record conversations (for use in this book, but not for attribution) with government officials, local and regional newspapers, radio program transcripts, websites posted by the various states, and more.

Two of the most widely circulating weekly publications, *Coin World* and *Numismatic News*, have followed each quarter dollar program from the beginning. Each has printed comments from collectors, as well as from artists whose work had either been chosen or rejected. Each features sketches of proposed designs, and more. These were prime sources for *unofficial* but real information. *COINage, Coins* magazine, and the *Numismatist,* each covered the new quarters as well.

Coverage was more intensive for the 1999 to 2008 State quarters than for the later issues. No publication saw fit to send a reporter to the Northern Mariana Islands to cover the 2009 launch ceremony there. Most of us, including me, don't know much about them or even where they are located—somewhere in the vast reaches of the South Pacific.

In writing about the State quarters I devoted a section to each of the 50 issues. I have tried to give an objective view even with certain issues that swirled with hot controversy (Missouri and California are prime examples). I have no vested interest in the outcome, save that I enjoy my own collection of these quarters. I have simply tried to relate the facts as I see them.

Some are quite fascinating. Did you know that a *frog* pushed the button on a coining press to launch the 2000 Connecticut quarter? This is the same quarter that has the wrong tree depicted on the reverse. Is that a toilet shown on the Hot Springs National Park quarter of 2010, as some have suggested? No, it is a basin on the front of a building built in the 1930s. And why the heck is a flycatcher used on the Oklahoma quarter? Some quarters have mottoes in Latin, others in English, and some in native languages. In my opinion there are endless interesting aspects to these issues.

Two people can view the same set of circumstances differently. What do *you* think? In any event, you are welcome to take any of my remarks with a grain of salt. The key is to *enjoy* these quarters, as I do. Collectively, the coins are wonderful, and I congratulate the U.S. Mint on two of the finest programs in numismatic history. By now the sculptor-engravers at the Mint must feel like leading actors in a Broadway play—many plaudits mixed with comments from people who do not like the designs, applause and bouquets mixed with boos and tossed eggs. That goes with the territory—part of creativity. Occasionally, when I write a provocative column in *Coin World,* I get my share of slings and arrows. Collectively, independent coin designers who are part of the Artistic Infusion Program (AIP), Mint sculptor-engravers, and Mint staff include some of the nicest people I have met. We are all fortunate that many of them are frequent attendees at coin conventions.

I have had close ties with the Mint as a researcher and writer for most of the time since the 1960s and intermittently before that. The degree of closeness has varied with the warmth of the current director and his or her appreciation, or lack thereof, for numismatic scholarship. It has been a *quid pro quo* relationship—I've answered a lot of questions about Mint and coinage history, and the Mint has given me access to files, old coin models, visits to engraving and coining operations, and the like. In my files I have a nice handwritten letter from Angela M. "Bay" Buchanan, treasurer of the United States from 1981 to 1983, thanking me for the assistance I had furnished the Treasury Department over a period of years, including testifying before Congress in order to help prevent a private company from taking over the marketing of numismatic products made by the Mint. When on April 3, 1992, the Mint celebrated the 200th anniversary of the Mint Act of April 2, 1792, I was invited to be the keynote speaker.

As to Washington quarters *before* 1999, the regular issues, these have their own fascination as well, sprinkled with a few mysteries. In quite a few books and other sources it is stated that Secretary of the Treasury Andrew W. Mellon, who made the decision as to the final design for the 1932 Washington quarter, rejected the best one in favor of a poor substitute. The best, according to the Commission of Fine Arts at the time, was one done by Laura Gardin Fraser, a sculptor of great talent, who with her husband, James Earle Fraser, created many motifs. They did the 1926 Oregon Trail Memorial half dollar, the design voted the most beautiful of all by members of the Society for United States Commemoratives.

The reason for Mellon's rejection of Fraser's art? Not because of artistic quality or beauty, but supposedly because *she was a woman*. Mellon was a sexist, this per modern conventional wisdom, vastly expanded by this comment by Walter Breen (*Complete Encyclopedia of U.S. and Colonial Coins*, p. 7), which has achieved wide circulation: "His male chauvinism partly or wholly motivated his unwillingness to let a woman win." This 1988 statement has been picked up and repeated many times. The only problem with this is that in checking contemporary records, correspondence, Mint documents in the National Archives, and more, I find no such scenario. Further, Mellon, secretary of the Treasury since 1921, appointed Mary M. O'Reilly assistant director of the Mint in 1923, the first woman ever to serve in that post. Mellon worked closely with her on many matters. No record has been found of Mellon being sexist in the presidency of the Mellon National Bank, or anything else. Credit the whole story as a modern fairy tale.

Another discrepancy is this: Why are 1932-D quarters, with a mintage slightly higher than the 1932-S, several times rarer in choice Mint State grade? I have always wondered, and I do not know the answer.

Time was when numismatists collected Washington quarters in routine date and mint sequence. Then came recognition of the Light Motto variety of 1934. Then, through the efforts and publicity of the "Collectors' Clearinghouse" column in *Coin World*, the writing of Herbert Hicks, John Feigenbaum, James Wiles, and others, and the popularity of the *Cherrypickers' Guide to Die Varieties* by Bill Fivaz and J.T. Stanton, interest spread beyond dates and mintmarks. When the "Extra Leaf Low" and "Extra Leaf High" varieties of the 2004-D Wisconsin quarter made headlines and created a lot of excitement in January 2005, I was as thrilled as anyone—and, in fact, bought several, including one for my set of quarters. Bill Fivaz was excited as well. On the other hand some dismissed them as unimportant. The doubling of some letters in ELLINGTON in the 2009 District of Columbia quarter was important to some numismatists, irrelevant to others. This goes to show that in numismatics, for one action there is sometimes an opposite reaction. Such spice adds to the hobby. Again, what do *you* think about these curious quarters?

To the preceding aspects of enjoying the history of quarters can be added the quest for ultra-high grades. This, too, is a new aspect of Washington quarters. Time was when the 1932-D and S sold for premium prices because they were key dates, but not much attention was paid to the other varieties. Beginning in a large way with the popularity of the Professional Coin Grading Service (PCGS, launched in 1986), there has been a scramble to obtain the highest possible certified grades of various coins. If a high-mintage issue of the 1950s is as common as can be in, say, Mint State-65 grade, but only a few are known in the MS-69 category, the MS-69 can be worth thousands of dollars. These are called *condition rarities*, or coins that are worth a high price only if they are in an unusually high grade.

The aspect of attractive toning is another relatively new consideration. If a Washington quarter dollar in a nice high grade, say MS-65 or higher, but not necessarily the highest grade known, is attractively toned it can be worth a strong premium. Both condition rarity and attractive toning give a lot of collectors bragging rights, especially in registry sets and various commentaries on the Internet. There is something special about listening to two collectors discuss the merits of a gem 1940-D quarter, a coin that I sold years ago by the roll, never doing more than quickly glancing at the coins to be sure that in fact they were basically Uncirculated.

When I began collecting coins as a young teenager in 1952 and started dealing in them in 1953, Washington quarters were a routine series—not much to notice except that the 1932-D and S were rare. It puzzled me that choice Mint State 1932-S quarters were readily available, even in an occasional roll, but the slightly higher mintage 1932-D was hard to find. All the others were available in roll quantities, particularly those after 1934, although the 1936-D was not seen often. A few years later, Jim Ruddy and I noticed that the mintage of the 1937-S was low as was the price, and we spent a couple years or so hoarding them—finding a few dozen rolls. Today, Washington quarters comprise hundreds of date and mintmark varieties, with four mint and metal varieties of each state quarter adding to the panorama.

Certainly, today Washington quarters are the most diverse series in American numismatics and one of the most interesting, something that could not have been said before the parade of 50 state coins commenced. There are no impossible rarities from 1932 to date, although the 1932-D and S remain key issues. All are affordable, and most issues of recent generations are very inexpensive. Often, the State, territorial, and America the Beautiful (to date) are offered in attractive albums.

There are still some mysteries to unravel, including the origin of the extra leaves on the 2004-D Wisconsin quarter, the subject of an internal investigation by the Mint. You can be your own art critic. Which of the state quarters are gorgeous? Which are not? In any event, you will want one of each. The current America the Beautiful program is still history in the making, as new designs are created and new coins released.

Even before state quarters were dreamed of, a Washington quarter could nip someone with numismatic virus, for which there is no known cure. In 1955 in Dallas, Harry W. Bass Jr., a bank director, heard that the low-mintage 1955-D quarters might become scarce, and bought a $10 roll for face value. This opened the door to his forming one of the greatest collections of U.S. *gold* coins ever gathered, plus many other series as well. The Harry W. Bass, Jr., Library at the American Numismatic Society in New York City bears his name, as does the incredible gallery of gold coins at the American Numismatic Association Headquarters in Colorado Springs. All because of a Washington quarter!

I enjoyed writing this book. I hope you will enjoy reading it.

Q. David Bowers
Wolfeboro, New Hampshire

How to Use This Book

Each Washington quarter date and mintmark has its own listing. I give general and specific comments concerning rarity, availability, and other aspects as a key to collecting each. For some issues, interesting repunchings or other die varieties are described, these being a few of my favorites—the ones I consider to be the most significant—from the latest edition of the Fivaz-Stanton *Cherrypickers' Guide to Rare Die Varieties*. FS numbers refer to this text. For even more varieties, refer to the *Cherrypickers' Guide* itself or the three books by James Wiles (see Selected Bibliography).

The prices for this edition have been compiled by the pricing team at our sister company, Greysheet, based on their CPG™ (Collector's Price Guide) dataset. You can find a comprehensive database of values for all U.S. coins and paper money at www.greysheet.com. More than one million prices are updated multiple times daily, with access to 3.1 million auction prices, and 7.6 million images. Subscriptions are required. Learn more at www.greysheet.com/allproducts.

The advanced collector who wishes to create a choice and gem Mint State or Proof set should learn to seek out what I call the "optimal collecting grade." Consider the highest grades available for a given issue (generally in the 64 to 65 range for Washington quarters through 1998), and note which one offers exceptional market value at current prices, compared to the next highest grade. If budget is a constraint, a general rule is that a grade such as MS-63 or PF-63, carefully selected, is ideal for the silver issues from 1932 through 1964, except for certain of the rare issues, which can be obtained in lower grades according to your budget requirements. Most clad issues from 1964 to date are sufficiently plentiful that MS-65 and PF-65 are within reach of just about everyone.

For modern series beginning with the State quarters, MS-65 is a good goal for circulation strikes and PF-66 is good for Proofs—and Proofs, carefully made, usually occur in PF-66 or better.

Abbreviations in the Listings

Breen number: The numbering system of varieties in *Walter Breen's Complete Encyclopedia of U.S. and Colonial Coins*, 1988. Example: Breen-4285.

FS (Fivaz-Stanton) number: The numbering system in the *Cherrypickers' Guide to Rare Die Varieties* (sixth ed., vol. 2, Whitman, 2024), by Bill Fivaz and J.T. Stanton. This replaces the old FS system (conversion information is given in the 2006 edition). This is the popular standard guide in the hobby. Example: FS-25-1950-601A.

Grading abbreviations: See the Official American Numismatic Association Grading Standards described in chapter 7 for a complete explanation. Examples: AU-50, MS-65.

Rarity Scales and Abbreviations

Since the 1850s, various systems for describing rarity have been devised. Adjectival descriptions such as "very rare" "I have only seen two in 35 years of experience," "extremely rare," "one of the most elusive varieties," and so on, have little meaning in an absolute sense. We cannot tell if "extremely rare" means just two are known, or 23, or 46.

To simplify matters, rarity scales are based on the number of coins known or estimated to exist by experts in a given series. However, it is likely that for most varieties there are more examples in existence, but which have not been seen by numismatists. By way of analogy, if on a drive through a national park you see 17 elk, there may be 804 more that you haven't seen. If you go to a baseball game and do not see Irene, she may have been there anyway. This concept is very important.

Numeric rarity scales have been devised to assign meaning to estimates. One popular measurement is the Universal Rarity Scale (URS) used in many numismatic texts and occasionally referenced herein:

The Universal Rarity Scale (URS) is used in the Fivaz-Stanton *Cherrypickers' Guide to Rare Die Varieties*, the several books by James Wiles, and other specialized texts for rarity and is employed in the present book in connection with such varieties:

Universal Rarity Scale

URS-0 = None known	URS-8 = 65 to 124
URS-1 = 1 known, unique	URS-9 = 125 to 249
URS-2 = 2 known	URS-10 = 250 to 499
URS-3 = 3 or 4	URS-11 = 500 to 999
URS-4 = 5 to 8	URS-12 = 1,000 to 1,999
URS-5 = 9 to 16	URS-13 = 2,000 to 3,999
URS-6 = 17 to 32	URS-14 = 4,000 to 7,999
URS-7 = 33 to 64	

And so on. As the popularity of collecting die varieties spreads, more bank-wrapped rolls of coins will be examined, and more overmintmarks, doubled dies, and the like will come to light. Paying an extremely high price for a newly discovered variety may be risky, for when it is publicized, chances are excellent that more will be found. It takes time for the rarity of a variety to be evaluated and for prices to stabilize.

Look up your coins and currency using GSID℠ today!

Visit greysheet.com/coin-prices

Enter GSID in search box

View live results - FREE

Subscribe for pricing

GSID℠ is a service offered through Greysheet® that identifies and links all coins and currency in our catalog across the entire family of Whitman Brands™ products, such as the Greysheet® online pricing tool, mobile app, CDN Exchange, and much more!"

John F. Flanagan
(1865–1952)
Designer of the Washington Quarter

1

Setting the Scene in 1932

INTRODUCTION

The Washington quarter dollar was born in the very depths of the Depression, when the nation was struggling for economic survival. The issuance of coins had slowed nearly to a halt the previous year, and the outlook for 1932 was no better. However, the bicentennial of George Washington's 1732 birth was at hand, and Americans wanted to celebrate it. The exposition and world's fair that had been envisioned during the heady times of the Roaring Twenties were set aside in face of reality.

Washington quarter struck at the Denver Mint in 1932, the first year of the new design. (shown at 125%)

The quarter was created, but not easily.

NEWS AND EVENTS OF 1932

American Life

The Great Depression had its beginnings in 1928 and 1929, when banks experienced slow repayments on loans, and the momentum of the great boom in real estate, art, and other prices began to slow. The stock market kept rising, and national focus was on this phenomenon. Behind the scenes, many financiers were worried, but just about everyone proclaimed that the American economy was robust. In commerce, being anything less than optimistic was apt to bring great criticism from one's peers.

In October 1929 the stock market crashed, and banks began to fail at a staggering rate. Production lines in factories slowed nearly to a halt, with total output for the year only a third of what it had been in 1929. More than 20,000 businesses closed their doors. The Dow-Jones Industrial Average touched bottom at 41.22 on July 28, 1932, the low point for the Depression years. This was in contrast to its record high of 381.17 on September 3, 1929. By 1932, one out of every four persons in the labor force was unemployed. Throngs lined up in breadlines and outside soup kitchens in the cities. Those who were lucky enough to be employed took home an average weekly paycheck of $17, as compared to $28 in 1929. These figures, while interesting enough in themselves, also have a connection to numismatics; they explain why, when Washington quarters were released in 1932, they were not widely saved as novelties.

The Political Scene

Herbert Hoover was president; his vice president was Charles Curtis. The national population was about 125,000,000. Every night when Hoover was at home in the White House, he partook of an elegant seven-course dinner, never mind the hard times. He had considered practicing frugality, including in the kitchen, but stated that it would be "bad for the country's morale." Hoover commented, "Nobody is actually starving. The hoboes, for example, are better fed than they have ever been. One hobo in New York got ten meals in one day." To this, *Fortune* magazine in its September issue called Hoover a liar and stated that the real situation was "twenty-five million people in want."[1] Schoolchildren were chanting:

Herbert C. Hoover, elected to the presidency in 1928 and inaugurated in 1929, grappled with the Great Depression. (American Bank Note Co. vignette)

Mellon pulled the whistle,
Hoover rang the bell,
Wall Street gave the signal,
And the country went to hell.

Overall federal spending for 1932 was $4.66 billion. Among proposals for reviving the solvency of American commerce was the federally funded Reconstruction Finance Corporation, approved on January 22, to stimulate banking and business. By year's end, $1.5 billion in loans had been placed, mostly to businesses seeking to restore their former solidity. The average citizen, however, received nothing. Proposals to give direct aid to the millions of unemployed fell on deaf ears. A proposal by Hoover to create a corps of paid civilian workers for government construction and other jobs was not passed by Congress.

Hoover felt that to dole out funds to the indigent would create an underclass of citizens who would become permanently reliant on the government, as they would have no incentive to work. His comments such as "Prosperity cannot be restored by raids upon the public treasury" and "The sole function of government is to bring about a condition of affairs favorable to the beneficial development of private enterprise" did little to cheer the common man or woman.

Hoover vs. Roosevelt

In the meantime, attention was focused on the forthcoming presidential election. Hoover, though he was an educated, talented man of many accomplishments, was simply out of his element in dealing with the worst economic depression the nation had ever seen. His prediction for prosperity had not come true, and his wait-and-see policy was wearing thin. Shantytowns where the unemployed and poor tried to eke out an existence were popularly called *Hoovervilles*, and *Hoover blankets* were newspapers under which the destitute huddled for warmth.

Franklin D. Roosevelt was chosen as the Democratic nominee over Al Smith, the 1928 candidate. "I pledge you, I pledge myself, to a new deal for the American people,"

Roosevelt stated in his acceptance speech. *New deal* later became synonymous with the early Roosevelt administration.

Roosevelt's campaign publicity portrayed him as having ideas to restore prosperity, offering hope to a country with an unemployment rate of about 25%. Hoover tried to paint his opponent as a wild-eyed extremist who would plunge the country into ruin. Hoover did not converse with homeless men in the streets of Washington or console a former executive who was now selling apples for a nickel apiece. The radio could provide a fine forum to reach the people, but Hoover dismissed the idea, apparently as being below his dignity. Instead, he kept up a steady pace of elegant dinners at the White House, often with several dozen guests present. William Allen White, renowned editor of the Kansan *Emporia Gazette*, wrote: "Without leaders, the people grow blind, and without vision, the people perish."[2]

Franklin D. Roosevelt won the November 1932 election in a landslide. (American Bank Note Co. vignette}

Matters were not helped for Hoover by his poor relationship with the press. He campaigned by defending his record, suggesting that without him things could have been worse—something difficult for citizens to envision. To this he added constant criticism of Roosevelt, pointing out inconsistencies. Meanwhile, Roosevelt charmed the electorate, offering them hope, not excuses.

To the populace, Roosevelt seemed more promising. On November 8, 56.9% of registered voters went to the polls and elected him president in a landslide victory, tallying 22,821,857 votes, compared to Hoover's 15,761,841.

Thus the Hoover administration soon came to an end. It was a different ballgame after Roosevelt's inauguration on March 4, 1933.

NUMISMATICS IN 1932

New and Old Coinage of the Era

From the standpoint of new issues, 1932 was a rather barren numismatic year. Production of Lincoln cents was small, and only at the Philadelphia and Denver mints. No nickels, dimes, half dollars, dollars, or commemorative coins were minted. Gold $10 and $20 coins were made, but few people could afford to collect them; even in more prosperous times in the 1920s, fewer than a dozen specialists aspired to keep up with current date and mintmark releases of these denominations.

Coins in general circulation bore dates back into the 19th century. Indian Head cents were common, with most dated from 1878 onward. Liberty Head nickels were plentiful, and well-worn Shield nickels were seen on occasion. All varieties of Indian Head or Buffalo nickels were in pocket change, although the earlier years from 1913 onward were apt to show extensive wear. Mercury and Barber dimes were the order of the day in the ten-cent series, with some earlier Liberty Seated issues seen now and then. Quarters and half dollars dated back to the 1870s as a rule.

Silver dollars, not popular with collectors, were available from banks or through the Federal Reserve System. Many of the coins dated back as early as 1878, the first year of the Morgan design, and many were in brilliant Mint State preservation. They had been stored for decades (as backing for Silver Certificates) because people did not like using them in commerce. The availability of certain dates and mintmarks was erratic for the few who sought them. Carson City coins were seldom encountered, and certain San Francisco issues seemed rare.

Gold coins were available through banks and included five-, ten-, and twenty-dollar coins dated as early as the 1840s and 1850s, including five-dollar coins minted at Charlotte and Dahlonega. Gold dollars and three-dollar coins were not to be seen, for dealers such as New York City's Thomas L. Elder had been paying small premiums to bank officers and tellers for any they could find. Quarter eagles, minted as recently as 1929, were not available for face value either, but could be bought for a small premium, such as 25¢, from tellers who received them in the course of business.

Most gold coins were held by the government. Official gold-related figures for the year, as issued by the Treasury Department, are as follows:

> *Gold coins minted in 1932 ($10 and $20 coins):* $66,665,000; these consisted of 4,463,000 $10 coins and 1,101,750 $20 coins, all struck at Philadelphia.
>
> *Gold coins held by the Treasury Department:* $964,795,000.
>
> *Gold coins in Federal Reserve Banks:* $410,760,000.
>
> *Gold coins in National Banks:* $12,753,000.
>
> *Other gold coins in the United States:* $455,726,000.
>
> *Total gold coins held domestically:* $1,844,034,000; including bullion: $4,513,001,000.
>
> *Gold coins imported in 1932:* $196,539,282.
>
> *Gold coins exported in 1932:* $163,863,560.

A Treasury Bonanza

The Treasury Department in Washington, D.C., endeavored to be helpful to numismatists, as it had been for many years. Examples of current coinage were available for face value plus a handling charge. In 1932, Charles W. Foster, librarian and curator of the American Numismatic Association (ANA), issued a notice to all coin collectors and dealers, detailing how to request new coins from the Mint. He emphasized the need to include not only the price of the coins but also the price of postage, including separate postage if the applicant wanted coins from different mints. Foster also detailed the holdings of each mint:

> *Denver Mint coinage:* 1907 half eagles, 1909 half eagles, 1914 eagles, 1921 Morgan silver dollars, 1922 Peace dollars, 1925 double eagles, 1926 double eagles, Peace dollars, 1927 double eagles, 1928 quarters, 1929 halves, quarters, dimes, nickels, 1930 cents, 1931 double eagles, dimes, cents, 1932 cents.
>
> *Philadelphia Mint coinage:* 1921 Morgan and Peace dollars, 1924 Peace dollars, 1925 Peace dollars, 1926 Peace dollars, 1927 Peace dollars, 1928 Peace dollars,

1929 half eagles, quarters, dimes, nickels, cents, 1930 quarters, dimes, nickels, cents, 1931 double eagles, dimes, cents, 1932 double eagles, eagles, cents.

San Francisco Mint coinage: 1921 Morgan dollars, 1922 Peace dollars, 1923 Peace dollars, 1924 Peace dollars, 1925 double eagles, Peace dollars, 1926 double eagles, Peace dollars, 1927 double eagles, Peace dollars, 1928 Peace dollars, quarters, 1929 halves, quarters, dimes, nickels, cents, 1930 double eagles, eagles, quarters, dimes, nickels, cents, 1931 dimes, nickels, cents.

This list yields delights for present-day readers and also gives insights as to coin-holding policies of the Treasury Department. Silver dollars and gold coins were stored as backing for Silver Certificates and Gold Certificates. The 1927 Denver double eagle, available in any quantity desired in 1932, would prove to be a rarity to a later generation of collectors. Official records state that just 110 coins were paid out. This issue, and most other Denver double eagles of the 1920s, were melted in the 1930s. Very few were ever released into circulation.

Among Philadelphia Mint coins, the gold double eagles would prove to be rare and valuable, but in 1932 there was little demand for them. The large quantities of copper, nickel, and silver coins from San Francisco reflected merely a backup of supply. With no call for these coins in circulation, they were simply held by the Treasury Department until needed. Soon, the low-mintage 1931-S cents and nickels would be recognized as potential rarities, and Treasury supplies would be cleaned out. The pleasing result is that both of these issues are plentiful in Mint State today.

The stock of quarter dollars at all three mints indicates why no new coins of this particular denomination had been struck in 1931.

Collecting Coins

Numismatics remained a strong hobby in 1932. Prices weakened for certain rare and expensive coins, simply because few people had money to buy them. Interest remained intense for affordable coins, including commemorative half dollars dating back to 1892 and dates and mintmarks of current low denominations.

M.L. Beistle of Shippensburg, Pennsylvania, had marketed a line of coin album pages since 1928, and these had become popular. However, most collectors kept their coins in 2x2-inch paper envelopes or in coin cabinets, with envelopes being preferred. Information about each coin was written or typed on the face, and the envelopes were then sorted in order, often in long, cardboard, piano-roll-style boxes. These were easy to store.

There were no regularly issued guides to prices, although Wayte Raymond, who conducted the Coin Department of Scott Stamp & Coin Co. in New York City, produced a slim guide with meager information, which was a predecessor to the *Standard Catalogue of United States Coins* (a larger, more elaborate production that created a sensation when it was launched in 1934). Raymond also sold Beistle's album pages, soon developing them into an extensive line under the National name.

The American Numismatic Society (ANS), New York City, had lapsed into a fairly quiet mode, with curators and members concentrating on ancient and world coins, with little interest in the American series. This was due in large part to the collecting preferences of its major benefactor, Archer Huntington, who had paid for its new building in 1908 and its expansion two decades later. The once-dynamic *American Journal of Numismatics* had evolved into a series of occasional, specialized monographs, and lacked mainstream interest for U.S. collectors.

In the meantime, the ANA, founded in 1891, was the main focus group in the hobby. Its magazine, *The Numismatist*, was the only monthly numismatic periodical in 1932 and was the main source for auction, convention, and other information. Coin clubs were active in many towns and cities, and reports of their activities were published each month.

In New York City, the Chase National Bank Collection of Money of the World continued to be a prime tourist attraction, introducing many to the hobby. The curator was Farran Zerbe, who had sold the collection to the bank several years earlier.

Frank Duffield, editor of *The Numismatist*, discussed trends and changing preferences in the hobby in the September 1932 issue. He included this passage:

> Collectors of all series of coins cannot fail to have noted the increasing number of those who collect the small United States cents in the higher grades of preservation and the consequent advance in prices of Uncle Sam's humble coin. Much of this is probably due to an increase in the number of collectors who began a few years ago to form collections of cents from coins found in circulation, many of whom later became dissatisfied with the condition of their coins after they had been obliged to purchase a few of the rarer dates in a high state of preservation, and finally accepted Uncirculated or Proof as their standard.

Wooden Nickels and Commemoratives

A nationwide fad was started in the small town of Tenino, Washington. The local bank had closed its doors, and there was a shortage of small change. The Chamber of Commerce intervened and produced its own money—"coins" of thin wooden veneer cut into the size of silver dollars. Though they were imprinted with denominations of 25¢, $1, $5, and $10, they were called *wooden nickels*.

Local merchants agreed to accept the "nickels," and normal business was soon restored. Word of the novelty spread nationwide through newspaper accounts, and the townsfolk were offered up to twice face value for any they wanted to sell. The genie was out of the bottle, and since that time many towns, businesses, and coin clubs have issued their own styles of wooden nickels.

No new commemorative coins had been issued since 1928, when Hawaiian and Oregon Trail half dollars were struck. The Hawaiian halves sold out, but the Oregon Trail Memorial Association had a glut of unsold 1926 coins on hand and did not release the 1928-dated pieces. In 1932 there was a call by collectors for these 1928 coins. The association said it would keep the 1928s in reserve until thousands of the unwanted 1926 coins found buyers.

It was Treasury policy in the 1920s to mint commemorative coins for committees and organizations that had received congressional permission to sell the issues. The Treasury charged face value plus a die-making charge and shipping—but the commissions could charge whatever they wanted to. As can be imagined, there were many abuses. Production of the Oregon Trail coins, considered by collectors to be very beautiful, recommenced in 1933 and did not wind down until 1939. The deceptions practiced by their sellers prompted Congress to curtail any later commemorative coins. No more were made until 1946.

The American Numismatic Association

The grading of coins was a hot topic in 1932, just as it remains today. In the June issue of *The Numismatist*, Frank Duffield stated that ever since 1907, descriptions of coin conditions had been controversial. Although it had been suggested that the ANA prepare a list of official grading standards, this would not solve the problem.

> The difficulty is not in preparing such a standard classification, because there is very little difference of opinion among collectors on this point. The apparently insurmountable objection to it is that no one would feel compelled to adhere to it once adopted. Many dealers and cataloguers who have been selling coins for years have their own standards, which they have been using for years and which they honestly believe to be fair and just to all concerned.

Duffield concluded by agreeing with a recent correspondent that the best policy would be to get to know the dealers, after which "the customers will soon learn where to send for Uncirculated and Proofs when they get what they order." At the time, many "Uncirculated" coins were what might be called About Uncirculated today. The lure was that these bore cheaper prices.

In 1932 the annual convention of the ANA was held in Los Angeles from August 20 to 26. The Biltmore Hotel served as the headquarters for the gathering of 50 collectors. It was generally agreed that if the show had been held in the East, more would have attended. George J. Bauer, a highly regarded dealer from Rochester, New York, was president. At the convention, votes in the recent ANA election were reported, and Alden Scott Boyer, a Chicago manufacturer of chemicals and cosmetics, was announced as the incoming president.

Affairs of the ANA were in good order, with strong finances and only a small dip in membership. "The general business depression has affected *The Numismatist* only slightly," Duffield reported. "With renewed interest in collecting with the coming of fall and more hopeful conditions in the business world, the outlook for the coming year is bright."

Among the Dealers

Reflective of hard times worldwide, the advertisement of Spink & Son of London in the January issue of *The Numismatist* included this wording:

> A Happy and Prosperous New Year is the wish we extend to all numismatists the world over, and, although it is an old, old wish, we believe it will be said with greater sincerity than ever this year.
>
> Times are difficult, and have been for some months, but we feel sure that the old adage, "Hope springs eternal in the human breast," is still true, and that with the advent of the New Year we are all looking forward with renewed optimism to a general if gradual improvement in world affairs.

But if we are to expect this improvement we must be ready and eager to put our shoulders with yet greater energy to the wheel, whatever our sphere of life, and, as the work may become harder, we venture to say that numismatics will prove still further that it is unsurpassed as a hobby and a relaxation from the daily round.

We should therefore like to offer our services and experience to all numismatists, old or young, novices or experts, in furthering their interest and researches in this fascinating pursuit.

B. Max Mehl, of Fort Worth, Texas, basking in the great sales of his dollar-priced *Star Rare Coin Encyclopedia*, was accounting for more than half of the incoming mail at the post office in his city. He was also occupied with more serious numismatic matters, including the sale on consignment of the large and valuable coin collection formed by Waldo C. Newcomer, a Baltimore banker. In January, Mehl took 75 of the most impressive coins and made them available for members of the Dallas Coin Club to examine and discuss. In gratitude, William A. Philpott, representing the club, presented Mehl with a leather album of Fractional Currency specimen notes originally made by Spencer M. Clark, of the National Currency Bureau, for President Andrew Johnson.[3]

Early in the year, William Hesslein, a prominent dealer in Connecticut for many years, but then located in Boston, absconded with coins and other property belonging to his clients, leaving behind a string of debts and a bewildered family.

The numismatic estate of Virgil M. Brand was being disposed. The collector had died in 1926, leaving more than 350,000 coins, including multiple specimens of many rarities. His brothers Armin and Horace were the sole heirs, and soon became involved in wrangling. Large quantities of high-denomination gold and paper money were cashed in for face value. The rare material was appraised by dealers Henry Chapman, of Philadelphia, and Burdette G. Johnson, of St. Louis. In 1932, much of the paper money was sold to B. Max Mehl. Other segments of the estate would be filtered into the market through the 1980s.

During the year, more than 30 mail-bid and auction sales of American numismatic items were conducted. Sellers included J.C. Morgenthau & Co. (a division of Scott Stamp & Coin; the sales were cataloged by James G. Macallister and Wayte Raymond), Wayte Raymond (separately), Barney Bluestone, B. Max Mehl, Thomas L. Elder, M.H. Bolender, and several others.

Bluestone, a newcomer to the auction field, held four sales in 1932, none of particular note. M.H. Bolender, a schoolteacher who dabbled in coins in his spare time, ran eight mail-bid sales (again, none of lasting memory). The Morgenthau sales comprised five offerings, notable among them being a consignment from Waldo C. Newcomer (patterns, an original 1861 Confederate cent, and colonial paper money) and the collection of William Festus Morgan, containing remarkable large copper cents. Raymond's standalone sale included outstanding world coins from the G.P. Morosini Collection. Mehl held just two mail-bid sales, both unimportant.[4] Elder announced that his New York City business was for sale and began to wind down his affairs. No buyers were forthcoming, so in 1932 Elder renewed his business interest, including auctions. He was also a frequent correspondent to various publications such as *Hobbies* magazine, which had a special section for coins.

2
Early Quarter Dollars

BACKGROUND

"Two-Bit" Pieces

Today, *two bits* remains a nickname for quarter dollars, including the newest Washington state-reverse varieties. The term has been in use for more than two centuries, a remarkable record of endurance.

In the early days, before U.S. quarter dollars were first minted (in 1796), many if not most monetary transactions were denominated in Spanish-American coins. The Continental Currency paper issues of 1775 to 1779 were payable in Spanish milled dollars. There was no federal monetary system yet in place.

The Spanish-American coins, minted of silver and gold mined in Mexico, Central America, and South America, were denominated in *reales* and escudos. Silver coins of one *real* were valued at 12-1/2¢ and were familiarly called *bits*. The 8-*real* piece was called a *dollar*, or *Spanish dollar*, and became the foundation of the federal system when it was established in 1792 (but in revised form, with decimal equivalents).

Most popular of the smaller denominations was the 2-*real* coin, or *two bits*, worth 25¢; these were also called *quarters*. It was logical that when Uncle Sam began making his own twenty-five-cent pieces, people would call them two bits. Other popular Spanish-American silver coins included the 1/2-*real*, called a *medio*, worth 6-1/4¢; and the four-*real* piece.

A selection of silver coins, which are about the size of a quarter dollar, in circulation in the United States in 1850. The illustrations are from *The Coin Chart Manual* of that date, with exchange values printed below each (only one side is shown of each coin). Bankers and merchants kept charts and guides on hand to aid in transactions when foreign coins were tendered for payment.

Certain of these foreign silver and gold coins remained legal tender in the United States until the passage of the Act of February 21, 1857, even though federal coins had been produced for more than six decades. This legislation provided for the legal-tender status to expire in two years, later extended for a further six months.

Early U.S. Quarters

The Mint Act of April 2, 1792, provided for the establishment of a federal coining facility. The legislation also established a monetary system based on dollars and the decimal system, and gave weights and finenesses for various issues from the copper half cent to the gold $10 coin, or eagle. Although the act authorized the quarter dollar, no coins of this denomination were made until 1796, the same year that the silver dime and gold $2.50 quarter eagle made their debut.

George Washington was president of the United States but would soon leave the office. After his inauguration in 1789, he lived in New York City for a year until the seat of the federal government was moved to Philadelphia. The Federal City, known today as Washington, D.C., was still in the planning stages.

In this era the Mint did not coin silver or gold coins for its own account. Instead, when depositors brought precious metal to the Mint, they specified what denominations they wanted. For silver coins, this usually meant dollars, as they were more popular for export and large transactions than were equivalent values in half dimes, dimes, quarters, or half dollars.

The first quarter dollar of 1796 featured the Draped Bust obverse in combination with the Small Eagle reverse. Only 6,146 were made, after which no more of this denomination were struck until 1804. In that year a new reverse was employed, the Heraldic Eagle style, modeled after the Great Seal of the United States. Coins of this design were produced through 1807. As demand for

The first U.S. quarter dollars were made in 1796, and only to the extent of 6,146 pieces. Many were saved as novelties, with the result that several hundred high-grade examples exist today. Due to their status as a one-year type, such coins today are expensive and highly sought-after.

The Draped Bust obverse design was combined with the Heraldic Eagle reverse to coin quarters from 1804 to 1807, including the 1805 shown here.

Quarter dollar of the Capped Bust type, motto on reverse, large diameter, of the style made from 1815 to 1828.

Quarter dollar of the Capped Bust type, no motto, reduced diameter, as made from 1831 to 1838.

this denomination was low, and depositors continued to request larger coins, no more quarters were made until 1815, when a new motif was used: John Reich's Capped Bust style in combination with a perched eagle on the reverse. Coinage was intermittent until a modification to the design was made in 1831, after which quarters of this type were made continuously until 1838.

Liberty Seated and Barber Quarters

The Liberty Seated quarter, designed by Christian Gobrecht, was introduced in 1838 and made continuously through 1891 with several modifications to the weight and design details. In 1866 the motto IN GOD WE TRUST was added. Until 1838, all U.S. coinage had been made at the Philadelphia Mint. In that year, branches opened at Charlotte, North Carolina; Dahlonega, Georgia; and New Orleans, Louisiana. Charlotte and Dahlonega struck only gold coins, each with a C or D mintmark, respectively; these mints made no quarter dollars. Silver and gold coins were produced at New Orleans. In 1854 the San Francisco Mint opened for business. Coins made there had an S mintmark. The next branch mint was Carson City (mintmark CC), which operated from 1870 to 1893.

An 1870 Liberty Seated quarter dollar. In various modifications, Liberty Seated quarters were minted from 1838 to 1891.

A 1907 quarter of the Barber design, made from 1892 to 1916.

In 1862, the second year of the Civil War, the outcome of the conflict was uncertain, and the public hoarded coins of all kinds, including quarters. It was expected that silver coins would become abundant in circulation after the war ended. In April 1865 the Confederate States of America surrendered, but coins remained in hiding. Due to political and economic uncertainties, plus a large flood of Legal Tender Notes and other paper money that the public considered to be of less value than coins, quarter dollars and other silver pieces continued to be hoarded. It was not until April 20, 1876, that coins began to circulate in large quantities once again, although beginning in 1873, small numbers were seen in larger cities and elsewhere. Federal Legal Tender Notes and other paper currency sold at discounts in relation to gold and silver coins.

In 1892 the Liberty Head design by Chief Engraver Charles E. Barber made its debut. Known as Barber quarters today, these were produced until 1916. The Denver Mint began operations in 1906 and used a D mintmark.

Standing Liberty Quarters

In 1916 the silver dime, quarter, and half dollar denominations were redesigned. For this dramatic event, artists in the private sector submitted designs—their submissions constituted a first in these denominations, for it had been the responsibility of Mint engravers to routinely create designs. The Standing Liberty quarter dollar motif by artist Hermon A. MacNeil became the new standard and was described by the Mint in an official press release on the afternoon of May 30, 1916:

Standing Liberty quarter dollar of 1917. This is the Type I design made in 1916 and early 1917. In 1917 the Mint modified the design by encasing Miss Liberty in a suit of armor and rearranging the stars on the reverse.

A 1920-S quarter of the modified design used from 1917 to 1930.

The design of the twenty-five cent piece is intended to typify in a measure the awakening of the country to its own protection. The law specified that on the obverse of the coin not only the word "liberty," but a representation of Liberty shall be shown.

In the new design Liberty is shown as a full length figure, front view, with head turned toward the left, stepping forward to the gateway of the country, and on the wall are inscribed the words "In God We Trust." The left arm of the figure of Liberty is upraised, holding the shield in the attitude of protection, from which the covering is being drawn. The right hand bears the olive branch of peace. On the field above the head is inscribed the word "Liberty," and on the step under her feet, "1916."

The reverse of this coin necessitates by law a representation of the American eagle, and is here shown in full flight with wings extended, sweeping across the coin. Inscription "United States of America" and "E Pluribus Unum" and "Quarter Dollar" below. Connecting the lettering above on outer circle are olive branches with ribbon that is stirred by the breeze as the bird flies.[1]

The coins distributed later in the year differed slightly from that just described (a pattern version) in that there were neither olive branches nor a ribbon.

Quarters of the Standing Liberty design were made continuously from 1916 to 1930, with the exception of 1922. In 1931, no quarter dollars were minted, as in this Depression year there was no call for them. Thus was set the stage for the Washington quarter dollar of 1932.

The Isabella Quarter

In 1892 the first American silver commemorative coin was created, a half dollar to be issued in conjunction with the World's Columbian Exposition. At the beginning this and other commemorative issues were officially designated *souvenirs* (the *commemorative* nomenclature became popular later). The World's Columbian Exposition inspired the production not only of half dollars dated 1892 and 1893, but of the first and only commemorative twenty-five-cent piece, the 1893 Isabella quarter, which was made at the behest of society matron Mrs. Potter Palmer.

The Isabella quarters had a late start. An act of March 3, 1893, specified that the production of these quarters would not exceed 40,000 and that the pieces would be of standard weight and fineness. Like the Columbian half dollars, the quarters would be made from metal taken from uncurrent silver coins held by the Treasury Department.

The Isabella quarters were sold for $1 each in the Woman's Building at the World's Columbian Exposition. (From a stereoview published by J.F. Jarvis)

For the obverse, a depiction of Queen Isabella of Spain was suggested, for King Ferdinand and Queen Isabella furnished the financing for Columbus's voyage of discovery, Isabella vowing to pledge her crown and jewels if necessary (according to popular legend). In April 1893 the Treasury Department responded by submitting its own two obverse designs to the Board of Lady Managers; one sketch (the one eventually chosen) showed Isabella as a young queen, while the other depicted a facing head of Isabella in later years. Thus the Isabella quarter was the first legal-tender U.S. coin to depict a foreign monarch. The sketch for the reverse design depicted a woman kneeling, holding a distaff, signifying woman's industry, although an alternative suggestion was that an illustration of the Woman's Building at the fair would be appropriate. The models and dies for the Isabella quarter were prepared by Chief Engraver Charles E. Barber, who also designed the obverse of the Columbian half dollar.

Production of the coins began at the Philadelphia Mint on June 13, 1893. Soon afterward they were placed on sale in the Woman's Building at the exposition. Priced at $1 each, they drew little attention, for the 1892 and 1893 Columbian half dollars at the same price seemed to be a better value. Sales languished, and even considering 10,000 coins bought by Mrs. Palmer Potter, only 24,214 were distributed. Quantities remained on the numismatic market through the 1920s. Today, they are widely dispersed, popular, and in strong demand.

3

The Life of George Washington

GENTLEMAN AND PLANTER

The subject of the new quarter, George Washington, was born on February 11, 1732,[1] on a farm later known as Wakefield, in Westmoreland County, Virginia. An ancestor, John Washington, had settled in Virginia in 1657. His descendants followed farming, real estate, milling, iron founding, and other trades, generally with success. The family was viewed as prosperous. George's father, Augustine Washington, had four children in a previous marriage and six with George's mother, Mary Ball. From 1735 to 1738 the family lived at Little Hunting Creek, later the site of Mount Vernon. In 1738 the Washingtons moved to Ferry Farm, on the Rappahannock River opposite Fredericksburg. His father died when George was 11, leaving an estate that included several farms. George's half-brother, Lawrence, inherited the Mount Vernon tract, where he built the main part of what would become a famous mansion. Wakefield went to another half-brother, Augustine, and Ferry Farm was kept by George's mother (after her death it passed to George).

General George Washington as engraved for the National Portrait Gallery of Distinguished Americans, by Asher B. Durand, 1834.

In comfortable circumstances, young George went to local schools but never had an advanced education. At an early age he was trained in the manners and morals of a gentleman of the era. He learned the trade of a surveyor by age 15, and at age 16 he was hired to survey the Shenandoah Valley for Thomas, Lord Fairfax. He was a skilled traveler on horseback and was familiar with life in the wilderness. In 1749 he took his first job in public service, as surveyor for Culpeper County. In 1751 and 1752 he went with his half-brother and mentor, Lawrence, to Barbados, where the latter sought relief from his tuberculosis. George was infected with smallpox, which permanently scarred his face. Lawrence, in failing health, died shortly after their return. Mount Vernon was leased by George Washington in 1754, and 1761 it became George's by inheritance after the passing of Lawrence's widow, Anne Fairfax Lee.

In 1753, Governor Robert Dinwiddie of Virginia sent Washington and a small group to Fort Le Boeuf, in Waterford, Pennsylvania, to confront French troops stationed there and, in so doing, to assert Britain's claim to the district. Washington returned to report that the French commander had no intention of backing down. His description of the wilderness and his winter travels to and from the French fort solidified his reputation as a man of strength and courage. In 1754 he was commissioned as a lieutenant colonel and then colonel in the militia, and he saw action in the early skirmishes of the conflict that evolved into the French and Indian War. Disillusioned with British military practices, he resigned in 1754 and went back to Mount Vernon. He reentered military service with the courtesy title of colonel in 1755, as an aide to General Edward Braddock. In that service he narrowly escaped with his life several times: four bullets tore his coat, and two horses were shot from under him. For his bravery, he was rewarded with his colonelcy and command of the militia forces in Virginia. He resigned his commission in 1758. His war experience to this point was, in the balance, unsatisfactory, with confused instructions and criticism from his British superiors and a lot of political intervention.

Washington returned to manage the farming lands around Mount Vernon, overlooking the Potomac River. On January 6, 1759, he married Martha Dandridge Custis, a widow with two children, whom George adopted: George Washington Custis, age four, called Jacky; and Eleanor Parke Custis, age two, called Patsy. The couple never had children of their own.

He became a member of the Virginia House of Burgesses in 1758, which necessitated lengthy stays away from home, and served until 1774. His main crop on the Mount Vernon lands was tobacco. As a producer of raw goods, Washington was forced to deal with British regulations on exports that required him to buy all finished goods from Britain. The imbalance between imports and exports with Britain increased Washington's distaste for that country. Increasingly, he thought of himself as an American, not a citizen under British authority. He turned to other activities. With slave labor, he turned cloth into finished goods.[2] He raised wheat and operated a gristmill. His commercial fishery on the Potomac proved to be profitable. Many of his products were exported to the West Indies, one of the most active maritime trading areas in the New World. Real estate transactions brought additional profits.

The Revolutionary War

In the meantime, Great Britain levied increasing restrictions on commerce and conduct in the Virginia colony, without the advice or consent of the population. The Townshend Revenue Act, the Stamp Act, and other offensive decrees were enforced by British troops in America, some of whom stayed in private homes as uninvited guests. Washington and others felt that the self-rule of the colonies was being eroded, and that America would soon be subjected to outright tyranny. By the early 1770s, most political figures in Virginia were anti-British. In May 1774, Washington joined other burgesses in Virginia to propose the establishment of a continental congress to further the rights of citizens. In September, he was a Virginia delegate to the First

Continental Congress in Philadelphia. Returning to Virginia, he helped organize independent military companies that could possibly be used to fight the British.

In other colonies the fires of revolution were burning as well, with Massachusetts being the focal point after the Boston Massacre of March 5, 1770; the Boston Tea Party; and the citizens' continuing resentment of British troops. On February 2, 1775, the British House of Commons declared Massachusetts to be in rebellion. British Army troops took charge of Boston, but were encircled by American militiamen on the outskirts.

After convening in Philadelphia on May 20, 1775, the Second Continental Congress elected Washington as commander in chief of the Continental Army on June 17. In Cambridge, Massachusetts, on July 3, he assumed command of his troops, most of whom had plenty of patriotic spirit, but little in the way of formal training. On August 3, King George III signed the Royal Proclamation of Rebellion and charged Washington with treason, subject to punishment. Although certain members of the Continental Congress hoped for appeasement and formation of a satisfactory arrangement with Britain, Washington felt that the colonies had no choice but to become independent. In the summer of 1776 the Declaration of Independence was signed.

For six years, until the surrender of British General Cornwallis at Yorktown, Virginia, in 1781, General Washington overcame many adversities, losses, and tragedies, which were punctuated by triumphs. The story of the Revolution is beyond the scope of the present numismatic text but is easily found elsewhere. Washington's first victory was the ouster of British troops from Boston in March 1776.

Jean Antoine Houdon's bust of George Washington. Many copies of this sculpture were made in bronze, marble, and plaster.

Portrait of General Washington, painted from life by Charles Willson Peale, 1784. (Nassau Hall, Princeton University)

Perhaps the low point was the winter at Valley Forge in 1777 and 1778 as the war raged on. In February 1778, France joined as an ally, providing troops, naval vessels, and equipment. At first vastly outnumbered by British troops and warships, but later gaining strength and achieving notable victories, Washington secured the independence of the united colonies, soon called the United States of America. In 1783, Congress voted to give officers of the Revolution full back pay. As a

To finance the Revolution, the Continental Congress issued vast amounts of paper money. This $1 note of January 14, 1779, (shown reduced) is representative.

postscript to history, during the bicentennial celebrations in 1976, Congress voted to designate Washington as a six-star general, so that he would permanently rank over all of his successors.

Washington went back to Mount Vernon, where he hoped to continue life as a gentleman farmer. The main house was enlarged and other improvements were made. At the request of Benjamin Franklin and Thomas Jefferson, in October 1785, French sculptor Jean Antoine Houdon (1741–1828) visited Mount Vernon, took a life-mask impression, and spent two weeks modeling a marble bust. Afterward, he went back to Paris, where the bust was completed years later. In 1796 it was installed in the state capitol in Richmond, Virginia. In 1786, Pierre Simon Duvivier used the work, not yet completed by Houdon, to model the Washington Before Boston medal authorized by the U.S. Congress.[3] The Duvivier depiction was copied by many others, most notably Charles Cushing Wright in the 19th century. From 1775 to 1789, Houdon sculpted the busts of many well-known figures in Europe and America, including Jefferson (the bust used on the 1801 Indian peace medal, the 1903 commemorative gold dollar, and the 1938 nickel five-cent piece) and Franklin (the bust used on the 1963 half dollar).

WASHINGTON AS PRESIDENT

With a constant eye on the political situation, George Washington realized the fledgling government had problems operating under the Articles of Confederation. He became a prime mover in the formation of the Constitutional Convention held in Philadelphia in 1787. When the Constitution was completed and ratified, the Electoral College elected him as the first president of the United States.

On April 30, 1789, on the balcony of the Federal Hall on Wall Street, New York City, George Washington took his oath of office. In 1790 the seat of the government was moved from New York to Philadelphia, where it remained for the ensuing decade.

The first American medals bearing an authentic portrait of Washington were sold in 1790 by J. Manly & Co. in Philadelphia, and by Peter Rynberg in Wilmington, Delaware. Struck on cast planchets from dies cut by Samuel Brooks, these were offered for

$2 in a brass composition and $4 in silver. Gold strikings were also available, priced according to weight. The brass version proved to be immensely popular.

In 1792, Washington was reelected president unanimously by electoral vote. In the same year, residing in Philadelphia, he may have participated in the groundbreaking for the Mint on July 31. Earlier in the same month he is thought by some to have furnished silver for the striking of 1,500 half dismes, the first circulating coins made by the government. Equipment was on hand for the new Mint, but it was stored in local craftsman and saw-maker John Harper's coach house, where the coins were struck.

Washington contended with many challenges during his administration. England and France were at war, and each side sought the alliance of the United States. Washington issued a proclamation of neutrality on April 22, 1793. Matters became tense, and a war with England seemed imminent, due to British interference with American shipping and the impressing (kidnapping) of American sailors. The treaty of November 19, 1794, signed in London by American emissary John Jay, soothed matters with the British, but angered the French. The latter engaged in attacks on and seizures of American ships in 1799 and 1800 in the so-called Undeclared War with France. Decades later, in the 1830s, reparations by France brought large quantities of gold coins to the Philadelphia Mint. Washington successfully guided the expansion of the western frontier, trade on the Mississippi River (involving negotiations with Spain), the forging of relationships and policies between the states and the federal government, and other dynamic challenges. He worked with Congress to establish and define the new executive office of the government, to establish an effective judiciary system, and to put a diplomatic corps in place.

In 1789, as a unification measure, he traveled throughout the Northeast, and in 1791 through the South, often staying at private residences. The "George Washington slept here" phrase arose mainly from these trips.

In his farewell address of September 17, 1796, the president urged elected officials to support the Constitution and federal laws, to strengthen and support the public financial system, to avoid entangling alliances with foreign countries, to maintain friendship with other nations, and to discourage political parties favoring a certain section of the United States. Washington left the office in 1797. His vice president, John Adams, was elected the next president of the United States.

The Manly medal, 1790, features the earliest true portrait of Washington on a medal made in America.

Retirement

George Washington returned to Mount Vernon, where he enjoyed his surroundings and received many visitors. One of these was Daniel Eccleston, an Englishman who some years later, in 1805, produced a large medal with his portrait.

In 1798 he agreed to command an American army should a war with France erupt, but hostilities remained limited to maritime commerce in the aforementioned Undeclared War. In the same year he opposed the Virginia and Kentucky Resolutions, which sought to supersede the Constitution with certain laws of their own.

In December 1799 Washington caught a cold, which worsened. He went to bed, and blood was drawn from him by the use of leeches (a common practice at the time). On December 14, 1799, he died, following an illness of two days.

Father of His Country

Memorials

George Washington's passing, a national loss, was widely mourned. In Newburyport, Massachusetts, silversmith and inventor Jacob Perkins struck a series of silver medals, about the diameter of a copper cent, with the inscription HE IS IN GLORY, THE WORLD IN TEARS on the obverse. The reverse gives life dates and events in abbreviated form, with a funeral urn at the center. In Massachusetts, the *Essex Journal*, January 10, 1800, printed this notice (dated January 7):

A gold funeral medal honoring Washington, made by Jacob Perkins and sold in 1800. The hole permitted it to be hung by a cord or ribbon. (Dwight N. Manley)

> Jacob Perkins takes leave to inform the public that he will now be able to answer orders for the medals in memory of the late illustrious Gen. WASHINGTON, from any part of the continent, and to any amount, executed in gold, silver, or white metal, with punctuality and dispatch—from 3 to 5 thousand can be made daily. A liberal discount will be made to those who purchase quantities to sell again.

These funeral medals (as numismatists refer to them today) were holed at the top for suspension on a cord or ribbon. Many were worn at memorial services held in January 1800, and in parades held on the anniversary of Washington's birthday, February 22, 1800. In 1832, the centennial of his birth, there were extensive celebrations and remembrances, and several varieties of medals were struck.

Washington Honored

From 1804 to 1807, *The Life of George Washington*, by John Marshall (famed as chief justice of the Supreme Court), was published in five volumes, followed in 1843 by a work of the same title by Jared Sparks. The latter's main source was 10 folio volumes of Washington's collected correspondence. After extracting what he wanted, Sparks distributed many pages and documents to friends and acquaintances, without making copies first. A later generation of historians lamented the action.[4]

In 1824 and 1825, Marquis de LaFayette, French hero of the American Revolution, revisited America and toured each of the states. Congress honored him as "The Nation's Guest." Many souvenirs depicting Washington were made in connection with this event, perhaps the most famous being the Washington/Lafayette counterstamps applied to current coins, mostly copper cents and silver half dollars.

In the early 1850s a group of women organized under the leadership of Ann Pamela Cunningham; they would come to be known as the Mount Vernon Ladies Association of the Union. In 1858 the association, for about $200,000, payable in installments, acquired Mount Vernon and 200 acres. A campaign was mounted to raise the necessary funds.

Commemorative pitcher made in Liverpool, England, 1800, with designs similar to those on the Perkins medal. (Larry Stack)

Edward Everett, famous Massachusetts legislator and orator, became the champion of the cause. He traveled widely and gave nearly 200 speeches on the subject. In the meantime, Benson J. Lossing's two-volume *Pictorial Field-Guide of the Revolution*, published in 1852, went through multiple printings. Superbly illustrated by hundreds of engravings, the work showcased the leadership of Washington and depicted most of the Revolutionary War battle sites with accompanying narrative.

Other publishers hastened to issue books about the Revolution and the president. Prints of Washington achieved wide sale. His portrait was featured on many notes issued by state-chartered banks, and his life was a popular subject for articles in illustrated weekly magazines, an innovation of the decade.

Washington memorial funeral procession on High Street in Philadelphia.

Numismatics to the Forefront

The Act of February 21, 1857, eliminated the copper large cent and half cent, phased out foreign coins as legal tender, and authorized the copper-nickel small cent. On May 25 the first of the new cents, with a flying eagle design, were released into circulation.

A wave of nostalgia swept across America. The familiar, warm copper "pennies" of childhood would soon be gone. Thousands of citizens checked their change, looked in drawers, and hunted elsewhere in an effort to collect as many different dates as possible. It was soon realized that a well-worn cent of 1793 or 1799 could be sold for several dollars, that and certain other dates had value as well. Numismatics became a popular hobby. Inquiries about the value of old coins were published in newspapers, and *Historical Magazine* published articles on old money. Jewelers, art dealers, and others found that a few old coins on display found ready sale.

In early 1858 the Philadelphia Numismatic Society—the first such club in America—was formed. In March of the same year, the American Numismatic Society was organized by Augustus B. Sage (a teenager at the time) and his collector-friends. Auctions of coins soon drew wide interest and participation.

The Mint Cabinet

Numismatics, formerly the purview of a few hundred collectors scattered across the United States, now encompassed thousands. The Philadelphia Mint received increasing inquiries for Proofs, patterns, and other items. Mint Director James Ross Snowden was happy to comply, at first selling or exchanging pieces with most applicants.

A numismatist himself, Snowden contemplated adding Washington medals to the Mint Cabinet, to build a first-class display. The cabinet had been formed in June 1838, and since that time had been augmented with yearly coinage—interesting pieces obtained from bullion and exchange offices and by trade with collectors. However, only a few Washington medals had been acquired.

With all of the current interest in the life of George Washington and his times, a great demand arose for the medals that had been produced over the years, dating back to the Manly medal of 1790 and the even earlier Voltaire medal, the latter with a fictitious portrait of Washington (as in France his actual appearance was not known).

Director Snowden contemplated the possibilities, but rued that the Mint Cabinet had so few pieces. In 1859 Snowden began placing medallic memorials of Washington in the cabinet of the National Mint. At first he knew of 20 Washington memorials, but investigation soon ascertained that at least 60 different such medals existed. By the time the collection was formally inaugurated on February 22, 1860, 138 pieces resided in the cabinet.[5]

The Voltaire medal of Washington, struck in Paris in 1778, bore an imaginary portrait of the American general as no image was on hand. This is believed to be the earliest of the medals relating to Washington, initiating a series that would eventually comprise hundreds of different versions of his likeness in the coming century.

Washingtoniana

In the late 1850s and early 1860s, many new Washington medals were struck to accommodate the increasing demand. George H. Lovett, of New York City, was perhaps the most prolific engraver of dies of such pieces. His brother, Robert Lovett Jr., of Philadelphia, also turned out many. A half dozen or more other diesinkers added to the supply. Inscriptions on certain of these are wonderful to contemplate today, and reflect the esteem in which Washington was held. Some of the more innovative include *How Abject Europe's Kings Appear by the Side of Such a Man*; *Freedom's Favorite Son*; *Hail Immortal Washington*; *Time Increases His Fame*; *George the Great Whom All Do Honor*; *While We Enjoy the Fruit Let Us Not Forget Him That Planted the Tree*; *Though Lost to Sight to Memory Dear*; *Hero of Freedom*; *Emancipator of America*; and *Providence Left Him Childless That the Nation Might Call Him Father*.

Of course, Jacob Perkins started it all in 1800, with his HE IS IN GLORY, THE WORLD IN TEARS funeral medal.

In the auction salesroom, Washington tokens and medals led the market. Collectively known as *Washingtoniana* (or, in modern times, often shortened to *Washingtonia*), the coins, medals, prints, books, and other items relating to the first president found ready sale.

In the meantime, Director Snowden authorized the restriking of many rare coins, the making of curious patterns and die combinations, and the creation of other special pieces for the numismatic trade. While some were used in trade for Washington pieces needed for the Mint Cabinet, most were sold into the coin market. The latter activity was done in secret, with the profits going to the Mint officials involved. No records were kept, and inquiries were met with denials or false information. In the process, thousands of rare coins were made; these constitute most of the existing pattern issues of that era.

On February 22, 1860, the Washington Cabinet section of the Mint Cabinet was dedicated in a special ceremony. A large and handsome medal was struck for the occasion, in copper and silver, from dies by Anthony C. Paquet.

In the 1860s, pattern two-cent pieces and nickel five-cent pieces were made with Washington's portrait, but no circulating coinage materialized. Federal paper money was issued in quantity, beginning with the Demand Notes of 1861, followed by other issues, including Legal Tender Notes. From that era to the present, Washington's portrait has been a popular subject for currency, and is today on the $1 bill.

In 1885, *Medallic Portraits of Washington*, by W.S. Baker, was published. By that time the market for Washingtoniana had diminished, and many prices were lower than they had been in the late 1850s and early 1860s. Still, the book sold widely.

The centennial of Washington's inauguration, 1889, saw the production of many new medals. Over a period of years, Washington's was a popular portrait on many tokens and medals, aggregating into hundreds of different interpretations by the early 20th century. Although the investment-and-speculation fever of the late 1850s and early 1860s was never regained, Washington pieces remained a popular specialty through the 1920s and into the early 1930s, when the Washington quarter was created.

The Georgivs Triumpho token dated 1783 was likely made in Birmingham, England. As to whether it applies to George Washington of America or to King George III of England is a matter of debate. Likely, Washington was intended, despite the imaginary portrait, as 1783 is the year that the peace treaty was signed, and it was George Washington who was triumphant (Triumpho) in the Revolution. The reverse shows Britannia (a figure used on contemporary British halfpence) restrained by a grate of 13 vertical bars, a significant number. The fleur-de-lis emblems at the corners of the grate represent France, which aided America in the conflict. These tokens were made in large numbers and are readily available today.

Copper store card (advertising token) issued by Augustus B. Sage, New York City, in 1859, from dies by George H. Lovett. Sage, a teenaged dealer and collector, was instrumental in founding the American Numismatic Society in March 1858. The obverse of the medal is based on the Houdon bust, but with Washington draped with the top of a toga, in classic Roman style. (shown at 125%)

Washington Cabinet medal by Anthony C. Paquet, 1860. The obverse features Houdon's bust as adapted by DuVivier on the 1776-dated Washington Before Boston medal. The reverse depicts Washington tokens and medals on display.

Pattern nickel five-cent piece of 1866 (Judd-473). The obverse portrait is an adaptation of the familiar Houdon bust.

4

History of the Washington Quarter

Planning for the Washington Bicentennial

Getting Ready

In 1924 in America, times were good. The financial recession of 1921 was over, and banks and businesses were taking advantage of growth opportunities. Money flowed freely—to buy elegant automobiles, waterfront estates, and other luxuries of life. The stock market had not yet gone into fever heat, but lots of action was provided by the land boom in Florida—buyers fell all over themselves to stake out options and buy properties across the state. Never mind that some land was swamp, at best.

Ahead on the calendar was 1932, the bicentennial of Washington's birth. How to celebrate the occasion in proper and memorable fashion was anyone's guess. On December 2, 1924, Congress formed the United States George Washington Bicentennial Commission to do some planning. President Calvin Coolidge was on the commission ex officio and was joined by an impressive lineup of other politicos. The private sector was represented by leading citizens, the most prominent being Henry Ford.

After the initial announcements, not much was done—although various statements were made about a commemorative medal and a related half dollar, stamps, and the importance of various sites in Washington's life, such as Mount Vernon and Valley Forge. Some even talked of holding a world's fair, the likes of the Panama-Pacific International Exposition of 1915. However, the Sesquicentennial Exposition held in Philadelphia in 1926 was a financial dud, and thoughts of a similar event in 1932 soon died.

Herbert Hoover's Veto

After his inauguration in 1929, President Herbert Hoover became the chairman of the United States George Washington Bicentennial Commission. While Hoover is not remembered as a numismatist, he did have an awareness of recent commemorative issues, perhaps including the large, still-undistributed quantities of Oregon Trail Memorial half dollars, which had found no buyers.

In early 1930, a commemorative coin bill passed by Congress was presented for his signature. Hoover vetoed it on April 21. In his memorandum to Congress on the matter, the president discussed the number of commemorative coins minted in the previous 10 years, as well as the number of pending bills for coinage and additional requests in earlier stages. His argument against further commemorative coins centered on maintaining the integrity of the U.S. monetary system.

Hoover worried that the minting of commemoratives would lead to more success with passing counterfeit coins. Without standard coinage, the public would be unable to determine which coins were real and which were not. In addition, he pointed out that Congress had already addressed this issue when it provided that "No change in the design or die of any coin shall be made oftener than once in twenty-five years from and including the year of the first adoption of the design, model, die, or hub from the same coin."[1]

Aware that many events deserved the recognition that commemorative coins afforded, Hoover concluded: "The government would be glad to assist such celebrations in the creation of appropriate medals which do not have coinage functions."

In 1930 there was talk about making a commemorative coin to honor the 200th anniversary of Washington's birth. A careful reading of Hoover's veto dashed any hopes on the subject.

Behind the Scenes at the Treasury Department

The Design Competition for a Half Dollar

On February 21, 1930, a new group, titled the George Washington Bicentennial Committee and established by an act of Congress, seemingly took the place of the United States George Washington Bicentennial Commission established in 1924. Associate directors were Lieutenant Colonel U.S. Grant III and Representative Sol Bloom, the latter from New York and with an interest in past expositions, celebrations, and related memorabilia.

In the same year the Bicentennial Commission went into action to create an appropriate *regular-issue* half dollar, not a commemorative, to observe the Washington bicentennial. The half dollar was the logical coin of choice, as the largest regularly circulating silver denomination. Although Peace-type silver dollars were current and had last been minted in 1928, they were not seen in everyday commerce, except in certain Rocky Mountain states.

Following several precedents, it was decided to open a competition for designs that would serve for both a commemorative coin and a medal. Perhaps reflective of the sometimes unfocused motifs used on commemorative coins up to this point, the commission published guidelines specifying the nature of the art, these being under the direction of Secretary of the Treasury Andrew W. Mellon:

> That, subject to the approval of Congress, the coinage of the United States silver half dollars during the calendar year 1932 shall have a commemorative character. That the obverse shall bear a head of Washington based on the Houdon bust at Mount Vernon.

That the design of the reverse is left to the sculptor, with the proviso that it shall be national in conception.

That one sculptor be selected to design both the coin (if Congress shall provide) and the medal (already provided for).

That each competitor shall submit in plaster for one design for each the obverse and reverse of the medal. The designs for the coin will be considered when and if Congress shall so provide.

Secretary Mellon (1855–1937) was one of America's best-known collectors of art, and no one questioned his choice of the Houdon image.[2] Making this decision as well as approving the final art was his option. Representative Bloom secured a photograph of the Houdon bust and sent copies to artists who expressed interest in the competition. This avoided free-style ideas as to what the Father of Our Country should look like. It was up to the artist to create a reverse design.

A copy of the famous Houdon bust, this one in the unusual medium of papier maché made from macerated paper money. (Steve Tanenbaum and Steve Hayden)

The Houdon bust was already the most familiar coin and medal representation of Washington, having been used on the 1900 Lafayette dollar, 1926 Sesquicentennial half dollar, and hundreds of tokens and medals. On coins and medals dating back as early as the Washington Before Boston medal, the Houdon bust was modified by adding a peruke (wig) of long hair tied by a ribbon. All entries were to be submitted by October 27, 1930, at which time they would be reviewed by the Commission of Fine Arts—an advisory group whose members would make recommendations to the Treasury Department.

The Washington Before Boston medal, copper striking from original dies, Paris Mint. The medal was commissioned by Congress. Pierre Simon DuVivier cut the dies in 1786, using the Houdon bust as a model.

A reading of the above reflects that while the design for the half dollar was to be commemorative in nature, the motif was to take the place of the current style (the Liberty Walking design by Adolph A. Weinman, used since 1916) and was to be a circulating issue. Due to the slow economic times, there had been no need for half dollars, and none had been coined since 1929.

In due course, selections were received and reviewed, and one by Laura Gardin Fraser was selected by the Commission of Fine Arts as being the best.

A Quarter Dollar Instead

On February 9, 1931, Representative Perkins introduced HR 16973 to change the design to the *quarter* dollar, instead of the half dollar. From this arose plan B, so to speak. The House of Representatives Coinage Committee issued a memorandum on February 13, 1931, addressing several issues, including the ban on changing design more often than once every 25 years. The proposed legislation was required in order to overcome that prohibition. The memorandum concluded:

> As the new design would replace the present type of quarter dollar, it would be in no sense a "special coin," and the issue thereof would not be contrary to the Department's policy of opposing the issue of "special coins."

The plan would serve several purposes:

1. It would replace an unsatisfactory design now being issued.
2. It would be in a popular denomination; and
3. It would permit the Treasury Department to contribute a notable feature to the coming celebration.

Present-day numismatists who specialize in Standing Liberty quarters (minted 1916–1930) might not agree with purpose number one above! However, that was the view at the time, and the design was discontinued.

Charles Moore, chairman of the Commission of Fine Arts, wrote to the chairman of the House Committee on Coinage, Weights, and Measures on February 12, 1931, to protest the switch of denominations, stating that his commission plus the George Washington Bicentennial Medal Committee each preferred the half dollar. Moreover, the medal committee had already chosen a design for its medal, and this could just as well be used on a coin also. This had been done by Laura Gardin Fraser, with whom the medal committee had a contract. It seemed natural that she would create a coin to match.

Ignoring the Commission of Fine Arts, on March 4, 1931, Congress authorized a quarter dollar, following the memorandum quoted above. Chairman Moore of the commission would not remain silent, and a letter written on April 21, 1931, by David E. Finley (Treasury Department point person for this situation) for Secretary Mellon's signature, pointed out that the Treasury Department was not a party to any program or any agreements made by the Medal Committee or the Commission of Fine Arts. While the Treasury desired to cooperate, it alone was in charge of the final decision.

A New Competition

To reflect the change of denomination, the Treasury Department decided that a new competition was in order. Mary M. O'Reilly, assistant director of the Mint (a post she had held since 1923), courteously contacted Chairman Moore of the Commission of Fine Arts to ask for recommendations. Moore protested that a competition had already been held, and that another was not necessary. The half dollar designs could be used for quarters just as well, with some changes in the lettering. He was overridden by Secretary Mellon. By June 16, 1931, mimeographed invitations were sent out. The second competition attracted more than 100 entries by 98 artists, a few of whom submitted more than one design, as they were allowed to do.

About the Commission of Fine Arts

The Commission of Fine Arts, established by Congress on May 17, 1910, had its offices in the Department of the Interior Building in Washington. Members in 1931 included Chairman Charles Moore, Ferruccio Vitale, Benjamin Morris, Adolph A. Weinman, Ezra Winter, John L. Mauran, John W. Cross, and Egerton Swartwout.

An unadopted entry in the 1932 competition, by Thomas Cremona. The obverse photo is of a modern medal made from the Cremona design by the Patrick Mint. The reverse photo is of the original Cremona design. (Jesse Patrick photographs)

The commission, formed of recognized people in the arts and architecture, had been involved in earlier designs, as in the case of the commemoratives for the Panama-Pacific International Exposition in 1915. It was not easy for the commission, due to the extreme resentment that Chief Engraver Charles E. Barber had toward outside artists, including those recommended by the commission. He had assumed that it was his right to design them all. The commission also held design competitions for various national medals, buildings, and federally controlled open spaces.

A decade before the Washington-quarter era, on July 28, 1921, President Warren G. Harding had issued an executive order assigning to the commission the right to pass on all coinage designs. It was not to have a veto power, but still the influence was hoped to be very great for the final design. This action would come to the fore in the design-selection process for the 1932 Washington quarter.

Outside the circle of numismatic historians, the Commission of Fine Arts is little understood today. Through the years, the group has acted as advisers on designs, including the original as well as the state-reverse Washington quarters, but quite often its recommendations were ignored. Some writers (including those on the topic of the Washington quarter), seemingly unaware of the purely advisory nature of the commission, have viewed the nonacceptance of commission guidelines as a travesty or even a minor crime. For a long time, like it or not, the secretary of the Treasury has had the final say in most instances. A pleasing exception is found in the state-quarter program, in which the governor of each state made the choice; but ultimately that decision was approved by the secretary of the Treasury.

The Commission and the Quarter Design

Commission members selected number 56, a model by Laura Gardin Fraser, but noted that it would need some refinement. On November 2, 1931, Secretary of the Treasury Andrew W. Mellon reviewed the submissions, including the commission's favorite, but selected a different model, number 84. The commission asked Mellon whether Fraser could restudy her design and perhaps improve it to the secretary's liking. His response was that if this opportunity were given to one contest entrant, it should be given to all. On November 4, Mellon sent the commission photographs of the models he preferred.

On the same day, Chairman Moore responded, reiterating the strong preference for model number 56 based on specific criteria set by the Commission of Fine Arts and with guidance from renowned American sculptor Adolph Weinman. Mellon again disagreed and advised Chairman Moore accordingly. On November 10, the commission, reluctant to give up on the matter, advised Mellon that its members had reviewed Mellon's further ideas, but they still preferred model number 56.

Reduced illustration of an original plaster model by Laura Gardin Fraser for an unadopted reverse of the 1932 quarter, marked on the back, "Oct. 10, 1931." Diameter 10-3/4 inches. (Richard Jewell photograph)

The Fraser Choice

Accommodatingly, the Treasury sent a letter to Laura Gardin Fraser on November 12, 1931, noting the aspects of her design that did not conform to the requirements for the new coin and inviting her to "submit a restudy of your design, if you so desire."

In her November 14 reply, Fraser readily agreed to comply with the request and set out how she planned to proceed, including a visit to the Treasury to work out the remaining ambiguities. The correspondence between Fraser and Treasury officials continued until her new models were submitted in January 1932.

Coming to a Conclusion

Commission Chairman Moore doggedly pursued his advocacy of model number 56, and on January 20, 1932, wrote a three-page letter to Secretary Mellon, repeating much of what had been sent before, plus expanded praise of model number 56. Then, the matter of Mellon's own favorite (no. 84) was taken up:

> The Commission, however, found in a design [no. 84] which called for detailed examination a lack of simplicity and vigor in the head, and an artistically unfortunate and also an unnatural arrangement of the hair which became conspicuous in the reduced size representing the actual coin. The reverse was pictorial rather than medallic in character. For these reasons the Commission felt that the design lacked those very elements of universality and permanence which the quarter dollar should embody.
>
> The Commission also considered a suggestion that the Saint-Gaudens eagle on the twenty-dollar gold piece be used for the reverse. They considered that to use a design that had been used on another coin would be unfortunate and sure to provoke criticism.[3] Moreover, the eagle as it now appears on the coin has lost that essential quality which Saint-Gaudens gave to it. In reducing the relief vigor has been lost. Now the eagle has the quality of an engraving; it has become a picture instead of an emblem.

Commission wishes notwithstanding, Secretary Mellon persisted with his choice of number 84. Mellon left office on February 12, 1932, to take up an appointment as ambassador to Great Britain.

His successor was Ogden L. Mills, who served as secretary of the Treasury from February 12, 1932, until March 3, 1933.

On March 2, 1932, Secretary Mills had a meeting with O'Reilly in which he was briefed on the whole matter of the new quarter, former secretary Mellon's views, the correspondence with the Commission of Fine Arts, and other documents. David E. Finley, who had worked with and advised Mellon on the project, continued to advise Mills.

On March 8, the Treasury sent John Flanagan, creator of design number 84, a letter requesting minor model alterations on his portrait of Washington. The same letter informed him confidentially that while the final decision had not been made, the secretary of the Treasury preferred Flanagan's design.

Chairman Moore, who was becoming a nuisance to the Treasury by this time, sought to have Mills change the selection to the Fraser design. The matter was ended by a letter from Mills, dated April 11, 1932, in which he noted that while Chairman Moore's concerns prompted him to request changes from the artist, he would adhere to Mellon's decision. He went on to say that "the duty of making the selection falls upon the secretary of the Treasury and not upon the Commission of Fine Arts, the function of that body being purely advisory."

The official choice was made, and on April 16, the name of competition winner John Flanagan was publicly disclosed. John Sinnock, chief engraver at the Mint, prepared the final models needed for the process of creating working dies.

On August 20, Martin, acting superintendent under Superintendent Freas Styer of the Philadelphia Mint, sent this official description of the design to the director of the Mint:

Quarter Dollar

OBV: Portrait head of Washington to left; above, around the border LIBERTY; below the bust, around the border, 1932; in left field, IN GOD WE / TRUST.

REV: Eagle with wings spread, standing on a bundle of arrows; above around the border, UNITED STATES OF AMERICA and within this, E PLURIBUS / UNUM below around the border QUARTER DOLLAR; in lower field, two sprays of olive.

Laura Gardin Fraser

In recent generations many comments have reached print to the effect that Laura Gardin Fraser's work was rejected by Mellon because the artist was a *woman*. That concept is difficult to reconcile, inasmuch as during Mellon's tenure as secretary of the Treasury, several fine legal-tender commemorative coins were created by women, including Fraser. Moreover, no correspondence from the Treasury or other contemporary source, nor any published articles of the time, corroborate this theory. It seems to belong in the category of modern numismatic fiction.

The talent of Fraser is unquestioned. With her husband, James Earle Fraser (best known for the 1913 Indian Head or Buffalo nickel and for his sculpture *The End of the Trail*), she created many memorable works, including the 1926 Oregon Trail Memorial half dollar, which years later the members of the Society for United States Commemorative Coins voted as being the most beautiful in that series. On her own, Laura Gardin Fraser designed other coins and medals, including the 1922 Grant commemorative half dollar and gold dollar.

In 1999 the Fraser designs for the 1932 quarter dollar were adapted by Mint sculptor-engraver William C. Cousins to create a commemorative $5 gold half eagle. In 2022, exclusively for the duration of the American Women quarters program, Fraser's bust of Washington supplanted the Flanagan bust; the coins thus honor exceptional American women on both the obverse and the multiple reverses.

JOHN F. FLANAGAN

Flanagan, Medalist

John F. Flanagan (1865–1952), a sculptor and medalist born in Newark, New Jersey, created the winning design for the 1932 Washington quarter. Although the artist seems to have been well regarded in his own time, modern scholars have been less kind. Part of this has been due to a curious circumstance: he has been confused with another sculptor, John Bernard Flannagan (1895–1942), a ne'er-do-well whose art is less than memorable, who had a life of self-inflicted travails, and who died a suicide.[4]

John F. Flanagan was a studio assistant to sculptor Augustus Saint-Gaudens from 1885 to 1890. Flanagan learned from the master the techniques of creating human figures in plaster, metal, and stone. In particular, he worked on the Saint-Gaudens statue of Lincoln that now stands in Lincoln Park, Chicago.

For the World's Columbian Exposition, opened to the public in Chicago in 1893, Flanagan assisted Frederick MacMonnies in the creation of the Columbia Fountain. Alas for MacMonnies, he never created a commemorative or circulating coin. Thus, his name is not familiar in popular numismatics today. However, MacMonnies is well remembered by medal specialists. Importantly, he considered John F. Flanagan to be "the leading medalist of America."[5] In the 1890s, Flanagan lived in Europe and spent most of his time there. In Paris, he became internationally known for his relief work. In 1902 he settled in New York City, where he remained for the rest of his career.

In 1904, at the Louisiana Purchase Exposition, several of Flanagan's works were on display. Working in his New York City studio, Flanagan created many highly acclaimed medals and plaques, including the official award medal for the Panama-Pacific International Exposition. To reduce certain of his models he employed the Janvier portrait lathe, which was owned by the Deitsch brothers, New York City medalists and badge manufacturers, and was considered to be the latest in technology at the time.[6] By use of this pantograph-type machine, an original model in plaster or hardened clay, or a galvano impression of such a model, of large size, could be reduced to create a smaller medal, plaque, or other work of art. At the time, the Philadelphia Mint was making do with a Hill portrait lathe purchased in 1866 and put into service on May 2, 1867. It would be 1906 before the Mint would install its own Janvier device, and 1918 before a Mint engraver would be able to use it properly (when John Sinnock, who later became chief engraver, employed it in making the Illinois Centennial commemorative half dollar).[7]

In 1905, Flanagan went to Cornish, New Hampshire, and modeled a portrait of Saint-Gaudens from life. The art remained unfinished at Saint-Gaudens's death in 1907. In 1920, he resumed work, now with a commission from New York University's Hall of Remembrance for American Artists.

Flanagan joined the American Numismatic Society on November 17, 1909, this being the year after it moved into its well-appointed building on Audubon Terrace on Broadway between West 155th and West 156th streets. This building was a meeting place for sculptors and artists interested in medals. Victor D. Brenner, creator of the Lincoln cent of 1909, had been a member of the society since 1894.

In 1909, Flanagan created a medal for the Massachusetts Horticultural Society, depicting a kneeling gardener with a greenhouse in the background—evocative of a fine estate. After the sinking of the *Titanic* on April 15, 1912, Congress voted that a gold medal be made to honor Captain Arthur Henry Rostron, whose crew helped rescue many survivors, and Flanagan won the design competition. In 1915, Flanagan was named as an associate member of the Academy of Design. In the same year, several of his sculptures were on view, by invitation, at the Tower of Jewels at the Panama-Pacific International Exposition in San Francisco. In 1920 he created a medal, *From the People of the United States to the City of Verdun*.[8]

John Flanagan's *Philosopher* statue on view at the 1915 Panama-Pacific International Exposition, San Francisco.

Flanagan in the 1930s and 1940s

In the 1920s and 1930s Flanagan's address was 1931 Broadway, New York City. By that time his list of accomplishments was lengthy. For the Library of Congress, he created a monumental clock. For the Knickerbocker Hotel, famous in its time, he sculpted a highly acclaimed marble relief of Aphrodite. A bronze portrait of Samuel Pierpont Langley, aviation pioneer, was made on commission for the Smithsonian Institution.[9] It seems that he was kept continually busy with a stream of public and private projects, at least through the heady economic times extending to the late 1920s. Included were dozens of portrait plaques of artists, notable Americans, and commissioned subjects. After that time, new work became scarce, although many buildings and civic projects authorized before 1930 were carried to completion.

In 1935, Congress authorized the minting of commemorative half dollars to observe the 150th anniversary of the founding of the city of Hudson, New York. Representative Philip A. Goodwin of New York wrote Charles Moore, who was still holding his post as chairman of the Commission of Fine Arts, to ask his advice in the selection of a medalist to create the design. Moore strongly recommended Laura Gardin Fraser, stating that she "stands in the very first rank of medalists," and that she had been involved with several earlier commemoratives. Other of Moore's recommendations included John Sinnock, Chester Beach, Francis H. Packer, and Paul Manship. It can be conjectured that Moore had animus toward Flanagan, perhaps left over from the events of 1931 and 1932. While this was going on, Frank Wise, mayor of Hudson, did his own investigations and concluded that John Flanagan would be the best choice. In the end, however, it was Chester Beach who got the nod.

In 1946, Flanagan resided at 1947 Broadway, New York City. His name was mentioned in connection with the design of two new commemoratives. However, the work for the Iowa Centennial and the Booker T. Washington half dollars went to others.

THE WASHINGTON QUARTER BECOMES A REALITY
The Final Design

Although the Flanagan portrait is usually described as a close copy of the Houdon bust, in fact it is not. The outline of the head is different, as is the treatment of the hair. Flanagan added a heavy roll of curled hair above the neck, artistic license that does not seem to have been widely commented upon at the time, except, perhaps, behind closed doors at the Commission of Fine Arts and in the earlier-quoted correspondence to the Treasury Department.[10] Laura Gardin Fraser's version is much closer to the original. Both the Flanagan and the Fraser portraits show a peruke of long hair tied by a ribbon, similar to that used on many earlier tokens, coins, and medals, whereas the hair on the Houdon bust lacks this feature. The heavy roll of curled hair was distinctive to Flanagan's interpretation, although some early adaptations of Houdon's bust do have a light roll of hair.

The head is well positioned on the new quarter. On the 1932 issue, the letters in the lower left obverse field are not bold (per numismatic terminology, they are in the *Light Motto* style). Early in 1934 (no quarters were made in 1933), after more Light Motto coins were made, the letters were strengthened to create the Heavy Motto, in effect from that time onward.

On the reverse the national bird is depicted as especially bold, with heavy wings opened and extending downward. The eagle is firmly perched on a bundle of arrows. Similar bold eagles in the art deco style were popular as architectural ornaments at the time. A wreath below completes the arc of the eagle's wings and adds a nice effect. Above the eagle's head is the motto E PLURIBUS / UNUM in small letters on two lines. UNITED STATES OF AMERICA is around the top border, and QUARTER DOLLAR is at the lower border.

Mintmarks, D or S, were placed below the wreath on silver issues struck at Denver and San Francisco, respectively, from 1932 to 1964. No mintmarks were used from 1965 to 1967, when the Treasury Department, under Mint Director Eva Adams, sought to "punish" numismatists for supposedly creating a nationwide coin shortage. Later issues, made of clad metal, have a D or S mintmark, later joined by P when the Philadelphia Mint used this letter. The location is on the obverse to the right of the ribbon at the lower part of Washington's hair.

At long last, the Mint had a new coin design that had *no* problems in striking! The heads of Washington and the eagle are both arranged with the relief spread over a large area, with no high-relief points. Accordingly, the vast majority of Washington quarters of the 1932-to-1998 era are well struck. This aspect, although not widely mentioned in numismatic texts, is a blessing for collectors.

Minting the Coins

Production commenced in the summer of 1932, but there was no need for more quarter dollars in commerce at that time. None had been made since 1930, when 5,632,000 of the Standing Liberty design were struck at the Philadelphia Mint and 1,556,000 at the San Francisco Mint.

Money was scarce in people's pockets in 1932, and the Mint had no plans for a generous production. By year's end, the Philadelphia Mint had struck 5,404,000 coins, Denver had made 436,800, and San Francisco had produced 408,000. On August 1, 1932, the quarters were released into circulation.

In September, *The Numismatist* printed a report on the new coin. The article reminded readers that it carried a new design to commemorate the 200th anniversary of Washington's birth, and was not a "commemorative" coin in numismatic terms. It pointed out that the Washington quarter corrects the problem of wear that had plagued the design it replaced, and that had earned the Standing Liberty motif "almost universal objection." In conclusion:

> All in all, it is an attractive coin. The bust of Washington stands out in strong relief in contrast to the reverse, which appears somewhat crowded, particularly the part above the eagle's head. But sculptors are better judges of such things than laymen.

THE CONTINUING STORY

The 1930s and Beyond

The supply of 1932 quarters was sufficient that no more were made in 1933. This was the very depth of the Depression. In 1934, coinage of the quarter resumed, with the Philadelphia, Denver, and San Francisco mints producing coins each year for the rest of the decade (except for San Francisco in 1938).

The coinage from each of the three mints continued through 1954, with the exception of San Francisco in 1949. The year 1954 marked the end of making quarter dollars for the San Francisco Mint; and, after coining cents and dimes in 1955, it was announced that the facility would discontinue operations as a mint and would serve only as an assay office and storage facility. From 1955 through 1964, quarters were made each year at the Philadelphia and Denver mints.

In 1936 the Philadelphia Mint offered Proof sets for sale; it was the first such coinage since 1916. Each contained a Lincoln cent, Buffalo nickel, Mercury dime, Washington quarter, and Liberty Walking half dollar. Sets were sold at $1.81 each, and single coins could also be ordered. In the first year, 3,837 Proof quarters were made, in comparison to 5,569 cents. Proof sets continued to be produced through and including 1942, then were discontinued due to the exigencies of World War II. In 1942 the mintage of Proof quarters was 21,123, compared to 32,600 cents.

During this period, quarters were also less popular than the other denominations with regard to collecting circulation strikes. The cent, nickel, and dime were regarded as inexpensive, and the higher-denomination Liberty Walking half dollar was admired for its artistry. Washington quarters fell betwixt and between.

Under the administration of President John F. Kennedy, Eva Adams was director of the Mint. As many (but not all) Mint directors have done, she visited an annual convention of the American Numismatic Association. In 1962 in Detroit she made a good impression and was given a warm welcome, and at the convention banquet she was honored with a one-of-a-kind gold convention medal from the ANA-CNA [Canadian Numismatic Association] and Medallic Arts Company. "When she finally gave her sincere 'Thank you,' all knew it was from a full heart and . . . all rejoiced with and for her."[11] No one predicted that these mutual good feelings would change for the worse.

The "Changing Dimes" of 1964

In 1964 the Kennedy half dollar was launched. The obverse, designed by Chief Engraver Gilroy Roberts (who soon resigned his position to take an executive post with the Franklin Mint), featured the portrait of the recently martyred president. The reverse was an adaptation of the Great Seal of the United States, by Frank Gasparro, who succeeded to the post of chief engraver after Roberts's departure.

The public went wild when the coins were released. Immediately, supplies given to banks had to be rationed, then they dried up entirely. Those fortunate to have bought quantities could sell them for twice face value or more. Demand was great in other parts of the world. In Europe the going rate was the equivalent of $5. By year's end, more than 400,000,000 had been minted—more than one each for every American citizen—yet no Kennedy halves were to be found in circulation.

At the ANA convention in Cleveland, Ohio, in the summer of 1964, Director Adams gave a talk with the pun title "These Changing Dimes." In that speech, Adams lamented the effect that the leading edge of the baby boom was having on the U.S. coin supply. She alluded to the impact John F. Kennedy's assassination had had, with the reaction to the half dollars minted in his honor. She told of cash-department layoffs at the Federal Reserve because coins were not flowing back to the banks in usual numbers. Adams announced that the Proof program had to be scrapped so all the Mint's efforts could be turned to producing coinage for circulation. With this speech, she began to hold the numismatic community responsible for the shortfall:

> I need not remind you that there are probably 43 billion coins in circulation now, or in your piggy banks or dresser drawers, or wherever they may be. Someday we just won't have a coin shortage; I think it will be very soon. And so I hope none of you are depending on making any tremendous profit on those vaults full of coins. I really don't think any of you here have them, and I hope the people who are doing it will stop.[12]

Increasingly, Director Adams and others in the government blamed coin collectors (numismatists, that is) for hoarding coins. In actuality, relatively few numismatists were interested in squirreling away quantities of current coins that were being produced in immense quantities. The culprits, if they should be called that, were everyday citizens who had learned of the shortages and were seeking to make some profit by buying whatever coins they could.

The Great Confusion of 1965–1967

In 1964, the price of silver was rising on international markets, and was seemingly headed to the point that it would cost more than face value to mint silver dimes, quarters, and half dollars (the higher denominations then being made). The Treasury Department made a sweeping change: beginning in 1965, silver coins would no longer be made, except for half dollars, which would have a sharply reduced silver content. Thus a tradition of minted silver coins that had started in 1794 came to an end. Later, some silver coins would be made for collectors and sold at a premium. In 1971 silver was dropped from the half dollars.

The substitute metal was a clad composition. The planchet was a metal sandwich with an outer layer of copper-nickel (75% copper and 25% nickel, the same alloy used for five-cent pieces) bonded to a core of 100% copper.

In 1965 the public was still agog about coins. Lincoln cents, Jefferson nickels, and all other denominations were being hoarded, especially the lower values. Cents were scarce at supermarkets and stores, and some advertised to pay a few cents' premium for every 100 coins brought to them. In the meantime, Kennedy half dollars continued to be minted, but all were hoarded by the public. For *years* afterward, despite mintages of hundreds of millions of coins, the Kennedy half dollars did not circulate. The quarter dollar became the highest-value circulating coin of the United States.

This was a dynamic change. In time, as new vending machines were developed, and when arcade machines (Pac Man, Donkey Kong, and the like) became a passion for the younger set, their slots took quarters. Half dollars remained out of circulation. To this day they are rarely seen in commerce.

In 1965, Mint Director Eva Adams continued to blame coin collectors for the coin shortage—an erroneous view that was loudly protested by the numismatic press. Numismatists did not cause the problem, the general public did, in combination with sluggishness in the Federal Reserve System's distribution process.

To punish coin collectors, Director Adams, backed by Congress, carried out the decree that Proof sets would no longer be made and that mintmarks (D for Denver) would be removed from coins. Moreover, the Silver Bullion Depository at West Point, on the grounds of the Military Academy (and later called the West Point Bullion Depository), was equipped with coining presses to turn out cents, but without mintmarks. The San Francisco Mint, now known as the San Francisco Assay Office, once again began to produce coins for circulation, its first since 1955 (when it had last made cents and dimes). Adams declared that no mintmark would be used. Included were *silver* quarters dated 1964 and without mintmark. The San Francisco Assay Office / Mint began in 1966 to produce Special Mint Sets (SMS)—quasi-Proofs—that were dated 1965. Special Mint Sets were also made in 1966 and 1967 with dates of those two years.

In 1965, Assistant Secretary of the Treasury Robert A. Wallace visited the ANA convention held in Houston. He gave a mixed message, including this:

> I would like to emphasize one basic point: the Treasury Department is for coin collectors. I won't say that you have not caused us any problems. When there is a coin shortage, any coins held back from commercial transactions cannot help but add to the tightness of our supplies. But in the case of coin collectors, these problems are peripheral even if there are 10 million collectors, and some estimates place the figure

this high. If each collector takes one of each coin from each mint this would shrink the supply of coins by 100 million pieces. With an estimated 65 billion coins in circulation this would represent less than two-tenths of one percent of the supply. Of course, 100 million coins is still a substantial number and this is one of the reasons that the Treasury sought and obtained authority to continue the 1964 date on all of our current coins.

Our basic problem last year was not the coin collector but the coin speculator who bought up coins by the roll and by the bag in the hopes of an increase in their value. If anyone thinks these coins will be valuable because they are rare, let me say that we have made over 10.5 billion of them and we are still going strong. Nor are the coins dated 1961, '62 and '63 particularly rare, there having been from almost three to almost four billion minted in each of those years. . . . We have pretty much put [speculators] out of business by our huge production programs and we hope to keep it that way.[13]

At a subsequent private luncheon with Assistant Secretary Wallace and Mint Director Eva Adams, the ANA board of governors passed a motion suggesting that coin collectors wait several months after new coins were released before adding them to their collections.

In 1966 the report of a joint Treasury–Federal Reserve Board committee expressed this under the heading "Hoarding": "The Treasury consider hiring an outside research group to develop and carry out a proposal for sampling coin dealers and collectors for the purpose of obtaining a representative indication of their holdings."[14]

Despite numerous pronouncements by Treasury officials to the contrary, the numismatic community felt that it was receiving the lion's share of the blame, while virtually nothing was being done to discourage everyday citizens from hoarding coins.

The topsy-turvy mintmarkless and date-mix situation lasted until 1968, when Denver coins got their mintmarks back. In the same year, the mintmark position changed to be on the obverse, at the lower right, opposite the end of Washington's wig. From 1968 onward, the figures in *Mint Reports* reflected where the coins were struck, and, generally, with the date on the coin matching the calendar date.[15]

A peculiar thing then happened with Mint Director Adams. Around 1967 or 1968 she "got religion," became active in the affairs of the ANA, and in time was elected to the board of governors, where she served from 1971 to 1975. To the great puzzlement of many members of the Numismatic Literary Guild (NLG), in 1974 she was given the group's highest honor, the Clemy Award, awarded in recognition of writing skill, a sense of humor, and dedication to numismatics and the NLG. However, no one was or is aware of anything she ever wrote of a numismatic nature—other than routine *Mint Reports*, with even these being written by staff.

In 1975, Adams sought election as ANA vice president, but was beaten by Grover Criswell. Criswell became president in the 1977 election. During his inaugural speech at the ANA convention banquet in August 1977, with ex-director Adams in attendance, Criswell excoriated the Treasury Department and Adams on their actions against and attitudes concerning coin collectors in the 1960s. Many on hand were uncomfortable with the remarks and felt that the forum was inappropriate.

Trying to soothe hurt feelings, at an open meeting with the ANA board held the next day, certain members present offered up a resolution that the board extend a formal apology for Criswell's remarks. In Criswell's opinion, however, he had simply spoken the truth, for indeed there had been a "war" against coin collectors. Those with memories extending back to 1964 and 1965 undoubtedly remembered when collectors were made scapegoats for the coin shortage. However, by 1977 that unpleasant situation had been forgotten by some. Many new ANA members did not even know of it, and relations with the Bureau of the Mint and the Treasury Department had improved greatly.

President Criswell stood by his remarks and called for each member of the board to vote by mail. The resolution died from lack of support. Obviously, the board agreed with what Criswell had said.[16]

The Quarter Remains Dominant

In the late 1960s the price of silver rose, and silver coins in circulation became worth more than face value. The public rushed to sell them to coin dealers, bullion brokers, and others, who sent them to refineries. By the early 1970s, no more were to be seen in commerce. In the meantime, half dollars old and new disappeared from circulation, and the quarter dollar remained established as the largest denomination in wide use.

In 1968, Proof sets were again made. This time they were produced by the San Francisco Assay Office, as it was now called (the term *Mint* was later restored), instead of by the Philadelphia Mint. The Proofs were struck on slow, knuckle-style presses, some of them dating back to the 19th century. Though old, they were very effective for the job. Each coin was struck twice in rapid eye-blink succession, to bring up the details fully. Each coin bore an S mintmark. From that time to the present day, Proof sets with quarters have been issued—a continuous run except for the year 1975.

The Bicentennial

To observe the Bicentennial of American Independence in 1976 the Treasury Department announced that three coin denominations—the quarter dollar, half dollar, and dollar—would have obverses of regular style, but dated 1776 • 1976 (commonly described in numismatic literature as *1776–1976*), combined with reverses of a commemorative nature.

The National Bicentennial Coin Design Competition was launched, and many professional artists entered. The winner for the quarter dollar was Jack L. Ahr, of Arlington Heights, Illinois, whose motif of a colonial drummer boy was considered by numismatists to be very attractive.

On Wednesday, April 24, 1974, the three winners were hosted at the White House by Anne L. Armstrong, counselor to President Gerald Ford; John W. Warner of the American Revolution Bicentennial Administration; and Mint Director Mary Brooks. Virginia Culver, president of the ANA, was also an invited guest, and signed up the three artists as ANA members. After the reception, Secretary of the Treasury William E. Simon presented each of the winners with a $5,000 check. (Brooks, the successor to Director Eva Adams, was from the outset interested in coin collectors.)

Two days later, the artists visited the Philadelphia Mint to meet with the staff of the Engraving Department and view the process of transforming a design to models, then through the Janvier transfer lathe, to smaller size to make hubs. Director Brooks stated that she expected that 1.4 billion quarters, 400 million half dollars, and 225 million dollars would be minted with the new motifs. Clad metal was to be used for coins struck at all three mints, plus silver for special pieces to be made only at San Francisco.

During the following year, 1975, the mints struck regular-design quarters from 1974 as well as many coins with the 1776–1976 date. Thus the mints in 1975 were *re*-striking and *pre*-striking, but were making no quarters dated 1975!

The Bicentennial coins were released in 1976. It was a slump time in the coin market, and sales of Proof coins and silver versions were so sluggish that the Mint had supplies on hand for sale for several years afterward.

Later Issues

The regular Washington quarter dollar design was resumed in 1977. From then until 1998, circulation-strike coinage took place at the Philadelphia and Denver mints, and Proofs were made at San Francisco. Under changing administrations at the Treasury Department and the Bureau of the Mint (later designated the U.S. Mint), relations with the coin-collecting community became warm and friendly, and the Eva Adams era of the mid-1960s was forgotten.

From 1992 through 1998, special silver Proofs were made at San Francisco, these in addition to regular clad Proofs of the same years. In 1999 the 50 State Quarters® Program was inaugurated. For the next 10 years, five states per year would be honored with a special reverse design on the quarter dollar. The order was the same as the sequence in which each acquired statehood, beginning with Delaware. The program was extended for one year to include six U.S. territories. Following this program, the America the Beautiful Program was created to honor a site of "national or historic significance" from each state, the District of Columbia, and five U.S. territories. The program may be extended in 2021 to honor an additional site from each area. Detailed information about the State and Territories quarters and the Crossing the Delaware quarter is given in chapter 9. Detailed information about the America the Beautiful and the Crossing the Delaware quarters is given in chapter 10; and about the American Women quarters in chapter 11.

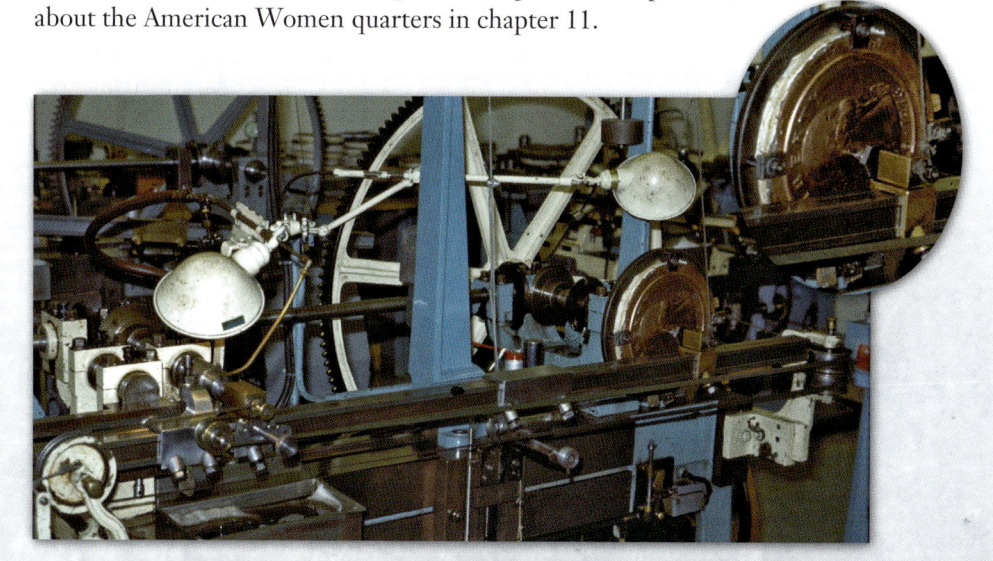

Janvier transfer or portrait lathe reducing the galvano with the 1776–1976 obverse for the bicentennial quarter, photographed at the Philadelphia Mint, June 15, 1974, by R.W. Julian with the permission of Mint Director Mary Brooks and Chief Engraver Frank Gasparro. Detail shows the galvano, an epoxy-coated model with its features in relief.

5

Die Changes and Technicalities

INTRODUCTION

Most collectors of Washington quarters aspire to obtain one of each different date and mintmark from the years 1932 to 1998, and one of each of the later state-quarter varieties. Beyond that, there are many different varieties that can be explored. Some are very significant, such as the 1950-D, D over S, overmintmark and the related 1950-S, S over D. Others are subtle, such as slight changes in the obverse or reverse hub.

Whether to collect these varieties is a matter of preference. Many use as a roadmap the issues listed in *A Guide Book of United States Coins* (popularly known as the *Red Book*), these being but a small fraction of the varieties listed in the *Cherrypickers' Guide to Rare Die Varieties*. An attractive aspect of the varieties not listed in the *Red Book* is that they can often be acquired for no more cost than regular examples of a given date and mintmark. Herbert P. Hicks's study, "The Washington Quarter Reverse: A Die-Variety Bonanza,"[1] *The Numismatist*, gives extensive descriptions of subvarieties, particularly for Variety C (to be discussed shortly). *Walter Breen's Complete Encyclopedia of U.S. and Colonial Coins* (1988) is important as well. James Wiles has issued three copiously illustrated books covering die varieties of certain years of Washington quarters, with more books on the way.

This chapter gives a chronological overview of many of the changes and developments in the Washington-quarter series. All coins are shown enlarged for visibility of details. For specific collecting information and listings as well as specific die varieties, see the entries under the different dates and mints in chapters 8 through 11.

DIE AND OTHER CHANGES, 1932–2001

1932: *Obverse:* All of the quarters of 1932 have IN GOD WE TRUST in faint or "Light Motto" letters. This was per John Flanagan's original design. *Reverse:* The Variety A (Breen nomenclature is *Type A*; Hicks nomenclature is *Variety I*) reverse is from an original design by John Flanagan. The relief is low, and the E and S in STATES nearly touch. The border between the field and the edges of the letters and motif is often indistinct. There is only one bold leaf to the left of the arrowheads, and the leaf above the A in DOLLAR is very weak and hardly visible. This reverse was used on circulation strikes from 1932 to 1958 and on Proofs of 1936. See comments under 1937.

A 1932 Washington quarter, first year of issue. All coins of this year are of the Light Motto style.

Generally, the issues from 1932 through 1935 have wider rims, which better "frame" the design, than do later issues.

1934: *Obverse:* There were two obverse hub changes this year, the "Medium Motto" and the "Heavy Motto." The Medium Motto was used for just a short time in 1934, then for all coinage of 1935. The Heavy Motto was introduced in June 1934 and was used on 1934 and 1934-D coins, and in 1936. Later it became the standard. Light, Medium, and Heavy Motto varieties exist for 1934. Medium and Heavy Motto varieties exist for 1934-D.

Light Motto: The central peak of the W in WE is *lower* than the sides. The letters and field blend without strong differentiation of the letter edges. Used for 1932, 1932-D, 1932-S, and some 1934 coins.

Medium Motto: The central peak of the W in WE is *lower* than the sides. It has the same style as the Light Motto, but the letters are stronger and are not faded into the field. This was used for some 1934 and 1934-D coins and all 1935 coinage.

Heavy Motto: The central peak of the W in WE is *higher* than the sides, and the letters are heavier (thicker) than the those on the other 1934 varieties. This was used for some 1934 and 1934-D coins; then it became standard beginning in 1936.

Reverse: David W. Lange writes

A fact I've never seen mentioned in print and which may have escaped observation to this point is that the original reverse hub of 1932 was never used after that date. It featured a much higher border that shielded the reverse from the rapid wear typical of all later issues through the end of silver coin production. This distinction is very difficult to discern from the Uncirculated coins that most collectors seek, yet it becomes readily apparent when studying worn pieces. [The] 1932 quarters from all three mints wear quite evenly front and back, while silver issues 1934 and later will still show complete obverse borders long after the reverse border is worn deeply into the lettering. This is true even of the 1934 Light Motto quarters.[2]

1937: *Reverse:* Variety B (Breen Type B, Hicks Variety II) was introduced this year. The relief was strengthened by a lowering of the field. In this variety, the E and S in STATES appear distinctly separated. There are two bold leaves to the left of the arrowheads; the stronger leaf touches or nearly touches top of the A in DOLLAR. The leaf touches on some Proofs, and nearly touches on dies that were more extensively relapped. Stronger than on Variety A. Certain letters and the edges of feathers were retouched. This reverse was used on Proofs of 1937 to 1964 and on circulation strikes from 1959 to 1964. Details on the Proofs are sharper than on circulation strikes.

Herbert Hicks writes:

> High-relief dies are not desirable for business strikes because of production problems, including greatly shortened die life, difficulty in bringing up the full relief, and stacking problems.
>
> However, these same dies, with their ability to withstand repeated polishing, would outlast low-relief dies on the Proof line and produce a much more attractive coin. Extra pressure and double striking brought up full relief with all the design showing. Thus began the modern Mint system of using different artwork for Proof and circulation strikes.[3]

1938: *Obverse:* The profile details of Washington were strengthened slightly.

1944: *Obverse:* The profile details of Washington were strengthened slightly and minor changes were made in the peruke and ribbon. The initials of the designer, JF, became slightly distorted.

1945: *Obverse:* The initials JF were corrected.

1964: *Reverse:* Variety C (Breen Type C, Hicks Variety III) was introduced this year. It is similar to Variety A (see 1932) in general relief. Leaf details include the centers for the first time. The leaf above the A in DOLLAR is short and does not touch the letter. This variety was probably made in anticipation of the clad coinage that commenced in 1965, but it is known on some of the silver 1964-D coins.

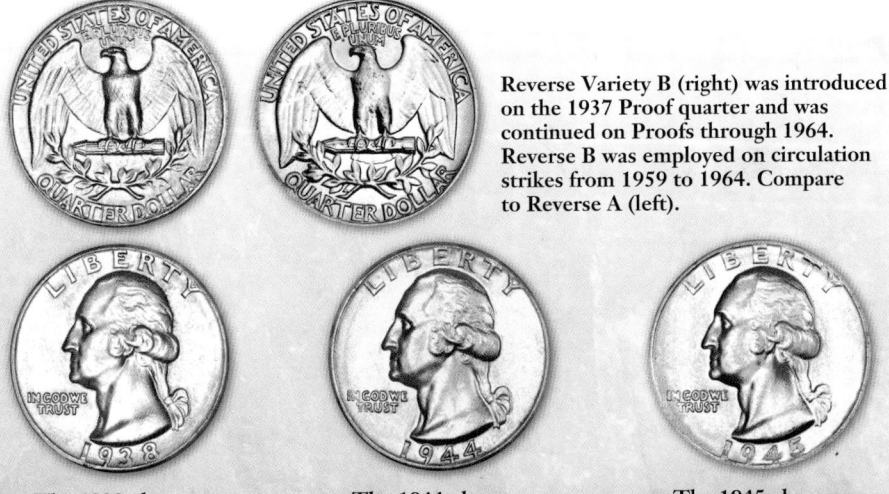

Reverse Variety B (right) was introduced on the 1937 Proof quarter and was continued on Proofs through 1964. Reverse B was employed on circulation strikes from 1959 to 1964. Compare to Reverse A (left).

The 1938 obverse.

The 1944 obverse.

The 1945 obverse.

Herbert Hicks describes the difference:

> The new reverse variety . . . was the clearest design to date, although it is the lowest in relief. You can think of it as a two-dimensional drawing rather than a three-dimensional sculpture. Leaf centers have detail for the first time. These quarters also have stacking problems: they will teeter when two obverses meet.[4]

1965–1967: *Obverse:* In 1965, a new obverse hub was introduced for the clad coinage. The relief was slightly lower than on the earlier silver issues. ***Reverse:*** Variety C (described under 1964) was introduced for regular coinage.

In the three years from 1965 to 1967, the Mint did not issue Proofs for collectors, but instead made Special Mint Sets containing coins that were struck from lightly polished dies, but were not deeply mirrored.

1974: *Obverse:* In 1974, a new obverse hub was introduced, with a slight lowering of the relief and sharpening of some details.

1976: *Obverse:* Another new obverse hub was introduced, with a slight lowering of the relief and sharpening of some details. The double date 1776 • 1976 was used for this year. ***Reverse:*** The Bicentennial motif of a colonial drummer boy was used only this year.

1977: *Obverse:* In 1976, Mint engraver Matthew Peloso reworked certain details of the quarter dollar obverse, including a lowering of the relief. ***Reverse:*** The reverse relief was lowered and the lettering and feathers were sharpened. The revised dies were first used in 1977.

1982–1983: *Obverse:* The diameter of the design elements (but not of the coin itself) was reduced slightly, as elements on the periphery had "migrated" closer to the rim. The details were sharpened slightly.

It had been the practice of the Mint to sell *Mint Sets*, or sets of circulation-strike coins, each year, so collectors could maintain their collections. The Mint was busy starting its new program of

Reverse C was first used for circulation on certain 1964-D quarters.

Obverse of the 1965 quarter. Close-up shows motto style used from 1965 onward, somewhat similar to the Medium Motto of 1934. Note that the center of the W in WE is lower than the sides.

The 1974 obverse.

The 1776–1976 Bicentennial quarter (a 1976-S silver coin is illustrated).

In 1977 the obverse and reverse were altered slightly, a style continued until 1983.

commemorative coins, beginning with the Washington half dollar in 1982 and expanding to include Olympic Games coins in 1983. In 1982 and 1983, no Mint Sets were sold. Accordingly, high-grade Mint State coins of these two years are scarcer than are those of the surrounding years.

1987: *Obverse:* The hairline and curls were sharpened.

1988: *Obverse:* The hairline and curls were sharpened further.

1992: *Obverse:* The hairline and curls were sharpened even further. The border of the coin was widened slightly, and the relief was slightly reduced.

1993: *Reverse:* The relief of the reverse was lowered and the lettering and feathers were sharpened.

1994–1998: *Obverse:* The relief was further lowered ever so slightly and at intervals during the next several years, and the hairline and curls were sharpened.

1999: Mint sculptor-engraver William Cousins modified the obverse design to meet the production demands of the State quarters program. The relief is noticeably flatter and the hair details are greatly sharpened. The date was moved to the reverse, and all of the legends and mottoes were relocated in some fashion to leave most of the reverse open for the new design elements.

2000: At the Philadelphia Mint, an undated obverse die for the Washington state-quarter coinage was combined with an undated Sacagawea "golden dollar" flying-eagle reverse. Examples were

The 1983 obverse.

The 1987 obverse.

The 1988 obverse.

The 1992 obverse.

The 1993 reverse.

By the time of the 1994 obverse modification, the hair details were quite different from those on the first quarter dollars of 1932.

The 1999 obverse.

The 2010 obverse.

The 2021 obverse.

The 2022 obverse.

struck on a dollar press using regular manganese-brass clad-dollar planchets. Likely, they were struck in April or May 2000. It may have been that some strikings were from an accidental muling (putting an incorrect front and back together) of two unrelated dies. At least three die pairs were involved.

The first specimen that came to light is believed to have been from an unintentional error at the Mint. It was discovered in late May of 2000 by Frank Wallis, who found it in a roll of Sacagawea dollars he bought for face value from the First National Bank & Trust in Mountain Home, Arkansas. This coin was auctioned in 2001 by Bowers & Merena for $29,900. Another was found in a roll in September 2000 by Greg Senske, a Missouri collector. Interest increased, and transactions as high as $70,000 took place later.

Some of the mulings, but not the two mentioned above, were made secretly by Mint employees, and two coining-press operators were arrested. One pleaded guilty to a federal charge, and the other became a fugitive. The charge was not for minting the coins, as this was not proved, but for selling such coins for their private profit. The sentence for the man with the guilty plea was restitution of $5,000—the price he had received for a coin—and five years' probation.

A "mule" struck on a Sacagawea planchett bearing a Washington quarter dollar obverse and a Sacagawea reverse.

Between 11 and 14 confirmed examples exist. At least eight of these are owned by Tommy Bolack, a New Mexico collector. For a time, according to Paul Gilkes of *Coin World*, more examples were held in private hands, but were kept secret for fear they would be confiscated. According to precedent the error coins that were released accidentally through normal channels, such as the discovery coin from Arkansas, are legal to own, but those purposely created by Mint employees and sold for a personal profit are another story. The Treasury Department has issued no specific policy on the subject.[5]

2001: New Schuler presses were brought into service. These, plus the use of riddler machines (circular sieves), dramatically reduced the number of misstruck and other error coins that left the mints. The 2001 Rhode Island quarter is the first for which relatively few off-center strikes and other oddities are known.

2010: For the America the Beautiful quarters program, the Mint produced "a restored version of the 1932 portrait of George Washington, including subtle details and the beauty of the original model." The other design elements were unchanged from the State and the D.C. and Territories programs.

2021: For the one-year Crossing the Delaware quarter issues, the obverse reverted "to the same design containing an image of President Washington" that preceded the State quarters, including the original placement of date, legends, and mottoes.

2022: For the first time since 1932, John Flanagan's bust of Washington was removed from the quarter. For the duration of the American Women quarters program (lasting through 2025), the obverse features the right-facing bust designed by Laura Gardin Fraser for the quarter dollar design competition in 1930.

6

The Minting of Washington Quarters

DIE-MAKING: FROM MODEL TO WORKING DIE

After John F. Flanagan made plaster models of the obverse and reverse of the Washington quarter in 1932, these were sent to the Philadelphia Mint. All of the features were in raised relief. The models, each probably about 10 inches or so in diameter, were used by Chief Engraver James R. Sinnock to make new models and finesse the details.

The finished plaster models were lightly coated with oil; plaster was then poured on top of them, creating versions with the features incuse, or intaglio. From these were made copper electrotypes called *galvanos*, with the features in relief once again.

The Master Hub (Positive, Features in Relief)

The finished galvanos were examined by Sinnock, and any roughness was smoothed or cut away. The metal model was then placed in a Janvier transfer lathe (a.k.a. portrait lathe); as the model slowly rotated, its surface topography was traced by a stylus that was connected with a pantograph arm to a tiny cutting head. The cutting head worked on a soft steel master hub that rotated in synchrony with the model, creating a small version of the model known as a *master hub*. The process usually took more than a day, sometimes two. All of the features on the master hub were raised, as on the larger version.

The small version in soft steel was examined and, if necessary, touched up. It was then heated to a high, sustained temperature, after which it was suddenly quenched to harden the crystalline structure. After being examined again and finessed to remove any further scaling or debris, the master hub, with most (but not all) of the design elements, was now finished.

The Master Die (Negative, Features Incuse)

The next step was to press the master hub into a soft shank of steel to create the master die, with the features incuse, or recessed. When this soft master die was completed, the engraver punched the numerals of the date into the surface (if the die was for an obverse). In the first year of the Washington quarter these were the digits 1, 9, 3, and 2. The undated master hub was then placed in storage for use in later years.

The Working Hub (Positive, Features in Relief)

In a repeat of the transfer process, the working hub was created in soft steel—in relief, a copy of the finished coin with all details. The obverse working hub was complete with the date. After hardening, the working hub was used to make as many working dies as needed.

The Working Die (Negative, Features Incuse)

Going through the process again, the hardened working hub was impressed into many working dies of soft steel, one at a time. Often, two or more blows were required to bring up the detail. If the later blow was slightly off register, a *doubled die* was created—with doubled outlines to certain of the features. This happened only occasionally.

Unhardened working dies for the Denver and San Francisco mints were taken to the Engraving Department of the Philadelphia Mint, where a staff member punched a D or S mintmark into each, using a punch about the size of a short pencil. D and S punches of various sizes were kept on hand. Sometimes different-size or style punches were used within a given year, creating varieties of interest to numismatists. It required two or more taps of a small hammer to impress the mintmark into a reverse die. If the punch slipped before the second tap, a *repunched mintmark* was created. This happened often in the Washington quarter series. Beginning in 1968, the mintmarks, now including a P for Philadelphia, were punched into the obverse die at the lower right. There was no jig to position the mintmark punch, although a sketch on the wall outlined the general area in which the mintmark was to be placed on each die. The punch was set visually by a trained engraver.

After this, the working dies for use at the Philadelphia Mint were hardened by the usual process, and then dressed by grinding or lapping of the field. For Proof coins, such dies were given a high polish. The dies were then ready for coining use. Unhardened dies were shipped to Denver and San Francisco. At the branch mints the hardening and finishing process took place in the machine shop.

Each die was heated to a cherry red and maintained for a time at that temperature, after which it was plunged into cold water or oil to harden it. After the quenching, the surface of the die was apt to have some scale or irregularities, so it was finished by grinding or basining (grinding with a circular motion). This resulted in tiny lines in the die, called *striae*. On Washington quarters these tiny, raised, parallel striae are most often seen in the open areas of the obverse field. For Proofs, the polishing process by basining removed the striae.

Changes in the process were made in the 1990s. The P, D, and S mintmarks were added to the master die. This ended the era of repunched mintmarks and other variations. A die shop was opened at the Denver Mint to share some of the work done formerly at Philadelphia.

The Coining Process

Preparing the Planchet

Quarter dollars as well as other coins are struck on planchets—circular discs of slightly smaller diameter than the finished coins. To make planchets for quarters, Mint workers first cut blanks out of long strips of silver alloy (90% silver and 10% copper), much as a cookie cutter would punch out pieces of dough. After 1964, the quarters were made of a clad composition, in which the strip has a solid copper core with a layer of copper-nickel (75%-25%, respectively) bonded to each side. In time, the process whereby blanks were cut one at a time from single strips of alloy gave way to a more efficient system, in which wider strips and gang punches are used to stamp out multiple blanks in one blow. This is a very noisy operation, as is coining, and visitors to the Mint must wear ear coverings.

In the early years of the Washington quarter, silver strips were made at the various mints from metal refined on the premises. Today, strips for the clad quarters are purchased in large coils from outside contractors.

Each individual blank must be of a specified diameter and with a weight of 96.45 grains, with a maximum 1.5-grain variation allowed (or, put another way, with a variation of plus or minus about 1.5%, totaling 3% overall).

After the circular blank is ready, it is put into a milling or upsetting machine and run at high speed between a roller and an edge, in an area in which the diameter decreases slightly, forcing the metal up on ridges on both sides of the coin. This process creates what is called a *planchet*. The resultant planchet is blank on both sides but has raised rims.

Although processes have varied, in the past it has been customary to anneal the planchets by heating, followed by slow cooling, to soften the metal. Afterward they are cleaned in a soapy or acidic mixture (dilute sulphuric acid), rinsed, and then dried by tumbling in sawdust or corncobs or by exposure to currents of air. Once dry, the planchets are ready for coining. Tumbling around in a cleaning machine imparts countless nicks and marks to both sides. It is hoped that these will be obliterated during the squeezing and compression of the planchet in the coining press. In practice, many times the dies did not come completely together in the coining press, and the deepest areas of the dies—representing the highest areas on the finished coins—were not completely struck, with the result that marks from the original planchets were still visible in these areas. On Washington quarters this is much more obvious on the clad coins from 1965 to date than on the earlier silver pieces, as silver metal flowed more readily into the die recesses.

Striking the Coins

The working dies are fitted to a coining press powered by an electric motor that is either fitted to the press, as with new equipment, or connected by shafts and pulleys, on older presses. Today's presses use gang dies and spew out coins at a rapid rate. Old-style presses, driven by connection to an electric motor, are still in use at the San Francisco Mint for the striking of Proofs. These use single pairs of dies.

An old-style press, used to make the early silver issues in the Washington series as well as Proofs today, is vertical with a more-or-less elliptical frame. An open area at the center holds the dies. The hammer (top) and anvil (bottom) dies can be removed at will when they become worn or damaged. The hammer die is fixed to a matrix that moves up and down as the flywheel on the press rotates and actuates a cam. This general type of press is called a *knuckle press*.

On a single die-pair press used years ago, the blank planchets were placed into a receptacle at the front, and mechanical fingers fed them one by one into a circular collar just above the anvil die. This collar, the size of a finished coin, was vertically reeded on the inside. After placing the blank, the fingers retracted automatically, and the hammer die came down, stamping the obverse and reverse of the coin and forcing the metal to the edge of the collar, the reeded pattern of which was impressed on the coin's edge. The finished coin, measuring 19/20" (or 24.3 mm) in diameter, was then forced from the collar and ejected by the mechanical fingers.

An old-style coining press.

At that point, the coin went down a slide at the back of the press and dropped into a little hopper or bin. Presses of this type were brought back into service and used during the coin shortage of the 1960s. Later, more-automated processes were developed. Proof coins are made with a slightly different process, which will be described later.

In recent times, a "riddler" machine—essentially a sieve with openings slightly larger than a quarter—has been used to check the finished coins. Oversized pieces will not fall through; thus many double-struck coins and certain other types of mint errors are caught. These errors are mutilated by being run through a press, creating so-called waffle coins.

Allowing for Variances

It was and still is the intention of the Philadelphia, Denver, and San Francisco mints to produce the largest number of quarter dollars in the least possible time and with the least possible effort. There was and is no consideration whatsoever to please the numismatists who might later collect such coins.

The sharpness of a finished Washington quarter depends on the technician who adjusts the press as well as on the weight of the planchet and how it is prepared. If the dies are fit precisely the right distance apart, and a planchet is of precisely the correct weight and has been annealed to the proper softness, a coin with every detail as sharp as on the original engraver's model will be the result. This represents the idea situation.

Bear in mind, however, that a 3% latitude in weight is permitted by law, and that problems will occur if an overweight planchet is introduced. If a too-heavy (though still legal) planchet is fed into the press, the excess metal will have nowhere to go into the dies and will be forced out the edge, creating a wire rim (called a *fin* in mint jargon) and wearing out the die in the process, or worse, cracking the die.

The obvious answer is to space the dies slightly farther apart than optimum, so that slightly overweight planchets can be accommodated and coined at high speed without attention. Under this arrangement, only overweight planchets will produce perfectly struck coins, while correct-weight and underweight planchets will create coins with areas of weakness. This fact has played havoc with most other 20th-century coins. Lincoln cents are often weak on Lincoln's shoulder; Indian Head or Buffalo nickels are nearly always without full details on the bison's head and shoulder; Jefferson nickels often lack full steps on Monticello; Mercury dimes sometimes are weak at the center of the reverse and also near the date; Standing Liberty quarters rarely have full details on the head and shield; Liberty Walking halves are usually lightly struck at the obverse center; and Franklin halves sometimes lack full bell lines.

The original Washington quarter design, used from 1932 to 1998, was in low relief at the high points. As a result, it is the rule, not the exception, that Washington quarters of this period show all of the few details intended. Any lightness in the striking process is compensated for by the lack of details on the original design. This was an ideal situation for the Mint—but one that, curiously, is not mentioned in any reports or other publicity I have seen. Not so with the state quarters, as certain features with fine details are significantly raised on the coin. Many 2004-D Michigan quarters have areas of light striking on the reverse. No sooner did the 2005 California quarters come out than it was noticed that, on some coins, one leg of John Muir was not fully struck-up. In addition, the hardness of improperly annealed planchets, poor metal flow, and design peculiarities can contribute to weakness.

Incidentally, the Roosevelt dime, minted since 1946, is similar to the Washington quarter in that its design permits some tolerance in the coining process, and still yields excellent coins. Similarly, the lack of detail on the portrait of Franklin on the 1948 to 1963 half dollar masks any lightness of striking.

Other Aspects of Quality

While it has been and still is a general rule that planchets should be bright and clean, sometimes defective planchets with stains, flakes, or the like have been used. In the nickel five-cent piece series, discolored planchets are common, especially for the 1950s and 1960s, but nearly all silver quarter-dollar planchets have been of high quality as to brightness. It is not unusual to see a mint-fresh clad metal quarter—1965 to date, including the state-reverse issues—with many nicks in the obverse field from the original planchet.

After the box receiving newly minted quarters at the back of the coining press is filled, it is taken by an attendant and dumped into a hopper and mixed with other coins. Afterward the coins, still mixed together, are run through the "riddler" or sieve, then mixed together again and taken to a mechanical counting machine. Next, they are put into cloth bags and tossed into a vault in bags heaped on the floor, later to be shipped away by truck. At no time, past or present, has any care been taken to prevent nicks and marks on planchets, nor has any effort been made to reduce damage during the storage, riddling, bagging, shipping, and delivery processes.

The result of this is that very few production-run quarter dollars ever emerged as Mint State–65 or higher quality when they finally reached the user. A banker viewing a bag of quarters might find few coins any nicer than MS-63 to MS-64 or so. As illogical as it might seem now, decades ago, few numismatists cared if a coin had numerous nicks. The vast majority of surviving Mint State examples of the two rarest regular varieties, the 1932-D and 1932-S, have nicks and marks, usually most prominent on the obverse.

Many of the later clad quarters, including state issues, that are certified in higher grades such as MS-66, 67, and even 68, are apt to have at least a few obvious marks, including (especially on the obverse) marks remaining from the original planchet. There seems to be some looseness in grading interpretations.

Producing Proof Quarters

Proof coins have been and are still being made in a different manner from the process used to make circulation strikes. The die-production steps are essentially the same, except that the face of each Proof from 1936 to date has been given a high degree of polish to create brilliant or mirror surfaces. Exceptions are certain early 1936 Proofs, which are not as mirrorlike as those made later in the same year.

A pair of dies was fitted into a hand-fed press of the old knuckle-action style located in the Medal Department of the Philadelphia Mint. A planchet was placed into the collar by an attendant in front of the press, the press actuated, and a coin struck. In some years, including in the present generation, the press struck each coin twice in quick succession to bring up all details sharply. The finished coin was then removed by hand and a new planchet inserted. These old presses, once used for high-speed regular coinage, are operated slowly when Proofs are struck.

In the early era of Washington quarters, planchets for Proof coins were always inspected (although sometimes not carefully) to be sure they did not have chips, flakes, discoloration, or damage. After annealing, they also went through a special cleaning process, after which they were dried.

Beginning in 1968, the making of Proofs was transferred to the San Francisco Mint. In addition, Special Mint Sets were made at the San Francisco Mint from 1965 through 1967; these bore no mintmark. At the San Francisco Mint in the 1970s, when I took a tour, camera in hand, the finished Proof coins of each denomination were carefully stacked on top of each other in small piles in a tray. Most Proofs made since 1968 have frosty or "cameo" designs set against deeply mirrored backgrounds. Cameo-style Proofs for certain earlier Washington quarters are very rare.

Today, the quality of Proof coins is superb. Nearly all can be graded PF-68 to PF-70 with cameo contrast. The packaging is very attractive as well.

The 1936 Proof quarter was the first Proof of this denomination struck for collectors since 1915, the last year of Proof Barber quarter coinage.

In 1968 the making of Proof coins was transferred to the San Francisco Mint. From that point onward, Proofs display the S mintmark on the obverse, as on this 1974-S.

Mints and the Distribution of Quarters

Quantities Minted

Quarter dollars cost less than face value to produce, and, accordingly, they have always been a source of profit for the Mint. The profit margin soared when silver was eliminated, beginning in 1964. The profit, called *seignorage*, has contributed heavily to the operating profits of the various mints and, accordingly, the production of such pieces has been highly encouraged. This was quite unlike the situation for silver and gold coins in the early days, when gold was of full intrinsic value, and for a long time (until 1873) silver was likewise, resulting in little if any profit for the Mint.

After the initial production of Washington quarters in 1932, no more were struck until 1934, as in this Depression era enough coins were already on hand. In fact, quantities of Standing Liberty quarters from the 1920s still were in bank vaults, awaiting distribution. As the economy pulled out of its slump in the late 1930s, demand for quarters increased. At the time, half dollars were the highest-denomination silver coins regularly used in circulation. Dollars were plentiful at banks, but circulated widely only in the Rocky Mountain district.

During World War II, mintages of all coins increased sharply. After the war, quantities remained high, but not at the levels of the early 1940s. By this time, quarters increasingly replaced half dollars in circulation, although the latter remained plentiful. It seemed more convenient to have a pocketful of quarters than of halves. In many ways, this was and is a coin of ideal size for handling.

The advent of the Kennedy halves in 1964 was the beginning of the end of the half dollar denomination. Later Kennedy halves were mostly hoarded, and even today they are hardly ever seen in commerce. I have not received one in change for several years. The rise in the price of silver in the late 1960s made half dollars profitable to melt down. The result was that, by the 1970s, there were very few halves in circulation.

The quarter dollar became the largest coin of the realm to see active use. When arcade machines, turnpike toll machines, and other devices became popular, they were fitted to take quarters. Today, the quarter remains secure as the highest-value coin normally seen, despite occasional challenges, such as the Eisenhower, Anthony, and "golden" dollars, none of which have ever been popular. The reasons for this are simple: paper dollars are also current. Eliminate the paper dollars and dollar coins will circulate. Further, most coin-operated machines will not accept dollar coins.

The Philadelphia Mint

By the time Washington quarters were first made, in 1932, the Philadelphia Mint had been relocated in the third facility to bear that name,

The third Philadelphia Mint in the early 20th century. Within its walls the Washington quarter designs were finalized and dies were made.

in a building first occupied in autumn 1901. Much new equipment had been installed, and operations, some of which had been conducted by steam power earlier, were now electrified. This structure remained in use until the fourth Philadelphia Mint was inaugurated in 1967.

During these transitions the Philadelphia Mint remained the center for creating designs and making dies. Later, in the 1990s, some die-making was assigned to the Denver Mint. The Engraving Department was and is headquartered in Philadelphia. The facility is staffed with talented sculptor-engravers, as they are known, but has lacked a chief engraver since Elizabeth Jones departed in 1992.

The Denver Mint

Construction of the Denver Mint began in 1904, and in 1906 it struck its first coins, these being in silver and gold. It was not until 1911 that the first cents were made there and not until 1912 that nickels were first struck. When Washington quarters were inaugurated in 1932, the Denver Mint coined an allotment, as it has ever since.

The Denver Mint, opened in 1906, has produced Washington quarters nearly continuously since 1932.

The facility was enlarged in 1937. Today, the same structure is in use, although with many improvements in technology. In recent years, limited die-making operations have been set up there, but they do not involve the design process.

The San Francisco Mint

The San Francisco Mint joined the other two mints in producing Washington quarters in 1932. Afterward it produced them nearly continuously. At that time, the facilities were located in the second building to bear that name—an impressive structure nicknamed the Granite Lady, in which operations had commenced in 1874. In 1937 a new facility, a modern fortress-like structure, was occupied on Duboce Street in the same city.

In 1955 the Treasury Department announced that the San Francisco Mint would close its coining operations forever, and designated it the San Francisco Assay Office. In that particular year, 1955-S Lincoln cents and Roosevelt dimes were made, but no Washington quarters, the last being the 1954-S. Later, the San Francisco Mint did resume coinage of some lower denominations, but not quarters, except for special silver-content and Proof coins sold at premiums to collectors and others. It also got back its Mint designation.

The second San Francisco Mint—nicknamed the Granite Lady—opened in 1874 and remained in use until 1937.

7

Secrets of Being a Smart Buyer

COLLECTING AND THE MARKETPLACE

In the Early Years

In 1932, there was little collector interest in Washington quarters. Economic times were difficult, and while the public saved many as souvenirs, they spent most of them once the novelty passed. A quarter could buy a meal in a typical restaurant, or furnish an evening's entertainment at a movie or vaudeville show.

Collecting coins by date and mintmark was not popular. M.L. Beistle of Shippensburg, Pennsylvania, had launched a series of coin album pages that had circular openings, faced on each side with cellulose acetate slides, but they were not yet widely popular. There is no recorded instance in which any collector or dealer set aside a quantity of coins for investment, although some dealers routinely added them to inventory. William Pukall was particularly active. Since about 1914 had he acquired multiple rolls of each date and mintmark in the quarter series.[1] Tatham Stamp & Coin Co., in Springfield, Massachusetts, also squirreled rolls away in the early period of Washington quarters.

The date-and-mintmark syndrome had yet to occur. In 1932, Standing Liberty quarters were not widely collected, either, and no one cared that, for example, the 1927-S had a very low mintage.

Changes of 1934 and 1935

In 1934, that all changed. Wayte Raymond, a leading New York City dealer, obtained a license to sell the Beistle album pages, which he did with great publicity. Raymond's first issue of the *Standard Catalogue* came out this year as well. Hobbies were a nationwide fad, and coin collecting caught on rapidly. A catalyst was the low-mintage 1931-S cent, affordable to just about everyone. In Neenah, Wisconsin, J.K. Post began selling "penny boards" made for him by Western Publishing Company of Racine. Later, Post's interest was bought by Western through a subsidiary, Whitman Coin Products—the precursor to today's Whitman Publishing, LLC, maker of the *Guide Book*.

While cents and nickels were the most popular series to collect, quarters soon developed a following. With an eye on the future, many dealers, collectors, and investors stashed away bank-wrapped rolls. However, these were saved in smaller quantities than were lower-value cents, nickels, and dimes. In autumn 1935 the great commemorative craze began with wild speculation in the 1935-D and S Daniel Boone Bicentennial half dollars with a small 1934 on the reverse; these coins had multiplied in value by year's end. The low-mintage Hudson Sesquicentennial and Old Spanish Trail halves of 1935, with mintages of 10,000 each, quickly sold out and rose sharply in value.

The *Numismatic Scrapbook* made its debut in 1935 under the brilliant editorship of Lee F. Hewitt, of Chicago. Hewitt was a collector and had a keen sense of what the public wanted. This magazine, written with human-interest items, fillers, and the like, quickly surpassed *The Numismatist*, the official magazine of the ANA, which was considered to be quite dull in comparison. (Today, the magazine known simply as *Numismatist* is a showcase of interesting articles and excellent graphics.)

When I first started dealing in rare coins as a teenager in 1953, the typical Washington quarter set owned by an advanced collector was housed in Raymond "National" album pages. All coins from 1932 to date were typically in Uncirculated grade, except for 1932-D and S, which were usually About Uncirculated (AU). The latter two grades were what people would have found in circulation when the coin-hobby boom started in a large way in 1934. Many of the large-mintage 1932-P coins were readily available from pieces kept as souvenirs. For some reason, the 1932-D slipped through the cracks. Few were saved, and from the outset this was considered the key to the series.

In addition, and even more popular in numismatics in 1953, were sets currently taken from circulation and housed in blue Whitman folders. Such coins usually included well-worn examples from the early 1930s, increasing in quality as the years progressed, with recent dates in Uncirculated and About Uncirculated grades. All could be found in circulation, although the 1932-D and S were scarce. In 1953, bank-wrapped rolls of quarters could be found in dealers' stocks with ease for all dates except 1932, 1932-D, 1932-S, 1934-D, and 1936-D. The 1932 Philadelphia coins were very common, but usually came in groups other than rolls.

Into the 1940s

The production of Washington quarters slipped into a routine in the 1930s—Philadelphia, Denver, and San Francisco minted coins each year, with the exception of 1938, when San Francisco did not participate. There was never an investment boom, promotion, or razzle-dazzle. The series was quietly collected by those who wanted to maintain continuing sets of current coinage. Dealers with good over-the-counter or mail-order retail trade stowed rolls away in quantity, and investors continued to do so as well.

In 1936, Proofs were struck for the first time since 1916. These were available singly as well as in sets. Quarters were the least popular of the five denominations included. Proofs were not minted after 1942, due to the war efforts.

In July 1939, Wayte Raymond offered quarters for sale in *The Numismatist*. A complete date run of Proof quarter dollars of the Liberty Seated and Barber issues from 1858 to 1915 cost $125, a complete set of Uncirculated Barber quarter dollars except the 1901-S cost $200, a complete set of Uncirculated Standing Liberty quarters cost $275, and a complete collection of Washington quarters from 1932 to date cost $12.50. Today, to replicate all of these sets in gem Mint State and Proof would cost more than $500,000, and the $12.50 set of Washington quarters from 1932 to 1939 would cost several tens of thousands of dollars, mainly because of the 1932-D.

In June 1944, the Bebee Stamp & Coin Company of Chicago offered a complete set of Uncirculated Washington quarters of 1932 through 1944 for $30. In the 1950s I met Aubrey and Adeline Bebee, who by that time had moved to Omaha. Later, I handled much of their personal collection and inventory in a series of auctions. It was the policy of the Bebees to maintain a minimum stock of 100 coins in popular series from the 1930s onward. For Washington quarters they did this, except for 1932-D, which they were always scrambling to find.

The 1950s and 1960s

In January 1953, M. Hirschhorn, of Long Island City, New York, listed Uncirculated 40-coin rolls of Washington quarters of many dates. Sample prices include these: 1935, $42.50; 1936-S, $60; 1937-D, $34; 1937-S, $90; and 1939-S, $50.

Prices continued to rise, but gradually. In June 1954, Chicago dealer Ruth Green offered an Uncirculated set of Washington quarters from 1932 to date for $140. The Greens and the earlier-mentioned Bebees were among the dealers who delivered good quality. Some others fudged a bit, and a 1932-D or S quarter that was offered as Uncirculated might upon examination be found to have friction. In all instances, even the top-rated dealers sold what they could find in rolls. Accordingly, the typical set would grade MS-63 to MS-65 by today's standards.

From the 1930s through the 1950s, coins were simply graded as Uncirculated, period. No numbers, no differentiation in price between bagmarked coins and those we would call gems today. Similarly, a Proof was simply a Proof. There were no grading standards or regulations, as a perusal of the advertisements in *The Numismatist* or the *Numismatic Scrapbook* from the 1940s would show. Often, buffed or chrome-plated circulation-strike quarters would be offered as "Proofs," with an enticing low price. Then as now, bottom-feeders and bargain hunters usually ended up with the poorest quality.

In 1950, Proofs were again struck at the Philadelphia Mint. Most quarters from this year are not as deeply mirrorlike as those of later times. Soon, Proof sets became very popular for investment purposes. Proof coins were no longer offered singly. Production increased, and the Mint placed restrictions on how many sets could be ordered. Prices rose dramatically, a set of 1936 Proof coins going from the $300 or so to a peak of $600 in 1956. Then the market crashed; there were many sellers, but few buyers. In time, interest revived, and by 1960 Proofs were popular once again.

From 1960 through 1964 there was a tremendous boom in the rare-coin market, ignited by the great excitement over the 1960 Small Date Lincoln cent (bags of $50 face value soared to $12,000 or more) and the launching of *Coin World*, the first weekly numismatic publication. The Teletype system connecting dealers added to the enthusiasm, as did the *Coin Dealer Newsletter*, first published in 1963.

The market then slumped, and it remained in the doldrums for several years. Not all series suffered—tokens, medals, colonials, and many other series remained as popular as ever, and even grew. Washington quarters were never prominent in any of these cycles, but they did go up and down with the tide.

LATER TIMES

The market became hot again in the early 1970s, this time spurred by the rising price of gold. In mid-decade it slumped. The 1976 bicentennial coincided with a slack period in investment interest. For this reason, special Proofs and silver strikings laid a big fat egg. The Mint had unsold quantities on hand for several years afterward.

In the late 1970s the rising price of silver and gold bullion carried rare-coin prices along with it, but the market slumped in early 1980. Again, Washington quarters were not darlings of the market or the subject of any special interest, but were carried along with the rest. In 1992, a new product—*silver* strikings of quarter dollars—was added to the Mint menu of things offered to collectors. Similar to current Proofs, these were struck at the San Francisco Mint.

In the meantime, commercial grading services took hold in the market, the first big player being the American Numismatic Association Certification Service (ANACS) launched in the late 1970s, with Tom DeLorey running the division. Coins were split-graded, with a separate number assigned to each side, based on the new *Official American Numismatic Association Grading Standards for United States Coins*. Photographs were taken, and the coin and a photograph certificate were returned to the submitter.

The venture was so profitable that the ANA had an embarrassment of riches—as a nonprofit organization. The money was put to good use, with an expansion of the headquarters building in Colorado Springs and other expenditures beneficial to the hobby. Later, ANACS was sold to Amos Press, parent company of *Coin World*, and still later to Anderson Press, which today is also the parent of Whitman Publishing.

During the early years of ANACS, numerical grading increased in popularity, with Uncirculated now called Mint State and divided into several categories, finally into 11, from MS-60 to 70 (see the expanded discussion under "Official ANA Grading Standards" later in this chapter).

In 1986, the Professional Coin Grading Service (PCGS) revolutionized commercial grading by promoting and popularizing sealed plastic holders. In 1987, the Numismatic Guaranty Corporation of America (NGC) went into the same business. Soon, ANACS played catch-up and adopted holders as well. Then, in 1999, the new state-reverse quarters changed everything. All of a sudden, and for the first time in their entire history, Washington quarters were hot! Now, finally, attention was being paid to the scarcer early dates. In addition, a great demand arose for any Washington quarter—common or rare—that was in an ultra-high grade certified by a leading service. This popularity extends to the present day.

Ways to Collect Washington Quarters
By Type

Since 1932 there have been many different types of quarters produced, the "many" being the result of all of the different state types since 1999. The basic types are these:

1932–1964: Eagle Reverse, struck in silver.

1965–1974; 1977–1998: Eagle Reverse, struck in clad metal.

1975–1976: Bicentennial coin, dated 1776–1976.

1999–2009: State, D.C., and Territories designs.

2010–2021: America the Beautiful designs.

2022: Crossing the Delaware design.

2022–2025: American Women designs.

Additional silver strikes were made for sale to collectors in 1975–1976 and from 1992 to date.

One of Each Variety

This is the most deluxe way to go. Such a collection includes one of each date and mintmark from 1932 to 1998, plus Proofs of the various issues. Special Mint Set coins of 1965 to 1967 are part of such a set. In addition, the silver-content quarters of 1992 to 1998 are included.

The modern series from 1999 to date are essential elements, including circulation strikes from the Philadelphia and Denver mints and Proofs in clad metal and silver from the San Francisco Mint.

In the aggregate, the preceding includes hundreds of different dates, mintmarks, and other variations, to which five new America the Beautiful quarters are being added each year through 2021, each with four varieties—or a total of 20 new coins annually.

A set such as the preceding is extensive and impressive.

State, D.C., Territories, America the Beautiful, Crossing the Delaware, and American Women Quarters

Quarters from these programs can be collected on their own, and many people do just that. Such a collection could focus on any one program or all of them, although the Crossing the Delaware issues by themselves would make for a very small collection! The circulation strikes can be collected from pocket change, or purchased inexpensively. Sets of the Philadelphia and Denver Mint issues are the most popular—anyone can collect them, and easily. The clad and silver Proofs made in San Francisco play to a different and more dedicated audience, defined in numbers by about 3 million or so of each clad issue and slightly less than a million of each silver issue.

In sharp contrast to the limited-edition Proofs and silver issues, the clad-metal circulation strikes seem to be popular with just about everybody. At the launch ceremony for the 2005 California quarter, Mint Director Henrietta Holsman Fore stated that 140 million citizens were collecting them—wow!

CHOOSING WHAT IS RIGHT FOR YOU

Factors Affecting Price

What at first glance seems to be a simple pursuit—obtaining one of each of the quarters you desire—is actually quite challenging and, in some aspects, complex. In the simpler world of, say, the 1950s, basic rarity determined price. In the Washington quarter series, the 1932-D and 1932-S were the most expensive, because they had the lowest mintages and, across all grades, were the hardest to find.

There was one—just one—notable exception: the high-mintage 1936-D was expensive, but only in Uncirculated condition. Worn examples were very common. Although saving bank-wrapped rolls was a popular thing to do from 1934 onward, the 1936-D was overlooked by most dealers and investors. It did not seem to be rare in 1936, and focus was on buying commemorative coins, the hot spot of the market at the time. A few years later, collectors and dealers looked around and, surprisingly, found that rolls of 1936-D quarters were very rare—while both 1936 Philadelphia and 1936-S could be bought by the dozens of rolls, simply by writing a check.

Thus was introduced the concept of *condition rarity* in the Washington series. A variety could be common and of low value in one grade, but could be rare and expensive in a high grade.

Today, Uncirculated and Proof grades are each divided into 11 categories. In Mint State, these range from MS-60 continuously through MS-70. A Washington quarter can be worth a dollar or two in MS-60, but be priced in the hundreds of dollars, or even far more, if approaching MS-70 when few others are certified at that level.

Today, basic rarity affects price. However, condition rarities sell for very high prices if they are in high grades. Condition rarity is the hot ticket for now. If someone were to mention on an Internet forum that he owned a 1932 Philadelphia quarter in the ultimate MS-70 grade there would be lots of buzz. A mention that he had an MS-64 1932-D would attract no attention at all! Personally, basic rarity appeals more to me—perhaps because that is the way I grew up in the hobby. I would rather have a whole collection of silver Washington quarters in MS-63 grade than a single common date that grades as the only known MS-69 or 70, this being valued at the same price. I am in the minority in my view. High-grade coins are where the action is at the moment, basic rarity not being as important.

Choices

One of the first things to do when contemplating purchases is to review market prices. This book gives an excellent overview, which can be supplemented by current listings in the weekly coin papers and elsewhere.

Evaluate the depth of your interest as well as your budget. For me—and I say again that I may not be typical in the current market—I see excellent value in obtaining all of the varieties in MS-65 and PF-65. By their very nature, the more recent Proofs will be graded higher than that, due to improved manufacturing and quality-control procedures.

This set will cost several tens of thousands of dollars, with the 1932-D being the key issue, and the 1932-S and 1936 Proof being expensive as well.

On second thought, I would probably critique my plan a bit more carefully, to see what a set in MS-64 and PF-64 would cost for the silver issues. The price would fall off sharply. Being a careful buyer by training and tradition, and having some patience in the matter, I am confident that by cherrypicking for quality, my 64 set would be as good as if not nicer than a collection put together quickly by simply buying holders labeled 65.

Other variations suggest themselves, such as buying all the scarcer early dates in MS-63 grades, and the other silver issues in MS-64 or 65. It doesn't cost much to have the clad issues from 1965 to date in MS-65. Such a set would be far less than $10,000.

There is also the aspect of how you want to spend your money. If I had $100,000 to spend, I would still go for an MS-65 and PF-65 set, and use the leftover amount to buy something else—a set of silver commemoratives, or a type set of gold, or whatever.

GRADING BY THE NUMBERS
Grading Washington Quarters

The grade of a Washington quarter or other coin reflects the amount of handling or wear it has received. Most collectors, dealers, and commercial grading services use the book published by Whitman: *Official American Numismatic Association Grading Standards for United States Coins*. Another fine guide is *Grading Coins by Photographs*, by Q. David Bowers. PCGS, NGC, and *Coin World* have each issued information-filled grading texts.

The ANA standards were codified in 1977 by Kenneth E. Bressett and Abe Kosoff, with input from many hobby leaders and the ANA board of governors.[2] I wrote the introductory material. Many collectors and professionals provided information and suggestions. The standards have been updated several times over the years, and the official publication has added color imagery to aid users.

OFFICIAL ANA GRADING STANDARDS
Washington Quarter Dollars, 1932 to Date

The following standards are from the *Official American Numismatic Association Grading Standards for United States Coins*, edited by Kenneth Bressett, with narrative by Q. David Bowers.

MINT STATE
Absolutely no trace of wear.

MS-70: A flawless coin exactly as it was minted, with no trace of wear or injury. Must have full mint luster and brilliance or light toning.

MS-67: Virtually flawless, but with very minor imperfections.

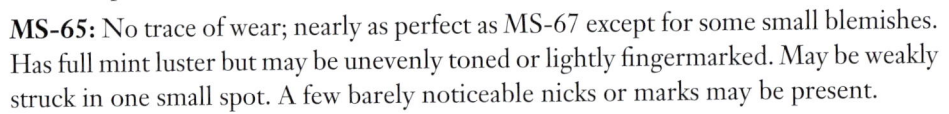

MS-65: No trace of wear; nearly as perfect as MS-67 except for some small blemishes. Has full mint luster but may be unevenly toned or lightly fingermarked. May be weakly struck in one small spot. A few barely noticeable nicks or marks may be present.

MS-63: A Mint State coin with attractive mint luster, but noticeable detracting contact marks or minor blemishes.

MS-60: A strictly Uncirculated coin with no trace of wear, but with blemishes more obvious than for MS-63. May lack full mint luster, and the surface may be dull, spotted, or heavily toned.

ABOUT UNCIRCULATED
Small trace of wear visible on highest points.

AU-58 *(Very Choice)*: Has some signs of abrasion: high points of cheek, hair in front and back of ear; tops of legs and details in breast feathers.

AU-55 *(Choice)*: *Obverse:* Only a trace of wear shows on highest points of hair in front and back of ear. *Reverse:* A trace of wear shows on highest spots of breast feathers. *Surface:* Nearly all of the mint luster is still present.

AU-50 *(Typical)*: *Obverse:* Traces of wear show on hair in front and in back of ear. *Reverse:* Traces of wear show on legs and breast feathers. *Surface:* Three-quarters of the mint luster is still present.

EXTREMELY FINE

Light wear on most of the highest points.

EF-45 *(Choice)*: *Obverse:* Slight wear shows on high points of hair around ear and along hairline up to crown. Hair lines are sharp and detailed. *Reverse:* High points of legs are lightly worn. Breast feathers are worn but clearly defined and fully separated. *Surface:* Half of the mint luster is still present.

EF-40

EF-40 *(Typical)*: *Obverse:* Wear shows on high points of hair around ear and at hairline up to crown. *Reverse:* High points of breast, legs, and claws are lightly worn, but all details are clearly defined and partially separated. *Surface:* Part of the mint luster is still present.

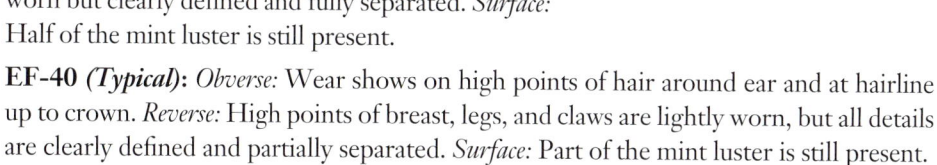

VERY FINE

Light to moderate even wear. All major features are sharp.

VF-30 *(Choice)*: *Obverse:* Wear spots show on hair at forehead and ear, cheek, and jaw. Hair lines are weak but have nearly full, visible details. *Reverse:* Wear shows on breast but some of the details are visible. All vertical wing feathers are plain. Most details in the leg are worn smooth.

VF-20

VF-20 *(Typical)*: *Obverse:* Three-quarters of the lines still show in hair. Cheek lightly worn but bold. Some hair details around ear are visible. *Reverse:* Wear shows on breast but a few feathers are visible. Legs are worn smooth. Most details on the wings are clear.

FINE

Moderate to considerable even wear. Entire design is clear and bold.

F-12: *Obverse:* Details show only at back of hair. Motto is weak but clearly visible. Part of cheek edge is worn away. *Reverse:* Feathers on breast and legs are worn smooth. Leaves show some detail. Parts of wings are nearly smooth.

F-12

VERY GOOD

Well worn. Design is clear but flat and lacking details.

VG-8: *Obverse:* Entire head is weak, and most details in hair are worn smooth. All letters and date are clear. Rim is complete. *Reverse:* About half of the wing feathers are visible. Breast and legs are only outlined. Leaves show very little detail. Rim is flat in spots but nearly complete.

GOOD

Heavily worn. Design and legend are visible but faint in spots.

G-4: *Obverse:* Hair is well worn with very little detail remaining. Half of motto is readable. LIBERTY and date are weak but visible. Rim merges with letters. *Reverse:* Eagle is worn nearly flat but is completely outlined. Leaves, breast, and legs are worn smooth. Legend is all visible but merges with rim.

ABOUT GOOD

Outlined design. Parts of date and legend are worn smooth.

AG-3: *Obverse:* Head is outlined with nearly all details worn away. Date is readable but worn. Traces of motto are visible. Legend merges into rim. *Reverse:* Entire design and lettering are partially worn away. Rim merges into legend.

NOTES

Keep the following issues in mind when analyzing and selecting coins:

> The obverse motto is always weak on coins of 1932 and early issues of 1934.
>
> The obverse rim is especially thick on coins of 1932 through 1935, protecting the obverse and often resulting in split grades (e.g., VG/AG) on well-worn examples.
>
> The reverse rim and lettering tend to be very weak, particularly on coins dated 1934-D, 1935-D, 1935-S, 1936-D, 1936-S, 1937-D, 1937-S (especially), 1938-S, 1939-D, 1940-D, 1940-S, 1941-S, 1943-S, and 1944-S.
>
> Clad pieces are often weakly struck in spots.
>
> Bicentennial coins and the modern series from State quarters onward can be graded by obverse and surface quality.[3]
>
> The mintmark on many of the earlier issues tends to be filled.

Significance of Grading Numbers

Grading numbers are simply shorthand for the rating that one person, group of people, or commercial certification service assigns to a particular coin at a particular time. The system is highly subjective, not scientific. For a rare 1932-S Washington quarter for which a small difference in grade can mean a large difference in price, Grader A might call it MS-64. Grader B may be more liberal and suggest MS-65. Grader C may consider it to be MS-63.

Differences of a point or two among experts are not unusual. In fact, via the practice of *resubmission*, many numismatists send certified coins back to the same services that graded them, and often the coins are returned with higher grades. This verifies that grading is a matter of opinion—an art, not a science. If it were scientific, the rules would be easy to follow, and all grading services would assign precisely the same number to a given coin, as would a collector or dealer using the grading descriptions. Under a scientific system, anyone with a copy of the ANA Grading Standards, a good light, and a good magnifying glass could come to precisely the same grade as that assigned by a commercial service.

In my opinion, it is easy to learn to grade Washington quarters. The ANA Standards given here are an outline. For a reality check, you need to examine coins in person. The best way to do this is to visit a coin convention or a friendly local coin dealer, and look at the coins on display. Most sellers are happy to "talk coins" and give you some advice. It is courtesy to buy a few coins or a few books from the person who helps you.

After an hour or two of immersion, examining certified as well as "raw" coins, you will be able to evaluate Washington quarters on your own.

Certification Services

Over the years, many companies, generally called *certification services* or *grading services*, have been established to assign grades to coins that are submitted. Since 1986, the year PCGS was established, more than 100 have been set up. Most have faded from the scene. PCGS was the first to make a large, successful business by encapsulating coins in tamper-resistant holders. ANACS began a large trade in the late 1970s, but did not use sealed holders until the late 1980s.

In alphabetical order, the leading grading services today are ANACS, Certified Acceptance Corporation (CAC) Grading, Independent Coin Graders (ICG), Numismatic Guaranty Company (NGC), and PCGS. There are other grading services as well. Many collectors and dealers have preferences. Before selecting a favorite, it would be good to ask around for advice. Some are services stricter than others.

In very high grades, opinions can vary widely, and you should proceed with caution. One person's MS-67 can be another's MS-69. If you are contemplating paying a high price for a condition rarity—a Washington quarter that is common in MS-65 or 66, but very expensive in MS-69—it would be wise to show the coin to others and seek opinions. Also read about market trends and fads.

However, within a certain range, the leading services are very good. If you sent the same Washington quarter to the four mentioned previously, you might get opinions such as these: MS-65, 65, 66, and 66. It is highly unlikely that you would get an MS-62, if three called the coin MS-65 or 66. Before the advent of such services, there were many overgraded, processed, cleaned coins advertised as "choice," "gem," or the like, often with the sellers assigning ANA numbers. Traps such as chrome-plated pseudo-Proofs are easily caught by the services, but might fool you in the beginning stages of your knowledge.

Among Washington quarters, the majority of dates and mintmarks are inexpensive. The result is that it costs more to have a coin certified than the coin is worth. This is particularly true of issues from the 1940s onward, including the state quarters. In addition, the hundreds of holders needed for a full set would weigh many pounds and take up a lot of space. Probably a good compromise is to buy certified examples of the rarer issues, but to acquire "raw" specimens of the usual inexpensive varieties. To do the latter you will either need to learn grading on your own, or buy from a trustworthy dealer. To store and display a high-grade, expensive set, a notebook-type album with plastic pages permitting a mix of certified holders and plain plastic holders may be a good way to go.

Being a Smart Buyer

If you've read some of my other books you know that buying coins in some series can be very complex. Washington quarters, for a change, are straightforward.

Step 1: The Numerical Grade

Following my earlier advice, look at market listings and determine what grades you would like to buy for each of the coins you need. This will be a combination of your budget plus the desire to obtain good value for your money. Generally, this means that if the next-higher grade of a coin is multiples of the price, it may not be a good value.

If you are typical, you will probably have a high grade in mind for most if not all issues from the 1960s onward, and perhaps slightly lower grades for earlier, more expensive varieties. Make up a want-list with each variety and the hoped-for grade, and cross off each as you acquire it. Except for the handful of rare issues, a first-class collection can be made with MS-64 and 65 coins for the dates before 1940, and MS-65 and 66 after 1940. As to the 1932-D and S, contemplate these separately and form a buying plan.

If your budget calls for an MS-60 1932-D, and if you are at a coin show, ask to see pieces in the MS-60 category. There is no particular point in asking for an MS-64 or EF-40. Consider the offered coin and the grade assigned to it. If you can do so, verify with your own knowledge, or ask to show it to a friend, to be sure it is correct. Most dealers welcome outside consultation when making a sale. Better yet, spend an hour or two learning how to grade coins on your own, as mentioned earlier. Then with confidence you can buy most of the pieces you need. It would be advisable, however, to seek an experienced friend's opinion on the more valuable pieces if they are not certified.

Immediately, you can see if the coin at hand is in the numerical grade you are seeking and qualifies for further consideration. Otherwise, hand it back and look at something else. It is likely that most of the Washington quarters you are offered will not be certified, but most will have grading numbers assigned to them.

If you see an offering on the Internet or a catchpenny printed advertisement of "a nice gem," or "a really choice Mint State," ask the buyer to translate that into ANA numbers. If he or she won't, you should walk. There are lots of other coins around.

Step 2: Eye Appeal at First Glance

At this point take a quick glance at the coin. Is it "pretty"? Is the toning (if present) attractive, or is it dark or blotchy? Is the coin stained? If it is brilliant, is it attractively lustrous, or is it dull and lifeless?

For all the Washington quarters you will be considering for your collection, there are many opportunities in the marketplace. It is not at all necessary in any instance to compromise on eye appeal! Even the rarest of the rare 1932-D can be found with excellent eye appeal with just a little bit of patience.

If it is not attractive, then reject it and go on to look at another. An ugly coin graded as MS-65 is still ugly, and if it were my decision I would not buy it for half of the current market price! Avoid price-bargains; most are overgraded, lack eye appeal, or have some other problem. The market for quality Washington quarters is very strong, and there is no such thing as "below wholesale" for a problem-free coin. If the coin is attractive to you, then in some distant future when you sell it, the piece will be attractive to other buyers. Among Washington quarters from the 1940s to date, *most* have good eye appeal—a situation not at all true for many other series (Jefferson nickels, for example). For modern Proof coins 1968-S to date, including the state issues, you can almost buy with your eyes closed—the quality is that nice!

Step 3: Evaluating Sharpness and Related Features

At this point you have a coin that has excellent eye appeal and that you believe to be in the numerical grade assigned. The next step is to take out a magnifying glass and evaluate its sharpness. In 90% of silver issues from 1932 to 1964 there will be no problem. For clad coins 1965 to 1998, there can be some weakness that often manifests itself by the presence of tiny nicks and marks on the high parts of the portrait, while the surrounding fields are essentially mark-free. The marks on the high areas are marks on the original planchet that did not become obliterated by striking pressure at that deep point in the die.

State and later quarters are usually well struck, but some are not. Check the high parts of Washington's portrait for planchet marks. Also check the points in highest relief in the reverse design. If you need a reference point, examine a Proof of the same variety—these are nearly always needle-sharp in detail, and you can tell which design features should be present.

As part of step 3, look at the planchet and surface quality. Silver issues usually pass with flying colors, but clad coins can be dull, or have a lot of nicks from the original planchet, particularly on the obverse. Take your time, even when buying inexpensive issues.

In other instances, coins were struck from "tired" dies that had been used in some instances to strike more than 200,000 pieces, and may show graininess or metal flow. This can be problematic with quarters of the 1932-to-1998 era, but is less so for the modern quarters.

Examine your prospective coin carefully, and reject it if there are any problems with the surface or planchet. No compromise of any kind need be made.

Step 4: Establishing a Fair Market Price

For starters, use one or several handy market guides for a ballpark estimate. This book is a handy guide, but should be verified with one of the weekly or monthly listings, such as those in *Coin Values*, the "Coin Market" feature of *Numismatic News*, or the *Coin Dealer Newsletter*. Nearly all Washington quarters in grades up to MS-65 have standard values and trade within certain ranges. There will be more variation with such scarce varieties as the 1932-D, 1932-S, and high-grade examples of 1936-D.

If the coin is common enough in a given grade, with sharp strike, with fine planchet quality, and with good eye appeal, then be sure the coin is offered for about the going market price. If the going price is $25, and you are at a convention or coin shop and are offered a nice one for $27, buy it anyway—your time and the opportunity have value. If it is priced at $40, you can wait. If it is offered for $15, better look at it more carefully!

Most of the modern quarters are so plentiful that they are almost a commodity. Probably a good way to get all or most is to pick a dealer you like, with reasonable prices, and buy as many as you can from this single source—then fill in any open spaces later.

8

Washington Quarters, 1932–1998: Analysis by Date and Mintmark

Eagle Reverse, 1932–1974

Designer: *John Flanagan.* **Weight:** *Silver (1932–1964)—6.25 grams; copper-nickel clad (1965–1974)—5.67 grams.* **Composition:** *Silver (1932–1964)—.900 silver, .100 copper (net weight .18084 oz. pure silver); copper-nickel clad (1965–1974)—outer layers of copper nickel (.750 copper, .250 nickel) bonded to inner core of pure copper.* **Diameter:** *24.3 mm.* **Edge:** *Reeded.* **Mints:** *Philadelphia, Denver, and San Francisco.*

1932

Circulation-Strike Mintage: 5,404,000
GSID: 5609

Key to Collecting: The 1932 Philadelphia Mint Washington quarter has always been popular as the first year of issue. Mint State coins are readily available, but are certainly scarce in comparison to dates after 1934. The typical coin graded at MS-63 or higher is apt to be lustrous and have good eye appeal. Quite a few are around in About Uncirculated and lower Mint State grades. When marks are present, they are usually most noticeable on the portrait and the left obverse field.

Numismatic Notes: All 1932 quarters are of the Light Motto variety with the edges of the letters in the motto IN GOD WE TRUST blending into the field.

Quarters of this new design were released into circulation on August 1, 1932. There was considerable interest at first, and many were saved as souvenirs. However, in this deep Depression year few bank-wrapped rolls or other quantities were saved by anyone. Later, Mint State examples would prove to be plentiful on the numismatic market, but they were usually offered one or a few at a time, never in quantity.

In the July 1980 issue of *Coin Dealer Newsletter Monthly Supplement*, Allen Harriman wrote, "Of all the P-mints, this is the one most often encountered in AU-55 'slider' and MS-60 condition." Such pieces represent coins saved by the public at the time of release, but spent afterward when the novelty had passed. All quarters of this date have a higher rim on the reverse than do later silver quarters issued 1934 to 1964.

VG-8	F-12	VF-20	EF-40	AU-50	MS-60	MS-63	MS-65	MS-66
$8.70	$9.50	$10.50	$11.50	$16.00	$32.50	$57	$273	$650

1932-D

Circulation-Strike Mintage: 436,800
GSID: 5646

Key to Collecting: The Denver Mint issue of the year is far and away the key issue of the series.

Although the mintage figure of the 1932-D is slightly higher than for 1932-S (408,000), in grades of MS-63 or better the 1932-D is at least 5 to 10 times rarer than the 1932-S. As such, it is far and away the key issue of the series. In the dawn days of rare-coin activity on the Internet (in the 1990s), Elliot Goldman, who operated Allstate Coin Co. in Tucson, Arizona, specialized in Washington quarters. He and I conversed often on the 1932-D, as we both recognized their rarity and recommended them to clients (many of whom couldn't figure out why we would be excited about such an inactive series!). Today, with collectors' interest catalyzed by the state quarters, the classic 1932-D in a grade such as MS-63 or MS-64 (never mind the even rarer MS-65) is a magnet for bidders in an auction sale.

When the 1932-D was minted and distributed, no effort was made to handle the coins gently. As a result, most pieces saved in Mint State in 1932 and surviving to the present day are apt to be in MS-60 to MS-62 grades. As with other coins in the series, nicks and marks are most obvious on the portrait and in the left obverse field. Such marks generally get lost on the reverse and are not distracting there.

In worn grades, the 1932-D is available in proportion to its mintage and is seen about as often as is the 1932-S. Examples in such grades as Good and Very Good were occasionally found in circulation in the early 1950s, after which they disappeared almost entirely. Due to the high price of Mint State coins, circulated examples enjoy a wide market. Many fakes with D mintmarks added to Philadelphia Mint coins do exist. Seeking the advice of an expert when buying one is good practice; better yet, purchase a specimen that has been certified by one of the leading services.

Numismatic Notes: All 1932-D quarters are of the Light Motto variety with the edges of the letters in the motto IN GOD WE TRUST blending into the field. The D mintmark on genuine coins is often small and in high relief, and is sometimes filled at the center. The small D had been the standard for the entire Standing Liberty quarter production at the Denver Mint from 1917 to 1929. A ghost outline of a larger D, an artifact of machine damage doubling, is seen north and east of the final D.

All quarters of this date have a higher rim on the reverse than do later silver quarters issued 1934 to 1964.

VG-8	F-12	VF-20	EF-40	AU-50	MS-60	MS-63	MS-65	MS-66
$76	$100	$136	$214	$312	$1,000	$1,500	$8,750	$90,000

1932-S

Circulation-Strike Mintage: 408,000
GSID: 5647

Key to Collecting: In *worn grades* the 1932-S is slightly scarcer than the 1932-D, as evidenced by finds in circulation decades ago. However, the 1932-D is priced higher (makes no sense!). There are many About Uncirculated 1932-S quarters around—pieces that were plucked from circulation in 1932 and 1933, then spent in the days just before collecting dates and mintmarks became wildly popular, starting in 1934.

Among Mint State coins, most are in lower grades, again representing pieces saved by the public. Quite a few of the About Uncirculated and lower Mint State level 1932 quarters from each of the mints have yellowish toning and/or black specks and freckles, why I don't know. This coloration is not often seen among later dates. Perhaps it is because most of the later ones were taken from bank-wrapped rolls, whereas the 1932 coins were saved one at a time. Mint State 1932-S quarters are more available than are those of 1932-D.

With the 1932-D, the 1932-S is a key to the series—far outranking any other later dates and mints.

Numismatic Notes: All 1932-S quarters are of the Light Motto variety with the edges of the IN GOD WE TRUST letters blending into the field.

All quarters of this date have a higher rim on the reverse than do later silver quarters issued 1934 to 1964.

VG-8	F-12	VF-20	EF-40	AU-50	MS-60	MS-63	MS-65	MS-66
$73	$94	$101	$122	$162	$43	$545	$2,500	$42,000

1934

Circulation-Strike Mintage: 31,912,052
GSID: Light Motto, 374321; Medium Motto, 374322; Heavy Motto, 374323

Key to Collecting: The 1934 quarter is readily available in Mint State, although hardly common. Years ago there were only a few bank-wrapped rolls on the market at any given time, and the issue was ranked as quite scarce in comparison to later Philadelphia coins. Most coins have a distinctive satiny finish and are very attractive (the same satin is seen on Peace dollars of this date and mint, but not on other issues of this year). There are several varieties of this date listed below. While most collectors are satisfied with a single example to illustrate the date, the Light Motto, Heavy Motto (easy to find), and Doubled-Die Obverse are sought by many. The Medium Motto is not as popular.

Numismatic Notes: Edward S. Horowitz noted the motto differences as part of an article, "The Washington Quarter," published in *The Numismatist*, October 1944:

> The records of the Philadelphia Mint, which is the only one using the low relief die in 1934, show that on June 30, 1934, working dies were delivered to the Coining Department with the motto "In God We Trust" in higher relief, prepared on order of the director of the Mint. The records there further show that up to June 30, 6,432,000 pieces had been coined that year, all in May and June; and that 25,480,052 were coined from July to December inclusive.

Today, certain of the certification services are attributing 1934 quarters by the three motto differences.

Varieties: Light Motto *(FS-25-1934-401):* This variety was made through the first part of 1934, but was not widely saved (see Numismatic Notes). The same Light Motto style was used for all the coinage of 1932. The center of the W in WE is lower than the sides. As this variety is not widely noticed, there is ample opportunity for cherrypicking.

Medium Motto *(FS-25-1934-402):* This variety has the same general letter font as the 1932, with center of the W in WE is lower than the sides and somewhat blunt (not pointed as in the Light Motto), but in higher relief. It has thin letters compared to the 1934, Heavy Motto.

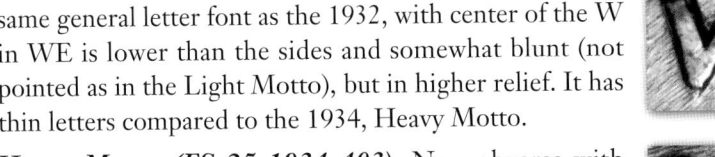

Heavy Motto *(FS-25-1934-403):* New obverse with thick, heavy letters in the motto. The center of the W in WE is higher than the sides.

Doubled Die Obverse *(FS-25-1934-101, Breen-4272):* Prominent doubling, especially at the (medium) motto. The reverse is slightly doubled, one of just a few doubled dies listed in the *Red Book*. Fivaz-Stanton state that this is "one of the strongest and most popular of all Washington quarter varieties." Quite a few have been run through the certification services, with the current population totaling over 500 pieces, mostly in circulated grades, but MS-64 is the most common Mint State grade.

Light Motto

VG-8	F-12	VF-20	EF-40	AU-50	MS-60	MS-63	MS-65	MS-66
$8.30	$8.70	$11.50	$15	$23	$47	$61	$208	$429

Medium Motto

VG-8	F-12	VF-20	EF-40	AU-50	MS-60	MS-63	MS-65	MS-66
$8.70	$11.00	$9.90	$11.50	$12.00	$27.00	$40.50	$70	$169

Heavy Motto

VG-8	F-12	VF-20	EF-40	AU-50	MS-60	MS-63	MS-65	MS-66
$8.30	$9.00	$12.00	$17.50	$27	$51	$61	$156	$364

1934-D

Circulation-Strike Mintage: 3,527,200
GSID: Medium Motto, 5648; Heavy Motto, 5649

Key to Collecting: Mint State coins are scarce in relation to most later issues, but enough are around that you will find one without difficulty. The luster is of a pleasing but unusual matte-satiny finish, as also used on Peace silver dollars of this year and mint. Dies were prepared at the Philadelphia Mint and shipped unhardened to Denver, where they were hardened and finished for use. Some special process must have been used for quarters and dollars of this date (but not cents, dimes, or nickels).

Medium and Heavy Motto varieties exist, but are not widely known or collected. Most numismatists are content to have just one example of this date and mint. See illustrations under 1932.

Although the 1934-D was minted to the extent of several million coins, this was a year deep in the Depression, and few were saved. This and the 1932-D are the only quarter dollars that I have never handled in roll quantities. I have always considered this to be a sleeper, but not many agree with me, as the published mintage figure is so generous.

Numismatic Notes: On a minority of coins the D mintmark is small and heavy, similar to that used on 1932-D. On most a large mintmark is seen.

Varieties: Medium Motto: This variety has the same general letter font as the 1932, with the center of the W in WE lower than the sides, but in higher relief. It has thin letters compared to other varieties of the year. Opinion is divided as to whether the Medium Motto is scarcer than the Heavy Motto, or vice versa. In his 1988 *Encyclopedia* Walter Breen estimated the production as 1,000,000 Medium Motto and 2,500,000 Heavy Motto, but in the marketplace the Medium Motto is seen more often. David W. Lange of NGC suggests that Breen's estimates should be reversed.[1] Estimated mintage for this variety is 2,000,000. Most 1934-D pieces have not been certified according to the motto style.

Heavy Motto: New obverse with thick, heavy letters in the motto. The center of the W in WE is higher than the sides. Estimated mintage: 1,500,000

Mintmark of 1932 *(FS-25-1934D-501)*: Small, heavy mintmark as on 1932-D, presumably from a leftover die.

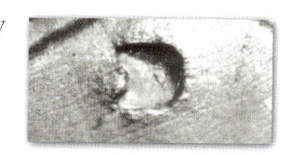

Medium Motto

VG-8	F-12	VF-20	EF-40	AU-50	MS-60	MS-63	MS-65	MS-66
$8.00	$11.30	$20	$34	$108	$195	$312	$455	$895

Heavy Motto

VG-8	F-12	VF-20	EF-40	AU-50	MS-60	MS-63	MS-65	MS-66
$9.70	$13.50	$24.50	$40.50	$122	$195	$247	$585	$1,020

1935

Circulation-Strike Mintage: 32,484,000
GSID: 5614

Key to Collecting: Beginning this year, bank-wrapped rolls were saved in quantity of all Washington quarters except 1936-D. The 1935 is plentiful today, but in view of the demand for such coins they are no longer seen in quantity. The typical coin is well struck and richly lustrous. An MS-65 coin, selected for eye appeal, will be just right for the advanced collector.

Numismatic Notes: All 1935 quarters from each of the mints are of the Medium Motto variety, even though the Heavy Motto had been created in 1934 and would become the standard from 1936 onward.

VG-8	F-12	VF-20	EF-40	AU-50	MS-60	MS-63	MS-65	MS-66
$8.00	$8.70	$9.50	$11.50	$13.50	$20.00	$32.50	$61	$81

1935-D

Circulation-Strike Mintage: 5,780,000
GSID: 5650

Key to Collecting: The 1935-D is easily enough available in an absolute sense, but is at least five times more elusive than the 1935 Philadelphia issue in choice and gem Mint State, MS-63 and above. Examples usually have rich frost and good eye appeal.

Numismatic Notes: All 1935 quarters from each of the mints are of the Medium Motto variety.

VG-8	F-12	VF-20	EF-40	AU-50	MS-60	MS-63	MS-65	MS-66
$8.00	$10.80	$17.50	$38	$128	$221	$286	$318	$468

1935-S

Circulation-Strike Mintage: 5,660,000
GSID: 5651

Key to Collecting: The 1935-S is similar to the 1935-D, but seen more often. Years ago, rolls of the 1935-S were easily found, while those of 1935-D required some searching. High-grade examples usually have excellent frost and good eye appeal.

Numismatic Notes: All 1935 quarters from each of the mints are of the Medium Motto variety.

VG-8	F-12	VF-20	EF-40	AU-50	MS-60	MS-63	MS-65	MS-66
$8.30	$9.4	$11	$19	$38	$78	$94	$182	$247

1936

Circulation-Strike Mintage: 41,300,000

Proof Mintage: 3,837

GSID: Circulation strike, 5615; Proof, 5847

Key to Collecting: In 1936, Proofs of Washington quarters first became available.

This is the first really common date in Mint State, with at least two or three times more known than of the 1935, which itself is plentiful. Occasionally, bags of these traded in the early 1950s, this being the earliest Washington quarter I ever encountered in this quantity. Today, millions of collectors later, such hoards have been dispersed and like most Washington quarters of the 1930s, the 1936 is usually seen singly or on small groups. Most are brilliant, lustrous, and attractive. Proofs are often seen on the market, but are the scarcest of any issue from this year to the present.

Numismatic Notes: Beginning in this year the Heavy Motto variety (used for some 1934 and 1934-D coinage) became the standard. Proofs were offered as part of five coin sets (cent, nickel, dime, quarter, half dollar) for $1.81 or could be purchased singly. This method of ordering prevailed through 1942.

Varieties: Doubled Die Obverse: *(FS-25-1936-101):* With very noticeable doubling in the motto, especially at the uprights of the I in IN and the first T in TRUST. Fivaz-Stanton write: "This very rare variety is always in very high demand." This is a good variety to cherrypick, as most 1936 quarters have not been checked for this feature.

EF-40	AU-50	MS-60	MS-63	MS-65	MS-66	MS-67	PF-63	PF-65	PF-67
$13	$16	$27	$34	$88	$108	$344	$520	$820	$6,250

1936-D

Circulation-Strike Mintage: 5,374,000

GSID: 5652

Key to Collecting: The 1936-D quarter has always been scarce in Mint State, but common in worn grades. Rolls of 1936-S were saved in quantity, but not 1936-D. Finding a lustrous, attractive 1936-D will take some doing, but will hardly be a problem, as at any given time there are examples on the market. Circulated coins are common, but in my opinion overpriced (see notes below).

Breen's *Encyclopedia* lists a 1936-D, D over Horizontal D (Breen-4285). The D mintmark was first punched into the die with the rounded part facing down, 90° to the right of normal. A correct D was then overpunched. Little has reached print about this variety. Bill Fivaz commented, "I do not believe this exists. It is not listed in the James Wiles book, nor have J.T. Stanton and I included it in the *Cherrypickers' Guide to Rare Die Varieties*."[2]

Numismatic Notes: In 1936 at the Denver Mint, 5,374,000 Washington quarters were produced, certainly a common coin by any consideration. Thus, numismatists did not bother to save them. Moreover, many were busy with the great commemorative coin craze. A number of years later, according to Lee F. Hewitt, founder and editor of the *Numismatic Scrapbook Magazine*, when Wayte Raymond's "National" holders had been popular for a few years and when Whitman and other holders became available in quantity, it was discovered that Uncirculated examples of this "common" variety were relatively scarce. Today, the 1936-D remains a key issue in Mint State. However, worn pieces are not at all difficult to find. They exist in proportion to their original mintage. There is no logical reason why a worn 1936-D in a grade such as Very Fine, Extremely Fine, or About Uncirculated should be priced more than a worn 1936-S. The only reason this has happened is that those who know that *Mint State* are scarce, assume *all* are scarce.

EF-40	AU-50	MS-60	MS-63	MS-65	MS-66	MS-67
$68	$162	$500	$605	$885	$1,080	$3,250

1936-S

Circulation-Strike Mintage: 3,828,000
GSID: 5653

Key to Collecting: Many rolls of 1936-S were saved in and around the year of issue, making quantities plentiful on the market until the 1960s, when the expansion of the hobby caused most rolls to be broken apart and distributed. The typical 1936-S is lustrous and attractive.

The 1936-S, Repunched Mintmark, has the final S dramatically punched over a previous S to the south-southeast and was discovered by Jose Cortez. A few pieces have been noticed by the certification services. Although this variety is not in great demand, if you want one, simply look through regular 1936-S quarters until you locate an example.

EF-40	AU-50	MS-60	MS-63	MS-65	MS-66	MS-67
$19	$51	$97	$115	$214	$247	$700

1937

Circulation-Strike Mintage: 19,696,000
Proof Mintage: 5,542
GSID: Circulation strike, 5616; Proof, 5850

Key to Collecting: The 1937 is plentiful in all Mint State categories up through 66, but somewhat scarcer above that. Most quarters of this date have not been run through a certification service, so be careful when contemplating paying a high price for a condition rarity. In the future, more will be certified.

Proofs of this year are the second scarcest date from 1936 to the present. The mintage of 5,542 coins was the lowest for any Proof denomination of the 1937 year.

Numismatic Notes: Reverse B was introduced on Proofs in 1937, while circulation strikes continued with Reverse A. The relief was strengthened by lowering the field, and the ES in STATES became distinctly separated. There are *two bold leaves to the left of the arrowheads. The stronger leaf touches or nearly touches the top of the A in DOLLAR.* The leaf touches on some Proofs and nearly touches on dies which were more extensively relapped. Stronger than on Variety A. Certain letters and the edges of feathers were retouched. Used on Proofs of 1937 to 1964 and circulation strikes from 1959 to 1964. Details on the Proofs are sharper than on circulation strikes.

Varieties: Doubled Die Obverse *(FS-25-1937-101, Breen-4287):* This variety has very noticeable doubling at the bases of the letters in the motto and at the date. Listed in the *Red Book*, most known pieces are in circulated grades. Gem Mint State coins are rare. Fivaz-Stanton say this is "considered one of the most important varieties in the series."

EF-40	AU-50	MS-60	MS-63	MS-65	MS-66	MS-67	PF-63	PF-65	PF-67
$20.00	$29.50	$40.50	$43	$88	$128	$481	$169	$292	$750

1937-D

Circulation-Strike Mintage: 7,189,600
GSID: 5654

Key to Collecting: The 1937-D is another date from the 1930s that was saved in roll quantities. The typical specimen is very lustrous and with good eye appeal.

EF-40	AU-50	MS-60	MS-63	MS-65	MS-66	MS-67
$23.00	$32.50	$76	$94	$130	$221	$585

1937-S

Circulation-Strike Mintage: 1,652,000
GSID: 5655

Key to Collecting: With its enticingly low mintage the 1937-S has always been high on the list of collectors' favorites. Mint State coins, while somewhat scarce, are available in the marketplace. Most are lustrous and very attractive. In the context of quarters of the 1930s, circulated coins are elusive.

Numismatic Notes: This is the third-lowest mintage issue in the series (after 1932-S and 1932-D). However, many were saved in roll quantities. James F. Ruddy and I sought to buy all the rolls we could find of these, circa the late 1950s, and were able to find only a few dozen. In contrast, it would have been possible to purchase hundreds of rolls of 1937 (in particular) and 1937-D.

In an article, "Investing in Washington Quarters," in *The Numismatist*, October 1944, Edward S. Horowitz included this: "Two later dates of Washington quarters are probably underrated, and may stage a surprise some day. They are the 1937-S quarter, with a total coinage of only 1,652,000, and the 1939-S quarter with a coinage of 2,628,000. In comparison with other recent coins of greater coinage, they are behind the market."

David W. Lange comments:

> Aside from its scarcity, there is something else that sets the 1937-S quarter dollar apart from every other issue in this long running series. For reasons now forgotten, the obverse rim of the 1937-S quarter was raised above the normal level. . . . It isn't really noticeable on Uncirculated coins. Since most collectors of the Washington series don't bother with worn examples, it's easy to overlook this phenomenon. Still, the obverse rim of 1937-S quarters is clearly higher than on other dates, a fact that becomes quite apparent when examining heavily worn coins. On all Washington quarters, the reverse typically wears more rapidly than the obverse. The inadequacy of the reverse rim in protecting this side from wear is a hallmark of the series. But on the 1937-S quarters the discrepancy in wear is almost ludicrous. The typical coin of this date grading Good on its reverse will grade anywhere from Very Good to Fine on its obverse. One grading as low as About Good on its reverse will still show a complete obverse rim.[3]

EF-40	AU-50	MS-60	MS-63	MS-65	MS-66	MS-67
$34	$94	$156	$202	$273	$377	$1,560

1938

Circulation-Strike Mintage: 9,472,000
Proof Mintage: 8,045
GSID: Circulation strike, 5618; Proof, 5853

Key to Collecting: The 1938 in Mint State has always been scarce, the key issue among Philadelphia Mint quarters in the series. The reason may be that as Proofs were available, not many rolls were saved. In the early 1950s, when roll and bag quantities of Uncirculated Washington quarters often traded among dealers, single rolls of the 1938 were hard to find. The typical coin is lustrous and attractive.

Proofs exist in proportion to their mintage, with probably 7,000 or so surviving from the original distribution of 8,045.

Numismatic Notes: Circulation strikes have the Variety A reverse; Proofs have the Variety B reverse (see chapter 5) used on Proofs from 1937 to 1964. Allen Harriman, writing in the *Coin Dealer Newsletter, Monthly Supplement*, July 1980, commented: "This low mintage issue is by far the scarcest of all the P-mint Washington quarters." I do not dispute this statement.

EF-40	AU-50	MS-60	MS-63	MS-65	MS-66	MS-67	PF-63	PF-65	PF-67
$24.50	$47	$94	$108	$122	$182	$416	$108	$156	$895

1938-S

Circulation-Strike Mintage: 2,832,000
GSID: 5656

Key to Collecting: The 1938-S is on the scarce side by virtue of its low mintage. Because of this it is a long time favorite. As is true of most other quarters of the era, Mint State coins are apt to be lustrous and with good eye appeal.

EF-40	AU-50	MS-60	MS-63	MS-65	MS-66	MS-67
$28.50	$54	$81	$105	$156	$195	$600

1939

Circulation-Strike Mintage: 33,540,000
Proof Mintage: 8,795
GSID: Circulation strike, 5619; Proof, 5856

Key to Collecting: Plentiful by virtue of its large mintage. Choice and gem Mint State examples abound. Proofs are scarce, but when found are usually of choice or gem quality.

Numismatic Notes: Circulation strikes have the Variety A reverse; Proofs have the Variety B reverse (see chapter 5) used on Proofs 1937 to 1964.

EF-40	AU-50	MS-60	MS-63	MS-65	MS-66	MS-67	PF-63	PF-65	PF-67
$10.00	$12.00	$24.50	$29.50	$58	$74	$162	$128	$136	$43

1939-D

Circulation-Strike Mintage: 7,092,000

GSID: 5657

Key to Collecting: Easily available in any grade desired.

Numismatic Notes: Some have a heavily punched mintmark with the center opening small, others have a lighter mintmark with the opening larger. Several varieties of repunched mintmarks are described by James Wiles.

EF-40	AU-50	MS-60	MS-63	MS-65	MS-66	MS-67
$13.50	$23.00	$44.50	$57	$81	$94	$43

1939-D, D over S

Circulation-Strike Mintage:
Small part of 1939-D mintage.

GSID: 374317

Key to Collecting: This is a very rare variety. If you opt to include overmintmarks as part of your date and mintmark collection, this will be a great challenge. The open center of the D mintmark shows the center curve of a previous S, and part of the left upper curve of the S can be seen to the left of the upright of D. Listed by Fivaz-Stanton as FS-25-1939D-501 at URS-7, indicating great rarity. However, as this overmintmark is not widely known, here is an opportunity for cherrypicking. Check all of the regular 1939-D quarters you can find.

Numismatic Notes: As the Fivaz-Stanton text points out, this is the *real* 1939-D, D over S. Some repunched D 1939-D coins have been illustrated as "1939-D, D over S."

MS-65	MS-66	MS-67
$650	$860	$1,250

1939-S

Circulation-Strike Mintage: 2,628,000
GSID: 5658

Key to Collecting: Although the 1939-S has the fourth lowest mintage figure in the series (after 1932-S, 1932-D, and 1937-S), many were saved in roll quantities, and on an absolute basis they are not *rare*. However, in the context of the several hundred varieties of Washington quarters made from 1932 to date, it is one of the scarcer issues.

Numismatic Notes: See 1937-S.

EF-40	AU-50	MS-60	MS-63	MS-65	MS-66	MS-67
$27	$61	$94	$176	$208	$273	$650

1940

Circulation-Strike Mintage: 35,704,000
Proof Mintage: 11,246
GSID: Circulation strike, 5620; Proof, 5859

Key to Collecting: Easily available, a comment that pertains to all other standard date and mintmark issues from this point forward. Proofs are slightly scarce, per the mintage.

Numismatic Notes: Circulation strikes have the Variety A reverse; Proofs have the Variety B reverse (see chapter 5) used on Proofs 1937 to 1964.

EF-40	AU-50	MS-60	MS-63	MS-65	MS-66	MS-67	PF-63	PF-65	PF-67
$12	$15	$32	$34	$46	$74	$169	$82	$108	$325

1940-D

Circulation-Strike Mintage: 2,797,600
GSID: 5659

Key to Collecting: In the context of quarters of the decade the 1940-D is slightly scarce. See the following notes.

Numismatic Notes: In "Grading Insights," *Coin World*, Randy Campbell commented:

> The 1940-D Washington quarter dollar, with a mintage of about 2.8 million, has always been popular with collectors and dealers. The typical 1940-D Washington quarter dollar displays a wide range of luster quality. Full gems will have blazing, original, mint frost. However, many examples of this date exhibit substandard luster that is impaired by cleaning, overdipping or improper storage. A significant percentage of 1940-D Washington quarter dollars will have worse than average surface abrasions. Those that are moderately contact marked tend to grade in the MS-63 to MS-64 range. Those with heavy contact marks usually grade MS-60 to MS-62 (if they are still Uncirculated).[4]

Varieties: Doubled Die Obverse *(FS-25-1940D-101):* With light doubling, most notable at the bases of the letters in the motto (more prominent on the motto). Fivaz-Stanton state: "This is a very attractive doubled die!"

Dramatically Repunched Mintmark *(FS-25-1940D-501):* The Final D mintmark is separated from and punched to the east of an earlier, lighter D. Fivaz-Stanton comment: "This is one of about 10 known repunched mintmarks [across all U.S. coin series] that are totally separated." Also see 1941-D from the same reverse die. Discovered by Lee Hiemke in recent times, this dramatic variety was overlooked by a generation of earlier collectors.

EF-40	AU-50	MS-60	MS-63	MS-65	MS-66	MS-67
$40.50	$88	$130	$156	$234	$260	$550

1940-S

Circulation-Strike Mintage: 8,244,000
GSID: 5660

Key to Collecting: A popular and easily available variety.

EF-40	AU-50	MS-60	MS-63	MS-65	MS-66	MS-67
$13.50	$20.00	$36.50	$51	$65	$94	$364

1941

Circulation-Strike Mintage: 79,032,000
Proof Mintage: 15,287
GSID: Circulation strike, 5621; Proof, 5862

Key to Collecting: Plentiful in Mint State. Proofs of this era usually show light gray or hazy toning unless they have been dipped.

Numismatic Notes: Circulation strikes have the Variety A reverse; Proofs have the Variety B reverse (see chapter 5) used on Proofs 1937 to 1964.

Varieties: Doubled Die Obverses *(FS-25-1941-101 and FS-25-1941-102):* With light doubling, most notable at GOD WE and UST in the motto. Several other doubled-die obverses exist for 1941.

FS-25-1941-101   FS-25-1941-102

EF-40	AU-50	MS-60	MS-63	MS-65	MS-66	MS-67	PF-63	PF-65	PF-67
$8.20	$8.20	$11	$16	$43	$68	$182	$74	$94	$195

1941-D

Circulation-Strike Mintage: 16,714,800
GSID: 5661

Key to Collecting: A popular and readily available issue.

Varieties: Doubled Die Reverse *(FS-25-1941D-801):* The doubling is most evident on STATES OF AMERICA, with a light spread on the D of UNITED and the AR of DOLLAR. It is considered rare and in demand by Washington variety enthusiasts.

EF-40	AU-50	MS-60	MS-63	MS-65	MS-66	MS-67
$9.50	$15	$47	$58	$76	$108	$468

1941-S

Circulation-Strike Mintage: 16,080,000
GSID: 5662

Key to Collecting: Readily available in choice and gem preservation.

Numismatic Notes: Large and small mintmark varieties per the *Red Book* and Breen *Encyclopedia*. The elusive Large S was used on at least four dies. The lower left serif is called the "trumpet tail" due to its shape. Some have the upper loop of the S filled. The *Cherrypickers' Guide to Rare Die Varieties* gives illustrations and details.

EF-40	AU-50	MS-60	MS-63	MS-65	MS-66	MS-67
$9.50	$12.00	$40.50	$48.50	$65	$81	$325

1942

Circulation-Strike Mintage: 102,096,000
Proof Mintage: 21,123
GSID: Circulation strike, 5622; Proof, 5865

Key to Collecting: Circulation strikes are plentiful. Proofs, while scarce in comparison to those of the 1950s and later, have the highest mintage of the early years, 1936 to 1942. No further Proofs were made until 1950.

Numismatic Notes: Circulation strikes have the Variety A reverse; Proofs have the Variety B reverse (see chapter 5) used on Proofs 1937 to 1964. Doubled-Die Reverses are known to exist for 1942 and are described in the *Cherrypickers' Guide to Rare Die Varieties*.

Varieties: Doubled Die Obverse *(FS 25-1942-101):* This variety doubles on the motto, especially on GOD and TRUST, and is listed in the *Red Book*.

EF-40	AU-50	MS-60	MS-63	MS-65	MS-66	MS-67	PF-63	PF-65	PF-67
$8.20	$8.50	$11.00	$14.00	$29.50	$81	$325	$74	$94	$195

1942-D

Circulation-Strike Mintage: 17,487,200
GSID: 5663

Key to Collecting: Popular and readily available wartime issue.

Varieties: Doubled Die Obverse *(FS-25-1942D-101):* Doubling on LIBERTY, the date, and the motto, this coin is one of just a few doubled-die varieties to be listed in the *Red Book*. Fivaz-Stanton praise the coin as "one of the 'Top 10' Washington quarter varieties."

EF-40	AU-50	MS-60	MS-63	MS-65	MS-66	MS-67
$8.20	$8.20	$21.50	$24.50	$43	$68	$429

1942-S

Circulation-Strike Mintage: 19,384,000
GSID: 5666

Key to Collecting: Popular and readily available wartime issue.

Numismatic Notes: Breen distinguishes between sharp-serif and knob-tailed S mintmarks.

EF-40	AU-50	MS-60	MS-63	MS-65	MS-66	MS-67
$12.00	$21.50	$61	$78	$103	$115	$429

1943

Circulation-Strike Mintage: 99,700,000
GSID: 5623

Key to Collecting: Easily available high-mintage issue. Beginning in this year, collectors, dealers, and investors set aside bank-wrapped rolls in much larger quantities than for earlier times. The Michael Higgy sale (Abe Kosoff, September 1943) saw record prices realized for scarce and rare coins of many denominations. This focused attention on current coins as well, resulting in an acceleration of investing interest. In addition, in this wartime period cash was plentiful and consumer goods were scarce. Current coins were a good place to park available funds.

Varieties: Doubled Die Obverse *(FS-25-1943-102):* Doubling on LIBERTY, the motto, and the date, this coin is one of just a few doubled-die varieties to be listed in the *Red Book*.

EF-40	AU-50	MS-60	MS-63	MS-65	MS-66	MS-67
$8.20	$8.20	$9.70	$12.50	$46	$94	$273

1943-D

Circulation-Strike Mintage: 16,095,600
GSID: 5667

Key to Collecting: Easily available in choice and gem Mint State. As a general rule for this era, the branch mint coins were saved in smaller quantities than were Philadelphia quarters. However, enough were set aside that all are plentiful today.

Varieties: D over Horizontal D *(Breen-4321):* D first punched into the die with rounded part facing up, 90° to the left of normal. A correct D was then overpunched.

EF-40	AU-50	MS-60	MS-63	MS-65	MS-66	MS-67
$11.50	$17.50	$31	$46	$59	$88	$24

1943-S

Circulation-Strike Mintage: 21,700,000
GSID: 5668

Key to Collecting: Plentiful and popular. Although quality is usually not a problem with quarters of the 1950s through 1964, cherrypicking for nice luster and eye appeal is worthwhile.

Varieties: Doubled Die Obverse *(FS-25-1943S-101):* Very strong doubling is evident on the motto, LIBERTY, the designer's initials, and the date. One of just a few doubled-die varieties to be listed in the *Red Book*, this variety has long been known to collectors.

EF-40	AU-50	MS-60	MS-63	MS-65	MS-66	MS-67
$9.50	$15.00	$40.50	$48.50	$108	$156	$43

1944

Circulation-Strike Mintage: 104,956,000
GSID: 5625

Key to Collecting: One of the most common issues of the era.

Numismatic Notes: All 1944 quarters show doubling on the earlobe and nostril from doubling of the master hub or master die.

EF-40	AU-50	MS-60	MS-63	MS-65	MS-66	MS-67
$8.20	$8.20	$9.70	$12.50	$29.50	$54	$234

1944-D

Circulation-Strike Mintage: 14,600,800
GSID: 5670

Key to Collecting: Choice and gem Mint State coins are readily available. As is true of most other quarters of this era, the typical Uncirculated coin taken from a bank-wrapped roll is apt to be MS-63 or MS-64.

Numismatic Notes: All 1944 quarters show doubling on the earlobe and nostril from doubling of the master hub or master die.

EF-40	AU-50	MS-60	MS-63	MS-65	MS-66	MS-67
$8.20	$8.20	$13.50	$20	$42	$70	$130

1944-S

Circulation-Strike Mintage: 12,560,000
GSID: 5671

Key to Collecting: Choice and gem Mint State coins are readily available.

Numismatic Notes: All 1944 quarters show doubling on the earlobe and nostril from doubling of the master hub or master die.

Varieties: Doubled Die Obverse *(FS-25-1944S-101):* This variety is also listed in the Breen *Encyclopedia*.

EF-40	AU-50	MS-60	MS-63	MS-65	MS-66	MS-67
$8.20	$8.50	$15.00	$22.00	$32.50	$61	$188

1945

Circulation-Strike Mintage: 74,372,000
GSID: 5626

Key to Collecting: Choice and gem Mint State coins are readily available.

Varieties: Doubled Die Obverse *(FS-25-1945-101):* This variety is also listed in the Breen *Encyclopedia*. It is tough to locate in a high grade.

EF-40	AU-50	MS-60	MS-63	MS-65	MS-66	MS-67
$8.20	$8.80	$9.80	$11.00	$40.50	$81	$292

1945-D

Circulation-Strike Mintage: 12,341,600
GSID: 5672

Key to Collecting: Choice and gem Mint State coins are readily available.

EF-40	AU-50	MS-60	MS-63	MS-65	MS-66	MS-67
$8.20	$8.80	$9.80	$27	$35	$61	$325

1945-S

Circulation-Strike Mintage: 17,004,001
GSID: 5673

Key to Collecting: Choice and gem Mint State coins are readily available.

Numismatic Notes: There are trumpet-tailed and knob-tailed S varieties.

EF-40	AU-50	MS-60	MS-63	MS-65	MS-66	MS-67
$8.20	$8.80	$9.80	$13.50	$34	$68	$286

1946

Circulation-Strike Mintage: 53,436,000
GSID: 5627

Key to Collecting: Although World War II was over, consumer goods remained scarce. Bank-wrapped rolls of quarters continued to be a popular investment. Today, choice 1946 quarters are easily found.

EF-40	AU-50	MS-60	MS-63	MS-65	MS-66	MS-67
$8.20	$8.50	$11	$14	$38	$88	$455

1946-D

Circulation-Strike Mintage: 9,072,800
GSID: 5674

Key to Collecting: Readily available, although the mintage is low for the era.

EF-40	AU-50	MS-60	MS-63	MS-65	MS-66	MS-67
$8.20	$8.50	$11	$15	$35	$54	$176

1946-S

Circulation-Strike Mintage: 4,204,000
GSID: 5675

Key to Collecting: The 1946-S was very popular in its time due to the restricted mintage of just 4,204,000 coins. A higher percentage of pieces than usual went to investors who anticipated they would become scarce. Today, the 1946-S is readily available.

Numismatic Notes: There are trumpet-tailed and knob-tailed S varieties.

EF-40	AU-50	MS-60	MS-63	MS-65	MS-66	MS-67
$8.20	$8.50	$11.00	$15.00	$32.50	$81	$214

1947

Circulation-Strike Mintage: 22,556,000
GSID: 5628

Key to Collecting: Easily available at different levels of Mint State. From this year through the very early 1950s, the interest in hoarding bank-wrapped rolls diminished. Accordingly, although there are enough 1947 quarters to go around, they and others of the next several years are not as common as are those of the earlier part of the decade.

EF-40	AU-50	MS-60	MS-63	MS-65	MS-66	MS-67
$8.20	$8.30	$9.50	$20.00	$32.50	$51	$234

1947-D

Circulation-Strike Mintage: 15,338,400
GSID: 5676

Key to Collecting: Choice and gem pieces are readily available.

EF-40	AU-50	MS-60	MS-63	MS-65	MS-66	MS-67
$8.20	$8.30	$9.50	$17.50	$38	$47	$162

1947-S

Circulation-Strike Mintage: 5,532,000
GSID: 5677

Key to Collecting: The rather low mintage for the 1947-S did not attract much attention at the time (unlike 1946-S). Mint State pieces are readily available.

Numismatic Notes: There are trumpet-tailed and knob-tailed S varieties.

EF-40	AU-50	MS-60	MS-63	MS-65	MS-66	MS-67
$8.20	$8.30	$9.50	$16	$27	$51	$176

1948

Circulation-Strike Mintage: 35,196,000
GSID: 5629

Key to Collecting: Choice and gem Mint State coins are readily available. Mintage figures trended upward this year.

EF-40	AU-50	MS-60	MS-63	MS-65	MS-66	MS-67
$8.20	$8.30	$9.50	$11.00	$24.50	$54	$156

1948-D

Circulation-Strike Mintage: 16,766,800
GSID: 5678

Key to Collecting: Choice and gem Mint State coins are readily available.

EF-40	AU-50	MS-60	MS-63	MS-65	MS-66	MS-67
$8.20	$8.30	$9.50	$19	$35	$54	$338

1948-S

Circulation-Strike Mintage: 15,960,000
GSID: 5679

Key to Collecting: Choice and gem Mint State coins are readily available.

EF-40	AU-50	MS-60	MS-63	MS-65	MS-66	MS-67
$8.20	$8.30	$9.50	$12.00	$44.50	$74	$234

1949

Circulation-Strike Mintage: 9,312,000
GSID: 5630

Key to Collecting: Choice and gem Mint State coins are readily available. This was a slump year in the coin market, a malaise that continued through 1951. Fewer rolls were saved than previously. However, on an absolute basis enough were set aside that they are not scarce today.

EF-40	AU-50	MS-60	MS-63	MS-65	MS-66	MS-67
$11	$17	$38	$46	$61	$92	$247

1949-D

Circulation-Strike Mintage: 10,068,400
GSID: 5680

Key to Collecting: Choice and gem Mint State coins are readily available.

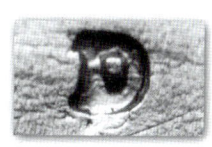

Varieties: D over S *(FS-25-1949D-601):* A 1949-D, D over S, overmintmark may exist, but it is not distinct and is not widely sought. Some believe it is actually a D over D variety, but Fivaz-Stanton say they believe studying an earlier die state of the variety proves conclusively that the earlier mintmark is an S.

EF-40	AU-50	MS-60	MS-63	MS-65	MS-66	MS-67
$11	$14	$22	$35	$43	$101	$228

1950

Circulation-Strike Mintage: 24,920,126
Proof Mintage: 51,386
GSID: Circulation strike, 5631; Proof, 5868

Key to Collecting: Choice and gem Mint State coins are readily available. Proofs were made this year for the first time since 1942. The earlier Proof strikings of 1950 are not as mirrorlike as the later ones made this year.

Numismatic Notes: Circulation strikes have the Variety A reverse; Proofs have the Variety B reverse (see chapter 5) used on Proofs 1937 to 1964.

EF-40	AU-50	MS-60	MS-63	MS-65	MS-66	MS-67	PF-63	PF-65	PF-67
$8.20	$8.20	$11	$16	$35	$57	$312	$47	$63	$108

1950-D

Circulation-Strike Mintage: 21,075,600
GSID: 5681

Key to Collecting: Choice and gem Mint State coins are readily available.

EF-40	AU-50	MS-60	MS-63	MS-65	MS-66	MS-67
$8.20	$8.20	$9.50	$20.00	$40.50	$89	$286

1950-D, D over S

Circulation-Strike Mintage: Small part of 1950-D mintage

GSID: 5682, 374348

Key to Collecting: This is a very interesting and desirable variety for the specialist. It is scarcer than market prices indicate, as the demand is not great (but is increasing).

Numismatic Notes: Listed widely, including as FS-25-1950D-601.

EF-40	AU-50	MS-60	MS-63	MS-65	MS-66	MS-67
$122	$162	$247	$780	$2,250	$3,000	$16,800

1950-S

Circulation-Strike Mintage: 10,284,004

GSID: 5683

Key to Collecting: Choice and gem Mint State coins are readily available.

Numismatic Notes: A variety with double-punched S is known.

EF-40	AU-50	MS-60	MS-63	MS-65	MS-66	MS-67
$8.20	$8.20	$9.50	$15.00	$36.50	$61	$312

1950-S, S over D

Circulation-Strike Mintage: Small part of 1950-D mintage

GSID: 5684, 374351

Key to Collecting: Another overmintmark that is somewhat scarce, highly interesting, and well worth owning.

Numismatic Notes: Now listed widely, including as FS-25-1950S-601.

EF-40	AU-50	MS-60	MS-63	MS-65	MS-66	MS-67
$214	$292	$364	$455	$1,220	$1,620	$7,500

1951

Circulation-Strike Mintage: 43,448,102
Proof Mintage: 57,500
GSID: Circulation strike, 5632; Proof, 5871

Key to Collecting: Choice and gem Mint State coins are readily available. The Proof mintage is higher than that of 1950. The market remained in a slump in 1951, but would awake soon.

Numismatic Notes: Circulation strikes have the Variety A reverse; Proofs have the Variety B reverse (see chapter 5) used on Proofs 1937 to 1964.

EF-40	AU-50	MS-60	MS-63	MS-65	MS-66	MS-67	PF-63	PF-65	PF-67
$8.20	$8.20	$9.50	$11.00	$24.50	$34.00	$162.00	$40.50	$54	$101

1951-D

Circulation-Strike Mintage: 35,354,800
GSID: 5685

Key to Collecting: Choice and gem Mint State coins are readily available.

Varieties: *D over D (FS-25-1951D-501):* A relatively strong repunched mintmark.

EF-40	AU-50	MS-60	MS-63	MS-65	MS-66	MS-67
$8.20	$8.20	$9.50	$11.00	$29.50	$40.50	$208

1951-S

Circulation-Strike Mintage: 9,048,000
GSID: 5686

Key to Collecting: Choice and gem Mint State coins are readily available.

EF-40	AU-50	MS-60	MS-63	MS-65	MS-66	MS-67
$8.20	$8.20	$9.50	$23	$38	$68	$130

1952

Circulation-Strike Mintage: 38,780,093

Proof Mintage: 81,980

GSID: Circulation strike, 5633; Proof, 5874

Key to Collecting: Choice and gem Mint State coins are readily available. Proofs were rapidly catching on with the public, and it was not unusual for dealers and investors to order five or 10 sets instead of just one. The coin market began to strengthen. In Iola, Wisconsin, Chet Krause launched *Numismatic News*, which went on to become the nucleus of the vast Krause Publications empire, a juggernaut by the 1980s.

Numismatic Notes: Circulation strikes have the Variety A reverse; Proofs have the Variety B reverse (see chapter 5) used on Proofs 1937 to 1964.

EF-40	AU-50	MS-60	MS-63	MS-65	MS-66	MS-67	PF-63	PF-65	PF-67
$8.20	$8.20	$9.50	$13.50	$32.50	$61	$115	$38	$47	$81

1952-D

Circulation-Strike Mintage: 49,795,200

GSID: 5687

Key to Collecting: Choice and gem Mint State coins are readily available.

EF-40	AU-50	MS-60	MS-63	MS-65	MS-66	MS-67
$8.20	$8.20	$9.50	$11	$35	$57	$860

1952-S

Circulation-Strike Mintage: 13,707,800

GSID: 5688

Key to Collecting: Choice and gem Mint State coins are readily available.

EF-40	AU-50	MS-60	MS-63	MS-65	MS-66	MS-67
$8.20	$8.20	$11.00	$20.00	$40.50	$68	$162

1953

Circulation-Strike Mintage: 18,536,120
Proof Mintage: 128,800
GSID: Circulation strike, 5634; Proof, 5877

Key to Collecting: Choice and gem Mint State coins are readily available. Proofs were ordered in such record numbers that the Mint became alarmed at the prospect. Soon, limits on orders were put in place, which in the next few years only served to fuel demand further. Beginning about this time, interest in saving bank-wrapped rolls of new coins went into high gear. Although most emphasis was on the lower denominations, particularly Lincoln cents, countless thousands of rolls and even bags of new quarters were set aside.

Numismatic Notes: Circulation strikes have the Variety A reverse; Proofs have the Variety B reverse (see chapter 5) used on Proofs 1937 to 1964.

EF-40	AU-50	MS-60	MS-63	MS-65	MS-66	MS-67	PF-63	PF-65	PF-67
$8.20	$8.20	$9.50	$12.00	$24.50	$34.00	$195.00	$21.50	$44.50	$61

1953-D

Circulation-Strike Mintage: 56,112,400
GSID: 5689

Key to Collecting: Attractive choice and gem Mint State coins are readily available.

Varieties: D over Inverted D *(FS-25-1953D-501):* Further study may determine the underlying D to be horizontal, but inverted is more likely. This variety is not widely known and is an excellent cherrypicking opportunity.

EF-40	AU-50	MS-60	MS-63	MS-65	MS-66	MS-67
$8.20	$8.20	$9.50	$13.50	$34	$61	$494

1953-D, D over S

Circulation-Strike Mintage:
Small part of 1953-D mintage
GSID: 374357

Key to Collecting: This curious overmintmark is actually 1953-D, with three impressions of the D punch, over two earlier S mintmarks! This variety is not well known, and thus can be a cherrypicker's delight.

Numismatic Notes: FS-25-1953D-601, Breen-4367.

MS-65
$292

1953-S

Circulation-Strike Mintage: 14,016,000
GSID: 5690

Key to Collecting: This variety is easily available in choice and gem Mint State.

EF-40	AU-50	MS-60	MS-63	MS-65	MS-66	MS-67
$8.20	$8.20	$9.50	$11.00	$29.50	$61	$176

1954

Circulation-Strike Mintage: 54,412,203
Proof Mintage: 233,300
GSID: Circulation strike, 5635; Proof, 5880

Key to Collecting: Easily available in choice and gem Mint State. Proofs were made in record high quantities, but nothing like the mintage figures of years to come.

Numismatic Notes: Circulation strikes have the Variety A reverse; Proofs have the Variety B reverse (see chapter 5) used on Proofs 1937 to 1964.

EF-40	AU-50	MS-60	MS-63	MS-65	MS-66	MS-67	PF-63	PF-65	PF-67
$8.20	$8.20	$8.30	$8.50	$16	$38	$169	$11	$20	$54

1954-D

Circulation-Strike Mintage: 42,305,500
GSID: 5691

Key to Collecting: This coin is easily available in choice and gem Mint State.

EF-40	AU-50	MS-60	MS-63	MS-65	MS-66	MS-67
$8.20	$8.20	$8.40	$10.50	$24.50	$61	$468

1954-S

Circulation-Strike Mintage: 11,834,722
GSID: 5692

Key to Collecting: This coin is easily available in choice and gem Mint State. This is the last of the San Francisco Mint silver quarters of the era.

EF-40	AU-50	MS-60	MS-63	MS-65	MS-66	MS-67
$8.20	$8.20	$8.50	$11.00	$20.00	$32.50	$195

1955

Circulation-Strike Mintage: 18,180,181
Proof Mintage: 378,200
GSID: Circulation strike, 5636; Proof, 5883

Key to Collecting: This coin is easily available in choice and gem Mint State. Proofs attained a record mintage.

Numismatic Notes: Circulation strikes have the Variety A reverse; Proofs have the Variety B reverse (see chapter 5) used on Proofs 1937 to 1964.

EF-40	AU-50	MS-60	MS-63	MS-65	MS-66	MS-67	PF-63	PF-65	PF-67
$8.20	$8.20	$8.30	$8.50	$29.50	$51.00	$422.00	$11.00	$19.00	$40.50

1955-D

Circulation-Strike Mintage: 3,182,400
GSID: 5693

Key to Collecting: This coin is easily available in choice and gem Mint State, despite a low mintage. The investment potential was widely recognized at the time, and many were saved. Hoarding rolls of all denominations was a passion by this time, driven by the ever-escalating price of the low-mintage 1950-D nickel. The entire market was robust.

EF-40	AU-50	MS-60	MS-63	MS-65	MS-66	MS-67
$8.20	$8.20	$8.30	$8.50	$34	$81	$9,000

1956

Circulation-Strike Mintage: 44,144,000
Proof Mintage: 669,384
GSID: Circulation strike, 5637; Proof, 5886

Key to Collecting: This coin is easily available in choice and gem Mint State. Proofs were especially hot in the market, with much excitement. Those who were lucky enough to have ordered sets under the restrictions in place could sell "futures" at a profit before the coins were delivered. Sol Kaplan, Cincinnati dealer, was in the forefront of the market and posted bid and ask prices, including on a chalkboard at conventions. Some prices for older sets changed *hourly*.

Numismatic Notes: Circulation strikes have the Variety A reverse; Proofs have the Variety B reverse (see chapter 5) used on Proofs 1937 to 1964.

EF-40	AU-50	MS-60	MS-63	MS-65	MS-66	MS-67	PF-63	PF-65	PF-67
$8.20	$8.20	$8.30	$8.50	$16.00	$29.50	$74.00	$8.50	$13.50	$29.50

1956-D

Circulation-Strike Mintage: 32,334,500
GSID: 5694

Key to Collecting: This coin is easily available in choice and gem Mint State.

Numismatic Notes: Variety A and B reverses, see 1937. Variety with D over horizontal D.

Varieties: D over Horizontal D *(Breen-4378):* The D was first punched into the die with the rounded part facing down, 90° to the right of normal. A correct D was then overpunched. This variety is not listed by Fivaz-Stanton.

EF-40	AU-50	MS-60	MS-63	MS-65	MS-66	MS-67
$8.20	$8.20	$8.30	$8.50	$20	$43	$312

1957

Circulation-Strike Mintage: 46,532,000
Proof Mintage: 1,247,952
GSID: Circulation strike, 5638; Proof, 5889

Key to Collecting: This coin is easily available in choice and gem Mint State. The Proof mintage crossed the million mark for the first time. However, the market for Proofs crashed by the time most people received their sets from the Mint, placing a damper on all investment in modern coins—Proof sets as well as rolls. Quantities of rolls saved were less from this point, continuing through 1959.

Numismatic Notes: Circulation strikes have the Variety A reverse; Proofs have the Variety B reverse (see chapter 5) used on Proofs 1937 to 1964.

EF-40	AU-50	MS-60	MS-63	MS-65	MS-66	MS-67	PF-63	PF-65	PF-67
$8.20	$8.20	$8.30	$8.50	$16.00	$29.50	$74.00	$8.50	$13.50	$27

1957-D

Circulation-Strike Mintage: 77,924,160
GSID: 5695

Key to Collecting: This coin is easily available in choice and gem Mint State.

Numismatic Notes: Variety A and B reverses, see 1937.

EF-40	AU-50	MS-60	MS-63	MS-65	MS-66	MS-67
$8.20	$8.20	$8.30	$8.50	$29.50	$47	$115

1958

Circulation-Strike Mintage: 6,360,000
Proof Mintage: 875,652
GSID: Circulation strike, 5639; Proof, 5892

Key to Collecting: This coin is easily available in choice and gem Mint State. The mintage of Proofs took a nosedive due to the weak market.

Numismatic Notes: Circulation strikes have the Variety A reverse; Proofs have the Variety B reverse (see chapter 5) used on Proofs 1937 to 1964.

EF-40	AU-50	MS-60	MS-63	MS-65	MS-66	MS-67	PF-63	PF-65	PF-67
$8.20	$8.20	$8.30	$8.50	$16.00	$29.50	$74.00	$8.50	$13.50	$27

1958-D

Circulation-Strike Mintage: 78,124,900
GSID: 5696

Key to Collecting: This coin is easily available in choice and gem Mint State.

Numismatic Notes: Variety A and B reverses, see 1937.

EF-40	AU-50	MS-60	MS-63	MS-65	MS-66	MS-67
$8.20	$8.20	$8.30	$8.50	$29.50	$48.50	$74

1959

Circulation-Strike Mintage: 24,384,000
Proof Mintage: 1,149,291
GSID: Circulation strike, 5640; Proof, 5895

Key to Collecting: This coin is easily available in choice and gem Mint State. Interest in Proofs revived to an extent, and the mintage was more than a million.

Numismatic Notes: Circulation strikes and Proofs have the Variety B reverse (see chapter 5).

EF-40	AU-50	MS-60	MS-63	MS-65	MS-66	MS-67	PF-63	PF-65	PF-67
$8.20	$8.20	$8.30	$8.50	$16.00	$43.00	$860.00	$7.50	$13.50	$40.50

1959-D

Circulation-Strike Mintage: 62,054,232
GSID: 5697

Key to Collecting: This coin is easily available in choice and gem Mint State.

Numismatic Notes: Variety A and B reverses, see 1937.

EF-40	AU-50	MS-60	MS-63	MS-65	MS-66	MS-67
$8.20	$8.20	$8.30	$8.50	$19	$74	$715

1960

Circulation-Strike Mintage: 29,164,000
Proof Mintage: 1,691,602
GSID: Circulation strike, 5641; Proof, 5898

Key to Collecting: This coin is easily available in choice and gem Mint State. The coin market was on fire, driven by the advent of *Coin World*, the first weekly publication in the field, and by the excitement of the 1960 Small Date Lincoln cent. All series benefited. The Library of Coins album series, marketed widely by the Coin and Currency Institute, proved to be a popular and attractive way to store and display sets of coins.

Numismatic Notes: Circulation strikes and Proofs have the Variety B reverse (see chapter 5).

EF-40	AU-50	MS-60	MS-63	MS-65	MS-66	MS-67	PF-63	PF-65	PF-67
$8.20	$8.20	$8.30	$8.50	$16.00	$47.00	$468.00	$7.90	$11	$20

1960-D

Circulation-Strike Mintage: 63,000,324
GSID: 5698

Key to Collecting: This coin is easily available in choice and gem Mint State.

Numismatic Notes: Variety A and B reverses, see 1937.

EF-40	AU-50	MS-60	MS-63	MS-65	MS-66	MS-67
$8.20	$8.20	$8.30	$8.50	$21.50	$51	$2,000

1961

Circulation-Strike Mintage: 37,036,000
Proof Mintage: 3,028,244
GSID: Circulation strike, 5642; Proof, 5901

Key to Collecting: This coin is easily available in choice and gem Mint State. Proof mintages continued to climb, and another record was set. The market was dynamic in all series. Interest spread to mint errors, die varieties, tokens, paper money, and other series outside of the mainstream (i.e., not listed in the *Red Book*).

Numismatic Notes: Circulation strikes and Proofs have the Variety B reverse (see chapter 5).

EF-40	AU-50	MS-60	MS-63	MS-65	MS-66	MS-67	PF-63	PF-65	PF-67
$8.20	$8.20	$8.30	$8.50	$24.50	$59.00	$2,500.00	$7.90	$11	$20

1961-D

Circulation-Strike Mintage: 83,656,928
GSID: 5699

Key to Collecting: This coin is easily available in choice and gem Mint State. Rolls were hoarded in unprecedented quantities from 1960 through 1964.

Numismatic Notes: Variety A and B reverses, see 1937.

EF-40	AU-50	MS-60	MS-63	MS-65	MS-66	MS-67
$8.20	$8.20	$8.30	$8.50	$29.50	$81	$3,120

1962

Circulation-Strike Mintage: 36,156,000

Proof Mintage: 3,218,019

GSID: Circulation strike, 5643; Proof, 5904

Key to Collecting: This coin is easily available in choice and gem Mint State. Market prices kept rising across the board. Proof production stabilized as slightly over three million, about the level that the Mint found comfortable to produce without having to place other facilities in use.

Numismatic Notes: Circulation strikes and Proofs have the Variety B reverse (see chapter 5).

EF-40	AU-50	MS-60	MS-63	MS-65	MS-66	MS-67	PF-63	PF-65	PF-67
$8.20	$8.20	$8.30	$8.50	$29.50	$47.00	$1,150.00	$7.90	$11.00	$13.50

1962-D

Circulation-Strike Mintage: 127,554,756

GSID: 5700

Key to Collecting: This coin is easily available in choice and gem Mint State.

Numismatic Notes: Variety A and B reverses, see 1937.

Varieties: D over Horizontal D *(Breen-4404):* The D was first punched into the die in a horizontal position. A correct D was then overpunched.

EF-40	AU-50	MS-60	MS-63	MS-65	MS-66	MS-67
$8.20	$8.20	$8.30	$8.50	$21.50	$68	$2,250

1963

Circulation-Strike Mintage: 74,316,000

Proof Mintage: 3,075,645

GSID: Circulation strike, 5644; Proof, 5907

Key to Collecting: Mint State coins are available in just about any level desired. The market continued its upward movement. The *Coin Dealer Newsletter* was launched, and included bid and ask prices for rolls and Proof sets.

Numismatic Notes: Circulation strikes and Proofs have the Variety B reverse (see chapter 5).

EF-40	AU-50	MS-60	MS-63	MS-65	MS-66	MS-67	PF-63	PF-65	PF-67
$8.20	$8.20	$8.30	$8.50	$27.00	$47.00	$560.00	$7.90	$11.00	$20

1963-D

Circulation-Strike Mintage: 135,288,184
GSID: 5701

Key to Collecting: Attractive choice and gem Mint State coins are readily available.

Numismatic Notes: Variety A and B reverses, see 1937. Doubled obverse die variety listed in Breen.

EF-40	AU-50	MS-60	MS-63	MS-65	MS-66	MS-67
$8.20	$8.20	$8.30	$8.50	$27	$61	$650

1964

Circulation-Strike Mintage: 560,390,585
Proof Mintage: 3,950,762
GSID: Circulation strike, 5645; Proof, 5911

EF-40	AU-50	MS-60	MS-63	MS-65	MS-66	MS-67	PF-63	PF-65	PF-67
$8.20	$8.20	$8.30	$8.50	$21.50	$40.50	$429.00	$7.90	$11.00	$13.50

Key to Collecting: Mint State coins are available in just about any level desired. The market continued its upward movement. *The Coin Dealer Newsletter* was launched, and included bid and ask prices for rolls and Proof sets.

Numismatic Notes: The year 1964 was the last in which circulation-strike Washington quarters were solid silver. Circulation strikes and Proofs have the Variety B reverse (see chapter 5). Possible Reverse C exists on circulation strikes per Breen "new hub of 1965; 2 leaves touch tops of AR," but this is not confirmed by Fivaz and Stanton.

The Philadelphia Mint continued striking silver 1964-dated quarters in early 1965. The date was not changed, per the "date freeze" mandate of Mint Director Eva Adams. She blamed coin collectors for the current coin shortage and sought to stymie the collecting of new coins. In 1965 the *San Francisco Mint* (then called the San Francisco Assay Office) struck more than 15,000,000 mintmarkless 1964-dated silver quarters in 1965 and a further 4,640,865 in early 1966.[5]

After 1964, solid silver Proof quarters would be discontinued, not to resume again until 1992.

1964-D

Circulation-Strike Mintage: 704,135,528
GSID: 5702

Key to Collecting: Choice and gem Mint State coins are readily available.

Numismatic Notes: Variety A and B reverses, see 1937. Also rare Variety C reverse, see above. The Denver Mint continued striking silver 1964-D quarters through 1965. The date was not changed, per the "date freeze" mandate of Mint Director Eva Adams.[6] The year 1964 was also the last in which the Washington quarter mintmark would appear on the reverse.

Varieties: Misplaced Mintmark *(FS-25-1964D-902)*: Fivaz-Stanton states: "On this very visually dramatic variety, a secondary D mintmark is evident protruding from the branch above the normal mintmark area. This is one of very few completely separated mintmark varieties."

Reverse C *(FS-25-1964D-901)*: Fivaz-Stanton: "A very small quantity of 1964-D coins is known to have the Type C reverse intended for use starting in 1965. Type C coins show the leaves above the AR in DOLLAR sharp and almost touching the letters, where the Type A is weak and the Type B is bold, but with the one leaf touching the A of DOLLAR. The tail feathers on Type C have a very distinct centerline. Additionally, the leaves below the tail feathers are sharp and barely touch those tail feathers. The leaf in front of the arrow tips comes to a distinct point in front of the arrow tips. On Type B, this leaf rises above the top arrow point, and the leaf end tips left. On Type A it is very weak."

EF-40	AU-50	MS-60	MS-63	MS-65	MS-66	MS-67
$8.20	$8.20	$8.30	$8.50	$24.50	$54	$292

1965

Circulation-Strike Mintage: 1,819,717,540
Special Mint Set Mintage: 2,360,000
GSID: Circulation strike, 5703; SMS, 5914; SMS Cameo, 5915; SMS Deep Cameo, 5916

Key to Collecting: Although clad quarters dated 1965 were made in unprecedented quantities, crossing the billion mark for the first time, there was scarcely any interest anymore in saving rolls, for clad metal, unlike silver, faced an uncertain future. For this year through the rest of the decade, very small quantities of quarter rolls were saved in proportion to the mintage figures.

Numismatic Notes: Examples are known on 90% silver planchet.

The mintage of this year set an all-time high record, not equaled since that time. This high figure is explained by the production of 1965-dated quarters into the year 1966, due to the "date freeze" set in place by Mint Director Eva Adams, and by the fact that Denver quarters bore no mintmark in 1965 and thus appeared identical to Philadelphia coins. The Denver Mint did not resume using the D mintmark until 1968.

Clad quarters were first released into circulation in November 1965.

Varieties: Special Mint Sets: 2,360,000 Special Mint Sets of coins dated 1965 were struck *in 1966* at the San Francisco Mint (but with no mintmark) for sale to collectors. These were carefully made and have a satiny, partially mirrored surface. Unless Special Mint Set coins have cameo contrast and are prooflike, they can be indistinguishable from regular issues. Thus they are not priced here.

Doubled Die Obverse *(FS-25-1965-101):* Fivaz-Stanton says: "The doubling is very strong on all obverse lettering, the eye, and the date. This variety is extremely rare and sells very quickly at auction."

Circulating Strikes

MS-63	MS-65	MS-66	MS-67
$4.05	$6.80	$34	$364

Special Mint Sets

SP-65	SP-67Cam	SP-67DC
$5.40	$325	$2,500

1966

Circulation-Strike Mintage:
821,101,500

Special Mint Set Mintage: 2,261,583

GSID: Circulation strike, 5704; SMS, 5917; SMS Cameo, 5918; SMS Deep Cameo, 5919

Key to Collecting: Mint State coins are readily available. Quality of 1966 and other early clad quarters is a different matter, and most coins have extensive marks (including from the original planchets), or striking, or eye appeal, or all of these considerations.

Varieties: Special Mint Sets: 2,261,583 Special Mint Sets of coins were struck at the San Francisco Mint (but with no mintmark) for sale to collectors. These were carefully made and have a partially mirrored surface. Unless Special Mint Set coins have cameo contrast and are prooflike, they can be indistinguishable from regular issues. Thus they are not priced here.

Circulating Strikes

MS-63	MS-65	MS-66	MS-67
$1.50	$9.50	$24.50	$214

Special Mint Sets

SP-65	SP-67Cam	SP-68DC
$5.40	$54	$3,750

1967

Circulation-Strike Mintage: 1,524,031,848

Special Mint Set Mintage: 1,863,344

GSID: Circulation strike, 5705; SMS, 5920; SMS Cameo, 5921; SMS Deep Cameo, 5922

Key to Collecting: Mint State coins are readily available, but cherrypicking is recommended to obtain quality.

Numismatic Notes: The mintage for this year is the second highest all-time record (1965 is highest).

Varieties: Special Mint Sets: 1,863,344 Special Mint Sets of coins were struck at the San Francisco Mint (but with no mintmark) for sale to collectors. These were carefully made and have a partially mirrored surface. Unless Special Mint Set coins have cameo contrast and are prooflike, they can be indistinguishable from regular issues. Thus they are not priced here.

Circulating Strikes

MS-63	MS-65	MS-66	MS-67
$5.40	$11	$20	$81

Special Mint Sets

SP-65	SP-68Cam	SP-68DC
$5.40	$208	$2,750

1968

Circulation-Strike Mintage: 220,731,500

GSID: 5706

Key to Collecting: Philadelphia Mint coins continued to display no mintmark until 1980.

Mint State coins are readily available on an absolute basis, although quality can be a problem. Clad coins continued to be ignored by investors.

MS-63	MS-65	MS-66	MS-67
$1.50	$8.10	$27	$59

1968-D

Circulation-Strike Mintage: 101,534,000
GSID: 5720

Key to Collecting: Through 1964, the mintmark appeared on the reverse. From 1965 through 1967, Washington quarters were made only in Philadelphia, and bore no mintmarks. Beginning with 1968's Denver coinage, the mintmark appeared on the obverse.

The same comment as for the 1968 Philadelphia quarters. Around this time Ken Bressett, editor of the *Red Book*, was one of the first to comment that clad coins, ignored by investors, might prove to be scarce someday.

MS-63	MS-65	MS-66	MS-67
$1.50	$5.40	$16	$57

1968-S

Proof Mintage: 3,041,506
GSID: 5923; Cameo, 5924; Deep Cameo, 5925

Key to Collecting: The mintmark on Proof Washington quarters of this period is likewise on the obverse. Beginning this year, Proofs were packaged attractive hard plastic holders. The quality was better than ever before, and from this point onward, cameo contrast became a feature of many (but not all) Proof coins.

Numismatic Notes: Doubled-die obverse and doubled-die reverse varieties are known and command a strong premium. Listed as FS-25-1968S-101 and 801, respectively.

PF-65	PF-67Cam	PF-68DC
$6.80	$13.50	$108

1969

Circulation-Strike Mintage: 176,212,000
GSID: 5707

Key to Collecting: Mint State coins are readily available. Cherrypicking for quality is advised. In this era plastic holders, such as those marketed by Capital Plastics, were a popular way to display sets of coins, including Washington quarters.

MS-63	MS-65	MS-66	MS-67
$1.50	$16	$74	$2,380

1969-D

Circulation-Strike Mintage: 114,372,000
GSID: 5721

Key to Collecting: Mint State coins are readily available. Cherrypicking for quality is advised. Clad coins continued to be ignored in their own time.

MS-63	MS-65	MS-66	MS-67
$2.65	$8.10	$14	$88

1969-S

Proof Mintage: 2,934,631
GSID: 5926; Cameo, 5927; Deep Cameo, 5928

Key to Collecting: Readily available and with good eye appeal.

Numismatic Notes: Doubled-die obverse listed as FS-25-1969S-101. Doubling on the lettering and date.

PF-65	PF-67Cam	PF-68DC
$6.80	$13.50	$68

1970

Circulation-Strike Mintage: 136,420,000
GSID: 5708

Key to Collecting: Mint State coins are readily available. Cherrypicking for quality is advised.

MS-63	MS-65	MS-66	MS-67
$1.50	$12	$34	$338

1970-D

Circulation-Strike Mintage: 417,341,364
GSID: 5722

Key to Collecting: Mint State coins are readily available. Cherrypicking for quality is advised.

MS-63	MS-65	MS-66	MS-67
$1.50	$5.40	$11	$47

1970-S

Proof Mintage: 2,632,810
GSID: 5929; Cameo, 5930; Deep Cameo, 5931

Key to Collecting: Attractive and of high quality— this is the general rule for coins in the marketplace today. Single Proof quarters are available from sets that have been taken apart.

Numismatic Notes: The writer purchased a 1970-S Proof quarter plainly struck over a 1900 Barber quarter. The coin was publicly offered and was seized by the Treasury Department. Apparently the concoction of a creative Mint employee, the piece somehow escaped into a 1970-S Proof set, no doubt initially baffling its discoverer.

PF-65	PF-67Cam	PF-68DC
$6.80	$13.50	$68

1971

Circulation-Strike Mintage: 109,284,000
GSID: 5709

Key to Collecting: Mint State coins are readily available. Cherrypicking for quality is advised.

MS-63	MS-65	MS-66	MS-67
$1.50	$6.80	$122	$3,120

1971-D

Circulation-Strike Mintage: 258,634,428
GSID: 5723

Key to Collecting: Mint State coins are readily available. Cherrypicking for quality is advised.

MS-63	MS-65	MS-66	MS-67
$1.50	$6.80	$19	$101

1971-S

Proof Mintage: 3,220,733
GSID: 5932; Cameo, 5933; Deep Cameo, 5934

Key to Collecting: Attractive and of high quality, as usual. The San Francisco Mint set new high standards in production.

PF-65	PF-67Cam	PF-68DC
$6.80	$13.50	$260

1972

Circulation-Strike Mintage: 215,048,000
GSID: 5710

Key to Collecting: Mint State coins are readily available. Cherrypicking for quality is advised.

MS-63	MS-65	MS-66	MS-67
$1.50	$5.40	$36.50	$780

1972-D

Circulation-Strike Mintage: 311,067,732
GSID: 5724

Key to Collecting: Mint State coins are readily available. Cherrypicking for quality is advised. As improbable as it may seem in retrospect, there was no emphasis on high quality. Bank-wrapped rolls were Uncirculated, and that was that—no sorting through to find gems. This situation remained in effect for much of the decade.

MS-63	MS-65	MS-66	MS-67
$1.50	$9.50	$13.50	$61

1972-S

Proof Mintage: 3,260,996
GSID: 5935; Cameo, 5936; Deep Cameo, 5937

Key to Collecting: High quality and beautiful appearance as usual.

PF-65	PF-67Cam	PF-68DC
$6.80	$10.80	$19

1973

Circulation-Strike Mintage: 346,924,000
GSID: 5711

Key to Collecting: Mint State coins are readily available. Cherrypicking for quality is advised.

MS-63	MS-65	MS-66	MS-67
$1.50	$5.40	$54	$390

1973-D

Circulation-Strike Mintage: 232,977,400
GSID: 5725

Key to Collecting: Mint State coins are readily available. Cherrypicking for quality is advised.

MS-63	MS-65	MS-66	MS-67
$1.50	$4.05	$27	$122

1973-S

Proof Mintage: 2,760,339
GSID: 5938; Cameo, 5939; Deep Cameo, 5940

Key to Collecting: Nice!

PF-65	PF-67Cam	PF-68DC
$6.80	$9.50	$12

1974

Circulation-Strike Mintage: 801,456,000
GSID: 5712

Key to Collecting: Mint State coins are readily available. Cherrypicking for quality is advised. The investment end of the coin market entered a slow period that would reach its nadir in 1976, after which it would become warm, then hot.

Numismatic Notes: Many of the 1974-dated Washington quarters were struck in 1975, pursuant to Public Law 93-531 (December 26, 1974). In 1975 most activities at the mints were in striking the 1776–1976 Bicentennial quarters. Accordingly, while no 1975-dated quarters were made, 1974 quarters were restruck, and 1776–1976 quarters were prestruck.

MS-63	MS-65	MS-66	MS-67
$0.80	$4.05	$20	$234

1974-D

Circulation-Strike Mintage: 353,160,300
GSID: 5726

Key to Collecting: Mint State coins are readily available. Cherrypicking for quality is advised.

MS-63	MS-65	MS-66	MS-67
$0.80	$4.05	$34	$150

1974-S

Proof Mintage: 2,612,568
GSID: 5941; Cameo, 5942; Deep Cameo, 5943

Key to Collecting: Beautiful and of high quality.

Numismatic Notes: One variety has a doubled S-mintmark.

PF-65	PF-67Cam	PF-68DC
$4.70	$6.80	$9.50

BICENTENNIAL REVERSE, 1975–1976

Designers: *John Flanagan (obverse) and Jack L. Ahr (reverse).* **Weight:** *Silver clad—5.75 grams; copper-nickel clad—5.67 grams.* **Composition:** *Silver clad—outer layers of .800 silver, .200 copper bonded to inner core of .209 silver, .791 copper (net weight .0739 oz. pure silver); copper-nickel clad—outer layers of .750 copper, .250 nickel bonded to inner core of pure copper.* **Diameter:** *24.3 mm.* **Edge:** *Reeded.* **Mints:** *Philadelphia, Denver, and San Francisco.*

Quarters minted in both 1975 and 1976 received the dual dates 1776–1976.

1776–1976

Circulation-Strike Mintage: 809,784,016
GSID: 5714

Key to Collecting: Mint State coins are readily available. Cherrypicking for quality is advised. Especially large quantities were saved.

MS-63	MS-65	MS-66	MS-67
$0.80	$4.05	$20	$68

1776–1976-D

Circulation-Strike Mintage: 860,118,839
GSID: 5727

Key to Collecting: Common in Mint State, although gems are in the minority. Many were saved.

Numismatic Notes: A doubled-die obverse variety is listed in Breen.

MS-63	MS-65	MS-66	MS-67
$0.80	$4.05	$20	$101

1776–1976-S, Copper-Nickel Clad

Proof Mintage: 7,059,099
GSID: Deep Cameo, 5947

Key to Collecting: Easily available due to the extraordinary high mintage. Sales fell short of expectation, and sets were still available from the Mint for several years afterward.

Numismatic Notes: In August 1974 at the American Numismatic Association convention held that year in Bal Harbour, Florida, visitors were given a preview of the Proof coinage. On view were examples of each of the three Bicentennial denominations, but *without* S mintmark. The whereabouts of these coins is not known today.

PF-65DC	PF-67DC	PF-68DC
$4.75	$5.40	$11

1776–1976-S, Silver Clad

Circulation-Strike Mintage: 7,000,000
Proof Mintage: 4,000,000
GSID: Circulation strike, 5728; Proof Deep Cameo, 5949

Key to Collecting: Choice and gem Mint State and Proof coins are easily obtained, but at a premium due to the silver content.

Numismatic Notes: Demand for the silver strikes was below Mint expectations. By December 31, 1982, only 4,294,000 of the circulation strike (Uncirculated format) coins had been released and only 3,262,970 of the proofs. Some Proofs were struck at the *Philadelphia* Mint before the mintmark was added to the dies.

MS-63	MS-65	MS-66	MS-67	PF-65DC	PF-67DC	PF-68DC
$2.95	$3.25	$13.50	$19.00	$8.10	$11	$15

EAGLE REVERSE RESUMED, 1977–1998

Designer: *John Flanagan.* **Weight:** *Clad issue—5.67 grams; silver Proofs—6.25 grams.*
Composition: *Clad issue—outer layers of copper nickel (.750 copper, .250 nickel)
bonded to inner core of pure copper; silver Proofs—.900 silver, .100 copper
(net weight .18084 oz. pure silver).* **Diameter:** *24.3 mm.*
Edge: *Reeded.* **Mints:** *Philadelphia, Denver, and San Francisco.*

1977

Circulation-Strike Mintage: 468,556,000
+ 7,352,000 West Point = 475,908,000
GSID: 5715

Key to Collecting: Mint State coins are readily available. Cherrypicking for quality is advised, although choice and gem coins are much more available from this era than from the late 1960s and early 1970s.

Numismatic Notes: Includes some examples struck at the West Point Mint.

MS-63	MS-65	MS-66	MS-67
$0.80	$4.05	$20	$68

1977-D

Circulation-Strike Mintage: 256,524,978
GSID: 5729

Key to Collecting: Choice and gem Mint State coins are common, but they are a minority of the Mint State coins in existence.

MS-63	MS-65	MS-66	MS-67
$0.80	$4.05	$24.50	$128

1977-S

Proof Mintage: 3,251,152
GSID: Deep Cameo, 5952

Key to Collecting: Readily available and of high quality.

Numismatic Notes: Normal- and thin-motto varieties listed by Breen.

PF-65DC	PF-67DC	PF-68DC
$4.75	$5.40	$6.80

1978

Circulation-Strike Mintage: 521,452,000
+ 20,800,000 West Point = 542,252,000
GSID: 5716

Key to Collecting: Choice and gem Mint State coins are easily available. The coin market was especially active, driven by rising prices of silver and gold bullion. The market would peak in early 1980. This passion did not extend to saving bank-wrapped rolls of clad quarters.

Numismatic Notes: Includes pieces struck at the West Point Mint.

MS-63	MS-65	MS-66	MS-67
$0.80	$4.05	$27	$130

1978-D

Circulation-Strike Mintage: 287,373,152
GSID: 5730

Key to Collecting: Choice and gem Mint State coins are readily available.

MS-63	MS-65	MS-66	MS-67
$0.80	$4.05	$27	$390

1978-S

Proof Mintage: 3,127,781
GSID: Deep Cameo, 5955

Key to Collecting: High quality and with great eye appeal, as usual.

PF-65DC	PF-67DC	PF-68DC
$4.75	$5.40	$6.80

1979

Circulation-Strike Mintage: 515,708,000
+ 22,672,000 West Point = 538,380,000
GSID: 5717

Key to Collecting: Choice and gem Mint State coins are easily available. The American Numismatic Association Certification Service (ANACS) was active in grading coins for a fee, popularizing an innovation that would be very profitable to the ANA and create a lot of attention among dealers and collectors. Coins were returned loose (not encapsulated)

with a photographic certification giving the grade separately for each side, such as MS-64/65. From here it was onward and upward in the search for high-grade coins.

Numismatic Notes: Mintage includes pieces struck at the West Point Mint.

MS-63	MS-65	MS-66	MS-67
$0.80	$4.05	$27	$143

1979-D

Circulation-Strike Mintage: 489,789,780
GSID: 5731

Key to Collecting: Choice and gem Mint State coins are easily available.

MS-63	MS-65	MS-66	MS-67
$0.80	$4.05	$24.50	$325

1979-S

Proof Mintage: 3,677,175
GSID: Type 1 Deep Cameo, 5959; Type 2 Deep Cameo, 5961

Key to Collecting: High quality, as expected.

Numismatic Notes: Filled-S (Type 1) and Clear-S (Type 2) mintmark varieties are known. The Clear S is the scarcer of the two.

Type 1 Mintmark

PF-65DC	PF-67DC	PF-68DC
$4.75	$5.40	$8.10

Type 2 Mintmark

PF-65DC	PF-67DC	PF-68DC
$5.10	$6.80	$8.10

1980-P

Circulation-Strike Mintage: 635,832,000
GSID: 5718

Key to Collecting: Choice and gem Mint State coins are easily available. Early in the year the general coin market went into a slump, where it would remain until the later years of the decade.

MS-63	MS-65	MS-66	MS-67
$0.80	$4.05	$19	$115

1980-D

Circulation-Strike Mintage: 518,327,487
GSID: 5732

Key to Collecting: Choice and gem Mint State coins are easily available.

MS-63	MS-65	MS-66	MS-67
$0.80	$4.05	$20	$182

1980-S

Proof Mintage: 3,554,806
GSID: Deep Cameo, 5964

Key to Collecting: Nearly all are of gem quality.

PF-65DC	PF-67DC	PF-68DC
$4.75	$5.40	$9.50

1981-P

Circulation-Strike Mintage: 601,716,000
GSID: 5734

Key to Collecting: Choice and gem Mint State coins are easily available.

MS-63	MS-65	MS-66	MS-67
$0.80	$4.05	$27	$195

1981-D

Circulation-Strike Mintage: 575,722,833
GSID: 5733

Key to Collecting: Choice and gem Mint State coins are easily available.

MS-63	MS-65	MS-66	MS-67
$0.80	$4.05	$20	$115

1981-S

Proof Mintage: 4,063,083

GSID: Type 1 Deep Cameo, 5968; Type 2 Deep Cameo, 5970

Key to Collecting: Gem quality is the rule.

Numismatic Notes: Two mintmark varieties (Type 1 and Type 2; see 1979-S) mentioned by Breen.

Type 1 Mintmark

PF-65DC	PF-67DC	PF-68DC
$4.75	$5.40	$9.50

Type 2 Mintmark

PF-65DC	PF-67DC	PF-68DC
$6.80	$9.50	$13.50

1982-P

Circulation-Strike Mintage: 500,931,000

GSID: 5736

Key to Collecting: Choice and gem Mint State coins are plentiful, but fewer are around than for recent earlier dates (see notes below).

Numismatic Notes: In 1982 and 1983, "Mint Sets" of current circulation strikes were not sold by the Mint. Accordingly, today the quarters of these two years are slightly scarcer than are others of this era.

MS-63	MS-65	MS-66	MS-67
$5.40	$38	$143	$364

1982-D

Circulation-Strike Mintage: 480,042,788

GSID: 5735

Key to Collecting: Choice and gem Mint State coins are plentiful on an absolute basis, but more elusive than for most other issues before and after 1982 and 1983.

Numismatic Notes: In 1982 and 1983, "Mint Sets" of current circulation strikes were not sold by the Mint. Accordingly, today the quarters of these two years are slightly scarcer than are others of this era.

MS-63	MS-65	MS-66	MS-67
$5.40	$27	$88	$208

1982-S

Proof Mintage: 3,857,479
GSID: Deep Cameo, 5973

Key to Collecting: Gem quality continues to be the rule. Quite a few Proof sets have been broken up, with the result that runs of Proof quarters are available from many mail-order dealers and coin shops.

PF-65DC	PF-67DC	PF-68DC
$5.10	$6.80	$9.50

1983-P

Circulation-Strike Mintage: 673,535,000
GSID: 5719

Key to Collecting: Choice and gem Mint State coins are easily available, but are scarcer than most other issues of the decade.

Numismatic Notes: In 1982 and 1983, "Mint Sets" of current circulation strikes were not sold by the Mint. Accordingly, MS-65 and finer quarters of these two years are slightly scarcer today than are others of this era.

MS-63	MS-65	MS-66	MS-67
$18.50	$54	$88	$650

1983-D

Circulation-Strike Mintage: 617,806,446
GSID: 5737

Key to Collecting: Same comment as 1983-P.

Numismatic Notes: In 1982 and 1983, "Mint Sets" of current circulation strikes were not sold by the Mint. Accordingly, MS-65 and finer quarters of these two years are slightly scarcer today than are others of this era.

MS-63	MS-65	MS-66	MS-67
$10	$34	$68	$650

1983-S

Proof Mintage: 3,279,126

GSID: Deep Cameo, 5976

Key to Collecting: Gem quality is easily available.

PF-65DC	PF-67DC	PF-68DC
$5.10	$6.80	$12

1984-P

Circulation-Strike Mintage: 676,545,000

GSID: 5739

Key to Collecting: Choice and gem Mint State coins are plentiful.

MS-63	MS-65	MS-66	MS-67
$0.80	$4.05	$34	$520

1984-D

Circulation-Strike Mintage: 546,483,064

GSID: 5738

Key to Collecting: Choice and gem Mint State coins are plentiful.

MS-63	MS-65	MS-66	MS-67
$0.80	$4.05	$38	$43

1984-S

Proof Mintage: 3,065,110

GSID: Deep Cameo, 5979

Key to Collecting: Easily available in gem preservation.

PF-65DC	PF-67DC	PF-68DC
$5.10	$6.80	$9.50

1985-P

Circulation-Strike Mintage: 775,818,962
GSID: 5741

Key to Collecting: Choice and gem Mint State coins are plentiful.

MS-63	MS-65	MS-66	MS-67
$0.80	$4.05	$29.50	$585

1985-D

Circulation-Strike Mintage: 519,962,888
GSID: 5740

Key to Collecting: Choice and gem Mint State coins are plentiful.

MS-63	MS-65	MS-66	MS-67
$0.80	$4.05	$29.50	$247

1985-S

Proof Mintage: 3,362,821
GSID: Deep Cameo, 5982

Key to Collecting: Gems are readily available from the sets.

PF-65DC	PF-67DC	PF-68DC
$5.10	$6.80	$9.50

1986-P

Circulation-Strike Mintage: 551,199,333
GSID: 5743

Key to Collecting: Choice and gem Mint State coins are plentiful. The Professional Coin Grading Service (PCGS) was launched, popularizing the grading of coins and encapsulating them in plastic.

MS-63	MS-65	MS-66	MS-67
$0.80	$4.05	$40.50	$1,620

1986-D

Circulation-Strike Mintage: 504,298,660
GSID: 5742

Key to Collecting: Choice and gem Mint State coins are plentiful.

MS-63	MS-65	MS-66	MS-67
$0.80	$4.05	$24.50	$390

1986-S

Proof Mintage: 3,010,497
GSID: Deep Cameo, 5985

Key to Collecting: Gems are plentiful.

PF-65DC	PF-67DC	PF-68DC
$4.75	$5.40	$8.10

1987-P

Circulation-Strike Mintage: 582,499,481
GSID: 5745

Key to Collecting: Choice and gem Mint State coins are easily available. The Numismatic Guaranty Corporation of America (NGC) began business with encapsulated coins and soon acquired a substantial market niche, second to PCGS.

MS-63	MS-65	MS-66	MS-67
$0.80	$4.05	$40.50	$260

1987-D

Circulation-Strike Mintage: 655,594,696
GSID: 5744

Key to Collecting: Choice and gem coins are common but constitute a minority of Mint State coins in existence, this being true of other clad quarters of the era. Many have extensive surface marks, especially prominent on the obverse.

MS-63	MS-65	MS-66	MS-67
$0.80	$4.05	$20	$260

1987-S

Proof Mintage: 4,227,728
GSID: Deep Cameo, 5988

Key to Collecting: Nearly all are of gem quality. There was an exceptionally high Proof mintage this year. The coin market was heating up, after being sluggish since early 1980.

PF-65DC	PF-67DC	PF-68DC
$4.75	$5.40	$6.80

1988-P

Circulation-Strike Mintage: 562,052,000
GSID: 5747

Key to Collecting: Choice and gem Mint State coins are plentiful.

MS-63	MS-65	MS-66	MS-67
$0.80	$4.05	$74	$1,560

1988-D

Circulation-Strike Mintage: 596,810,688
GSID: 5746

Key to Collecting: Choice and gem Mint State coins are plentiful.

MS-63	MS-65	MS-66	MS-67
$0.80	$4.05	$54	$715

1988-S

Proof Mintage: 3,262,948
GSID: Deep Cameo, 5991

Key to Collecting: Nearly all are gems.

PF-65DC	PF-67DC	PF-68DC
$4.75	$5.40	$8.10

1989-P

Circulation-Strike Mintage: 512,868,000
GSID: 5749

Key to Collecting: Choice and gem Mint State coins are plentiful. The coin market was very hot, spurred by much publicity about coins as an investment. Partnerships and funds were set up to invest, including one by Merrill Lynch. "Wall Street money" was said to be descending into the numismatic marketplace, or soon would be.

Numismatic Notes: In this year some Washington quarters were made without a mintmark, not a die preparation oversight, but due to grease or other material filling the mintmark in a working die. A flurry of media excitement included stories that they were worth $1,000 each. However, after a statement was given by the Philadelphia Mint as to the true nature of the coins, interest faded quickly.

MS-63	MS-65	MS-66	MS-67
$0.80	$11	$88	$1,500

1989-D

Circulation-Strike Mintage: 896,535,597
GSID: 5748

Key to Collecting: Choice and gem Mint State coins are plentiful.

MS-63	MS-65	MS-66	MS-67
$0.80	$4.05	$24.50	$280

1989-S

Proof Mintage: 3,220,194
GSID: Deep Cameo, 5994

Key to Collecting: Nearly all are gems.

PF-65DC	PF-67DC	PF-68DC
$4.75	$5.40	$6.80

1990-P

Circulation-Strike Mintage: 613,792,000
GSID: 5751

Key to Collecting: The investment market peaked, after which there was a crash in "investment-quality" coins, which were said to include choice and gem silver and gold coins. A set of MS-65 Peace silver dollars would fall to less than 25% of its 1990 high. Mainstream *collectors* were not affected. Wall Streeters who paid record prices were disillusioned. In time, Merrill Lynch liquidated its fund and investors suffered great losses.[7]

MS-63	MS-65	MS-66	MS-67
$0.80	$4.05	$27	$1,250

1990-D

Circulation-Strike Mintage: 927,638,181
GSID: 5750

Key to Collecting: Choice and gem Mint State coins are plentiful.

MS-63	MS-65	MS-66	MS-67
$0.80	$2.65	$13.50	$143

1990-S

Proof Mintage: 3,299,559
GSID: Deep Cameo, 5750

Key to Collecting: Nearly all are gems.

PF-65DC	PF-67DC	PF-68DC
$3.50	$4.05	$5.40

1991-P

Circulation-Strike Mintage: 570,968,000
GSID: 5753

Key to Collecting: Choice and gem Mint State coins are plentiful.

MS-63	MS-65	MS-66	MS-67
$0.80	$4.05	$43	$260

1991-D

Circulation-Strike Mintage: 630,966,693
GSID: 5752

Key to Collecting: Choice and gem Mint State coins are plentiful.

MS-63	MS-65	MS-66	MS-67
$0.80	$4.05	$57	$1,810

1991-S

Proof Mintage: 2,867,787
GSID: Deep Cameo, 6000

Key to Collecting: Nearly all are gems.

PF-65DC	PF-67DC	PF-68DC
$3.50	$4.05	$5.40

1992-P

Circulation-Strike Mintage: 384,764,000
GSID: 5755

Key to Collecting: Choice and gem coins are plentiful. By this time PCGS, NGC, and certain other grading services were very popular, but mostly for use in encapsulating earlier coins. There was hardly any interest in having current Mint State quarters certified, due to the high cost of the services in relation to the value of the coins.

MS-63	MS-65	MS-66	MS-67
$0.80	$4.05	$68	$266

1992-D

Circulation-Strike Mintage: 389,777,107
GSID: 5754

Key to Collecting: Choice and gem coins are plentiful.

MS-63	MS-65	MS-66	MS-67
$0.80	$4.05	$61	$650

1992-S, Copper-Nickel Clad

Proof Mintage: 2,858,981
GSID: Deep Cameo, 6006

Key to Collecting: Virtually all are gems.

PF-65DC	PF-67DC	PF-68DC
$3.50	$4.05	$5.40

1992-S, Silver

Proof Mintage: 1,317,579
GSID: Deep Cameo, 6004

Key to Collecting: This marked the first year of special Proof coins struck in the old alloy of 90% silver and 10% copper. These are not easily distinguished from the clad examples, except by looking at the coins edge-on to see full silver color. On clad coins, the copper core is seen.

PF-65DC	PF-67DC	PF-68DC
$8.90	$10.50	$12

1993-P

Circulation-Strike Mintage: 639,276,000
GSID: 5757

Key to Collecting: Choice and gem coins are plentiful.

MS-63	MS-65	MS-66	MS-67
$0.80	$4.05	$24.50	$122

1993-D

Circulation-Strike Mintage: 645,476,128
GSID: 5756

Key to Collecting: Choice and gem coins are plentiful.

MS-63	MS-65	MS-66	MS-67
$0.80	$4.05	$47	$234

1993-S, Copper-Nickel Clad

Proof Mintage: 2,633,439

GSID: Deep Cameo, 6012

Key to Collecting: Nearly all are gems.

PF-65DC	PF-67DC	PF-68DC
$3.50	$4.05	$5.40

1993-S, Silver

Proof Mintage: 761,353

GSID: Deep Cameo, 6010

Key to Collecting: Nearly all are gems. The mintage dropped sharply from that of 1992, primarily because at quick glance the silver coins could not be differentiated easily from the clad coins, unless the edge was inspected.

PF-65DC	PF-67DC	PF-68DC
$8.90	$10.50	$13.50

1994-P

Circulation-Strike Mintage: 825,600,000

GSID: 5759

Key to Collecting: Choice and gem coins are plentiful.

MS-63	MS-65	MS-66	MS-67
$0.80	$4.05	$36.50	$520

1994-D

Circulation-Strike Mintage: 880,034,110

GSID: 5758

Key to Collecting: Choice and gem coins are plentiful.

MS-63	MS-65	MS-66	MS-67
$0.80	$4.05	$61	$1,150

1994-S, Copper-Nickel Clad

Proof Mintage: 2,484,594
GSID: Deep Cameo, 6018

Key to Collecting: Nearly all are gems.

PF-65DC	PF-67DC	PF-68DC
$3.50	$4.05	$5.40

1994-S, Silver

Proof Mintage: 785,329
GSID: Deep Cameo, 6016

Key to Collecting: Nearly all are gems.

PF-65DC	PF-67DC	PF-68DC
$8.90	$10.50	$13.50

1995-P

Circulation-Strike Mintage: 1,004,336,000
GSID: 5761

Key to Collecting: Choice and gem coins are plentiful.

Numismatic Notes: The circulation strikes at the Philadelphia and Denver mint this year crossed the billion mark for the first time since the 1960s.

MS-63	MS-65	MS-66	MS-67
$0.80	$4.05	$20	$68

1995-D

Circulation-Strike Mintage: 1,103,216,000
GSID: 5760

Key to Collecting: Choice and gem coins are plentiful.

MS-63	MS-65	MS-66	MS-67
$0.80	$4.05	$24.50	$81

1995-S, Copper-Nickel Clad

Proof Mintage: 2,117,496

GSID: Deep Cameo, 6024

Key to Collecting: Virtually all are gems.

PF-65DC	PF-67DC	PF-68DC
$3.50	$4.05	$5.40

1995-S, Silver

Proof Mintage: 679,985

GSID: Deep Cameo, 6022

Key to Collecting: Nearly all are gems. Silver Proof quarters continued to generate lukewarm interest in comparison to the clad issues that were part of sets.

PF-65DC	PF-67DC	PF-68DC
$8.90	$10.50	$12

1996-P

Circulation-Strike Mintage: 925,040,000

GSID: 5763

Key to Collecting: Choice and gem coins are plentiful.

MS-63	MS-65	MS-66	MS-67
$0.80	$2.65	$11	$27

1996-D

Circulation-Strike Mintage: 906,868,000

GSID: 5762

Key to Collecting: Choice and gem coins are plentiful.

MS-63	MS-65	MS-66	MS-67
$0.80	$2.65	$11	$20

1996-S, Copper-Nickel Clad

Proof Mintage: 1,750,244
GSID: Deep Cameo, 6030

Key to Collecting: Nearly all are gems.

PF-65DC	PF-67DC	PF-68DC
$3.50	$4.05	$5.40

1996-S, Silver

Proof Mintage: 775,021
GSID: Deep Cameo, 6028

Key to Collecting: Nearly all are gems.

PF-65DC	PF-67DC	PF-68DC
$8.90	$12.00	$14.50

1997-P

Circulation-Strike Mintage: 595,740,000
GSID: 5765

Key to Collecting: Choice and gem coins are plentiful.

MS-63	MS-65	MS-66	MS-67
$0.80	$2.65	$20	$68

1997-D

Circulation-Strike Mintage: 599,680,000
GSID: 5764

Key to Collecting: Choice and gem coins are plentiful. By this time the certification of current quarter dollars had become popular. Increasingly, collectors were aspiring to own grades beyond MS-65.

MS-63	MS-65	MS-66	MS-67
$0.80	$2.65	$16	$61

1997-S, Copper-Nickel Clad

Proof Mintage: 2,055,000
GSID: 6036

Key to Collecting: Nearly all are gems.

PF-65DC	PF-67DC	PF-68DC
$3.50	$4.05	$5.40

1997-S, Silver

Proof Mintage: 741,678
GSID: 6034

Key to Collecting: Nearly all are gems.

PF-65DC	PF-67DC	PF-68DC
$8.90	$10.50	$12

1998-P

Circulation-Strike Mintage: 896,268,000
GSID: 24989

Key to Collecting: Choice and gem coins are plentiful. Last of the old-style quarters with the basic obverse and reverse design of 1932.

MS-63	MS-65	MS-66	MS-67
$0.80	$2.65	$11.00	$21.50

1998-D

Circulation-Strike Mintage: 821,000,000
GSID: 24990

Key to Collecting: Choice and gem coins are plentiful.

MS-63	MS-65	MS-66	MS-67
$0.80	$2.65	$40.50	$182

1998-S, Copper-Nickel Clad

Proof Mintage: 2,086,507

GSID: Deep Cameo, 6042

Key to Collecting: Gem coins are plentiful.

PF-65DC	PF-67DC	PF-68DC
$3.50	$4.10	$5

1998-S, Silver

Proof Mintage: 878,792

GSID: Deep Cameo, 6040

Key to Collecting: Nearly all are gems.

PF-65DC	PF-67DC	PF-68DC
$8.90	$10.50	$12

9

State, D.C., and Territories Quarters, 1999–2009: Analysis by Date and Mintmark

THE 50 STATE QUARTERS® PROGRAM

In numismatics, observers have come to expect the unexpected. After the 1776–1976 Bicentennial quarter faded into history, production of this denomination continued routinely. Circulation strikes were made in large quantities at the Philadelphia and Denver mints, and at the San Francisco Mint, Proofs were struck for collectors. Among collectors the series remained fairly humdrum, attracting little attention. Lincoln cents, Jefferson nickels, Roosevelt dimes, and even Franklin half dollars were more popular. Eisenhower dollars came in for their share of attention as well, as did, in time, the Susan B. Anthony mini-dollar of 1979.

Commemorative coins had not been produced since 1954, when the lengthy Carver/Washington half dollar series ended. Unpopular though that series had been, the collecting community soon missed having new issues of commemoratives. Proposals were made, including by spokespeople for the American Numismatic Association (ANA) and the Professional Numismatists Guild (PNG). Articles advocating new commemoratives appeared in periodicals. There was no interest on the part of Congress, however, to pass enabling acts, and no encouragement from the Treasury Department.

Finally, in 1982, under the administration of Mint Director Donna Pope, the George Washington 250th Anniversary commemorative half dollars were made, from designs by Chief Engraver Elizabeth Jones. Pieces with frosty or "Mint State" finish were struck at the Denver Mint, to the extent of 2,210,458 coins, and 4,894,044 Proofs were made at San Francisco. The numismatic community gave the new commemoratives a warm reception, but it was more than a year before all were sold.

Other commemorative designs followed. Some issues were of single denominations, such as a silver dollar, while others consisted of several. All were sold at premiums considerably over face value, for amounts often significantly in excess of their metal or intrinsic values. Many complaints were voiced in the coin papers about how expensive it was just to keep current with new issues.

There was a quiet call for a "people's commemorative"—an issue, or issues, that would circulate as regular coinage. I suggested that the reverse of the Kennedy half dollar, a denomination not often seen in circulation, would be an ideal matrix for a series of designs depicting American events. Harvey G. Stack thought that quarter dollars could be made as commemoratives. Other ideas were discussed and written about, as well.

In the summer of 1996, Representative Michael N. Castle (R-Delaware) introduced HR 3793, the 50 States Commemorative Coin Program Act. Under its provisions, the Mint was to produce five new "commemorative" quarter dollars each year, for 10 years, with each coin depicting motifs relating to one of the states. The innovative concept was that these were to be circulating coins, to be placed into the channels of commerce at face value.

The news was greeted with enthusiasm by the numismatic hobby, but with a degree of caution. Memories were still clear regarding the 1979 Susan B. Anthony mini-dollar, publicized as a great innovation in coinage. The program was a flop. The earlier Bicentennial coins—the quarter, half dollar, and dollar with the dates 1776–1976—had not lived up to their expectations, either. Would it be different with the State quarters?

The concept became a reality with the signing by President Bill Clinton of PL 105-124 in December 1997. The U.S. Mint revised the name slightly and launched the 50 State Quarters® Program. This name was registered, and a symbol was used, for in recent times there had been all sorts of private sales organizations—some with minting facilities, but most without—advertising themselves as "mints." Some of these had names suggesting an official or government connection, gulling many buyers into thinking they were buying from the source. The 50 State Quarters® Program was to be the property of the U.S. Mint, and no one else.

In 1994, President Clinton appointed Philip N. Diehl to be director of the Mint, succeeding Donna Pope, who had held the post since 1992. Under Diehl's watch as Mint director, the quarter dollar became the circulating commemorative that so many had wanted. Since that time, the program was expanded to include Washington, D.C., and five territories, and a new program was implemented, celebrating sites of national and historic importance, called the America the Beautiful coin program.

The Program Plan

Under the 50 State Quarters® Program, each year five states of the Union were to suggest designs for the reverse of the quarter dollar, with motifs to depict some aspect of history, tradition, nature, or fame. Prohibitions included busts, state seals, state flags, logotypes, and depictions of living people or of "organizations whose membership or ownership is not universal." Although rules varied over a period of time, these were in effect in 2004:

> Designs shall maintain a dignity befitting the nation's coinage. Designs shall have broad appeal to t he citizens of the state and avoid controversial subjects or symbols

The 1999 Delaware State quarter, the first issue of a 50-coin series. The obverse was completely restyled from earlier versions and no longer bears the date. (shown at 125%)

that are likely to offend. . . . The states are encouraged to submit designs that promote the diffusion of knowledge among the youth of the United States about the state, its history and geography, and the rich diversity of our national heritage.

Generally, citizens were invited to submit art and written suggestions to be reviewed by the governor and advisors, after which up to five semifinal designs would be selected. These would be sent to the Mint, where artists would modify the art to their own specifications. The Mint art would then be submitted to the Commission of Fine Arts and the Citizens Commemorative Coin Advisory Committee (usually referred to as the Citizens Coin Advisory Committee), after which the Mint might make some modifications. In the next step, the state would make a choice among the semifinal motifs. Usually, state citizens would be invited to select their favorites. Sometimes the first-place design would be approved by the governor. In other instances, the governor would have the absolute right to select the motif he or she wanted, regardless of public opinion. The secretary of the Treasury reserved the right to reject any design he or she considered inappropriate, and in all cases would have the final say.

Each year, five quarters were released in the order in which the states joined the Union (by ratifying the Constitution), with appropriate launch ceremonies attended by Mint officials and dignitaries. The launch times were generally spaced throughout the year. Circulation strikes were made at the Philadelphia and Denver mints, while at the San Francisco Mint Proofs were struck for collectors and others, in clad composition as well as silver. The general policy was to strike coins of a given design, beginning about a month before general release, and continuing until it was necessary to prepare for the next design. Once a design was finished, no additional coins were made later. However, Proofs were often struck early, so that a year-set of these could be distributed before certain related circulation strikes were released. The quantities of circulation strikes varied widely, mostly dependent on the general need for new quarter dollars in commerce, not on the popularity of a given state.

Since the inception of the 50 State Quarters® Program in 1999, the Mint had been creative with its marketing (witness the use of Kermit the Frog, of Muppets fame, as the "Mint Spokesfrog"). Many other new ideas were implemented, like offering individual issues in rolls and in 100-coin and 1,000-coin bags. Other innovative programs were devised under the watch of Mint Director Diehl and continued with Jay Johnson. These included the American Spirit Collection of state dolls and related items by

Hallmark, promotions with *Reader's Digest* and *National Geographic*, and other entrepreneurial ventures.[1]

From a financial and popularity viewpoint, the entire program was a spectacular success—absolutely brilliant, in my opinion. And although there were a few problems involving communication and timely responses,[2] the U.S. Mint did much in its outreach to collectors in recent years. This included the administrations of Mint directors Philip Diehl, Jay Johnson, and Henrietta Holsman Fore during the quarters program from 1999 to 2005. Collectors and writers were warmly welcomed, exhibits were mounted at conventions, and much information was supplied to numismatic periodicals, although not all questions were answered.

Director Johnson Remembers

Jay Johnson, director of the Mint in 2000 and 2001, shared some reminiscences for readers of this book:

> One of my favorite lines I gave in speeches about the state quarters was that they were both *collectible* coins and *circulating* coins. I used to refer folks (if the audience was old enough to remember) to that old commercial for a breath mint (get it? Mint Director talking about mints!) that said, "Is it a *breath* mint or a *candy* mint? It's both. It's two, it's two, it's two mints in one!"
>
> That's what I used to say of the quarters—as I held a coin in each hand and clicked them together: "Is it a circulating coin, or a commemorative coin? It's both, it's two, it's two coins in one!"
>
> Anyone who remembered the Certs commercial got the connection, and it was an easy way of explaining "circulating" and "commemorative" coins to the non-numismatist.
>
> Non-numismatic audiences also got a smile out of a line I used to use in speeches after talking about the popularity of the 50 state quarters and the numbers of people collecting them. I would add, "Why, these days, practically everybody is calling himself a numismatist!" To many people who couldn't think of even pronouncing *numismatist*, it got a nice smile. Hopefully, it even helped people think about joining the American Numismatic Association.[3]

Artistic Infusion

In 2004 the U.S. Mint implemented the novel Artistic Infusion Program, an effort to bring the talents of private-sector artists under the wing of the government. Eighteen "master" designers and six "associate" designers were selected from applications received, to create motifs for American coins and medals. Only *one* of the master designers was credited with having any coin experience: Bill Krawczewicz of Severna Park, Maryland, was listed as a bank-note designer, currently with Bureau of Engraving and Printing, and said to be a "designer of U.S. commemorative coins and state quarter dollars."

An orientation meeting was held at the Philadelphia Mint in February of the same year. "Together, we will invigorate the artistry of coin design in America," Mint Director Henrietta Holsman Fore announced.

Each master designer is to receive $1,000 for each sketch submitted, while associates are to receive $500. In contrast, Daniel Carr, a private-sector artist, was paid $2,500 for each of his sketches used on quarters. How this "infusion" will affect the quality of the state quarter program remains to be seen. There is some good news (concerning regular coins and medals) and bad news (state quarters):

The Artistic Infusion Program artists will also receive other new coin and medal assignments as they become available. The initials of both the artists and the engravers will be on all coins and medals, except the 50 state quarters, which will carry only the sculptor-engravers' initials.[4]

Daniel Carr, who designed three of the State quarters and was paid by the Mint for doing so, but whose name did not appear on the coins.

This nonrecognition of private artists who create designs caused a lot of criticism. The Mint then went a few steps further to ensure internal control of the artwork on the State quarters. Perhaps stung by the Missouri quarter controversy (see pages 185–186), the Mint rewrote the rules to completely eliminate outside art, to be effective with the 2005 designs:

New Rules of 2005

Stage 1: The United States Mint will initiate the formal state design process by contacting the state governor approximately 24 months prior to the beginning of the year in which the state will be honored. The governor, or such other state officials or group as the state may designate, will appoint an individual to serve as the state's liaison to the United States Mint for this program.

Stage 2: The state will conduct a concept selection process as determined by the state. The state will provide to the United States Mint at least three, but no more than five, different concepts or themes emblematic of the state; each concept or theme will be in narrative format. The narrative must explain why the concept is emblematic of the state and what the concept represents to the state's citizens. A narrative that merely describes a particular design is not acceptable.

Stage 3: Based on the narratives, the United States Mint will produce original artwork of the concepts, focusing on aesthetic beauty, historical accuracy, appropriateness and coinability. If the state has not provided at least three concepts, the United States Mint may produce additional concepts for the state.

Stage 4: The United States Mint will contact the state to collaborate on the artwork. The state will appoint an historian, or other responsible officials or experts, to participate in this collaboration to ensure historical accuracy and proper state representation of the artwork. The United States Mint will refine the artwork before forwarding it to the advisory bodies.

Stage 5: The Citizens Coinage Advisory Committee and the U.S. Commission of Fine Arts will review the candidate designs and make recommendations, and the United States Mint may make changes to address such recommendations.

Stage 6: The United States Mint will present the candidate designs to the Secretary of the Treasury for review and approval.

Stage 7: The United States Mint will return to the state all candidate designs approved by the Secretary of the Treasury.

Stage 8: From among the designs approved by the Secretary, the state will recommend the final design through a process determined by the state, within a time frame specified by the United States Mint.

Stage 9: The United States Mint will present the state's recommended design to the Secretary for final approval.[5]

These rules were viewed by some as taking from the states the right to select art created within that state, and leaving it up to staff artists and engravers at the Mint to create final art from "concepts." From the viewpoint of artistic integrity, things went from bad to worse. In any event, an exception was granted to California for its 2005 quarter dollar.

Diversity in Designs

If anything, the State quarter designs are diverse. No two are alike, but closest to being twins are the issues of North Carolina (2001) and Ohio (2002), both of whose motifs include a Wright brothers biplane (though a later plane on the Ohio version). Many include inscriptions familiar only to state citizens or players of Trivial Pursuit. Do you know which state selected "The Crossroads of America"? What about "Foundation in Education," or "Corps of Discovery," or "Crossroads of the Revolution"? I knew none of these until I saw them on the coins (answers, in order: Indiana, Iowa, Missouri, and New Jersey). On the other hand, I and most others know that the Bay State is Massachusetts and the Lone Star State is Texas.

In each and every state, there were challenges to overcome with regard to the design-selection process. In 2004, when Governor Arnold Schwarzenegger made the final selection for the forthcoming 2005 California quarter, the design featured naturalist John Muir. Among other entries was one depicting an assortment of objects relating to the Gold Rush. When this was rejected, its designer wrote letters to newspapers and otherwise charged that the decision had been unfair. These things happen, and will continue to. Perhaps if a strong central motif, instead of scattered objects, had been suggested, a Gold Rush theme would have won. All's well that ends well, and almost everyone liked the final version when they saw it—a motif with Muir in Yosemite Valley, with Half Dome in the distance and a condor overhead. (The designer, Garrett Burke, contributed the foreword to this book.)

In addition, each and every design has had both its detractors (some more than others) and its fans. In that regard, *Coin World* columnist Michele Orzano wrote this bit of philosophy and opinion:

> What would you answer if someone stops you on the street tomorrow and asks, "How would you define the spirit of your state?"
>
> Now think about that question in light of the 26 State quarter dollar designs currently in circulation. The 2004 Michigan design shows the outline of the state and the Great Lakes. There's not an automobile in sight, yet that's what most Americans would probably say is the defining symbol—that of Motown.

From Concept to Coin

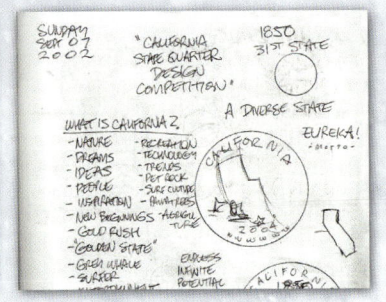

California State quarter designer Garrett Burke (pictured here with his wife Michelle, a coin collector) started with a question: "What does California mean to me?"

His notes led to rough sketches centering on natural themes, with writer/poet/conservation-ist John Muir connecting man to Nature.

Burke's final contest entry (left) was finessed at the Mint (center). Their final rendering (right) led to the California State quarter, one of the most popular coins in the series.

California governor Arnold Schwarzenneger (shown with design review committee member Dwight Manley, coin collector Penny Marshall, and wife Maria Shriver) praised the "beautiful, beautiful design."

Consider the design for the 2002 Mississippi quarter dollar. The design depicts two magnolia blossoms and leaves with the inscription THE MAGNOLIA STATE. But wouldn't many Americans think of riverboats and the tales Mark Twain told in his *Life on the Mississippi*, published in 1883?

Does the image of the Old Man of the Mountain truly define New Hampshire as depicted on its 2000 State quarter dollar? What would archeologists in the future discern from looking at that image? Would they surmise that the folks who populate New Hampshire all have craggy facial features?

The 1999 Georgia quarter dollar features the outline of the state enclosing a peach, with a banner featuring the state motto WISDOM, JUSTICE, MODERATION and a border of live oak sprigs. Does that design capture the full flavor of a state that's given the world and the nation Vidalia onions and the Okefenokee Swamp?

Bottom line: Not everyone is going to be happy with every design. Does that mean the state quarter dollar program is without merit? No. It just means that in a land like America, we're given the privilege to have an opinion and express it. It's clear that no matter the design, collectors are continuing to enjoy the program and will for many years to come.[6]

Well stated, Michele!

Comments on Designs

Some basic information about the state-reverse quarters was difficult to find. No single source seemed to have everything—rather surprising, as I thought that details on the launch ceremonies and the creators of the designs or concepts in each state as well as the identities of the Mint artists who made the final sketches and designs would be common knowledge.

What was envisioned as an easy procedure turned into a fairly lengthy search involving the use of numismatic articles, interviews, and comments from those involved, usually adding much to the official information issued by the U.S. Mint.

Concerning my quest for information, and also why some information in print does not reveal what *really* happened, this commentary from *Coin World* editor Beth Deisher may be of interest:

> In the early years, most of the states announced "winners" of their design concept competitions. If that happened, it is reported in news stories. For many of the state quarters, there is no specific person identified as the "concept" designer. Let's use Ohio as an example:
>
> Ohio invited the public to submit design concepts. Although 7,298 were received, none depicted exactly what was finally used on Ohio's quarter. The final design consists of elements selected by the Ohio Quarter Committee that were rendered into a sketch by an artist hired by the committee. Although that artist was introduced at the Ohio launch ceremony, he is not considered the "concept designer" because he did not develop the concept. So officially, *no individual* is credited with the design concept. The most accurate statement is that the Ohio quarter was literally designed by the committee. Proceedings were extensively reported in Ohio daily newspapers, as all meetings of the Ohio committee were open to the public.

It is easier to identify those at the Mint who sculpted the models. The Mint considers the sculptor-engraver who made the model (based on the design concept submitted by the state) to be the designer, and that person's initials appear on the coin.

At the same time, various newspaper articles as well as information on the U.S. Mint website suggest that for some designs, specific people were indeed involved in creating final sketches before they were submitted to the Mint staff. For example, Daniel Miller, a graphic artist from Arlington, Texas, was identified as the creator of the design selected from about 2,700 others to be used on the 2004 Texas quarter. Much publicity was given to Garrett Burke, designer of the aforementioned 2005 California quarter with the Muir motif. As to whether the limelight for an artist in the private sector was turned on or switched off, that seemed to be up to the Mint.

Credit Where Credit Is Due?

Michele Orzano noted this in one of her *Coin World* columns (excerpted):

> ### Inconsistency Dogs Designer Credit
> Future numismatists researching the identities of the designers of the State quarter dollars may get different answers, depending on the sources of their information. Since the beginning of the program in 1999, the U.S. Mint has only credited its staff engravers who created the models for the coins, by placing their initials on the State quarter designs—regardless of whether a state has identified the "designer" or the U.S. Mint paid the designer.
>
> "The policy has been just to have the engravers' initials on the coins because often the design concept is something other people have also submitted," according to Michael White, a spokesman for the U.S. Mint. In many cases, individuals have submitted different versions of the same design theme. . . . The decision to credit only the engravers and none of the original designers, even when their identities are known, is a change for the Mint. In the 20th century, the Mint generally acknowledged artists by placing their initials on the coins.[7]

Indeed, in the early 1980s Mint Director Donna Pope, realizing that for the 1984 Olympic commemorative $10 gold coin, the motif had been designed by one person (James Peed) and the models for dies engraved by another (John Mercanti), sought to recognize both on the coin. Both JM and JP initials appear at the lower left, a double signature, which resulted from a conversation Pope and I had. At the time, I was president of the ANA, and Pope maintained an excellent relationship and continuing dialogue not only with the ANA but with numismatic publications and the entire collecting fraternity. She inquired whether it was accepted practice to include the initials of the designer as well as the engraver, and I cited several examples from history,[8] after which she decided to employ the initials on the 1984 Olympic gold coins.

The decision not to recognize these artists cost them an economic opportunity. Previously, retired Mint artist-sculptors (e.g., William Cousins) whose initials appear on regular or commemorative coins, inked profitable contracts by signing holders containing their coins. Some past Mint directors had also inked contracts to autograph coin holders. Those who designed coins, but whose initials did not appear, landed some contracts as well, but their identities were little known to most people. For example, Daniel Carr, an independent artist from Colorado, was paid by the Mint to design the reverses of the 2001 New York and Rhode Island quarters, and was later involved with the 2003 Maine issue—but he received no recognition on the coins and was not featured at launch ceremonies, and Mint publicity did not acknowledge his existence. Garrett Burke, on the other hand, although not allowed to sign his art, was (quite deservedly) feted at the 2005 California quarter ceremony. Would that other artists could have the same honor.

There was one final inconsistency to the whole non-recognition policy. The famous works of old masters are sometimes the source for coin designs. On the 2004 Iowa quarter, the name of Grant Wood, the artist of the *Arbor Day* painting, is displayed in very large letters on the reverse—larger than on any previous American coin! In contrast, Emmanuel Leutze, painter of *Washington Crossing the Delaware*, received no credit on the Delaware quarter.

Obverse Changes

In 1999, to accommodate the creative designs intended for the reverse of the State quarters, the inscriptions UNITED STATES OF AMERICA and QUARTER DOLLAR, were relocated to the obverse above and below the portrait, respectively. LIBERTY and IN GOD WE TRUST were moved to new positions. At the same time, the Mint decided to "improve" the portrait of Washington by adding little curlicue-and-squiggle hair details (apparently, there had been complaints that the portrait details were unclear, and this was the Mint's solution).

In 1999, the name of the Mint engraver who created the new die, William Cousins, was memorialized by the addition of his initials, WC, next to JF (for John Flanagan, the original designer in 1932) on the neck truncation. The initials now appear to run together as JFWC. The W is of unusual appearance and is not very legible.

It is probably correct to call this the Cousins portrait. Perhaps one day the Mint will bring back a classic portrait of Washington—perhaps the 1786 version on the Washington Before Boston medal by Pierre Simon Duvivier (after Houdon, but with peruke added) or the 19th-century portrait by Charles Cushing Wright (after Duvivier).

NUMISMATIC ASPECTS OF STATE QUARTERS
Basic Information

As planned, the various State quarters were made in circulation-strike format (Mint State) at the Philadelphia and Denver mints, and in Proof format, both in clad metal and in 90% silver, at the San Francisco Mint. In all instances, circulation-strike mintages ran into the hundreds of millions, clad proofs to the extent of several million, and silver Proofs into the high hundreds of thousands. Accordingly, the four varieties of each issue were readily available in their years of mintage, and after that time the market supply was generous.

For each issue described on the following pages, mintage figures are given for circulation strikes and for Proofs. It is normal practice to pay out circulation strikes through banks and the Federal Reserve. Such coins quickly reach circulation all over the United States, not just in the honored state. Proofs are sold at a premium, and at year's end, remaining coins are withdrawn. Usually, the U.S. Mint delays publishing Proof mintage quantities until two years or so after the striking.

Information is also given about the creation of the design, the minting of the coins, and their distribution. Selected information is given about the featured subjects and the state honored. For the states, certain related aspects of numismatic history and interest are given.

STRIKING AND APPEARANCE

Circulation strikes require checking as to sharpness. Planchet quality can vary, and some have marks from the original planchet that did not flatten out during the striking process. For some issues, the obverse can be marked and nicked, while the reverse has fewer such indications. There are so many State quarters around that finding a choice piece will be easy. For a few issues, Denver Mint coins are not sharp in certain areas of the lettering. The 2004-D Michigan quarter usually exhibits lightness, and for this particular issue, cherrypicking is necessary.

Some have interesting die cracks, an example being a 2002-P Tennessee with a large crack from the neck through Q of QUARTER to the border, and another die crack from the forehead through the first S of STATES; others could be cited. Quite a few Mint errors, such as off-center strikings, are available and are interesting to see. Fred Weinberg, a California dealer, has made a specialty of these, and many other professionals have handled them as well. Weinberg advised me that the best time to find significant errors is soon after the coins are released. Not many new discoveries are made in later years.

Nearly all Proofs were well struck and handled with care at the Mint. Grades commonly are PF-66 and higher, all the way to PF-70. On some Proofs, over-polishing of dies eliminated some details, as on part of the WC initials on certain 1999 Delaware pieces. Some Proofs show die cracks. Ken Potter, columnist for *Numismatic News*, filed a series of stories on these.

Designers: *John Flanagan (obverse); see individual entries for reverse designers.*
Weight: *Clad issue—5.67 grams; silver Proofs—6.25 grams.* **Composition:** *Clad issue—Outer layers of copper-nickel (.750 copper, .250 nickel) bonded to inner core of pure copper; silver Proofs—.900 silver, .100 copper (net weight .18084 oz. pure silver).* **Diameter:** *24.3 mm.* **Edge:** *Reeded.* **Mints:** *Clad issue—Philadelphia, Denver, and San Francisco; silver Proofs—San Francisco.*

1999, Delaware

Circulation-Strike Mintage, Philadelphia: 373,400,000
Circulation-Strike Mintage, Denver: 401,424,000
Proof Mintage, San Francisco, Clad: 3,713,359
Proof Mintage, San Francisco, Silver: 804,565
GSID: Circulation-strike, Philadelphia, 5772; Circulation-strike, Denver, 5767; Proof Clad Deep Cameo, 6045; Proof Silver Deep Cameo, 6046

Specifics of the Reverse Design

Description: The coin features a rider on horseback headed to the left, with CAESAR / RODNEY near the left border. At the upper right is THE / FIRST / STATE, signifying Delaware's position. The top and bottom border inscriptions are standard.

Designer: Per information given by the Public Information Office of the U.S. Mint in early 1999, the designer was Eddy Seger, an art and drama teacher. However, after reading this statement in *Coin World* (February 15, 1999), certain officials from the state of Delaware stated that no single person deserved the credit, and that at least six different sketches depicted the equestrian Rodney theme.[9] *Mint sculptor-engraver who made the model:* William Cousins. *Engraver's initials and location:* WC conjoined, with the top of the C missing on some impressions due to over-polishing of the die, giving the initials the appearance of "WL." The initials are located to the left, between the horse's extended hoof and the border.

Story of the Design
A REVOLUTIONARY WAR PATRIOT

The first coin out of the gate, so to speak, was widely appreciated by collectors. Depicted on this coin is Caesar Rodney on horseback, on an 80-mile ride to Philadelphia (then the seat of the Continental Congress). On July 1, 1776, despite severe discomfort and illness, as a delegate from the colony of Delaware he cast the deciding vote that called for independence from England. This bold yet simple design, with the horse and rider quickly catching the eye, is in my opinion one of the best in the entire series. This view is shared by many others. The artistic bar was raised high at the outset, and many later designs could not come up to it.

To start the design-selection process, citizens of the state were invited to send ideas for the design to the Delaware Arts Council, resulting in more than 300 entries. Certain of these were sent to the Mint, where they were converted into drawings. Three concepts were selected, these being Caesar Rodney, an allegorical Miss Liberty, and a quill-and-pen design. The office of Governor Thomas R. Carper conducted a limited email and telephone poll, garnering 1,519 votes, of which 948 were for Rodney, 235 for Miss Liberty, and 336 for the writing materials.

Finally, on December 7, 1998, "Delaware Day" was held at the Philadelphia Mint.[10] On hand were Citizens Commemorative Coin Advisory Committee members, Delaware state officials, and Mint officers and personnel, including Mint Director Philip N. Diehl and U.S. Treasurer Mary Ellen Withrow. All guests were invited to join coining-press operator John Hill in striking their very own Delaware quarters. These were set aside to be mailed to the participants early in 1999, after the official release.

Nearly a month later, on January 4, 1999, the first coins went into circulation.

Numismatic Aspects of the State of Delaware

Colonial era: The state issued many types of currency. *1936:* The Delaware Tercentenary commemorative half dollar was issued.

1999-P, Delaware

MS-64	MS-65	MS-66	MS-67	MS-68	MS-69
$0.50	$0.80	$4.05	$11	$860	—

1999-D, Delaware

MS-64	MS-65	MS-66	MS-67	MS-68	MS-69
$0.50	$0.80	$4.05	$11	—	—

1999-S, Delaware, Proof, Clad

PF-67DC	PF-68DC	PF-69DC
$1.50	$4.05	$9.50

1999-S, Delaware, Proof, Silver

PF-67DC	PF-68DC	PF-69DC
$11.00	$16.00	$40.50

1999, Pennsylvania

Circulation-Strike Mintage, Philadelphia: 349,000,000

Circulation-Strike Mintage, Denver: 358,332,000

Proof Mintage, San Francisco, Clad: 3,713,359

Proof Mintage, San Francisco, Silver: 804,565

GSID: Circulation-strike, Philadelphia, 5775; Circulation-strike, Denver, 5770; Proof Clad Deep Cameo, 6051; Proof Silver Deep Cameo, 6052

Specifics of the Reverse Design

Description: At the center is an outline of the state, with the goddess Commonwealth prominent at the center, holding a standard topped by an eagle. She is elegantly styled and would serve well as a large motif on any coin. At the upper left of the map is a keystone in pebbled bas-relief, representing "the Keystone State," a motto used on license plates and elsewhere. The motto reflects both Pennsylvania's position near the center of the original 13 colonies and, as a Mint release suggests, "the key position of Pennsylvania in the economic, social, and political development of the United States." To the right of the map is a more formal motto, VIRTUE / LIBERTY / INDEPENDENCE, on three lines.

Designer: Concept by Donald Carlucci. *Mint sculptor-engraver who made the model:* John Mercanti. Roland Hinton Perry is deserving of some small part of the credit for his statue of Commonwealth. *Engraver's initials and location:* JM, placed immediately below the bottom border of the state and to the right of the goddess's leg.

Story of the Design

The design of the 1999 Pennsylvania quarter is a small collage of items relating to the state. The design, an outline map, includes a representation of the 14-foot statue from the top of the State Capitol building, a keystone, and a motto, and ties the elements together.

The statue itself was relatively unknown prior to its appearance here, and probably not one in a thousand residents of the state could identify it as *Commonwealth*, by an obscure New York sculptor. The U.S. Mint gives this information:

The statue *Commonwealth*, designed by New York sculptor Roland Hinton Perry, is a bronze-gilded 14' 6" high female form that has topped Pennsylvania's State Capitol dome in Harrisburg, Pennsylvania since May 25, 1905. Her right arm extends in kindness and her left arm grasps a ribbon mace to symbolize justice. The image of the keystone honors the state's nickname, "The Keystone State." At a Jefferson Republican victory rally in October 1802, Pennsylvania was toasted as "the keystone in the federal union."

I am not quite sure what a ribbon mace is, but it sounds important. A keystone is the top stone in an arch, and is the final stone placed during construction.

The design-selection process began when Governor Tom Ridge established the Commemorative Quarter Committee to furnish guidance and solicit designs.[11] More than 5,300 sketches and other submissions were received from residents of the state.

Five final designs were selected by the Pennsylvania Commemorative Quarter Committee; the eventual motif was selected from these five designs.

THE FIRST-EVER STATE-QUARTER LAUNCH CEREMONY

On March 9, 1999, at the Philadelphia Mint, the official launch ceremony was held. Governor Tom Ridge, U.S. Treasurer Mary Ellen Withrow, Mint Deputy Director John Mitchell, and others were on hand. About two dozen fifth-graders from the General George A. McCall Elementary School were invited guests. Many of those on hand were allowed to push a button to actuate an 82-ton press to strike a quarter.

At the launch ceremony on March 9, 1999. Left to right: Govenor Thomas Ridge, Mint sculptor-engraver John Mercanti, and Donald Carlucci.

By the day of the launch ceremony, March 9, millions of Pennsylvania quarters had been struck by both the Philadelphia and Denver mints. On the same day as the ceremony these were released from storage and placed into circulation.

Numismatic Aspects of the State of Pennsylvania

Colonial era: The state issued many types of currency. *1775:* Continental Currency was first issued at Philadelphia, the seat of the federal government. It was printed by Hall & Sellers, who also printed bills for colonies and states. *1776:* The Continental Congress is believed to have issued pewter Continental dollars. *1782:* The Bank of North America, the first significant commercial bank in America, was chartered. It issued paper money over a long period of time. *1783:* Nova Constellatio pattern copper and silver coins were made to test coinage concepts for use at the North America Mint; no further action occurred. *1791–1811:* The first Bank of the United States was headquartered in Philadelphia. *1792:* The Philadelphia Mint was established. *Circa 1810–1840:* Philadelphia was the leading center for bank-note engraving and printing. *1816–1836:* The Second Bank of the United States was headquartered in Philadelphia. *1833:* The Second Philadelphia Mint building was occupied. *1858:* The Philadelphia Numismatic Society, the first such organization in the United States, was founded. (It was soon followed by the American Numismatic Society, New York.) *1870s:* A vast hoard of silver coins was discovered in the town of Economy. *1901:* The Third Philadelphia Mint building was occupied. *1913:* The Philadelphia Federal Reserve Bank was established under the Federal Reserve Act. Currency issued there bears the letter C. *1926:* The Sesquicentennial of American Independence commemorative half dollar and $2.50 gold piece were issued to help fund the Sesquicentennial Exposition, held in Philadelphia. *1936:* The Battle of Gettysburg Anniversary commemorative half dollar was issued. *1967:* The Fourth (present) Philadelphia Mint building was occupied. *1990:* The Eisenhower Centennial commemorative silver dollar, featuring the Eisenhower home in Gettysburg on the reverse, was issued. *1992:* On April 2, a ceremony was held to observe the 200th anniversary of the Mint Act of April 2, 1792. Many numismatists were present.

1999-P, Pennsylvania

MS-64	MS-65	MS-66	MS-67	MS-68	MS-69
$0.50	$0.80	$4.05	$11	$750	—

1999-D, Pennsylvania

MS-64	MS-65	MS-66	MS-67	MS-68	MS-69
$0.50	$0.80	$4.05	$54	$520	—

1999-S, Pennsylvania, Proof, Clad

PF-67DC	PF-68DC	PF-69DC
$1.50	$4.05	$9.50

1999-S, Pennsylvania, Proof, Silver

PF-67DC	PF-68DC	PF-69DC
$7.20	$8.50	$11

1999, New Jersey

Circulation-Strike Mintage, Philadelphia: 363,200,000

Circulation-Strike Mintage, Denver: 299,028,000

Proof Mintage, San Francisco, Clad: 3,713,359

Proof Mintage, San Francisco, Silver: 804,565

GSID: Circulation-strike, Philadelphia, 5774; Circulation-strike, Denver, 5769; Proof Clad Deep Cameo, 6049; Proof Silver Deep Cameo, 6050

Specifics of the Reverse Design

Description: The design features George Washington and accompanying soldiers in a rowboat crossing the Delaware River from Pennsylvania to New Jersey, adapted from an Emmanuel Leutze painting that is now a prized holding of the Metropolitan Museum of Art, New York City. A soldier is seated on the prow and is pushing an ice floe with his foot. The Father of Our Country and at least one other person are standing in the vessel, (seemingly a rather risky thing to do in the dark on a river filled with drifting ice). Moreover, Washington's foot is blocking an oarlock that could be used effectively by the paddler in the bow, who is forced to do without one. Below is the two-line inscription CROSSROADS OF THE / REVOLUTION. The top and bottom border inscriptions are standard.

Designer: Adapted from a painting created by Emmanuel Leutze. *Mint sculptor-engraver who made the model:* Alfred F. Maletsky. *Engraver's initials and location:* AM, located between the end of the boat and the rim on the right. The initials are tiny.

Story of the Design

The 1999 New Jersey quarter furnished the first truly familiar motif on a state coin—the well-known scene taken from the 1851 painting by Emmanuel Gottlieb Leutze (1816–1868), Washington Crossing the Delaware, also used in 1976 for 13¢ stamps in connection with the bicentennial. Generations earlier, it was part of the face design for $50 National Bank Notes of the Original Series, Series of 1875, and the Series of 1882. Accordingly, it might have been proper to credit Leutze as the designer of the coin, but this was not done. Mint policy proved to be erratic in this regard—see the discussion of the 2005 Iowa quarter, which prominently features the name of artist Grant Wood.

The process of creating this design began on November 17, 1997, when the New Jersey Commemorative Coin Design Commission was authorized. This committee of 15 citizens was appointed to review ideas for the quarter design. It is to the everlasting credit of this and many other state committees that experienced coin collectors were invited to join these advisory groups. The 15 advisors settled on five concepts to be sent to the Mint to be developed into drawings. These designs were subsequently reviewed by the Commission of Fine Arts and the secretary of the Treasury, after which three were returned to Governor Christine Todd Whitman, who consulted with her advisors and made the final selection (although she could have made the choice on her own).

Numismatic Aspects of the State of New Jersey

May 1682: The Legislature made Irish St. Patrick's coinage legal tender in the colony. *Colonial era:* New Jersey issued many types of currency. *1786–1788:* New Jersey coppers were produced under private contract. *1850s:* The Toms River and Cape May areas became centers for fraudulent banks that issued paper money. *2004:* A commemorative silver dollar honoring Thomas A. Edison, the "Wizard of Menlo Park", was issued.

1999-P, New Jersey

MS-64	MS-65	MS-66	MS-67	MS-68	MS-69
$0.50	$0.80	$4.05	$11	$1,000	—

1999-D, New Jersey

MS-64	MS-65	MS-66	MS-67	MS-68	MS-69
$0.50	$0.80	$4.05	$40.50	$1,020	—

1999-S, New Jersey, Proof, Clad

PF-67DC	PF-68DC	PF-69DC
$1.50	$4.05	$9.50

1999-S, New Jersey, Proof, Silver

PF-67DC	PF-68DC	PF-69DC
$7.20	$8.50	$11

1999, Georgia

Circulation-Strike Mintage, Philadelphia: 451,188,000
Circulation-Strike Mintage, Denver: 488,744,000
Proof Mintage, San Francisco, Clad: 3,713,359
Proof Mintage, San Francisco, Silver: 804,565
GSID: Circulation-strike, Philadelphia, 5773; Circulation-strike, Denver, 5768; Proof Clad Deep Cameo, 6047; Proof Silver Deep Cameo, 6048

Specifics of the Reverse Design

Description: An outline map of Georgia with a peach (for Georgia's nickname, "the Peach State") at the center, with a leaf attached to a stem. To the left and right are branches of live oak (the state tree). A loosely arranged ribbon bears the motto WISDOM JUSTICE MODERATION in three sections. Top and bottom border inscriptions are standard.

Designer: Bill Fivaz (peach on the state outline) and Caroline Leake (motto and wreath), sketch by Susan Royal. *Mint sculptor-engraver who made the model*: T. James Ferrell. *Engraver's initials and location*: TJF in italic capitals. Below the lower side of the branch stem on the right.

Story of the Design

The 1999 Georgia quarter features a montage of topics relating to the state, similar in concept to the Pennsylvania issue.[12] An outline map has at the center a peach, the best-known symbol of the state. The official state tree, the live oak, is represented by branches at each side. On a flowing ribbon is the motto WISDOM JUSTICE MODERATION—seemingly good precepts for anyone to observe.

The Georgia Council for the Arts was enlisted to receive and develop motifs. The council brought together a committee consisting of Caroline Leake, executive director of the council; Danny Robinson, then-president of the Georgia Numismatic Association; Bill Fivaz, well-known numismatist and author; and Susan Royal, a local graphic artist who joined the committee at the end to render the designs for submission. The committee met in February and March 1999, choosing five designs, which they narrowed down to four. Governor Roy Barnes selected the winner.

Numismatic Aspects of the State of Georgia

Colonial era: The state issued many types of currency. *1830:* Templeton Reid, assayer and coiner, struck $2.50, $10, and $20 coins at Milledgeville, then at Gainesville. *1838:* The Dahlonega Mint opened and coined gold continuously until 1861. *1913:* The

Atlanta Federal Reserve Bank was established under the Federal Reserve Act. Currency issued there bears the letter E. *1925:* The Stone Mountain Memorial commemorative half dollar was issued. *1995:* To recognize the XXVI Olympiad, held in Atlanta, commemorative half dollars, silver dollars, and $5 gold pieces were issued. *2013:* To recognize the Girl Scouts of the U.S.A. Centennial, a commemorative silver dollar was issued; the organization was founded in Savannah.

1999-P, Georgia

MS-64	MS-65	MS-66	MS-67	MS-68	MS-69
$0.50	$0.80	$4.05	$11	$650	—

1999-D, Georgia

MS-64	MS-65	MS-66	MS-67	MS-68	MS-69
$0.50	$0.80	$4.05	$11	$650	—

1999-S, Georgia, Proof, Clad

PF-67DC	PF-68DC	PF-69DC
$1.50	$4.05	$9.50

1999-S, Georgia, Proof, Silver

PF-67DC	PF-68DC	PF-69DC
$7.20	$8.50	$11

1999, Connecticut

Circulation-Strike Mintage, Philadelphia: 688,744,000
Circulation-Strike Mintage, Denver: 657,880,000
Proof Mintage, San Francisco, Clad: 3,713,359
Proof Mintage, San Francisco, Silver: 804,565
GSID: Circulation-strike, Philadelphia, 5771; Circulation-strike, Denver, 5766; Proof Clad Deep Cameo, 6043; Proof Silver Deep Cameo, 6044

Specifics of the Reverse Design

Description: A rather bushy-appearing tree, with a small trunk, and leafless (presumably from the frost of winter). Above the ground at the lower left is THE / CHARTER OAK. The top and bottom border inscriptions are standard.

Designer: Andy Jones. *Mint sculptor-engraver who made the model:* T. James Ferrell. *Engraver's initials and location:* TJF in italic capitals, located on the border to the right of M in UNUM.

Story of the Design

The design on the Connecticut quarter is an image of the state's famous Charter Oak—a tree of significance not only to the state of Connecticut but to the nation as well.[13] A U.S. Mint news release tells of the following:

> If not for the famed "Charter Oak," Connecticut—and this country in general—might be a very different place than it is today! On the night of October 31, 1687, Connecticut's Charter was put to a test. A British representative for King James II challenged Connecticut's government structure and demanded its surrender. In the middle of the heated discussion, with the Charter on the table between the opposing parties, the candles were mysteriously snuffed out, darkening the room. When visibility was reestablished, the Connecticut Charter had vanished. Heroic Captain Joseph Wadsworth saved the Charter from the hands of the British and concealed it in the safest place he could find—in a majestic white oak.

The 1935 Connecticut Tercentenary commemorative half dollar, with a rendition of the Charter Oak on the reverse.

In 1855, Charles Dewolf Brownell painted the tree from life. By that time, the tree was thought to be more than 400 years old. It had been described by *Niles' Register* (May 7, 1825) as measuring 28 feet in circumference near its base, and about 70 feet in height, with branches extending nearly 40 feet. Such was the gnarled and aged tree depicted by Brownell, and it was his image that was later used on the 1935 Connecticut Tercentenary half dollar, on a commemorative stamp, and elsewhere.

With this gnarled image in mind, many people have found fault with the bushy, youthful-looking tree on the back of the Connecticut quarter. (One numismatist even suggested that it was the *root system* of the Charter Oak being shown, upside down!) Perhaps it illustrates a young Charter Oak, quite unlike the appearance of the same tree when it blew down in a storm in 1856. Whether the image is an accurate representation of the young tree is not known; variations of younger versions appeared on notes of the Charter Oak Bank (Hartford) and in 1859 on a medal issued by coin dealer Augustus Sage. In any case, the design on the State quarter is completely *original*.

When Governor John G. Rowland set up the Connecticut Coin Design Competition, 19 of the more than 100 entries depicted the Charter Oak. Apparently, five were selected from those 19, sent off to the Mint, reviewed, and reviewed again, after which one was picked.

Numismatic Aspects of the State of Connecticut

Colonial era: The state issued many types of currency. *1737–1739:* The Higley threepence coins were struck from native metal in Granby. *1785–1788:* The state issued copper coins. *19th century:* Scovill Manufacturing Co., Waterbury, was a major maker of Hard Times tokens, encased postage stamps, and Civil War tokens. *1935:* The Connecticut Tercentenary commemorative half dollar was issued. *1936:* The Bridgeport Centennial commemorative half dollar was issued.

1999-P, Connecticut

MS-64	MS-65	MS-66	MS-67	MS-68	MS-69
$0.50	$0.80	$4.05	$11	$468	—

1999-D, Connecticut

MS-64	MS-65	MS-66	MS-67	MS-68	MS-69
$0.50	$0.80	$4.05	$11	$429	—

1999-S, Connecticut, Proof, Clad

PF-67DC	PF-68DC	PF-69DC
$1.50	$4.05	$9.50

1999-S, Connecticut, Proof, Silver

PF-67DC	PF-68DC	PF-69DC
$7.20	$8.50	$11

2000, Massachusetts

Circulation-Strike Mintage, Philadelphia: 628,600,000
Circulation-Strike Mintage, Denver: 535,184,000
Proof Mintage, San Francisco, Clad: 4,020,172
Proof Mintage, San Francisco, Silver: 965,421
GSID: Circulation-strike, Philadelphia, 5792; Circulation-strike, Denver, 5786; Proof Clad Deep Cameo, 6057; Proof Silver Deep Cameo, 6058

Specifics of the Reverse Design

Description: An outline map of Massachusetts with a stippled background, and with French's *Minuteman* statue superimposed. The location of Boston is noted by a raised, five-pointed star. At the right, offshore in the ocean, is the three-line inscription THE / BAY / STATE. The top and bottom border inscriptions are standard.

Designer: Two schoolchildren illustrated the famous Minuteman statue by Daniel Chester French. Their identities were withheld. Mint sculptor-engraver who made the model: Thomas D. Rogers. Engraver's initials and location: TDR, located below the bottom left side of the map.

Story of the Design

If you have a 1925 Lexington-Concord commemorative half dollar depicting Daniel Chester French's Minuteman statue on the obverse, then you'll recognize the same motif on the back side of the 2000 Massachusetts quarter. The statue itself stands not far from the "rude bridge that arched the flood," evocative of the early days of the American Revolution. On the new coin, the statue is shown with a textured outline map of THE / BAY / STATE (per the legend), complete with such details as Nantucket and Martha's Vineyard islands (among others) and a star indicating the location of Boston.

It was February 1998 when Governor Paul Cellucci began the process leading to the creation of a suitable design, after which more than 100 youngsters provided sketches. Only children were invited (a novel approach and, so far, a unique one in the quarter program). Ten members on an advisory council narrowed the 100 or so entries down to five. In June 1999, Governor Cellucci and Lieutenant Governor Jane Swift announced the winning design.

A 2000-P Massachusetts quarter struck over a 1999-P Georgia quarter! This is the only multistate overstrike known in the State quarter series. (Fred Weinberg photograph)

Considering that the same motif had been used on a commemorative coin, postage stamps, savings stamps, and elsewhere, setting up a 10-member advisory council and engaging in other hoopla may have been wasted effort. But for the two school kids, one in the sixth grade and the other in the seventh, who had the same idea and shared the recognition, the hoopla was welcome. They were featured guests at the official launch ceremony—a heartwarming situation for them and their classmates, all of whom were invited to be on hand at the event in Boston's historic Faneuil Hall. They were illustrated on the Mint website, but their names were not disclosed.

Numismatic Aspects of the State of Massachusetts

1652–1682: The state issued silver coins in the New England, Willow Tree, Oak Tree, and Pine Tree series. *1690:* The state issued the first paper money in the Western World. Many types of colonial currency were issued, including some from plates engraved by Paul Revere. *1776:* Pattern copper coins were made. The Washington Before Boston medal also bears this date. *1787–1788:* Copper half cents and cents were minted. *1790s–early 19th century:* Jacob Perkins of Newburyport issued medals and devised the Patent Stereotype Steel Plate for printing paper money. *1860:* The Boston Numismatic Society, today the second oldest society (after the ANS), was founded. *1913:* The Boston Federal Reserve Bank was established under the Federal Reserve Act. Currency issued there bears the letter A. *1920–1921:* Pilgrim Tercentenary commemorative half dollars were issued. *1925:* The Lexington-Concord Sesquicentennial commemorative half dollar was issued.

2000-P, Massachusetts

MS-64	MS-65	MS-66	MS-67	MS-68	MS-69
$0.50	$0.80	$4	$11	$68	—

2000-D, Massachusetts

MS-64	MS-65	MS-66	MS-67	MS-68	MS-69
$0.50	$0.80	$4.05	$11	$234	—

2000-S, Massachusetts, Proof, Clad

PF-67DC	PF-68DC	PF-69DC
$1.50	$4.05	$9.50

2000-S, Massachusetts, Proof, Silver

PF-67DC	PF-68DC	PF-69DC
$7.20	$8.50	$11

Various Massachusetts Colonial Coinage

From 1652 to 1682 Massachusetts issued silver coins in the NE, Willow Tree, Oak Tree, and Pine Tree series, and in 1690 the colony issued the first paper money in the Western World. In 1787 and 1788 the state minted copper half cents and cents.

2000, Maryland

Circulation-Strike Mintage, Philadelphia: 678,200,000
Circulation-Strike Mintage, Denver: 556,532,000
Proof Mintage, San Francisco, Clad: 4,020,172
Proof Mintage, San Francisco, Silver: 965,421

GSID: Circulation-strike, Philadelphia, 5791; Circulation-strike, Denver, 5785; Proof Clad Deep Cameo, 6055; Proof Silver Deep Cameo, 6056

Specifics of the Reverse Design

Description: Wooden dome and supporting structure on the Maryland State House in Annapolis, with THE OLD / LINE STATE in two lines, and with branches of white oak to each side. The top and bottom border inscriptions are standard.

Designer: Bill Krawczewicz. Mint sculptor-engraver who made the model: Thomas D. Rogers. Engraver's initials and location: TDR, located below an acorn and above the M in UNUM.

Story of the Design

In the opinion of many collectors, Maryland—the Old Line State, as proclaimed on the coins—laid an egg with the design of this quarter dollar. Featuring the top part of the State House (a "striking dome" in Mint terminology), this supposedly wonderful subject that used up Maryland's once-in-a-lifetime coin opportunity is also "the country's largest wooden dome built without nails." In addition, there are two branches from a white oak—the state tree—complete with a few acorns (but no squirrels).

A Mint news release gave these details of the design-selection process:

> After Governor [Parris N.] Glendening received design concepts from all Maryland residents, including schoolchildren, the 17-member Maryland Commemorative Coin Committee evaluated all of the submissions. The committee narrowed the options down to five selections from which the Governor picked the state house. "In our view, the state house best favors Maryland's rich history, and the unique role the state has played in our nation's history," said Glendening.[14]

But what about the seemingly unfamiliar motto, "the Old Line State"? Lori Montgomery, writer for the *Washington Post*, wrote this in March 2000:

> [The] slogan, emblazoned on the tail side of the latest coin in the U.S. Mint's series of 50 state quarters, is raising puzzled brows even in Maryland, the state in question.
> . . . [It seems that] Tom D. Rogers Sr., a sculptor and engraver with the U.S. Mint in Philadelphia, found the dome a bit stark. So he added clusters of white oak, the state tree, and "The Old Line State." The words made a nice design, but even Rogers didn't know what it meant. "I pulled it out of a book or off the Internet someplace," he said. "I know I got it somewhere official." . . .
> It seems Washington himself bestowed the nickname on Maryland after the Battle of Long Island in August 1776, when a line of Maryland troops held off the British while Washington retreated. Thousands died, and many Maryland soldiers

were buried in Brooklyn, said Maryland state archivist Edward C. Papenfuse. Thereafter, Washington referred to Maryland troops as "the old line"—meaning they were always there, reliable, Papenfuse said. . . .[15]

Numismatic Aspects of the State of Maryland

1658–1659: Silver fourpence, sixpence, and shilling coins are struck at the Tower Mint, London, for circulation in the Maryland colony. *Colonial era:* Maryland issued many types of currency. *1783:* Annapolis silversmith John Chalmers issued silver threepence, sixpence, and shilling coins. *1790:* Standish Barry, Baltimore silversmith, issued a threepence coin. In the same era he produced a gold "doubloon" of Spanish-American design.[16] *1934:* The Maryland Tercentenary commemorative half dollar was issued. *2012:* The Star-Spangled Banner commemorative half dollar, silver dollar, and $5 gold piece were issued.

2000-P, Maryland

MS-64	MS-65	MS-66	MS-67	MS-68	MS-69
$0.50	$0.80	$4.05	$11	$88	—

2000-D, Maryland

MS-64	MS-65	MS-66	MS-67	MS-68	MS-69
$0.50	$0.80	$4.05	$11	$260	—

2000-S, Maryland, Proof, Clad

PF-67DC	PF-68DC	PF-69DC
$1.50	$4.05	$9.50

2000-S, Maryland, Proof, Silver

PF-67DC	PF-68DC	PF-69DC
$7.20	$8.50	$11

2000, South Carolina

Circulation-Strike Mintage, Philadelphia: 742,576,000

Circulation-Strike Mintage, Denver: 566,208,000[17]

Proof Mintage, San Francisco, Clad: 4,020,172

Proof Mintage, San Francisco, Silver: 965,421

GSID: Circulation-strike, Philadelphia, 5794; Circulation-strike, Denver, 5788; Proof Clad Deep Cameo, 6062; Proof Silver Deep Cameo, 6061

Specifics of the Reverse Design

Description: Outline map of South Carolina with a Carolina wren (the state bird) and yellow jessamine flowers (the state flower) to the left; a palmetto (the state tree) with severed trunk is shown to the right. THE / PALMETTO / STATE appears in three lines at the upper left. A raised five-pointed star indicates the position of Columbia, the state capital. The top and bottom border inscriptions are standard.

Designer: Unknown. *Mint sculptor-engraver who made the model:* Thomas D. Rogers. *Engraver's initials and location:* TDR. Below the right side of the palmetto ground.

Story of the Design

The South Carolina Numismatic Society had a hand in picking this design. The motif is the most natural (in the botany and zoology sense) seen to date in the series, what with a palmetto tree, a Carolina wren, and some yellow (we are told) jessamine flowers. These motifs and the motto THE / PALMETTO / STATE are on and around an outline map of South Carolina.[18]

Somebody must have designed this coin, or come up with the concept. Here is what the Mint stated:

> Beginning in 1998, the South Carolina Department of Parks, Recreation and Tourism (PRT) accepted quarter design suggestions. Contributions came from PRT's offices, school children and the South Carolina Numismatic Society. From these contributions, PRT compiled five semi-finalist design concepts. The Citizens Commemorative Coin Advisory Committee and the Fine Arts Commission narrowed these five semi-finalist design concepts down to three choices.
>
> Governor Jim Hodges then made his final decision, indicating that the Palmetto Tree represents South Carolina's strength; the Carolina Wren's song symbolizes the hospitality of the state's people; and the Yellow Jessamine, a delicate golden bloom—a sign of coming spring—is part of South Carolina's vast natural beauty.

Perhaps the designer will step forward someday and make a statement. Then, numismatists can wonder if the revelation is fact or fiction.

I am reminded of Irene MacDowell, who, years after the fact, stated that *she*, rather than the usually named Dora Doscher, modeled for the 1916 Standing Liberty quarter dollar. By that time there was no way to check the story, for the others involved were no longer living. We do know that Thomas D. Rogers Sr., a fine engraver at the Mint, made the models for the South Carolina State quarter from designs done by some hitherto unknown person. I consider it very important to learn the identities of the designers of State quarters—such as the school kids who created the Massachusetts quarter motif—before such information becomes lost, and impostors arise to claim the credit.

State emblems of South Carolina. (James McCabe Jr., *A Centennial View of Our Country and Its Resources*, 1876)

Numismatic Aspects of the State of South Carolina

Colonial era: The state issued many types of currency. *1936:* Columbia Sesquicentennial commemorative half dollars, struck at the Philadelphia, Denver, and San Francisco mints, were issued.

2000-P, South Carolina

MS-64	MS-65	MS-66	MS-67	MS-68	MS-69
$0.50	$0.80	$4.05	$11	$38	—

2000-D, South Carolina

MS-64	MS-65	MS-66	MS-67	MS-68	MS-69
$0.50	$0.80	$4.05	$11	$38	—

2000-S, South Carolina, Proof, Clad

PF-67DC	PF-68DC	PF-69DC
$1.50	$4.05	$9.50

2000-S, South Carolina, Proof, Silver

PF-67DC	PF-68DC	PF-69DC
$7.20	$8.50	$11

2000, New Hampshire

Circulation-Strike Mintage, Philadelphia: 673,040,000
Circulation-Strike Mintage, Denver: 495,976,000
Proof Mintage, San Francisco, Clad: 4,020,172
Proof Mintage, San Francisco, Silver: 965,421
GSID: Circulation-strike, Philadelphia, 5793; Circulation-strike, Denver, 5787; Proof Clad Deep Cameo, 6059; Proof Silver Deep Cameo, 6060

Specifics of the Reverse Design

Description: The Old Man of the Mountain, a.k.a. the Great Stone Face, on the right side of the coin, extending to the center, gazes upon a field in which the state motto, LIVE / FREE / OR DIE, appears in three lines. Nine stars, representing the state's order of ratifying the Constitution, are at the left border.

Designer: Unknown, one of many traditional versions of the famous icon used in many places, including on a commemorative stamp. Adapted from a quarter-size brass token used until December 31, 2005, on routes I-93, I-95, and the Everett Turnpike in the state. *Mint sculptor-engraver who made the model:* William Cousins. *Engraver's initials and location:* WC, located below the Old Man of the Mountain and above the M in UNUM.

Story of the Design

As a resident of the Granite State, I find this quarter is one of my favorites. I was responsible, in a way, for the final design, although I did not create it. By the way, of all state motifs this is one of the most criticized by others—those from out-of-state just don't understand why we like the thing!

Ideas for depictions on the quarter were aplenty. Finally, the choice narrowed down to just two: (1) a wooden spire–topped "meetinghouse" of the type said to have been a forum for town meetings generations ago, and in many New Hampshire communities, still used today; and (2) a covered bridge crossing a stream.

A New Hampshire turnpike token, the inspiration for the State quarter.

These sketches were sent to Philadelphia, where the ideas were reviewed at the Mint. Committee member Ken Bressett, a long-time friend of mine and, at the time, the long-term editor of the *Red Book*, sent me copies of several variations of these two final contenders.

I was rather disappointed. To me, the meetinghouse with four spires resembled a standard design for a Baptist church of the old days, not a nonsectarian town hall. As to the covered bridge, while there are dozens in the state, they do not immediately pop to mind as emblematic of the place. Of Vermont, perhaps. Of New Hampshire, no. I mentioned these concerns, then suggested to Ken:

"Why not use the Old Man of the Mountain?"

This referred to the Great Stone Face, as it is (or was) sometimes called—a 40-foot rocky outcrop on Cannon Mountain in Franconia Notch that had been the symbol of the state for a long time. It even attracted the attention of Daniel Webster, who penned a commentary reproduced on a large sign near the site. Ken said that the idea had been considered but the Mint had stated that the motif was too heavy on one side, not balanced. I found this curious, as for years the New Hampshire State Turnpike Commission had been using tokens with the Old Man of the Mountain on them—and they were well struck and durable.[19] I sent some of these to Ken, he saw that coining was practical, and soon the Old Man was adopted.

AN INADVERTENT COMMEMORATIVE

Unfortunately, on May 3, 2003, the rocky outcrop crumbled to rubble, the victim of thousands of years of weathering—warm summers alternating with icy winters. The Old Man was no more, giving the coin the unwanted distinction of being the first State quarter that depicted something in existence when the coin was struck, but now, in effect, a commemorative of times past, but not forgotten.

Numismatic Aspects of the State of New Hampshire

Colonial era: The state issued many types of currency. *1776:* Pattern copper coins were made. *1792–1865:* State-chartered banks were among the most sound in America, with very few failures. *1863:* Just one variety of Civil War token was issued in the state, by A.W. Gale of Concord, who operated a restaurant in the Concord railroad station.

2000-P, New Hampshire

MS-64	MS-65	MS-66	MS-67	MS-68	MS-69
$0.50	$0.80	$4.05	$11	$195	—

2000-D, New Hampshire

MS-64	MS-65	MS-66	MS-67	MS-68	MS-69
$0.50	$0.80	$4.05	$11	$780	—

2000-S, New Hampshire, Proof, Clad

PF-67DC	PF-68DC	PF-69DC
$1.50	$4.05	$9.50

2000-S, New Hampshire, Proof, Silver

PF-67DC	PF-68DC	PF-69DC
$7.20	$8.50	$11

Vignette From a New Hampshire Bank Note.
From 1792 to 1865, the state-chartered banks of New Hampshire were among the most sound in the nation, with very few that failed. This illustration of an Indian Princess is from a $5 note of the Strafford Bank in Dover.

2000, Virginia

Circulation-Strike Mintage, Philadelphia: 943,000,000
Circulation-Strike Mintage, Denver: 651,616,000
Proof Mintage, San Francisco, Clad: 4,020,172
Proof Mintage, San Francisco, Silver: 965,421
GSID: Circulation-strike, Philadelphia, 5796; Circulation-strike, Denver, 5790; Proof Clad Deep Cameo, 6065; Proof Silver Deep Cameo, 6066

Specifics of the Reverse Design

Description: Three ships under sail en route to a destination that would become known as Jamestown. At the upper left is the inscription JAMESTOWN / 1607–2007, and beneath the seascape is the word QUADRICENTENNIAL. The top and bottom border inscriptions are standard.

Designer: Paris Ashton, a graphic artist, was credited by the Independent Coin Grading (ICG) Company as the designer. *Mint sculptor-engraver who made the model:* Edgar Z. Steever. *Engraver's initials and location:* EZS, located on the surface of the ocean at the lower right corner of that feature.

Story of the Design

The center of the 2000 Virginia quarter is graced by a pleasing little flotilla of boats—the Susan Constant, Godspeed, and Discovery—carrying brave emigrants on their way to what would become Jamestown, the first permanent English settlement in the New World. Under a charter granted to the Virginia Company by King James on April 10, 1606, the vessels left London on September 20 of the same year. On May 12, 1607, the group of 104 men and boys landed on an island in the James River about 60

Ruins of an ancient church at Jamestown, Virginia. (Rau Studios, 1920s)

miles into the Chesapeake Bay from the ocean. This was 13 years prior to the better-known arrival of the Pilgrims at Massachusetts, far to the north. The Virginia quarter bears legends relating to the 400th anniversary of the event—an observance somewhat premature, but there were no complaints.

To choose a design for the 2000 Virginia quarter, Susan F. Dewey, state treasurer, was appointed as the liaison to the U.S. Mint. Several different state agencies and offices as well as many citizens joined the effort. Thousands of ideas and sketches were submitted. Finally, Governor James S. Gilmore III made the final selection, and the Treasury Department nodded its approval.

Although the Mint remained mum on the subject, it is generally thought that Paris Ashton (Ashton-Bressler), a graphic designer, created the winning motif. She is a 1985 Bachelor of Fine Arts graduate of the Virginia Commonwealth University, Richmond.

RECORD MINTAGE

The mintage figures for Virginia quarters shattered all records, with 943 million for the 2000-P and 651.6 million for the 2000-D. The Mint's dynamic marketing program left no sales opportunity untouched. In print and on television, the State quarters were in view, accompanied by interesting pictures and stories. Congressmen, perhaps not fully aware that the Mint was earning a great profit for the government, squawked about the expenditures, and publicity for the State quarters was cut back dramatically, seemingly costing the Treasury hundreds of millions of dollars in lost revenue.

As to the Virginia production, Paul M. Green contributed this to *Numismatic News* in 2004 as part of a retrospective:

> The massive production that was seen for issues in 2000 and even early 2001 was bound to catch up with the program. The Virginia mintage from Philadelphia represented at least three 2000-P Virginia quarters for every man, woman and child in the United States. No matter how much you love Virginia, that sort of total is on the high side. With over 651 million more from Denver, the combination for just one of the five quarters that year was easily in the range of the normal quarter production in recent times for an entire year. Consequently, there was certain to be something of a backlog at the Mint, especially in an economy that was beginning to slow down.[20]

Numismatic Aspects of the State of Virginia

Colonial era: Virginia issued many types of currency. *1773:* Copper halfpence of this date were struck in England for distribution in Virginia. *1861–1865:* Richmond was the capital of the Confederate States of America. Most CSA paper money was issued with this imprint. *1936:* The Lynchburg Sesquicentennial commemorative half dollar was issued. *1936:* The Norfolk Bicentennial commemorative half dollar was issued. *1937:* The Roanoke Island 350th Anniversary commemorative half dollar was issued. *1937:* The Battle of Antietam Anniversary commemorative half dollar was issued. *1946–1951:* Booker T. Washington Memorial commemorative half dollars, struck at the Philadelphia, Denver, and San Francisco mints, were issued. *1982:* The George Washington 250th Anniversary of Birth commemorative half dollar was issued. *1993:* The Bill of Rights commemorative silver half dollar, silver dollar, and $5 gold piece were issued. *1993:* The Thomas

Jefferson commemorative silver dollar was issued. *1994:* The Women in Military Service for America Memorial commemorative silver dollar was issued; the memorial is located in Arlington. *1999:* The Dolley Madison commemorative silver dollar, featuring the Madison home in Montpelier on the reverse, was issued. *1999:* The George Washington Death Bicentennial commemorative $5 gold piece was issued. *2007:* The Jamestown 400th Anniversary commemorative silver dollar and $5 gold piece were issued.

2000-P, Virginia

MS-64	MS-65	MS-66	MS-67	MS-68	MS-69
$0.50	$0.80	$4.05	$11	$130	—

2000-D, Virginia

MS-64	MS-65	MS-66	MS-67	MS-68	MS-69
$0.50	$0.80	$4.05	$11	$325	—

2000-S, Virginia, Proof, Clad

PF-67DC	PF-68DC	PF-69DC
$1.50	$4.05	$9.50

2000-S, Virginia, Proof, Silver

PF-67DC	PF-68DC	PF-69DC
$7.20	$8.50	$11

2001, New York

Circulation-Strike Mintage, Philadelphia: 655,400,000

Circulation-Strike Mintage, Denver: 619,640,000

Proof Mintage, San Francisco, Clad: 3,094,140

Proof Mintage, San Francisco, Silver: 889,697

GSID: Circulation-strike, Philadelphia, 5804; Circulation-strike, Denver, 5798; Proof Clad Deep Cameo, 6070; Proof Silver Deep Cameo, 6071

Specifics of the Reverse Design

Description: Consisting of a textured map of New York State (with apparent topological relief, but not to scale), the design shows a recessed line showing the Hudson River and Erie Canal waterway (at the same level, with no locks in the Erie Canal). The river is shown only to the point at which it joins the canal. The Statue of Liberty is to the left, and to the right, the inscription GATEWAY / TO / FREEDOM. This phrase is not a replacement for the time-honored EXCELSIOR motto, or even for THE EMPIRE STATE, but is seemingly a comment on the fact that New York City harbor, home of the statue, was an entry port for those emigrating from distant lands. Eleven stars are added at the upper left and right borders, past NEW YORK, nicely complementing the design and representing the order in which the state ratified the Constitution. This is the second quarter design to use this symbolism (New Hampshire's was the first).

Designer: Daniel Carr. *Liberty Enlightening the World* was designed by French sculptor Frédéric Auguste Bartholdi, and thus he should get some peripheral credit or at least a slight nod. *Mint sculptor-engraver who made the model:* Alfred F. Maletsky. *Engraver's initials and location:* AM in italic capitals below the left border of the map.

Story of the Design

The first of the 2001 issues, the New York State quarter continued the map concept used for the 1999 Pennsylvania and Georgia and the 2000 Massachusetts and South

Carolina issues. The map of the Empire State has some geographical details, including lines added to reflect the course of a waterway using part of the Hudson River and all of the Erie Canal. The Statue of Liberty is on the left side, nicely balancing the heavier map area to the right. However, to some collectors, the statue was a tired motif, in view of its extensive use on 1986 commemorative coins, among other places (including by that time nearly 30 different varieties of postage stamp). This, probably the most famous icon of America, stands on Liberty Island (formerly Bedloe's Island) in the harbor of New York City. It was officially dedicated on October 28, 1886, with President Grover Cleveland doing the honors. At the 1876 Centennial Exhibition in Philadelphia the detached uplifted arm of Liberty had been a great attraction, displaying part of the work in progress.

In keeping with procedures used elsewhere, the governor of the state called for designs from the public, attracting many entries. On June 19, 2000, Governor George E. Pataki unveiled the five semifinal designs as created by Mint artists. These included the aforementioned statue as well as Henry Hudson and his *Half Moon* ship, a scene depicted on the historical *Battle of Saratoga* painting, and the Federal Building on Wall Street, New York City.

Present-day numismatists may know that the 1909 Hudson-Fulton celebration in New York spawned a number of medals with Hudson and the *Half Moon*, but no commemorative coins. The Federal Building is important in numismatic history for its connection with the Treasury Department and the inauguration of George Washington. As to the *Battle of Saratoga*, this is less well known to collectors and probably to state residents as well. However, it was once proposed as the main design for the first Legal Tender Note of 1862 and was used on the back of the rare $500 National Bank Note, Original Series and Series of 1875.

Citizens of the state were invited to cast their ballots for their favorite via email or letter to the governor's office. The winner garnered an impressive 76% of responses.

Daniel Carr's design was chosen from among those of 14 artists who were invited to submit proposed designs. The Mint "paid Carr for his work, [but] it did not credit him as designer. The engravers' initials appear on the coins, but not those of Carr...."[21]

The New York State quarters were released in January 2001. At the inaugural ceremony it seems that little-noticed giveaways were New York State quarters in *chocolate*. Numismatist Frank S. Robinson recalled:

The Statue of Liberty, formally known as *Liberty Enlightening the World*, was dedicated in 1886. (American Bank Note Co. vignette)

I took my daughter to the launching ceremony here in Albany, they had a bowl full of the chocolate quarters. Some were left behind untaken at the end, so I took them, and actually sold them on my list (for a very modest sum). I believe I heard somewhere that chocolati-zing was repeated elsewhere too.[22]

Numismatic Aspects of the State of New York

Colonial era: The state issued many types of currency. *1786:* Nova Eborac and related copper coins were minted. *1786–1787:* Ephraim Brasher, a New York City goldsmith, struck doubloons. *1786–1789:* Machin's Mills in Newburgh made many counterfeit coins that were widely circulated. *1790:* First Presbyterian Church in Albany issued copper "church pennies." *1826:* The Erie Canal medal, by C.C. Wright, was an early product of the famous engraver. *1854:* The New York Assay Office opened. *1858:* The American Bank Note Co. was formed by the consolidation of eight firms, to become world's largest printer of currency. *1858:* The American Numismatic Society was founded by Augustus B. Sage and friends. *1859:* The National Bank Note Co. was founded in New York City. *1862:* The Continental Bank Note Co. was founded in New York City. *1862:* John Gault, New York City, issued encased postage stamps. *1863:* New York City diesinkers produced Civil War tokens in quantity. *1913:* The New York Federal Reserve Bank was established in New York City under the Federal Reserve Act. Currency issued there bears the letter B. *1924:* The Huguenot-Walloon Tercentenary commemorative half dollar was issued. *1935:* The Hudson Sesquicentennial commemorative half dollar was issued. *1936:* The Albany Charter commemorative half dollar was issued. *1936:* The Long Island Tercentenary commemorative half dollar was issued. *1938:* The New Rochelle 250th Anniversary commemorative half dollar was issued. *1986:* The Statue of Liberty commemorative half dollar, silver dollar, and $5 gold piece were issued. *2002:* The West Point Bicentennial commemorative silver dollar was issued. *2014:* Specially struck in a concave/convex fashion to mimic a baseball glove and baseball, respectively, half dollar, silver dollar, and $5 gold piece commemoratives were issued to recognize the National Baseball Hall of Fame, located in Cooperstown.

The Erie Canal at Lockport, New York. (Bartlett, *American Scenery*, 1840)

2001-P, New York

MS-64	MS-65	MS-66	MS-67	MS-68	MS-69
$0.50	$0.80	$4.05	$11	$35	$960

2001-D, New York

MS-64	MS-65	MS-66	MS-67	MS-68	MS-69
$0.50	$0.80	$4.05	$11	$560	—

2001-S, New York, Proof, Clad

PF-67DC	PF-68DC	PF-69DC
$1.50	$4.05	$9.50

2001-S, New York, Proof, Silver

PF-67DC	PF-68DC	PF-69DC
$7.20	$8.50	$11

2001, North Carolina

Circulation-Strike Mintage, Philadelphia: 627,600,000
Circulation-Strike Mintage, Denver: 427,876,000
Proof Mintage, San Francisco, Clad: 3,094,140
Proof Mintage, San Francisco, Silver: 889,697
GSID: Circulation-strike, Philadelphia, 5805; Circulation-strike, Denver, 5799; Proof Clad Deep Cameo, 6072; Proof Silver Deep Cameo, 6069

Specifics of the Reverse Design

Description: The first manned flight at Kitty Hawk, North Carolina, is depicted as adapted from a famous photograph. The Wright biplane, flying toward the right, has Orville lying on his stomach, operating the controls. Above is FIRST FLIGHT. In the foreground are a bench and the large standing figure of Wilbur Wright (much larger than on the original photograph). The top and bottom border inscriptions are standard.

Designer: Mary Ellen Robinson, "who submitted a drawing based upon the famous photograph," was credited by ICG as the designer.[23] One might also grant posthumous credit to the 1903 photographer, John P. Daniels. *Mint sculptor-engraver who made the model:* John Mercanti. *Engraver's initials and location:* JM, located above the far right side of the ground.

Story of the Design

The 2001 North Carolina quarter depicts the Wright brothers' airplane that, on December 17, 1903, flew a distance of 120 feet among the sand dunes of Kitty Hawk, on the seacoast of the state.[24] Although S.P. Langley, backed by many assertions from the Smithsonian Institution, claimed that he was first in the manned flight of a self-propelled heavier-than-air machine, most historians have credited the Wrights.

The image on the coin is loosely adapted from a contemporary photograph by John P. Daniels, now with the standing figure of Wilbur Wright larger in the foreground, as he observes the historic flight with brother Orville lying flat on his stomach at the controls. Concepts for the plane were developed and the craft constructed in Ohio, home of the Wright brothers, who operated a bicycle shop. Henry Ford, who collected all sorts of things, later bought the shop operated by the Wrights in Dayton, and moved it to Greenfield Village in Dearborn, Michigan, where it can be seen today. Later, in 2002, Ohio also memorialized the Wright brothers on its State quarter, but with a different airplane.

Ideas for the coin design were solicited by the North Carolina Department of Cultural Resources, which set up the North Carolina Commemorative Coin Committee.

The resultant publicity drew many submissions. Alternate motifs included the Wright biplane superimposed on an outline map of the state, the Cape Hatteras lighthouse (also on a map), and the same seashore prominence but with a sand dune and seagulls. As Okracoke Inlet, nearby, is famous for its supposed buried treasure, it might have been interesting to add a chest of doubloons.

On June 5, 2000, the Committee and Governor James B. Hunt picked the "First Flight" motif, as it was called—Hunt's choice from three semifinal designs. The FIRST FLIGHT inscription, eventually appearing on the coin, caused some confusion as a slightly different version, FIRST IN FLIGHT, had been used on state license plates since 1981.

Numismatic Aspects of the State of North Carolina

Colonial era: The state issued many types of currency. *1830:* Christopher Bechtler and family opened a private mint and assay office in Rutherfordton to coin $1, $2.50, and $5 pieces. Their mint operated until 1852. *1838–1861:* The Charlotte Mint produced gold coins of $1, $2.50, and $5 denominations. *2003:* The First Flight Centennial commemorative half dollar, silver dollar, and $5 gold piece were issued.

2001-P, North Carolina

MS-64	MS-65	MS-66	MS-67	MS-68	MS-69
$0.50	$0.80	$4.05	$11	$61	$1,250

2001-D, North Carolina

MS-64	MS-65	MS-66	MS-67	MS-68	MS-69
$0.50	$0.80	$4.05	$11	$122	—

2001-S, North Carolina, Proof, Clad

PF-67DC	PF-68DC	PF-69DC
$1.50	$4.05	$9.50

2001-S, North Carolina, Proof, Silver

PF-67DC	PF-68DC	PF-69DC
$7.20	$8.50	$11

The Deco-style Wright Brothers Memorial was dedicated in November 1932, as depicted both on this cachet (printed design) on an air mail cover and seen on the 2003 half dollar First Flight Centennial commemorative.

2001, Rhode Island

Circulation-Strike Mintage, Philadelphia: 423,000,000
Circulation-Strike Mintage, Denver: 447,100,000
Proof Mintage, San Francisco, Clad: 3,094,140
Proof Mintage, San Francisco, Silver: 889,697
GSID: Circulation-strike, Philadelphia, 5806; Circulation-strike, Denver, 5800; Proof Clad Deep Cameo, 6073; Proof Silver Deep Cameo, 6074

Specifics of the Reverse Design

Description: A sailboat shown heading to the left before the wind is the main central feature of the motif. Deck details are visible, but no people are obvious. The boat was modeled after the *Reliance*, the 1903 winner of the America's Cup, a craft built in Bristol, Rhode Island, by the famous Herreshoff Manufacturing Co. In the distance is the Pell Bridge, of the suspension type, with THE / OCEAN / STATE above. The top and bottom border inscriptions are standard.

Designer: Daniel Carr. *Mint sculptor-engraver who made the model:* Thomas D. Rogers. *Engraver's initials and location:* TDR, located at an angle on the surface of the waves at the lower right corner of this feature.

Story of the Design

The Rhode Island quarter of 2001 is inscribed OCEAN STATE, reflecting the importance of the sea, including Narragansett Bay, a vast inlet of the Atlantic.[25] The motif illustrates a vintage sailboat gliding across the waves before the wind, evocative of the America's Cup races centered there for more than a half century. In the distance is the Pell Bridge.

Governor Lincoln Almond authorized the Rhode Island State Council on the Arts to set up the Coin Concept Advisory Panel. Citizens of the state were invited to submit ideas, and more than 500 were received. The choice was narrowed down to three designs, after which it was open voting via libraries, the State House, and the Internet. Of the 34,566 votes cast, 57% were for the sailboat design. Governor Almond did not use his right to change the results and substitute a favorite. He seconded the will of the voters, and this became a people's coin.

Daniel Carr's sketch for the 2001 Rhode Island quarter as submitted to the Mint, after which the design was modified by a Mint artist. (Daniel Carr photo)

The Mint hired Daniel Carr, the highly talented Colorado artist responsible for the 2001 New York quarter, to create the motif used on the coin, an effort that most numismatists considered to be a great success. For some unexplained reason the Mint did not credit Carr in any way. This coin completed the honoring of the 13 original colonies.

Numismatic Aspects of the State of Rhode Island

Colonial era: the state issued many types of currency. *1778–1779:* The Rhode Island ship medal bearing this date was struck in Europe. *1805–1809:* The Farmers Exchange Bank of Gloucester issued large amounts of worthless paper money—the first major bank

Maritime themes have long been used on the coinage and currency of Rhode Island, as reflected on the illustrated Rhode Island Ship Medal, circa 1778–1779, and $1 note issued by the Commericial Bank in Providence in the 1860s (a proof example is shown).

fraud in the United States. *1863–1864:* Many Civil War tokens of a distinctive style were issued, mostly in Providence. *1936:* Providence Tercentenary commemorative half dollars, struck at the Philadelphia, Denver, and San Francisco mints, were issued.

2001-P, Rhode Island

MS-64	MS-65	MS-66	MS-67	MS-68	MS-69
$0.50	$0.80	$4.05	$11	$68	—

2001-D, Rhode Island

MS-64	MS-65	MS-66	MS-67	MS-68	MS-69
$0.50	$0.80	$4.05	$24.50	$169	—

2001-S, Rhode Island, Proof, Clad

PF-67DC	PF-68DC	PF-69DC
$1.50	$4.05	$9.50

2001-S, Rhode Island, Proof, Silver

PF-67DC	PF-68DC	PF-69DC
$7.20	$8.50	$11

2001, Vermont

Circulation-Strike Mintage, Philadelphia: 423,400,000

Circulation-Strike Mintage, Denver: 459,404,000[26]

Proof Mintage, San Francisco, Clad: 3,094,140

Proof Mintage, San Francisco, Silver: 889,697

GSID: Circulation-strike, Philadelphia, 5808; Circulation-strike, Denver, 5802; Proof Clad Deep Cameo, 6077; Proof Silver Deep Cameo, 6078

Specifics of the Reverse Design

Description: Two maple trees, truncated at the top, stand alone, with an empty field or plain in the distance, beyond which is Camel's Hump, a prominence in the Green

Mountain range. A standing man has his right hand at the top of one of four sap buckets in evidence. To the right is FREEDOM / AND / UNITY. The top and bottom border inscriptions are standard.

Designer: Sarah-Lee Terrat. *Mint sculptor-engraver who made the model:* T. James Ferrell. *Engraver's initials and location:* TJF, in italic capitals located above the ground at the far right.

Story of the Design

In 1785 and 1786, Vermont, an independent entity, issued copper coins with the legend STELLA QUARTA DECIMA, or the 14th star. Vermont had hoped to achieve statehood by this time, but opposition from nearby New York, with which there were intense boundary disputes, prevented this from happening. Finally, in 1791 Vermont became the 14th star in the flag, as its citizens had hoped.

The 2001 Vermont quarter dollar features a scene of two maple trees in early spring, not in the usual grove, but standing all by themselves. Perhaps the grove is out of sight behind the observer. Maple sugaring is in progress, with sap buckets affixed to trees. Camel's Hump, the eponymous 4,083-foot landmark in the northern part of the Green Mountains range (from which the name Vermont was derived), forms the background. Maple sugar production, earlier done by Native Americans, became an important industry in the state. The theme on the quarter offers a change from motifs earlier seen on Vermont-related coins, including the sun-and-forested-ridge "landscape" design of the aforementioned 1785 and 1786 coppers, and the Ira Allen / catamount design of the 1927 Vermont Sesquicentennial commemorative half dollar.

Governor Howard Dean named the Vermont Arts Council to coordinate the quarter design. This group created five concepts, each including Camel's Hump, after which a casual survey was conducted by radio. Governor Dean made the final choice, based on artwork by Sarah-Lee Terrat (artist and principal owner of YeloDog Design in Waterbury, Vermont), and sent it to the Treasury Department. The identity of Terrat was unknown to viewers of the coins, and only the initials of William Cousins, who altered the motif and made the models, were featured.[27]

Numismatic Aspects of the State of Vermont

April 14, 1781: An act authorized the issuance of paper money, eventually amounting to £25,155 in total face value; these are rarities today. *1785–1787:* Vermont copper

State emblems of Vermont. (James McCabe Jr., *A Centennial View of Our Country and Its Resources, 1876*)

coins were struck under contract at a private mint on Millbrook, in Pawlet. *1787–1788:* Vermont copper coins were struck at Machin's Mills, Newburgh, New York. *1806:* The Vermont State Bank was authorized, and eventually had four branches. This was the first state-operated bank in the country. *1835:* Gustin & Blake, Chelsea, issued the state's only Hard Times token. *1927:* The Vermont Sesquicentennial commemorative half dollar was issued.

2001-P, Vermont

MS-64	MS-65	MS-66	MS-67	MS-68	MS-69
$0.50	$0.80	$4.05	$11	$47	$364

2001-D, Vermont

MS-64	MS-65	MS-66	MS-67	MS-68	MS-69
$0.50	$0.80	$4.05	$11	$74	—

2001-S, Vermont, Proof, Clad

PF-67DC	PF-68DC	PF-69DC
$1.50	$4.05	$9.50

2001-S, Vermont, Proof, Silver

PF-67DC	PF-68DC	PF-69DC
$7.20	$8.50	$11

2001, Kentucky

Circulation-Strike Mintage, Philadelphia: 353,000,000
Circulation-Strike Mintage, Denver: 370,564,000
Proof Mintage, San Francisco, Clad: 3,094,140
Proof Mintage, San Francisco, Silver: 889,697
GSID: Circulation-strike, Philadelphia, 5803; Circulation-strike, Denver, 5797; Proof Clad Deep Cameo, 6067; Proof Silver Deep Cameo, 6068

Specifics of the Reverse Design

Description: High on a rise, the two-story Federal Hill house is shown, with 11 five-pointed stars erratically spaced on its sides, either an artistic gaffe on the coin or the result of very sloppy carpentry on the building way back when. In the foreground, a sleek and handsome horse stands behind a wooden fence. Above its head is "MY OLD / KENTUCKY / HOME" in quotation marks, which indicate the inscription as a song title. The top and bottom border inscriptions are standard.

Designer: Seemingly the design is one suggested by Kentucky citizen Ronald J. Inabit, although uncredited. ICG signed a contract with contest entrant Benjamin Blair to sign "slabs" containing the coins, crediting him as the "concept artist."[28] *Mint sculptor-engraver who made the model:* T. James Ferrell. *Engraver's initials and location:* TJF, in italic capitals located below the ground at the far right.

Story of the Design

The 2001 Kentucky quarter dollar illustrates a hilltop mansion with a thoroughbred racehorse behind a fence in the foreground.[29] The U.S. Mint described the design:

> Kentucky was the first state on the western frontier to join the Union and is one of four states to call itself a "commonwealth." Kentucky is home of the longest running annual horse race in the country, the Kentucky Derby. The famous Kentucky bluegrass country is also grazing ground for some of the world's finest racehorses.

Also featured on the new quarter is another prominent symbol of Kentucky, Federal Hill, which has become known as My Old Kentucky Home. The design shows a side view of the famous Bardstown home where Stephen Foster wrote the state song, *My Old Kentucky Home*.[30]

It may be of numismatic interest to mention that the portrait of Foster is depicted on the obverse of the 1936 Cincinnati commemorative half dollar. The composer roved widely, and called several places home. In 1852 he visited Judge John Rowan (a cousin) in Bardstown, Kentucky, and stayed in his house, built in 1818. While there he wrote the memorable song.

IDEAS INVITED

Governor Paul E. Patton appointed his wife, Judi, to lead the Kentucky Quarter Project Committee. Designs were solicited, and about 1,800 were received. These were narrowed to 12 final motifs which were displayed in the Capitol building and shown on the Internet for people to review. By this time the Internet played an important role in disseminating information during the design process. The semifinalists for Kentucky's quarter dollar included "horse behind plank fence in field, house in background," "Birthplace of Lincoln," "My Old Kentucky Home with sunlight surrounding it," "Thoroughbred running with jockey aboard," and "Daniel Boone with long rifle, dog under tree."[31]

More than 50,000 votes were received. The selection was further reduced to just two: one featuring the birthplace of Abraham Lincoln and the other a racing horse. Regarding the Lincoln motif, a spokesperson for the state commented, "The commission threw it out, saying it was artistically unsophisticated."[32]

CONFUSION AND DISSATISFACTION

Kay Harrod, who coordinated much of the project, went with other committee members to Washington to visit Mint officials and discuss the racehorse motif. However, the reception proved to be disappointing. In her words:

> They would not look at our drawings. We were just reeling. We thought we had done all the right things. We had been working ourselves to death, our tongues wagging. Why even bother it?
>
> They made up the rules as they went along. The language began to change when we got up there with our design. The word "concept" came up. The words began to change.[33]

An August 22 memo sent by the state, on behalf of the committee, to artists participating in the design took the position that Kentucky would not officially recognize *any* designer, stating:

> The finished art on the coin was done by Mint engraver Jim Ferrell and is a reflection of many entries with horses and *My Old Kentucky Home*. [These] influenced the decision of our committee, Governor Patton and First Lady Judi Patton, who chaired Kentucky's committee. . . .
>
> The art is done by the engravers at the U.S. Mint. In fact, when our committee met with engravers at the Mint in June 1999, the representatives of the Mint did not

look at or accept our drawings that we took with us to that meeting, citing legal reasons. Instead they asked our committee members to discuss the look we wanted.[34]

Apparently the "drawings" that the committee took to the Mint were not to be credited to anyone. Bob Farmer, the state's liaison person to the U.S. Mint in matters concerning design selection, cautioned artists from becoming involved with "coin entrepreneurs" who might seek to sell signed coin products crediting particular individuals. In reality, artists as well as former Mint directors profited by making deals with "coin entrepreneurs" to sign holders featuring coins they had created or, in the case of the directors, coins that were made under their administrations (as discussed near the beginning of this chapter).

Numismatic Aspects of the State of Kentucky

1792–1794: A British Conder token, widely collected in America, is called the Kentucky token, as it depicts a pyramid with 15 state abbreviations, with K (for Kentucky) at the top. *1796:* The P.P.P. Myddelton token of this date bears inscriptions for the British Settlement [in] Kentucky and is related to a colonization scheme. These were made at the Soho Mint (England) from dies engraved by Conrad Küchler, were struck in copper and silver, and are rare today. *1934–1938:* Daniel Boone commemorative half dollars, with examples struck at the Philadelphia mint in 1934, and at the Philadelphia, Denver, and San Francisco mints from 1935–1938, were issued.

2001-P, Kentucky

MS-64	MS-65	MS-66	MS-67	MS-68	MS-69
$0.50	$0.80	$4.05	$11	$47	$1,880

2001-D, Kentucky

MS-64	MS-65	MS-66	MS-67	MS-68	MS-69
$0.50	$0.80	$4.05	$29.50	$108	—

2001-S, Kentucky, Proof, Clad

PF-67DC	PF-68DC	PF-69DC
$1.50	$4.05	$9.50

2001-S, Kentucky, Proof, Silver

PF-67DC	PF-68DC	PF-69DC
$7.20	$8.50	$11

2002, Tennessee

Circulation-Strike Mintage, Philadelphia: 361,600,000
Circulation-Strike Mintage, Denver: 286,468,000[35]
Proof Mintage, San Francisco, Clad: 3,084,245[35]
Proof Mintage, San Francisco, Silver: 892,229

GSID: Circulation-strike, Philadelphia, 5820; Circulation-strike, Denver, 5814; Proof Clad Deep Cameo, 6089; Proof Silver Deep Cameo, 6090

Specifics of the Reverse Design

Description: A collage at the center includes a trumpet (this was a year for trumpets, and one would also be used on the 2002 Louisiana quarter, both with errors in the design details), a guitar with five strings (but with six pegs, and intended to be a six-string guitar), a violin (or fiddle), and a music book. Three large, pointed stars are in an arc above and to the sides; below, the inscription MUSICAL HERITAGE is on a ribbon. The top and bottom border inscriptions are standard.

Designer: Shawn Stookey, a teacher at Lakeview Elementary in New Johnsonville, Tennessee, was publicly credited by the Mint for his winning design. Mint sculptor-engraver who made the model: Donna Weaver. Engraver's initials and location: DW, located above the ribbon end at the right.

Story of the Design

The motif of the 2002 Tennessee quarter is a course in the musical history of the state:

> The design incorporates musical instruments and a score with the inscription "Musical Heritage." Three stars represent Tennessee's three regions, and the instruments symbolize each region's distinct musical style.
>
> The fiddle represents the Appalachian music of East Tennessee, the trumpet stands for the blues of West Tennessee for which Memphis is famous, and the guitar is for Central Tennessee, home to Nashville, the capital of country music.[36]

Following the direction of Governor Don Sundquist, a statewide contest for designs was launched in the spring of 2000, with the nearly 1,000 entries being evaluated by the seven members of the Tennessee Coin Commission. That group picked three favorite themes, including Musical Heritage, Ratification of the 19th Amendment, and Sequoyah (the creator of the Cherokee writing system).

On June 28, 2000, these were sent to the U.S. Mint. Nearly a year later, on June 26, 2001, the Mint sent five "approved renditions" of these ideas, from which Governor Sundquist exercised his prerogative and picked the one to be used. The Mint website included this desirable information: "The winning design was submitted by Shawn Stookey, a teacher at Lakeview Elementary in New Johnsonville, Tennessee." (Kudos to the Mint for showcasing Stookey!)

A CURIOUS GUITAR

After the coin design was released, it was seen that the guitar had six pegs but only five strings. Actually, there are six strings from the tuning pegs to the fretboard, but the sixth string disappears above the sound hole.

There was some controversy about the details of the depicted trumpet, with the bell and leadpipe on the same side as the valves on the instrument. The same error is on the 2002 Louisiana quarter. Errors in design details contribute to the enjoyment of numismatics and are always amusing to contemplate.

Numismatic Aspects of the State of Tennessee

1860s: Civil War tokens were issued by several merchants. Today they range from scarce to rare.

2002-P, Tennessee

MS-64	MS-65	MS-66	MS-67	MS-68	MS-69
$0.50	$0.80	$4.05	$11	$38	$195

2002-D, Tennessee

MS-64	MS-65	MS-66	MS-67	MS-68	MS-69
$0.50	$0.80	$4.05	$11	$61	$520

2002-S, Tennessee, Proof, Clad

PF-67DC	PF-68DC	PF-69DC
$1.50	$4.05	$9.50

2002-S, Tennessee, Proof, Silver

PF-67DC	PF-68DC	PF-69DC
$7.20	$8.50	$11

2002, Ohio

Circulation-Strike Mintage, Philadelphia: 217,200,000[37]
Circulation-Strike Mintage, Denver: 414,832,000
Proof Mintage, San Francisco, Clad: 3,084,245
Proof Mintage, San Francisco, Silver: 892,229
GSID: Circulation-strike, Philadelphia, 5818; Circulation-strike, Denver, 5812; Proof Clad Deep Cameo, 6085; Proof Silver Deep Cameo, 6085

Specifics of the Reverse Design

Description: Against an outline map of Ohio, the Wright *Flyer* is shown high in the air with a pilot sitting (or, rather, lying prone) at the controls. BIRTHPLACE / OF AVIATION / PIONEERS appears in three lines below. To the lower right is an Apollo-era astronaut standing in a space suit on the moon, facing forward. The top and bottom border inscriptions are standard. The numismatic community was well represented in the creation of the design.

Designer: Unknown. *Mint sculptor-engraver who made the model:* Donna Weaver. *Engraver's initials and location:* DW, located below the lower left side of the map.

Story of the Design

The history of the 2002 Ohio quarter is especially well documented, as professional numismatist Tom Noe chaired the committee evaluating the designs, and among the members were *Coin World* editor Beth Deisher and Bill Kamb, president of the Columbus Numismatic Society.

Originally, the committee recommended BIRTHPLACE OF AVIATION as the inscription on the coin, this matching what was on Ohio state license plates. On the coin this was changed to BIRTHPLACE OF AVIATION PIONEERS. Mint Director Jay Johnson said that he had no idea why the change was made, and Governor Bob Taft was surprised. Actually, the Commission of Fine Arts had suggested the change, as there was some question as to where aviation itself was actually "born," as the first flight had taken place in North Carolina and had already been depicted on the quarter of that state. Moreover, aviation in the form of lighter-than-air balloons dated back more than a century before the Wright brothers.

This is what the Mint had to say:

> The Ohio quarter, the second quarter of 2002 and seventeenth in the series, honors the state's contribution to the history of aviation, depicting an early aircraft and an astronaut, superimposed as a group on the outline of the state. The design also includes the inscription "Birthplace of Aviation Pioneers."
>
> The claim to this inscription is well justified—the history making astronauts Neil Armstrong and John Glenn were both born in Ohio, as was Orville Wright, co-inventor of the airplane. Orville and his brother, Wilbur Wright, also built and tested one of their early aircraft, the 1905 *Flyer III*, in Ohio.[38]

The Toledo Blade reported that the astronaut depicted was created at the Mint by using a photograph taken by Neil Armstrong of Colonel Edwin "Buzz" Aldrin Jr., a native of New Jersey—a clear violation of Mint rules that no living person be used as a motif.[39] Accordingly, an alteration was made. The plane depicted is the Wright Flyer III of 1905, although some have mistaken it for the 1903 plane used at Kitty Hawk. Why the original craft was not used was not explained. On the original Mint design there was an error, per this comment from Ohio Governor Bob Taft to Secretary of the Treasury Paul O'Neill, May 11, 2001:

> The designs developed by the Mint show the plane in reverse, which is a common error. What appears to be the tail is actually the front of the aircraft, and the committee feels it is appropriate to show the Wright Flyer emerging from Ohio to show outward growth and progress.

"LAUNCHED" IN SPACE

On March 1, before the official release of the Ohio State quarters, four Ohio quarters were placed on the space shuttle Columbia during an 11–day mission to repair the Hubble telescope. The quarters were carried by Ohioans Lt. Col. Nancy Currie and Dr. Richard Linnehan, DVM, both of whom were graduates of Ohio State University. On their return to earth, one quarter each was kept by Currie and Linnehan, and the remaining two quarters were given to the U.S. Air Force Museum in Dayton, Ohio.

U.S. Mint Director Henrietta Holsman Fore congratulated the astronauts, "I am delighted that NASA has chosen to send four Ohio quarters on Space Shuttle Columbia's mission that began this morning. Colonel Currie and Dr. Linnehan join an illustrious group, from Orville Wright and Eddie Rickenbacker, to John Glenn, Neil Armstrong, and Judith Resnik, as Ohio's latest aviation pioneers." The Ohio quarter was released into general circulation on March 11th, with an official ceremony on March 18th at the U. S. Air Force Museum in Dayton, where the quarters from the shuttle mission were displayed.

Numismatic Aspects of the State of Ohio

1913: The Cleveland Federal Reserve Bank was established under the Federal Reserve Act. Currency issued there bears the letter D. *1916–1917:* McKinley Memorial commemorative gold dollars were issued. *1922:* Grant Memorial commemorative half dollars and gold dollars were issued. *1936:* Cincinnati Music Center commemorative half dollars, struck at the Philadelphia, Denver, and San Francisco mints, were issued. *1936:* The Cleveland Centennial / Great Lakes Exposition commemorative half dollar was issued. *1960: Coin World* was launched in Sidney.

2002-P, Ohio

MS-64	MS-65	MS-66	MS-67	MS-68	MS-69
$0.50	$0.80	$4.05	$11.00	$29.50	$156

2002-D, Ohio

MS-64	MS-65	MS-66	MS-67	MS-68	MS-69
$0.50	$0.80	$4.05	$11	$34	—

2002-S, Ohio, Proof, Clad

PF-67DC	PF-68DC	PF-69DC
$1.50	$4.05	$9.50

2002-S, Ohio, Proof, Silver

PF-67DC	PF-68DC	PF-69DC
$7.20	$8.50	$11

2002, Louisiana

Circulation-Strike Mintage, Philadelphia: 362,000,000
Circulation-Strike Mintage, Denver: 402,204,000
Proof Mintage, San Francisco, Clad: 3,084,245
Proof Mintage, San Francisco, Silver: 892,229
GSID: Circulation-strike, Philadelphia, 5816; Circulation-strike, Denver, 5810; Proof Clad Deep Cameo, 6081; Proof Silver Deep Cameo, 6082

Specifics of the Reverse Design

Description: A full outline of the contiguous 48 United States is shown, with the Louisiana Purchase Territory represented in a stippled map (with no topological features), in relief slightly higher than the rest of the country. At the bottom of the stippled area, a line separates what is now the state of Louisiana. Above is a trumpet with three musical notes, said by some to have included a design mistake (see commentary under the Tennessee-quarter trumpet) and by others to be simply a "cartoon" illustration of a trumpet. To the right is the inscription LOUISIANA / PURCHASE, and to the lower left is a standing brown pelican, apparently with its beak empty. The top and bottom border inscriptions are standard.

Designer: Unknown. *Mint sculptor-engraver who made the model:* John Mercanti. *Engraver's initials and location:* JM, located in the Gulf of Mexico below the Florida panhandle.

Story of the Design

The 2002 Louisiana quarter features a textured area indicating the Louisiana Purchase as a part of an outline map of the United States, the acquisition having been made for a cost of $15,000,000 in 1803, during the presidency of Thomas Jefferson.[40] The brown pelican, the state bird of Louisiana, is also depicted on the quarter, as are a trumpet and musical notes—honoring the tradition of jazz in New Orleans.

This design was the result of considerable effort, beginning in a significant way when Governor M.J. "Mike" Foster Jr. established the Louisiana Commemorative Coin Advisory Commission. The motif

The pelican has long served as the state emblem. (Vignette from a stock certificate, Louisiana National Bank of Baton Rouge)

was to "be easily understood by both the youth of the state of Louisiana and the youth of other states." In time, the commission reviewed 1,193 design suggestions, about 80% of which were submitted by schoolchildren, paralleling in part the design process for the 2000 Massachusetts quarter. Five concepts were given to the U.S. Mint, which developed designs. Governor Foster made the final choice, not at all his personal preference, which had been "a pelican facing right roosting on a pier piling and a paddle-wheel riverboat traveling west over an outline of the state."[41]

Coin World columnist Michele Orzano said the final motif didn't play out very well:

One design that doesn't "work," or offers a mixed message at best, is the 2002 Louisiana quarter dollar design. The coin features the outline of a map of the United States with a highlighted area designating the Louisiana Purchase and text stating LOUISIANA PURCHASE. That's a message all by itself, but the design gets complicated because a pelican is depicted below the map and a trumpet with musical notes is depicted above the map.[42]

Aesthetic considerations aside, these quarters were avidly sought by numismatists to add to their growing collections, which reflect the diversity of the program.

Numismatic Aspects of the State of Louisiana

1830s: Ten-dollar notes were issued in New Orleans; imprinted DIX (ten in French), they are thought to have been the inspiration for the "land of dixes," or Dixie. *1838:* The New Orleans Mint opened; it continued coinage until 1861. *1879:* The New Orleans Mint reopened, and continued operations until 1909.

2002-P, Louisiana

MS-64	MS-65	MS-66	MS-67	MS-68	MS-69
$0.50	$0.80	$4.05	$11.00	$24.50	$240

2002-D, Louisiana

MS-64	MS-65	MS-66	MS-67	MS-68	MS-69
$0.50	$0.80	$4.05	$11	$88	—

2002-S, Louisiana, Proof, Clad

PF-67DC	PF-68DC	PF-69DC
$1.50	$4.05	$9.50

2002-S, Louisiana, Proof, Silver

PF-67DC	PF-68DC	PF-69DC
$7.20	$8.50	$11

Two "Dix" $10 notes from the Citizens' Bank in New Orleans. The first, issued in the 1840s and 1850s, showed "Dix" on the face of the note as well as the back; by the 1860s, when the second note was issued, "Dix" appeared only on the back, but now embedded in an intricate design.

2002, Indiana

Circulation-Strike Mintage, Philadelphia: 362,600,000
Circulation-Strike Mintage, Denver: 327,200,000
Proof Mintage, San Francisco, Clad: 3,084,285
Proof Mintage, San Francisco, Silver: 892,229
GSID: Circulation-strike, Philadelphia, 5815; Circulation-strike, Denver, 5809; Proof Clad Deep Cameo, 6079; Proof Silver Deep Cameo, 6080

Specifics of the Reverse Design

Description: Against the top part of a stippled outline map (without topological features) a powerful Indianapolis 500 race car is shown, facing forward and slightly right. As Indy 500 race cars and the race itself are commercial, this seems to have been in violation of Treasury rules. CROSSROADS OF AMERICA is below. To the left are 18 stars arranged in a partial circle, with a stray star in the field within, making a total of 19, representing the order of the state's admission to the Union. The top and bottom border inscriptions are standard.

Designer: Josh Harvey. *Mint sculptor-engraver who made the model:* Donna Weaver. *Engraver's initials and location:* DW, located below the lower right of the map.

Story of the Design

The Indiana quarter of 2000 includes 19 stars as part of the motif. The primary image is an outline map of the state, over which is superimposed a race car of one of the types used in the famous Indianapolis 500 races, held every year from 1911 to date (except during World Wars I and II). The angle and strength of the car image make it appear to almost be speeding toward the viewer—one of the most dynamic visual effects on any State quarter dollar, it violates the Mint rule that no commercial item be used as a motif. The inscription CROSSROADS OF AMERICA reflects the status of the state as a focus of transportation.

Governor Frank O'Bannon asked his wife, Judy, to solicit designs for the quarter, beginning at the Indiana State Fair on August 17, 1999. Eventually 3,737 ideas were received. The Indiana Quarter Design Committee selected 17 of these and submitted them to a referendum of state citizens. After tallying the responses, the committee selected four semifinalists and sent them to the Mint. A news release from the governor's office, May 5, 2000, told the story up to that point:

> A basketball player and a racecar superimposed over the state's outline: That's the design Governor Frank O'Bannon recommended today for Indiana's commemorative quarter. The design, created by 17-year-old Josh Harvey of Centerville, was also the first pick among the more than 156,000 ballots cast either online or by mail for the 17 semifinalists in a statewide competition. . . .
>
> O'Bannon is forwarding Harvey's design to the Mint today along with these three others: The state outline with a cardinal, 19 stars and the Crossroads of America logo, submitted by Joan Butler of Rushville; the state outline beside the

torch and stars from the state flag, submitted by Seth Fulkerson of Evansville; and Chief Little Turtle, submitted by Zac Shuck of Kokomo.

"Josh did a great job capturing the images that people most identify with Indiana," the governor said. "Our love of basketball and motor racing is world-famous, and I think that when people see our quarter, they'll know immediately that it represents Indiana."

The Mint reviewed the designs, made changes, and sent the revisions back to O'Bannon. On July 18, 2001, the governor made the final choice based on Josh Harvey's design, but now without Harvey's basketball player (in the air or on tiptoe, about to make a shot), with the stars in a different position, and with the racecar from a different perspective. The Commission of Fine Arts recommendation of an entirely different design, one featuring Chief Little Turtle of the Miami Indian nation, was ignored.

AN INSIDE VIEW
Well-known numismatic scholar and historian R.W. Julian was part of the committee to advise the governor about the design. The following account gives certain information that never reached print or official news releases:

> Central States Numismatic Society president Ray Lockwood and I were on the Indiana Quarter Dollar Commission. It was our impression that the Treasury banned reference to a private business, which is exactly what was done here. The Indianapolis 500 is a privately owned entity, whose owners contributed to the O'Bannon political campaigns.

The committee preferred a design showing George Rogers Clark wading through the icy water, holding a gun over his head. The committee knew that it was dead in the water when the governor's official representative on the committee looked at it and said "Oh my God, he's carrying a gun!" The other designs were chosen because of pressure from the governor for a sports or Indian design. The public voting on the designs was designed to get votes for the governor in the forthcoming 2000 election; one of his appointees on the committee actually gave stump speeches the first several meetings, stating that a good design would get O'Bannon a lot of votes!

> The governor had considered scrapping the racecar and using the Little Turtle design instead (and had called a special meeting of the committee to discuss the point), but this was abandoned when someone on the committee pointed out that Little Turtle's background did not bear close scrutiny. There were some red faces at the governor's office over this incident because, as his representative on the committee never tired of telling us, Indiana history was the governor's favorite pastime reading.[43]

Numismatic Aspects of the State of Indiana
Hoosier tame cat became a slang term (ca. 1837–1838) for a bank note originating in Indiana, often worthless.[44] Later, Indiana developed a well-organized state banking system, of which Hugh McCulloch was a vital part. He would become the first Comptroller of the Currency for the U.S. Treasury.

2002-P, Indiana

MS-64	MS-65	MS-66	MS-67	MS-68	MS-69
$0.50	$0.80	$4.05	$11	$16	$234

2002-S, Indiana, Proof, Clad

PF-67DC	PF-68DC	PF-69DC
$1.50	$4.05	$9.50

2002-D, Indiana

MS-64	MS-65	MS-66	MS-67	MS-68	MS-69
$0.50	$0.80	$4.05	$13.50	$43	$240

2002-S, Indiana, Proof, Silver

PF-67DC	PF-68DC	PF-69DC
$7.20	$8.50	$11

2002, Mississippi

Circulation-Strike Mintage, Philadelphia: 290,000,000

Circulation-Strike Mintage, Denver: 289,600,000

Proof Mintage, San Francisco, Clad: 3,084,245

Proof Mintage, San Francisco, Silver: 892,229

GSID: Circulation-strike, Philadelphia, 5817; Circulation-strike, Denver, 5811; Proof Clad Deep Cameo, 6083; Proof Silver Deep Cameo, 6084

Specifics of the Reverse Design

Description: Magnolia blossoms and leaves dominate the single-subject coin, with *The / Magnolia / State* in italic letters in three lines at the above right. The top and bottom border inscriptions are standard.

Designer: Unknown. *Mint sculptor-engraver who made the model:* Donna Weaver. *Engraver's initials and location:* DW, incuse on the lowest leaf at the right—the first incuse or recessed signature in the State series.

Story of the Design

The Mississippi quarter of 2002, with its bold treatment of the state flower and the inscription "The Magnolia State," is simple and effective in its concept—reflecting a tried-and-true symbol. Variety is the spice of life, and the reiteration of familiar motifs is not always desirable, but in this instance the depiction of Magnolia grandiflora scored an artistic success, although it is best appreciated when viewed close-up, not at a distance.

Virtually nothing was publicized nationally about the design-creation process. The U.S. Mint gives this:

> In response to the United States Mint's request for design concepts for the Mississippi quarter, Governor Ronnie Musgrove submitted three concepts on June 22, 2000, a Magnolia flower with a branch, a Mockingbird and "Mississippi—The Magnolia State." The United States Mint provided Governor Musgrove with three candidate designs from which he chose "The Magnolia State" on July 3, 2001.[45]

The motif is unusual in that the magnolia is both the state tree (made official on April 1, 1938, by vote of the state legislature) and the state flower (February 26, 1952). The magnolia is not native, but was introduced from Asia. Its name is derived from that of Pierre Magnol, a French botanist.

Numismatic Aspects of the State of Mississippi

1995: The Civil War Battlefield Preservation commemorative half dollar, silver dollar, and $5 gold piece were issued; funds generated from the sales of these coins went to the Civil War Trust, which has helped preserve land from the 1863 Siege of Vicksburg.

2002-P, Mississippi

MS-64	MS-65	MS-66	MS-67	MS-68	MS-69
$0.50	$0.80	$4.05	$11.00	$40.50	$1,220

2002-D, Mississippi

MS-64	MS-65	MS-66	MS-67	MS-68	MS-69
$0.50	$0.80	$4.05	$16	$94	$240

2002-S, Mississippi, Proof, Clad

PF-67DC	PF-68DC	PF-69DC
$1.50	$4.05	$9.50

2002-S, Mississippi, Proof, Silver

PF-67DC	PF-68DC	PF-69DC
$7.20	$8.50	$11

Victors of the siege of Vicksburg. Pictured are Major-General McPherson, of Grant's army, and his chief engineers (from a sketch by Theo. R. Davis, in *Harper's Weekly*, August 1, 1863).

Settling the terms of surrender. Shown is an interview between generals Grant and Pemberton (*Harper's Weekly*, August 1, 1863).

2003, Illinois

Circulation-Strike Mintage, Philadelphia: 225,800,000
Circulation-Strike Mintage, Denver: 237,400,000
Proof Mintage, San Francisco, Clad: 3,408,516
Proof Mintage, San Francisco, Silver: 1,125,755
GSID: Circulation-strike, Philadelphia, 5829; Circulation-strike, Denver, 5823; Proof Clad Deep Cameo, 6095; Proof Silver Deep Cameo, 6096

Specifics of the Reverse Design

Description: An outline map of Illinois encloses most of the standing figure of Abraham Lincoln, holding a book in his right hand and a small object in his left. The state motto, *Land / of / Lincoln*, is in three lines to the left, and *21st / State / Century* in three lines to the right, all in upper- and lowercase italic characters. At the upper left of the field is an outline of a farmhouse, barn, and silo. At the upper right is an outline of the Chicago skyline, dominated by the Sears Tower, the last a possibly against-the-rules instance of a commercial icon appearing on a State quarter. At the left and right borders, 21 stars represent the order in which the state was admitted to the Union. The top and bottom border inscriptions are standard.

Designer: Tom Ciccelli was important in this regard.[46] *Mint sculptor-engraver who made the model:* Donna Weaver. *Engraver's initials and location:* DW, located to the right of the bottom of the map. On some coins the initials are indistinct.

One of the most famous statues of Abraham Lincoln, not used on the State quarter, is by Augustus Saint-Gaudens and is in Lincoln Park in Chicago. (Century magazine, June 1897)

Story of the Design

An outline map of Illinois sets the background for the design of this state's 2003 quarter.[47] A young Abraham Lincoln, as taken from the statue The Resolute Lincoln, by Avard Fairbanks, is seen inside the map, while other motifs, quite diverse, include a farm and the Chicago skyline. Around the border are 21 stars, reflecting the state's sequence in joining the Union on December 3, 1818. The 1918 Illinois Centennial commemorative half dollar also featured Lincoln, but as a facial portrait.

In January 2001, Governor George Ryan launched the Governor's Classroom Contest encouraging youngsters to submit ideas for the quarter. In time, more than 6,000 were submitted, of which about 5,700 were from schoolchildren. A 14-person committee then reviewed the suggestions and narrowed them down to three categories: state history, agriculture and industry, and symbols of the state. The Mint created five different designs from these, from which Governor Ryan made the final decision.

Numismatic Aspects of the State of Illinois

1891: The American Numismatic Association was formed at a meeting in Chicago. *1892–1893:* The World's Columbian Exposition commemorative half dollars were issued. *1893:* The World's Columbian Exposition Isabella commemorative quarter dollar was issued. *1913:* The Chicago Federal Reserve Bank was established under the Federal Reserve Act. Currency issued there bears the letter F. *1918:* The Illinois Centennial commemorative half dollar was issued. *1936:* The Elgin Centennial commemorative half dollar was issued.

2003-P, Illinois

MS-64	MS-65	MS-66	MS-67	MS-68	MS-69
$0.50	$0.80	$4.05	$16	$228	—

2003-D, Illinois

MS-64	MS-65	MS-66	MS-67	MS-68	MS-69
$0.50	$0.80	$4.05	$21.50	$436	—

2003-S, Illinois, Proof, Clad

PF-67DC	PF-68DC	PF-69DC
$1.50	$4.05	$9.50

2003-S, Illinois, Proof, Silver

PF-67DC	PF-68DC	PF-69DC
$7.20	$8.50	$11

2003, Alabama

Circulation-Strike Mintage, Philadelphia: 225,000,000

Circulation-Strike Mintage, Denver: 232,400,000

Proof Mintage, San Francisco, Clad: 3,408,516

Proof Mintage, San Francisco, Silver: 1,125,755

GSID: Circulation-strike, Philadelphia, 5827; Circulation-strike, Denver, 5821; Proof Clad Deep Cameo, 6091; Proof Silver Deep Cameo, 6092

Specifics of the Reverse Design

Description: A three-quarters view of Helen Keller seated in a chair, facing to the right, with her fingers on the surface of a Braille book in her lap. SPIRIT *of* COURAGE is on a ribbon below. Her name appears in Braille in the field to the right, with HELEN / KELLER in two lines immediately below it. A long-leaf pine branch is at the left border, and camellia flowers (called a "magnolia branch" by the Mint; see previous narrative). The top and bottom border inscriptions are standard.

Designer: Unknown. *Mint sculptor-engraver who made the model:* Norman E. Nemeth. *Engraver's initials and location:* NEN, placed in the field below the SPI in SPIRIT.

Story of the Design

The 2003 Alabama quarter design features Helen Keller (1880–1968), the world-famous author, lecturer, and Radcliffe College graduate (with honors) who lost her sight, hearing, and speech from illness at the age of 19 months. Eventually, an arrangement was made whereby she consulted Alexander Graham Bell, who helped form a relationship between Keller and Anne Sullivan, who remained to work with her for 50 years. The play Miracle Worker is based on this partnership. The coin features Keller's name in English as well as in Braille. At the sides are a long-leaf pine branch and mysterious flowers, while a banner inscribed SPIRIT OF COURAGE typifies Keller's life.

The use of Keller as a motif was unexpected to many citizens, who did not consider her to be a recognizable icon to represent the state. This was no reflection on her accomplishments—many numismatists expressed the same surprise. As for the flowers, the Mint calls this part of the design a *magnolia* branch, per a specification in a letter of April 27, 2001, from Governor Don Siegelman. However, six professors of horticulture at the College of Agriculture at Auburn University stated that, in fact, *red camellias* were depicted—not a surprise, since the camellia is the state flower, and Alabama is known as the Camellia State.

EDUCATION THE THEME

Governor Siegelman called for schoolchildren to create ideas for the quarter dollar, based on the theme "Education: Link to the Past, Gateway to the Future." From the entries received he selected topics including social movements in the state, social and economic history, and Helen Keller. The Commission of Fine Arts and the Citizens Commemorative Coin Advisory Committee both preferred a design featuring the State Capitol in Montgomery, while the choice of the governor was a design "bearing state symbols."[48]

Sketches were produced at the Mint and sent to the governor, who made the final selection, one not among the favorites mentioned earlier. Again, the advisory commissions were ignored.

Numismatic Aspects of the State of Alabama

1861: Montgomery was the first capital of the Confederacy. "Montgomery Notes" in denominations of $50, $100, $500, and $1,000 bear this imprint. *1860s:* White & Swann, in Huntsville, were the only merchants in Alabama to issue Civil War tokens. *1921:* Alabama Centennial commemorative half dollars were issued, two years after the actual centennial.

2003-P, Alabama

MS-64	MS-65	MS-66	MS-67	MS-68	MS-69
$0.50	$0.80	$11.00	$29.50	—	—

2003-D, Alabama

MS-64	MS-65	MS-66	MS-67	MS-68	MS-69
$0.50	$0.80	$11.00	$29.50	$182	—

2003-S, Alabama, Proof, Clad

PF-67DC	PF-68DC	PF-69DC
$1.50	$4.05	$9.50

2003-S, Alabama, Proof, Silver

PF-67DC	PF-68DC	PF-69DC
$7.20	$8.50	$11

Some 1921 Alabama Centennial commemorative half dollars have "2X2" on the obverse (the "22" representing Alabama's status as the 22nd state of the Union, and the X representing the St. Andrews cross which appears on the state flag), while the majority were issued without.

2003, Maine

Circulation-Strike Mintage, Philadelphia: 217,400,000
Circulation-Strike Mintage, Denver: 231,400,000[49]
Proof Mintage, San Francisco, Clad: 3,408,516
Proof Mintage, San Francisco, Silver: 1,125,755
GSID: Circulation-strike, Philadelphia, 5830; Circulation-strike, Denver, 5824; Proof Clad Deep Cameo, 6098; Proof Silver Deep Cameo, 6099

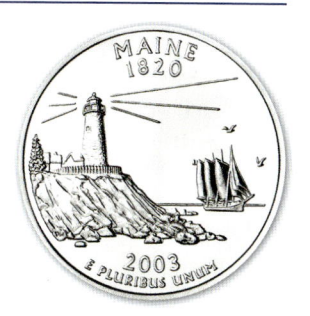

Specifics of the Reverse Design

Description: On the left, high on the rocky shore, the Pemaquid Lighthouse casts beams to the left and right. At its base is the fenced-in residential compound of the lighthouse keeper. At sea in the distance to the right is the three-masted schooner *Victory Chimes*, with two seagulls nearby. The top and bottom border inscriptions are standard.

Designer: Daniel J. Carr with Leland and Carolyn Pendleton. *Mint sculptor-engraver who made the model:* Donna Weaver. *Engraver's initials and location:* DW, incuse on a shore rock at the edge of the design at lower left.

Story of the Design

The Maine quarter of 2003 was the last for the six New England States. The design shows a lighthouse on the rockbound Atlantic coast.

The Commission on the Maine State Quarter Design was established by Governor Angus King in March 2001. More than 200 sketches and ideas were received. These were narrowed to three and sent to the governor, who added a fourth. The candidates then stood as "Nation's First Light," "Where America's Day Begins," Mt. Katahdin, and the lighthouse at Pemaquid Point.

"Nation's First Light," the suggestion of the governor, depicted West Quoddy Head Light in Lubec, Maine, near the easternmost part of the contiguous 48 states, giving the earliest view of the sunrise. "Where America's Day Begins" was of similar theme, but differently executed, featuring an outline map of the state, with the sun rising above the ocean. The 16 rays of the sun represented the number of counties in the state. To the left of the sun, the North Star—a part of the Maine State Arms—was depicted.

A BEAUTIFUL DESIGN AND ITS PROBLEMS

A Mt. Katahdin design, as first submitted by Brian Kent, was one of the most beautiful I had seen thus far in preliminary sketches for the various quarters. A stately pine to the left overlooked a lake with a solitary canoeist, with Mt. Katahdin rising in the distance. In fact, among numismatists who were communicating with me on the subject of State quarters, everyone was enthusiastic—a truly splendid work of coinage art was in the offing!

The Mint made dramatic changes, rendering the design bilaterally symmetrical, more or less, now with the canoe in the center and with five people aboard (an unusually heavy load), pine trees to each side, and a "generic" mountain (not resembling Katahdin) in the distance. The artist found the alterations "disgusting," and the design work "an abomination." Indeed, all of the Mint redoings of the Maine sketches were "so bad they were sent back." By this time a storm of protest had already been mounted by the winning artist of the Missouri quarter (see the following coin description).[50]

DANIEL CARR AND THE MINT SAVE THE DAY

More than 100,000 citizens voted on the Maine sketches, and the Pemaquid Lighthouse was the most popular. Daniel J. Carr, a Colorado artist, submitted the lighthouse design. In its original form on the sketch, it appeared as a bold structure on the right side of the coin, with rays streaming to the left and the right, a pine tree to the far right, and at sea to the left a three-masted schooner, Victory Chimes, a 170-foot ship in service since 1954. The motif was created in cooperation with Leland and Carolyn Pendleton of Rockland, Maine, the coastal port home of the Victory Chimes. This was done in technical conformity to the rules that the motif must be by a Maine resident—and although Carr was from out of state, the "guidelines also indicated that collaborations between groups and individuals were allowed. My submission was a collaboration between the Pendletons and myself."[51] In its final form, as revised by the Mint, the lighthouse is smaller and to the left. In my view, this Mint version was a great improvement, creating one of the finer motifs to date—a splendid blending of Carr's talent with the artistry of Mint engraver-sculptor Donna Weaver.

Daniel Carr's final design, here in the form of a simulated coin, as submitted to the Mint. (Daniel Carr)

Again, art is in the eye of the beholder; the *Bangor Daily News* commented, "The Mint's treatment of the original drawing by Daniel J. Carr of this coastal landmark is shabby and inexplicable. Mis-proportion and clutter seem to be consistent elements of Mint style." The paper further suggested that the schooner "resembles Maryland's *Pride of Baltimore II* more than it resembles the *Victory Chimes*." As if that were not enough, the writer went on to state that in real life the Pemaquid Lighthouse is *not* on a rocky cliff![52]

Oh, well!

Numismatic Aspects of the State of Maine

1820: Maine, a district of Massachusetts, became a separate state. Banks issuing currency with the Massachusetts imprint afterward issued Maine notes, creating banks that were located first in one state, then in another, without moving an inch! *1840:* The famous Castine hoard of Massachusetts silver and other coins was found. *1863:* Just one merchant—R.S. Torrey, inventor of the Maine State Bee Hive—issued Civil War tokens. *1920:* The Maine Centennial commemorative half dollar was issued. *1936:* The York County Tercentenary commemorative half dollar was issued.

2003-P, Maine

MS-64	MS-65	MS-66	MS-67	MS-68	MS-69
$0.50	$0.80	$11.00	$38	$43	—

2003-D, Maine

MS-64	MS-65	MS-66	MS-67	MS-68	MS-69
$0.50	$0.80	$11.00	$24.50	$935	—

2003-S, Maine, Proof, Clad

PF-67DC	PF-68DC	PF-69DC
$1.50	$4.05	$9.50

2003-S, Maine, Proof, Silver

PF-67DC	PF-68DC	PF-69DC
$7.20	$8.50	$11

2003, Missouri

Circulation-Strike Mintage, Philadelphia: 225,000,000
Circulation-Strike Mintage, Denver: 228,200,000
Proof Mintage, San Francisco, Clad: 3,408,516
Proof Mintage, San Francisco, Silver: 1,125,755
GSID: Circulation-strike, Philadelphia, 5831; Circulation-strike, Denver, 5825; Proof Clad Deep Cameo, 6100; Proof Silver Deep Cameo, 6101

Specifics of the Reverse Design

Description: The Gateway Arch at St. Louis forms the center of the design, with three men in a pirogue in the water in front of it, headed toward the lower left. At each side is a riverbank with trees. Above is the inscription CORPS OF DISCOVERY and the dates 1804 and 2004. The top and bottom border inscriptions are standard.

Designer: Paul Jackson, whose original concept was greatly modified by the Mint. Mint sculptor-engraver who made the model: Alfred F. Maletsky. Engraver's initials and location: A.M., in script capital letters, located in the field below the ground at the right.

Story of the Design

The process for determining the design for Missouri's own coin began in February 2001, when Governor Bob Holden named 12 citizens to the Missouri Commemorative Quarter Design Committee. A statewide competition was announced, and about 3,300 submissions were eventually received. From these, a dozen semifinal motifs were chosen and posted on the Internet for voting. About 175,000 responses were received, the results narrowing the field down to five concepts. Finally, a sketch by Paul Jackson, a Missouri artist, was selected.

In its original form, the Gateway Arch (official name: Jefferson National Expansion Monument) at St. Louis was small in the distance, above center, with a river in the foreground and wooded banks to each side. At the center was a canoe with Lewis and Clark paddling. At the time, the design attracted little admiration in numismatic circles, and many felt its artistic quality would be no better than average, if even that.

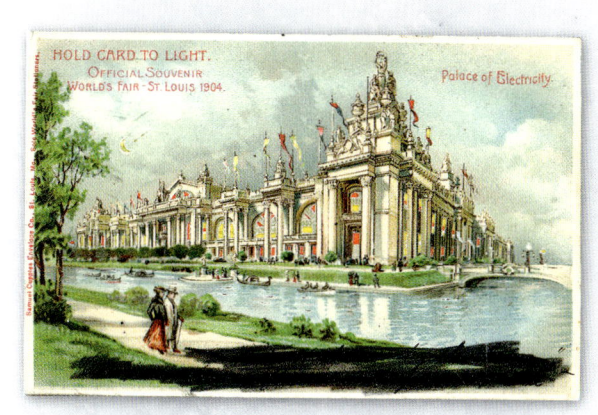

The Louisiana Purchase Exposition (St. Louis World's Fair) of 1904 honored the accomplishments of Lewis and Clark, the same theme as used on the 2003 quarter. Shown is a postcard of the Palace of Electricity at that event.

This design was altered by the Mint to move the arch to the center, to change the appearance of the riverbank trees, to substitute a heavy rowboat (a pirogue) with six men and an American flag, and to add the inscription CORPS OF DISCOVERY and the dates 1804 and 2004. Controversy erupted when artist Jackson found that the Mint had grossly modified the design without consultation, stating, "Entrants were told that the winning design would appear on the reverse of Missouri's quarter. Now it appears as if the competition was nothing more than a hoax. The U.S. Mint never intended to use our designs."

The Mint revision was given to the Commission of Fine Arts for review. The Commission members "felt more comfortable with a design featuring a single theme rather than conflicting motifs." Moreover, one member thought that the arch resembled "the handle coming out of an Easter basket."[53] The idea of different elements thrown in, as originally presented in the Jackson art and in different form by the Mint, seemed to please very few people—a double whammy.

Jackson protested the changes and appeared widely to publicize his views, including on the *Morning Edition* program of National Public Radio on August 26, 2002, and on CBS television's *Up to the Minute* news program the next day. According to a story in *Coin World*, by Michele Orzano, Jackson visited the Mint headquarters, but a public-affairs officer would not meet with him. When CBS contacted the Mint for information, "No comment" was the reply. After articles appeared in the *Washington Post* on the 28th and the *Baltimore Sun* on the 29th, the Mint contacted Jackson to finally arrange a meeting.[54]

Although some further changes were made in the design (e.g., the rowboat—somewhat resembling a rubber lifeboat, or, as some said, a bathtub—was revised to have just three men), the Mint's version essentially prevailed. The entire situation was played out at length in the numismatic as well as the public press. The affair was a first-class headache for just about everyone involved, creating a quarter that many observers found to be one of the poorest motifs so far in the series. Mint Director Jay Johnson later reminisced, "I still remember the remark that the design looked like three men in a tub rowing between two clumps of broccoli!"[55]

This regrettable controversy was the catalyst for the U.S. Mint's revision of its rules. Future quarter designs for 2005 and later would be created by the Mint itself—no outside talent wanted. Instead, concepts were to be submitted in writing, and the Mint would do the artistry.

Early in 2005, it was announced that an unknown quantity of misstruck 2004-P Missouri quarters had been run through a crushing machine to disfigure the pieces and make them unfit for circulation.[56] Afterward these were sold as scrap. Rather than going to the melting pot, large quantities ended up in numismatic hands, including many in holders made by NGC. A campaign was mounted to offer these as collectibles, and there was extensive press coverage at the time.

While the Missouri quarter garnered scarcely any praise or admiration, it became part of the series, and today it is especially interesting to contemplate as a reminder of a specific State quarter project that started going wrong in its early stages. If it is any consolation to Missourians, a few years later the 2005 Westward Journey Nickel Series™ focusing on Lewis and Clark drew unstinted praise from just about everyone.

Numismatic Aspects of the State of Missouri

1904: The Louisiana Purchase Exposition (St. Louis World's Fair) saw the issuance of commemorative gold dollars dated 1903, one with McKinley and the other with a

Jefferson portrait. *1913:* The St. Louis Federal Reserve Bank was established under the Federal Reserve Act. Currency issued there bears the letter G. *1921:* Missouri Centennial commemorative half dollars were issued.

2003-P, Missouri

MS-64	MS-65	MS-66	MS-67	MS-68	MS-69
$0.50	$0.80	$11	$24.50	$1,310	—

2003-D, Missouri

MS-64	MS-65	MS-66	MS-67	MS-68	MS-69
$0.50	$0.80	$4.05	$11	$61	—

2003-S, Missouri, Proof, Clad

PF-67DC	PF-68DC	PF-69DC
$1.50	$4.05	$9.50

2003-S, Missouri, Proof, Silver

PF-67DC	PF-68DC	PF-69DC
$7.20	$8.50	$11

2003, Arkansas

Circulation-Strike Mintage, Philadelphia: 228,000,000
Circulation-Strike Mintage, Denver: 229,800,000
Proof Mintage, San Francisco, Clad: 3,408,516
Proof Mintage, San Francisco, Silver: 1,125,755
GSID: Circulation-strike, Philadelphia, 5828; Circulation-strike, Denver, 5822; Proof Clad Deep Cameo, 6093; Proof Silver Deep Cameo, 6094

Specifics of the Reverse Design

Description: A collage of Arkansas-iana greets the eye, with a faceted diamond in the air above a group of pine trees, and with a marsh or lake in the foreground. A mallard duck to the right, with wings upraised, seems to be rising (for its feet are not extended, as they would be if it were about to alight on the water). To the left are stalks of rice. The motif includes no motto or sentiment apart from the required state name, dates, and E PLURIBUS UNUM. The top and bottom border inscriptions are standard.

Designer: Ariston Jacks of Pine Bluff, Arkansas. *Mint sculptor-engraver who made the model:* John Mercanti. *Engraver's initials and location:* JM, incuse on a raised water detail at the lower right.

Story of the Design

The Arkansas quarter of 2003 features a collage of items relating to the state, including a cut diamond, rice stalks, a lake, and a mallard.[57] The suite is arranged to be heavy at the sides, and light at the middle, somewhat distracting to the eyes of some observers. The Mint commented on the appropriateness of the design choice, given that Arkansas is "the Natural State," with abundant waterways; its status as a prime area for hunting mallard ducks; its Crater of Diamonds State Park (with what is said to be the oldest North American diamond mine); and its agricultural importance as a rice-growing state.[58]

The search for a design was launched by Governor Mike Huckabee in January 2001 under the name of the Arkansas Quarter Challenge. In two weeks, 9,320 entries were received. The field was subsequently narrowed to three, whose creators each received $1,000 in cash, but whose names were not publicized. The Mint then made its own sketches and submitted them to the governor, who made the final choice. The motif by Ariston Jacks, modified at the Mint, was the winner.

The Crescent Hotel in Eureka Springs, Arkansas. While the state has an abundance of natural resources as epitomized on the State quarter, it also has rich scenery and has been a magnet for tourists, as here. (*Harper's Weekly*, December 18, 1886)

Numismatic Aspects of the State of Arkansas

1935–1939: Arkansas Centennial commemorative half dollars, with examples struck at the Philadelphia, Denver, and San Francisco mints for all years, were issued. *1936:* The Arkansas Centennial–Robinson commemorative half dollar was issued. *2007:* The Little Rock Central High School Desegregation commemorative silver dollar was issued.

2003-P, Arkansas

MS-64	MS-65	MS-66	MS-67	MS-68	MS-69
$0.50	$0.80	$4.05	$11	$228	—

2003-D, Arkansas

MS-64	MS-65	MS-66	MS-67	MS-68	MS-69
$0.50	$0.80	$4.05	$16	$61	$780

2003-S, Arkansas, Proof, Clad

PF-67DC	PF-68DC	PF-69DC
$1.50	$4.05	$9.50

2003-S, Arkansas, Proof, Silver

PF-67DC	PF-68DC	PF-69DC
$7.20	$8.50	$11

2004, Michigan

Circulation-Strike Mintage, Philadelphia: 233,800,000
Circulation-Strike Mintage, Denver: 225,800,000[59]
Proof Mintage, San Francisco, Clad: 2,740,684
Proof Mintage, San Francisco, Silver: 1,769,786
GSID: Circulation-strike, Philadelphia, 5841; Circulation-strike, Denver, 5835; Proof Clad Deep Cameo, 6108; Proof Silver Deep Cameo, 6109

Specifics of the Reverse Design

Description: An outline map of the five Great Lakes dominates the center, with the state of Michigan set apart in bas-relief seemingly representing actual topology. GREAT / LAKES / STATE is in three lines to the upper right. The top and bottom border inscriptions are standard.

Designer: Unknown. *Mint sculptor-engraver who made the model:* Donna Weaver. *Engraver's initials and location:* DW, located on the Ohio shore (not indicated as such) on the southern edge of Lake Erie.

Story of the Design

The effort to select a design representative of the state began on November 28, 2001, when Governor John Engler established the Michigan Quarter Commission with 25 members, including numismatists. Residents of the state were encouraged to submit ideas, and 4,300 were received. Four of the semifinalists were "Michigan State Outline, with Great Lakes and State Icons," "Michigan State Outline, with Great Lakes and the Mackinac Bridge," "Michigan State Outline, with the Mackinac Bridge and Automobile," and "Michigan State Outline, with Great Lakes and Automobile."

Daniel Carr's proposal for a Michigan quarter, shown here in the form of a simulated coin. (Daniel Carr)

The fifth was simply the Michigan state outline with the outlines of the Great Lakes, a motif similar in concept to the Cleveland Centennial commemorative half dollar of 1936. Michigan borders on four of these lakes and, per Mint publicity, "Standing anywhere in the state, a person is within 85 miles of one of the Great Lakes."[60] In September 2003, Governor Jennifer Granholm, in consultation with designer Steven M. Bieda, selected this as the winner.

The final design engendered quite a bit of controversy, both in numismatic periodicals and in Michigan newspapers. Among various state designs, it seemed to be among the least pleasing to many people. By this time, critiquing the designs had become a pastime for many citizens, including numismatists. One observer, Ken Anderson, wrote this to *Coin World*:

Plaster mold for the reverse of the 2004 Michigan quarter. (Stephen Bieda photograph)

> I congratulate Governor Jennifer Granholm in regards to the Michigan State quarter design. Her comment of the state outline being the most recognizable characteristic when viewed from space is not justification for portraying only the outline on our quarter.

Out of the first 50 quarters the Michigan quarter is the only quarter that does not depict something of interest within the state, the people of Michigan, or any major accomplishments of its citizens. Next time we are all in space we must remember to look for the outline of Michigan.[61]

There were problems with striking the 2004-D coins, in that the dies were spaced too far apart. Collector Brett Lothrop reported that he had to go through 20 rolls (800 coins) to find *one* that had all of the details sharply defined. As to whether this proportion is true of the whole population of the issue remains to be determined.[62]

Numismatic Aspects of the State of Michigan

1836: The Gobrecht silver dollar featured 26 stars on the reverse, in anticipation of Michigan's becoming the 26th state. *1837–1838:* Dozens of "wildcat" banks were formed in the state, often by fraudsters with no financial banking. By 1840 most were defunct. *1888:* George F. Heath of Monroe launched *The Numismatist*, later to become the official magazine of the ANA. *1863:* Many merchants in Detroit issued Civil War tokens.

2004-P, Michigan

MS-64	MS-65	MS-66	MS-67	MS-68	MS-69
$0.50	$0.80	$4.05	$11	$47	$520

2004-D, Michigan

MS-64	MS-65	MS-66	MS-67	MS-68	MS-69
$0.50	$0.80	$4.05	$11	$16	$273

2004-S, Michigan, Proof, Clad

PF-67DC	PF-68DC	PF-69DC
$1.50	$4.05	$9.50

2004-S, Michigan, Proof, Silver

PF-67DC	PF-68DC	PF-69DC
$7.20	$8.50	$11

2004, Florida

Circulation-Strike Mintage, Philadelphia: 240,200,000
Circulation-Strike Mintage, Denver: 241,600,000[63]
Proof Mintage, San Francisco, Clad: 2,740,684[64]
Proof Mintage, San Francisco, Silver: 1,769,786
GSID: Circulation-strike, Philadelphia, 5839; Circulation-strike, Denver, 5833; Proof Clad Deep Cameo, 6104; Proof Silver Deep Cameo, 6105

Specifics of the Reverse Design

Description: The sea is suggested by the presence of a Spanish galleon at the left and a shore with two palm trees to the right. GATEWAY TO DISCOVERY is below. Above the palm trees is a space shuttle at an angle, nose upward, as if coming in for a landing. The top and bottom border inscriptions are standard.

Designer: Ralph Butler, a resident of Bayonet Point, Florida; his design was vastly altered. *Mint sculptor-engraver who made the model:* T. James Ferrell. *Engraver's initials and location:* TJF, in italic capitals, located on the shore below the rightmost palm tree.

Story of the Design

To get the coin project underway, Governor Jeb Bush appointed the nine-person Florida Commemorative Quarter Committee on April 9, 2002.[65] Gary E. Lewis, a collector residing in Cape Coral in the state, was named as chairman. Lewis would later serve as president of the American Numismatic Association, 2003 to 2005.

In time, more than 1,500 ideas were received, a field narrowed by the committee to 25, then to 10. These were sent to the governor, who selected five semifinalists. Themes remaining after this cut included "The Everglades," "Gateway to Discovery," "Fishing Capital of the World," "St. Augustine," and "America's Space-

Daniel Carr's proposal for a Florida quarter, one of 10 semi-finalists in the competition, shown here in the form of a simulated coin. (Daniel Carr)

port." The final choice was put to the vote of the citizens, who chose "Gateway to Discovery." Bush had hoped for a great white heron standing in sawgrass, but deferred to his constituents.

The art as originally accepted—the galleon on the sea[66] with billowing clouds overhead, two palm trees on the shore to the right, and a somewhat oversize shuttle in the sky—presented a unified picture. However, the design was executed (pun intended) at the Mint, and the three subjects appear disjointed. Perhaps if the sea had been retained, connecting the galleon and the shore, artistic harmony would have been improved. Perhaps an alligator, a bolt of lightning, or some large central theme, a focal point for the eyes, would have helped.

Public opinion of the design was poor, but at least Ralph Butler, the designer of this quarter (its original scenic version, not the later, scattered-objects version), was publicly acknowledged. Early the next year, at the Florida United Numismatists Convention in Fort Lauderdale, January 2005, he was featured and signed souvenirs for show attendees.

Numismatic Aspects of the State of Florida

The East Coast of Florida and the Florida Keys have yielded many silver and gold coins sunk when fleets of Spanish galleons encountered hurricanes in the 18th century. *1935:* The Old Spanish Trail commemorative half dollar was issued; the route depicted began in Florida. *1955:* The Florida United Numismatists (FUN) organization was established. Today it is perhaps the strongest state numismatic club.

2004-P, Florida

MS-64	MS-65	MS-66	MS-67	MS-68	MS-69
$0.50	$0.80	$4.05	$11	$101	$585

2004-D, Florida

MS-64	MS-65	MS-66	MS-67	MS-68	MS-69
$0.50	$0.80	$4.05	$11.00	$24.50	$364

2004-S, Florida, Proof, Clad

PF-67DC	PF-68DC	PF-69DC
$1.50	$4.05	$9.50

2004-S, Florida, Proof, Silver

PF-67DC	PF-68DC	PF-69DC
$7.20	$8.50	$11

Early 20th century "alligator border" Florida postcard showing part of the fort on the coast at Augustine. The old Spanish fort was one motif considered for the State quarter. One of two launch ceremonies was held there.

Ralph Butler, designer of the original version of the quarter, signs a souvenir at the Florida United Numismatists convention, January 2005. (Fred Lake photograph)

2004, Texas

Circulation-Strike Mintage, Philadelphia: 278,800,000
Circulation-Strike Mintage, Denver: 263,000,000
Proof Mintage, San Francisco, Clad: 2,740,684
Proof Mintage, San Francisco, Silver: 1,769,786
GSID: Circulation-strike, Philadelphia, 5843; Circulation-strike, Denver, 5837; Proof Clad Deep Cameo, 6110; Proof Silver Deep Cameo, 6111

Specifics of the Reverse Design

Description: Against a stippled map of the state (no topographical features) a bold, five-pointed star, with ridges to each ray, is shown. In the field to the lower left is "The / Lone Star / State" on three lines in upper- and lowercase block letters. Arclike lengths of rope, said to represent a lariat, are placed individually at the left and right. The top and bottom border inscriptions are standard.

Designer: Daniel Miller, a graphic artist from Arlington, Texas. Certain art by Nancy Boren influenced the final version.[67] *Mint sculptor-engraver who made the model:* Norman E. Nemeth. *Engraver's initials and location:* NEN, located in the Gulf of Mexico (to the right of the lower tip of the state).

Story of the Design

The Republic of Texas, which had used the lone-star emblem on its flag beginning in 1839, joined the Union in 1845, becoming the 28th state.[68] Its State quarter reflects this tradition, with an outline map of the state, a large single star, and the inscription "The Lone Star State." The two sections of rope around the border represent the cattle-and-cowboy tradition of Texas.

There was no lack of motifs to consider, what with the Alamo, oil wells, longhorn steers, armadillos, tumbleweeds, and chili cookouts! It is an interesting fact that the district has been under the flags of Spain, France, Mexico, Republic of Texas, United States of America, Confederate States of America, and United States of America again, which equates to six *different*, giving rise to the Six Flags amusement park in the late 20th century, which eventually expanded to use the name in other states. The state name is derived from *Tejas*, an Indian word meaning *friends*, a logical connection to the present-day motto "Friendship."

In August 14, 2000, Governor George W. Bush, with his eye on the November presidential election, found time to appoint 15 people to the Texas Quarter Dollar Coin Advisory Committee.

This group wisely enlisted the Texas Numismatic Association to supervise a contest that resulted in the submission of more than 2,500 ideas, these only from natives of the state or those who had lived there for at least a year as of May 11, 2001. The association selected 17 finalists and submitted them to the committee, and five semifinalists emerged. Governor Rick Perry selected the winner, a sketch made by Daniel Miller, a graphic artist from Arlington, Texas.

All in all, the Texas State quarter design-selection process was a textbook example of a well-run scenario. The program seemed to flow well, the motif was widely appreciated, and the artist was credited in publicity (although not on the coin).

Numismatic Aspects of the State of Texas

1836: The Republic of Texas was formed, and issued paper money. *1900:* B. Max Mehl (1884–1957) began in the rare coin business; in time he became America's most famous dealer. *1913:* The Dallas Federal Reserve Bank was established under the Federal Reserve Act. Currency issued there bears the letter J. *1934–1938:* Texas Independence Centennial commemorative half dollars, with examples struck at the Philadelphia mint in 1934, and at the Philadelphia, Denver, and San Francisco mints from 1935–1938, were issued. *1935:* The Old Spanish Trail commemorative half dollar was issued; the route depicted terminated in Texas.

2004-P, Texas

MS-64	MS-65	MS-66	MS-67	MS-68	MS-69
$0.50	$0.80	$4.05	$11	$47	—

2004-D, Texas

MS-64	MS-65	MS-66	MS-67	MS-68	MS-69
$0.50	$0.80	$4.05	$11.00	$24.50	$292

2004-S, Texas, Proof, Clad

PF-67DC	PF-68DC	PF-69DC
$1.50	$4.05	$9.50

2004-S, Texas, Proof, Silver

PF-67DC	PF-68DC	PF-69DC
$7.20	$8.50	$11

2004, Iowa

Circulation-Strike Mintage, Philadelphia: 213,800,000[69]
Circulation-Strike Mintage, Denver: 251,400,000
Proof Mintage, San Francisco, Clad: 2,740,684[70]
Proof Mintage, San Francisco, Silver: 1,769,786
GSID: Circulation-strike, Philadelphia, 5840; Circulation-strike, Denver, 5834; Proof Clad Deep Cameo, 6106; Proof Silver Deep Cameo, 6107

Specifics of the Reverse Design

Description: A one-room clapboard schoolhouse is shown at the center and to the left, with a door, two windows, and steps on the front and three windows on the right side. To the right, a teacher in a long flowing dress stands holding the hand of a child with her right hand and the trunk of a tree approximately ten feet tall in her left. The tree, with a very heavy clump of roots, is on the ground, near a hole for it. A kneeling child has both hands on the root clump, while another child is seated, sprawling, on the ground to the right. A fourth child is sitting on the schoolhouse steps. In the distance can be seen a road, a fence, and undulating farmland. The legend FOUNDATION / IN EDUCATION is at the upper right. An oversized inscription, GRANT WOOD, in capitals, is in the field at the lower right. The top and bottom border inscriptions are standard.

Designer: Loosely adapted from *Arbor Day*, a painting by Grant Wood. *Mint sculptor-engraver who made the model:* John Mercanti. *Engraver's initials and location:* JM, located in the field below the lower left of the design.

Story of the Design

In May 2002, Governor Thomas J. Vilsack set up the Iowa Commemorative Quarter Commission, with 16 announced members (number later reduced to 13), to advise on the design of the 2004 quarter dollar. Included were two numismatists: Tom Robertson and Brian Fanton. Libraries, banks, and credit unions were used as information-gathering sources for the designs submitted by citizens—about 5,000 ideas in all. These were narrowed down by the commission to five themes: "American Gothic," "Foundation in Education," "Feeding the World," "Sullivan Brothers," and "Beautiful Land."

Much controversy ensued. The theme concerning the five Sullivan brothers, of Waterloo (who died heroically in November 1942 when their ship, the USS *Juneau*, was sunk), drew fire from critics who said that certain of the brothers had been juvenile delinquents before they went into service. Corn seemed to be a logical—indeed, the one and only—choice for many Iowans, and certainly the "Feeding the World" concept would reflect favor on the state. *American Gothic*, Grant Wood's famous painting that is widely reproduced today, including in parodies, was a strong favorite. The stern-visaged elderly couple with a pitchfork and, behind them, and austere farmhouse symbolized agriculture and hard work.

Vilsack took matters into his own hands, and on May 5, 2003, at PMX Industries in Cedar Rapids (a supplier of certain metal to the mints), he declared that "Foundation in Education" would be the topic.

The Iowa State quarter was the first to host a striking ceremony at the Denver Mint before the release of the coin. The ceremony was held on July 12, 2004.[71]

Daniel Carr's proposal for an Iowa quarter, shown here in the form of a simulated coin. (Daniel Carr)

ARBOR DAY

To implement the theme of education, the Iowa quarter displays a one-room schoolhouse with a teacher and students planting a large tree, a motif based on an obscure and somewhat surrealistic Grant Wood painting, Arbor Day. While just about everyone knew about Wood's American Gothic, the chosen painting was considered by some to be a strange choice, not on a par artistically with its more-famous counterpart. On the coin, the inscriptions FOUNDATION IN EDUCATION and GRANT WOOD are prominent.

Many details of Wood's painting are altered on the coin: the school outhouse (privy) is omitted, and the small tree the students were planting has been replaced by a seemingly very large tree (perhaps 10 feet high) with a root clump that must weigh hundreds of pounds—in real life a bit heavy for little school kids to move around! Also missing from the coin are most of the people in the Grant painting, including the driver of a two-horse team who, it seems, could have been helpful in planting the tree. A reviewer in the *Numismatist* took no notice of such things, and gushed about the sentimental, old-fashioned images depicted on the coin.[72] For my part, I do not think the connection with education seems particularly unique or representative of Iowa, as a cornfield would have been.

What *is* unquestionably unique about this coin, at least so far, is that the name of the artist, GRANT WOOD, on the reverse is the largest inscription of an artist found on any legal tender U.S. coin from 1793 to date! Again, Mint rules for quarter dollars were made to be broken. This contributes to the interesting character of each coin in the series—just about all have some sort of a twist in the stories of their creation and implementation.

Numismatic Aspects of the State of Iowa

1863: First National Bank of Davenport was the first National Bank to open its doors for business. *1946:* The Iowa Centennial commemorative half dollar was issued.

2004-P, Iowa

MS-64	MS-65	MS-66	MS-67	MS-68	MS-69
$0.50	$0.80	$11	$38	$468	—

2004-D, Iowa

MS-64	MS-65	MS-66	MS-67	MS-68	MS-69
$0.50	$0.80	$4.05	$11	$34	$585

2004-S, Iowa, Proof, Clad

PF-67DC	PF-68DC	PF-69DC
$1.50	$4.05	$9.50

2004-S, Iowa, Proof, Silver

PF-67DC	PF-68DC	PF-69DC
$7.20	$8.50	$11

2004, Wisconsin

Circulation-Strike Mintage, Philadelphia: 226,400,000
Circulation-Strike Mintage, Denver: 226,800,000[73]
Proof Mintage, San Francisco, Clad: 2,740,684
Proof Mintage, San Francisco, Silver: 1,769,786
GSID: Circulation-strike, Philadelphia, 5844; Circulation-strike, Denver, 5838; Proof Clad Deep Cameo, 6112; Proof Silver Deep Cameo, 6113

Specifics of the Reverse Design

Description: At the left, the head and neck of a cow, wearing a cowbell on a strap, faces right, with its nose nearly touching a large wheel of cheese from which a section has been cut (not very carefully, with the deepest part of the cut noticeably off center). Behind the cheese is an unshucked ear of corn, placed vertically. FORWARD is on a ribbon at the bottom of the design. The top and bottom border inscriptions are standard.

Designer: Adapted from a drawing by Wisconsin resident Rose Marty, who lives on a farm in Monticello. *Mint sculptor-engraver who made the model:* Alfred F. Maletsky. *Engraver's initials and location:* AM, located in the field below the D in FORWARD.

Story of the Design

In December 2001, Governor Scott McCallum named 23 people to the Wisconsin Commemorative Quarter Council.[74] Over the allotted period of time for submissions, the council received 9,608 ideas, mostly from schoolchildren, which were narrowed to six.[75] These were further reduced, by a statewide referendum, to three: "Scenic Wisconsin," "Agriculture/Dairy/Barns," and "Early Exploration and Cultural Interaction." Council member Leon A. Saryan had this to say:

> Essentially, the selection process was flawed from the beginning. There is an inherent conflict between, on the one hand, a written design idea (for example, put a cow on the coin), and on the other hand an actual, professionally created piece of artwork (a clear drawing showing how a cow would actually look on a coin). The latter will win every time, because our product, in the final analysis, is not a written dissertation on the glories of this state, but a simple picture, severely limited in size and scope, not more than an inch in diameter.[76]

The preceding commentary is poignant and points out a fatal flaw in the policy of submitting "concepts" rather than actual pictures. Concepts are utterly *meaningless* from an art viewpoint. The *Mona Lisa* is not famous because it is a concept of "woman with scenic background," but because of the *art* involved. To one person, the concept "black-and-white drips and splatters" might conjure an image of a birdcage liner—but to Jackson Pollock it might conjure artwork that would sell for a small fortune.

Far better, in my opinion, is for the state committees to require sketches and other art in the submissions, and for the Mint to faithfully translate this art into coinage. In that way we have Wisconsin art, or Florida art, or whatever. The talent of the Mint's sculptor-engravers could enhance the art submitted to them.

In 2003, Governor Jim Doyle, who had unseated Governor McCallum in the latest election, submitted the three semifinal concepts to voters on the Internet, drawing about 36,000 responses. "Agriculture/Dairy/Barns," a single concept with three elements, was the people's choice.

The governor accepted this referendum. Accordingly, the Wisconsin quarter features the head of a cow and a wheel of cheese, echoing the state motto, "America's Dairyland" (which was not used on the coin, although another motto, FORWARD, was). An ear of corn was also depicted, possibly making Iowans jealous!

The secretary of the Treasury approved the design on October 9, 2003, after which the Mint began design and production plans. Mint sculptor-engraver Alfred F. Maletsky prepared models. This project was his swan song, for he retired on December 31.

THOSE CURIOUS "EXTRA LEAF" VARIETIES

The first "gold rush" in the State quarter series occurred in January 2005, when word spread of two curious die varieties discovered among 2004-D Wisconsin quarters. As these are the only varieties among State quarters that have thus far captured the fancy of thousands of collectors, I devote extra space to them here.

Ben Weinstein, manager of the Old Pueblo Coin Exchange in Tucson, explained how the varieties were first found. On December 11, Bob Ford brought in two quarters he had found with die breaks. A regular customer in his 70s, Ford often bought loose change to look through for treasure. He showed his latest find to Rob Weiss, the owner, and then to Weinstein. They bought a set of the quarters from Ford and contacted *Coin World* editor Bill Gibbs. By mid-January 2005, their efforts had spread the word to the numismatic community.

It seems that estimates of known pieces are about 2,000 or so of the Extra Leaf Low and about 3,000 of the Extra Leaf High. Distribution of the coins stopped earlier in the year. I am not aware of any significant hoards or new finds. Original distribution seems to have been mainly in Southern Arizona, centered in Tucson, although some turned up at Flagstaff in the north and some in Kerrville, Texas.

On December 20, 2005, J.T. Stanton sent the following excerpt from the manuscript of the *Cherrypickers' Guide to Rare Die Varieties* (fourth edition, vol. 2):

> It is our belief that the additional lines on this and the next variety of the Wisconsin quarters were deliberately added to the reverse dies. Apparently a tool with a rounded edge was impressed into the working dies to create the images that were

not a part of the intended design. Many collectors, dealers, etc. refer to these as an "extra leaf" variety. However, the lines are not the image of a leaf. . . .

It is our belief that someone in the Denver Mint may have been celebrating their retirement (or celebrating something) a little early by intentionally adding an additional image to some dies. The reasons behind our thoughts are as follows:

1. These additional images are concentric, very similar in appearance, and do appear in a place that would become interesting. The mathematical odds of this occurring totally by accident are too astronomical to be considered.

2. These concentric lines would have likely been caused by an implement such as a small nut driver or other similar instrument. It would be very easy to make an impression into a working die with such a tool.

3. These lines would not necessarily be the same length, depending upon the angle and pressure in which the implement was placed against the die.

4. Some error/variety specialists have noted that only a die-room worker could have done this. We totally disagree, as anyone in the Mint with access to the dies at any time could have caused these.

5. The added knowledge of a 2004-D dime with a very similar size and shape mark near the ear is virtually conclusive evidence these were made intentionally as a form of entertainment by a Mint worker.

In our opinion, the lines on the reverse of the Wisconsin quarters in no way appear to be a form of adding a leaf to the corn husk. The location was likely chosen almost at random, yet allowing for the added images to be identified. . . . Our feelings are very simple—if you like the coins as varieties, consider adding them to your collection. If you don't like them, don't consider a purchase. But it's very clear these varieties are here to stay. And if you're wondering, *we love 'em!*

The Mint Police investigated the situation, and concluded that some unknown person or persons "engaged in a sequence of criminal acts to intentionally alter and/or mutilate an unknown quantity of Wisconsin quarters from the Denver Mint, and in furtherance of their scheme, caused the release of those coins to the public."[77]

Wisconsin State reverse with normal leaves.  **Extra Leaf High variety.**  **Extra Leaf Low variety.**

Numismatic Aspects of the State of Wisconsin

1863: State merchants were important issuers of Civil War tokens. *1936:* The Wisconsin Territorial Centennial commemorative half dollar was issued. *1952: Numismatic News* was founded in Iola.

2004-P, Wisconsin

MS-64	MS-65	MS-66	MS-67	MS-68	MS-69
$0.50	$0.80	$8.10	$29.50	$1,150	—

2004-D, Wisconsin

MS-64	MS-65	MS-66	MS-67	MS-68	MS-69
$0.50	$0.80	$4.05	$11.00	$44.50	$960

2004-S, Wisconsin, Proof, Clad

PF-67DC	PF-68DC	PF-69DC
$1.50	$4.05	$9.50

2004-S, Wisconsin, Proof, Silver

PF-67DC	PF-68DC	PF-69DC
$7.20	$8.50	$11

2005, California

Circulation-Strike Mintage, Philadelphia: 257,200,000
Circulation-Strike Mintage, Philadelphia, Satin Finish: 1,160,000
Circulation-Strike Mintage, Denver: 263,200,000
Circulation-Strike Mintage, Denver, Satin Finish: 1,160,000
Proof Mintage, San Francisco, Clad: 3,262,960
Proof Mintage, San Francisco, Silver: 1,678,649

GSID: Circulation-strike, Philadelphia, 15342; Satin Finish Philadelphia, 15343; Circulation-strike, Denver, 15352; Satin Finish Denver, 15353; Proof Clad Deep Cameo, 15362; Proof Silver Deep Cameo, 15363

Specifics of the Reverse Design

Description: The standing figure of John Muir with a scene of Yosemite National Park in the background showing Half Dome. A California condor, an endangered species, flies overhead. The top and bottom border inscriptions are standard.

Designer: Garrett Burke, with the inspiration of his wife, numismatist Michelle. *Mint sculptor-engravers who made the model:* The design was finessed by Alfred Maletsky at the Mint and was sculpted by Don Everhart II. *Engraver's initials and location:* DE, located at the base of the mountain.

Story of the Design

Much interest centered about the selection of a motif for California's quarter dollar, scheduled to be the first State coin launched in 2005. Although the Mint had announced earlier that no more sketches were wanted—only written concepts—an exception was made for California (a good idea, in my opinion).[78]

Submissions were received by Governor Gray Davis's office in Sacramento from September 9, 2002 (Admissions Day, the anniversary of California statehood in 1850) to November 9. A committee appointed by the governor screened the entries and chose 20 considered to be of special merit. These were presented on an Internet poll from December 31, 2002, to January 31, 2003. After reviewing the results, but not necessarily abiding by them (this being the governor's prerogative), the governor selected five motifs. These were displayed publicly, and comments were invited.

This was a time of political chaos in California. Governor Davis, a Democrat, was charged by some with mismanaging certain of the state's affairs, including the costs of energy. He faced a recall election, and was tossed out of office. Arnold Schwarzenegger, a Republican, was his successor in November 2003.

The five semifinal concepts included the Golden Gate Bridge, a gold miner and implements from the Gold Rush, John Muir and the Yosemite Valley, waves and the sun, and the giant sequoia tree. Public input was invited but, as it turned out, was ignored.

Many numismatists and quite a few others, including the majority of Californians who cast votes for their favorite, supposed that the gold miner would be a shoo-in, a no-brainer. I received much correspondence on this, and while most favored a Gold Rush motif, others said that it had been overdone, and still others said that the semi-final art was more of a group of scattered objects on a plate than a unified artistic scene, not at all on an artistic par with the similarly themed 1925 California Diamond Jubilee commemorative half dollar.

SURPRISE!

Much to the surprise of many citizens of California, in 2004 Governor Schwarzenegger announced that the forthcoming 2005 State quarter would not feature the Gold Rush at all. Instead, John Muir, a famous naturalist, was to be depicted against a background of Yosemite National Park. It would have been the governor's prerogative to choose a cow jumping over the moon, but in the brouhaha that followed, many people forgot this. History shows that the personal choices of governors for State quarters (and even Treasury Secretary Andrew Mellon's choice for Flanagan's quarter-dollar design in 1932) have been common and proper.

The Sierra Club campaigned intensely for the Muir/Yosemite motif and was backed by a sketch that many found highly artistic. This well-organized effort was viewed as unfair by many who hoped for a Gold Rush motif, although the Gold-Rushers were not organized and mounted no publicity effort at all.

The winning designer was Garrett Burke, whose biography was soon posted on the website of the Sierra Club and elsewhere, with a sketch of the design. At the launch ceremony, Schwarzenegger told how he made the final selection:

> We have our landmarks, our discoveries and, of course, all the great achievements, so we couldn't decide. Should it be the Golden Gate Bridge that should be on the coin? Should it be a camera that represents Hollywood, as the entertainment capital of the world? Or should it be the beautiful ocean, the coastline? Should it be the sun, because we have more sunshine than any other place in the world? What should it be? . . .
>
> And the more we went through the five designs, the more we decided that Garrett's design is really the most beautiful one and it says it all. With Yosemite, with the California condor, with John Muir—I thought it was spectacular. A beautiful, beautiful design and a beautiful coin. Muir lit the torch of conservation in our state, and he has inspired generations of Californians to preserve our natural beauty, and this is what makes him so special.[79]

Complaints about the final choice filled many paragraphs of newspapers in California as well as numismatic periodicals, but in the end, this comment from Robert Holbrook, a reader of *Coin World*, is a fair assessment of the matter: "Muir and Yosemite might not 'be California,' but the design is aesthetic. Both are certainly identified with the state by the whole world outside the state and would do the state proud on one of the few tastefully designed coins in the series."[80]

Numismatic Aspects of the State of California

1848: The discovery of gold at Sutter's Mill on the American River, by John Marshall, on January 24, was the catalyst for the Gold Rush. *1849–1855:* Private gold coins were minted. Assay offices produced ingots. *1854:* The San Francisco Mint opened. *1874:* The Second San Francisco Mint building opened. *1913:* The San Francisco Federal Reserve Bank was established under the Federal Reserve Act. Currency issued there bears the letter K. *1915:* The Panama-Pacific International Exposition commemorative half dollar, gold dollar, gold $2.50 piece, and gold $50 piece (in both round and octagonal) were issued. *1923:* The Monroe Doctrine Centennial commemorative half dollar, released in conjunction with a motion picture exposition organized by the California film industry, was issued. *1925:* The California Diamond Jubilee commemorative half dollar was issued. *1935–1936:* The California Pacific Exposition commemorative half dollar was issued. *1936:* The San Francisco–Oakland Bay Bridge Opening commemorative half dollar was issued. *1937:* The Third San Francisco Mint building opened. *1983–1984:* Los Angeles Olympiad commemorative silver dollars and $10 gold pieces were issued. *2006:* The San Francisco Old Mint Centennial commemorative silver dollar and $5 gold piece were issued.

2005-P, California

MS-64	MS-65	MS-66	MS-67	MS-68	MS-69
$0.50	$0.80	$4.05	$11	$650	$2,500

2005-P, California, Satin Finish

MS-64	MS-65	MS-66	MS-67	MS-68	MS-69
$2.65	$2.65	$4.05	$11.00	$20.00	$29.50

2005-D, California

MS-64	MS-65	MS-66	MS-67	MS-68	MS-69
$0.50	$0.80	$8.10	$24.50	$390	—

2005-D, California, Satin Finish

MS-64	MS-65	MS-66	MS-67	MS-68	MS-69
$2.65	$2.65	$4.05	$11.00	$20.00	$29.50

2005-S, California, Proof, Clad

PF-67DC	PF-68DC	PF-69DC
$1.50	$4.05	$9.50

2005-S, California, Proof, Silver

PF-67DC	PF-68DC	PF-69DC
$7.20	$8.50	$11

A magnificent array of temporary structures were created for the Panama-Pacific International Exposition, held in San Francisco in 1915. This postcard pictures the Peristyle, the columned entranceway to the Palace of Fine Arts.

2005, Minnesota

Circulation-Strike Mintage, Philadelphia: 239,600,000
Circulation-Strike Mintage, Philadelphia, Satin Finish: 1,160,000
Circulation-Strike Mintage, Denver: 248,400,000
Circulation-Strike Mintage, Denver, Satin Finish: 1,160,000
Proof Mintage, San Francisco, Clad: 3,262,960
Proof Mintage, San Francisco, Silver: 1,678,649
GSID: Circulation-strike, Philadelphia, 15344; Satin Finish Philadelphia, 15345; Circulation-strike, Denver, 15354; Satin Finish Denver, 15355; Proof Clad Deep Cameo, 15364; Proof Silver Deep Cameo, 15365

Specifics of the Reverse Design

Description: Lake scene with a loon in the foreground, a motorboat with two fishermen not far away to the right, and a shore wooded with pines in the distance. Somewhat incongruously, a map of the state is placed vertically in the lake, to the left of the boat, and bears the inscription, LAND / OF / 10,000 / LAKES. The top and bottom border inscriptions are standard.

Designer: Unknown. *Mint sculptor-engraver who made the model:* Charles L. Vickers. *Engraver's initials and location:* CLV (very subtle), located at lower right, at the tip of an islet in front of the loon.

Story of the Design

Minnesota is called the Land of 10,000 Lakes, a motto bespeaking nature and tranquility. As to how many lakes there actually are, the number is 11,842, according to the Minnesota Department of Natural Resources.[81] The U.S. Mint differs and says, "The Land of 10,000 Lakes actually contains more than 15,000 such bodies of water. . . ."[82] Counting the number of lakes is a subjective matter. First, there has to be a definition of the size of a lake—somewhere between a puddle and an ocean. Second, once size is defined, when it is a dry season, some lakes will shrink to below requirements. When it is rainy, some puddles will be definable as lakes. Uncertainties such as this are interesting to contemplate and in a way are reflective of many elements of the State quarter program. In any event, "10,000 lakes" was bound to be a part of the Minnesota quarter theme considerations.

The Minnesota Quarter Dollar Commission was set up in May 2003 to review design ideas for the 2005 quarter. Included was numismatist Bill Himmelwright, of Minneapolis. The group was charged with receiving comments from the public and narrowing the

State emblems of Minnesota. (James McCabe Jr., A Centennial View of Our Country and Its Resources, 1876)

choices to five, to be submitted to the governor. Schools were given lesson plans on the subject from material prepared by the U.S. Mint, but with the proviso that this was only an exercise—the ideas obtained from it were not to be reviewed for consideration. Many of the drawings were posted in a hallway in the State Capitol.[83] Posters encouraged ideas from the public that were to be part of the selection process. The Mint wanted only narratives, not sketches or any other art—with the result that many impossible-to-visualize concepts like "State With Symbols" and "Fisherman Lake Recreation" were submitted.[84] As before, the "concepts-only concept" was roundly attacked by members of the numismatic press, who sought recognition of artists and the preparation of actual art.

In due course, the commission made its choice of five designs. These were sent to the Mint, which rejected one (a depiction of a single snowflake). That left four: (1) a plow, snowflake, and loon superimposed on an outline map of the state; (2 and 3) two versions of a lake with trees and a loon; and (4) the Mississippi River and its headwaters. An exhibit was set up in the huge Mall of America in Burlington so the public could review and comment upon and the semifinalist sketches from the Mint.

On May 14, Governor Tim Pawlenty announced the choice recommended by his commission: a fishing scene on a Minnesota lake as part of the "10,000 Lakes" theme. Depicted was an outline of the state, a forest of pine trees in the distance, and, in the foreground a small motorboat with two fishermen, with a loon swimming in the foreground. (When Canada pictured a loon on its dollar coin, they immediately became called *loonies*. So far, this has not happened to the Minnesota quarters.) The Treasury Department approved of the design on June 15, 2004.

"When people from around the world see our quarter," commented the governor, "they will immediately associate Minnesota with the beautiful woods and waters of our natural resources."[85] Appropriately, the decision was revealed in Baudette, Minnesota, on the eve of the opening day of fishing season there.

Numismatic Aspects of the State of Minnesota

1913: The Minneapolis Federal Reserve Bank was established under the Federal Reserve Act. Currency issued there bears the letter H.

Varieties: "Spiked Head": Certain clad Proof examples of the 2005-S Minnesota quarters have a die break running from the top of Washington's head to the border. Similar cracks are known for Tennessee, Iowa, Florida, and Texas quarters (the Texas crack is in a different location). Such pieces have an additional value.[86]

2005-P, Minnesota

MS-64	MS-65	MS-66	MS-67	MS-68	MS-69
$0.50	$0.80	$4.05	$11	$780	$2,500

2005-P, Minnesota, Satin Finish

MS-64	MS-65	MS-66	MS-67	MS-68	MS-69
$2.65	$2.65	$4.05	$11.00	$20.00	$29.50

2005-D, Minnesota

MS-64	MS-65	MS-66	MS-67	MS-68	MS-69
$0.50	$0.80	$4.05	$11	$358	$2,000

2005-D, Minnesota, Satin Finish

MS-64	MS-65	MS-66	MS-67	MS-68	MS-69
$2.65	$2.65	$4.05	$11.00	$20.00	$29.50

2005-S, Minnesota, Proof, Clad

PF-67DC	PF-68DC	PF-69DC
$1.50	$4.05	$9.50

2005-S, Minnesota, Proof, Silver

PF-67DC	PF-68DC	PF-69DC
$7.20	$8.50	$11

2005, Oregon

Circulation-Strike Mintage, Philadelphia: 316,200,000
Circulation-Strike Mintage, Philadelphia, Satin Finish: 1,160,000
Circulation-Strike Mintage, Denver: 404,000,000
Circulation-Strike Mintage, Denver, Satin Finish: 1,160,000
Proof Mintage, San Francisco, Clad: 3,262,960
Proof Mintage, San Francisco, Silver: 1,678,649
GSID: Circulation-strike, Philadelphia, 15346; Satin Finish Philadelphia, 15347; Circulation-strike, Denver, 15356; Satin Finish Denver, 15357; Proof Clad Deep Cameo, 15366; Proof Silver Deep Cameo, 15367

Specifics of the Reverse Design

Description: A panorama of Crater Lake, is shown from the south rim. Pines are in the foreground. In the distance is seen Wizard Island, whose size increases and decreases depending on the water level.

Designer: Unknown. *Mint sculptor-engraver who made the model:* Donna Weaver. *Engraver's initials and location:* DW, located at the lower right near the trunk of the rightmost pine tree.

Story of the Design

In the summer of 2003, Governor Ted Kulongoski received many suggestions for his state's coin motifs: Mount Hood, salmon, beavers, Tom McCall, a woman, Crater Lake, a lighthouse, and Sacagawea, among others (this per his press secretary, Mary Ellen Glynn). In the meantime, he was selecting candidates to sit on the 18-member Oregon Commemorative Coin Commission, "which will include a high-school teacher, a numismatist, a member of an Oregon tribe, a historian, a student, a Republican and a Democrat from both the state Senate and state House, the state treasurer, and the governor himself."[87]

On May 7, 2004, the commission reviewed its past work and the semifinal design submissions. These included Crater Lake, a salmon leaping up a waterfall, Mount Hood, and a historical scene including an Indian village or encampment and a covered wagon. The salmon and historical scene were the first to be eliminated, and Crater Lake defeated Mount Hood 10-8 in the final vote.[88]

On May 24, 2004, Kulongoski endorsed the choice of the commission and announced that Crater Lake would form the motif, and the Treasury approved the design on July 13. An account in *Coin World* told this:

> The Crater Lake design features a view of the lake from the south rim, with conifer trees in the foreground, Wizard Island rising from the lake waters and the opposite rim. Crater Lake is the caldera of a volcano, Mount Mazama; the lake was formed following a cataclysmic eruption approximately 7,700 years ago. The lake is the deepest in the United States and seventh deepest [at 1,949 feet] in the world.[89]

When the mintages were totaled, 720,200,000 circulation strikes had been produced at the Philadelphia and Denver mints—the highest figure since the 2000 Louisiana quarter of 764,205,000. These figures compare to an average of slightly more than 497,000,000 for the issues from 2002 to this point. By this time, the all-time record was held by the 2000 Virginia quarter, with an overwhelming 1,594,616,000 coins. The low point was registered by the 2000 Maine, with just 448,000,000.[90]

The design was widely appreciated by numismatists as one of the finest in the series. The elements were all part of a single scene, giving artistic value to the motif.

Numismatic Aspects of the State of Oregon

1790: The ships *Columbia* and *Washington* reached and discovered the Columbia River. The vessels carried 1787-dated medals and Massachusetts copper coins; some were distributed to Native Americans. *1820:* The North West Token, which depicted a beaver, was used for trade. *1845:* A.L. Lovejoy and F.W. Pettygrove were pioneers at a settlement but could not decide on a name. Lovejoy, from Massachusetts, wanted to call it Boston, while Pettygrove, from Maine, wanted Portland. An 1835-dated cent was flipped, and Portland was the choice. *1849:* The Oregon Exchange Co. minted $5 and $10 gold coins. *1864:* On July 4, the 38th Congress passed "An Act to establish a Branch Mint of the United States at Dalles City in the state of Oregon for the coinage of gold and silver." To provide for planning and construction, the sum of $100,000 was appropriated. A fine Mint building was constructed, but never used. *1904–1905:* A commemorative gold dollar was issued for the Lewis and Clark Exposition in Portland. *1907:* Gold discs were issued as money in Baker City. At the time, there was a gold rush in the district, centered in nearby Sumpter. *1926–1939:* Oregon Trail Memorial commemorative half dollars were issued at various mints over the listed span of years. *2005:* Nickel five-cent pieces in the Westward Journey Nickel Series™ feature the sighting of the Pacific by Lewis and Clark at the mouth of the Columbia River.

2005-P, Oregon

MS-64	MS-65	MS-66	MS-67	MS-68	MS-69
$0.50	$0.80	$4.05	$11.00	$24.50	$44.50

2005-P, Oregon, Satin Finish

MS-64	MS-65	MS-66	MS-67	MS-68	MS-69
$2.65	$2.65	$4.05	$101	$130	$195

2005-D, Oregon

MS-64	MS-65	MS-66	MS-67	MS-68	MS-69
$0.50	$0.80	$4.05	$11	$325	—

2005-D, Oregon, Satin Finish

MS-64	MS-65	MS-66	MS-67	MS-68	MS-69
$2.65	$2.65	$4.05	$11.00	$20.00	$29.50

2005-S, Oregon, Proof, Clad

PF-67DC	PF-68DC	PF-69DC
$1.50	$4.05	$9.50

2005-S, Oregon, Proof, Silver

PF-67DC	PF-68DC	PF-69DC
$7.20	$8.50	$11

Portland hosted a world's fair in 1905 called the Lewis and Clark Exposition, celebrating the centennial of their historic journey. The Bridge of All Nations led to the various pavilions.

2005, Kansas

Circulation-Strike Mintage, Philadelphia: 263,400,000
Circulation-Strike Mintage, Philadelphia, Satin Finish: 1,160,000
Circulation-Strike Mintage, Denver: 300,000,000
Circulation-Strike Mintage, Denver, Satin Finish: 1,160,000
Proof Mintage, San Francisco, Clad: 3,262,960
Proof Mintage, San Francisco, Silver: 1,678,649
GSID: Circulation-strike, Philadelphia, 15348; Satin Finish Philadelphia, 15349; Circulation-strike, Denver, 15358; Satin Finish Denver, 15359; Proof Clad Deep Cameo, 15368; Proof Silver Deep Cameo, 15369

Specifics of the Reverse Design

Description: An American bison, the state animal (chosen in 1955), stands on a small patch of ground, facing forward and slightly to the right. To the left are three large sunflowers. The top and bottom border inscriptions are standard.

Designer: Unknown. *Mint sculptor-engraver who made the model:* Norman E. Nemeth. *Engraver's initials and location:* NEN, located at the lower right in the turf.

Story of the Design

To select a design for the State quarter, Kansas Governor Kathleen Sebelius invited participation from all citizens, including students.[91] Per current Mint policy, no art was welcome, just concepts. More than 1,600 were received by the 16-member Kansas Commemorative Coin Commission. Concepts were varied and included bison, wheat, one or more Indians, the statue atop the state capitol, sunflowers singly and in combination with other objects, and outline maps of the state. One had a sunflower with a banner across it labeled "There's no place like home." Another, with a farmer in overalls standing in a sea of wheat with two children, was flatly rejected by the Mint and was eliminated from final consideration. High-school students voted to select the final motif.

The winning concept for the 2005 Kansas quarter, turned into a design at the Mint, was announced by Sebelius on May 6, 2004. Featured was a standing bison (popularly but incorrectly called a *buffalo* by most Americans) with a group of sunflowers to the left. No special inscriptions beyond the standard were shown on a publicized sketch. The three runners-up all featured sunflowers as well.[92]

State emblems of Kansas. (James McCabe Jr., *A Centennial View of Our Country and Its Resources, 1876*)

On the winning design, the horns of the animal were pointing forward, "but as any bison rancher knows, the horns should be pointing up," one observer commented.[93] Perhaps in Philadelphia there weren't any bison handy for Mint artists to check. State officials suggested some modifications, including raising the bison's head, fixing the horn problem, and making the ground appear more natural.[94] These things were done, preventing the coin from being listed among the design errors in the series.

As to the *bison*-versus-*buffalo* terminology, the correct name of the animal is a bison. A buffalo is a different species and is not the animal of our Wild West. Numismatists call the 1901 $10 Legal Tender issue the "Bison Note," and the 2004 five-cent pieces were called "Bison Nickels" by collectors and the Mint alike. However, collectors love their Buffalo nickels, minted from 1913 to 1938, and never call them Bison nickels. Far and away, *buffalo* is the favorite word Americans use.

Numismatic Aspects of the State of Kansas

1860s: Adolph Cohen, a clothier in Leavenworth, was the only Kansas merchant to issue Civil War tokens. *1913:* The Kansas City Federal Reserve Bank was established under the Federal Reserve Act. Currency issued there bears the letter I. *2013:* The 5-Star Generals commemorative half dollar, silver dollar, and $5 gold piece were issued, honoring both the depicted generals and the Command and General Staff College Foundation, located at Fort Leavenworth.

2005-P, Kansas

MS-64	MS-65	MS-66	MS-67	MS-68	MS-69
$0.50	$0.80	$4.05	$11	$16	$38

2005-P, Kansas, Satin Finish

MS-64	MS-65	MS-66	MS-67	MS-68	MS-69
$2.65	$2.65	$4.05	$11.00	$20.00	$29.50

2005-D, Kansas

MS-64	MS-65	MS-66	MS-67	MS-68	MS-69
$0.50	$0.80	$4.05	$11	$390	—

2005-D, Kansas, Satin Finish

MS-64	MS-65	MS-66	MS-67	MS-68	MS-69
$2.65	$2.65	$4.05	$11.00	$20.00	$29.50

2005-S, Kansas, Proof, Clad

PF-67DC	PF-68DC	PF-69DC
$1.50	$4.05	$9.50

2005-S, Kansas, Proof, Silver

PF-67DC	PF-68DC	PF-69DC
$7.20	$8.50	$11

2005, West Virginia

Circulation-Strike Mintage, Philadelphia: 365,400,000
Circulation-Strike Mintage, Philadelphia, Satin Finish: 1,160,000
Circulation-Strike Mintage, Denver: 356,200,000
Circulation-Strike Mintage, Denver, Satin Finish: 1,160,000
Proof Mintage, San Francisco, Clad: 3,262,960
Proof Mintage, San Francisco, Silver: 1,678,649

GSID: Circulation-strike, Philadelphia, 15350; Satin Finish Philadelphia, 15351; Circulation-strike, Denver, 15360; Satin Finish Denver, 15361; Proof Clad Deep Cameo, 15370; Proof Silver Deep Cameo, 15371

Specifics of the Reverse Design

Description: An almost three-dimensional scenic view that features the New River Gorge Bridge and the inscription NEW RIVER GORGE. The bridge abutments or banks are missing at the ends of the bridge. This must have been an oversight.

Designer: Unknown. *Mint sculptor-engraver who made the model:* John Mercanti. *Engraver's initials and location:* JM, located in the waterway at the lower right.

Story of the Design

The governor's office invited citizens to submit ideas for the new quarter. Students at the Governor's School for the Arts were tapped to review more than 1,800 design concepts received.[95] The field was narrowed to include New River Gorge and the related Bridge Day / New River Gorge, River Rafters, Appalachian Warmth, and Mother's Day / Anna Jarvis. Probably, to an outsider, Appalachian Warmth might well reflect the hills, rusticity, and fine people of the state, or as John Denver put it in his "Country Roads" song, "almost heaven."

On March 31, 2004, Governor Bob Wise announced his selection of a motif—a depiction of the New River Gorge and the bridge over it. A sketch showed the river in the foreground and in the distance a steel bridge arching over forested slopes to each side of the waterway. The New River Gorge Bridge, arching 876 feet above the waterway, is the world's second-longest steel span at 3,030 feet. The bridge and gorge are part of the National Park System and are collectively designated the New River Gorge National River. When the bridge was completed in 1977, a 40-mile trip over twisting roads was reduced to one minute.

Numismatic Aspects of the State of West Virginia

After statehood, banks formerly in Virginia had West Virginia addresses, as reflected on changing imprints on currency of banks of the district, similar to the situation in Maine in 1820.

2005-P, West Virginia

MS-64	MS-65	MS-66	MS-67	MS-68	MS-69
$0.50	$0.80	$4.05	$11	$34	—

2005-P, West Virginia, Satin Finish

MS-64	MS-65	MS-66	MS-67	MS-68	MS-69
$2.65	$2.65	$4.05	$11.00	$20.00	$29.50

2005-D, West Virginia

MS-64	MS-65	MS-66	MS-67	MS-68	MS-69
$0.50	$0.80	$4.05	$24.50	$650	—

2005-D, West Virginia, Satin Finish

MS-64	MS-65	MS-66	MS-67	MS-68	MS-69
$2.65	$2.65	$4.05	$11.00	$20.00	$29.50

2005-S, West Virginia, Proof, Clad

PF-67DC	PF-68DC	PF-69DC
$1.50	$4.05	$9.50

2005-S, West Virginia, Proof, Silver

PF-67DC	PF-68DC	PF-69DC
$7.20	$8.50	$11

2006, Nevada

Circulation-Strike Mintage, Philadelphia: 277,000,000
Circulation-Strike Mintage, Philadelphia, Satin Finish: 847,361
Circulation-Strike Mintage, Denver: 312,800,000
Circulation-Strike Mintage, Denver, Satin Finish: 847,361
Proof Mintage, San Francisco, Clad: 2,882,428
Proof Mintage, San Francisco, Silver: 1,585,008
GSID: Circulation-strike, Philadelphia, 77565; Satin Finish Philadelphia, 70498; Circulation-strike, Denver, 77566; Satin Finish Denver, 70499; Proof Clad Deep Cameo, 65099; Proof Silver Deep Cameo, 65104

Specifics of the Reverse Design

Description: Three galloping mustang horses at the center and to the foreground, representing a species for which the state is known. In the distance is a mountain range with a sun and resplendent rays behind it. To the left and right are sagebrush branches, and THE SILVER STATE appears on a curved ribbon below.

Designer: Unknown. Mint sculptor-engraver who made the model: Don Everhart II. Engraver's initials and location: DE, located near tip of ribbon at lower right; D and E each lean left.

Story of the Design

In June 2004 it was announced that Nevada State Treasurer Brian Kolicki had been placed in charge of a group with a particularly lengthy name: Great Nevada Commemorative Quarter Quest Advisory Panel. The panel was created to help select the design for the 2006 quarter. Among those appointed was Phil Carlino, a long-time numismatist. Kolicki noted that the decision would not be easy:

> There are so many different things in Nevada. The history of mining, railroads, Lake Tahoe, Lake Mead, The Strip, the Biggest Little City in the World [Reno], Yucca Mountain, the good, the bad, the test site, the mushroom cloud, wild horses—you name it. There's so many things that are Nevada and its history and again we have to capture that essence and put it on a small piece of metal.[96]

Once again, no *art* from the state was acceptable. Desired were words. Treasurer Kolicki's office maintained a website to receive concepts and to provide information about the program. Five motifs were posted. In early 2003, votes on the design were solicited until 5:00 p.m. on May 30. The popular choice:

> Residents selected the design called "Morning in Nevada." It depicts the sun behind the Sierra Nevada Mountains with three wild mustangs at center, flanked by sagebrush branches. At the bottom of the design is a ribbon inscribed THE SILVER STATE.[97]

Daniel Carr's proposal for a Nevada quarter, shown here in the form of a simulated coin. (Daniel Carr)

CAN A RAM HAVE A PHILOSOPHY?

On January 25, 2004, the Commission of Fine Arts selected a favorite from among five designs done for Nevada by Mint staff. It did not correspond with what the citizens of Nevada preferred. An account in *Coin World* noted:

> CFA Historian Sue Kohler said commission members unanimously selected the design of the bighorn sheep for the 2006 Nevada quarter dollar, but recommended modifications. Kohler said commission members suggested that the image of the ram be reduced in size so that the Sierra Nevada Mountain range could be slightly more prominent in the foreground.[98]
>
> It was also suggested, although the inscription all for our country in the left field of the coin design is the Nevada state motto, that it be removed because it makes it appear the ram is espousing that philosophy.

The sheep design follows Nevada's design concept representing "Nevada Wilderness." A close second among the Nevada designs was a design representing the theme "The Silver State." The design features a waist-up portrait of a miner with a pickaxe held in his right hand, a shovel in his left, with elements of a mine in the background and the inscription the silver state in the lower left field.

The Nevada designs not selected represented the themes "Morning in Nevada," depicting the sun rising from behind the Sierra Nevada Mountains, three wild mustangs at the center, flanked by sagebrush branches, with a ribbon below inscribed the silver state; "Nevada's Early Heritage," showing an outline of the state with American Indian petroglyphs, a Dat-So-La-Lee basket, a tule duck decoy and the inscription nevada's heritage; and "Mother Nature's Nevada," showing crossed miner's axes with a star below for Carson City that separates sagebrush branches, with the sun rising at the center from behind a ribbon inscribed the silver state.[99]

The final motif as used on the coin was ramless. The art was arranged more or less symmetrically, with a sun in the distance, over mountains, three galloping wild mustang horses near the center, THE SILVER STATE on a curved ribbon below, and with sagebrush branches to each side. The elements were nicely tied in with each other, with a horse's leg overlapping a sagebrush branch, and the most distant horse against the mountains. Accordingly,

Hoisting works at the Yellow Jacket Silver Mining Co., Gold Hill, Nevada, circa 1880. The Comstock Lode, discovered in 1859, yielded hundreds of millions of dollars in gold and silver in the district centered around Virginia City, giving rise to "The Silver State" motto.

The Palace, a saloon and gambling emporium, did a lively business in Reno in 1908. The gambling and entertainment industry, so important to Nevada today, did not figure in motifs selected for the 2006 State quarter.

the common complaint of collage designs—elements scattered on a background and not connected—was not applicable here. This closely follows a design chosen as the favorite by citizens, but rejected by the Committee of Fine Arts, described above.

WILD HORSES GALLOP INTO HISTORY ON NEVADA QUARTER

On January 31, 2006 the U.S. Mint issued the following press release on the coin's launch ceremony:

United States Mint, Governor And
State Treasurer Launch Quarter In Carson City

Carson City, Nevada—Wild horses on the run, sagebrush and the sun rising behind snow-capped mountains grace the Nevada commemorative quarter-dollar coin, the newest coin in the United States Mint's popular 50 State Quarters® Program. United States Mint Acting Director David A. Lebryk, Nevada Governor Kenny C. Guinn, and State Treasurer Brian K. Krolicki launched the Nevada quarter-dollar today on the steps of the State Capitol Building in Carson City.

"The trio of wild horses galloping across the Nevada quarter captures the freedom of the American spirit and the bold and rugged beauty of Nevada," said Acting Director Lebryk.

Nevada is home to most of the Nation's wild horses, and they are mentioned in the journals of settlers dating back nearly 200 years. Below the horses on the coin is a banner reading "The Silver State," Nevada's nickname.

On October 31, 1864, Nevada became the 36th state to be admitted into the Union, and the Nevada quarter is the 36th coin in the 50 State Quarters Program.

Following the launch ceremony featuring McAvoy Layne as Mark Twain and the delivery of Nevada quarters by the Carson City Pony Express, Acting Director Lebryk, Governor Guinn, and Treasurer Krolicki handed out shiny, new Nevada quarters to the children in the crowd. Adults lined up to exchange their bills for $10 rolls of Nevada quarters.

The Governor declared January 31, 2006, through March 2006, as a time to celebrate the Nevada quarter in the classroom. Free United States Mint lesson plans about the Nevada quarter-dollar may be downloaded at www.usmint.gov/kids.

The United States Mint also hosted a Coin Collectors Forum in Reno on the eve of the launch at which the public was asked to share ideas on coin programs and design....

The Nevada quarter is available in two-roll sets (40 coins per roll), including one roll each from the United States Mint at Philadelphia and Denver, and in bags of 100 and 1,000 coins, at the United States Mint website at www.usmint.gov. The two-roll sets are $32.00, bags of 100 coins are $35.50, and bags of 1,000 coins are $300.00.

Numismatic Aspects of the State of Nevada

1870–1893: The Carson City Mint produced silver and gold coins, mostly Morgan silver dollars and gold double eagles. From 1942 to date the structure has housed the Nevada State Museum, which includes a numismatic display. *20th century:* Casino chips become a popular collectible.

2006-P, Nevada

MS-64	MS-65	MS-66	MS-67	MS-68	MS-69
$0.50	$0.80	$4.05	$11	$51	$520

2006-P, Nevada, Satin Finish

MS-64	MS-65	MS-66	MS-67	MS-68	MS-69
$2.65	$2.65	$4.05	$11.00	$20.00	$29.50

2006-D, Nevada

MS-64	MS-65	MS-66	MS-67	MS-68	MS-69
$0.50	$0.80	$8.10	$19	$390	$960

2006-D, Nevada, Satin Finish

MS-64	MS-65	MS-66	MS-67	MS-68	MS-69
$2.65	$2.65	$4.05	$11.00	$20.00	$29.50

2006-S, Nevada, Proof, Clad

PF-67DC	PF-68DC	PF-69DC
$1.50	$4.05	$9.50

2006-S, Nevada, Proof, Silver

PF-67DC	PF-68DC	PF-69DC
$7.20	$8.50	$11

2006, Nebraska

Circulation-Strike Mintage, Philadelphia: 318,000,000
Circulation-Strike Mintage, Philadelphia, Satin Finish: 847,361
Circulation-Strike Mintage, Denver: 273,000,000
Circulation-Strike Mintage, Denver, Satin Finish: 847,361
Proof Mintage, San Francisco, Clad: 2,882,428
Proof Mintage, San Francisco, Silver: 1,585,008
GSID: Circulation-strike, Philadelphia, 70793; Satin Finish Philadelphia, 285875; Circulation-strike, Denver, 70794; Satin Finish Denver, 285876; Proof Clad Deep Cameo, 65096; Proof Silver Deep Cameo, 65101

Specifics of the Reverse Design

Description: Historic Chimney Rock to the right, with terrain in the foreground and a covered wagon drawn by two oxen to the left, depicting a scene of pioneers in the 19th century. The sun is in the sky to the left.

Designer: Rick Masters. *Mint sculptor-engraver who made the model:* Charles L. Vickers. *Engraver's initials and location:* CLV, located in the field to the left, below the edge of the terrain.

Story of the Design

Every State quarter had its procedures, complications, reviews, and so on. Because the scenarios for Nebraska and Colorado are perhaps representative of the others, and because they are the most recent (as of press time), I have chosen the Nebraska scenario for expanded coverage.

In 2003, John Gale, Nebraska secretary of state and chairman of the Nebraska State Quarter Design Committee, posted a notice outlining the quarter program as carried out by other states in the past and suggesting guidelines for the Nebraska issue. He concluded by noting, "This is an opportunity for all Nebraskans to show pride in their state by submitting a design."[100] Actually, the more accurate word would have been *concept*. Again, no *art* was wanted from residents of the state.

The first meeting of the committee was held in the State Capitol two days later. Minutes of meetings were subsequently posted on the Internet, making it possible for anyone to follow the deliberations. The May 30 narrative included this information, giving an excellent overview of the process then in effect. Particularly notable is the comment that a *single motif* is the most desirable:

> *U.S. Mint Guests:* Secretary Gale introduced Gloria Eskridge, associate director sales and marketing and Jean Gentry, deputy chief counsel, both from the Department of the Treasury, U.S. Mint. Ms. Eskridge relayed a little of the history of the program and how the Treasury Department has discovered the importance of working very early and often with the states as they work through the process of their quarter design development. One of the big elements of this program is to educate people across the nation on history in each state. Ms. Gentry stated there are three elements the Mint will be looking for in a design; these are as follows:
>
> 1. Coinability (something that can be reproduced in a large quantity, can be used in vending machines, etc. etc.)
>
> 2. Historical accuracy (the Mint will work very closely with the state to make sure every element on the design is historically accurate)
>
> 3. Appropriateness (should be dignified and not frivolous). Ms. Eskridge and Ms. Gentry gave some general guidelines for elements that should NOT be used on the quarters. One of the things they mentioned is [that] something that is popular now but is only a fad should not be used. It is inappropriate to use any depiction of a religion or a sport. No state flag or seal may be used; however, parts of the flag or seal can be used. No head or shoulders/bust of any person living or dead may be used and no portrait of any living person may be used. There should be no symbol used that can be seen as an endorsement for any commercial product or brand. Even the depiction of a car, tractor, etc., should be completely generic.

It was explained that in submitting concepts in a narrative form, it gets away from setting an expectation from an artist that their design will be reproduced exactly as they had submitted it. It gives the state a lot more latitude in the final design.

They suggested that as a normal rule a simple design is a better design. A single element that stands out usually looks better than several elements in the small space. They did say that wording can be used; and in fact, most quarters do have some wording identifying an element on the coin. The Mint will request source material to support the narrative. Photographs may be used for this.

In time, more than 6,500 concepts were received. Chimney Rock, an icon for Forty Niners on the way to California, was represented. Farming and homesteading motifs, reflective of the early years of the territory that became a state in 1906, included fields, tractors, crops, and sod huts.

DECISIONS

After the May 1, 2004, deadline, the committee was given until September 30 to select concepts to be forwarded to the U.S. Mint. In the meantime, 25 of the concepts were posted on the Internet, and Nebraskans were invited to vote. From August 20 to the September 30 end date, 138,649 did. The 10 most popular were Chimney Rock and westward migration, Standing Bear, the State Capitol, The Sower, the state outline, agriculture, sandhill cranes, frontier travel, transportation and communication, and homesteading.

Numismatic News told what happened next:

> On September 28, the Nebraska Quarter Design Committee sent four narratives to the U.S. Mint for rendering for its 2006 state quarter design. Prior to a September 22 meeting, the NQDC had opted for five narratives. However, at the meeting, the design of Chimney Rock with the State Capitol was eliminated.
>
> The committee also slightly altered two other narratives at that meeting. The State Capitol with text "The Unicameral State" was changed to "Home of the Unicameral State," and the Capitol's *Sower* with the text "The Arbor Day State" was changed to the similar "Home of Arbor Day." The designs will now go to Mint sculptor-engravers. Nebraska officials expect the design renderings next spring for final selection.[101]

This narrative from *Coin World* reveals internal processes of the committee, which was struggling with Mint-created art rather than art submitted by Nebraskans—a continuing bone of contention in the State quarter program:

> In December [on the 15th] the Nebraska State Quarter Design Committee suggested some minor changes to the first round of U.S. Mint approved designs for its 2006 State quarter dollar. The four design concepts and the committee's recommended changes are:
>
> A depiction of a covered wagon with the Chimney Rock formation in the background and a sun overhead. The text CHIMNEY ROCK appears to the right. Chimney Rock is a naturally occurring rock formation located in the valley of the North Platte River. It is considered one of the state's most famous landmarks and was seen by those traveling along the Oregon Trail. The rock formation stands 325 feet from base to tip. The committee asked the Mint to make the wagon, oxen and family members smaller so Chimney Rock is the more dominant image in the design.

A depiction of the statue *The Sower*, a 19.5-foot bronze sculpture that has stood atop the 400-foot tower of the state Capitol since 1930. The text HOME OF ARBOR DAY appears above and to the right of the image while THE SOWER appears below and to the left of the image and the first initial and last name of the sculptor, Lee Lawrie, appears just to the right and below the depiction of the statue. The committee asked that the name of the sculptor be dropped from the design. The committee also asked that the figure's legs be extended to just below the knee to avoid an amputated look to the legs as on the current Mint designs.

The state Capitol with the text HOME OF THE UNICAMERAL STATE and STATE CAPITOL flank the depiction of the building. The word "unicameral" refers to Nebraska being the only single-house state legislature in the country. The committee requested Mint artists to add details to the north entrance of the Capitol building to show the building's grandeur.

A portrait of Chief Standing Bear of the Ponca tribe with the state's motto EQUALITY BEFORE THE LAW to the right of the portrait and the words CHIEF STANDING BEAR to the left of his portrait. The only change sought by the committee was to increase the size of the state motto and the legend CHIEF STANDING BEAR from 10 to 15 percent.[102]

The Commission of Fine Arts added its commentary:

> A desert bighorn sheep ram, state capitol building and grazing bison appear on the designs recommended Jan. 25 by the Commission of Fine Arts for the reverses of the 2006 State quarter dollars. . . .
>
> For Nebraska, commission members selected a design showing the State Capitol building in Lincoln that was designed by renowned architect Bertram Grosvenor Goodhue, who also designed the National Academy of Sciences Building in Washington, D.C. [CFA historian Sue] Kohler said it was recommended that the inscription state capitol be moved from the right field on the design to below the building, with the date of completion, 1832, added. There was no mention about retaining or removing the inscription from the left field, home of the / unicameral, a reference to Nebraska being the only state with a single-body legislature.
>
> The designs not recommended were a rendition of *The Sower* statue that graces the dome of the State Capitol; a design showing Chimney Rock with a blazing sun rising behind an ox-drawn Conestoga wagon transporting a pioneer family; and a portrait of Standing Bear, a Ponca Indian chief whose 1879 trial in Omaha led to a decision by Judge Elmer Dundy that native Americans are "persons within the meaning of the law" and have the rights of citizenship.[103]

THE FINAL CHOICE

On June 1, 2005, the governor's office issued this statement:

> Gov. Dave Heineman announced Chimney Rock as his selection for the commemorative U.S. quarter to represent Nebraska. He was joined for the announcement by Secretary of State John Gale.
>
> The Chimney Rock design, which was one of four finalists presented to the Governor last month, features a pioneer family, a covered wagon and Chimney Rock, the

clay and sandstone natural wonder that served as a landmark for westward expansion and that today serves as a tourist destination and historical marker. The Governor has forwarded his choice to U.S. Treasury Secretary John Snow for final approval.

"I chose Chimney Rock because I felt it best represented our state's pioneering spirit and cultural heritage," Gov. Heineman said. "It reflected the resolve, persistence and incomparable work ethic that our forbearers brought to the plains."

The Commission of Fine Arts added another item to its long list of rejections of its choices for Washington quarters; the first had been way back in 1932 with the original design. In my opinion, the final design by the Mint is one of the most beautiful in the series—well integrated, with Chimney Rock being the main motif, the covered wagon being subsidiary and a part of the landscape, importantly connected to Chimney Rock by intervening terrain.

AN INTERVIEW WITH THE DESIGNER
Peter Lindblad contributed "Masters Designs Nebraska Quarter" to *Numismatic News*, December 20, 2005, an interview with the artist:

> Rick Masters is a Midwesterner, born and bred. And that Midwestern upbringing has served him well in his career as an artist, helping Masters come up with the design that will be featured on the 2006 Nebraska state quarter.
>
> "It's still kind of sinking in," said Masters, an associate professor of art and graphic design at the University of Wisconsin-Oshkosh. "It's something I've dreamed of for a long time. It's a one-in-a-million kind of thing. I always thought these kinds of things always happen to other people, not me."
>
> But it did, and for a kid who collected coins while growing up in Sioux City, Iowa, a city near the Iowa-Nebraska border, it's quite an honor. Masters is the only Midwestern artist in the U.S. Mint's Artistic Infusion Program. He applied for admission to the program in November 2003, when the Mint sent out a call for applicants. He found out about the recruiting plea in *Numismatic News*.
>
> "I was one of the lucky 18, out of the 300 who applied," said Masters. "I think they did most of their advertising on the East Coast. Being a subscriber to *Numismatic News*, that's where I found out about the application process." Applicants were required to have either taught art or worked as a professional artist for five years. Masters was excited to be selected.
>
> "I was one of those typical kids who started out with those blue Whitman folders," said Masters. "Coin collecting was a big phenomenon during the 1960s. I had a paper route, so I was seeing a lot of coins. I remember the transition from silver to clad."
>
> Masters lapsed as a collector until the boom in silver and gold prices. "I became an NN subscriber in 1982 and my interest in the hobby took off," said Masters. After joining the AIP, Masters and the other artists were assigned to work on the 2005 nickels that were part of the Westward Journey Nickel Series. Then, in the fall of 2004, the artists were divided into groups of five to come up with designs for the 2006 state quarters. They were asked if they had any preferences. Immediately, Masters said he wanted to work on the Nebraska design. He talked about how the assignment came about:

"The Mint modified the state quarter process a while back and asked that states not submit artwork for the quarters, but use narratives instead," said Masters. "Those narratives are fairly descriptive about what they want, and Chimney Rock was one thing they'd picked."

Along with Chimney Rock, the state wanted a covered wagon carrying pioneers. "I worked off some historic photographs," said Masters. "I read about Chimney Rock as well, and in the 20th century, Chimney Rock lost a part of its spire. Because of the pioneer family, it had it to be a 19th century image, so I wanted it to look like it did in the 19th century."

Masters submitted variations of the same theme. Two of Masters' designs were among the four finalists presented to . . . Heineman. "It was the same subject matter, but it "was kind of like rearranging the stage," said Masters. "There were just different compositions."

While Masters kept Chimney Rock in the same place, he moved the positions of the pioneer family and their wagon. The final design shows the ox-drawn wagon in the left-hand corner with the sun shining directly behind it. It came as a surprise to Masters when his design was picked. "I was not that optimistic," said Masters. "I had an old professor at the University of Iowa who said that if you get selected into the final round of a contest, don't expect to win. It's a matter of luck because you're always at the mercy of the judges, so I didn't get too worked up about it."

That changed when his depiction was selected. "It's been an incredible experience working with the Mint," said Masters, who is currently on sabbatical and working on projects that aren't related to numismatics. "I went out there for two symposiums and the Mint was just a first-class organization."

THE LAUNCH

The release ceremony was held in Lincoln, Nebraska, the state capital, on April 7, 2006, starting at 9:45 in the morning. This event followed a forum the night before at the Bennett Martin Public Library. This and related forums in the series allowed collectors and others to discuss Mint programs and designs.

The venue for the official launch was the Bob Devaney Sports Center. Dignitaries included U.S. Mint Acting Director David A. Lebryk, Treasury Assistant Secretary Sandra L. Pack, Nebraska Governor David Heineman, and First Lady Sally Ganem. The governor had proclaimed April 7 as "Nebraska State Quarter Day in the Classroom."

Lebryk reviewed the coins:

> When we hold this new Nebraska quarter, we all share the wonder of our ancestors as they glimpsed Chimney Rock for the first time during the westward expansion. This quarter captures America's pioneering spirit and the joy those trailblazers must have felt as they reveled in the beauty of this new land.

Entertainment was provided by Terry Lane impersonating Buffalo Bill Cody, Matthew Jones as Sitting Bear, and three groups of musicians. After the ceremony Lebryk, Heineman, and Ganem passed out free coins to the younger set, and adults were allowed to buy $10 rolls of the coins—the standard procedure.

On the same day celebrations of the new coin took place at the University of Nebraska and at the Five Rocks Amphitheatre in Gering at 1:30 p.m. In keeping with standard practice, quarters could be ordered from the U.S. Mint website. Two-roll sets with Denver and Philadelphia coins cost $32, bags of 100 coins from either mint were priced at $35.50, and 1,000-coin bags cost $300.

Numismatic Aspects of the State of Nebraska

The Durham Western History Museum in Omaha houses much of the Byron Reed collection, including an 1804 silver dollar. In the 1960s the City of Omaha featured this collection in a bid to be the headquarters city for the American Numismatic Association, but Colorado Springs was the ANA's final choice.

2006-P, Nebraska

MS-64	MS-65	MS-66	MS-67	MS-68	MS-69
$0.50	$0.80	$8.10	$34	$960	—

2006-P, Nebraska, Satin Finish

MS-64	MS-65	MS-66	MS-67	MS-68	MS-69
$2.65	$2.65	$4.05	$11.00	$20.00	$29.50

2006-D, Nebraska

MS-64	MS-65	MS-66	MS-67	MS-68	MS-69
$0.50	$0.80	$8.10	$34	$520	—

2006-D, Nebraska, Satin Finish

MS-64	MS-65	MS-66	MS-67	MS-68	MS-69
$2.65	$2.65	$4.05	$11.00	$20.00	$29.50

2006-S, Nebraska, Proof, Clad

PF-67DC	PF-68DC	PF-69DC
$1.50	$4.05	$9.50

2006-S, Nebraska, Proof, Silver

PF-67DC	PF-68DC	PF-69DC
$7.20	$8.50	$11

2006, Colorado

Circulation-Strike Mintage, Philadelphia: 274,800,000
Circulation-Strike Mintage, Philadelphia, Satin Finish: 847,361
Circulation-Strike Mintage, Denver: 294,200,000
Circulation-Strike Mintage, Denver, Satin Finish: 847,361
Proof Mintage, San Francisco, Clad: 2,882,428
Proof Mintage, San Francisco, Silver: 1,585,008
GSID: Circulation-strike, Philadelphia, 68433; Satin Finish Philadelphia, 82071; Circulation-strike, Denver, 77567; Satin Finish Denver, 68407; Proof Clad Deep Cameo, 65100; Proof Silver Deep Cameo, 65105

Specifics of the Reverse Design

Description: Landscape scene with pines in the foreground and the Rocky Mountains in the distance. The inscription COLORFUL COLORADO is on a ribbon below.

Designer: Leonard Buckley. *Mint sculptor-engraver who made the model:* Norman E. Nemeth. *Engraver's initials and location:* NEN in the branches of a pine tree at the lower right.

Story of the Design

In preparation for the state's turn in the coin lineup, the Colorado Commemorative Quarter Advisory Commission was organized to review and recommend designs.[104]

Residents of the state were then invited to submit written concepts to the governor's office. Art was also allowed, even though art was not to be considered by the Mint. In the early months of 2004, Frances Owens, first lady of Colorado, began a tour to introduce schoolchildren and others to the State quarter concept, inviting designs to be submitted. To listeners in Pueblo she had the following to say:

> "This is an opportunity for you to become a part of history," Mrs. Owens told students in Michael Divelbiss' seventh-grade social studies class. "This is something in your lifetime and my lifetime that the Mint may never do again, so I encourage you to participate. We want your ideas on what you think should be on the Colorado quarter," Mrs. Owens said. "I encourage you to keep it very simple but at the same time design something that you think makes Colorado special."[105]

Reminiscent of the Sierra Club's publicity efforts for the 2005 California quarter design, in Morrison, Colorado, the Friends of Red Rocks, a group supporting the Red Rocks Park and Amphitheatre, began a campaign. A petition was made available for people to sign, and residents of the state were encouraged to write to the governor, proposing Red Rocks Park for the quarter design. The group's website proclaimed:

> Red Rocks is the singular icon that differentiates Colorado from all others. Colorado like many other states has amazing mountains and incredible skiing. What does Colorado have that no other state can claim? Creation Rock and Ship Rock, the two majestic red monoliths creating a place so magical and original, that no other place on earth can replicate.

NARROWING THE FOCUS

Design ideas were accepted until May 10, 2004. By this time, more than 1,500 concepts had been submitted. On March 9, 2005, Governor Bill Owens and First Lady Frances Owens unveiled the semifinal concepts, translated into sketches by Mint staff, at a press conference in Denver. The governor commented:

> With a state as beautiful as ours, it is not at all surprising that we have five wonderful designs. Each of these coins uniquely presents the beauty and tradition of Colorado. One of the designs features mountains and foothills behind a large capital C partially encircling the inscription THE CENTENNIAL STATE. A cluster of columbine flowers rests atop a portion of the large C. The columbine is the state flower of Colorado.
>
> Another design features a representation of Mesa Verde's famous Cliff Palace, located in the 52,000-acre site of the Mesa Verde National Park, near Cortez, Colo. From A.D. 600 to 1300, groups of people built stone villages in the alcoves of the canyon walls. These cliff dwellers, as they are known today, eventually disappeared without a trace of explanation, leaving behind their homes.
>
> Another design features Pikes Peak, a mountain that has become a Colorado landmark, with a miner's pick and shovel below the central device. The inscription

Daniel Carr's proposal for a Colorado quarter was a semi-finalist, shown here in the form of a simulated coin. (Daniel Carr)

PIKES PEAK OR BUST appears above the date 2006. The mountain peak became the symbol of the 1859 Colorado gold Rush, through that slogan. A trip up the 14,000-plus foot mountain peak by poet Katherine Lee Bates in the 19th century served as the inspiration for her poem "America the Beautiful."

A third quarter dollar design depicts an alpine soldier skiing downhill with the inscription BIRTHPLACE OF THE 10TH MOUNTAIN DIVISION. A training camp was constructed in early 1942 at Camp Hale, high in the Rocky Mountains near Pando, Colo. The camp became home to the U.S. Army 10th Light Division (Alpine) on July 13, 1943. The Army unit was redesignated the 10th Mountain Division on November 6, 1944.

A fourth design under consideration for the State quarter dollar shows a rugged mountain backdrop above a banner bearing the inscription COLORFUL COLORADO.

Colorado residents submitted more than 1,500 written and visual descriptions of their design concepts. The visual representations were used to help the commission evaluate the written explanations but were not passed along to Mint officials per their request.[106]

THE CITIZENS COINAGE ADVISORY COMMITTEE

Citizens Coinage Advisory Committee weighed in with its suggestions. The appointed chairman was Tom Noe, a rare coin dealer from Ohio who had especially strong political ties reaching up to the governor of his state and with connections to the George W. Bush White House.[107] The committee of seven members had been established under PL 108-15 on April 23, 2003, to advise the secretary of the Treasury as to coin designs, suggest events and topics to be commemorated, and to provide estimated coinage levels, among other duties. The same law abolished the Citizens Commemorative Coin Advisory Committee, a predecessor group that had advised on State quarters and certain other coin designs. Concerning the Colorado quarter, Bill McAllister, in an exclusive story filed with *Coin World*, described the inner workings of the committee:

> Members of the Citizens Coinage Advisory Committee couldn't agree on whether the mountains on designs for the 2006 Colorado quarter dollar were mountainous enough or whether the coin needs a "the" in the legend THE CENTENNIAL STATE on the proposed design. But in the end, the panel voted overwhelmingly at a March 15 meeting for a design that features that slogan.
>
> Unable to reach a firm consensus on disputed parts of the design, the committee suggested that others will have to decide about the mountains and wording of the state's nickname. The CCAC-favored design, one of five selected by state officials, features a view of the craggy Rocky Mountains rising from a forested valley. It also carries a large letter "C" partially inter-wreathed with the state flower, the columbine, and bears the nickname THE CENTENNIAL STATE. The design drew 20 out of a possible 30 points in balloting by the 10 members of the panel. Each member could give up to three points for a favored design under the panel's procedures. A design with another view of mountains and the state's other nickname, COLORFUL COLORADO, on a scroll drew 14 points.

A design with a view of Pikes Peak, perhaps the state's best-known mountain, drew 13 points to finish in third place. It carries the slogan PIKES PEAK OR BUST and features two snowflakes and the crossed pick and shovel of a miner. A design that features the cliff dwellings at Mesa Verde National Park in southwestern Colorado drew only five points with several members complaining the design is too crowded. A design that features a skiing soldier from the Army's famed 10th Mountain Division, a unit formed in the state during World War II, drew no votes at all from the committee members. . . .

Some CCAC members questioned whether the Colorado designs accurately depicted the state's mountains. "It's mountains, mountains, mountains," groused historian Robert Remini, who complained the designs could have represented any mountain state. "Why, Pikes Peak doesn't even have a peak," Remini exclaimed.

But Bill Fivaz, a Dunwoody, Ga., coin collector, responded that the design is "a good representation of the mountain that overlooks the city of Colorado Springs. "It *doesn't* have a peak," he explained. Fivaz had spent much time within view of Pikes Peak.[108] He was a former board member of the American Numismatic Association, which has its headquarters in Colorado Springs. The panel's newest member at the time, Ken Thomasma of Jackson, Wyo., sought to assure the committee that the designs are accurate. "Those mountains look a lot like the mountains of Colorado," said Thomasma, adding he had climbed some of them.

Some panel members clearly liked the designs. Rita Laws called the recommended design "very dramatic" and Mitchell Sanders said "mountains are clearly important" to Colorado. Colorado officials had acknowledged on March 9 when the five designs were disclosed by Governor Bill Owens that they, too, questioned the images of the mountains as created by Mint artists. "They're not used to mountains in Washington," Sean Duffy, Owens's deputy chief of staff, told the *Rocky Mountain News*. "In one drawing the mountain looked like an anthill."

Pikes Peak as shown on a postcard from the early 20th century.

Except for Pikes Peak no specific Colorado mountains were used on the coins, the state officials said. They also said that artists took liberties by showing Mesa Verde National Park with high mountains in the immediate background.[109] That point troubled some members of the CCAC, which gave low marks to that design.

Committee chairman Thomas W. Noe, a coin dealer from Maumee, Ohio, thought that the panel's comments had indicated that most members wanted to drop the word "the" from the phrase "The Centennial State" in an effort to reduce the wording on the coin. Some members also wanted to drop the first C from CENTENNIAL and reduce the size of the large letter "C" from the coin. But the consensus over dropping the word "the" evaporated after Ute Wartenberg, executive director of the American Numismatic Society, suggested that Colorado may have specifically included the "the" to point out that Colorado was the only state to join the Union in the year 1876, the nation's centennial. The Colorado state government's website reports the state nickname begins with a "the."[110]

THE COMMISSION OF FINE ARTS
The selections went next to the Commission of Fine Arts. Paul Gilkes reported this in *Coin World*:

> Two of the final five proposed designs for the 2006 Colorado quarter dollar were approved March 17 by the Commission of Fine Arts, as acceptable, but neither without recommended revisions to simplify the sketches.
>
> CFA historian Sue Kohler said commission members favor the PIKES PEAK OR BUST design that prominently features the 14,110-foot elevation peak outside Colorado Springs. It was recommended that the peak itself be sharpened and be more defined, Kohler said. Commission members also recommended the removal of the PIKES PEAK OR BUST inscription, the flanking snowflake icons, and the crossed miner's shovel and pick axe.
>
> Also considered acceptable was a design featuring mountains looming out of the forest with the inscription COLORFUL COLORADO in a wavy ribbon below. Kohler said it was recommended should this design be chosen, that the ribbon and inscription be removed and the taper at the base of the mountain range be leveled off. Kohler said commission members liked the sharp details of the mountain range as presented.
>
> The commission meeting was attended for the first time by U.S. Mint Director Henrietta Holsman Fore at the suggestion of CFA Chairman David M. Childs. Kohler said Fore introduced herself to CFA members before the meeting and briefly addressed them just before the presentation of the Colorado quarter dollar designs for review. Kohler said Fore discussed the popularity of the State quarter dollar program.[111]

AND THE ENVELOPE, PLEASE. . . .
On May 31, 2005, Governor Bill Owens announced his personal choice, which became the adopted design. The central motif featured the Rocky Mountains and the inscription COLORFUL COLORADO, the one favored by many Coloradoans and voted as number one by the Citizens Coinage Advisory Committee. The design was of a scenic nature, with all elements tied together—the type of motif that, in my opinion, is most pleasing to the eye.

THE LAUNCH

The official launch ceremony for the Colorado quarter took place in Denver on June 14, 2006. On the night before the Mint hosted a collectors' forum at the Auraria Campus.

On the launch day the scene began with a stagecoach leaving the Denver Mint five blocks away and arriving at the State Capitol. On hand as greeters were U.S. Mint Deputy Director David A. Lebryk, Assistant Secretary of the Treasury Sandra L. Pack, Governor Bill Owens, First Lady Frances Owens, and Denver Mayor John Hickenlooper.

Lybryk addressed the audience:

> Colorado's rainbow of beauty and color is what the anthem America the Beautiful calls the "purple mountains majesty." Today, we celebrate the launch of a beautiful addition to the 50 State Quarters program, and the centennial anniversary of the United States Mint at Denver, one of two proud facilities that together will make up to 650 million "Colorful Colorado" quarters.

After the ceremony Lebryk, Pack, Owens, and Hickenlooper passed out quarters to those 18 years old and younger while others were allowed to buy $10 rolls of coins at a separate stand.

Numismatic Aspects of the State of Colorado

With its extensive history of gold and silver mining, the state is closely interwoven with numismatics. *1860–1861:* During the gold rush to Colorado, a mint was operated by Clark, Gruber & Co. in Denver, and produced $2.50, $5, $10, and $20 coins, the 1860 versions of the largest two denominations featured a fanciful depiction of Pikes Peak. *1861:* J.J. Conway & Co. in Georgia Gulch produced a small number of $2.50, $5 and $10 gold coins. *1861:* John Parsons & Co. struck a small number of $2.50 and $5 coins near Tarryall. *1862:* The Treasury Department bought the operation of Clark, Gruber & Co. and renamed it the Denver Mint, using that terminology in Annual Reports. However, the government did not strike coins there. *1900–1901:* In Victor, Joseph Lesher issued octagonal medals or "Lesher dollars" as a private venture. Most of these bore the advertisements of regional merchants. *1906:* The Denver Mint, in a new building under construction since 1904, opened for business. *1964:* The American Numismatic Association Headquarters was established in Colorado Springs.

2006-P, Colorado

MS-64	MS-65	MS-66	MS-67	MS-68	MS-69
$0.50	$0.80	$8.10	$27	$390	—

2006-P, Colorado, Satin Finish

MS-64	MS-65	MS-66	MS-67	MS-68	MS-69
$2.65	$2.65	$4.05	$11.00	$20.00	$29.50

2006-D, Colorado

MS-64	MS-65	MS-66	MS-67	MS-68	MS-69
$0.50	$0.80	$4.05	$34	$715	—

2006-D, Colorado, Satin Finish

MS-64	MS-65	MS-66	MS-67	MS-68	MS-69
$2.65	$2.65	$4.05	$11.00	$20.00	$29.50

2006-S, Colorado, Proof, Clad

PF-67DC	PF-68DC	PF-69DC
$1.50	$4.05	$9.50

2006-S, Colorado, Proof, Silver

PF-67DC	PF-68DC	PF-69DC
$7.20	$8.50	$11

2006, North Dakota

Circulation-Strike Mintage, Philadelphia: 305,800,000
Circulation-Strike Mintage, Philadelphia, Satin Finish: 847,361
Circulation-Strike Mintage, Denver: 359,000,000
Circulation-Strike Mintage, Denver, Satin Finish: 847,361
Proof Mintage, San Francisco, Clad: 2,882,428
Proof Mintage, San Francisco, Silver: 1,585,008
GSID: Circulation-strike, Philadelphia, 69116; Satin Finish Philadelphia, 69117; Circulation-strike, Denver, 69118; Satin Finish Denver, 82072; Proof Clad Deep Cameo, 65098; Proof Silver Deep Cameo, 65103

Specifics of the Reverse Design

Description: Two bison facing left, one running and the other grazing. The top of a mesa is seen in the distance, with a stylized sun outline and rays to the left.

Designer: Stephen Clark. *Mint sculptor-engraver who made the model:* Donna Weaver. *Engraver's initials and location:* DW in the sod at the lower right.

Story of the Design

Serious planning for the state's 2006 quarter began on April 14, 2004, when the North Dakota Quarter Design Selection Commission was formed under Governor John Hoeven. Lieutenant General Dalrymple was chair of the nine-member group composed of historians, state politicians, educators, and tourism officials. A website was set up to keep interested people abreast of events. North Dakotans were invited to submit written concepts of up to 50 words before the July 1 deadline.

The invitation generated nearly 400 entries. Chairman Dalrymple sorted them into five thematic categories: agriculture, American Indian culture, Badlands, International Peace Gardens, and landscape.[112] Theodore Roosevelt did not make the list of finalists, but he was featured on the America the Beautiful quarter design for North Dakota. "Rough Rider State," one of North Dakota's nicknames, refers to Roosevelt, who resided there when he was a young man.

These written concepts were sent to the Mint to be turned into art. In December 2004 the Citizens Coinage Advisory Committee met to review what they received from the Mint, and suggested several revisions. Three were picked as favorites and returned.

Next, the Commission of Fine Arts had its say of the three, and selected one with two grazing bison with a backdrop of the sun rising behind Badlands buttes. The commission requested that the two bison be placed farther apart, that the sun be eliminated, and that the buttes made taller.

The citizens of North Dakota followed, as they were asked to choose from the bison design (with sun remaining in place) and one depicting geese flying over typical terrain of the state with a rising sun in the distance. Governor John Hoeven had the right to make the final choice. On June 3, 2005, he picked the "Badlands with Bison."[113]

THE LAUNCH

The launch ceremony of the quarter was held at the Civic Center in Bismarck on August 30, 2006. President Theodore Roosevelt was represented by impersonator Clay Jenkinson.

The lead representative for the Mint was Deputy Director David A. Lebryk, a regular attendee at such events. Joining him were Governor John Hoeven, First Lady Mikey Hoeven, and Lieutenant Governor Jack Dalrymple. The Medora Musical Singers entertained the crowd, as did a song presented by the Cannon Ball Singers from the Standing Rock Sioux Tribe.

The dignitaries as well as members of the 17th Infantry Regiment and Company H handed out "shiny new" quarters to the younger set, while not far away adults stood in line to purchase $10 rolls of the coins.

Per the usual program, on the night before the ceremony a Coin Collectors Forum was held, this time in the state capitol building. Collectors and interested others were invited to share comments and ideas on the State quarters and other Mint programs. In connection with the release the Mint made rolls and bags of the coins available through its Internet site. Proofs for this and other State quarters were sold separately by mail and at Mint shops in groups of five, covering all issues of the years.

Numismatic Aspects of the State of North Dakota

National Bank Notes from this state are considered by collectors to be especially scarce.

2006-P, North Dakota

MS-64	MS-65	MS-66	MS-67	MS-68	MS-69
$0.50	$0.80	$13.50	$47	—	—

2006-P, North Dakota, Satin Finish

MS-64	MS-65	MS-66	MS-67	MS-68	MS-69
$2.65	$2.65	$4.05	$11.00	$20.00	$29.50

2006-D, North Dakota

MS-64	MS-65	MS-66	MS-67	MS-68	MS-69
$0.50	$0.80	$8.10	$24.50	$1,500	—

2006-D, North Dakota, Satin Finish

MS-64	MS-65	MS-66	MS-67	MS-68	MS-69
$2.65	$2.65	$4.05	$11.00	$20.00	$29.50

2006-S, North Dakota, Proof, Clad

PF-67DC	PF-68DC	PF-69DC
$1.50	$4.05	$9.50

2006-S, North Dakota, Proof, Silver

PF-67DC	PF-68DC	PF-69DC
$7.20	$8.50	$11

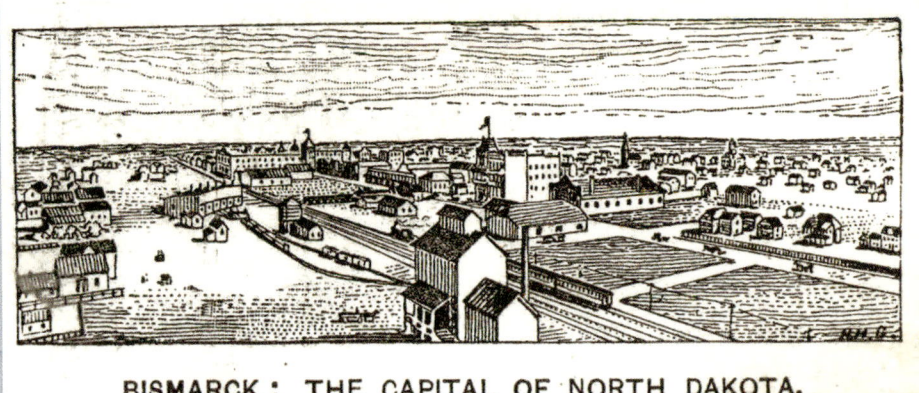

Panoramic view of Bismark, North Dakota.
(*King's Handbook of the United States*, 1891)

2006, South Dakota

Circulation-Strike Mintage, Philadelphia: 245,000,000
Circulation-Strike Mintage, Philadelphia, Satin Finish: 847,361
Circulation-Strike Mintage, Denver: 265,800,000
Circulation-Strike Mintage, Denver, Satin Finish: 847,361
Proof Mintage, San Francisco, Clad: 2,882,428
Proof Mintage, San Francisco, Silver: 1,585,008
GSID: Circulation-strike, Philadelphia, 65267; Satin Finish Philadelphia, 65268; Circulation-strike, Denver, 65269; Satin Finish Denver, 65270; Proof Clad Deep Cameo, 65097; Proof Silver Deep Cameo, 65102

Specifics of the Reverse Design

Description: The state bird, the Chinese ring-necked pheasant, is depicted flying over the Mount Rushmore National Memorial. Heads of wheat are at the border.

Designer: Michael Leidel. *Mint sculptor-engraver who made the model:* John Mercanti. *Engraver's initials and location:* JM on lower part of rock, below and to the left of Lincoln.

Story of the Design

A five-member committee set up for the South Dakota quarter considered 50 concepts, before settling on five of them. These were: Mount Rushmore framed by two heads of wheat, Mount Rushmore with a bison in the foreground, Mount Rushmore with a pheasant in the foreground, a bison framed by wheat, and a pheasant framed by wheat.[114] These were sent to the Mint to be turned into artwork. Mount Rushmore was considered by numismatists to be a tired motif, for they had a serving of three different Mount Rushmore commemoratives in 1991, none being particularly popular at the time.

Emblems of South Dakota.
(*King's Handbook of the United States, 1891*)

The Commission of Fine Arts reviewed the motifs and selected a bison standing on a grassy mound, facing right, with its head slightly toward the viewer. Heads of wheat were to each side, somewhat reminiscent of the early design of the Lincoln cent reverse. *Coin World* writer Paul Gilkes said that the CFA was having a "love fest" with bison. One had recently appeared on a commemorative dollar, another on the 2005 Kansas quarter, and still another on the 2005 nickel five-cent piece.[115]

The Citizens Coinage Advisory Commission met under chairman Tom Noe in Washington, D.C., in December 2004, to discuss commemorative designs and other matters. Member Rita Laws stated that Native Americans in the state considered Mount Rushmore to be an insult. With this sensitivity in mind, the sculptured mountain design was out, and the winner became the motif with the ring-necked pheasant (the state bird).

The CCAC was required to meet six times a year. To this point, telephone conferencing had been permitted, but no longer. Any member who missed three meetings would now be dropped. Candidates for future appointments, which had been political patronage in the past, now had to include not just one person, but "several" names, so the secretary of the Treasury could make the final choice.[116]

State Special Projects Coordinator John G. Moisan stated soon afterward that residents of the state who learned about Laws's comment had emailed and telephoned his office to protest the possible removal of Mount Rushmore for consideration.[117]

MOUNT RUSHMORE, AGAIN

On January 12, 2005, Governor M. Michael ("Mike") Rounds unveiled the Mint staff art for the five final design options. Beginning on this date, public input was requested, until April 15. The governor said he would abide by the people's choice. Residents cast nearly 172,000 votes. The winner with 65,766 votes was a design with Mount Rushmore, a single stalk of wheat to each side, and an out-of-proportion (so it seems) Chinese ring-necked pheasant flying in the foreground. The image was not much different from the 1991 Mount Rushmore commemorative dollar, except for the giant pheasant—suggesting that a lot of time and effort could have been saved by simply modifying that motif.

Coming in second with 49,203 votes was the Mount Rushmore design with bison. This image featured two unrelated subjects—Mount Rushmore and a bison against a plain background (no terrain or connection). Once again, the Commission of Fine Arts' preference was ignored, ditto for the other choice of the Citizens Coinage Advisory Committee, ditto any feelings Native Americans may have had, this time by the voters of the state.

An April 20, 2005, news release from the governor's office included this: "As the state quarter projects across the nation have evolved since the program's inception, states have moved away from a single image or figure representing the state in favor of multiple images highlighting the diversity of the various states." Such a comment flies in the face of what collectors and most people with a sense of art prefer—scenic designs, unified, not scattered objects. On April 27, Governor Rounds picked the "Mount Rushmore and Pheasant" motif.

THE LAUNCH

"U.S. Presidents Witness Launch of South Dakota Quarter at Mount Rushmore National Monument," was the title on a U.S. Mint news release covering the November 13, 2006, launch ceremony. The presidents said not a word. They were, of course, the stony faces of Washington, Jefferson, Lincoln, and Roosevelt carved in the mountainside high above. The event was held out in the open in the Amphitheater. On hand to represent the Mint was Director Edmund C. Moy, who would become a familiar face at such events. Joining him were Governor M. Michael Rounds, South Dakota First Lady Jean Rounds, and Rapid City Mayor Jim Shaw. A Native American drum group, the Star Nation, treated the audience to an honor song. After the ceremony Director Moy and other notables passed out free quarters to those under 18 years of age, while all were invited to purchase $10 rolls of the coins at a nearby stand.

On the night before the event Director Moy held the traditional Coin Collectors Forum, this time at the Dahl Art Center in Rapid City.

Numismatic Aspects of the State of South Dakota

1991: The Mount Rushmore Golden Anniversary commemorative half dollar, silver dollar, and $5 gold piece were issued.

2006-P, South Dakota

MS-64	MS-65	MS-66	MS-67	MS-68	MS-69
$0.50	$0.80	$4	$47	$1,250	—

2006-P, South Dakota, Satin Finish

MS-64	MS-65	MS-66	MS-67	MS-68	MS-69
$2.65	$2.65	$4.05	$11.00	$20.00	$29.50

2006-D, South Dakota

MS-64	MS-65	MS-66	MS-67	MS-68	MS-69
$0.50	$0.80	$4.05	$13.50	$195	—

2006-D, South Dakota, Satin Finish

MS-64	MS-65	MS-66	MS-67	MS-68	MS-69
$2.65	$2.65	$4.05	$11.00	$20.00	$29.50

2006-S, South Dakota, Proof, Clad

PF-67DC	PF-68DC	PF-69DC
$1.50	$4.05	$9.50

2006-S, South Dakota, Proof, Silver

PF-67DC	PF-68DC	PF-69DC
$7.20	$8.50	$11

2007, Montana

Circulation-Strike Mintage, Philadelphia: 257,000,000
Circulation-Strike Mintage, Philadelphia, Satin Finish: 895,628
Circulation-Strike Mintage, Denver: 256,240,000
Circulation-Strike Mintage, Denver, Satin Finish: 895,628
Proof Mintage, San Francisco, Clad: 2,374,778
Proof Mintage, San Francisco, Silver: 1,313,481
GSID: Circulation-strike, Philadelphia, 69652; Satin Finish Philadelphia, 82073; Circulation-strike, Denver, 68978; Satin Finish Denver, 82074; Proof Clad Deep Cameo, 68617; Proof Silver Deep Cameo, 68618

Specifics of the Reverse Design

Description: A bison skull hangs in the sky over a Montana mountain range.

Designer: Don Everhart, who was also the sculptor-engraver who made the model. *Engraver's initials and location:* DE on the right edge of the landscape.

Story of the Design

Montana residents were invited to submit written narratives suggesting motifs for their State quarter, with the deadline set at August 31, 2005. The concepts were to be reviewed by the Montana Quarter Design Commission, after which residents would be allowed to vote for their favorite.

Governor Brian Schweitzer and the commission selected four designs and sent them to the Mint in October 2005. In April 2006, the governor invited the residents to vote for their favorites among the four designs approved by the Mint. One design featured a bull elk at the center with the plains extending back to a rock formation and the sun rising in the distance. A second design featured the skull of a bison at the upper two-thirds of the coin, with plains and distant mountains below and the words BIG / SKY / COUNTRY to the right. A third concept pictured a landscape with a mountain range in the distance, a river, a large expanse of sky with a few clouds, and the inscription BIG SKY COUNTRY in the sky. The fourth design enclosed mountains, plains, and a dramatic sunrise in an outline of the state, with BIG SKY COUNTRY on a ribbon above. The second design was the final selection.

THE LAUNCH

The launch ceremony of the Montana quarter took place on January 29, 2007, at the Helena Civil Center. The night before a forum for collectors was held.

Mint Director Edmund C. Moy joined Governor Brian Schweitzer, his wife Nancy, Gary Marks (a member of the Montana Quarter Design Selection Commission), and Blackfoot singer and songwriter Jack Gladstone to introduce the launch event. Music was provided before, during, and after the ceremony by several groups.

In his welcome Director Moy noted:

> Montana's history recalls a state composed of vast landscapes, mountains and high plains, big sky and bison, all of which are represented on the Montana quarter we launch today. The bison skull is an evocative image of the American West, its bounty and hardships, familiar to Montanans as a symbol of their own rugged and resilient nature.

After the ceremony Moy and the governor and first lady went through the audience and handed out quarters to the younger set. In a separate facility adults exchanged paper bills for $10 rolls of quarters.

Numismatic Aspects of the State of Montana

Montana has several traditions relating to gold and numismatics, the first with a curious political twist. On May 26, 1863, two prospectors, Bill Fairweather and Henry Edgar, discovered gold near Alder Creek. They could not contain their excitement, and within a short time many others were in the area. A district was organized to sort out and regulate claims. The area became lawless as dozens of robbers, called road agents, stole from the miners and killed those with gold. The Vigilance Committee of Alder Gulch was organized and hanged more than a dozen of the perpetrators, including the local sheriff.

The United States Assay Office in Helena was a repository for many Morgan silver dollars that, upon their release in the 1960s, proved to be scarce issues.

2007-P, Montana

MS-64	MS-65	MS-66	MS-67	MS-68	MS-69
$0.50	$0.80	$12.00	$24.50	—	—

2007-P, Montana, Satin Finish

MS-64	MS-65	MS-66	MS-67	MS-68	MS-69
$2.65	$2.65	$4.05	$11.00	$20.00	$29.50

2007-D, Montana

MS-64	MS-65	MS-66	MS-67	MS-68	MS-69
$0.50	$0.80	$11.00	$40.50	$650	—

2007-D, Montana, Satin Finish

MS-64	MS-65	MS-66	MS-67	MS-68	MS-69
$2.65	$2.65	$4.05	$11.00	$20.00	$29.50

2007-S, Montana, Proof, Clad

PF-67DC	PF-68DC	PF-69DC
$1.50	$4.05	$9.50

2007-S, Montana, Proof, Silver

PF-67DC	PF-68DC	PF-69DC
$7.20	$8.50	$11

2007, Washington

Circulation-Strike Mintage, Philadelphia: 265,200,000
Circulation-Strike Mintage, Philadelphia, Satin Finish: 895,628
Circulation-Strike Mintage, Denver: 280,000,000
Circulation-Strike Mintage, Denver, Satin Finish: 895,628
Proof Mintage, San Francisco, Clad: 2,374,778
Proof Mintage, San Francisco, Silver: 1,313,481
GSID: Circulation-strike, Philadelphia, 77584; Satin Finish Philadelphia, 82075; Circulation-strike, Denver, 68979; Satin Finish Denver, 82076; Proof Clad Deep Cameo, 68621; Proof Silver Deep Cameo, 68622

Specifics of the Reverse Design

Description: A leaping king salmon is seen in front of Mount Rainier.

Designer: Charles L. Vickers, who was also the sculptor-engraver who made the model. *Engraver's initials and location:* CLV appears under the right edge of Mount Rainier.

Story of the Design

The Washington State Quarter Advisory Commission invited written suggestions from the public for the design of their State quarter. The deadline was set as July 30, 2005. By that time, the commission had received 1,150 entries. Governor Christine Gregoire planned to select her favorites by September 30, then to submit three to five written concepts for the Mint to turn into art.

This was done, and the five concepts were a salmon; Mount Rainier and an apple within an outline of Washington state; an apple within the outline of Washington state; an outline of Washington State with Mount Rainier centered; a salmon breaching the water with Mount Rainier as a backdrop; and a Northwest Native American stylized orca. It was suggest that the motto *The Evergreen State* be included in at least some of the designs.[118]

After the art was returned by the Mint, a public opinion poll was held. The winning design was that of the salmon breaching at the left of the coin, with Mount Rainier in the background to the right and the motto beneath the mountain.

THE LAUNCH

Mint Director Edmund C. Moy, new in that office, went to Seattle for the launch ceremony of the Washington State quarter on April 11, 2007. Moy would prove to be one of the most active directors with regard to attending these events. Governor Chris Gregoire told the audience that this was "the first 100 percent Washington quarter," in that Washington the president was on one side and Washington the state was on the other.

After the ceremony Moy and Gregoire went among the audience and passed out quarters to the younger set. As usual, adults went to a special station where they could exchange paper money for $10 rolls of the new quarters.

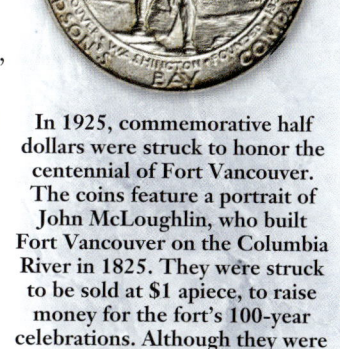

In 1925, commemorative half dollars were struck to honor the centennial of Fort Vancouver. The coins feature a portrait of John McLoughlin, who built Fort Vancouver on the Columbia River in 1825. They were struck to be sold at $1 apiece, to raise money for the fort's 100-year celebrations. Although they were struck in San Francisco, they do not bear the S mintmark. The coin's models were prepared by Laura Gardin Fraser, a talented artist whose husband had created the Buffalo nickel design.

Numismatic Aspects of the State of Washington

1925: The Fort Vancouver Centennial commemorative half dollar was issued. These were struck at the San Francisco Mint, but the usual S mintmark was omitted in error.

1962: The American Numismatic Association held its annual summer convention in Seattle in the same year that the World's Fair was held there. As hotel rooms were in short supply, ANA members were directed to lodge in private homes and other non-standard rental facilities.

2007-P, Washington

MS-64	MS-65	MS-66	MS-67	MS-68	MS-69
$0.50	$0.80	$4.05	$38	$1,560	—

2007-P, Washington, Satin Finish

MS-64	MS-65	MS-66	MS-67	MS-68	MS-69
$2.65	$2.65	$4.05	$11.00	$20.00	$29.50

2007-D, Washington

MS-64	MS-65	MS-66	MS-67	MS-68	MS-69
$0.50	$0.80	$4.05	$47	$1,560	—

2007-D, Washington, Satin Finish

MS-64	MS-65	MS-66	MS-67	MS-68	MS-69
$2.65	$2.65	$4.05	$11.00	$20.00	$29.50

2007-S, Washington, Proof, Clad

PF-67DC	PF-68DC	PF-69DC
$1.50	$4.05	$9.50

2007-S, Washington, Proof, Silver

PF-67DC	PF-68DC	PF-69DC
$7.20	$8.50	$11

2007, Idaho

Circulation-Strike Mintage, Philadelphia: 294,600,000
Circulation-Strike Mintage, Philadelphia, Satin Finish: 895,628
Circulation-Strike Mintage, Denver: 286,800,000
Circulation-Strike Mintage, Denver, Satin Finish: 895,628
Proof Mintage, San Francisco, Clad: 2,374,778
Proof Mintage, San Francisco, Silver: 1,313,481
GSID: Circulation-strike, Philadelphia, 77585; Satin Finish Philadelphia, 82077; Circulation-strike, Denver, 68980; Satin Finish Denver, 82078; Proof Clad Deep Cameo, 68615; Proof Silver Deep Cameo, 68616

Specifics of the Reverse Design

Description: A peregrine falcon appears to the left of an outline of the state.

Designer: Donna Weaver. *Mint sculptor-engraver who made the model:* Don Everhart. *Engraver's initials and location:* DE is in the feathers on the peregrine's breast.

Story of the Design

Governor Dirk Kempthorne tapped the Idaho Commission of the Arts to oversee the design-submission process and to review ideas. Citizens of the state were invited to submit written concepts of up to 150 words each until September 9, 2005. To encourage more participation, residents were also invited to submit art, but the governor hastened to say that no art would be sent to the Mint. Multiple submissions from the same person were allowed. To get the ball rolling, he stated:

Emblems of Idaho.
(*King's Handbook of the United States, 1891*)

Idaho is truly a gem among the states. The spirit of our people is unmatched. Our industrious heritage is rich. The pristine beauty of our mountains, lakes, canyons and rivers is world famous. Idaho shines from the Rocky Mountain bighorns and proud white pines on the high alpine ridges to the crystal clear streams and great sturgeon in our deep desert canyons. Just like our state, the Idaho quarter will stand out among the rest.

Sample submission suggestion: The peaks of the snow-capped Sawtooth Mountains stretch across the top of the coin. A majestic bull elk grazes on the edge of a clear mountain lake in the foreground, his breath steaming in the cold mountain air. Behind the elk, a single tall, straight Western white pine stands on the right side of the coin. In capital, block letters, the words "The Sawtooths" are written in the surface of the lake.[119]

Further, "Simplicity should be emphasized; designs that include too many elements become cluttered and are discouraged."

In late September the governor reported that more than 1,200 ideas had been received. The commission sorted through them and selected 10 to be presented to Governor Kempthorne, who then narrowed the field down to five. These were a peregrine falcon with the state motto ESTO PERPETUA; the Sawtooth Mountains; farmland tapestry showing an aerial view of cropland; two lines from the state song *Here We Have Idaho* flanking an outline of the state; and "bold and distinctive," the latter having the word IDAHO prominently across the center of the coin.[120] The design with the falcon was the eventual winner.

THE LAUNCH

On August 3, 2007, Dirk Kempthorne, who as governor of Idaho had been involved in the design, attended the official launch ceremony under his new title, secretary of the Interior of the United States. Joining him was secretary of the Treasury Henry M. Paulson Jr., the first time that two Cabinet members attended a State quarters event. Joining them were Mint Director Edmund Moy and State Treasurer Ron G. Crane. The venue was the Boise Depot, long a popular railroad stop.

In prepared remarks Secretary Paulson said, "Today we celebrate a distinctive state quarter and the recovery of the peregrine falcon. Millions of Americans will have the chance to collect the Idaho quarter and learn more about this spectacular bird." To this Secretary Kempthorne added, "When our children hold Idaho's quarter, it will serve as our promise to do better to conserve species." It was then Director Moy's turn: "The Idaho quarter contains many lessons in a very small space. State geography, history, a little Latin, and a big reminder of Idaho's part in the remarkable comeback of the fastest bird in the world."

After the ceremony the officials did the usual and handed out free quarters to the younger set while adults lined up to buy $10 rolls of the coins for face value. In the meantime quantities were available for a premium and could be ordered on the Mint website.

Numismatic Aspects of the State of Idaho

Miller's Brewery & Bakery, Idaho City, was the only Idaho merchant to issue Civil War tokens. Dated 1865, these are rare today.

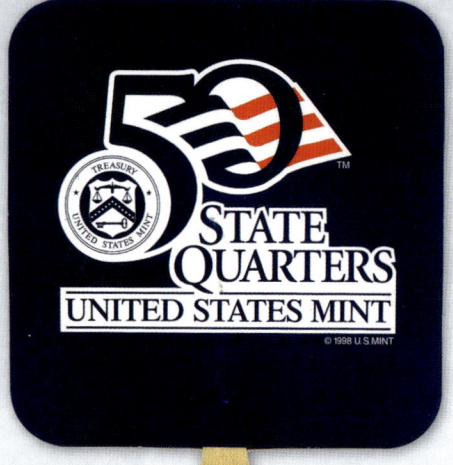

Fans like this were distributed to attendees at the official launch of the Idaho State quarter.

2007-P, Idaho

MS-64	MS-65	MS-66	MS-67	MS-68	MS-69
$0.50	$0.80	$16	$81		

2007-P, Idaho, Satin Finish

MS-64	MS-65	MS-66	MS-67	MS-68	MS-69
$2.65	$2.65	$4.05	$11.00	$20.00	$29.50

2007-D, Idaho

MS-64	MS-65	MS-66	MS-67	MS-68	MS-69
$0.50	$0.80	$4.05	$19	$156	

2007-D, Idaho, Satin Finish

MS-64	MS-65	MS-66	MS-67	MS-68	MS-69
$2.65	$2.65	$4.05	$11.00	$20.00	$29.50

2007-S, Idaho, Proof, Clad

PF-67DC	PF-68DC	PF-69DC
$1.50	$4.05	$9.50

2007-S, Idaho, Proof, Silver

PF-67DC	PF-68DC	PF-69DC
$7.20	$8.50	$11

2007, Wyoming

Circulation-Strike Mintage, Philadelphia: 243,600,000
Circulation-Strike Mintage, Philadelphia, Satin Finish: 895,628
Circulation-Strike Mintage, Denver: 320,800,000
Circulation-Strike Mintage, Denver, Satin Finish: 895,628
Proof Mintage, San Francisco, Clad: 2,374,778
Proof Mintage, San Francisco, Silver: 1,313,481
GSID: Circulation-strike, Philadelphia, 68962; Satin Finish Philadelphia, 82079; Circulation-strike, Denver, 68963; Satin Finish Denver, 82080; Proof Clad Deep Cameo, 68623; Proof Silver Deep Cameo, 68624

Specifics of the Reverse Design

Description: The coin features the outline of a cowboy riding a bucking horse.

Designer: Norman E. Nemeth, who was also the sculptor-engraver who made the model. *Engraver's initials and location:* NEM appears in the field.

Story of the Design

Governor David D. Freudenthal set up the Wyoming Coinage Advisory Committee and appointed stamp collector Jack Rosenthal as chairman. Rosenthal had chaired the U.S. Postal Service's Citizens' Stamp Advisory Committee in Washington, D.C. News items did not state whether a numismatist was anywhere in sight on the committee.

The committee's first meeting was in Cheyenne on January 13, 2005. The goal was to collect and finalize designs by September, at which time no more than five were to be submitted to the Mint, where art would be created—this being the usual process since the 2005 California quarter (the last time that an artist from the honored state was allowed to contribute talent and be recognized).

Residents were allowed to submit words only, up to 50 of them, by completing the statement, "I think the back of the Wyoming quarter should show . . ." The deadline was April 30. More than 1,300 people filled out the form. The committee selected five designs, four of which depicted a bucking horse with rider, with various differences in the background and details. This symbol has been a Wyoming icon for a long time and has been featured on license plates since 1936. The fifth concept was the Old Faithful geyser in Yellowstone National Park, as illustrated on a stamp issued in 1934. The horse won. Old Faithful would have its day in the numismatic sun years later as part of the America the Beautiful quarter series.

THE LAUNCH

The official launch ceremony was held on September 14, 2006, at the Cheyenne Civic Center. Mint Director Edmund Moy and Governor Dave Freudenthal hosted the event. Music was provided by the University of Wyoming Marching Band. By that time the coins had been released into circulation, starting on September 4.

Director Moy stated, "The Wyoming quarter embodies ideals that our Nation reveres: a pioneering spirit and equal opportunity for all. The U.S. Mint is especially proud of this quarter because Wyoming's first woman governor, Nellie Tayloe Ross, also served as the U.S. Mint's first woman director."

After the remarks had concluded, members of the University of Wyoming Cowgirls women's basketball team helped Moy and Freudenthal pass out free coins to those who declared themselves to be 18 years of age or younger. All were able to buy, for face value, $10 rolls set up at a separate display. As per usual, a Coin Collectors Forum had been held the night before, this time at the Cheyenne Depot.

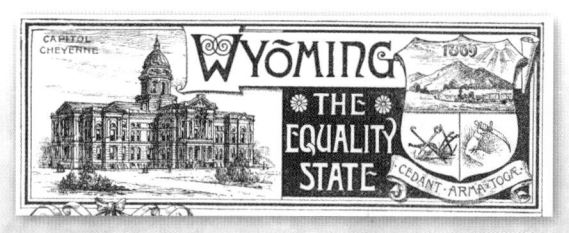

Emblems of Wyoming. (*King's Handbook of the United States, 1891*)

In 1999 the Mint struck commemorative silver dollars honoring Yellowstone National Park. The design shows a geyser in full blast, with Yellowstone's park landscape surrounding. (The park has more geysers, hot springs, steam vents, and mud spots than exist in the rest of the world combined.) On the reverse, an American bison—the largest animal in the park's ecosystem—dominates the motif, with mountains and the rising sun in the background. Yellowstone is the nation's first (and the world's oldest) national park; it was dedicated by an act of Congress, signed by President Ulysses Grant, on March 1, 1872. Half the proceeds from the sale of this coin went to support Yellowstone, with the other half assigned to other national parks.

Numismatic Aspects of the State of Wyoming

1999: The Yellowstone National Park commemorative silver dollar was issued.

2007-P, Wyoming

MS-64	MS-65	MS-66	MS-67	MS-68	MS-69
$4.05	$16	$68	$234	$1,500	—

2007-P, Wyoming, Satin Finish

MS-64	MS-65	MS-66	MS-67	MS-68	MS-69
$2.65	$2.65	$4.05	$11	$20	$162

2007-D, Wyoming

MS-64	MS-65	MS-66	MS-67	MS-68	MS-69
$0.50	$0.80	$16	$43	$442	—

2007-D, Wyoming, Satin Finish

MS-64	MS-65	MS-66	MS-67	MS-68	MS-69
$2.65	$2.65	$4.05	$11	$20	$29.50

2007-S, Wyoming, Proof, Clad

PF-67DC	PF-68DC	PF-69DC
$1.50	$4.05	$9.50

2007-S, Wyoming, Proof, Silver

PF-67DC	PF-68DC	PF-69DC
$7.20	$8.50	$11

2007, Utah

Circulation-Strike Mintage, Philadelphia: 255,000,000
Circulation-Strike Mintage, Philadelphia, Satin Finish: 895,628
Circulation-Strike Mintage, Denver: 253,200,000
Circulation-Strike Mintage, Denver, Satin Finish: 895,628
Proof Mintage, San Francisco, Clad: 2,374,778
Proof Mintage, San Francisco, Silver: 1,313,481
GSID: Circulation-strike, Philadelphia, 68961; Satin Finish Philadelphia, 82081; Circulation-strike, Denver, 68960; Satin Finish Denver, 82082; Proof Clad Deep Cameo, 68619; Proof Silver Deep Cameo, 68620

Specifics of the Reverse Design

Description: Two locomotives advance toward each other, with a golden spike in the air between them.

Designer: Joseph F. Menna, who was also the sculptor-engraver who made the model. *Engraver's initials and location:* JFM appears under the back wheel of the right-hand locomotive.

Story of the Design

On September 17, 2004, Utah Governor Olene Walker created the Utah Quarter Dollar Commemorative Coin Commission. He appointed as chairman H. Robert Campbell, Salt Lake City numismatist, past president of the ANA, and owner of the All About Coins shop. The commission had just three other members: Frank McEntire, director of the Utah Arts Council; Patti Harrington, superintendent of public instruction of the Utah State Office of Education; and Phil Notarianni, director of the Utah State Historical Society. Three other committees were set up with other connections with the quarter: the Special Events Committee, the Public Affairs Committee, and the Education and Curriculum Committee.[121]

The public were invited to send concepts until March 1, 2005, after which the commission would select five favorites to be submitted to the governor, who would select up to five to send on to the Mint. Members of the commission said that they preferred the design to have a single theme, rather than a mix or collage of symbols. About 5,000 entries were received, a remarkable number, 90% of which were from schoolchildren.

The commission presented its five choices to Governor Jon Huntsman on July 29, 2005, this being one of a number of instances in which there were changes of governor during the quarter-dollar design-selection process. Huntsman picked out three designs and sent them to the Mint. One motif illustrated the 1869 transcontinental railroad ceremony at Promontory Point. Another showed a beehive, symbol of industry and long an icon associated with the district, including on the Mormon $5 gold coin of 1860. The third illustrated winter sports, reflecting the state's prominence in that field and its 2002 hosting of the Winter Olympics, and featured a female snowboarder flying through the air.

When Mary Kaye Huntsman, wife of the governor, showed the design to about two-dozen children and their parents, the most excitement by far was for the winter scene. A report of the event noted:

> The snowboarder appears to jump off the quarter as she catches big air with rugged, snowcapped mountains in the background. With a beaming smile, she joyfully stretches her right arm overhead and bends to clutch her snowboard with her left hand in a high-flying maneuver called a ``front grab." Next to her are the words, "The World is Welcome."

After concerns about the girl lacking proper headgear, the design was modified to show the girl wearing a knit cap. Mrs. Hunt said, "If that were my daughter, she would be wearing a helmet." Indeed, she spoke from experience as her daughter engaged in that sport.

Although the beehive is the state symbol, Commission members thought many citizens would view it as a Mormon Church symbol. This concern was run by the Mint attorneys in Washington, who allowed that it was more a cultural than a religious icon and would be okay to use.

Concerning the third motif, the Commission stated:

Emblems of Utah.
(King's Handbook of the United States, 1891)

The golden spike design depicts the meeting of two steam locomotives at Promontory, Utah, in 1869, where the nation's first transcontinental railroad was linked. Hovering above is a ceremonial golden spike officials used to mark the occasion, and the words, "Crossroads of the West." The event, officials said, marked the uniting of the nation following the Civil War and helped transform Utah Territory from an agrarian to a more industrial economy.

Commission member Bob Campbell suggested that "This was the 19th century equivalent of man landing on the moon." Not stated was the fact that the original photograph of the May 10, 1869, meeting of the locomotives of the Central Pacific and Union Pacific railroads showed three celebratory bottles of champagne being held aloft, presumably excluded from the coin on the basis of political correctness. No problem, it turned out. Where the bottle had been in real life was a gigantic vertical spike on the coin. Artistic license had long been a part of coin motifs.

The locomotives were chosen.

THE LAUNCH

The official launch ceremony was held on November 9, 2007, at the Rio Grande Railroad Depot in Salt Lake City, fitting in with the railroad and golden spike theme. That rail line depicted on the coin was now defunct and had been replaced by Amtrak years earlier.

At the event Director Moy was nowhere to be seen, and in his place was Senior Mint Official Gloria C. Eskridge. She was well known to those who had been following recent Mint releases, such as the Westward Journey nickels, for which she gave programs and set up exhibits. Governor Jon M. Huntsman and First Lady Mary Kaye Huntsman were among the other dignitaries on hand. The emcee was Ken Verdoia of Station KUED, the local PBS affiliate. The Bonneville Elementary School fourth grade class serenaded the audience with *Iron Wheels a Rollin'—the Golden Spike Song*.

Per usual, quarters were given out free to the younger set, and all attendees could buy $10 face-value rolls at a nearby stand. In the evening before, the standard Coin Collectors Forum was held, this time at the Discovery Gateway Museum. Coins had already been released through the Federal Reserve System.

Numismatic Aspects of the State of Utah

1849–1850: Mormon gold coinage in denominations of $2.50, $5, $10, and $20 was minted. *1860:* Mormon gold coinage in the $5 denomination was minted. *2002:* The Salt Lake Olympic Games commemorative silver dollar and $5 gold piece were issued.

2007-P, Utah

MS-64	MS-65	MS-66	MS-67	MS-68	MS-69
$0.50	$0.80	$8.10	$162	—	—

2007-P, Utah, Satin Finish

MS-64	MS-65	MS-66	MS-67	MS-68	MS-69
$2.65	$2.65	$4.05	$11.00	$20.00	$29.50

2007-D, Utah

MS-64	MS-65	MS-66	MS-67	MS-68	MS-69
$0.50	$0.80	$13.50	$81	$1,380	—

2007-D, Utah, Satin Finish

MS-64	MS-65	MS-66	MS-67	MS-68	MS-69
$2.65	$2.65	$4.05	$11.00	$20.00	$29.50

2007-S, Utah, Proof, Clad

PF-67DC	PF-68DC	PF-69DC
$1.50	$4.05	$9.50

2007-S, Utah, Proof, Silver

PF-67DC	PF-68DC	PF-69DC
$7.20	$8.50	$11

2008, Oklahoma

Circulation-Strike Mintage, Philadelphia: 222,000,000
Circulation-Strike Mintage, Philadelphia, Satin Finish: 745,464
Circulation-Strike Mintage, Denver: 194,600,000
Circulation-Strike Mintage, Denver, Satin Finish: 745,464
Proof Mintage, San Francisco, Clad: 2,078,112
Proof Mintage, San Francisco, Silver: 1,192,908
GSID: Circulation-strike, Philadelphia, 69023; Satin Finish Philadelphia, 70547; Circulation-strike, Denver, 69024; Satin Finish Denver, 70551; Proof Clad Deep Cameo, 69060; Proof Silver Deep Cameo, 69061

Specifics of the Reverse Design

Description: The state bird, a scissor-tailed flycatcher, flies above the state wildflower, the Indian blanket, amid a field of wildflowers.

Designer: Susan Gamble. *Mint sculptor-engraver who made the model:* Phebe Hemphill. *Engraver's initials and location:* PH appears below the bottom-right flower.

Story of the Design

The design process began in early 2006 when citizens were invited to submit written essays up to 100 words (no graphics or artwork) giving their ideas, to be received by Governor Brad Henry and the Oklahoma Centennial Commission. One essay per person was allowed. Entries were to be archived by the Oklahoma Historical Society and not returned. Acceptable themes included Oklahoma landmarks, landscapes, historically significant buildings, symbols of Oklahoma resources or industries, the state's official flora and fauna, and state icons. March 31 was the deadline for entries.

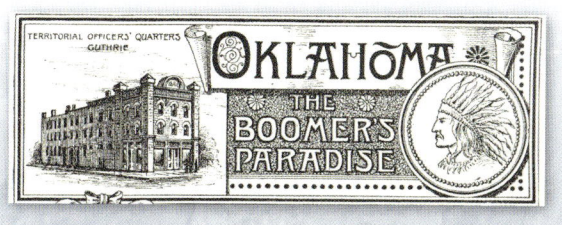

Emblems of Oklahoma.
(*King's Handbook of the United States, 1891*)

By late summer 10 semi-final designs were chosen from over 1,000 submissions, with the oil industry being the most popular motif. Among the selected ideas, eight included an outline of the state, four had gushing oil derricks, and three showed the *Pioneer Woman*, a 17-foot tall bronze statue in Ponca City depicting a woman wearing a sunbonnet, carrying a Bible, and leading a young boy by the hand. Artistic renderings of these were created and posted on the Internet. Interested observers could vote for up to five favorites by September 20.

Governor Henry sent the winning subjects to the Mint, where official sketches were created, differing from the original artwork.

At the Citizens Coinage Advisory Committee meeting held in Washington on January 23, 2007, semi-final designs for each of the five 2008 State quarters were reviewed, according to Bill McAllister of *Coin World*. Four of the five semi-final designs for Oklahoma featured the Pioneer Woman statue with various elements added. The CCAC members strongly favored one that showed the statue in front of an outline map, with an Indian peace pipe as part of the motif. It earned 21 out of a possible 24 points in the committee's rating system. In contrast the Commission of Fine Arts favored what turned out to be the winning design, the state bird, the scissor-tailed flycatcher, and the state flower, the Indian blanket.

The CCAC recommendations and those of the CFA were then sent to Treasury Secretary Henry M. Paulson, who made the final decision for the State quarters and picked the flycatcher.

NATIVE AMERICANS CONSIDERED

Oklahoma became a state on November 16, 1907. The name of the state itself is from Choctaw words *okla* and *humma* meaning "red person." Earlier it had been known as Indian Territory and belonged to Native Americans, many of whom had been forcibly evicted from the Southeast under the Indian Removal Act of 1830, implemented during the later administration of Martin Van Buren—the infamous "Trail of Tears" in which 4,000 unfortunate souls died in a forced 2,000-mile march. The Indian Appropriations Act of 1889 opened the land to white settlers and other homesteaders, many of whom rushed across the line before the authorized date—giving rise to the name of *Sooners*, the nickname today for state residents.

Coin World ran a detailed history of the Trail of Tears, along with feedback from collectors and others who felt that the Native Americans of Oklahoma history should have been acknowledged on the coin design instead of a bird. Unfortunately the bird remained.

THE LAUNCH

The official launch ceremony took place on January 28, 2008, at the Oklahoma History Center in Oklahoma City, the capital and largest city. U.S. Mint Acting Deputy Director Dan Shaver joined Governor and Mrs. Brad Henry in hosting the festivities. Shaver told the crowd, mostly comprised of schoolchildren:

> 2007 was an exciting year for the Sooner State, celebrating its centennial. Today's issuance of this beautiful Oklahoma quarter serves as an encore to the State's centennial, and the coin itself will serve as a lasting, nationwide tribute to Oklahoma, its heritage, and its people.

Free coins were given to the younger set, and all attendees were welcome to buy $10 rolls for face value. On the night before Shaver hosted the Coin Collectors Forum in the Chesapeake Room of the same building.

MONROE DOLLAR ERROR

The Oklahoma quarters earned a footnote in the history of the Presidential Dollar program when it was learned that many 2008 Monroe dollar coins had been struck on planchets intended for the Oklahoma quarter. Many of these errors were caught by the Mint before its shipping contractor, Coin Wrap Inc., of Harrisburg, Pennsylvania, shipped them in paper rolls to the Federal Reserve Banks.

A correct Monroe dollar measures 26.5 mm in diameter, weighs 8.1 grams, and is in manganese-brass. An Oklahoma quarter properly made measures 24.26 mm in diameter, weighs 5.67 grams, and are copper-nickel clad. The striking process of the error dollars changed the diameter on some pieces, but such pieces can be distinguished by having the weight and color of a quarter. On February 18, 2008, *Coin World* reported that from its sources it learned that "tens of thousands of the errors were struck—possibly as many 70,000 to 140,000 error coins."

Numismatic Aspects of the State of Oklahoma

National Bank Notes from the Territory of Oklahoma, before statehood, are especially highly prized.

Based on a photograph, this engraving showing the formation of early cities in Oklahoma was published in *Harper's Weekly* in **1889**.

2008-P, Oklahoma

MS-64	MS-65	MS-66	MS-67	MS-68	MS-69
$0.50	$0.80	$4.05	$19	$260	—

2008-P, Oklahoma, Satin Finish

MS-64	MS-65	MS-66	MS-67	MS-68	MS-69
$2.65	$2.65	$4.05	$11.00	$20.00	$29.50

2008-D, Oklahoma

MS-64	MS-65	MS-66	MS-67	MS-68	MS-69
$0.50	$0.80	$5.40	$38	$680	—

2008-D, Oklahoma, Satin Finish

MS-64	MS-65	MS-66	MS-67	MS-68	MS-69
$2.65	$2.65	$4.05	$11.00	$20.00	$29.50

2008-S, Oklahoma, Proof, Clad

PF-67DC	PF-68DC	PF-69DC
$1.50	$4.05	$9.50

2008-S, Oklahoma, Proof, Silver

PF-67DC	PF-68DC	PF-69DC
$7.20	$8.50	$11

2008, New Mexico

Circulation-Strike Mintage, Philadelphia: 244,200,000
Circulation-Strike Mintage, Philadelphia, Satin Finish: 745,464
Circulation-Strike Mintage, Denver: 244,400,000
Circulation-Strike Mintage, Denver, Satin Finish: 745,464
Proof Mintage, San Francisco, Clad: 2,078,112
Proof Mintage, San Francisco, Silver: 1,192,908
GSID: Circulation-strike, Philadelphia, 69025; Satin Finish Philadelphia, 70549; Circulation-strike, Denver, 69026; Satin Finish Denver, 70552; Proof Clad Deep Cameo, 69062; Proof Silver Deep Cameo, 69063

Specifics of the Reverse Design

Description: The Zia Sun symbol is engraved into a topographical map of the state. The symbol represents the giver of all good, who provided gifts in groups of four. The circle in the center of the symbol represents life and love without beginning or end, while the four rays represent the four directions, four seasons, four phases of the day, and the four divisions of life. The symbol is superimposed over a topographical outline of the state.

Designer: Don Everhart, who was also the sculptor-engraver who made the model. *Engraver's initials and location:* DE is on the lower-right corner of the state's map.

Story of the Design

Governor Bill Richardson set up a website for citizens to download information about the New Mexico coin and to see the special logo he and the New Mexico Coin Commission set up for the project in the governor's office in the State Capitol Building. Participants were invited to submit design ideas in writing, up to 150 words, by May 12, 2006. Responses were evaluated and then sent to the Mint.

Emblems of New Mexico.
(King's Handbook of the United States, 1891)

From there sketches were sent to the Commission of Fine Arts and the Citizens Coinage Advisory Committee. At a two-hour meeting of the latter in January 2007 multiple designs were reviewed, all of which were accepted after due review. The only exception was the New Mexico quarter with all sketches using an outline map and the Zia symbol. Member Sheryl Joseph Winters, a former sculptor-engraver at the Mint, expressed disappointment that multiple designs were not offered, a complaint registered by some other members as well. Committee chairman Mitch Sanders stated that if that is what state officials wanted, so be it. As was custom, the final design was reviewed by Secretary of the Treasury Henry M. Paulson Jr.

THE LAUNCH

The official launch ceremony was held on April 7, 2008, in the Rotunda of the State Capitol in Santa Fe. The event began at 11 in the morning. Mint Director Edmund Moy joined Governor Bill Richardson in welcoming the public, including a large contingent of schoolchildren. Music provided by the Santa Fe All-Stars entertained the crowd. Director Moy's remarks included this:

> The New Mexico quarter's Zia sun symbol design speaks to your state's history and diversity. Your quarter will be immediately recognizable and serve New Mexico as an ambassador to the nation.

This was followed by the traditional free handout of coins to younger attendees and the sale of $10 face value rolls. Nationwide release of the new quarters by the Federal Reserve System took place the same day.

On the night preceding the launch Director Moy gave comments and fielded questions at the Coin Collectors Forum at the National Hispanic Cultural Center of New Mexico in Albuquerque.

Numismatic Aspects of the State of New Mexico

National Bank Notes from the Territory of New Mexico, before statehood, are especially highly prized.

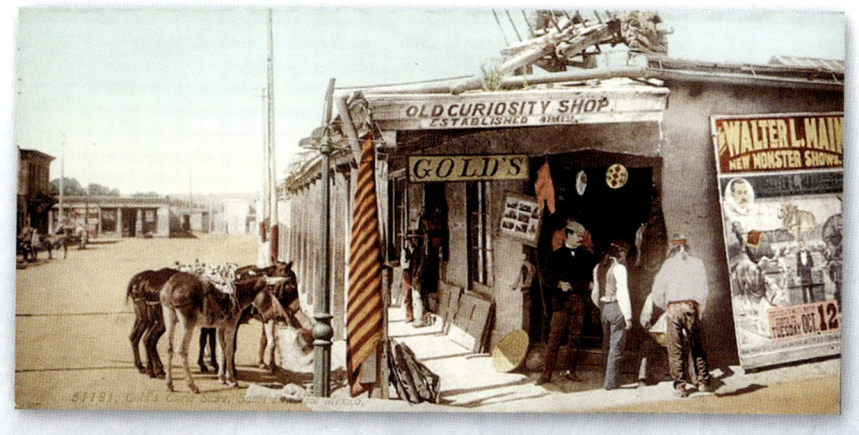

This colorized photograph of Gold's Curio Shop displays the mix of vibrancy and bareness to be found in Santa Fe, New Mexico, circa 1897.

2008-P, New Mexico

MS-64	MS-65	MS-66	MS-67	MS-68	MS-69
$0.50	$0.80	$5.40	$38	—	—

2008-P, New Mexico, Satin Finish

MS-64	MS-65	MS-66	MS-67	MS-68	MS-69
$2.65	$2.65	$4.05	$11	$34	$358

2008-D, New Mexico

MS-64	MS-65	MS-66	MS-67	MS-68	MS-69
$0.50	$0.80	$24.50	$68	$845	—

2008-D, New Mexico, Satin Finish

MS-64	MS-65	MS-66	MS-67	MS-68	MS-69
$2.65	$2.65	$4.05	$11	$27	$234

2008-S, New Mexico, Proof, Clad

PF-67DC	PF-68DC	PF-69DC
$1.50	$4.05	$9.50

2008-S, New Mexico, Proof, Silver

PF-67DC	PF-68DC	PF-69DC
$7.20	$8.50	$11

2008, Arizona

Circulation-Strike Mintage, Philadelphia: 244,600,000
Circulation-Strike Mintage, Philadelphia, Satin Finish: 745,464
Circulation-Strike Mintage, Denver: 265,000,000
Circulation-Strike Mintage, Denver, Satin Finish: 745,464
Proof Mintage, San Francisco, Clad: 2,078,112
Proof Mintage, San Francisco, Silver: 1,192,908
GSID: Circulation-strike, Philadelphia, 69706; Satin Finish Philadelphia, 70548; Circulation-strike, Denver, 69707; Satin Finish Denver, 82083; Proof Clad Deep Cameo, 69064; Proof Silver Deep Cameo, 69065

Specifics of the Reverse Design

Description: The design features a depiction of the Grand Canyon, one of the Seven Wonders of the World and part of the United States National Park Service. A Saguaro cactus and various other flora can be seen in the foreground.

Designer: Joel Iskowitz. *Mint sculptor-engraver who made the model:* Joseph F. Menna. *Engraver's initials and location:* JFM appears under the cactus.

Story of the Design

In November 2005, Governor Janet Napolitano of Arizona established a commission to recommend designs for the new State quarter. On December 13 she announced that 22 members had been chosen. The panel was composed of representatives from the State Legislature, historical and art societies, school students and teachers, and members of the general public. The governor wanted students in particular to take part. Two coin collectors were named to the commission, Earl Quintel and Thomas Trompeter. Others

Emblems of Arizona.
(*King's Handbook of the United States, 1891*)

in the diverse lineup included fourth grader Matthew Rounis, several school teachers and administrators, and James I. Bowie, a senior researcher in Northern Arizona University's Social Research Laboratory. Bowie had conducted a survey in 2005 that showed that most citizens preferred natural subjects such as the Grand Canyon in particular, and also the saguaro cactus. Few wanted historical or cultural symbols.

In the autumn the committee's five favorite designs were sent to the Mint to be converted into official sketches for review by the Commission of Fine Arts and the Citizens Coinage Advisory Committee. From there the design traveled to the secretary of the Treasury, then into production at the Mint.

THE LAUNCH

On June 2, 2008, the official launch ceremony for the Arizona quarter was conducted on the Senate Lawn of the State Capitol in Phoenix. Mint Director Edmund C. Moy and Governor Janet Napolitano led a contingent of dignitaries in the event. Music was provided by Mariachi Aguila de Marcelino Cervantes, a Phoenix band. The Southwest Association of Buffalo Soldiers was in attendance. Director Moy observed that "When Americans pull this coin out of their pockets, they'll immediately think of Arizona." Further, "This quarter celebrates the breathtaking natural beauty of Arizona, from its rare Saguaro cactus to the awe-inspiring Grand Canyon,"

Each member of the younger set received a free 2008-D quarter, and all interested attendees could buy $10 rolls for face value.

The night before the ceremony the usual Coin Collectors Forum was held, this time at the Carnegie Center in Phoenix.

Numismatic Aspects of the State of Arizona

The state motto, Ditat Deus, translates to "God enriches." The name of the state is said to have come from Aztec words meaning "silver bearing." National Bank Notes from the Territory of Arizona, before statehood, are especially highly prized. Superstition Mountain, near Phoenix, is said to be the hiding place for a vast gold treasure.

As grand as the Grand Canyon may be, the cactus is equally prominent on the Arizona State quarter, just as it is on this vintage postcard featuring Native Americans.

2008-P, Arizona

MS-64	MS-65	MS-66	MS-67	MS-68	MS-69
$0.50	$0.80	$5.40	$38	—	—

2008-P, Arizona, Satin Finish

MS-64	MS-65	MS-66	MS-67	MS-68	MS-69
$2.65	$2.65	$4.05	$11.00	$20.00	$29.50

2008-D, Arizona

MS-64	MS-65	MS-66	MS-67	MS-68	MS-69
$0.50	$0.80	$16	$47	$1,380	—

2008-D, Arizona, Satin Finish

MS-64	MS-65	MS-66	MS-67	MS-68	MS-69
$2.65	$2.65	$4.05	$11	$27	$234

2008-S, Arizona, Proof, Clad

PF-67DC	PF-68DC	PF-69DC
$1.50	$4.05	$9.50

2008-S, Arizona, Proof, Silver

PF-67DC	PF-68DC	PF-69DC
$7.20	$8.50	$11

2008, Alaska

Circulation-Strike Mintage, Philadelphia: 251,800,000
Circulation-Strike Mintage, Philadelphia, Satin Finish: 745,464
Circulation-Strike Mintage, Denver: 254,000,000
Circulation-Strike Mintage, Denver, Satin Finish: 745,464
Proof Mintage, San Francisco, Clad: 2,078,112
Proof Mintage, San Francisco, Silver: 1,192,908
GSID: Circulation-strike, Philadelphia, 69648; Satin Finish Philadelphia, 69650; Circulation-strike, Denver, 69649; Satin Finish Denver, 69651; Proof Clad Deep Cameo, 69066; Proof Silver Deep Cameo, 69067

Specifics of the Reverse Design

Description: A grizzly bear emerging from a stream with a salmon in its jaws.

Designer: Susan Gamble. *Mint sculptor-engraver who made the model:* Charles L. Vickers. *Engraver's initials and location:* CLV appears to the right of the bear's paw.

Story of the Design

The Alaska Commemorative Coin Commission, established in 2005, was composed of 11 members. The agendas of its meetings, held in Anchorage the first Thursday of each month, were posted on the Internet as were the minutes. Residents of the state were invited to submit design concepts in writing from January 1 to February 28, 2006. These were to be reviewed by the 11 members of the Alaska Commemorative Coin Commission appointed by Governor Frank Murkowski.

On April 23, 2007, Governor Sarah Palin, successor to Murkowski in that office, announced her choice. *Coin World* described it as: "a bear emerging from a stream after catching a salmon. To the right is the great land. A single star, representing the North Star, will appear to the right of the word ALASKA at the top of the design. A view of spruce trees above a waterfall is also part of the design."

A fanciful vignettte of Alaskan hunting culture prior to statehood. (E.C. Kropp Educational Series, 1906)

Emblems of Alaska.
(*King's Handbook of the United States, 1891*)

Michele Orzano, staff writer for *Coin World*, commented:

> Throughout the 50 State quarter program, some states have made the process easier for residents to access than some others have. One of the items in the minutes indicates Alaskan officials have talked with officials in other states about what worked for them while setting up a review process. Those kinds of alliances can help the Alaskan commissioners to sort through submissions and understand the overall process more quickly.
>
> Many of the states have learned that a simple, one-topic design works best. Most states have figured out that naming a "winning designer" is not the best approach to take in selecting designs. Accepting design concepts from the public and including their opinions in a non-binding Internet-based survey are two ways to encourage public participation.

THE LAUNCH

On August 29, 2008, on the Colony Stage at the Alaska State Fair the launch ceremony drew a crowd. While the new quarters were the featured attraction, *Numismatic News* reported that the buzz throughout the crowd had to do with Senator John McCain's recent selection of Governor Palin as his running mate on the Republican ticket for the presidential election to be held in November. This set the scene for unending media coverage of her personal and political life from the summer through the autumn.

Governors had routinely launched State quarters in other states, but that was not to be this time. Although the governor's office did proclaim "49th State Quarter Day." Lieutenant Governor Sean Parnell officiated at the ceremony. He was joined on the Colony Stage by U.S. Mint Deputy Director Andrew Brunhart (in the quarter program the term "deputy director" was attached to any Mint official who was assigned to cover a launch ceremony). Brunhart gave the usual type of statement, "The bear gripping a salmon firmly in its jaws as it emerges from rapids captures the essence of your state. When Americans pull this coin out of their pockets, they will think of Alaska—America's last frontier."

Brunhart and Parnell passed out quarters for free to the younger set. Attendees could buy $10 bank-wrapped rolls for face value at a nearby stand.

On the night before the Public Coin Forum was hosted by Brunhart at the Alaska Heritage Museum in Anchorage. By that evening the coins had been in general release for three days.

Numismatic Aspects of the State of Alaska

1935: Tokens of the Alaska Rural Rehabilitation Corporation were issued; these are listed in the *Guide Book of United States Coins* today.

2008-P, Alaska

MS-64	MS-65	MS-66	MS-67	MS-68	MS-69
$0.50	$0.80	$5.40	$38	—	—

2008-P, Alaska, Satin Finish

MS-64	MS-65	MS-66	MS-67	MS-68	MS-69
$2.65	$2.65	$4.05	$11	$27	$195

2008-D, Alaska

MS-64	MS-65	MS-66	MS-67	MS-68	MS-69
$0.50	$0.80	$5.40	$38	$520	—

2008-D, Alaska, Satin Finish

MS-64	MS-65	MS-66	MS-67	MS-68	MS-69
$2.65	$2.65	$4.05	$11	$27	$234

2008-S, Alaska, Proof, Clad

PF-67DC	PF-68DC	PF-69DC
$1.50	$4.05	$9.50

2008-S, Alaska, Proof, Silver

PF-67DC	PF-68DC	PF-69DC
$7.20	$8.50	$11

2008, Hawaii

Circulation-Strike Mintage, Philadelphia: 254,000,000
Circulation-Strike Mintage, Philadelphia, Satin Finish: 745,464
Circulation-Strike Mintage, Denver: 263,600,000
Circulation-Strike Mintage, Denver, Satin Finish: 745,464
Proof Mintage, San Francisco, Clad: 2,078,112
Proof Mintage, San Francisco, Silver: 1,192,908
GSID: Circulation-strike, Philadelphia, 69708; Satin Finish Philadelphia, 70550; Circulation-strike, Denver, 69709; Satin Finish Denver, 70553; Proof Clad Deep Cameo, 69068; Proof Silver Deep Cameo, 69069.

Specifics of the Reverse Design

Description: A statue of King Kamehameha I appears to the right of raised Hawaiian Islands. The inscription includes Hawaii's state motto "UA MAU KE EA O KA 'AINA I KA PONO" ("The life of the land is perpetuated in righteousness").

Designer: Don Everhart, who was also the sculptor-engraver who made the model. *Engraver's initials and location:* DE appears to the right of the statue's base.

Story of the Design

To set the scene on February 14, 2006, Governor Linda Lingle announced the formation of the Hawai'i Commemorative Quarter Advisory Commission, with the state name spelled in an traditional manner with an apostrophe before the final letter. Jonathan Johnson, project manager for the Hawaii State Foundation on Culture and the Arts, was named as chair. Among others selected was Greg Hunt, president of the Honolulu Coin Club and a member of the Hawaii Numismatic Association. Perhaps in recognition of the state's order in the Union the commission was not to exceed 50 members.

On April 23, 2007. Governor Lingle announced her choice: a full-length portrait of King Kamehameha I with his arm extended toward the outlines of the eight larger Hawaiian Islands, his left hand holding a spear. Kamehameha had unified the various islands into a kingdom. At a quick glance the concept of the standing figure was not much different from that of a standing Hawaiian chief in full regalia used on the 1928 Hawaiian Sesquicentennial commemorative half dollar.

THE LAUNCH

At 10 in the morning of October 4, 2008, Hawaii Governor Linda Lingle was at the Denver Mint for the first striking for circulation of 2008-D Hawaii quarters.

The launch ceremony for the 50th coin in the State quarter series was held five weeks later at noon on November 10, 2008, in downtown Honolulu, one week after the Federal Reserve had made them available in quantity to member banks. Unlike the Alaska ceremony, the Hawaii event drew the top officials: Mint Director Edmond C. Moy and Governor Linda Lingle. Moy addressed the end of the program rather than the coin making its debut:

> Long after the last coin in the 50 State Quarters Program rolls off the presses at the United States Mint, we will remember the wonderful things we accomplished with this 10-year initiative. Americans gained a renewed sense of pride in their respective states. More of us were inspired to explore our nation's history through the unique story that each quarter dollar tells. Because of the 50 State Quarters Program, a geography lesson will jingle in our pockets for years to come.

The event included a keiki hula performance with Hawaiian music, the usual quarter distribution, and a program given the night before at the Kanaina Building on Iolani Palace grounds for a forum of collectors and others interested in the Mint's programs.

Hawaii became a state on August 21, 1959, following years of agitation for such by many interests. Parallel to this, many citizens of the Territory of Puerto Rico had the same objective, but without success. Beginning in 1959 there were 50 stars in the flag, as there are today.

Numismatic Aspects of the State of Hawaii

1847: Copper cents were issued by King Kamehameha; they were struck in Massachusetts. *1883:* Silver dimes, quarter dollars, half dollars, and dollars (total face value $1 million) were struck in San Francisco (but with no mintmark) for Hawaii. *20th century:* National Bank Notes with territorial address are especially popular with collectors. *1928:* The Hawaii Sesquicentennial commemorative half dollar was issued. It is the rarest of the basic design types in the classic commemoratives silver series from 1892 to 1954. *1940s:* $1, $5, $10, and $20 bills with HAWAII overprints were issued during World War II.

2008-P, Hawaii

MS-64	MS-65	MS-66	MS-67	MS-68	MS-69
$0.50	$0.80	$5.40	$38		

2008-P, Hawaii, Satin Finish

MS-64	MS-65	MS-66	MS-67	MS-68	MS-69
$2.65	$2.65	$4.05	$11	$34	$143

2008-D, Hawaii

MS-64	MS-65	MS-66	MS-67	MS-68	MS-69
$0.50	$0.80	$5.40	$38		

2008-D, Hawaii, Satin Finish

MS-64	MS-65	MS-66	MS-67	MS-68	MS-69
$2.65	$2.65	$4.05	$11	$20	$122

2008-S, Hawaii, Proof, Clad

PF-67DC	PF-68DC	PF-69DC
$1.50	$4.05	$9.50

2008-S, Hawaii, Proof, Silver

PF-67DC	PF-68DC	PF-69DC
$7.20	$8.50	$11

THE 1999–2008 STATE QUARTERS: A RETROSPECTIVE

The State Quarters Program, first suggested by Harvey Stack and shepherded into law and reality by Representative Michael Castle, was launched in the order that the states ratified the Constitution and became part of the Union. It concluded with the Hawaii quarter in 2008, by which time 50 states had each been honored with a differently distinctive reverse design. Some of the motifs were quickly identified with the state. Others (the scissortail flycatcher for Omaha comes to mind) had hardly any popular recognition.

As related, the typical procedure called for the state governor to appoint a committee to solicit designs from the public. In the earlier times these were often sketches sent in by schoolchildren (in particular) and others. Most later designs were required to be in short narrative form. The governor, sometimes with the advice and consent of others in the state, selected from one to several semi-final designs. These were sent to the Engraving Department at the Philadelphia Mint, where official sketches were professionally created.

The sketches were reviewed by the Commission of Fine Arts and, separately, by the Citizens Coinage Advisory Committee. Neither group did more than furnish preferences and suggestions. The secretary of the Treasury made the final call, sometimes ignoring the recommendations furnished.

Representative Castle's 2006 estimate that the program might earn the United States Treasury department $3.4 billion was based on the difference between the cost of manufacture and the face value that the Federal Reserve System paid. When all was said and done, the profit was about $6.1 billion!

The numismatic press, including the weekly *Coin World* and *Numismatic News*, endeavored to provide detailed coverage from the first design ideas through to the official launch ceremonies and distribution. This was often a warm hand-in-hand situation, but in some instances the press was stonewalled when details were requested. The current director of the Mint and Mint staff dictated policy on this point, which varied.

Interest was intense at the beginning, but it faded over time. Quantities of later quarters were much smaller than those for the first years. Distribution was curiously erratic from a numismatic viewpoint. The Federal Reserve System distributed coins to fill requests from member banks, which usually had little to do with the states being honored. For instance, in 2013 the White Mountain National Forest (New Hampshire) quarter was not in general circulation in the Granite State as supplies of coins there were already adequate. Many if not most were distributed in Maryland and Virginia!

In *Coin World*, Jeff Starck described the program's success as of December 29, 2008:

> With mintages known for 49 of the 50 states, the total number of coins struck numbers about 34.3 billion, or about $8.5 billion face value, according to the U.S. Mint. According to the Mint, the $6.1 billion figure is about $2.7 billion to $2.9 billion more than it could have been expected to generate through production of the 25-cent denomination without the program. According to the Mint, it produced 19.4 billion more coins during the 10-year period of the program compared to the previous 10-year period ending in 1998 (34.28 billion compared to 14.8 billion).

That doesn't account for any population growth, which would certainly fuel demand for coinage in circulation, but the numbers are still staggering, and staggering evidence of the program's success.

Adding to the above, the U.S. Mint registered many millions of dollars in profit from the sale of State quarters in Proof sets, in silver strikings, and in other packaging and programs not for general circulation.

Numismatics benefited immensely from the program. The relations between the Mint and collectors reached a new level of communication as directors Henrietta Holsman Fore, Philip Diehl, Jay Johnson, and Edmund Moy in succession attended launch ceremonies as well as numismatic events. It was win-win for all concerned.

SEQUEL TO THE STATE QUARTERS PROGRAM

When the State Quarters Program was first envisioned in 2006, it was anticipated that in time all 50 states would be showcased, one at a time at the rate of five designs per year, starting in 1999. The program was a great success and concluded in 2008, as described in the previous section. The earlier issues were more popular than the later ones, but overall the public, as well as members of the numismatic community, were satisfied.

As the program neared its end there was a movement to extend it by including the District of Columbia and the American territories. The former in particular had long hoped to gain some of the privileges of the states, such as having representatives in Congress. In the end it was decided that the places to be honored were the District of Columbia; the commonwealths of Puerto Rico and the Northern Mariana Islands; and the territories of Guam, the U.S. Virgin Islands, and American Samoa.

One incorporated territory was omitted—Palmyra Atoll. One reason may be because the area has no permanent residents so it has no citizens to propose designs. A dozen or two scientific sorts cycle in and out as visitors to the 12-square-mile island. Palmyra has its share of stories—as a quick Internet search revealed—ranging from buried gold coins and buried pirate treasure waiting to be discovered, to being the southernmost place owned by the United States, to a foul modern ship capture and murder. However, interpretations of these and other motifs will never happen in coin form. Other forgotten places, called "minor islands" by the government, include Baker Island, Howland Island, Jarvis Island, Johnston Atoll, Kingman Reef, Midway Atoll, and Wake Island in the Pacific Ocean, and Navassa Island in the Caribbean Sea. Wake Island and Midway in particular figure in the history of World War II. On December 11, 1941, Wake Island was invaded by the Japanese. Navassa Island, discovered by Christopher Columbus in 1504, has been the subject of a territorial dispute with Haiti since 1801. Such are the interesting footnotes in the history of remote places.

Enabling Legislation

The concept of the extended coinage found favor in the House of Representatives during the 106th through the 108th Congresses, but each time died in the Senate. In the 109th Congress the House passed H.R. 3885 by voice vote in the early morning house of December 9, 2006, and adjourned shortly after. This was followed by the adjournment of the Senate without acting on it. On January 10, 2007, at the inception of the 110th Congress Eleanor Holmes Norton (Democrat-D.C.), on hand as a *delegate*, introduced HR-392. This was passed by the House on January 23. It was approved by the Senate on September 6 and was signed into law by President George W. Bush on December 26. A provision inserted into the act allowed any territory that became a state in the meantime to be honored on the 51st state quarter. As reflected by the long title, the new coins were to be similar to those of the states and would be placed into circulation for face value. Not stated was that Proofs would also be made for collectors.

Without much input from the numismatic community, it was stated in the halls of Congress that the six new quarters, all to be issued in 2009, would bring over $400 million in additional revenue to the United States Treasury and that the public's interest, which had been waning toward the end of the state series, would be regenerated by books and albums expected to be issued by many publishers.

The secretary of the Treasury and the Mint developed the design evaluation and selection process, which included these elements:

> **Step One:** The United States Mint will initiate the formal design process by contacting the chief executive of the District of Columbia or the territory being honored. The chief executive, or such other officials or group as the chief executive officer of the District of Columbia or the territory may designate for such purpose, will appoint an individual to serve as the liaison to the United States Mint for this Program.
>
> **Step Two:** The District of Columbia and each territory will conduct a concept selection process as determined by the District of Columbia and each territory. The District of Columbia and each territory will provide to the United States Mint at least two, but no more than three, different concepts or themes emblematic of the District of Columbia or the territory; each concept or theme will be in narrative format. The narrative must explain why the concept is emblematic of the District of Columbia or the territory and what the concept represents to its citizens. A narrative that merely describes a particular design is not acceptable.
>
> **Step Three:** Based on the narratives, the United States Mint will produce at its discretion one or more original candidate designs for each concept, focusing on aesthetic beauty, historical accuracy, appropriateness and coinability.
>
> **Step Four:** The United States Mint will contact the District of Columbia and each territory to collaborate on the candidate designs. The District of Columbia and each territory will appoint an historian, or other responsible officials or experts, to participate in this collaboration to ensure historical accuracy and proper representation of the candidate designs. The United States Mint will refine the candidate designs, as necessary, before presenting them to the Citizens Coinage Advisory Committee (CCAC) and the Commission of Fine Arts (CFA).

Step Five: The CCAC and the CFA will review the candidate designs and make recommendations, and the United States Mint, in consultation with the District of Columbia and each territory, may make changes to address such recommendations.

Step Six: From among the final candidate designs, the District of Columbia and each territory will recommend its primary and secondary candidate design choices through a process determined by the District of Columbia and each territory, within a time frame specified by the United States Mint.

Step Seven: The United States Mint will present the primary recommended design from the District of Columbia and each territory to the Secretary of the Treasury for approval.

On December 15, 2008, the U.S. Mint released the final designs as approved by Secretary of the Treasury Henry M. Paulson Jr. As with other coinage programs, the Commission of Fine Arts, the Citizens Coinage Advisory Committee, members of Congress, and many others had their opinions, but it fell to the secretary of the Treasury to personally make the final decision.

At the top of the reverse the name of the geographical subject appeared, permitting instant identification. E PLURIBUS UNUM was at the bottom of the border.

News from the Mint

A Mint news release dated December 27, 2007, included an estimate as to the number of collectors of quarters and gave an overview:

> The District of Columbia and the five U.S. territories will get their own commemorative quarter–dollars in 2009, under new legislation signed by President Bush.
>
> "The 50 State Quarters® Program has been the most popular coin program in U.S. history, generating billions of dollars that have been used to pay down the National debt," said United States Mint Director Ed Moy. "We look forward to honoring the District of Columbia and the U.S. Territories by minting and issuing six quarters in 2009 that will build upon the success of a program that has educated a generation in state geography and history."
>
> An estimated 147 million people collect the 50 State Quarters coins, a ten–year program introduced in 1999 that will end in late 2008 with the issuance of the Hawaii commemorative quarter, marking the 50th State to be honored.
>
> Congress has now added a provision to the 2008 Consolidated Appropriations Act that calls on the United States Mint to produce six newly designed quarters in 2009 honoring the District of Columbia and the five U.S. territories: the Commonwealth of Puerto Rico, Guam, American Samoa, the United States Virgin Islands and the Commonwealth of the Northern Mariana Islands. The new quarter program will continue to feature images of President George Washington on the obverse (heads side) of each quarter. The image on the reverse (tails side) will commemorate the history, geography or traditions of the District of Columbia and each territory.
>
> The first quarter to be issued in the 2009 program will be the one honoring the District of Columbia. The five United States territories will follow throughout 2009.

2009, District of Columbia

Circulation-Strike Mintage, Philadelphia: 83,600,000
Circulation-Strike Mintage, Philadelphia, Satin Finish: 784,614
Circulation-Strike Mintage, Denver: 88,800,000
Circulation-Strike Mintage, Denver, Satin Finish: 784,614
Proof Mintage, San Francisco, Clad: 2,113,478
Proof Mintage, San Francisco, Silver: 996,548
GSID: Circulation-strike, Philadelphia, 70027; Satin Finish Philadelphia, 82084; Circulation-strike, Denver, 70028; Satin Finish Denver, 82085; Proof Clad Deep Cameo, 70666; Proof Silver Deep Cameo, 70667

Specifics of the Reverse Design

Description: The famous jazz musician and composer Duke Ellington, who was born and raised in the District of Columbia, is seen sitting next to the keyboard of a grand piano. The sculptor's initials can be found on the leg of the piano, to the right.

Designer: Joel Iskowitz. *Mint sculptor-engraver who made the model:* Don Everhart. *Engraver's initials and location:* DE is on the leg of the piano, to the right.

Story and Background of the Design

The design of the District of Columbia quarter was not without an element of controversy. It was suggested by several people that the inscription include NO TAXATION WITHOUT REPRESENTATION, or a similar message reflecting that citizens of the District did not have the right to elect representatives to Congress. Such wording had been popular for a long time on stickers on automobiles in the area. This idea did not find favor with the Treasury Department, which stated that there was no place on coins for controversial messages or ideas. The District revised the text to JUSTICE FOR ALL; a saying which they thought would be less controversial.

Mayor Adrian M. Fenty established the District of Columbia Quarter Design Advisory Committee, which reviewed more than 300 sketches and other ideas submitted by artists and the general public. The motifs were condensed to three—Duke Ellington, Benjamin Bannker (who worked with the original survey of the district), and the District flag. The last was replaced by Frederick Douglass, the famous abolitionist and statesman. The artistic renderings were then proposed to the District. The citizens were allowed to give their preferences, and Ellington was selected. The Ellington choice was finalized by the secretary of the Treasury, creating America's first non-commemorative coin to depict an African-American man.

Numismatic Commentary

Gone were the days of standardized launch ceremonies for each coin in the series, with crowds attending, with music and entertainment, and a forum the night before. In comparison the ceremony for the first of the 2009 quarter was a simple affair held on February 24 at the Smithsonian Institution's National Museum of American History, a short walk from the White House. The president was nowhere to be seen, nor had any other sitting presidents been present at earlier ceremonies. The only two chief executives in American history to show an interest and spend significant time with coins were

George Washington and Ronald Reagan. In several tours of the four mints in recent years it was learned that no president in office had visited one in modern times. Several had been at Independence Square in Philadelphia with the Mint across the street.

The subject of the reverse, Edward Kennedy ("Duke") Ellington was born in Washington, D.C., on April 29, 1899, and lived there until 1923, when he moved to New York City. There he furthered his career as a performing musician that he had started at the age of 17. Ellington became a popular figure in nightclubs and later formed his own band. Many famous musicians played alongside him, including Louis Armstrong, Ella Fitzgerald, John Coltrane, and Billy Strayhorn, to give a short list. In a career that spanned 50 years he composed more than a thousand melodies, made countless recordings, and received many honors. He died in New York City on May 24, 1974.

On May 4, 2009, a 2009-D District of Columbia doubled die quarter was reported in *Coin World*, most prominent with strong doubling of ELL in ELLINGTON. The finder was Lee Maples, a collector from Texas who filed the first report on the Collectors Universe Message Boards.[122]

The new series laid an egg in comparison to even the less popular issues of the State Quarter Series. This was due to the obscurity of most of the six subjects and, possibly even more important, the sliding of the American economy into a recession that would last for several years. Beyond that, no special albums were issued for this series, and numismatic interest was minimal.

2009-P, District of Columbia

MS-64	MS-65	MS-66	MS-67	MS-68	MS-69
$0.50	$0.80	$2.65	$9.50	—	—

2009-P, District of Columbia, Satin Finish

MS-64	MS-65	MS-66	MS-67	MS-68	MS-69
$2.65	$2.65	$4.05	$8.10	$13.50	$24.50

2009-D, District of Columbia

MS-64	MS-65	MS-66	MS-67	MS-68	MS-69
$0.50	$0.80	$2.65	$9.50	—	—

2009-D, District of Columbia, Satin Finish

MS-64	MS-65	MS-66	MS-67	MS-68	MS-69
$2.65	$2.65	$4.05	$8.10	$16	$68

2009-S, District of Columbia, Proof, Clad

PF-67DC	PF-68DC	PF-69DC
$1.50	$4.05	$9.50

2009-S, District of Columbia, Proof, Silver

PF-67DC	PF-68DC	PF-69DC
$7.20	$8.50	$11

2009, Puerto Rico

Circulation-Strike Mintage, Philadelphia: 53,200,000
Circulation-Strike Mintage, Philadelphia, Satin Finish: 784,614
Circulation-Strike Mintage, Denver: 86,000,000
Circulation-Strike Mintage, Denver, Satin Finish: 784,614
Proof Mintage, San Francisco, Clad: 2,113,478
Proof Mintage, San Francisco, Silver: 996,548

GSID: Circulation-strike, Philadelphia, 71268; Satin Finish Philadelphia, 82086; Circulation-strike, Denver, 71269; Satin Finish Denver, 82087; Proof Clad Deep Cameo, 71265; Proof Silver Deep Cameo, 70670

Specifics of the Reverse Design

Description: A view of the seas as seen from a sentry box in Old San Juan with hibiscus flowers to the right. The sculptor's initials can be found below the flowers on the right.

Designer: Joseph F. Menna, who was also the sculptor-engraver who made the model. *Engraver's initials and location:* JFM appears below the flowers on the right.

Story and Background of the Design

The background of the Puerto Rico quarter, similar to the stories that unfolded for the other territorial coins, is far simpler than that for the earlier state issues. In view of the impending coinage, the Senate of Puerto Rico resolved in June 2008 to urge the Mint to select a depiction of the Arecibo Observatory, a wonder of astronomical radio science that had figured in many important discoveries. In actuality, the Mint would have little to do with the final design; that was the prerogative of the secretary of the Treasury.

This design idea fell by the wayside when a commission established by Governor Aníbal Acevedo-Vilá and chaired by the director of the Puerto Rico Culture Institute had its own ideas—the Palacio de Catalina, which is the residence of the governor today, and the sentry box. The Mint created drawings. The governor picked the sentry box and on July 31, 2008, it was given final approval by the secretary of the Treasury.

The Mint described the motif as a bartizan (sentry turret) and a view of the ocean from Old San Juan, a Flor de Maga (Maga tree flower), and the motto "Isla del Encanto," meaning "Island of Enchantment." The Puerto Rico quarter is the first U.S. coin with an inscription in Spanish.

Numismatic Commentary

On April 2, 2009, a launch ceremony evocative of some of the state quarter events took place in Old San Juan. Mint Director Ed Moy and Governor Luis Fortuño were joined by other dignitaries. The director commented, "Puerto Rico's striking quarter design evokes its tropical beauty, rich history, and bilingual culture. San Juan Bay as the background of the coin, the hibiscus flower, and 16th century sentry box remind us that Puerto Rico stands for 'rich port.'"

Coins were released into circulation on March 30, and on that day collectors and others could order quantities from the Mint. Proofs of San Francisco quarters could be ordered in sets, similar to the case for state quarters.

Christopher Columbus landed in Puerto Rico in 1493. It was added to the captured Spanish possessions in the New World and was developed as a military post. Over a long period of years it was attacked by other empire builders including France, Holland, and England, but it remained under Spanish dominance until it was taken over in 1898 in the short-lived Spanish-American War. This imperialist period in American history also yielded other island possessions including Cuba, the Philippines, and Guam.

After being ceded to the United States, it gained importance with the mainland, including the establishment of National Banks that issued their own currency. Residents became official American citizens in 1917. On July 3, 1950, Congress allowed Puerto Rico to draft its own Constitution. Under an act of July 25, 1952, it became a commonwealth. Many proposals for statehood have been made over years, but none have come close to passage.

2009-P, Puerto Rico

MS-64	MS-65	MS-66	MS-67	MS-68	MS-69
$0.50	$0.80	$2.65	$9.50	—	—

2009-P, Puerto Rico, Satin Finish

MS-64	MS-65	MS-66	MS-67	MS-68	MS-69
$2.65	$2.65	$4.05	$8.10	$13.50	$34

2009-D, Puerto Rico

MS-64	MS-65	MS-66	MS-67	MS-68	MS-69
$0.50	$0.80	$2.65	$9.50	—	—

2009-D, Puerto Rico, Satin Finish

MS-64	MS-65	MS-66	MS-67	MS-68	MS-69
$2.65	$2.65	$4.05	$8.10	$24.50	$195

2009-S, Puerto Rico, Proof, Clad

PF-67DC	PF-68DC	PF-69DC
$1.50	$4.05	$9.50

2009-S, Puerto Rico, Proof, Silver

PF-67DC	PF-68DC	PF-69DC
$7.20	$8.50	$11

2009, Guam

Circulation-Strike Mintage, Philadelphia: 45,000,000
Circulation-Strike Mintage, Philadelphia, Satin Finish: 784,614
Circulation-Strike Mintage, Denver: 42,600,000
Circulation-Strike Mintage, Denver, Satin Finish: 784,614
Proof Mintage, San Francisco, Clad: 2,113,478
Proof Mintage, San Francisco, Silver: 996,548
GSID: Circulation-strike, Philadelphia, 70796; Satin Finish Philadelphia, 82088; Circulation-strike, Denver, 70797; Satin Finish Denver, 82089; Proof Clad Deep Cameo, 71266; Proof Silver Deep Cameo, 70668

Specifics of the Reverse Design

Description: An outline of the island of Guam along with two symbols associated with the island—at the left is a sailing vessel known as the "Flying Proa" for its great speed, and on the right is a Latte, a stone pillar used in ancient houses. The legend GUAHAN I TANO MANCHAM ORRO ("Guam, Land of the Chamorro") is placed to the right of the center of the coin's reverse.

Designer: David Westwood. *Mint sculptor-engraver who made the model:* Jim Licaretz. *Engraver's initials and location:* DL is to the right of the latte stone.

Story and Background of the Design

Guam Governor Felix P. Camacho invited citizens to submit design ideas. He reviewed several hundred and selected two as semi-finalists: (1) The outline of the Island of Guam with a flying proa and latte stone, and (2) A flying proa at sail, a coconut tree bending toward the water, and Two Lovers Point in the background. These were sent to the U.S. Mint, and the engraving department in Philadelphia prepared two sketches. Both were put up to vote in Guam, and the first was suggested. This was approved by the secretary of the Treasury on July 31, 2008.

Numismatic Commentary

At 9:00 a.m. on Thursday, June 4, 2009, the ceremonial launch was held for the Guam quarter at Skinner Plaza in Hagåtña, Guam. Governor Felix Camacho, First Lady Joann Camacho, and other dignitaries were on hand. Mint Director Edmund C. Moy, quite possibly the most enthusiastic launch ceremony attendee in Mint history, was on hand, and local entertainment enlivened the scene. After the ceremony those 18 years old or younger received free quarters handed out by the governor and the Mint director. The 18-year limit varied for different ceremonies over the years. For some, those who obtained quarters had to be *under* 18 (legal age). In practice, the youngsters who raised their hands received coins without question. Rolls with a face value of $10 were available for purchase at face value.

On the afternoon before, starting at noon, Moy hosted a Coin Collectors Forum at the University of Guam's Leon Guerrero School of Business and Public Administration Building. By that time the Guam quarter had already been released to banks and collectors on May 26, 2009. From the U.S. Mint website, 100-coin and 1,000-coin bags from the Philadelphia and Denver mints were available, as were sets of two $10 face value rolls, one from each mint.

Guam, in the South Pacific at the southern end of the Mariana Islands, was occupied by Chamorro natives for millennia. The first Europeans landed there in 1521 with explorer Ferdinand Magellan. Spain claimed possession. From 1668 to 1815 the remote island was a supply and rest stop for Spanish ships on the route from Acapulco, Mexico, to Manila in the Philippines. When the United States won the Spanish-American War in 1898 it took possession of Guam as part of territorial expansion, rather than returning it to the natives. The same was true of many other places, although control of Cuba and the Philippine Islands was later relinquished.

During World War II Japan occupied he island for two years, until it was recaptured by American forces in 1944. It played a large role in the Pacific theater. In 1950 the residents of Guam were given American citizenship, and an island government was established.

2009-P, Guam

MS-64	MS-65	MS-66	MS-67	MS-68	MS-69
$0.50	$0.80	$2.65	$9.50	—	—

2009-P, Guam, Satin Finish

MS-64	MS-65	MS-66	MS-67	MS-68	MS-69
$2.65	$2.65	$4.05	$8.10	$16	$81

2009-D, Guam

MS-64	MS-65	MS-66	MS-67	MS-68	MS-69
$0.50	$0.80	$2.65	$9.50	—	—

2009-D, Guam, Satin Finish

MS-64	MS-65	MS-66	MS-67	MS-68	MS-69
$2.65	$2.65	$4.05	$8.10	$16	$81

2009-S, Guam, Proof, Clad

PF-67DC	PF-68DC	PF-69DC
$1.50	$4.05	$9.50

2009-S, Guam, Proof, Silver

PF-67DC	PF-68DC	PF-69DC
$7.20	$8.50	$11

2009, American Samoa

Circulation-Strike Mintage, Philadelphia: 42,600,000
Circulation-Strike Mintage, Philadelphia, Satin Finish: 784,614
Circulation-Strike Mintage, Denver: 39,600,000
Circulation-Strike Mintage, Denver, Satin Finish: 784,614
Proof Mintage, San Francisco, Clad: 2,113,478
Proof Mintage, San Francisco, Silver: 996,548

GSID: Circulation-strike, Philadelphia, 71270; Satin Finish Philadelphia, 82090; Circulation-strike, Denver, 71271; Satin Finish Denver, 82091; Proof Clad Deep Cameo, 71262; Proof Silver Deep Cameo, 71263

Specifics of the Reverse Design

Description: Items typically used in special Samoan ceremonies are seen in the foreground against a background image of the coastline. The items include the ava bowl, a whisk, and a staff. The ava bowl is used to make a ceremonial drink during important events. The whisk and staff represent the rank of a Samoan orator. The lettering includes the motto, "Samoa Muamua Le Atua," which means "Samoa, God is First" in the Samoan language.

Designer: Stephen Clark. *Mint sculptor-engraver who made the model:* Charles L. Vickers. *Engraver's initials and location:* CLV is underneath the whisk.

Story and Background of the Design

American Samoa Governor Togiola T.A. Tulafono solicited design ideas from the public and received about 60, which he and his review committee narrowed down to three. These included: (1) The ava bowl, whisk and staff and coconut tree, (2) A native with traditional Samoan tattoo holding an ava bowl, and (3) A traditional Samoan guest house with a head-dress and ava bowl. These were sent to the Mint, where sketches were created. Governor Tulafono picked his choice. That was forwarded to the secretary of the Treasury and approved on July 31, 2008.

Numismatic Commentary

The release of the American Samoa quarter through the Federal Reserve System took place on July 27, 2009. Perhaps as a testimony to the remote location of the island group the official launch ceremony did not take place until September 3. The event began at 10:00 in the morning on Utelei Beach on the island of Pago Pago. Deputy Director Andrew Brunhart represented the Mint. Governor Togiola T.A. Tulafono, First Lady Mary Ann Tulafono, and other dignitaries were on hand. Free quarters were given to those under 18 years of age. Rolls of $10 face value coins were available for purchase.

American Samoa is comprised of a group of five islands and two coral atolls in the far reaches of the South Pacific about 2,300 miles southwest of Hawaii and 2,700 miles northeast of Australia. The islands had been populated by natives for millennia until Europeans began arriving in the early 18th century and introducing their ways. In the 1830s it was visited by members of the London Missionary Society and by traders. In 1899 under the Treaty of Berlin, the United Kingdom and Germany gave the United States rights to the eastern islands area, with rights to the western islands retained by Germany, with acts of cession in 1900 and 1904. The United States established a military base. These acts of cession officially ratified years later in 1929. Most residents can speak both English and the Samoan language.

2009-P, American Samoa

MS-64	MS-65	MS-66	MS-67	MS-68	MS-69
$0.50	$0.80	$2.65	$9.50	$960	—

2009-P, American Samoa, Satin Finish

MS-64	MS-65	MS-66	MS-67	MS-68	MS-69
$2.65	$2.65	$4.05	$8.10	$16	$81

2009-D, American Samoa

MS-64	MS-65	MS-66	MS-67	MS-68	MS-69
$0.50	$0.80	$2.65	$9.50	—	—

2009-D, American Samoa, Satin Finish

MS-64	MS-65	MS-66	MS-67	MS-68	MS-69
$2.65	$2.65	$4.05	$8.10	$13.50	$47

2009-S, American Samoa, Proof, Clad

PF-67DC	PF-68DC	PF-69DC
$1.50	$4.05	$9.50

2009-S, American Samoa, Proof, Silver

PF-67DC	PF-68DC	PF-69DC
$7.20	$8.50	$11

2009, U.S. Virgin Islands

Circulation-Strike Mintage, Philadelphia: 41,000,000
Circulation-Strike Mintage, Philadelphia, Satin Finish: 784,614
Circulation-Strike Mintage, Denver: 41,000,000
Circulation-Strike Mintage, Denver, Satin Finish: 784,614
Proof Mintage, San Francisco, Clad: 2,113,478
Proof Mintage, San Francisco, Silver: 996,548
GSID: Circulation-strike, Philadelphia, 71272; Satin Finish Philadelphia, 82092; Circulation-strike, Denver, 71273; Satin Finish Denver, 82093; Proof Clad Deep Cameo, 71264; Proof Silver Deep Cameo, 70671

Specifics of the Reverse Design

Description: A bird, known as the banana quit, is pictured next to the Yellow Cedar flower. Behind the bird is a tyre palm, a tree native to the islands. The background includes an outline of the three main islands. The motto "United in Pride and Hope" is lettered on the reverse.

Designer: Joseph F. Menna, who was also the sculptor-engraver who made the model. *Engraver's initials and location:* JFM appears below the right tip of the island.

Story and Background of the Design

Governor John P. de Jongh Jr. established a review committee and encouraged citizens to submit design ideas in writing. Three were semi-finalists: (1) Yellow Breast and Yellow Cedar ("Virgin Islands Beauty"), (2) A male conch shell blower, and (3) Three women symbolizing the three major islands. These were sent to the Mint.

Sketches were returned and submitted to citizens for voting, with Virgin Islands Beauty being the favorite. The secretary of the Treasury approved the design on July 31, 2008.

Numismatic Commentary

The Federal Reserve released the new quarters on September 28, 2009, in advance of the official launch ceremony on October 9. The event began at 9:30 in the morning at Emancipation Gardens in the town of Charlotte Amalie on St. Thomas. On hand was

Deputy Director Andrew Brunhart representing the Mint, U.S. Congresswoman Donna Christensen, and Governor John P. de Jongh Jr. Lieutenant Governor Francis gave a talk outlining the history of the islands, including:

> Our rich culture and history has been memorialized on a coin that will be in circulation for generations. Be proud that you can carry a piece of Virgin Islands history in your pocket and let that be an inspiration to do everything we can to keep our islands clean and beautiful, to keep our community safe, to work together towards progress and to continue to be people who are united in pride and hope.

After the ceremony and entertainment that included music and dance performances, free quarters were given out to the younger set. Reflective of modern technology, highlights of the event were made available on YouTube, this being true of certain other launch ceremonies as well.

On the evening before, a one-hour Coin Collectors Forum was held starting at 6:00 in the evening at the University of the Virgin Islands, Administration and Conference Center, #2 John Brewers Bay, St. Thomas.

The islands now known as the United States Virgin Islands are in the Caribbean Sea east of Puerto Rico. They were first explored by Christopher Columbus in 1493. Home to the Arawak, Taino, and later the Carib Indians, they were colonized by Denmark beginning in 1666 and became known as the Danish West Indies.

During the Napoleonic Wars in the early 19th century the islands were occupied by the British intermittently from 1801 to 1815. In 1917 for $25 million the United States purchased three large islands—St. Croix, St. Thomas, and St. John—and about 50 islets. In 1927 residents were granted American citizenship. Under a congressional act of 1954 the islands were given a large degree of self-government, with executive, legislative, and judicial branches. For many years tourism has been the main industry and in recent times accounted for about 70 percent of employment.

2009-P, U.S. Virgin Islands

MS-64	MS-65	MS-66	MS-67	MS-68	MS-69
$0.50	$0.80	$2.65	$9.50	—	—

2009-P, U.S. Virgin Islands, Satin Finish

MS-64	MS-65	MS-66	MS-67	MS-68	MS-69
$2.65	$2.65	$4.05	$8.10	$13.50	$34

2009-D, U.S. Virgin Islands

MS-64	MS-65	MS-66	MS-67	MS-68	MS-69
$0.50	$0.80	$2.65	$9.50	—	—

2009-D, U.S. Virgin Islands, Satin Finish

MS-64	MS-65	MS-66	MS-67	MS-68	MS-69
$2.65	$2.65	$4.05	$8.10	$19	$108

2009-S, U.S. Virgin Islands, Proof, Clad

PF-67DC	PF-68DC	PF-69DC
$1.50	$4.05	$9.50

2009-S, U.S. Virgin Islands, Proof, Silver

PF-67DC	PF-68DC	PF-69DC
$7.20	$8.50	$11

2009, Northern Mariana Islands

Circulation-Strike Mintage, Philadelphia: 35,200,000
Circulation-Strike Mintage, Philadelphia, Satin Finish: 784,614
Circulation-Strike Mintage, Denver: 86,000,000
Circulation-Strike Mintage, Denver, Satin Finish: 784,614
Proof Mintage, San Francisco, Clad: 37,600,000
Proof Mintage, San Francisco, Silver: 996,548
GSID: Circulation-strike, Philadelphia, 71274; Satin Finish Philadelphia, 82094; Circulation-strike, Denver, 71275; Satin Finish Denver, 82095; Proof Clad Deep Cameo, 71267; Proof Silver Deep Cameo, 70669

Specifics of the Reverse Design

Description: A two-piece stone pillar known as a Latte appears amongst coconut trees, wild plants, native birds, and a sailing vessel. A teibwo (Pacific basil) frames the design.

Designer: Richard Masters. *Mint sculptor-engraver who made the model:* Phebe Hemphill. *Engraver's initials and location:* PH is to the right of the teibwo.

Story and Background of the Design

The Northern Mariana Islands Quarter Commission was established and invited the public to submit written ideas of motifs. These were narrowed down to three semifinalists. Two showed the Latte stone with a Carolinian canoe and the third depicted the World War II landing of the U.S. Marines and an amphibious tractor on a beach with a destroyer outside a reef. Governor Benigno R. Fitial made the choice, which was forwarded to Washington and approved by the secretary of the Treasury on July 31, 2008.

Numismatic Commentary

The new quarters were released by the Federal Reserve System on November 30, 2009, well in advance of the launch ceremony held on December 9. That event took place in American Memorial Park in Garapan on the island of Saipan. The celebration started at 8:00 in the evening, an unusual time of day for such.

On hand were Deputy Mint Director Andrew Brunhart and Governor Fitial, each wearing a "mwar," symbolic of the islands' tradition. Music and other entertainment were provided by local groups.

The 15 islands in the western Pacific Ocean were held by Spain until 1898, after which they were sold to Germany. In 1914 Japan seized them, a takeover officially recognized in 1921 by the League of Nations. During World War II American forces occupied them. In 1947 they were included in the U.S. Trust Territory of the Pacific Islands. In 1975 residents of the islands approved the status as a United States commonwealth, which was made official by the signature of President Gerald Ford in 1976.

2009-P, Northern Mariana Islands

MS-64	MS-65	MS-66	MS-67	MS-68	MS-69
$0.50	$0.80	$2.65	$9.50	$715	$2,190

2009-D, Northern Mariana Islands

MS-64	MS-65	MS-66	MS-67	MS-68	MS-69
$0.50	$0.80	$2.65	$9.50	$845	$1,500

2009-S, Northern Mariana Islands, Proof, Clad

PF-67DC	PF-68DC	PF-69DC
$1.50	$4.05	$9.50

2009-P, Northern Mariana Islands, Satin Finish

MS-64	MS-65	MS-66	MS-67	MS-68	MS-69
$2.65	$2.65	$4.05	$8.10	$16	$68

2009-D, Northern Mariana Islands, Satin Finish

MS-64	MS-65	MS-66	MS-67	MS-68	MS-69
$2.65	$2.65	$4.05	$8.10	$13.50	$47

2009-S, Northern Mariana Islands, Proof, Silver

PF-67DC	PF-68DC	PF-69DC
$7.20	$8.50	$11

10

America the Beautiful and Crossing the Delaware Quarters, 2010–2021: Analysis by Date and Mintmark

THE AMERICA THE BEAUTIFUL PROGRAM

Aware of the wonderful success of the 50 State Quarters Program, even including the somewhat lackluster interest in the D.C. and territories coins at the end, Representative Michael Castle initiated and promoted a new series. This became H.R. 6184—America's Beautiful National Parks Quarter Dollar Coin Act of 2008. This became PL 110-456 and was signed by President George W. Bush on December 23, 2008.

Oops!

After the fact it was realized that some states did not have a national park!

Behind the scenes regrouping took place, and these became known as America the Beautiful quarters. States that did not have national parks were searched for a national something-or-other, such as a national historic site, or river way, or wildlife preserve.

This resulted in the showcasing of many places that hardly anyone had ever heard of—the Chickasaw National Recreation Area (2011), El Yunque National Forest (2011), Kisatchie National Forest (2015), and Bombay Hook National Wildlife Refuge (2015) being several examples. As mentioned in my introduction, many of these places would be unknown even to winners of *Jeopardy!*

This was and is a plus situation for anyone who receives a quarter who is interested in learning more. We all know about Yellowstone, Yosemite, Grand Canyon, and some other subjects, but the obscure places invite study.

Some designs do not tell all. For example, the 2013 New Hampshire quarter only says WHITE MOUNTAIN. Depicted is a mountain with a lake in the foreground. There is no peak called White Mountain. Shown is Mount Chocorua, not mentioned either on the coin or the official Mint news releases concerning it. What is intended is the White Mountain National Forest, a range of peaks of which Mount Washington is one of the highest and Mount Chocorua is one of the lowest.

Such things add a lot to the enjoyment of collecting the quarters.

On the negative side, quarters with places few had ever heard of did not engender much public interest. Mintages of the various issues fell far below those of the State quarters issues. Not simplifying matters is the Federal Reserve System's program—which in a way makes sense—of supplying new quarters to member banks that request them. If a bank needs coins it is sent the supply currently on hand, which like it or not has nothing to do with the location of the bank in relation to the showcased subject. When the New Hampshire quarters were released in 2013 I did not learn of a single bank in the state that received a supply—as no new coins were needed.

Beginning with Hot Springs National Park in 2010, the America the Beautiful subjects were issued in the chronological order in which they came under national protection. The Hot Springs were protected under federal authority beginning in 1832, the first such location. However, private businesses exploited the location by setting up private bathhouses (warm-water spas). It was not named as a national park until 1921. The illustration on the coin is of a modern (1936) building. Go figure, as they say! Again, all of this adds interest to the series for anyone who seeks to explore the coins in depth.

Beyond the complications mentioned, the selection of designs was often controversial, as reflected in this article by Debbie Bradley in *Numismatic News*, February 9, 2010:

Design Dilemma

The very features American parks have in common—mountains, streams, meadows—make them difficult to distinguish on coins. That's what the Commission of Fine Arts is wrestling with as it recommends designs for the 2011 coins in the "America the Beautiful" quarter series. At its January 21 meeting, the CFA reviewed reverse designs for quarters honoring Gettysburg National Military Park in Pennsylvania, Glacier National Park in Montana, Olympic National Park in Washington, Vicksburg National Military Park in Mississippi and Chickasaw National Recreation Area in Oklahoma. It recommended designs for only three of the quarters—Gettysburg, Glacier and Olympic—while giving support to a design for Vicksburg and asking for a redesign of the Chickasaw quarter.

CFA Secretary Tom Luebke said the CFA doesn't support what appears to be a tendency to take photographic images and use them as the basis for the coin design. That results in excessive detail and realism, which isn't appropriate for medallic design, he said. Coin design could instead emphasize key elements and possibly an abstraction or stylization of the iconic elements to convey the essence of the subject, he said… Although the U.S. Mint has adopted a template for the "America the Beautiful" quarters, the CFA is not pleased with the straight bottom in the design area because it is often in conflict with the design composition, Luebke said. And the placement of the state name and E PLURIBUS UNUM presents odd symmetry, he said. "But members acknowledged that is water under the dam," Luebke said.

In summary, for anyone with intellectual curiosity in combination with numismatic enthusiasm, these quarters have a lot to offer!

2010, Hot Springs National Park (AR)

Circulation-Strike Mintage, Philadelphia: 35,600,000
Circulation-Strike Mintage, Philadelphia, Satin Finish: 583,897
Circulation-Strike Mintage, Denver: 34,000,000
Circulation-Strike Mintage, Denver, Satin Finish: 583,897
Proof Mintage, San Francisco, Clad: 1,402,889
Proof Mintage, San Francisco, Silver: 859,417
GSID: Circulation-strike, Philadelphia, 70924; Satin Finish Philadelphia, 82096; Circulation-strike, Denver, 70925; Satin Finish Denver, 82097; Proof Clad Deep Cameo, 71179; Proof Silver Deep Cameo, 71180

Specifics of the Reverse Design

Description: The Park Headquarters building is shown in the background with a thermal-spring fountain in the foreground. The building in the Spanish Colonial Revival style was completed in 1936. Shown to the right of the Headquarters door is the National Park Service (NPS) emblem.

Designer: Don Everhart. *Mint sculptor-engraver who made the model:* Joseph F. Menna. *Designers's initials and location:* DE is on the bottom left of the base of the fountain. *Engraver's initials and location:* JLM is on the bottom right of the base of the fountain.

Story and Background of the Design

Descriptions were created for four different designs and sent to the Commission of Fine Arts and the Citizens Coin Advisory Committee. The CFA favored the one that was adopted, as did Mint Director Edmund C. Moy. The CCAC liked one that showed the fountain as well as trees and grass. Secretary of the Treasury Tim Geithner consulted with Moy and endorsed his suggestion that became the final design.

Numismatic Commentary

The launch ceremony was held on April 20, 2010, the 178th anniversary of federal oversight on this popular resort. On hand were Mint Director Edmund Moy, Hot Springs National Park Superintendent Josie Fernandez, and other officials. Single coins were given free to those who indicated they were under 18 years and younger of age. $10 rolls of coins could be purchased for face value. Coin sales began the night before at a forum for collectors and others interested.

The U.S. Mint offered coins by mail in two-roll sets of one $10 roll from the Philadelphia and Denver Mints, $32.95 for $20 face value. Bags of 100 coins from either mint were priced at $39.95. Shipping of $4.95 per order was extra.[1]

This design was also used for the first of the continuing entries in the 5-ounce silver bullion program.

The design drew mixed reviews. Why a relatively modern building from 1936 was used instead of a classical bathhouse was questioned by some. One irreverent reader of *Coin World* sated that the motif appeared to show "a toilet sitting in front of a mausoleum."[2]

Hot Springs National Park is unique among national parks in that it is in the middle of a city and mainly consists of commercial buildings. Located in the Zig Zag Mountains about 55 miles northwest of the state capital of Little Rock, the Hot Springs were a popular spa and resort destination in the 19th century, continuing into the 20th. Today, Bathhouse Row, as it is called, extends along Central Avenue. The facilities are restored to their appearance of years ago.

In a 10-acre spread, 47 underground springs emerge through the rocks to issue water at temperatures up to 143 degrees Fahrenheit. The output of about 700,000 gallons daily is gathered at a central part and is distributed by pipes to bathhouses and fountains.

The area has a rich history dating from quarrying and other activities by Native Americans who called it the "Valley of the Vapors." It was "discovered" by Hernando DeSoto in the 16th century, but attracted little notice. The Dunbar-Hunter Expedition dispatched by President Thomas Jefferson in 1803, following the purchase of the Louisiana Territory in 1803, reported on the area. It became known for alleged healing power from its warm water, and was designated as a national site in 1832, a place on the calendar that gave it the number one spot in the new program of quarters. This designation did not do much to prevent exploitation of the area, and private interests set up bathhouses. Some federal regulation began in 1877, to regulate the flow to the bath houses. In retrospect that is what spawned great commercial growth in the area. Had it been left alone as a nature preserve its appearance today would be much different as would be the motif on the quarter. In 1921 Congress changed the name of the area to Hot Springs National Park.

Today the large town of Hot Springs continues to provide accommodations and other resources for visitors and it remains a popular tourist attraction.

2010-P, Hot Springs National Park (AR)

MS-64	MS-65	MS-66	MS-67	MS-68
$0.50	$0.80	$2.65	$16	—

2010-P, Hot Springs National Park (AR), Satin Finish

MS-64	MS-65	MS-66	MS-67	MS-68
$2.65	$4.05	$4.75	$6.80	$9.50

2010-D, Hot Springs National Park (AR)

MS-64	MS-65	MS-66	MS-67	MS-68
$0.50	$0.80	$2.65	$16	—

2010-D, Hot Springs National Park (AR), Satin Finish

MS-64	MS-65	MS-66	MS-67	MS-68
$2.65	$4.05	$4.75	$6.80	$9.50

2010-S, Hot Springs National Park (AR), Proof, Clad

PF-67DC	PF-68DC	PF-69DC
$1.50	$4.05	$9.50

2010-S, Hot Springs National Park (AR), Proof, Silver

PF-67DC	PF-68DC	PF-69DC
$7.20	$8.50	$11

2010, Yellowstone National Park (WY)

Circulation-Strike Mintage, Philadelphia: 33,600,000
Circulation-Strike Mintage, Philadelphia, Satin Finish: 583,897
Circulation-Strike Mintage, Denver: 34,800,000
Circulation-Strike Mintage, Denver, Satin Finish: 583,897
Proof Mintage, San Francisco, Clad: 1,404,259
Proof Mintage, San Francisco, Silver: 859,417
GSID: Circulation-strike, Philadelphia, 70926; Satin Finish Philadelphia, 82098; Circulation-strike, Denver, 70927; Satin Finish Denver, 82099; Proof Clad Deep Cameo, 71181; Proof Silver Deep Cameo, 71182

Specifics of the Reverse Design

Description: Old Faithful geyser and two bison—one mature in the foreground and another located closer toward the middle scenery alongside the geyser.

Designer: Don Everhart, who was also the sculptor-engraver who made the model.
Engraver's initials and location: DE is to the left of the foreground bison, beneath the geyser.

Story and Background of the Design

The Yellowstone National Park quarter had three design candidates that made it to the final round to be reviewed by the Commission of Fine Arts and the Citizens Coinage Advisory Committee, among other parties. The Commission of Fine Arts outright rejected all design candidates for the coin, stating that all were of poor quality, though they did agree that the use of Old Faithful was appropriate. The CCAC showed a strong preference for the first design candidate, which features bison in the foreground and the background, as well as the Old Faithful geyser mid-eruption. They felt the design beautifully showcased both the landscape and the wildlife of the park; Secretary Geithner agreed, choosing this design for the official park quarter.

Numismatic Commentary

The official launch ceremony took place on June 3, 2010, within the park, two days after the coins were released into circulation through the Federal Reserve. The venue was the Recreation Hall in the Old Faithful Lodge, a change from the intended outdoor ceremony in front of the Old Faithful geyser, dictated by the weather.

The logistics presented challenges—as bison freely roam the park and the nearest banks that could help with the distribution were each a two-hour drive away—one in West Yellowstone, Montana, and the other in Cody, Wyoming. In a change from the normal, the distribution was done by Xanterra, the park management company.

Representing the Mint at the ceremony were Director Ed Moy and several others from his office. Superintendent Suzanne Lewis of Yellowstone Park welcomed visitors. A Yellowstone historian, Paul Schullery, spoke about the traditions of the park.

At the ceremony $44,000 of the new quarters were given out at face value to the crowd in attendance, except for individual coins presented for free to those 18 years or younger. The post office set up a facility in which the paper wrappers on rolls could receive a special cancellation, and about 1,100 rolls were so imprinted.

An ugly incident occurred when an authorized person appeared and tried to sell the attendees Hot Springs National Park quarters that he had brought with him. The problem was that he did not have the license required to vend things on federal property. He was arrested and his coins and sales proceeds were confiscated.

Unlike many of the later America the Beautiful quarter subjects, Yellowstone was very familiar to the American public. This popularity no doubt accounted for the mintage figures being higher than for the first coin in the America the Beautiful series.

Production of the Yellowstone quarters was completed in July 2010, after which the three mints switched their efforts to the next issue, for Yellowstone National Park.

In a letter to *Coin World*, July 12, 2010, Jerome Diekmann, who had visited this and Yosemite several times, took issue with both designs. "There are no mountain peaks behind old Faithful, as shown on the coin. All the surrounding territory consists of rolling hills." Further, what with the bison depicted on the 2005 nickels, on some of the State quarters, and on gold remakes of the 1913 nickel, anyone from a foreign country contemplating our coins might think that our country was overrun with these animals!

Yellowstone National Park, mainly located in the State of Wyoming, but with some acreage in Montana and Idaho, was established as such by legislation signed by President Ulysses S. Grant on March 1, 1872. It was the first national park in America. The area of 3,468 square miles is a wonderland of natural features, most prominently thermal springs and geysers. Of the last the best known is Old Faithful, which at intervals throws a high column of steam and water into the sky, to the delight of tourists.

Wildlife are another attraction, with American bison roaming freely throughout the park along with grizzly bears, wolves, elk, and many other species. Over 1,000 archaeological sites have been studied by scientists. Hotels and other facilities accommodate and serve tourists in this, one of the most popular National Parks.[3]

2010-P, Yellowstone National Park (WY)

MS-64	MS-65	MS-66	MS-67	MS-68
$0.50	$0.80	$2.65	$16	—

2010-P, Yellowstone National Park (WY), Satin Finish

MS-64	MS-65	MS-66	MS-67	MS-68
$2.65	$4.05	$4.75	$6.80	$9.50

2010-D, Yellowstone National Park (WY)

MS-64	MS-65	MS-66	MS-67	MS-68
$0.50	$0.80	$2.65	$16	—

2010-D, Yellowstone National Park (WY), Satin Finish

MS-64	MS-65	MS-66	MS-67	MS-68
$2.65	$4.05	$4.75	$6.80	$9.50

2010-S, Yellowstone National Park (WY), Proof, Clad

PF-67DC	PF-68DC	PF-69DC
$1.50	$4.05	$9.50

2010-S, Yellowstone National Park (WY), Proof, Silver

PF-67DC	PF-68DC	PF-69DC
$7.20	$8.50	$11

2010, Yosemite National Park (CA)

Circulation-Strike Mintage, Philadelphia: 35,200,000
Circulation-Strike Mintage, Philadelphia, Satin Finish: 583,897
Circulation-Strike Mintage, Denver: 34,800,000
Circulation-Strike Mintage, Denver, Satin Finish: 583,897
Proof Mintage, San Francisco, Clad: 1,401,522
Proof Mintage, San Francisco, Silver: 859,417

GSID: Circulation-strike, Philadelphia, 70928; Satin Finish Philadelphia, 82100; Circulation-strike, Denver, 70929; Satin Finish Denver, 82101; Proof Clad Deep Cameo, 71183; Proof Silver Deep Cameo, 71184

Specifics of the Reverse Design

Description: The obverse depicts the historic El Capitan, which rises more than 3,000 feet, above the Yosemite Valley floor and is the largest monolith of granite in the world. Half Dome, another Yosemite icon, was depicted on the California State quarter of 2005.

Designer: Joseph F. Menna, based on a photograph taken by park ranger Scott Gediman's wife, Bethany Gediman. *Mint sculptor-engraver who made the model:* Phebe Hemphill. *Designers's initials and location:* JFM is at the bottom of the log. *Engraver's initials and location:* PH is beneath the trees on the right.

Story and Background of the Design

Four design ideas were given to the Mint, and sketches were prepared by them. These were reviewed by the Commission of Fine Arts and the Citizens Coinage Advisory Committee. The CFA liked the Yosemite El Capitan motif the best, but suggested some changes, which were made. The motif was somewhat redundant as Yosemite had already been showcased on the 2005 California State quarter that depicted Half Dome. With dozens of national historic sites in the state, many wondered why Yosemite was chosen over such possibilities as the Redwood Forest, sites in the Gold Rush Country, or even Death Valley. Secretary of the Treasury Geithner approved the El Capitan motif, after which dies were made and coinage took place.

In a letter to *Coin World,* July 12, 2010, Jerome Diekmann criticized the published designs of the Yellowstone (see previous listing) and Yosemite quarters. For the last he said that El Capitan was shown with a slanted face rather than the correct vertical, the still water pond (?) in the foreground probably was intended to represent the rushing Merced River, and that other details were confusing. "If the Mint wants to show off our nation's parks, they should at least get them as they are."

The portrait of Washington was improved slightly in early 2010 by using the original plasters made in 1932 for John Flanagan's quarter, these adopted from Jean Antoine Houdon's bust of Washington taken from life at Mount Vernon in 1785. In *Coin World* Paul Gilkes commented:

> The most noticeably differing detail has often been the appearance of Washington's hair, sometimes derided as spaghetti-like on pre-2010 versions. Washington's hair has a softer look on the 2010 portrait, as it did on the original 1932 portrait. There was also a difference on the frosted devices in the 2010 version.[4]

Numismatic Commentary

The launch ceremony for the new coin took place at 11:00 in the morning on July 29, 2010, in front of the Yosemite Visitor's Center. Director Edmund C. Moy represented the Mint and was joined by other dignitaries, but no high government officials. Park Superintendent Don Neubacher commented: "This new quarter is yet another way that Yosemite's legacy will live on by reminding those who take home the Yosemite National Park quarter how special America's National Parks are."

Historian Tom Bopp was on hand to deliver the keynote speech telling of the park's background and legacy. About 1,200 people were on hand. Those 18 and younger were given free quarters. $10 bank-wrapped rolls were available for face value. The Federal Reserve had released the coins three days earlier on July 26.

Yosemite National Park in the Sierra Mountains in Northern California ranks with Yellowstone and Grand Canyon as extensive Western scenic areas under federal protection and open to the public. It covers 1,168 square miles and is comprised of forest, rocky prominences including El Capitan and Half Dome (earlier depicted on the California

State quarter), scenic waterfalls, and a rushing river. In 2016 for the first time in its history the park welcomed over five million visitors.

2010-P, Yosemite National Park (CA)

MS-64	MS-65	MS-66	MS-67	MS-68
$0.50	$0.80	$2.65	$16	—

2010-P, Yosemite National Park (CA), Satin Finish

MS-64	MS-65	MS-66	MS-67	MS-68
$2.65	$4.05	$4.75	$6.80	$9.50

2010-D, Yosemite National Park (CA)

MS-64	MS-65	MS-66	MS-67	MS-68
$0.50	$0.80	$2.65	$16	—

2010-D, Yosemite National Park (CA), Satin Finish

MS-64	MS-65	MS-66	MS-67	MS-68
$2.65	$4.05	$4.75	$6.80	$9.50

2010-S, Yosemite National Park (CA), Proof, Clad

PF-67DC	PF-68DC	PF-69DC
$1.50	$4.05	$9.50

2010-S, Yosemite National Park (CA), Proof, Silver

PF-67DC	PF-68DC	PF-69DC
$7.20	$8.50	$11

2010, Grand Canyon National Park (AZ)

Circulation-Strike Mintage, Philadelphia: 34,800,000

Circulation-Strike Mintage, Philadelphia, Satin Finish: 583,897

Circulation-Strike Mintage, Denver: 35,400,000

Circulation-Strike Mintage, Denver, Satin Finish: 583,897

Proof Mintage, San Francisco, Clad: 1,401,462

Proof Mintage, San Francisco, Silver: 859,417

GSID: Circulation-strike, Philadelphia, 70930; Satin Finish Philadelphia, 82102; Circulation-strike, Denver, 70931; Satin Finish Denver, 82103; Proof Clad Deep Cameo, 71185; Proof Silver Deep Cameo, 71186

Specifics of the Reverse Design

Description: A portion of the Grand Canyon can be seen, particularly the granaries above the Nankoweap Delta in Marble Canyon near the Colorado River. This official description was probably lost on most readers. The scene depicts canyon walls with the river below. The granaries were used ages earlier by Native Americans to store seeds.

Designer: Phebe Hemphill, who was also the sculptor-engraver who made the model. *Engraver's initials and location:* PH appears at the bottom of the design, above the second 0 in 2010.

Story and Background of the Design

Of the four design candidates for the Grand Canyon National Park quarter, one stood out as particularly exceptional to both the Commission of Fine Arts and the Citizens Coinage Advisory Committee. It shows views of the Colorado River with the canyon walls surrounding it. Both groups approved it as did the secretary of the Treasury.

Numismatic Commentary

On the South Rim of the Grand Canyon with the vast expanse of much of the national park in the background the official launch ceremony was conducted on September 21, 2010. Mint Director Edmund C. Moy was on hand, and with his usually cheery mien joined Steve Martin, park superintendent, and others. The area is a popular tourist spot located between the Hopi House and the Verkamp's Visitor Center, with a small airport and extensive parking nearby.

Quarters were given for free to the younger set, and all could purchase $10 rolls for face value. The official release into circulation by the Federal Reserve took place on September 20. Per usual, a Coin Collectors Forum was held the night before.[5]

Grand Canyon National Park is perhaps America's most famous scenic attraction from a global viewpoint. It is often considered to be one of the Seven Natural Wonders of the World. Comprising 1,902 square miles, it is, in essence, the Colorado River, the banks of which have been sculpted by millennia of erosion. In 2016 the park received nearly six million visitors, second only to the Great Smoky Mountains National Park in terms of national park attendance. The two are not directly comparable, for the first is in a relatively remote area, and the second is close to many population centers. In 1903 President Theodore Roosevelt visited and later wrote:

> The Grand Canyon fills me with awe. It is beyond comparison—beyond description; absolutely unparalleled through-out the wide world . . . Let this great wonder of nature remain as it now is. Do nothing to mar its grandeur, sublimity and loveliness. You cannot improve on it. But what you can do is to keep it for your children, your children's children, and all who come after you, as the one great sight which every American should see.

Through various steps under federal auspices, early efforts to make it a national park were not successful until 1919. In the meantime it was a magnet for tourists and was largely protected.

Today the area includes Lake Mead, created by the Hoover Dam, an engineering marvel. The water of the Colorado River is divided by legislation between various users, most importantly via aqueducts to California and parts of Arizona. Relatively little flow remains at the point at which it empties into the Gulf of Mexico.

2010-P, Grand Canyon National Park (AZ)

MS-64	MS-65	MS-66	MS-67	MS-68
$0.50	$0.80	$2.65	$16	—

2010-P, Grand Canyon National Park (AZ), Satin Finish

MS-64	MS-65	MS-66	MS-67	MS-68
$2.65	$4.05	$4.75	$6.80	$9.50

2010-D, Grand Canyon National Park (AZ)

MS-64	MS-65	MS-66	MS-67	MS-68
$0.50	$0.80	$2.65	$16	—

2010-D, Grand Canyon National Park (AZ), Satin Finish

MS-64	MS-65	MS-66	MS-67	MS-68
$2.65	$4.05	$4.75	$6.80	$9.50

2010-S, Grand Canyon National Park (AZ), Proof, Clad

PF-67DC	PF-68DC	PF-69DC
$1.50	$4.05	$9.50

2010-S, Grand Canyon National Park (AZ), Proof, Silver

PF-67DC	PF-68DC	PF-69DC
$7.20	$8.50	$11

2010, Mt. Hood National Forest (OR)

Circulation-Strike Mintage, Philadelphia: 34,400,000
Circulation-Strike Mintage, Philadelphia, Satin Finish: 583,897
Circulation-Strike Mintage, Denver: 34,400,000
Circulation-Strike Mintage, Denver, Satin Finish: 583,897
Proof Mintage, San Francisco, Clad: 1,398,106
Proof Mintage, San Francisco, Silver: 859,417

GSID: Circulation-strike, Philadelphia, 70932; Satin Finish Philadelphia, 70932; Circulation-strike, Denver, 70933; Satin Finish Denver, 82105; Proof Clad Deep Cameo, 71187; Proof Silver Deep Cameo, 71188

Specifics of the Reverse Design

Description: The Lost Lake is in the foreground with a large image of Mount Hood in the distance.

Designer: Phebe Hemphill, who was also the sculptor-engraver who made the model. *Engraver's initials and location:* PH appears below the treeline on the right.

Story and Background of the Design

Following what proved to be the typical scenario, designs selected to pick the honored topic were sent to the Mint to be made into official sketches. These were reviewed by the Commission of Fine Arts and the Citizens Coinage Advisory Committee. Readers of *Coin World* and *Numismatic News* often gave opinions and criticisms, but such outside commentary was not welcomed by the two committees.

The Mount Hood design was not at all controversial, and in due course the secretary of the Treasury gave it his approval.

Numismatic Commentary

The Federal Reserve System released the new Mount Hood National Park quarters beginning on November 15. The launch ceremony for the Mount Hood quarter took place two days later beginning at 10:00 in the morning on November 17, 2010. The venue was the World Forestry Center, 4033 S.W. Canyon Road, in Portland, not close to the mountain, but with the peak prominent in the distance to the east. This was a departure, for most such ceremonies were held near the park or other area honored.

About 700 people were on hand. Representing the Mint was Deputy Director Andrew D. Brunhart, a familiar figure at such events. Peter the Eagle, the Mint mascot was on hand. Kermit the Spokesfrog, used for certain earlier State quarters ceremonies, was history by then. Dignitaries included Gary Larsen, supervisor of Mount Hood National Forest; Oregon State Treasurer Ted Wheeler, representing Oregon Governor Ted Kulongoski; Hillary Barbour, field representative for U.S. Representative Early Blumenauer (D-Oregon); and Native Americans representing the Confederated Tribes of Warm Springs and the Confederated Tribes of Grand Ronde.[6]

Mount Hood, an ancient volcano, is the dominant landmark of its area. Located about 60 miles east of Portland, Oregon, it is visible for many miles in all directions

The national forest comprises over a million acres of mostly wilderness, of which about a third is devoted to old-growth forest. Part of the area was known as the Bull Run National Forest in 1892. After it was merged into the Cascade National Forest in 1908 it was called the Oregon National Forest. The present name was applied in 1924.

2010-P, Mt. Hood National Forest (OR)

MS-64	MS-65	MS-66	MS-67	MS-68
$0.50	$0.80	$2.65	$16	—

2010-P, Mt. Hood National Forest (OR), Satin Finish

MS-64	MS-65	MS-66	MS-67	MS-68
$2.65	$4.05	$4.75	$6.80	$9.50

2010-D, Mt. Hood National Forest (OR)

MS-64	MS-65	MS-66	MS-67	MS-68
$0.50	$0.80	$2.65	$16	—

2010-D, Mt. Hood National Forest (OR), Satin Finish

MS-64	MS-65	MS-66	MS-67	MS-68
$2.65	$4.05	$4.75	$5.40	$8.10

2010-S, Mt. Hood National Forest (OR), Proof, Clad

PF-67DC	PF-68DC	PF-69DC
$1.50	$4.05	$9.50

2010-S, Mt. Hood National Forest (OR), Proof, Silver

PF-67DC	PF-68DC	PF-69DC
$7.20	$8.50	$11

2011, Gettysburg National Military Park (PA)

Circulation-Strike Mintage, Philadelphia: 30,800,000
Circulation-Strike Mintage, Denver: 30,400,000
Proof Mintage, San Francisco, Clad: 1,273,068
Proof Mintage, San Francisco, Silver: 722,076

GSID: Circulation-strike, Philadelphia, 77700; Circulation-strike, Denver, 70935; Proof Clad Deep Cameo, 71189; Proof Silver Deep Cameo, 71190.

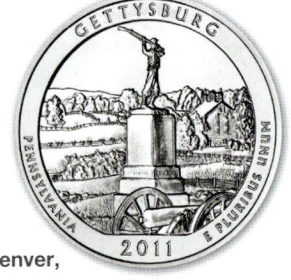

Specifics of the Reverse Design

Description: Depicted is the 72nd Pennsylvania Infantry Monument found on the battle line of the Union Army at Cemetery Ridge.

Designer: Joel Iskowitz. *Mint sculptor-engraver who made the model:* Phebe Hemphill. *Designers's initials and location:* JI is at the left, adjacent to the Y in Pennsylvania. *Engraver's initials and location:* PH is above the fence on the right.

Story and Background of the Design

At a meeting held in Washington on January 26, 2010, members of the Citizens Coinage Advisory Committee reviewed designs for the 2011 America the Beautiful quarters. Praise was heaped on most, but members were sharply divided on the Gettysburg design. Opponents suggested that all of the four designs submitted be rejected and thought that the artists at the Mint could come up with a more dramatic motif on their own.[7]

This had no practical effect, and Secretary of the Treasury Timothy Geithner picked the first choice of the CCAC, which became coinage reality. Many historians and numismatists groaned.

Numismatic Commentary

The official launch of the 2011 Gettysburg National Military Park quarter dollar took place at the Gettysburg National Military Park Visitor Center in Gettysburg. B.B. Craig, the Mint's associate director of sales and marketing, represented that institution. Other dignitaries included Governor Tom Corbett and first lady Susan Manbeck Corbett; Bob Kirby, superintendent of the park; and Barbara Finfrock, vice chairperson of the Gettysburg Foundation.

On the night before, Mint officials hosted a Collectors Coin Forum at the Ford Motor Company Fund Educational Center at the Gettysburg National Military Park Museum and Visitor Center.[8]

The Gettysburg National Military Park preserves the site of the 1863 Battle of Gettysburg, the pivotal event of the Civil War in which Confederate troops headed into Pennsylvania and the North were repelled by Union forces. The cost was thousands of lives.

Today the park includes the Gettysburg National Cemetery, monuments to the various divisions that engaged in combat, and a visitor center with tens of thousands of artifacts. Presently wooded areas are being restored to the mostly treeless landscape of 1863. It was in this location in 1864 that, following a two-hour oration by Edward Everett, President Abraham Lincoln gave his brief Gettysburg Address that he said would be little remembered.

Efforts to acquire additional land to expand the park continue. Interest in Civil War history has been intense for many years. More books have been written about Lincoln than for any other president and about the Civil War than for any other conflict. Curiously, most leading Civil War historians know very little about money of the era—Demand Notes, Legal Tender Notes, National Bank Notes, Civil War tokens, sutler tokens, Postage Currency, Fractional Currency, encased postage stamps, scrip, Confederate paper money, and other items—the richest area in American numismatics.

2011-P, Gettysburg National Military Park (PA)

MS-64	MS-65	MS-66	MS-67	MS-68
$0.50	$0.80	$2.65	$16	—

2011-D, Gettysburg National Military Park (PA)

MS-64	MS-65	MS-66	MS-67	MS-68
$0.50	$0.80	$2.65	$16	—

2011-S, Gettysburg National Military Park (PA), Proof, Clad

PF-67DC	PF-68DC	PF-69DC
$1.50	$4.05	$9.50

2011-S, Gettysburg National Military Park (PA), Proof, Silver

PF-67DC	PF-68DC	PF-69DC
$7.20	$8.50	$11

2011, Glacier National Park (MT)

Circulation-Strike Mintage, Philadelphia: 30,400,000

Circulation-Strike Mintage, Denver: 31,200,000

Proof Mintage, San Francisco, Clad: 1,269,422

Proof Mintage, San Francisco, Silver: 722,076

GSID: Circulation-strike, Philadelphia, 70936; Circulation-strike, Denver, 70937; Proof Clad Deep Cameo, 71191; Proof Silver Deep Cameo, 71192

Specifics of the Reverse Design

Description: A mountain goat is seen climbing along the rugged terrain of the Glacier National Park.

Designer: Barbara Fox. *Mint sculptor-engraver who made the model:* Charles L. Vickers. *Designers's initials and location:* BF is at the bottom right beneath the trees. *Engraver's initials and location:* CLV is beneath the goat's back hoof.

Story and Background of the Design

Only three design candidates were submitted to the Commission of Fine Arts and the Citizens Coinage Advisory Committee in January 2011 for review for the 2012 Glacier National Park quarter. Both groups chose the same design candidate to recommend to the secretary of the Treasury because they thought the combination of the iconic mountain goat with the mountains in the background would translate into a very appealing coin. The CFA also commented that the goat was emblematic of the park, and that its image in the foreground provides scale for the mountains in the background of the coin. For a change, a large quadruped other than a bison was chosen.

Numismatic Commentary

The launch ceremony for the new quarter was held starting at 1:00 in the afternoon of April 13, 2011, at Columbia Falls High School in Columbia Falls, Montana. Representing the Mint was B.B. Craig, the Mint's associate director for sales and marketing. Superintendent Charles Cartwright of the park joined others in greeting about a thousand people—an unusually large audience for a quarter in the America the Beautiful series.

Members of the younger set received free quarters. All were allowed to purchase $10 rolls of quarters for face value, maximum 10 rolls per person, at a stand set up by the Freedom Bank of Columbia Falls. A Coin Collectors Forum was held at 5:00 p.m. the day before at National Park Community Building within the park. By that time the quarters had been in general release by the Federal Reserve System since April 4.[9]

Glacier National Park in Montana is on the border with the Canadian provinces of Alberta and British Columbia. It comprises over 16,000 square miles of land and includes two sub-ranges of the Rocky Mountains, over 130 named lakes and hundreds of smaller ones, and many species of plants and animals—a natural paradise. In the mid-19th century there were about 150 glaciers of various sizes in the district, but due to global warming only about two dozen remain today. It has been predicted that if weather patterns persist, all may be gone by the year 2030.

The park was officially established by the government on May 11, 1910. The Great Northern Railway established hotels, chalets, and other facilities, and it has been a draw for tourists and vacationers ever since. The Going-to-the-Sun Road was completed in 1932 and later designated as a National Historic Civil Engineering Landmark.

The park is a magnet for tourists and nature lovers. About 350 structures, some still in use, are designated as National Historic Landmarks.

2011-P, Glacier National Park (MT)

MS-64	MS-65	MS-66	MS-67	MS-68
$0.50	$0.80	$2.65	$48.50	$780

2011-D, Glacier National Park (MT)

MS-64	MS-65	MS-66	MS-67	MS-68
$0.50	$0.80	$2.65	$40.50	—

2011-S, Glacier National Park (MT), Proof, Clad

PF-67DC	PF-68DC	PF-69DC
$1.50	$4.05	$9.50

2011-S, Glacier National Park (MT), Proof, Silver

PF-67DC	PF-68DC	PF-69DC
$7.20	$8.50	$11

2011, Olympic National Park (WA)

Circulation-Strike Mintage, Philadelphia: 30,400,000
Circulation-Strike Mintage, Denver: 30,600,000
Proof Mintage, San Francisco, Clad: 1,268,231
Proof Mintage, San Francisco, Silver: 722,076
GSID: Circulation-strike, Philadelphia, 77701; Circulation-strike, Denver, 70939; Proof Clad Deep Cameo, 71193; Proof Silver Deep Cameo, 71194

Specifics of the Reverse Design

Description: One of the park's most iconic creatures, the Roosevelt elk, is seen standing on a gravel bar of the Hoh River. In the distance is Mount Olympus.

Designer: Susan Gamble. *Mint sculptor-engraver who made the model:* Michael Gaudioso. *Designers's initials and location:* SG is to the right of the elk's rear hoof. *Engraver's initials and location:* MG is on the tip of the land to the right of the elk.

Story and Background of the Design

Four designs relating to the Olympic National Park were submitted to the Commission of Fine Arts and to the Citizens Coinage Advisory Committee. Both groups picked the same rendering. It was forwarded to Secretary of the Treasury Timothy Geithner, who met with Mint Director Edmund C. Moy, after which it was approved.

Numismatic Commentary

The launch ceremony for the new quarter was held on Flag Day, June 14, at the City Pier in Port Angeles, Washington. Children, who also received free quarters, led approximately 600 youngsters and an equal number of adults in the Pledge of Allegiance. Cool weather for the season and overcast skies were not a deterrent. On hand from the Mint was B.B. Craig, an associate director for sales and marketing, who commented:

> The beauty of Olympic National Park is in its biodiversity, three distinct ecosystems of sub-alpine, coastal and forest. There is no other national site like it, and the new Olympic National Park quarter will connect America to its natural splendor.

Vanessa Fuller of the Port Angeles Regional Chamber of Commerce was emcee. Mike Gregoire, first gentleman of the state (husband of the governor), was introduced. Park Superintendent Karen Gustin continued with more details, telling of the three distinct ecosystems. An advantage of the park was that visitors could see many different aspects of nature in a relatively short time.

In an unusual touch, Gregoire and Gustin were each given two quarters made at the Philadelphia and Denver mints on the first day of production, framed with a large image of the artwork and a souvenir—a very rare numismatic item!

Entertainment included a student band and a group of regional Native American musicians.[10]

Olympic National Park on the Olympic Peninsula in the state of Washington is remarkable for its varied weather, flora, and fauna. There are three ecosystems: (1) Sub-alpine forest and wildflower meadows, (2) Temperate forest, and (2) Rocky shore area of the Pacific Ocean. The entire area is well preserved, as nature intended. As such it is a magnet for tourists and scholars.

On March 2, 1909, President Theodore Roosevelt, with two days to go before he left office, designated it as the Mount Olympus National Monument. On June 29, 1938, President Franklin D. Roosevelt gave it national park status. In 1988 Congress marked about 95 percent of the park as the Olympic Wilderness.

2011-P, Olympic National Park (WA)

MS-64	MS-65	MS-66	MS-67	MS-68
$0.50	$0.80	$2.65	$16	—

2011-D, Olympic National Park (WA)

MS-64	MS-65	MS-66	MS-67	MS-68
$0.50	$0.80	$2.65	$16	—

2011-S, Olympic National Park (WA), Proof, Clad

PF-67DC	PF-68DC	PF-69DC
$1.50	$4.05	$9.50

2011-S, Olympic National Park (WA), Proof, Silver

PF-67DC	PF-68DC	PF-69DC
$7.20	$8.50	$11

2011, Vicksburg National Military Park (MS)

Circulation-Strike Mintage, Philadelphia: 30,800,000

Circulation-Strike Mintage, Denver: 33,400,000

Proof Mintage, San Francisco, Clad: 1,268,623

Proof Mintage, San Francisco, Silver: 722,076

GSID: Circulation-strike, Philadelphia, 77702; Circulation-strike, Denver, 70941; Proof Clad Deep Cameo, 71195; Proof Silver Deep Cameo, 71196

Specifics of the Reverse Design

Description: A depiction of the Civil War–era gunboat USS *Cairo* as it would have appeared steaming on the Yazoo River.

Designer: Thomas Cleveland. *Mint sculptor-engraver who made the model:* Joseph F. Menna. *Designers's initials and location:* TC is beneath the left of the ship. *Engraver's initials and location:* JFM is beneath the right side of the ship.

Story and Background of the Design

Four design candidates were presented to the Citizens Coinage Advisory Committee and Commission of Fine Arts for consideration for the Vicksburg National Military Park quarter. When presented with the design choices, the CCAC selected the second candidate, which was eventually chosen to be on the coin, due to its showcasing of the historical significance of the Navy in the Civil War. The CFA chose a different design candidate while also recommending that the design be simplified without attempting to depict a realistic landscape setting.

Numismatic Commentary

The official release ceremony for the Vicksburg National Military Park quarter was held on Tuesday, August 30, at 9:30 a.m. A large crowd was expected, and in anticipation of this there was no on-site parking. That took place in designated areas from which shuttle buses brought an amazing count of about 2,600 visitors—unprecedented to date in the America the Beautiful quarter program. The turnout was mainly of regional school students, about 2,000, most of which were well informed as to the history of the famous siege.

Representing the Mint and emceeing the event was Al Runnels, joined by Michael Madell, superintendent of the park.

The site was the USS *Cairo* Museum—a partial restoration of a Civil War gunboat (see notes). Children were given free quarters. All were allowed to buy $10 rolls for face value, maximum 10 rolls per person. At 7:00 in the evening before a Coin Collector's Forum was held at the Visitor Center Auditorium located on 3201 Clay Street. On that day, August 29, the Federal Reserve began the distribution of quarters to banks.

The Vicksburg National Military Park encompasses the large area on the east side of the Mississippi River where the Battle of Vicksburg and activities leading up to it took place from May 18 to July 4, 1863. Union forces put the city under a 47-day siege that wreaked hardship on its citizens and lead to the city's capitulation. The park is easily appreciated by a winding road 16 miles in length or, for the more rugged tourist, a 12-mile hiking trail. It comprises 1,325 markers and monuments, some quite large, mainly commemorating Union regiments and states, plus cannon emplacements and reconstructed trenches and battlements. The battle was pivotal for the Union. The victory here and at Port Hudson in Louisiana, gave it control of the Mississippi River.

The visitors' center features the USS *Cairo*, a partially-restored Union gunboat that sank in unrelated action on the Yazoo River on December 12, 1862. This was the first American ship in naval history to be sunk by a blast from a mine. The wreck was recovered from the Yazoo River in 1964. Other historic spots are available for tourists in the general area, including plantations. Some tour guides in those locations still falsely refer to the Civil War as the "War of Northern Aggression."[11]

2011-P, Vicksburg National Military Park (MS)

MS-64	MS-65	MS-66	MS-67	MS-68
$0.50	$0.80	$2.65	$16	—

2011-D, Vicksburg National Military Park (MS)

MS-64	MS-65	MS-66	MS-67	MS-68
$0.50	$0.80	$2.65	$16	—

2011-S, Vicksburg National Military Park (MS), Proof, Clad

PF-67DC	PF-68DC	PF-69DC
$1.50	$4.05	$9.50

2011-S, Vicksburg National Military Park (MS), Proof, Silver

PF-67DC	PF-68DC	PF-69DC
$7.20	$8.50	$11

2011, Chickasaw National Recreation Area (OK)

Circulation-Strike Mintage, Philadelphia: 73,800,000
Circulation-Strike Mintage, Denver: 69,400,000
Circulation-Strike Mintage, Denver, Satin Finish: 1,266,825
Proof Mintage, San Francisco, Silver: 722,076
GSID: Circulation-strike, Philadelphia, 77703; Circulation-strike, Denver, 70943; Proof Clad Deep Cameo, 71197; Proof Silver Deep Cameo, 71198

Specifics of the Reverse Design

Description: Depicted is the Lincoln Bridge, which can be found within the boundaries of the national recreational area. It was built in 1909 on the 100th anniversary of its namesake.

Designer: Donna Weaver. *Mint sculptor-engraver who made the model:* Jim Licaretz. *Designers's initials and location:* DW is hidden to the left of the river. *Engraver's initials and location:* JL is beneath the right side of the bridge.

Story and Background of the Design

Three very different design candidates for the Chickasaw quarter were prepared by the Mint artists and given to the Citizens Coin Advisory Committee and Commission of Fine Arts. While reviewing the designs the Commission of Fine Arts rejected every one of them, though they did like the bridge in design OK-02, but thought it needed to be further developed, and the design needed to be simplified to tone down or exclude the landscaping altogether. The Citizens Coin Advisory Committee liked design candidate OK-01 the best, but they also suggested editing the design as there was concern whether the person shown in the picture would be too small when scaled down for the coin. Secretary of the Treasury Timothy Geithner chose design OK-02 following its slight revision.

Numismatic Commentary

On November 16, 2011, the launch ceremony for the new quarter was held in Sulphur, Oklahoma—certainly one of the most memorable events in the small community's history. B.B. Craig, the Mint's associate director for sales, a familiar figure at such events, and Bruce Noble, superintendent of the recreation area were on hand. State Representative Wes Hilliard was master of ceremonies. Amanda Cobb-Greetham, administrator of the Chickasaw Nation Division of History and Culture, was among those who made remarks to the audience of about 800.

Those 18 years and younger received free quarters. Bank-wrapped $10 rolls were available for face value. The Federal Reserve had released coins into circulation two days earlier.[12]

The Chickasaw National Recreation Area comprises nearly 10,000 acres near the town of Sulphur in the foothills of the Arbuckly Mountains in south-central Oklahoma. It was established on July 1, 1902, as the Sulphur Springs Reservation, then renamed as the Platt National Park on June 29, 1906. It was combined with the Arbuckle Recreational Area and additional acreage and given its present name on

March 17, 1976. Accordingly, the area includes a national park that is no longer—an unusual situation among the places featured on the quarter coins.

The area was home to many Chickasaw Native Americans who, under the Martin Van Buren Administration in 1838, were forcibly removed from their Eastern property under the provisions of the Indian Removal Act of years earlier in 1830. Gold was being mined in quantity in North Carolina, and the Native Americans were considered to be a nuisance. The Trail of Tears features heavily in the history of Oklahoma but is not showcased.

2011-P, Chickasaw National Recreation Area (OK)

MS-64	MS-65	MS-66	MS-67	MS-68
$0.50	$0.80	$2.65	$16	—

2011-D, Chickasaw National Recreation Area (OK)

MS-64	MS-65	MS-66	MS-67	MS-68
$0.50	$0.80	$2.65	$16	—

2011-S, Chickasaw National Recreation Area (OK), Proof, Clad

PF-67DC	PF-68DC	PF-69DC
$1.50	$4.05	$9.50

2011-S, Chickasaw National Recreation Area (OK), Proof, Silver

PF-67DC	PF-68DC	PF-69DC
$7.20	$8.50	$11

2012, El Yunque National Forest (PR)

Circulation-Strike Mintage, Philadelphia: 25,800,000

Circulation-Strike Mintage, Denver: 25,000,000

Circulation-Strike Mintage, San Francisco: 1,680,140

Proof Mintage, San Francisco, Clad: 1,012,094

Proof Mintage, San Francisco, Silver: 608,060

GSID: Circulation-strike, Philadelphia, 77704; Circulation-strike, Denver, 71560; Circulation-strike, San Francisco, 77705; Proof Clad Deep Cameo, 77793; Proof Silver Deep Cameo, 77794.

Specifics of the Reverse Design

Description: A coqui tree frog sitting on a leaf is depicted with a Puerto Rican parrot behind an epiphyte plant and tropical flora in the background.

Designer: Gary Whitley. *Mint sculptor-engraver who made the model:* Michael Gaudioso. *Designers's initials and location:* GW is on the bottom left. *Engraver's initials and location:* MG is on the bottom right.

Story and Background of the Design

Representatives of the El Yunque National Forest were asked to submit ideas, leading to the Puerto Rican parrot, a highly endangered species unique to Puerto Rico, the bird that has been the focus of conservation efforts. This resulted in five sketches being prepared by Mint artists.

The Citizens Coinage Advisory Committee and the Commission of Fine Arts approved of the design, which was made official by the secretary of the Treasury.

Numismatic Commentary

This quarter inaugurated a new program of adding circulation-strike San Francisco Mint quarters to the coinage output of America the Beautiful coins. These were not placed into general circulation for face value, but were sold at a premium. This came as a surprise to many numismatists who now had one more coin to add to have completion for a given issue.

Representing the Mint at the launch ceremony for the new quarter was U.S. Treasurer Rosa Gumataotao Rios, a first for the holder of this high office at an America the Beautiful event. The venue was El Portal Rain Forest Visitor Center in Rio Grande at 10:00 in the morning of March 14, 2012. Rios commented:

> El Yunque National Forest is a perfect selection for the America the Beautiful quarters program. As Americans use this new quarter, they will connect to the stories of the endangered Puerto Rican parrot, the magnificent effort you are making to rescue this beautiful bird from extinction, and the biodiverse national treasure that is its home.—El Yunque National Forest.

Governor Luis Fortuno, El Yunque National Forest Supervisor Pablo Cruz, and Resident Commissioner Pedro Pierluisi were among the other dignitaries on hand. Channel 6 TV producer Maria Falcon served as master of ceremonies.

Quarters were given to the younger set, and rolls were available at face value. Perhaps due to Puerto Rico not being in the Continental United States, press coverage for the launch seems to have been minimal.

The El Yunque National Forest quarter dollar is the first in the America the Beautiful series to feature a territory. The lush tropical rain forest is the only such that is part of the National Forest System. The flora and fauna are a natural wonderland. The derivation of the name is uncertain and may refer to a Spanish adaptation of the aboriginal Taino word *yu-ke*, meaning "white lands," or it may have come from *yunque*, the Spanish word for anvil.

The second tallest mountain within the forest is also named El Yunque. The area encompasses 28,000 acres and is the largest area of public land in Puerto Rico. Trails enable visitors to enjoy the surroundings.

2012-P, El Yunque National Forest (PR)

MS-64	MS-65	MS-66	MS-67	MS-68
$0.50	$0.80	$2.65	$16	—

2012-D, El Yunque National Forest (PR)

MS-64	MS-65	MS-66	MS-67	MS-68
$0.50	$0.80	$2.65	$40.50	$358

2012-S, El Yunque National Forest (PR), Circulation Strike

MS-64	MS-65	MS-66	MS-67	MS-68
$0.50	$0.80	$2.65	$29.50	$128

2012-S, El Yunque National Forest (PR), Proof, Clad

PF-67DC	PF-68DC	PF-69DC
$1.50	$4.05	$9.50

2012-S, El Yunque National Forest (PR), Proof, Silver

PF-67DC	PF-68DC	PF-69DC
$7.20	$8.50	$11

2012, Chaco Culture National Historical Park (NM)

Circulation-Strike Mintage, Philadelphia: 22,000,000
Circulation-Strike Mintage, Denver: 22,000,000
Circulation-Strike Mintage, San Francisco: 1,389,020
Proof Mintage, San Francisco, Clad: 961,464
Proof Mintage, San Francisco, Silver: 608,060
GSID: Circulation-strike, Philadelphia, 71559; Circulation-strike, Denver, 77706; Circulation-strike, San Francisco, 77707; Proof Clad Deep Cameo, 77795; Proof Silver Deep Cameo, 77796

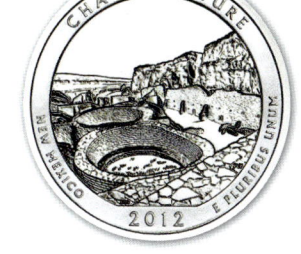

Specifics of the Reverse Design

Description: A view of Chaco Canyon to the west of two elevates kivas (enormous circular underground "houses") that are part of the Chetro Ketl Complex. Also depicted are the north wall of Chetro Ketl and the north wall of the canyon.

Designer: Donna Weaver. *Mint sculptor-engraver who made the model:* Phebe Hemphill. *Designers's initials and location:* DW is hidden in the stones on the bottom left. *Engraver's initials and location:* PH is hidden on the stones higher on the right.

Story and Background of the Design

Four designs were presented to the Citizens Coinage Advisory Committee and the Commission of Fine Arts for review. Based on the recommendations of these groups and upon his own review, the Treasury secretary made his decision. The chosen reverse design for the Chaco Culture National Historic Park features a view from above of two elevated kivas in the Chetro Ketl Complex. These rooms were used by Puebloans for religious and political meetings, and were central to the lives of the people of the American Southwest.

Numismatic Commentary

The launch ceremony for the latest America the Beautiful quarter was held on April 26, 2012, at the Chaco Culture National Historical Park Visitors Center. Dignitaries in attendance included Mint Deputy Director Richard A. Peterson, Park Superintendent Barbara West, and Theresa Pasqual of the Acoma Historic Preservation Office. Nearly 200 schoolchildren from around the region were part of the audience. A coin forum was held the night before.

The Chaco Culture National Historical Park is not well known, and no doubt the America the Beautiful quarter has called more attention to it than any other element in modern times. However, this is one quarter for which public access is limited in order to preserve the site. Located in a remote canyon cut by the Chaco Wash in northwestern New Mexico between Albuquerque and Farmington, it has the most extensive group of pre-Columbian ruins anywhere in the United States.

Phebe Hemphill with the plaster cast she created using Donna Weaver's design for the Chaco Culture National Historic Park quarter.

From about 900 to 1150 AD this was a major cultural center for Chacoans, an ancient Pueblo people. They brought lumber from a distance, quarried sandstone for building blocks, and erected 15 groups of structures. In the absence of recorded history it is thought that climate change beginning about 1130 forced the abandonment of the area. Archaeologists have found building alignments that coordinate with solar and lunar cycles, indicating the interest and knowledge of the inhabitants in astronomy. The "Sun Dagger" petroglyph at Fajada Butte is an example, but is not open to the general public.[13]

2012-P, Chaco Culture National Historical Park (NM)

MS-64	MS-65	MS-66	MS-67	MS-68
$0.50	$0.80	$2.65	$16	—

2012-D, Chaco Culture National Historical Park (NM)

MS-64	MS-65	MS-66	MS-67	MS-68
$0.50	$0.80	$2.65	$16	—

2012-S, Chaco Culture National Historical Park (NM), Circulation Strike

MS-64	MS-65	MS-66	MS-67	MS-68
$0.50	$0.80	$2.65	$27	$325

2012-S, Chaco Culture National Historical Park (NM), Proof, Clad

PF-67DC	PF-68DC	PF-69DC
$1.50	$4.05	$9.50

2012-S, Chaco Culture National Historical Park (NM), Proof, Silver

PF-67DC	PF-68DC	PF-69DC
$7.20	$8.50	$11

2012, Acadia National Park (ME)

Circulation-Strike Mintage, Philadelphia: 24,800,000

Circulation-Strike Mintage, Denver: 21,606,000

Circulation-Strike Mintage, San Francisco: 1,409,120

Proof Mintage, San Francisco, Clad: 962,038

Proof Mintage, San Francisco, Silver: 608,060

GSID: Circulation-strike, Philadelphia, 77709; Circulation-strike, Denver, 77710; Circulation-strike, San Francisco, 77711; Proof Clad Deep Cameo, 77797; Proof Silver Deep Cameo, 77798

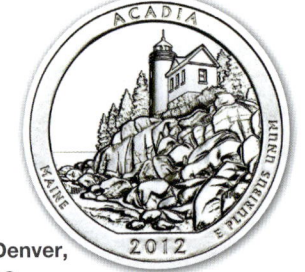

Specifics of the Reverse Design

Description: A view of Bass Harbor Head Light House with the coastline, pine trees, and the ocean.

Designer: Barbara Fox. *Mint sculptor-engraver who made the model:* Joseph F. Menna. *Designers's initials and location:* BF is to the left of the rocks. *Engraver's initials and location:* JFM is hidden in the rocks on the right.

Story and Background of the Design

The Mint presented five design candidates to interested parties, including the CCAC and the CFA, for consideration for the quarter honoring Acadia National Park. Designs were reviewed in late 2010, and on December 8, 2011, the final designs for all 2012 quarter dollars were presented to the public.

Foreword writer Barbara Fox designed the reverse of the coin, which features a stunning view of Bass Harbor Head Lighthouse. The lighthouse, located in the southwest portion of Mount Desert Island, dates back to 1855 and was officially added to the National Register of Historic Places on January 21, 1988, as Bass Harbor Head Light Station.

Numismatic Commentary

The Acadia quarter was launched on June 26, 2012, at the Hulls Cove Visitors Center in the park. WCSH–TV meteorologist Steve McKay was the master of ceremonies. Speakers included B.B. Craig, the Mint's associate director for sales and marketing; Park Superintendent Sheridan Steele; and Timothy Harrison, founder of the American Lighthouse Association. The history and appreciation of lighthouses is a subculture attracting many adherents, and those along the coasts and in the Great Lakes have attracted a lot of interest. Bill Green, host of WCSH-TV's "Bill Green's Maine," added to the scene.

An estimated 525 people were in attendance. Free quarters were given to the younger folks. Bank-wrapped $10 rolls were available for face value, about $19,000 worth was sold.[14]

Acadia National Park on the Atlantic coast in Maine is one of the most popular tourist areas in the Northeast. This largely dates from about 1855 and was sharply increased in 1868 with regular steamship service to and from Boston. On September 5, 1604, Samuel de Champlain, who was sailing down the coast, wrote in his diary:

> That same day we also passed near an island about four or five leagues in length, off which we were almost lost on a little rock, level with the surface of the water, which made a hole in our pinnace close to the keel. The distance from this island to the mainland on the north is not a hundred paces. It is very high and cleft in places, giving it the appearance from the sea of seven or eight mountains one alongside the other. The tops of them are bare of trees, because there is nothing there but rocks. The woods consist only of pines, firs, and birches.

He gave it the Mount Desert Island name. The park includes this and related small islands offshore and Cadillac Mountain (named for Antoine de la Mothe Cadillac who was granted territory by Louis XIV of France in 1688) and other acreage. The town of Bar Harbor is nearby and includes extensive facilities for the several million who visit there in a typical year. The history of the area includes a French missionary colony established on Mount Desert Island by the French in 1613, part of a rich but largely unappreciated narrative of European activities in North America between the settlement of Jamestown in 1607 and the Plymouth Colony in 1620. Most of the National Park remains in pristine condition.

2012-P, Acadia National Park (ME)

MS-64	MS-65	MS-66	MS-67	MS-68
$0.50	$0.80	$2.65	$40.50	—

2012-D, Acadia National Park (ME)

MS-64	MS-65	MS-66	MS-67	MS-68
$0.50	$0.80	$2.65	$195	—

2012-S, Acadia National Park (ME), Circulation Strike

MS-64	MS-65	MS-66	MS-67	MS-68
$0.50	$0.80	$2.65	$16	—

2012-S, Acadia National Park (ME), Proof, Clad

PF-67DC	PF-68DC	PF-69DC
$1.50	$4.05	$9.50

2012-S, Acadia National Park (ME), Proof, Silver

PF-67DC	PF-68DC	PF-69DC
$7.20	$8.50	$11

2012, Hawai'i Volcanoes National Park (HI)

Circulation-Strike Mintage, Philadelphia: 46,200,000
Circulation-Strike Mintage, Denver: 78,600,000
Circulation-Strike Mintage, San Francisco: 1,409,120
Proof Mintage, San Francisco, Clad: 962,447
Proof Mintage, San Francisco, Silver: 608,060

GSID: Circulation-strike, Philadelphia, 77712; Circulation-strike, Denver, 77713; Circulation-strike, San Francisco, 77714; Proof Clad Deep Cameo, 77799; Proof Silver Deep Cameo, 77800

Specifics of the Reverse Design

Description: An eruption on the east rift of Kilauea Volcano is shown.

Designer: Charles L. Vickers, who was also the sculptor-engraver who made the model. *Engraver's initials and location:* CLV appears on the right of the volcano.

Story and Background of the Design

Five proposal designs were submitted to the usual parties for review in 2010 for the Hawai'i Volcanoes National Park coin. The Hawaii design was not without controversy. A commentary by Bill McAllister in *Coin World*, November 15, 2010, included this:

> One member of the Citizens Coinage Advisory Committee said he might have guessed that the proposed coin for Hawai'i Volcanoes National Park is a campfire, not an erupting volcano. But his fellow committee members believed the unusual design for one of the new 2012 America the Beautiful quarter dollars is worth the risk. The committee voted overwhelmingly to recommend a coin design that many conceded they have doubts that the U.S. Mint could execute. If successful, it could be one of the "coins of the year," agreed Donald Scarinci, a medals specialist.
>
> "Give her a shot," said Roger Burdette, a numismatic researcher and writer. Karina Budow, the Mint's design manager for sales and marketing, said she and John Mercanti, the Mint's chief engraver, have no doubts about the design. "We're going to make it work," she assured the committee.

The committee's October 26 endorsement, which followed a similar recommendation by the Commission of Fine Arts, now goes to Treasury Secretary Timothy F. Geithner, who will have the final word.

This was done, and Secretary Geithner gave his approval. So far as is known the design caused no production problems.

Numismatic Commentary

The launch ceremony for the new quarter was held on August 29, 2012, at the Kahua Hula, south of the park's Kilauea Visitor Center on Hawaii's Big Island. Attendees included David Croft, plant manager of the Denver Mint representing the Mint, Senator Daniel Inouye, Park Superintendent Cindy Orlando, and other dignitaries. About 300 or so (published accounts ranged up to 500) attended. Inouye told of Pele, the goddess of volcanoes, and legends from ancient times and remarked that the drizzle of the day was a gift from Pele and other gods. The quarter exchange was conducted by the HFS Federal Credit Union. The forum was hosted the night before.

Hawai'i Volcanoes National Park, with an apostrophe in its official name, was established in 1916. Located on the island of Hawaii, it includes two active volcanoes that regularly make the news with lava flows. Mauna Loa is the world's largest shield-type volcano as measured from the floor of the Pacific Ocean. Kilauea, more popular with tourists, is among the most active anywhere. The park also includes rare flora and fauna. It is one of the more world-famous sites honored on America the Beautiful quarters.

2012-P, Hawai'i Volcanoes National Park (HI)

MS-64	MS-65	MS-66	MS-67	MS-68
$0.50	$0.80	$2.65	$21.50	$162

2012-D, Hawai'i Volcanoes National Park (HI)

MS-64	MS-65	MS-66	MS-67	MS-68
$0.50	$0.80	$2.65	$21.50	$228

2012-S, Hawai'i Volcanoes National Park (HI), Circulation Strike

MS-64	MS-65	MS-66	MS-67	MS-68
$0.50	$0.80	$2.65	$16	—

2012-S, Hawai'i Volcanoes National Park (HI), Proof, Clad

PF-67DC	PF-68DC	PF-69DC
$1.50	$4.05	$9.50

2012-S, Hawai'i Volcanoes National Park (HI), Proof, Silver

PF-67DC	PF-68DC	PF-69DC
$7.20	$8.50	$11

2012, Denali National Park and Preserve (AK)

Circulation-Strike Mintage, Philadelphia: 135,400,000

Circulation-Strike Mintage, Denver: 166,600,000

Circulation-Strike Mintage, San Francisco: 1,409,220

Proof Mintage, San Francisco, Clad: 959,602

Proof Mintage, San Francisco, Silver: 608,060

GSID: Circulation-strike, Philadelphia, 77715; Circulation-strike, Denver, 77716; Circulation-strike, San Francisco, 77717; Proof Clad Deep Cameo, 77801; Proof Silver Deep Cameo, 77802

Specifics of the Reverse Design

Description: A Dall sheep is seen in the foreground with Mount McKinley rising in the background.

Designer: Susan Gamble. *Mint sculptor-engraver who made the model:* Jim Licaretz. *Designers's initials and location:* SG is hidden on the bottom left. *Engraver's initials and location:* JL is to the right of the sheep's hooves.

Story and Background of the Design

Before the final selection was made by the secretary of the Treasury, five design candidates were created by Mint artists for consideration to the usual parties.

The Dall sheep depicted in the center of the reverse are commonly seen throughout the park, along with a variety of other birds and mammals, including grizzly bears, black bears, caribou, and Alaskan moose, among others. It is also home to over 450 species of flowering plants that can be viewed in bloom during the summer months.

Numismatic Commentary

The launch ceremony was November 15, 2012, at the Tri-Valley Community Center. Temperatures were in the single digits, yet more than 400 people attended. About half of attendees were from all three of the Denali Borough Schools and the local pre-school. Representing the Mint was David Croft. Jeff Mow, acting park superintendent, was on hand as was Jane Bryant, park historian. Croft hosted the forum the night before, giving participants the opportunity to learn first-hand about the operations of the Denver Mint.

Denali National Park and Preserve is located in the interior of Alaska and comprises more than six million acres. Denali, renamed from Mount McKinley in 2015, is the highest mountain in North America. The landscape is rugged and is best appreciated by visitors who enjoy camping in the outdoors. Grizzly bears are a hazard. The natural wonders include forest, tundra, and glaciers, the largest of the last being Kahiltna Glacier. Recreational activities in the winter season include dog-sledding, the use of snowmobiles, and cross-country skiing. On a typical year, over half a million people visit the park.

2012-P, Denali National Park and Preserve (AK)

MS-64	MS-65	MS-66	MS-67	MS-68
$0.50	$0.80	$2.65	$16	—

2012-D, Denali National Park and Preserve (AK)

MS-64	MS-65	MS-66	MS-67	MS-68
$0.50	$0.80	$2.65	$16	—

2012-S, Denali National Park and Preserve (AK), Circulation Strike

MS-64	MS-65	MS-66	MS-67	MS-68
$0.50	$0.80	$2.65	$16	—

2012-S, Denali National Park and Preserve (AK), Proof, Clad

PF-67DC	PF-68DC	PF-69DC
$1.50	$4.05	$9.50

2012-S, Denali National Park and Preserve (AK), Proof, Silver

PF-67DC	PF-68DC	PF-69DC
$7.20	$8.50	$11

2013, White Mountain National Forest (NH)

Circulation-Strike Mintage, Philadelphia: 68,800,000
Circulation-Strike Mintage, Denver: 107,600,000
Circulation-Strike Mintage, San Francisco: 1,606,900
Proof Mintage, San Francisco, Clad: 989,803
Proof Mintage, San Francisco, Silver: 467,691

GSID: Circulation-strike, Philadelphia, 77718; Circulation-strike, Denver, 77719; Circulation-strike, San Francisco, 77720; Proof Clad Deep Cameo, 77803; Proof Silver Deep Cameo, 77804

Specifics of the Reverse Design

Description: Mount Chocorua, the easternmost peak of the Sandwich Range, can be viewed framed by birch trees.

Designer: Phebe Hemphill, who was also the sculptor-engraver who made the model. *Engraver's initials and location:* PH appears on the bottom right.

Story and Background of the Design

In 2000 I covered the launch of the New Hampshire State quarter for *Coin World*. In 2013 it was an honor to do the same for the New Hampshire America the Beautiful quarter, after which the coin formed a chapter in my 2016 book, *Coins and Collectors: Golden Anniversary Edition*. With a nod to sculptor Phebe Hemphill and the staff of the Mint, I refer you to this book if you desire a particularly extensive coverage.

In a visit to the Philadelphia Mint on August 1, 2012, with camera and notepad in hand, I spent time at each of the departments. Over a long period of time I have documented the processes and activities of the four mints, leading in part to my 2016 *Guide Book of the United States Mint*. In 2012, realizing that the New Hampshire America the Beautiful quarter was on the list of upcoming coins for 2013, I visited the engraving department and found to my delight that Phebe Hemphill, a sculptor-engraver with a long list of credits, had the assignment and had already created two sketches, of which one had been selected from proposals submitted by several other talented Mint artists. She had in her office a clay model that more or less represented what the final product would be.

Later, as the launch time approached, I interfaced with Mint executive Tom Jurkowsky and Acting Mint Director Dick Peterson and arranged telephone conversations and discussions with Phebe, who consented to an interview. The result was a unique view of the creation of a quarter design, the 16th in the series, from the first concept down to completion, a procedure which, I believe, had never been outlined in print before and is in my book *Coins and Collectors: Golden Anniversary Edition*.

As to the design there had been multiple possibilities. Furnished to the Mint by the National Park Service were images of various peals and features of the White Mountain National Forest. The winning sketch by Phebe Hemphill showed Mount Chocorua in the distance with Chocorua Lake in the foreground. It was not identified in the art from which she worked, and she did not know the name of the mountain until I told her. To me it was instantly recognizable as I had viewed it many times from the same perspective along Route 16 in the town of Chocorua.

The mountain is a favorite in the National Forest, can be accessed by trails, and at one time had a small hotel near the summit. It blew down in a storm in 1917.

The design, recommended by the Commission of Fine Arts and the Citizens Coinage Advisory Committee, was approved by the secretary of the Treasury and was translated into dies and coinage.

Numismatic Commentary

The launch ceremony was held on Thursday, February 21, 2013, at Plymouth State University in Plymouth, in the heart of the White Mountains, eight miles from Campton, a small town in which the White Mountain National Forest headquarters is located. The venue was Hanaway Hall. As is Mint policy, the National Forest people were called upon to make arrangements with local and regional people to attend, including schoolchildren. It, like other launches, was truly "down home." Mint staffers conducted a Coin Collector's Forum in Campton the previous evening, with general discussions, but with no coins exchanged. Eighteen people were on hand.

At the ceremony most of the seats were filled—with hundreds of eager elementary school children from the area. Shortly after 10:30 a.m., Bill Dauer of the National Forest Service went to the podium and introduced guests and gave opening remarks. He was followed by Congresswoman Ann McLane Kuster. Acting Mint Director Richard A. Peterson came to the podium next. In contrast to the usual prepared remarks at such ceremonies, Peterson's comments were extemporaneous and personal. It turned out that he, a retired Navy official, used to be with the Portsmouth, New Hampshire, Naval Base, a headquarters for submarines. He and his family lived in the Granite State, enjoyed the surroundings from the seacoast to the White Mountains, and still reminisce about their experiences. Dick's remarks were more than just general—he even named his favorite restaurants.

He then shifted to numismatics, telling of President Theodore Roosevelt's desire in 1904 to enlist America's most accomplished sculptor and engraver to redesign the entire spectrum of American coinage from the cent to the $20 double eagle. The sculptor accepted the challenge and set about work in his studio in Cornish, New Hampshire.

"Who was that sculptor?" Peterson asked the audience. "Coin collectors are not allowed to answer!"

Someone in the distance shouted, "Saint-Gaudens!" Right choice. Dick continued with his reminiscences.

Over the years I have been to quite a few launch ceremonies dating back to commemoratives of the early 1980s, but this was the finest keynote speech by a Mint official I have ever heard.

Next in the program was Maggie Hassan, newly installed governor of New Hampshire, who told of her experiences among the peaks and her love for them. The ceremony then concluded, after which Kuster, Hassan, and Peterson went into the audience, each carrying a sack of quarters to hand out to hundreds of outstretched hands. Bank-wrapped $10 rolls were available for purchase for face value at a nearby stand.

The White Mountain National Forest with an expanse of 750,852 acres, mostly in New Hampshire but with 5.65% to the east in Maine, was established as such in 1918. To the south are the towns of Lincoln and North Woodstock, both with many tourist facilities. To the north are Franconia and Littleton.

Recreational activities include camping in season, skiing on Cannon Mountain, and taking the Auto Road or the Cog Railway up Mount Washington, the highest peak in the Northeast. At its top a year-round meteorological station is maintained for forecasting and scientific research. Other peaks over 4,000 feet high are within the area and are popular with hikers who seek to climb every one. Over 100 miles of the Appalachian Trail runs through the area. The Appalachian Mountain Club provides facilities for hikers. The Flume, a narrow rocky gorge; the Basin; and Echo Lake are other points of interest. The Old Man in the Mountain, the symbol of the State of New Hampshire, was an icon until it collapsed early in the present century.

2013-P, White Mountain National Forest (NH)

MS-64	MS-65	MS-66	MS-67	MS-68
$0.50	$0.80	$2.65	$16	—

2013-D, White Mountain National Forest (NH)

MS-64	MS-65	MS-66	MS-67	MS-68
$0.50	$0.80	$2.65	$19	$94

2013-S, White Mountain National Forest (NH), Circulation Strike

MS-64	MS-65	MS-66	MS-67	MS-68
$0.50	$0.80	$2.65	$16	—

2013-S, White Mountain National Forest (NH), Proof, Clad

PF-67DC	PF-68DC	PF-69DC
$1.50	$4.05	$9.50

2013-S, White Mountain National Forest (NH), Proof, Silver

PF-67DC	PF-68DC	PF-69DC
$7.20	$8.50	$11

2013, Perry's Victory and International Peace Memorial (OH)

Circulation-Strike Mintage, Philadelphia: 107,800,000
Circulation-Strike Mintage, Denver: 131,600,000
Circulation-Strike Mintage, San Francisco: 1,425,860
Proof Mintage, San Francisco, Clad: 947,815
Proof Mintage, San Francisco, Silver: 467,691
GSID: Circulation-strike, Philadelphia, 77721; Circulation-strike, Denver, 77722; Circulation-strike, San Francisco, 77723; Proof Clad Deep Cameo, 77805; Proof Silver Deep Cameo, 77806

Specifics of the Reverse Design

Description: The statue of Master Commandant Oliver Hazard Perry can be seen with the Peace Memorial in the distance.

Designer: Don Everhart, who was also the sculptor-engraver who made the model. *Engraver's initials and location:* DE appears on the bottom right.

Story and Background of the Design

Five design candidates in line-art form created by the Mint were submitted to the Committee of Fine arts and the Citizens Coinage Advisory Committee for review. As per usual, the final design was reviewed and approved by the secretary of the Treasury.

Numismatic Commentary

To attend the launch ceremony for the new quarter involved taking a ferry ride to Bass Island in Put-In-Bay—a first in any ceremony. On April 20, 2013, that did not deter over 600 people from braving rough water and cold temperatures, a number about three times the expected audience. On hand were J. Marc Landry, acting associate director of sales and marketing for the Mint; U.S. Representative Marcy Kaptur; and Blanca Alvarez Stansky, superintendent of the memorial. Greg Peiffer of WPIB/WPCR Radio was on hand to cover the event.

The unanticipated size of the crowd forced the First National Bank to cut the limit from ten $10 face-value rolls to five part way through the distribution, another first among launch incidents. A forum was held the night before.

The War of 1812 with England began in that year and continued until the peace treaty of December 1814. Unaware of the settlement, forces fought the Battle of New Orleans in January 1815. The present quarter as well as that honoring Fort McHenry in Maryland are the two coins reflecting that war.

The war took place on many fronts. The September 1813 Battle of Lake Erie in which Commodore Oliver Hazard Perry vanquished British ships near South Bass Island in Ohio did much to lift the spirit of citizens and allay fears of an invasion of the United States from troops coming from Canada. He is remembered for the wording on his flag, "Don't give up the ship," and for his comment after the battle, "We have met the enemy and they are ours." The monument commemorated on the coin is the world's most massive Doric column, extending 352 feet high. It was built from 1912 to 1915.

2013-P, Perry's Victory and International Peace Memorial (OH)

MS-64	MS-65	MS-66	MS-67	MS-68
$0.50	$0.80	$2.65	$16	—

2013-D, Perry's Victory and International Peace Memorial (OH)

MS-64	MS-65	MS-66	MS-67	MS-68
$0.50	$0.80	$2.65	$19	$74

2013-S, Perry's Victory and International Peace Memorial (OH), Circulation Strike

MS-64	MS-65	MS-66	MS-67	MS-68
$0.50	$0.80	$2.65	$16	—

2013-S, Perry's Victory and International Peace Memorial (OH), Proof, Clad

PF-67DC	PF-68DC	PF-69DC
$1.50	$4.05	$9.50

2013-S, Perry's Victory and International Peace Memorial (OH), Proof, Silver

PF-67DC	PF-68DC	PF-69DC
$7.20	$8.50	$11

2013, Great Basin National Park (NV)

Circulation-Strike Mintage, Philadelphia: 122,400,000

Circulation-Strike Mintage, Denver: 141,400,000

Circulation-Strike Mintage, San Francisco: 1,316,500

Proof Mintage, San Francisco, Clad: 945,777

Proof Mintage, San Francisco, Silver: 467,691

GSID: Circulation-strike, Philadelphia, 77724; Circulation-strike, Denver, 77725; Circulation-strike, San Francisco, 77726; Proof Clad Deep Cameo, 77807; Proof Silver Deep Cameo, 77808

Specifics of the Reverse Design

Description: A single bristlecone pine tree and the rocky glacial moraines where the trees grow.

Designer: Ronald D. Sanders. *Mint sculptor-engraver who made the model:* Renata Gordon. *Designers's initials and location:* RS is hidden on the horizon line at bottom left. *Engraver's initials and location:* RG is hidden on the horizon line at bottom right.

Story and Background of the Design

Similarly to past quarters, several designs were presented to the Commission of Fine Arts and the Citizens Coinage Advisory Committee and others for consideration. Their recommendations were then forwarded to the Treasury secretary before he chose a final design. The bristlecone pine featured in the center of the final design is famous for being the longest-lived species of tree—one of which is 5,000 years old!

Numismatic Commentary

Launch ceremony was on June 20, 2013, at the Great Basin Visitors Center in Baker, Nevada. Ron Harrigal represented the Mint. Andy Ferguson, former superintendent of the site, was emcee. Justin Brandenberg read aloud a message from Senator Harry Reid giving the history of the performance by Kiah Conrad of "Proud to be an American" fame, drew rousing applause. Coins from the First National Bank of Ely, Nevada, were given to the younger set and also made available for purchase. A forum was held the night before.

The Great Basin National Park established as such in 1986 is one of the newer of the national sites commemorated in the America the Beautiful quarter series. Not widely known, it is best accessed by State Route 487 and the small town of Baker. Comprising 77,180 acres the park is located near the border with Utah and is part of the mountainous region between the Sierra Nevada Range of California and the Wasatch Mountains of Utah.

Natural attractions include Wheeler Peak, Wheeler Peak Glacier, Lehman Caves, and groves of ancient bristlecone pines.

2013-P, Great Basin National Park (NV)

MS-64	MS-65	MS-66	MS-67	MS-68
$0.50	$0.80	$2.65	$16	—

2013-D, Great Basin National Park (NV)

MS-64	MS-65	MS-66	MS-67	MS-68
$0.50	$0.80	$2.65	$16	—

2013-S, Great Basin National Park (NV), Circulation Strike

MS-64	MS-65	MS-66	MS-67	MS-68
$0.50	$0.80	$2.65	$16	—

2013-S, Great Basin National Park (NV), Proof, Clad

PF-67DC	PF-68DC	PF-69DC
$1.50	$4.05	$9.50

2013-S, Great Basin National Park (NV), Proof, Silver

PF-67DC	PF-68DC	PF-69DC
$7.20	$8.50	$11

2013, Fort McHenry National Monument and Historic Shrine (MD)

Circulation-Strike Mintage, Philadelphia: 120,000,000
Circulation-Strike Mintage, Denver: 151,400,000
Circulation-Strike Mintage, San Francisco: 1,313,680
Proof Mintage, San Francisco, Clad: 946,380
Proof Mintage, San Francisco, Silver: 467,691

GSID: Circulation-strike, Philadelphia, 77727; Circulation-strike, Denver, 77728; Circulation-strike, San Francisco, 77729; Proof Clad Deep Cameo, 77809; Proof Silver Deep Cameo, 77810

Specifics of the Reverse Design

Description: The reverse depicts a scene during the "Defenders Day" celebration, with fireworks to the left and a prominent American flag on the right.

Designer: Joseph F. Menna, who was also the sculptor-engraver who made the model. *Engraver's initials and location:* JFM appears on the bottom right.

Story and Background of the Design

Several designs were created and presented by the Mint to the usual parties, including the Commission of Fine Arts and the Citizens Coinage Advisory Committee. The design chosen by the Treasury secretary depicts a scene during the "Defenders Day" celebration, which is considered to be the centerpiece annual event held at Fort McHenry. A legal holiday in the state of Maryland, Defenders Day commemorates the successful defense of the city of Baltimore on September 12, 1814, from the invading British forces during the Battle of 1812. Featured prominently in the design are two fireworks next to a billowing American flag, inspiration for the "The Star-Spangled Banner."

Numismatic Commentary

The launch ceremony was held on Friday, September 13, 2013, at Fort McHenry. About 600 people were in attendance—the same as for the Perry Memorial quarter. This was surprisingly low in view of Baltimore's central location and the ease of reaching the fort, but many potential visitors probably waited for the extensive program of events on Saturday and Sunday. The coin event was the starting point for three days set aside as the Star Spangled Banner Defenders' Day.

James C. Bailey was the emcee. Welcoming remarks were made Superintendent Tina Cappetta, who told of the fort's history. Senator Ben Cardin and U.S. representatives John Sarbanes and Dutch Ruppensberger each made brief remarks as did Mayor Stephanie Rawlings-Blake and U.S. Treasurer Rosa Rios.

Later events for the three-day weekend included the raising of a replica flag and fireworks on Saturday and a two-day "living history" encampment on Saturday and Sunday with military drills, cannon and musket firings, cooking demonstrations, and a parade. Boat tours in Chesapeake Bay were also held.

Fort McHenry, one of several historic star-shaped forts remaining on the Atlantic coast and inlets, in this instance on Chesapeake Bay in defense of Baltimore, is the best known of such structures. Watching the rockets' red glare, bombs bursting in air, and Old Glory still flying, he wrote the national anthem later titled, "The Star-Spangled Banner," putting words to the melody of an old English drinking song, "To Anachreon in Heaven."

In the late summer of 1814 British troops who had arrived by sea invaded Maryland and continued to Washington, where they burned the President's House, the Treasury Building, and other structures. Aboard their ships, the next stop was Baltimore. The bombardment of Fort McHenry on September 13, continuing through the night into the 14th, was unsuccessful. The ships gave up and returned to England, marking the end of the War of 1812.

The fort was built in 1798 and was used as a military post continuously through World War I, then by the Coast Guard in World War II. It was designated as a national park in 1924, then changed in 1939 to its present name.

2013-P, Fort McHenry National Monument and Historic Shrine (MD)

MS-64	MS-65	MS-66	MS-67	MS-68
$0.50	$0.80	$2.65	$16	—

2013-D, Fort McHenry National Monument and Historic Shrine (MD)

MS-64	MS-65	MS-66	MS-67	MS-68
$0.50	$0.80	$2.65	$19	$68

2013-S, Fort McHenry National Monument and Historic Shrine (MD), Circulation Strike

MS-64	MS-65	MS-66	MS-67	MS-68
$0.50	$0.80	$2.65	$27	$169

2013-S, Fort McHenry National Monument and Historic Shrine (MD), Proof, Clad

PF-67DC	PF-68DC	PF-69DC
$1.50	$4.05	$9.50

2013-S, Fort McHenry National Monument and Historic Shrine (MD), Proof, Silver

PF-67DC	PF-68DC	PF-69DC
$7.20	$8.50	$11

2013, Mount Rushmore National Memorial (SD)

Circulation-Strike Mintage, Philadelphia: 231,800,000
Circulation-Strike Mintage, Denver: 272,400,000
Circulation-Strike Mintage, San Francisco: 1,373,260
Proof Mintage, San Francisco, Clad: 958,853
Proof Mintage, San Francisco, Silver: 467,691

GSID: Circulation-strike, Philadelphia, 77730; Circulation-strike, Denver, 77731; Circulation-strike, San Francisco, 77732; Proof Clad Deep Cameo, 77811; Proof Silver Deep Cameo, 77812

Specifics of the Reverse Design

Description: Three men can be seen working on different spots on the faces of George Washington and Thomas Jefferson. The latter president's face is in the foreground with one of the men working on his eye, while the other two can be seen working on Washington's face in the background.

Designer: Joseph F. Menna, who was also the sculptor-engraver who made the model. *Engraver's initials and location:* JFM appears beneath the scaffolding on the left.

Story and Background of the Design

As Mount Rushmore had already appeared on a commemorative coin (the 1991 Mount Rushmore silver dollar), the challenge in creating this coin for the America the Beautiful program was designing something different this time around that didn't look too similar to the previous design. Several designs were submitted by the Mint to the CFA and CCAC for review before the Treasury secretary made his final decision. The chosen design was inspired by photographs of men as they added the final details to Thomas Jefferson's face.

Numismatic Commentary

The launch ceremony for the new quarter was held on November 6, 2013, at the National Guard Armory in the nearby town of Custer. Representing the Mint was David Croft. David Ressler, executive director of the Custer Chamber of Commerce was emcee. Park Superintendent Cheryl A. Schreiner told of the history of the sculptures. Governor Dennis Daugaard and U.S. Representative Krisi Noem were among the dignitaries present.

Quarters were distributed free to the younger set and were available to all for purchase at face value in $10 rolls. It had been planned to have had the ceremony in the theatre of Custer Middle and High School, but the venue was changed. A forum was held the night before at Carver's Café in the park.

2013-P, Mount Rushmore National Memorial (SD)

MS-64	MS-65	MS-66	MS-67	MS-68
$0.50	$0.80	$2.65	$16	—

2013-D, Mount Rushmore National Memorial (SD)

MS-64	MS-65	MS-66	MS-67	MS-68
$0.50	$0.80	$2.65	$16	—

2013-S, Mount Rushmore National Memorial (SD), Circulation Strike

MS-64	MS-65	MS-66	MS-67	MS-68
$0.50	$0.80	$2.65	$16	—

2013-S, Mount Rushmore National Memorial (SD), Proof, Clad

PF-67DC	PF-68DC	PF-69DC
$1.50	$4.05	$9.50

2013-S, Mount Rushmore National Memorial (SD), Proof, Silver

PF-67DC	PF-68DC	PF-69DC
$7.20	$8.50	$11

2014, Great Smoky Mountains National Park (TN)

Circulation-Strike Mintage, Philadelphia: 73,200,000
Circulation-Strike Mintage, Denver: 99,400,000
Circulation-Strike Mintage, San Francisco: 1,360,780
Proof Mintage, San Francisco, Clad: 881,896
Proof Mintage, San Francisco, Silver: 472,107

GSID: Circulation-strike, Philadelphia, 77733; Circulation-strike, Denver, 77734; Circulation-strike, San Francisco, 77735; Proof Clad Deep Cameo, 77813; Proof Silver Deep Cameo, 77814

Specifics of the Reverse Design

Description: A historic log cabin of the type found in the Great Smoky Mountains National Park, along with a segment of lush green forest and a hawk circling above, is seen on the reverse.

Designer: Chris Costello. *Mint sculptor-engraver who made the model:* Renata Gordon. *Designers's initials and location:* CTC is in the fence on the bottom left. *Engraver's initials and location:* RG is beneath the fence on the right.

Story and Background of the Design

The final design was selected from four candidates. After a review by the usual parties, the Treasury secretary decided which would be struck. The abundant greenery depicted in the background is one of the largest protected areas in the eastern United States, and is home to more than 200 species of bird, 50 species of fish, 39 species of reptiles, 43 species of amphibians, 100 species of trees, 1,400 flowering plant species, 4,000 non-flowering plant species, and dozens of species of mammals.

Numismatic Commentary

There was a lot of snow on the ground on January 29, 2014, when the launch ceremony for the new quarter was held in the Gatlinburg Convention Center in the city of the same name. The turnout was a modest 300 or so. On hand from the Mint was David Croft as acting associate director. Pedro Ramos, acting director of the park, gave remarks. Representatives on behalf of several elected officials were also on hand. Quarters were gifted to the younger folks. All could buy $10 rolls of quarters from a stand set up by the Citizens National Bank. The remarkable amount of $20,000 was paid out, equal to 80,000 coins.[15]

The Great Smoky Mountains National Park is far and away the most popular of the subjects in the America the Beautiful quarter series, as measured by the number of yearly visits. It includes the ridgeline of the Great Smoky Mountains, so-called from the haze seen in the warm summer months, emanating from the trees. It is on eastern side of Tennessee next to the border with North Carolina and is part of the Appalachian Mountain chain that extends to the north to Mount Katahdin in Maine. Hiking part or all of the Appalachian Trail is on the must-do list of many outdoors enthusiasts.

The park, which comprises the vast expanse of 522,419 acres, was chartered by Congress in 1924, and officially dedicated by President Franklin D. Roosevelt in 1940.

2014-P, Great Smoky Mountains National Park (TN)

MS-64	MS-65	MS-66	MS-67	MS-68
$0.50	$0.80	$2.65	$16	—

2014-D, Great Smoky Mountains National Park (TN)

MS-64	MS-65	MS-66	MS-67	MS-68
$0.50	$0.80	$2.65	$16	—

2014-S, Great Smoky Mountains National Park (TN), Circulation Strike

MS-64	MS-65	MS-66	MS-67	MS-68
$0.50	$0.80	$2.65	$16	—

2014-S, Great Smoky Mountains National Park (TN), Proof, Clad

PF-67DC	PF-68DC	PF-69DC
$1.50	$4.05	$9.50

2014-S, Great Smoky Mountains National Park (TN), Proof, Silver

PF-67DC	PF-68DC	PF-69DC
$7.20	$8.50	$11

2014, Shenandoah National Park (VA)

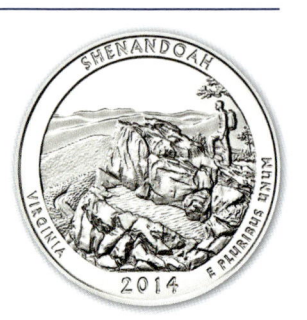

Circulation-Strike Mintage, Philadelphia: 112,800,000
Circulation-Strike Mintage, Denver: 197,800,000
Circulation-Strike Mintage, San Francisco: 1,260,700
Proof Mintage, San Francisco, Clad: 846,441
Proof Mintage, San Francisco, Silver: 472,107

GSID: Circulation-strike, Philadelphia, 77736; Circulation-strike, Denver, 77737; Circulation-strike, San Francisco, 77738; Proof Clad Deep Cameo, 77815; Proof Silver Deep Cameo, 77816

Specifics of the Reverse Design

Description: A day hiker can be seen taking in the view from Little Stony Man summit.

Designer: Phebe Hemphill, who was also the sculptor-engraver who made the model. *Engraver's initials and location:* PH appears hidden in the rocks on the right.

Story and Background of the Design

Five design candidates were presented by the Mint to the usual various groups, including representatives of the park, the Commission of Fine Arts, and the Citizens Coinage Advisory Committee. Based on recommendations from the mentioned parties and others, Secretary of the Treasury Jack Lew made the final decision on the design. The Little Stony Man trail, the summit of which is depicted in the design, offers views of beautiful wildflowers and is great for birdwatching.

Numismatic Commentary

The launch ceremony started at 10:00 in the morning of April 4, 2014, at the Skyline High School in Front Royal, Virginia. This guaranteed about 500 outstretched hands to receive gift quarters. In total, including citizens from the region, there were about 1,000 people in attendance—a large crowd. Mint Deputy Director Richard A. Peterson was on hand to direct the event. U.S. Senator Tim Kaine gave remarks as did Shenandoah National Park Superintendent Jim Northrup and Molly Ward, Virginia's secretary of natural resources. In the usual cash-for-quarters exchange for rolls about $30,000 face value was paid out.

A Coin Collecting Forum took place the night before at the Rappahannock County Library in Washington, Virginia.[16]

Similar to the area honored on the preceding Great Smoky Mountains quarter, the Shenandoah National Park coin showcases a large section of the Blue Ridge Mountains. In this case the area comprises 79,579 acres with the Shenandoah River and Valley to the west side of the ridge and the hills of the Piedmont Range to the east. The Skyline Drive runs along the ridge from near Front Royal to the northeast, 105 miles to near Waynesboro in the southeast. This scenic byway has been a popular tourist attraction for many years.

2014-P, Shenandoah National Park (VA)

MS-64	MS-65	MS-66	MS-67	MS-68
$0.50	$0.80	$2.65	$16	—

2014-D, Shenandoah National Park (VA)

MS-64	MS-65	MS-66	MS-67	MS-68
$0.50	$0.80	$2.65	$27	$228

2014-S, Shenandoah National Park (VA), Circulation Strike

MS-64	MS-65	MS-66	MS-67	MS-68
$0.50	$0.80	$2.65	$16	—

2014-S, Shenandoah National Park (VA), Proof, Clad

PF-67DC	PF-68DC	PF-69DC
$1.50	$4.05	$9.50

2014-S, Shenandoah National Park (VA), Proof, Silver

PF-67DC	PF-68DC	PF-69DC
$7.20	$8.50	$11

2014, Arches National Park (UT)

Circulation-Strike Mintage, Philadelphia: 214,200,000

Circulation-Strike Mintage, Denver: 251,400,000

Circulation-Strike Mintage, San Francisco: 1,235,940

Proof Mintage, San Francisco, Clad: 844,775

Proof Mintage, San Francisco, Silver: 472,107

GSID: Circulation-strike, Philadelphia, 77739; Circulation-strike, Denver, 77740; Circulation-strike, San Francisco, 77741; Proof Clad Deep Cameo, 77817; Proof Silver Deep Cameo, 77818

Specifics of the Reverse Design

Description: On the reverse is a depiction of the 65-foot freestanding Delicate Arch, the park's and Utah's most recognized landmark.

Designer: Donna Weaver. *Mint sculptor-engraver who made the model:* Charles L. Vickers. *Designers's initials and location:* DW is adjacent to the H in UTAH on the left. *Engraver's initials and location:* CLV is adjacent to the IB in PLURIBUM on the right.

Story and Background of the Design

Several design candidates were presented to the usual parties for review and recommendations. After Secretary Lew made his decision, the reverse designs for 2014 America the Beautiful quarters entered the die-making and coinage operations. The Delicate Arch seen in the design has also been depicted on Utah license plates and on a postage stamp commemorating Utah's centennial anniversary in 1996.

Numismatic Commentary

The launch ceremony for the Arches National Park took place on Friday, June 6, 2014, three days before the Federal Reserve System put them in general release. This was unusual, as the ceremonies were usually held a day or two or so after distribution to banks. Mint Deputy Director Richard A. Peterson, one of the most-informed Mint officials in the history of the various quarter programs, was on hand to make comments and to meet and greet attendees. "Having lived in Utah, I know from first-hand experience that Delicate Arch in Arches National Park is one of the Earth's very special geologic wonders and why it was chosen as the design for Utah's America the Beautiful quarter," said Peterson, and having lived in New Hampshire, made similar personal remarks during the launch for that state's quarter in 2013.

Mayor David Sakrison of the nearby town of Moab was master of ceremonies. Kate Cannon, park superintendent, told of the history and popularity of the region. Spencer J. Cox, lieutenant governor of Utah, was among the others making remarks.

About 400 people were on hand, including only about 40 of the younger set—the smallest such recorded attendance of those 18 and younger at any ceremony. About $20,000 in quarters were exchanged for face value. As can be seen from these various narratives, the attendance and coin distribution at ceremonies varied widely.

Arches National Park in eastern Utah is next to the Colorado River and is about 4 miles north of the town of Moab. The area is a scenic wonderland with over 2,000 natural sandstone arches sculpted by wind over countless millennia. These are an evolving feature of nature, and 47 have collapsed since 1977, per a survey. The park comprises 76,679 acres (119.8 square miles) in the high desert area of the Colorado Plateau. Only about 10 inches of rain fall per year. The area was designated as a National Monument in 1929 and as a National Park on November 12, 1971. A nicely equipped visitors' center welcomes tourists.

2014-P, Arches National Park (UT)

MS-64	MS-65	MS-66	MS-67	MS-68
$0.50	$0.80	$2.65	$16	—

2014-D, Arches National Park (UT)

MS-64	MS-65	MS-66	MS-67	MS-68
$0.50	$0.80	$2.65	$21.50	$94

2014-S, Arches National Park (UT), Circulation Strike

MS-64	MS-65	MS-66	MS-67	MS-68
$0.50	$0.80	$2.65	$16	—

2014-S, Arches National Park (UT), Proof, Clad

PF-67DC	PF-68DC	PF-69DC
$1.50	$4.05	$9.50

2014-S, Arches National Park (UT), Proof, Silver

PF-67DC	PF-68DC	PF-69DC
$7.20	$8.50	$11

2014, Great Sand Dunes National Park (CO)

Circulation-Strike Mintage, Philadelphia: 159,600,000

Circulation-Strike Mintage, Denver: 171,800,000

Circulation-Strike Mintage, San Francisco: 1,176,760

Proof Mintage, San Francisco, Clad: 843,238

Proof Mintage, San Francisco, Silver: 472,107

GSID: Circulation-strike, Philadelphia, 77742; Circulation-strike, Denver, 77743; Circulation-strike, San Francisco, 77744; Proof Clad Deep Cameo, 77819; Proof Silver Deep Cameo, 77820

Specifics of the Reverse Design

Description: A father and son are seen playing in the sand next to a creek bed. Mountains and sand dunes appear in the background.

Designer: Don Everhart, who was also the sculptor-engraver who made the model. *Engraver's initials and location:* DE appears on the small patch of land to the right.

Story and Background of the Design

Selected from among seven different design candidates, the accepted design features a father and son playing in the sand with massive sand dunes in the distance. The park itself includes 44,246 acres, and the preserve protects an additional 41,686 acres. It contains the tallest sand dunes in North America, the tallest of which rises to a maximum height of 750 feet from the floor of the San Luis Valley to the top and is referred to as "Star Dune."

Numismatic Commentary

On Thursday, September 4, 2014, a large crowd of about 3,000, including about 2,400 children, were on hand for the launch ceremony of the new quarter. The event took place in the Dunes Parking Lot near Mosca, Colorado, with picturesque scenery forming a dramatic backdrop.

"With its awe-inspiring combination of desert dunes, high mountain peaks, and flowing Medano Creek, I can see why Great Sand Dunes National Park and Preserve was chosen to represent the state of Colorado in the America the Beautiful Quarters Program," stated David Croft, plant manager for the Denver Mint (formerly called "superintendents," those in charge of the mints have this relatively new title). Croft presented first-day strike quarters from Denver and San Francisco to Park Superintendent Lisa Carrico.

Speakers included Erin Minks representing Senator Mark Udall, Brenda Felmlee representing Congressman Scott Tipton, and other dignitaries. Bill the Mint Buffalo, the Mint mascot, was on hand as well. Members of the younger set received free quarters, perhaps a record amount for any ceremony. Bank-wrapped rolls were available for purchase at face value.

The Great Sand Dunes National Park and Preserve is another site that is obscure to most Americans, and even when one thinks of Colorado it rarely comes to mind. As such, the America the Beautiful series has helped to publicize it. Located in the San Luis Valley in the western part of the state, it was named as a National Monument in 1932 and only recently, on September 13, 2004, as a national park, the newest site with such a numismatic honor.

The area includes over 85,000 acres. They are the tallest sand dunes in North America, rising to about 750 feet in some instances. They are relatively modern from a geological viewpoint. The formations are believed to have been started about 440,000 years ago from sand and particles of an ancient dry lake and from the Rio Grande River and its branches. The process is ongoing with the prevailing wind, and there are daily changes. Curiously, most of the ridges, even the higher ones, have damp sand less than a foot below their surfaces.

2014-P, Great Sand Dunes National Park (CO)

MS-64	MS-65	MS-66	MS-67	MS-68
$0.50	$0.80	$2.65	$16	—

2014-D, Great Sand Dunes National Park (CO)

MS-64	MS-65	MS-66	MS-67	MS-68
$0.50	$0.80	$2.65	$16	—

2014-S, Great Sand Dunes National Park (CO), Circulation Strike

MS-64	MS-65	MS-66	MS-67	MS-68
$0.50	$0.80	$2.65	$16	—

2014-S, Great Sand Dunes National Park (CO), Proof, Clad

PF-67DC	PF-68DC	PF-69DC
$1.50	$4.05	$9.50

2014-S, Great Sand Dunes National Park (CO), Proof, Silver

PF-67DC	PF-68DC	PF-69DC
$7.20	$8.50	$11

2014, Everglades National Park (FL)

Circulation-Strike Mintage, Philadelphia: 157,601,200
Circulation-Strike Mintage, Denver: 142,400,000
Circulation-Strike Mintage, San Francisco: 1,180,900
Proof Mintage, San Francisco, Clad: 856,139
Proof Mintage, San Francisco, Silver: 472,107

GSID: Circulation-strike, Philadelphia, 77745; Circulation-strike, Denver, 77746; Circulation-strike, San Francisco, 77747; Proof Clad Deep Cameo, 77821; Proof Silver Deep Cameo, 77822

Specifics of the Reverse Design

Description: An anhinga with outstretched wings is seen on a willow tree, with a roseate spoonbill visible in the mid-ground.

Designer: Joel Iskowitz. *Mint sculptor-engraver who made the model:* Joseph F. Menna. *Designers's initials and location:* JI is in the flora at bottom center. *Engraver's initials and location:* JFM is in the flora to the left of the foreground bird's tail.

Story and Background of the Design

Several design candidates were given to the usual parties for review before being sent to the Treasury secretary for his final decision. Two birds can be seen in the design—the anhinga (sometimes called "snakebird") and the roseate spoonbill. The former received its name due its appearance when swimming: only the neck appears above the water, making it look like a snake ready to strike. Like the American flamingo, the roseate spoonbill's pink color is diet-derived and can range from pale pink to bright magenta.

Numismatic Commentary

The launch ceremony for the new quarter was held on December 4, 2014, in the Sally Wood Barn Pavilion at Harris Field Park in Homestead, Florida. Representing the Mint was Beverly Babers, an administrative officer, who commented, "A vast mosaic of habitats that protects a thousand plant and bird species, Everglades National Park is the perfect choice to represent Florida in the America the Beautiful Quarters Program."

Over 1,000 onlookers were in attendance. Distinguished guests included Everglades National Park Acting Superintendent Bob Krumenaker, Homestead Mayor Jeff Porter, Vice-Mayor Stephen R. Shelley, and "Inside Homestead" host Josh Padgett.

The Community Bank of Homestead supplied about $21,000 in quarters in exchange for cash. By this time the coin had been in general circulation for a month, an exceptional advance period before a ceremony.

Everglades National Park, through which the popular Tamiami Trail road passes, is one of America's scenic wonders and is its largest tropical wilderness. The park comprises about 20 percent of what the area was generations ago prior to drainage and development. After Death Valley (nowhere observed on a federal coin to date) and Yellowstone (suitably honored in 2010), Everglades is the third largest National Park in the lower 48 states.

It is nourished by fresh water flowing south from Lake Okeechobee. Wildlife includes the well-known alligators and their rarer relatives, crocodiles, among about 50 species of reptiles, including the pesky pythons not native to the area, but which can grow to 12 feet or more in length. There are about 300 species of fresh and saltwater fish and about 40 different mammals, including the manatee. The park was established in 1934 to stem the continuing development of swampland to farming and residential uses by new canals and other drainage, and was officially dedicated in 1947.

2014-P, Everglades National Park (FL)

MS-64	MS-65	MS-66	MS-67	MS-68
$0.50	$0.80	$2.65	$16	—

2014-D, Everglades National Park (FL)

MS-64	MS-65	MS-66	MS-67	MS-68
$0.50	$0.80	$2.65	$16	—

2014-S, Everglades National Park (FL), Circulation Strike

MS-64	MS-65	MS-66	MS-67	MS-68
$0.50	$0.80	$2.65	$16	—

2014-S, Everglades National Park (FL), Proof, Clad

PF-67DC	PF-68DC	PF-69DC
$1.50	$4.05	$9.50

2014-S, Everglades National Park (FL), Proof, Silver

PF-67DC	PF-68DC	PF-69DC
$7.20	$8.50	$11

2015, Homestead National Monument of America (NE)

Circulation-Strike Mintage, Philadelphia: 214,400,000
Circulation-Strike Mintage, Denver: 248,600,000
Circulation-Strike Mintage, San Francisco: 1,153,840
Proof Mintage, San Francisco, Clad: 831,503
Proof Mintage, San Francisco, Silver: 490,829

GSID: Circulation-strike, Philadelphia, 77748; Circulation-strike, Denver, 77749; Circulation-strike, San Francisco, 77750; Proof Clad Deep Cameo, 77823; Proof Silver Deep Cameo, 77824

Specifics of the Reverse Design

Description: Emblematic of the Homestead National Monument of America, the design represents the three fundamentals of survival common to all homesteaders: food, shelter, and water.

Designer: Ronald D. Sanders. *Mint sculptor-engraver who made the model:* Jim Licaretz. *Designers's initials and location:* RS is in the corn on the left. *Engraver's initials and location:* JL is in the corn on the right.

Story and Background of the Design

Several designs were considered for the 2015 Homestead National Monument quarter dollar and were passed among the usual groups before recommendations were sent back to the Treasury secretary for a final decision. The design commemorates the Homestead Act of 1862, which stated, in exchange for five years of residence and the cultivation and improvement of the property, any qualified person was able to claim up to 160 acres of federally owned land.

Numismatic Commentary

The official launch ceremony for the latest quarter was held on February 10, 2015, with a crowd of 2,500 on hand, including about 1,800 school children in attendance, at Beatrice High School. David Croft, by now a familiar figure at these events, represented the Mint.

Guests included Lieutenant Governor Mike Foley, National Park Service Acting Regional Director Patty Trap, site Superintendent Mark Engler, and Mayor Stan Wirth of Beatrice.

Later, in its issue of May 12, 2015, *Numismatic News* reported a 2015-P Nebraska quarter with strong doubling on part of the reverse, a variety confirmed by Ken Potter, a specialist in such varieties. The feature is an additional handle to the water pump visible through the second window from the bottom write of the depicted historic Freeman school house. Other varieties of die doubling were later reported, some quite minor. These have not gained wide traction in the marketplace.

The Homestead National Monument of America, managed by the National Park System, commemorates (or otherwise observes) the Homestead Act of 1862 which allowed pioneers to claim up to 160 acres of federally-owned land if they developed it for farming and built a home. Eventually, 270 million acres went into private hands. The monument is four miles west of Beatrice, Nebraska.

2015-P, Homestead National Monument of America (NE)

MS-64	MS-65	MS-66	MS-67	MS-68
$0.50	$0.80	$2.65	$16	—

2015-D, Homestead National Monument of America (NE)

MS-64	MS-65	MS-66	MS-67	MS-68
$0.50	$0.80	$2.65	$16	—

2015-S, Homestead National Monument of America (NE), Circulation Strike

MS-64	MS-65	MS-66	MS-67	MS-68
$0.50	$0.80	$2.65	$16	—

2015-S, Homestead National Monument of America (NE), Proof, Clad

PF-67DC	PF-68DC	PF-69DC
$1.50	$4.05	$9.50

2015-S, Homestead National Monument of America (NE), Proof, Silver

PF-67DC	PF-68DC	PF-69DC
$7.20	$8.50	$11

2015, Kisatchie National Forest (LA)

Circulation-Strike Mintage, Philadelphia: 397,200,000
Circulation-Strike Mintage, Denver: 379,600,000
Circulation-Strike Mintage, San Francisco: 1,099,380
Proof Mintage, San Francisco, Clad: 762,407
Proof Mintage, San Francisco, Silver: 490,829
GSID: Circulation-strike, Philadelphia, 77751; Circulation-strike, Denver, 77752; Circulation-strike, San Francisco, 77753; Proof Clad Deep Cameo, 77825; Proof Silver Deep Cameo, 77826

Specifics of the Reverse Design
Description: A wild turkey can be seen flying over blue stem grass with long leaf pine trees in the background.

Designer: Susan Gamble. *Mint sculptor-engraver who made the model:* Joseph F. Menna. *Designers's initials and location:* SG is hidden in the grass on the left. *Engraver's initials and location:* JM is hidden in the grass on the right.

Story and Background of the Design
As with other America the Beautiful quarters, several designs were created by the Mint and passed around among the usual groups for their recommendations. Depicted in the design is a wild turkey in flight in Kisatchie, Louisiana's only national forest. The forest is home to 155 species of breeding birds, 48 mammal species, 56 reptile species, and 30 amphibian species. Rare animals in the area include the Louisiana pine snake, the red-cockaded woodpecker, the Louisiana black bear, and the Louisiana pearl shell mussel.

Numismatic Commentary
On Wednesday, April 22, 2015, the launch ceremony for the new quarter was held at the Alexandria Riverfront Center in downtown Alexandria, a town about a half-hour's drive from the National Forest. "We hope the Kisatchie National Forest quarter will inspire Louisianans to get outdoors and explore their national forest," said Jim Caldwell, public affairs officer for the forest.

About 1,500 people were on hand, including more than 850 children who received free quarters. Students told the story of famous author and horticulturist Caroline Dorman, who was important in natural preservation in the state. B.B. Craig represented the Mint and presented several dignitaries with quarters struck during the first day of mintage. The Pineville High School Choir sang and the Leesville High School JROTC Color Guard presented the colors. Rolls of quarters were supplied by the Red River Bank, and about $34,000 worth changed hands.

The Kisatchie National Forest is another site commemorated on an America the Beautiful quarter that is unknown except by a small percentage of Americans. As such, a quarter once again performs an educational function. The forest occupies about 604,000 acres of land, most of which is covered with longleaf pine and flatwoods vegetation and is home to many rare plant and animal species, including carnivorous plants and wild orchids. Areas of hardwoods and sections of bogs and marshes are also included. The National Forest was first designated as such in 1930 during the Herbert Hoover administration.

The Kisatchie quarter captured the Best Circulating Coin category at the 2017 Coin of the Year (COTY) Awards in Berlin.

2015-P, Kisatchie National Forest (LA)

MS-64	MS-65	MS-66	MS-67	MS-68
$0.50	$0.80	$2.65	$21.50	$130

2015-D, Kisatchie National Forest (LA)

MS-64	MS-65	MS-66	MS-67	MS-68
$0.50	$0.80	$2.65	$16	—

2015-S, Kisatchie National Forest (LA), Circulation Strike

MS-64	MS-65	MS-66	MS-67	MS-68
$0.50	$0.80	$2.65	$16	—

2015-S, Kisatchie National Forest (LA), Proof, Clad

PF-67DC	PF-68DC	PF-69DC
$1.50	$4.05	$9.50

2015-S, Kisatchie National Forest (LA), Proof, Silver

PF-67DC	PF-68DC	PF-69DC
$7.20	$8.50	$11

2015, Blue Ridge Parkway (NC)

Circulation-Strike Mintage, Philadelphia: 325,616,000
Circulation-Strike Mintage, Denver: 505,200,000
Circulation-Strike Mintage, San Francisco: 1,096,620
Proof Mintage, San Francisco, Clad: 762,407
Proof Mintage, San Francisco, Silver: 490,829

GSID: Circulation-strike, Philadelphia, 77754; Circulation-strike, Denver, 77755; Circulation-strike, San Francisco, 77756; Proof Clad Deep Cameo, 77827; Proof Silver Deep Cameo, 77828

Specifics of the Reverse Design

Description: The reverse design depicts the grace and curvature of the road hugging the side of a mountain. The American dogwood, which is the North Carolina state flower, appears in the foreground.

Designer: Frank Morris. *Mint sculptor-engraver who made the model:* Joseph F. Menna. *Designers's initials and location:* FM is in the road to the left. *Engraver's initials and location:* JM is in the dogwoods on the right.

Story and Background of the Design

Various designs were created for the Blue Ridge Parkway quarter and were dispersed to the usual groups for evaluation. The Treasury secretary made his selection and selected a design highlighting the grace and the curvature of the road hugging the side of a mountain. Standing out in the bottom right corner of the design are dogwood blossoms, the state flower of North Carolina. Dogwood trees can grow up to 33-feet tall and when mature, are often wider than they are tall.

Numismatic Commentary

On Thursday, June 25, 2015, officials from the U.S. Mint and National Park Service introduced the new Blue Ridge Parkway quarter-dollar to the public. The ceremony was held at Pack Square Park in Asheville, North Carolina, which is near the scenic national parkway that is commemorated on the new coin. David Holt, Grammy-award-winning musician and TV host, served as master of ceremonies. Music was provided by the Lightning Bolts.

"This new quarter stands now as a tribute to this national scenic byway—a cross section of Appalachian mountain history essential to the story of our nation, tying together diverse landscapes and rich history," said David Croft, plant manager at the Denver Mint.

Guests included Lieutenant Governor Dan Forest and Blue Ridge Parkway Superintendent Mark Woods. The Asheville Savings Bank exchanged $24,000 in quarters for face value, in addition to the free coins given out to the younger set.

The Blue Ridge Parkway is a cousin to the Skyline Drive of Virginia that is also featured on an America the Beautiful quarter. It is in America's longest linear park and winds its way for 469 miles through 29 counties in Virginia and North Carolina, much of which offers expansive views from the Blue Ridge Mountains. It was built to connect the Shenandoah National Park to the Great Smoky Mountains National Park.

2015-P, Blue Ridge Parkway (NC)

MS-64	MS-65	MS-66	MS-67	MS-68
$0.50	$0.80	$2.65	$16	—

2015-D, Blue Ridge Parkway (NC)

MS-64	MS-65	MS-66	MS-67	MS-68
$0.50	$0.80	$2.65	$16	—

2015-S, Blue Ridge Parkway (NC), Circulation Strike

MS-64	MS-65	MS-66	MS-67	MS-68
$0.50	$0.80	$2.65	$16	—

2015-S, Blue Ridge Parkway (NC), Proof, Clad

PF-67DC	PF-68DC	PF-69DC
$1.50	$4.05	$9.50

2015-S, Blue Ridge Parkway (NC), Proof, Silver

PF-67DC	PF-68DC	PF-69DC
$7.20	$8.50	$11

2015, Bombay Hook National Wildlife Refugee (DE)

Circulation-Strike Mintage, Philadelphia: 275,000,000
Circulation-Strike Mintage, Denver: 206,400,000
Circulation-Strike Mintage, San Francisco: 1,013,920
Proof Mintage, San Francisco, Clad: 762,407
Proof Mintage, San Francisco, Silver: 490,829
GSID: Circulation-strike, Philadelphia, 77757; Circulation-strike, Denver, 77758; Circulation-strike, San Francisco, 77759; Proof Clad Deep Cameo, 77829; Proof Silver Deep Cameo, 77830

Specifics of the Reverse Design

Description: A great blue heron is seen in the foreground with a great egret in the background.

Designer: Joel Iskowitz. *Mint sculptor-engraver who made the model:* Phebe Hemphill. *Designers's initials and location:* JI is hidden in the flora in the bottom left. *Engraver's initials and location:* PH is hidden in the flora in the bottom right, to the left of the foreground bird's leg.

Story and Background of the Design

This design was chosen from eight candidates, each of which showed birds (five standing and three in flight) by the usual parties and Secretary of the Treasury Lew. Featured in the design are two birds—the great blue heron and the great egret. The former is the largest North American heron and is roughly twice the size of the latter bird. Both birds seen in the design are standing in the midst of the refuge's tidal salt marsh.

Numismatic Commentary

The launch ceremony was held on Friday, September 19, 2015. Representing the Mint was the plant manager of the Philadelphia Mint, Mark Landry, who commented, "I'm uniquely excited about this launch because we are making these Bombay Hook quarters 67 miles north of here at our plant in Philadelphia. Some of the very people in our plant are Delaware residents, so this quarter carries a special meaning to the men and women of the United States Mint."

The event was held at the Bombay Hook National Wildlife Refuge Visitor Center. Dignitaries included both U.S. senators—Tom Carper and Chris Coons—former Governor and Representative Mike Castle (father of the quarter programs), and various officials connected with the refuge. Castle told the history of the original 50 State Quarter program and its segue into the America the Beautiful series, describing how each program was developed and his constant attention to be sure that each was on track.

Leilani Wall, a local singer and songwriter, provided entertainment before and after the event. Smyrna High School JROTC presented the colors and led the Pledge of Allegiance. An estimated 450 people were on hand, including, per the Mint news release, "several dozen" schoolchildren—this being one of the smallest turnouts of the younger set. Quarters were distributed as usual, including free coins for those 18 and younger.

There was not much to choose from in Delaware that was administered by the National Park Service, but the Bombay Hook National Wildlife Refuge filled the bill nicely. It is yet another America the Beautiful quarter with significant educational value. The rather small (as such things go) nature preserve occupies 15,987 acres of land on the coast of Delaware Bay.

The refuge was established on March 16, 1937, to preserve a landing area and breeding ground for migratory and other birds along the Atlantic Flyway. The cost of buying the land was paid for by funds generated by selling federal duck stamps to philatelists, a popular specialty.

The name of the place has nothing to do with Bombay, India (now named Mumbai), but is a corruption of the Dutch "Boompjes," or "Boompjes Hoeck," meaning "little-tree point." The general area has been a popular resort since the mid-19th century, especially for vacationing Philadelphia residents who stay at a hotel, later connected by steamship. A great storm in 1878, popularly known as the "great tidal wave," laid waste to the area, destroyed most cottages and other facilities, and rearranged the coastal dunes, vastly changing the biological nature of the area. From 1938 to 1942 the Civilian Conservation Corps, the highly effective make-work program of the Franklin D. Roosevelt administration, built a dike and causeway, erected buildings, created freshwater pools, and did much to restore the area to its original natural habitat for freshwater plants and animals.

During World War II the refuge was used for gunnery practice and for research on ordnance and rockets. Later it returned to its status as a wildlife area. New freshwater ponds were added. Today its continuation as a nature preserve seems assured.

2015-P, Bombay Hook National Wildlife Refugee (DE)

MS-64	MS-65	MS-66	MS-67	MS-68
$0.50	$0.80	$2.65	$16	—

2015-D, Bombay Hook National Wildlife Refugee (DE)

MS-64	MS-65	MS-66	MS-67	MS-68
$0.50	$0.80	$2.65	$16	—

2015-S, Bombay Hook National Wildlife Refugee (DE), Circulation Strike

MS-64	MS-65	MS-66	MS-67	MS-68
$0.50	$0.80	$2.65	$16	—

2015-S, Bombay Hook National Wildlife Refugee (DE), Proof, Clad

PF-67DC	PF-68DC	PF-69DC
$1.50	$4.05	$9.50

2015-S, Bombay Hook National Wildlife Refugee (DE), Proof, Silver

PF-67DC	PF-68DC	PF-69DC
$7.20	$8.50	$11

2015, Saratoga National Historical Park (NY)

Circulation-Strike Mintage, Philadelphia: 223,000,000

Circulation-Strike Mintage, Denver: 215,800,000

Circulation-Strike Mintage, San Francisco: 1,045,500

Proof Mintage, San Francisco, Clad: 791,347

Proof Mintage, San Francisco, Silver: 490,829

GSID: Circulation-strike, Philadelphia, 77760; Circulation-strike, Denver, 77761; Circulation-strike, San Francisco, 77762; Proof Clad Deep Cameo, 77831; Proof Silver Deep Cameo, 77832

Specifics of the Reverse Design

Description: A close up depiction of the moment when British General John Burgoyne surrendered his sword to General Horatio Gates is shown, a pivotal moment which was a turning point in the American Revolutionary War.

Designer: Barbara Fox. *Mint sculptor-engraver who made the model:* Renata Gordon. *Designers's initials and location:* BF is on the bottom of the sword. *Engraver's initials and location:* RG is at the bottom of the field, below the date 1777.

Story and Background of the Design

Designed by foreword author Barbara Fox and sculpted by Renata Gordon, the reverse design was chosen from among 10 design candidates. The design was presented to the usual parties, including the Commission of Fine Arts and Citizens Coinage Advisory Committee, for review before their recommendations were sent to the Treasury secretary and he made the final decision. The image depicts General Burgoyne surrendering his sword to General Gates, leading to Burgoyne never holding another active command again.

Numismatic Commentary

The official release ceremony for the latest quarter, the last of the 2015 year, took place on Tuesday, November 17, in the Schuylerville High School auditorium and gym near the park. Ron Harrigal represented the Mint. "You can't buy much with a quarter these days," Harrigal said. "Don't spend it. Put it away and pass it on to your grandchildren and tell them about the day you helped make history." More than 1,400 people were on hand, including about 500 school children. Barbara Fox, designer of the coin, was present—unusual for a quarter ceremony. The local *Saratogian News* reported:

> The design was done by U.S. Mint artist Barbara Fox, who lives in western New York. It's one of 17 coins she has done including two more for the American the Beautiful series, which show Glacier and Acadia national parks in Montana and Maine, respectively. "I wish I'd been chosen for the Hawaii coin," she said smiling. "I'd love to go there."

The auditorium was filled to capacity, and those in the overflow crowd watched a video screen. Amy Bracewell, park superintendent, told of the history of the shrine. WNYT-TV (Channel 13), the local NBC affiliate, live-streamed the quarter ceremony. Quarters were available free to the younger set and for sale in $10 rolls to all.

On the night before a coin forum attracted about 75 people, mostly numismatists.

Saratoga National Historical Park is located about 40 miles north of Albany in the town of Stillwater, in upstate New York. It is the site of the Battle of Saratoga—the military engagement with the British that were the first American victories during the Revolutionary War. The decisive win that forced British troops to surrender influenced France to recognize the United States as an independent nation and, later, to render assistance to American forces through the Marquis de Lafayette and others.

The area was first authorized as a New York State Historic Preserve in 1927, the 150th anniversary of the battle. In 1938 Congress made it the Saratoga National Historical Park. Visitors are guided by maps to various locations, including some outside of the park that played a role in the battle. The resort town of Saratoga Springs is not far distant—the summer getaway for many New York City residents, famed for its large hotels and many mineral springs.

2015-P, Saratoga National Historical Park (NY)

MS-64	MS-65	MS-66	MS-67	MS-68
$0.50	$0.80	$2.65	$16	—

2015-D, Saratoga National Historical Park (NY)

MS-64	MS-65	MS-66	MS-67	MS-68
$0.50	$0.80	$2.65	$16	—

2015-S, Saratoga National Historical Park (NY), Circulation Strike

MS-64	MS-65	MS-66	MS-67	MS-68
$0.50	$0.80	$2.65	$16	—

2015-S, Saratoga National Historical Park (NY), Proof, Clad

PF-67DC	PF-68DC	PF-69DC
$1.50	$4.05	$9.50

2015-S, Saratoga National Historical Park (NY), Proof, Silver

PF-67DC	PF-68DC	PF-69DC
$7.20	$8.50	$11

2016, Shawnee National Forest (IL)

Circulation-Strike Mintage, Philadelphia: 155,600,000
Circulation-Strike Mintage, Denver: 151,800,000
Circulation-Strike Mintage, San Francisco: 1,081,914
Proof Mintage, San Francisco, Clad: 696,564
Proof Mintage, San Francisco, Silver: 502,039

GSID: Circulation-strike, Philadelphia, 77763; Circulation-strike, Denver, 77764; Circulation-strike, San Francisco, 77765; Proof Clad Deep Cameo, 77833; Proof Silver Deep Cameo, 77834

Specifics of the Reverse Design

Description: The reverse shows a close view of Camel Rock with natural vegetation in the foreground and a red-tailed hawk soaring in the sky overhead.

Designer: Justin Kunz. *Mint sculptor-engraver who made the model:* Jim Licaretz. *Designers's initials and location:* JK is hidden in the trees on the bottom left. *Engraver's initials and location:* RG is at the base of the second tree down on the right.

Story and Background of the Design

Six design candidates were presented by the Mint to the regular parties for review, including the CFA and CCAC. After consulting the recommendations, Secretary Lew made his decision and chose the final design, announcing all 2016 designs in late 2015. Depicted on the coin is a view of Camel Rock, part of the Garden of the Gods of Wilderness area of Shawnee National Forest.

Numismatic Commentary

The official launch ceremony for the latest America the Beautiful quarter took place on February 4 at the Deaton Gymnasium at Southeastern Illinois College in Harrisburg. Representing the Mint was a new face, Dean Bidle, who was important in the fulfillment of quarters to collectors. He commented:

> Not only is the Shawnee National Forest quarter the 31st coin in the America the Beautiful Quarters Program–and the first quarter to be introduced into circulation in 2016–it also is the fifth and last national forest to be honored in the program. Millions of Americans will now have a reminder of the beauty of southern Illinois through a quarter designed in the national forest's honor.

About 1,300 people were on hand, including about 550 younger people from local schools, the Job Corps, and the Cub Scouts. Cindy Cain, executive director of the regional office of the Illinois Tourism Bureau was emcee. The Harrisburg High School Choral Ensemble led the singing of "The Star-Spangled Banner". U.S. Forest Service Chief Tom Tidwell delivered remarks on how proud the Forest Service was to be part of the program and to have Shawnee National Forest represented on the quarter for Illinois.

On the night previous about 70 numismatists and others were on hand at a forum explaining the quarter program. General release of the quarters took place a few days later on February 8—unusual as most Federal Reserve distributions took place before the launches.

The Shawnee National Forest is in the Ozark and Shawnee hills in southern Illinois. Consisting of about 280,000 acres it is the largest publicly owned land in the state. The parcel was acquired in sections, including many abandoned farms. It was designated as a national forest in September 1939. The Civilian Conservation Corps planted trees and helped rebuild the soil from the Dust Bowl conditions of the mid-1930s that prompted many residents to move to California and other parts in the West. The reclamation of the area has not been without controversy, as different people have differed on what was done and should be done. Supervised by forest rangers, the land is home to many birds and animals.

2016-P, Shawnee National Forest (IL)

MS-64	MS-65	MS-66	MS-67	MS-68
$0.50	$0.80	$2.65	$16	—

2016-D, Shawnee National Forest (IL)

MS-64	MS-65	MS-66	MS-67	MS-68
$0.50	$0.80	$2.65	$16	—

2016-S, Shawnee National Forest (IL), Circulation Strike

MS-64	MS-65	MS-66	MS-67	MS-68
$0.50	$0.80	$2.65	$16	—

2016-S, Shawnee National Forest (IL), Proof, Clad

PF-67DC	PF-68DC	PF-69DC
$1.50	$4.05	$9.50

2016-S, Shawnee National Forest (IL), Proof, Silver

PF-67DC	PF-68DC	PF-69DC
$7.20	$8.50	$11

2016, Cumberland Gap National Historic Park (KY)

Circulation-Strike Mintage, Philadelphia: 215,400,000
Circulation-Strike Mintage, Denver: 223,200,000
Circulation-Strike Mintage, San Francisco: 1,036,093
Proof Mintage, San Francisco, Clad: 666,857
Proof Mintage, San Francisco, Silver: 502,039

GSID: Circulation-strike, Philadelphia, 77766; Circulation-strike, Denver, 77767; Circulation-strike, San Francisco, 77768; Proof Clad Deep Cameo, 77837; Proof Silver Deep Cameo, 77838

Specifics of the Reverse Design

Description: A frontiersman is seen gazing across the mountains to the West.

Designer: Barbara Fox. *Mint sculptor-engraver who made the model:* Joseph F. Menna. *Designers's initials and location:* BF is beneath the end of the rifle. *Engraver's initials and location:* JFM is to the right on the pouch.

Story and Background of the Design

This image, designed by Barbara Fox and sculpted by Joseph Menna, was selected from among five candidates. After going through the conventional channels of review, the Treasury secretary chose this design for the reverse. Depicted is a frontiersman gazing to the mountains in the West. Many pioneers used the Cumberland Gap on their journeys into the western frontiers of Kentucky and Tennessee.

Numismatic Commentary

The launch ceremony for the second America the Beautiful quarter of 2016 took place on Monday, April 11, at the Park Visitors Center in Middlesboro, Kentucky. About 3,600 were on hand, including 2,700 schoolchildren—a remarkably large turnout of the younger set. Mark Landry, plant manager of the Philadelphia Mint, shared emcee duties with Hadden Landen and Makay Patterson, both fourth-grade students at Middlesboro Elementary School. More than 2,200 youngsters ages 5 to 13 were sworn in as junior rangers. Speakers included Park Superintendent Sula Jacobs; U.S. Representative Hal Rogers; National Park Service Deputy Director Peggy O'Dell; and others.

Quarters were given to the youngsters, and about $26,000 face value was sold in rolls by the Home Federal Bank. On the afternoon before the Mint hosted a coin forum at the C.V. Whitney Convention Center in Pine Mountain State Resort Park. This particular launch ceremony involved a particularly large number of local citizens.[17]

Established on June 11, 1940, Cumberland Gap National Historical Park is situated in Kentucky in the area near the borders of the states of Kentucky, Tennessee, and Virginia. It is a large natural gap in the Appalachian Mountains that in the early years of our country furnished the gateway to what was considered the American West, including what are now the states of Kentucky, Ohio, Indiana, and Illinois. For much of the time from the 1770s through the early 1900s, life in that district of Kentucky was very rural, often primitive by city standards, called "pioneer lifestyle," in one description. In time that changed.

The park covers 20,208 acres. The Visitor Center on Highway 25E, southeast of Middlesboro, Kentucky, the trails, and other features typically draw in the high hundreds of thousands of visitors each year, mainly in the warmer season.

2016-P, Cumberland Gap National Historic Park (KY)

MS-64	MS-65	MS-66	MS-67	MS-68
$0.50	$0.80	$2.65	$34	$468

2016-D, Cumberland Gap National Historic Park (KY)

MS-64	MS-65	MS-66	MS-67	MS-68
$0.50	$0.80	$2.65	$16	—

2016-S, Cumberland Gap National Historic Park (KY), Circulation Strike

MS-64	MS-65	MS-66	MS-67	MS-68
$0.50	$0.80	$2.65	$16	—

2016-S, Cumberland Gap National Historic Park (KY), Proof, Clad

PF-67DC	PF-68DC	PF-69DC
$1.50	$4.05	$9.50

2016-S, Cumberland Gap National Historic Park (KY), Proof, Silver

PF-67DC	PF-68DC	PF-69DC
$7.20	$8.50	$11

2016, Harpers Ferry National Historical Park (WV)

Circulation-Strike Mintage, Philadelphia: 434,630,000
Circulation-Strike Mintage, Denver: 424,000,000
Circulation-Strike Mintage, San Francisco: 1,050,185
Proof Mintage, San Francisco, Clad: 666,857
Proof Mintage, San Francisco, Silver: 502,039

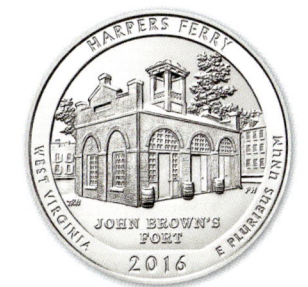

GSID: Circulation-strike, Philadelphia, 77769; Circulation-strike, Denver, 77770; Circulation-strike, San Francisco, 77771; Proof Clad Deep Cameo, 77839; Proof Silver Deep Cameo, 77840

Specifics of the Reverse Design
Description: John Brown's Fort is depicted.

Designer: Thomas R. Hipschen. *Mint sculptor-engraver who made the model:* Phebe Hemphill. *Designers's initials and location:* TRH is at the back left corner of the building. *Engraver's initials and location:* PH is at the back right corner of the building.

Story and Background of the Design
This design was selected by the Treasury secretary from among eight candidates. The chosen design features a rendition of John Brown's Fort, the site of the American abolitionist's last stand during his raid on the Harpers Ferry Armory in an attempt to start a liberation movement amongst the slaves. Brown believed that the only way to overthrow the institution of slavery was through armed insurrection and was eventually hanged for treason, murder, and inciting a slave insurrection.

Numismatic Commentary
The launch ceremony for the latest quarter took place on June 8, 2016, along the Shenandoah River in the Lower Town Historic District of Harpers Ferry. While the setting was tranquil, strong winds and a soaking downpour about halfway through the event added an unexpected element. As part of the ceremony a train came roaring down the tracks. Representing the Mint was William Norton, an officer in charge of legislative affairs, who, dripping wet on stage, commented:

> This new coin serves as a reminder that at a river-crossing established long before our country's struggle for independence, in a West Virginia town that played an integral role in our nation's Civil War, a diverse number of people and events came together to influence the course of our common history.

Thomas R. Hipschen, an Artistic Infusion Program member who designed the coin was on hand. Three members of Congress were represented by surrogates. Park Superintendent Rebecca Harriett was emcee for the event. She welcomed an estimated 1,100 attendees including about 400 children, and Vicky Bullett, an Olympic gold medalist for basketball and native of the area, who was well known to most in the audience. Local students led the Pledge of Allegiance and the presentation of the colors. After the ceremony the younger attendees received free quarters, and the Jefferson Security Bank paid out about $29,000 in Philadelphia Mint coins for face value. On the night before a coin forum was held.

Harpers Ferry National Historical Park is located where the Potomac and Shenandoah rivers meet, near the town of Harpers Ferry. This and other areas were part of Virginia until West Virginia separated from the Confederate States of America in 1863 to become its own state. The area was designated as a national monument in 1944 and as a national historical park in 1963. It is about 4,000 acres in extent.

Harpers Ferry is best remembered as the site of the raid by abolitionist John Brown on the federal armory there, a facility begun during the administration of George Washington. Much of the hardware and weaponry for the 1803–1805 Lewis and Clark expedition into the Louisiana Territory purchase was made there.

In 1859 Brown and his armed companions captured the Armory as part of plan to go farther south and enlist slaves to rebel against their oppression. He was arrested by federal troops under U.S. Army Colonel Robert E. Lee and was hanged shortly afterward. This was a time in the administration of President James Buchanan in which he and Congress tried to please the slave-holding South and the abolition-minded North and succeeded in satisfying neither. Anti-slavery sentiment had risen greatly in recent years, since the time of *Uncle Tom's Cabin* describing the life of the enslaved on plantations. Viewed as a criminal in 1859, today he is remembered as one of the great heroes in American civil rights. The melody of a popular song, "John Brown's Body," was later used for "The Battle Hymn of the Republic."

During the Civil War the town changed hands from Confederate to Union and back eight times. Today anyone acquiring one of the quarters and also spending a few hours reading history will find a visit to Harpers Ferry to be very educational and rewarding.

2016-P, Harpers Ferry National Historical Park (WV)

MS-64	MS-65	MS-66	MS-67	MS-68
$0.50	$0.80	$2.65	$16	—

2016-D, Harpers Ferry National Historical Park (WV)

MS-64	MS-65	MS-66	MS-67	MS-68
$0.50	$0.80	$2.65	$16	—

2016-S, Harpers Ferry National Historical Park (WV), Circulation Strike

MS-64	MS-65	MS-66	MS-67	MS-68
$0.50	$0.80	$2.65	$16	—

2016-S, Harpers Ferry National Historical Park (WV), Proof, Clad

PF-67DC	PF-68DC	PF-69DC
$1.50	$4.05	$9.50

2016-S, Harpers Ferry National Historical Park (WV), Proof, Silver

PF-67DC	PF-68DC	PF-69DC
$7.20	$8.50	$11

2016, Theodore Roosevelt National Park (ND)

Circulation-Strike Mintage, Philadelphia: 231,600,000

Circulation-Strike Mintage, Denver: 223,200,000

Circulation-Strike Mintage, San Francisco: 1,073,092

Proof Mintage, San Francisco, Clad: 666,857

Proof Mintage, San Francisco, Silver: 502,039

GSID: Circulation-strike, Philadelphia, 81977; Circulation-strike, Denver, 81978; Circulation-strike, San Francisco, 81979; Proof Clad Deep Cameo, 77841; Proof Silver Deep Cameo, 77842

Specifics of the Reverse Design

Description: A young Teddy Roosevelt on horseback is seen surveying the terrain near the Little Missouri River.

Designer: Joel Iskowitz. *Mint sculptor-engraver who made the model:* Phebe Hemphill. *Designers's initials and location:* JI is to the left on the bank. *Engraver's initials and location:* PH is on the right beneath the horse.

Story and Background of the Design

Six designs were presented by the Mint to the usual parties for review and recommendations. The final decision, as always, fell in the hands of the secretary of the Treasury. Depicted in the design is a young Teddy Roosevelt, whom dedicated much of his life to the conservation and preservation of America's natural parks, forests, and monuments.

Numismatic Commentary

At 10:00 in the morning of August 25 the launch ceremony for the Theodore Roosevelt National Park quarter took place—the date marking the 100th anniversary of the founding of the National Park Service. In contrast to the Harpers Ferry event, the weather in North Dakota was warm and under a cloudless sky. Representing the Mint was Principal Deputy Director Rhett Jeppson, new in the post, succeeding Richard A. Peterson. Similar to Peterson, Jeppson was interested in the numismatic fraternity. At the American Numismatic Association's annual World's Fair of Money held a few weeks earlier he was on hand to meet and greet the attendees.

Held at the park's Painted Canyon Visitor Center, the event attracted several dignitaries, including U.S. Senator John Hoeven and U.S. Congressman Kevin Cramer, each of whom gave remarks, as did Park Superintendent Windy Ross. About 900 people were on hand, including about 400 school children. The First State Bank of Golva exchanged $18,000 in Denver Mint quarters. A forum held the night before drew about 65 people.

Theodore Roosevelt National Park, comprising 70,446 acres, is located in areas of the Badlands in western North Dakota. It takes its name from the president who spent time in the area in his youth and was forever interested in the history of the American West, including writing a four-volume set of books on how it was "won" by suppressing Native Americans. He was a careful scholar, and his study of the War of 1812, published in 1882, became a standard text.

His first visit to the Badlands was in September 1883, where he shot his first bison and became impressed with the "strenuous life" (as he often put it) of the area. A man of means with an inheritance of $125,000, he invested $14,000 in the operating Maltese Cross Ranch seven miles south of Medora. After the unrelated deaths of his wife and mother (one in childbirth, the other naturally) in the same house on the same day, February 14, 1884, he went to his ranch to heal. He soon started on a second layout, the Elkhorn Ranch, 35 miles north of Medora. The later life of Roosevelt, including his involvement with sculptor Augustus Saint-Gaudens in coinage designs, is well known. By that time his life in North Dakota was but a fond memory.

2016-P, Theodore Roosevelt National Park (ND)

MS-64	MS-65	MS-66	MS-67	MS-68
$0.50	$0.80	$2.65	$16	—

2016-D, Theodore Roosevelt National Park (ND)

MS-64	MS-65	MS-66	MS-67	MS-68
$0.50	$0.80	$2.65	$16	—

2016-S, Theodore Roosevelt National Park (ND), Circulation Strike

MS-64	MS-65	MS-66	MS-67	MS-68
$0.50	$0.80	$2.65	$16	—

2016-S, Theodore Roosevelt National Park (ND), Proof, Clad

PF-67DC	PF-68DC	PF-69DC
$1.50	$4.05	$9.50

2016-S, Theodore Roosevelt National Park (ND), Proof, Silver

PF-67DC	PF-68DC	PF-69DC
$7.20	$8.50	$11

2016, Fort Moultrie at Fort Sumter National Monument (SC)

Circulation-Strike Mintage, Philadelphia: 154,400,000
Circulation-Strike Mintage, Denver: 142,200,000
Circulation-Strike Mintage, San Francisco: 979,566
Proof Mintage, San Francisco, Clad: 683,741
Proof Mintage, San Francisco, Silver: 502,039

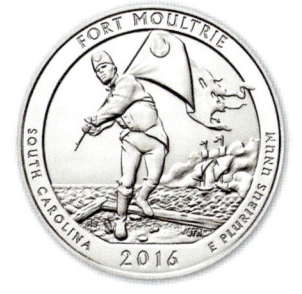

GSID: Circulation-strike, Philadelphia, 77772; Circulation-strike, Denver, 77773; Circulation-strike, San Francisco, 77774; Proof Clad Deep Cameo, 77835; Proof Silver Deep Cameo, 77836

Specifics of the Reverse Design

Description: Sergeant William Jasper is seen returning the regimental flag to the ramparts of Fort Moultrie in Charleston Harbor while under attack from a British ship.

Designer: Richard Scott. *Mint sculptor-engraver who made the model:* Joseph F. Menna. *Designer's initials and location:* RS is by the short wood beam on the left. *Engraver's initials and location:* JFM is at the right end of the long wood beam on the right.

Story and Background of the Design

The design for the 35th coin in the America the Beautiful series was selected from seven potential candidates. The usual parties received the designs and sent their recommendations to the Treasury secretary where he would make the final decision. Depicted on the coin is an image of Sergeant William Jasper running to return the regimental flag. Jasper distinguished himself at that moment during the defense of Fort Moultrie when he recovered and raised the South Carolina flag and held it under fire until a new flagstaff was installed.

Numismatic Commentary

The official launch ceremony began at 10:30 a.m. on Thursday, November 17, 2016, at Fort Moultrie, part of the Fort Sumter National Monument. Piper Hamrick, a fourth-grade student, led the audience in the Pledge of Allegiance. Mayor Pat O'Neil was on hand to welcome the crowd.

U.S. Mint Chief Counsel Jean Gentry was on hand to help with the distribution. National park staff members in period uniforms fired reproduction muskets to help set the historical scene. The Plantation Singers furnished entertainment before and after the ceremony. Park Superintendent Tim Stone and National Park Service Regional Deputy Director Sherri Fields were among the first recipients of the new quarters. Over a dozen other dignitaries were present.

About one thousand people were in attendance at the ceremony in nice weather. About 300 members of the younger set were each given a free coin. After the event about $24,000 in $10 rolls of Philadelphia Mint quarters was exchanged for cash.

On the night before a forum was held for interested collectors and others with 67 attending. By that time the quarters had been distributed by the Federal Reserve through member banks beginning on February 14.

Slightly fewer than 300 million Fort Moultrie quarters were minted—the lowest figure among the designs of 2016. There was no particular excitement within the numismatic community. Interested collectors added circulation strikes and Proofs to their sets.

To the Civil War historian, Fort Moultrie overlooking the harbor of Charleston, South Carolina, is where the Civil War began. When the Confederate States of America was formed in January 1861 by seven states that seceded from the Union, it was thought and hoped by many that the United States, or "the North," would recognize the CSA as a neighbor nation and that normal trade and relations would ensue. Not long afterward the CSA ordered its first paper money and bonds to be printed in New York City by the National Bank Note Company and the National Bank Note Company. That idea of tranquility disappeared on March 11 when batteries at Fort Moultrie began bombarding Fort Sumter in the distance across the water. The fort was reduced to rubble. The federal soldiers and their commander were allowed to depart safely under a white flag of truce. Thus the Civil War started, and would continue until April 1861, with a loss of over a million lives. This was the last time the fort's guns were fired in a war scenario.

This brief four-year chapter is only part of a large book on the fort, which has a history dating back to the Revolutionary War. Named after General William Moultrie, commander of the 1776 Battle of Sullivan's Island, the early fort was constructed of palmetto logs, giving rise to the flag motif and nickname of Palmetto State for South Carolina. It remained a bastion of seacoast defense continuously until it was decommissioned in 1947—the only such American fort with such a long service record. In 1960 the Department of Defense turned over to the National Park Service, which set up a program to interpret its history from early time though its use in World War II for potential coastal defense.

2016-P, Fort Moultrie at Fort Sumter National Monument (SC)

MS-64	MS-65	MS-66	MS-67	MS-68
$0.50	$0.80	$2.65	$16	—

2016-D, Fort Moultrie at Fort Sumter National Monument (SC)

MS-64	MS-65	MS-66	MS-67	MS-68
$0.50	$0.80	$2.65	$16	—

2016-S, Fort Moultrie at Fort Sumter National Monument (SC), Circulation Strike

MS-64	MS-65	MS-66	MS-67	MS-68
$0.50	$0.80	$2.65	$16	—

2016-S, Fort Moultrie at Fort Sumter National Monument (SC), Proof, Clad

PF-67DC	PF-68DC	PF-69DC
$1.50	$4.05	$9.50

2016-S, Fort Moultrie at Fort Sumter National Monument (SC), Proof, Silver

PF-67DC	PF-68DC	PF-69DC
$7.20	$8.50	$11

2017, Effigy Mounds National Monument (IA)

Circulation-Strike Mintage, Philadelphia: 271,200,000
Circulation-Strike Mintage, Denver: 210,800,000
Circulation-Strike Mintage, San Francisco: 945,853
Enhanced Uncirculated Mintage, San Francisco: 210,419
Proof Mintage, San Francisco, Clad: 692,129
Proof Mintage, San Francisco, Silver: 496,618
GSID: Circulation-strike, Philadelphia, 77775; Circulation-strike, Denver, 77776; Circulation-strike, San Francisco, 77777; Enhanced Uncirculated, 82106; Proof Clad Deep Cameo, 77843; Proof Silver Deep Cameo, 77844

Specifics of the Reverse Design

Description: An aerial view of the mounds in the Marching Bear Group is depicted on the reverse.

Designer: Richard A. Masters. *Mint sculptor-engraver who made the model:* Renata Gordon. *Designers's initials and location:* RAM is on the left beneath the bottom mound. *Engraver's initials and location:* RG is in the grass to the right.

Story and Background of the Design

After reviewing the recommendations from the routine channels, the Treasury secretary selected the final design from 13 design candidates. The coin depicts an aerial view of the Marching Bear Group of mounds at the monument. Effigy Mounds National Monument preserves more than 200 prehistoric mounds built by Native Americans mostly in the first millennium.

Numismatic Commentary

The launch ceremony for the latest America the Beautiful Quarter was held on February 7, 2017, at the Allamakee Community School District High School Gym in Waukon, Iowa. Representing the Mint was a familiar figure, J.J. Marc Landry, plant manager of the Philadelphia Mint. A unique aspect was the delivery of a video message by NASA astronaut and Iowa native Dr. Peggy Watson from the International Space Station. On hand was Richard Masters, a fourth-generation Iowan, the Mint's Artistic Infusion Program member who designed the quarter. Park Superintendent Jim Nepstad; Edmore Green, Tribal Chair of Sac and Fox Nation of Missouri in Kansas and Nebraska; and surrogates representing elected officials were also in attendance.

The audience was estimated at about 1,700 people, including 1,250 school children. The younger attendees received free 2017-D quarters, and representatives of the Kerndt Brothers Saving Bank exchanged about $23,000 worth for cash.

A coin forum was held the night before at the Effigy Mounds National Monument Visitor Center in Harpers Ferry, the Iowa town that in 1860 was named in honor of the John Brown raid location. About 75 attended.

Effigy Mounds National Monument is mostly located in Allamakee County. The visitors' center is in Harpers Ferry, Iowa, the new name for Winfield, with historic connections, given to it in 1860. The mounds made of sand number 206 and were made by Native Americans, mostly in the first millennium AD. They are in different areas within the 2,526-acre park. Of these 31 are in the outlines of animals, including birds and bears. The largest, Great Bear Mound, measures 42 meters from head to feet and rises one meter above the surrounding ground. An early explorer of earthworks was Dr. Montroville W. Dickeson, best remembered as the author of the *American Numismatical Manual*, 1859, and two later editions. These illustrated certain recovered fragments that may have been used as money in exchange.

2017-P, Effigy Mounds National Monument (IA)

MS-64	MS-65	MS-66	MS-67	MS-68
$0.50	$0.80	$2.65	$19	$94

2017-D, Effigy Mounds National Monument (IA)

MS-64	MS-65	MS-66	MS-67	MS-68
$0.50	$0.80	$2.65	$16	—

2017-S, Effigy Mounds National Monument (IA), Circulation Strike

MS-64	MS-65	MS-66	MS-67	MS-68
$0.80	$1.10	$2.65	$16	—

2017-S, Effigy Mounds National Monument (IA), Enhanced Unc.

MS-64	MS-65	MS-66	MS-67	MS-68
$2.65	$4.05	$4.75	$5.40	$8.10

2017-S, Effigy Mounds National Monument (IA), Proof, Clad

PF-67DC	PF-68DC	PF-69DC
$1.50	$4.05	$9.50

2017-S, Effigy Mounds National Monument (IA), Proof, Silver

PF-67DC	PF-68DC	PF-69DC
$7.20	$8.50	$11

2017, Frederick Douglass National Historic Site (DC)

Circulation-Strike Mintage, Philadelphia: 184,800,000

Circulation-Strike Mintage, Denver: 185,800,000

Circulation-Strike Mintage, San Francisco: 950,503

Enhanced Uncirculated Mintage, San Francisco: 210,419

Proof Mintage, San Francisco, Clad: 657,587

Proof Mintage, San Francisco, Silver: 496,618

GSID: Circulation-strike, Philadelphia, 81986; Circulation-strike, Denver, 81987; Circulation-strike, San Francisco, 81988; Enhanced Uncirculated, 82109; Proof Clad Deep Cameo, 77845; Proof Silver Deep Cameo, 77846

Specifics of the Reverse Design

Description: Frederick Douglass is depicted seated at a writing desk.

Designer: Thomas R. Hipschen. *Mint sculptor-engraver who made the model:* Phebe Hemphill. *Designers's initials and location:* TRH is on the left by the termination of Douglass's arm. *Engraver's initials and location:* PH is on the right below Douglass's forearm.

Story and Background of the Design

Six reverse design candidates were reviewed for the Frederick Douglass National Historic Site quarter dollar. Secretary of the Treasury Jack Lew chose the final design after consulting the recommendations of various groups, including the Commission of Fine Arts and the Citizens Coinage Advisory Committee. The coin depicts Frederick Douglass seated at his writing desk in front of his house, appearing to be looking at the person holding the coin.

Numismatic Commentary

The launch ceremony for the Frederick Douglass National Historic Site quarter was held beginning at 10:00 in the morning of April 4, 1917, at the Douglass home. The attendance was reported to be about 300, possibly a record low for any quarter launch. This included about 75 local schoolchildren. Showers had passed through the area earlier.

David Motl represented the Mint as deputy director, successor in that position to Rhett Jeppson and commented:

> Even at a young age, Frederick Douglass realized the value of literacy and the power of knowledge. This new coin honors one of the most influential African-American leaders of the 19th century, whose brilliant words will continue to inspire us for generations to come.

Thomas R. Hipschen, the Artistic Infusion Program member and former engraver at the Bureau of Engraving and Printing who designed the coin was on hand, joined by Site Superintendent Tara D. Morrison and Michael Reynolds, the last representing the National Park Service. Gabrielle Sutherland and Silas Montgomery, home-schooled students who were winners in the 2016 Frederick Douglass Oratorical Contest, told of his importance in history. Civil War–era music was provided by the Washington Revels Jubilee Voices, a local ensemble of four. The youngsters received free quarters, and the Industrial Bank exchanged about $11,000 in 2017-P quarters to anyone interested.

A coin forum was held the day before at the office of the U.S. Mint in the same city.

The Frederick Douglass National Historic Site quarter memorializes a city residence, unusual in the series. The building, designated as a national historic site in 1988, is located at 1411 West Street SE in the Anacostia district. It was built circa 1855 by John Van Hook. In 1878 it was purchased by Douglass, who expanded its 14 rooms to 21 and named it Cedar Hill. Earlier, he had hoped that incoming President Rutherford B. Hayes would appoint him as postmaster of Rochester, New York, or as the American ambassador to Haiti. Neither happened, and he was named as marshal for the District of Columbia—the first time that an African American had received a presidential appointment that required the approval of Congress.

Many of the duties of marshal were denied to him, and his role was mainly social—such as introducing visitors at formal gatherings in the White House. The position did bring financial stability. In his home he often hosted members of society. He was well known and highly acclaimed as a writer.

His wife Anna suffered a stroke and died on August 4, 1882. In January 1884 he married a white woman, Helen Pitts, a union that was criticized by both of their families. Douglass was one of the most prominent non-political figures in Washington and appeared at many events. On February 20, 1895, he died quietly at his home. After Douglass's death, his widow Helen founded the Frederick Douglass Memorial and Historical Association in 1900.

In 1916, the National Association of Colored Women's Clubs joined with the association and worked to help preserve the house for historical purposes. These groups owned the house until 1962, when the federal government took the deed through the National Park Service.

2017-P, Frederick Douglass National Historic Site (DC)

MS-64	MS-65	MS-66	MS-67	MS-68
$0.50	$0.80	$2.65	$16	—

2017-D, Frederick Douglass National Historic Site (DC)

MS-64	MS-65	MS-66	MS-67	MS-68
$0.50	$0.80	$2.65	$16	—

2017-S, Frederick Douglass National Historic Site (DC), Circulation Strike

MS-64	MS-65	MS-66	MS-67	MS-68
$0.80	$1.10	$2.65	$16	—

2017-S, Frederick Douglass National Historic Site (DC), Enhanced Unc.

MS-64	MS-65	MS-66	MS-67	MS-68
$2.65	$4.05	$4.75	$5.40	$8.10

2017-S, Frederick Douglass National Historic Site (DC), Proof, Clad

PF-67DC	PF-68DC	PF-69DC
$1.50	$4.05	$9.50

2017-S, Frederick Douglass National Historic Site (DC), Proof, Silver

PF-67DC	PF-68DC	PF-69DC
$7.20	$8.50	$11

2017, Ozark National Scenic Riverways (MO)

Circulation-Strike Mintage, Philadelphia: 203,000,000
Circulation-Strike Mintage, Denver: 200,000,000
Circulation-Strike Mintage, San Francisco: 921,747
Enhanced Uncirculated Mintage, San Francisco: 210,419
Proof Mintage, San Francisco, Clad: 657,587
Proof Mintage, San Francisco, Silver: 496,618

GSID: Circulation-strike, Philadelphia, 81983; Circulation-strike, Denver, 81984; Circulation-strike, San Francisco, 81985; Enhanced Uncirculated, 82108; Proof Clad Deep Cameo, 77847; Proof Silver Deep Cameo, 77848.

Specifics of the Reverse Design

Description: On the reverse is Alley Mill, a steel roller grist mill built in 1894.

Designer: Ronald D. Sanders. *Mint sculptor-engraver who made the model:* Renata Gordon. *Designers's initials and location:* RS is on the left riverbank. *Engraver's initials and location:* RG is on the right riverbank.

Story and Background of the Design

Nine design candidates were developed by the Mint for review by the usual parties, including the CFA and CCAC. After going over their recommendations, Secretary

Lew chose the final design for the coin. Featured on the coin is the Alley Mill, a steel roller mill built in 1894 to convert wheat into flour. The mill is a popular tourist destination with much of the original equipment still in place where it originally stood.

Numismatic Commentary

The launch ceremony for the Ozark National Scenic Riverways quarter dollar is scheduled for June 5, per a Mint news release. On the same day the Federal Reserve will release coins to member banks. The event is to be held in Eminence, Missouri, at the historic Alley Spring and Mill built in 1894. Quarters will be given free to the younger attendees, and the Security Bank of the Ozarks will have $10 rolls of 2017-D available for face value.

A coin forum will be held at 7:00 the evening before in the Nixon Room at Echo Bluff State Park in the same town.

The Ozark National Scenic Riverways located in the Ozark Mountains in southern Missouri is a National Park although it is not named as such. Comprising 80,000 acres it was created by Congress in 1964 to preserve the natural settings of the Current and Jacks Fork rivers and was formally dedicated in 1971. It is a popular recreation area with rafting, boating, birdwatching, and other activities and draws over a million visitors each year.

2017-P, Ozark National Scenic Riverways (MO)

MS-64	MS-65	MS-66	MS-67	MS-68
$0.50	$0.80	$2.65	$16	—

2017-D, Ozark National Scenic Riverways (MO)

MS-64	MS-65	MS-66	MS-67	MS-68
$0.50	$0.80	$2.65	$16	—

2017-S, Ozark National Scenic Riverways (MO), Circulation Strike

MS-64	MS-65	MS-66	MS-67	MS-68
$0.80	$1.10	$2.65	$16	—

2017-S, Ozark National Scenic Riverways (MO), Enhanced Unc.

MS-64	MS-65	MS-66	MS-67	MS-68
$2.65	$4.05	$4.75	$5.40	$8.10

2017-S, Ozark National Scenic Riverways (MO), Proof, Clad

PF-67DC	PF-68DC	PF-69DC
$1.50	$4.05	$9.50

2017-S, Ozark National Scenic Riverways (MO), Proof, Silver

PF-67DC	PF-68DC	PF-69DC
$7.20	$8.50	$11

2017, Ellis Island (Statue of Liberty National Monument) (NJ)

Circulation-Strike Mintage, Philadelphia: 234,000,000

Circulation-Strike Mintage, Denver: 254,000,000

Circulation-Strike Mintage, San Francisco: 973,147

Enhanced Uncirculated Mintage, San Francisco: 210,419

Proof Mintage, San Francisco, Clad: 657,587

Proof Mintage, San Francisco, Silver: 496,618

GSID: Circulation-strike, Philadelphia, 81980; Circulation-strike, Denver, 81981; Circulation-strike, San Francisco, 81982; Enhanced Uncirculated, 82107; Proof Clad Deep Cameo, 77849; Proof Silver Deep Cameo, 77850

Specifics of the Reverse Design

Description: An immigrant family can be seen approaching Ellis Island with a mixture of hope and uncertainty. The hospital building is in the background.

Designer: Barbara Fox. *Mint sculptor-engraver who made the model:* Phebe Hemphill. *Designers's initials and location:* BF is behind the child's elbow. *Engraver's initials and location:* PH is between the child and the flag.

Story and Background of the Design

Several design candidates were reviewed for the 2017 Ellis Island quarter dollar before the Treasury secretary chose the final design. Depicted on the coin is an immigrant family advancing towards Ellis Island. The young boy's face is full of hope, while his parents behind him seem much more apprehensive, the mother looking much more worried and almost regretful than the father. The main building reopened in 1990, while most of the remaining unrestored buildings were part of one of the first and largest public health hospitals in the United States.

Description of the Site

Ellis Island, located in New Jersey, is part of the Statue of Liberty National Monument that also includes the Statue of Liberty on Bedloe's Island in New York Harbor. From 1892 to 1954 the building on the island was the gateway for over 12 million immigrants, mostly from Europe, who came to America to seek a better life. Earlier, Castle Garden on the shore in southern Manhattan was the entry point. Of various processing centers, Ellis Island in its time handled more people than any other.

In 1990 a museum of immigration was opened there and soon proved to be a popular attraction. For most of its history Ellis Island was considered to be a part of New York. Without a landmark 1998 U.S. Supreme Court decision placing the location in New Jersey, neither this America the Beautiful quarter nor the Saratoga quarter would exist!

2017-P, Ellis Island (Statue of Liberty National Monument) (NJ)

MS-64	MS-65	MS-66	MS-67	MS-68
$0.50	$0.80	$2.65	$16	—

2017-D, Ellis Island (Statue of Liberty National Monument) (NJ)

MS-64	MS-65	MS-66	MS-67	MS-68
$0.50	$0.80	$2.65	$16	—

2017-S, Ellis Island (Statue of Liberty National Monument) (NJ), Circulation Strike

MS-64	MS-65	MS-66	MS-67	MS-68
$0.80	$1.10	$2.65	$16	—

2017-S, Ellis Island (Statue of Liberty National Monument) (NJ), Enhanced Unc.

MS-64	MS-65	MS-66	MS-67	MS-68
$2.65	$4.05	$4.75	$5.40	$8.10

2017-S, Ellis Island (Statue of Liberty National Monument) (NJ), Proof, Clad

PF-67DC	PF-68DC	PF-69DC
$1.50	$4.05	$9.50

2017-S, Ellis Island (Statue of Liberty National Monument) (NJ), Proof, Silver

PF-67DC	PF-68DC	PF-69DC
$7.20	$8.50	$11

2017, George Rogers Clark National Historical Park (IN)

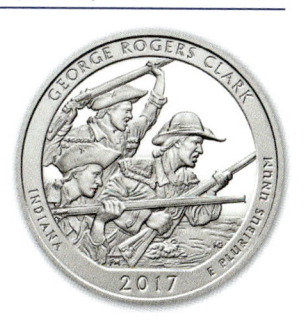

Circulation-Strike Mintage, Philadelphia: 191,600,000
Circulation-Strike Mintage, Denver: 180,800,000
Circulation-Strike Mintage, San Francisco: 933,150
Enhanced Uncirculated Mintage, San Francisco: 210,419
Proof Mintage, San Francisco, Clad: 675,757
Proof Mintage, San Francisco, Silver: 496,618

GSID: Circulation-strike, Philadelphia, 81989; Circulation-strike, Denver, 81990; Circulation-strike, San Francisco, 81991; Enhanced Uncirculated, 82110; Proof Clad Deep Cameo, 77851; Proof Silver Deep Cameo, 77852

Specifics of the Reverse Design

Description: George Rogers Clark is seen leading his men through the flooded plains approaching Fort Sackville.

Designer: Frank Morris. *Mint sculptor-engraver who made the model:* Michael Gaudioso. *Designers's initials and location:* FM is beneath the butt of the gun. *Engraver's initials and location:* MG is in the field to the right near PLURIBUS.

Story and Background of the Design

For the last coin released in 2017, many different design candidates were consulted before Secretary Lew made his design choice. Featured on the chosen reverse is an image of two men being led by George Rogers Clark through flooded plains. Clark is best known for his captures of Kaskaskia in 1778 and Vincennes in 1779 during the Illinois Campaign, greatly weakening the British influence in the Northwest.

Description of the Site

George Rogers Clark National Historical Park is in Vincennes, Indiana, on the banks of the Wabash River, at what is thought to have been the location of Fort Sackville in the Revolutionary War. It has been managed by the National Park Service since 1966. President Calvin Coolidge authorized a memorial, and the finished structure was dedicated by President Franklin D. Roosevelt in 1936. The visitors' center offers displays and what the National Park Services calls interpretative programs—an effort to educate most visitors to such places who know relatively little about American history. They will learn that February 25, 1779, Lieutenant Colonel George Rogers Clark led the capture of Fort Sackville and British Lieutenant Governor Henry Hamilton in the Illinois Campaign. Clark's troops marched in the depths of winter to achieve one of the most memorable victories of Revolution.

2017-P, George Rogers Clark National Historical Park (IN)

MS-64	MS-65	MS-66	MS-67	MS-68
$0.50	$0.80	$2.65	$16	—

2017-D, George Rogers Clark National Historical Park (IN)

MS-64	MS-65	MS-66	MS-67	MS-68
$0.50	$0.80	$2.65	$16	—

2017-S, George Rogers Clark National Historical Park (IN), Circulation Strike

MS-64	MS-65	MS-66	MS-67	MS-68
$0.80	$1.10	$2.65	$16	—

2017-S, George Rogers Clark National Historical Park (IN), Enhanced Unc.

MS-64	MS-65	MS-66	MS-67	MS-68
$2.65	$4.05	$4.75	$5.40	$8.10

2017-S, George Rogers Clark National Historical Park (IN), Proof, Clad

PF-67DC	PF-68DC	PF-69DC
$1.50	$4.05	$9.50

2017-S, George Rogers Clark National Historical Park (IN), Proof, Silver

PF-67DC	PF-68DC	PF-69DC
$7.20	$8.50	$11

2018, Pictured Rocks National Lakeshore (MI)

Circulation-Strike Mintage, Philadelphia: 186,714,000
Circulation-Strike Mintage, Denver: 182,600,000
Circulation-Strike Mintage, San Francisco: 931,220
Proof Mintage, San Francisco, Clad: 653,176
Proof Mintage, San Francisco, Silver: 461,048
Proof Mintage, San Francisco, Silver, Reverse Proof: 199,116

GSID: Circulation-strike, Philadelphia, 77778; Circulation-strike, Denver, 77779; Circulation-strike, San Francisco, 77780; Proof Clad Deep Cameo, 77853; Proof Silver Deep Cameo, 77854; Proof Silver Reverse Proof, 285284

Specifics of the Reverse Design

Description: The reverse design depicts Chapel Rock and the white pine tree that grows atop it. The design captures the northerly view from the Lake Superior shoreline. The white pine has survived for more than 250 years due to its roots extending across a narrow gap to the mainland, which provides nutrients and water.

Designer: Paul C. Balan. *Mint sculptor-engraver who made the model:* Michael Gaudioso. *Designer's initials and location:* PCB near the base of Chapel Rock. *Engraver's initials and location:* MG near the water's edge.

Story and Background of the Design

Pictured Rocks, established in 1966 as America's first national lakeshore, protects 42 miles of Lake Superior shoreline in Michigan's Upper Peninsula. The park's namesake comes from the colorful sandstone cliffs that stretch for about 15 miles, reaching heights of up to 200 feet and displaying stunning bands of red, orange, brown, and green created by mineral-rich groundwater seeping through the rock layers.

The site selection process involved consultation with park officials, geologists, and local historians to ensure the design would capture the park's geological and cultural significance. From multiple proposals featuring landmarks such as Miners Castle,

Grand Portal Point, and the Au Sable Light Station, the Chapel Rock design was chosen for its iconic representation of the park's unique geological features and demonstration of nature's resilience through the enduring white pine tree.

Numismatic Commentary

The first issue of 2018 and the 41st in the America the Beautiful series, the quarter was released at a launch ceremony on February 7, 2018, at Mather Elementary School in Munising, Michigan. The event drew over 500 attendees and featured traditional Native American music honoring the area's indigenous heritage. Local banks reported strong demand for the quarters, with many residents collecting them as souvenirs. Coin dealers noted particular interest from collectors due to the artistic rendering of the natural arch and tree on the small canvas of a quarter.

2018-P, Pictured Rocks National Lakeshore (MI)

MS-64	MS-65	MS-66	MS-67	MS-68
$0.50	$0.80	$2.65	$16	$74

2018-D, Pictured Rocks National Lakeshore (MI)

MS-64	MS-65	MS-66	MS-67	MS-68
$0.50	$0.80	$2.65	$16	—

2018-S, Pictured Rocks National Lakeshore (MI), Circulation Strike

MS-64	MS-65	MS-66	MS-67	MS-68
$0.80	$1.10	$2.65	$16	—

2018-S, Pictured Rocks National Lakeshore (MI), Proof, Clad

PF-67DC	PF-68DC	PF-69DC
$1.50	$4.05	$9.50

2018-S, Pictured Rocks National Lakeshore (MI), Proof, Silver

PF-67DC	PF-68DC	PF-69DC
$7.20	$8.50	$11

2018-S, Pictured Rocks National Lakeshore (MI), Reverse Proof, Silver

PF-67	PF-68	PF-69
$7.20	$8.50	$11

2018, Apostle Islands National Lakeshore (WI)

Circulation-Strike Mintage, Philadelphia: 223,200,000

Circulation-Strike Mintage, Denver: 216,600,000

Circulation-Strike Mintage, San Francisco: 889,080

Proof Mintage, San Francisco, Clad: 618,988

Proof Mintage, San Francisco, Silver: 461,048

Proof Mintage, San Francisco, Silver, Reverse Proof: 199,116

GSID: Circulation-strike, Philadelphia, 77781; Circulation-strike, Denver, 77782; Circulation-strike, San Francisco, 77783; Proof Clad Deep Cameo, 77857; Proof Silver Deep Cameo, 77858; Proof Silver Reverse Proof, 285386

Specifics of the Reverse Design

Description: The reverse features the sea caves at Devils Island with the lighthouse in the background and a kayaker paddling in the foreground. The design captures the experience of visiting the park's famous caves by kayak and witnessing the interaction between water and rock that has helped shape these historic cliffs.

Designer: Richard Masters. *Mint sculptor-engraver who made the model:* Renata Gordon. *Designer's initials and location:* RM near the water's edge. *Engraver's initials and location:* RG near the lighthouse base.

Story and Background of the Design

The Apostle Islands National Lakeshore, established in 1970, encompasses 21 islands and 12 miles of mainland along Lake Superior in northern Wisconsin. The park preserves a rich heritage, including the largest collection of lighthouses in the National Park System. Its history spans thousands of years, from indigenous Ojibwe settlements to European exploration, maritime commerce, and modern recreation.

The design selection process involved consultation with park staff, local historians, and maritime experts. The winning design was chosen for capturing multiple significant elements: the historic lighthouses, dramatic sea caves, and popular kayaking activities. The sea caves, formed over thousands of years by wave action, freezing, and thawing, transform into spectacular ice caves during winter months, drawing thousands of visitors when conditions permit safe access.

Numismatic Commentary

The launch ceremony for the second issue of 2018 was held on April 11, 2018, at the Legendary Waters Resort in Red Cliff, Wisconsin. The event took place on tribal lands of the Red Cliff Band of Lake Superior Chippewa and included traditional Native American blessing ceremonies, acknowledging the deep historical connection between the islands and indigenous peoples. The coin's release coincided with growing interest in kayaking at the park, leading to increased collector interest from outdoor enthusiasts. Numismatists praised the design's ability to incorporate multiple elements while maintaining visual clarity. It was the 42nd coin to be released in the series.

2018-P, Apostle Islands National Lakeshore (WI)

MS-64	MS-65	MS-66	MS-67	MS-68
$0.50	$0.80	$2.65	$21.50	$130

2018-D, Apostle Islands National Lakeshore (WI)

MS-64	MS-65	MS-66	MS-67	MS-68
$0.50	$0.80	$2.65	$16	—

2018-S, Apostle Islands National Lakeshore (WI), Circulation Strike

MS-64	MS-65	MS-66	MS-67	MS-68
$0.80	$1.10	$2.65	$16	—

2018-S, Apostle Islands National Lakeshore (WI), Proof, Clad

PF-67DC	PF-68DC	PF-69DC
$1.50	$4.05	$9.50

2018-S, Apostle Islands National Lakeshore (WI), Proof, Silver

PF-67DC	PF-68DC	PF-69DC
$7.20	$8.50	$11

2018-S, Apostle Islands National Lakeshore (WI), Reverse Proof, Silver

PF-67	PF-68	PF-69
$7.20	$8.50	$11

2018, Voyageurs National Park (MN)

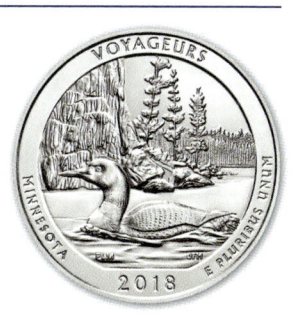

Circulation-Strike Mintage, Philadelphia: 237,400,000
Circulation-Strike Mintage, Denver: 197,800,000
Circulation-Strike Mintage, San Francisco: 867,400
Proof Mintage, San Francisco, Clad: 619,013
Proof Mintage, San Francisco, Silver: 461,048
Proof Mintage, San Francisco, Silver, Reverse Proof: 199,116
GSID: Circulation-strike, Philadelphia, 77784; Circulation-strike, Denver, 77785; Circulation-strike, San Francisco, 77786; Proof Clad Deep Cameo, 77861; Proof Silver Deep Cameo, 77862; Proof Silver Reverse Proof, 285288

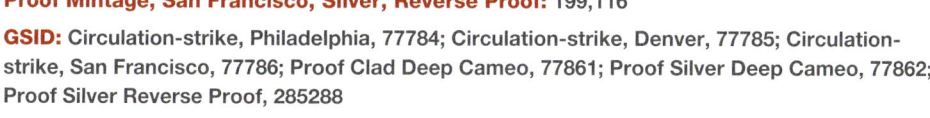

Specifics of the Reverse Design

Description: The reverse design depicts a common loon swimming in the crystal-clear waters of the park, with a rock cliff rising in the background. The design captures the essence of the park's wilderness character and its reputation as a premier destination for viewing and hearing loons.

Designer: Patricia Lucas-Morris. *Mint sculptor-engraver who made the model:* Joseph Menna. *Designer's initials and location:* PLM near the water's edge. *Engraver's initials and location:* JFM near the cliff base.

Story and Background of the Design

Voyageurs National Park, established in 1975, represents a unique chapter in American history, named for the French-Canadian voyageurs who traveled these waterways during the fur trade era. The park encompasses 218,055 acres, including four major lakes and 26 interior lakes, creating a maze of interconnected waterways shaped by ancient geological forces and glacial activity.

The design selection process considered the park's dual identity as both a historical site and modern wilderness area. The loon design was chosen for its ability to capture the park's wilderness character while nodding to Minnesota's cultural identity—the common loon being the state bird. The design also represents the park's crucial role in wildlife conservation, as Voyageurs provides essential habitat for numerous species and serves as part of an international wildlife corridor.

Numismatic Commentary

The launch ceremony for the Voyageurs quarter was held on June 14, 2018, at the Irvin L. Anderson Community Center in International Falls, Minnesota. The event drew attendees from both the United States and Canada, featuring presentations about voyageur history, conservation efforts, and traditional ceremonies by Native American representatives. Numismatists praised the design's artistic merit, particularly in the proof versions, where frosting techniques highlighted the fine details of the loon's plumage and cliff texture. This was the 43rd coin in the series and the third to be released that year.

2018-P, Voyageurs National Park (MN)

MS-64	MS-65	MS-66	MS-67	MS-68
$0.50	$0.80	$2.65	$16	$68

2018-D, Voyageurs National Park (MN)

MS-64	MS-65	MS-66	MS-67	MS-68
$0.50	$0.80	$2.65	$16	—

2018-S, Voyageurs National Park (MN), Circulation Strike

MS-64	MS-65	MS-66	MS-67	MS-68
$0.80	$1.10	$2.65	$16	—

2018-S, Voyageurs National Park (MN), Proof, Clad

PF-67DC	PF-68DC	PF-69DC
$1.50	$4.05	$9.50

2018-S, Voyageurs National Park (MN), Proof, Silver

PF-67DC	PF-68DC	PF-69DC
$7.20	$8.50	$11

2018-S, Voyageurs National Park (MN), Reverse Proof, Silver

PF-67	PF-68	PF-69
$7.20	$8.50	$11

2018, Cumberland Island National Seashore (GA)

Circulation-Strike Mintage, Philadelphia: 138,000,000
Circulation-Strike Mintage, Denver: 151,600,000
Circulation-Strike Mintage, San Francisco: 880,940
Proof Mintage, San Francisco, Clad: 618,725
Proof Mintage, San Francisco, Silver: 461,048
Proof Mintage, San Francisco, Silver, Reverse Proof: 199,116

GSID: Circulation-strike, Philadelphia, 77787; Circulation-strike, Denver, 77788; Circulation-strike, San Francisco, 77789; Proof Clad Deep Cameo, 77859; Proof Silver Deep Cameo, 77860; Proof Silver Reverse Proof, 285287

Specifics of the Reverse Design

Description: The reverse depicts a snowy egret perched on a branch on the edge of a salt marsh. The design showcases the critical ecosystem that the park protects, highlighting one of the many species of shore birds that can be found on the island.

Designer: Donna Weaver. *Mint sculptor-engraver who made the model:* Don Everhart. *Designer's initials and location:* DW in the marsh grass. *Engraver's initials and location:* DE near the water's edge.

Story and Background of the Design

Established in 1972, Cumberland Island National Seashore is one of the largest and most ecologically diverse barrier islands on the Atlantic coast. The park encompasses 9,800 acres of congressionally designated wilderness, including pristine maritime forests, undeveloped beaches, rolling dunes, and extensive salt marshes. The island's history spans multiple eras, from Native American settlements to Spanish missions, plantation agriculture, and the Carnegie family's winter retreat.

The design selection process involved consultation with wildlife biologists, park historians, and naturalists. From multiple candidates featuring the island's feral horses, historic Dungeness ruins, and wildlife species, the snowy egret design was chosen to represent the island's crucial role in protecting shore bird habitat. The salt marsh setting highlights these wetlands' vital role as nurseries for marine species and their importance in coastal protection.

Numismatic Commentary

Released as the fourth issue of 2018 and the 44th coin in the series, the launch ceremony the Cumberland Island quarter was launched in a ceremony on August 30, 2018, at Camden County High School in Kingsland, Georgia. The event drew over 1,000 attendees and featured presentations about the island's ecological significance. Local environmental organizations provided educational displays about shore bird conservation and barrier island ecology. Numismatists noted the artistic achievement in capturing the delicate details of the egret's feathers, with proof versions particularly praised for showcasing the subtle textures of the marsh grass.

2018-P, Cumberland Island National Seashore (GA)

MS-64	MS-65	MS-66	MS-67	MS-68
$0.50	$0.80	$2.65	$16	—

2018-D, Cumberland Island National Seashore (GA)

MS-64	MS-65	MS-66	MS-67	MS-68
$0.50	$0.80	$2.65	$16	—

2018-S, Cumberland Island National Seashore (GA), Circulation Strike

MS-64	MS-65	MS-66	MS-67	MS-68
$0.80	$1.10	$2.65	$40.50	—

2018-S, Cumberland Island National Seashore (GA), Proof, Clad

PF-67DC	PF-68DC	PF-69DC
$1.50	$4.05	$9.50

2018-S, Cumberland Island National Seashore (GA), Proof, Silver

PF-67DC	PF-68DC	PF-69DC
$7.20	$8.50	$11

2018-S, Cumberland Island National Seashore (GA), Reverse Proof, Silver

PF-67	PF-68	PF-69
$7.20	$8.50	$11

2018, Block Island National Wildlife Refuge (RI)

Circulation-Strike Mintage, Philadelphia: 159,600,000

Circulation-Strike Mintage, Denver: 159,600,000

Circulation-Strike Mintage, San Francisco: 854,940

Proof Mintage, San Francisco, Clad: 636,372

Proof Mintage, San Francisco, Silver: 461,048

Proof Mintage, San Francisco, Silver, Reverse Proof: 199,116

GSID: Circulation-strike, Philadelphia, 77790; Circulation-strike, Denver, 77791; Circulation-strike, San Francisco, 77792; Proof Clad Deep Cameo, 77855; Proof Silver Deep Cameo, 77856; Proof Silver Reverse Proof, 285385

Specifics of the Reverse Design

Description: The reverse design depicts a black-crowned night-heron flying over the beach at Cow Cove, with the North Light lighthouse in the background. The design captures the dual nature of the refuge as both a haven for migratory birds and a historic landmark.

Designer: Chris Costello. *Mint sculptor-engraver who made the model:* Phebe Hemphill. *Designer's initials and location:* CTC near the lighthouse base. *Engraver's initials and location:* PH in the beach area.

Story and Background of the Design

Block Island National Wildlife Refuge represents a crucial link in the chain of wildlife refuges along the Atlantic flyway. Located approximately 12 miles off the Rhode Island coast, the refuge's 134 acres provide critical habitat for migratory birds and other wildlife, encompassing diverse ecosystems including beaches, dunes, shrublands, and freshwater wetlands. It was established as a refuge in 1973.

The design selection process brought together wildlife biologists, lighthouse preservation specialists, and local historians. The final design was chosen for its integration of natural and cultural elements, representing the refuge's dual mission of wildlife conservation and historic preservation. The North Light lighthouse, dating back to 1867, connects the wildlife refuge to Block Island's broader maritime heritage, having served as a crucial navigational aid along the New England coast for over 150 years.

Numismatic Commentary

As the final release of 2018 and the 45th coin in the series, the Block Island quarter was launched on November 15, 2018, at the Mansion Beach on Block Island, Rhode Island. Despite challenging weather, the event drew significant attendance and featured presentations about the Atlantic Flyway's importance and the North Light's maritime significance. Collectors particularly appreciated the design's dynamic nature, with the flying heron creating movement while the lighthouse provided a stable anchor point. Proof versions were especially popular for their dramatic contrast between polished fields and frosted design elements.

2018-P, Block Island National Wildlife Refuge (RI)

MS-64	MS-65	MS-66	MS-67	MS-68
$0.50	$0.80	$2.65	$16	—

2018-D, Block Island National Wildlife Refuge (RI)

MS-64	MS-65	MS-66	MS-67	MS-68
$0.50	$0.80	$2.65	$16	—

2018-S, Block Island National Wildlife Refuge (RI), Circulation Strike

MS-64	MS-65	MS-66	MS-67	MS-68
$0.80	$1.10	$2.65	$47	—

2018-S, Block Island National Wildlife Refuge (RI), Proof, Clad

PF-67DC	PF-68DC	PF-69DC
$1.50	$4.05	$9.50

2018-S, Block Island National Wildlife Refuge (RI), Proof, Silver

PF-67DC	PF-68DC	PF-69DC
$7.20	$8.50	$11

2018-S, Block Island National Wildlife Refuge (RI), Reverse Proof, Silver

PF-67	PF-68	PF-69
$7.20	$8.50	$11

2019, Lowell National Historical Park (MA)

Circulation-Strike Mintage, Philadelphia: *165,800,000*
Circulation-Strike Mintage, Denver: *182,200,000*
Circulation-Strike Mintage, San Francisco: *909,080*
Circulation-Strike Mintage, West Point: *2,000,000*
Proof Mintage, San Francisco, Clad: *780,732*
Proof Mintage, San Francisco, Silver: *539,510*

GSID: Circulation-strike, Philadelphia, 81992; Circulation-strike, Denver, 81993; Circulation-strike, San Francisco, 81994; Circulation-strike, West Point, 81700; Proof Clad Deep Cameo, 82024; Proof Silver Deep Cameo, 82025

Specifics of the Reverse Design

Description: The reverse depicts a mill girl working at a power loom with its prominent circular bobbin battery. A view of Lowell's clock tower is seen through the window. The design represents the industrial heritage of the park and its role in America's Industrial Revolution.

Designer: Joel Iskowitz. *Mint sculptor-engraver who made the model:* Phebe Hemphill. *Designer's initials and location:* JI near the window frame. *Engraver's initials and location:* PH near the loom base.

Story and Background of the Design

Lowell National Historical Park, established in 1978, preserves the birthplace of America's Industrial Revolution. The park encompasses historic cotton mills, 5.6 miles of power canals, mill workers' boarding houses, and industrial machinery that tell the story of America's industrial transformation. Its significance extends beyond machinery to crucial social history, including labor rights, women's history, and immigration patterns.

The design selection process involved industrial historians, textile experts, and social historians. The final design was chosen for its ability to humanize the industrial revolution through the depiction of a mill girl at work while showcasing technological innovation. The clock tower visible through the window holds particular significance, as time management and strict scheduling represented a fundamental shift from agricultural to industrial work patterns.

Numismatic Commentary

Released as the first issue of 2019 and the 46th coin in the series, the launch ceremony was held on February 6, 2019, at the Lowell Memorial Auditorium. The event featured working loom demonstrations, presentations about mill girl life, and displays of original mill equipment. The ceremony included readings from mill girls' letters and diaries, providing personal context to the industrial history. Numismatists praised the design's technical accuracy in depicting the power loom, with proof versions particularly successful in capturing the machinery's intricate details.

2019-P, Lowell National Historical Park (MA)

MS-64	MS-65	MS-66	MS-67	MS-68
$0.50	$0.80	$2.65	$16	—

2019-D, Lowell National Historical Park (MA)

MS-64	MS-65	MS-66	MS-67	MS-68
$0.50	$0.80	$2.65	$16	—

2019-S, Lowell National Historical Park (MA), Circulation Strike

MS-64	MS-65	MS-66	MS-67	MS-68
$0.80	$1.10	$2.65	$16	—

2019-W, Lowell National Historical Park (MA)

MS-63	MS-64	MS-65	MS-66	MS-67	MS-68
$47	$68	$108	$156	$403	$6,250

2019-S, Lowell National Historical Park (MA), Proof, Clad

PF-67DC	PF-68DC	PF-69DC
$1.50	$4.05	$9.50

2019-S, Lowell National Historical Park (MA), Proof, Silver

PF-67DC	PF-68DC	PF-69DC
$7.20	$8.50	$11

2019, American Memorial Park (NMI)

Circulation-Strike Mintage, Philadelphia: *142,800,000*
Circulation-Strike Mintage, Denver: *182,600,000*
Circulation-Strike Mintage, San Francisco: *952,795*
Circulation-Strike Mintage, West Point: *2,000,000*
Proof Mintage, San Francisco, Clad: *712,674*
Proof Mintage, San Francisco, Silver: *539,510*

GSID: Circulation-strike, Philadelphia, 81995; Circulation-strike, Denver, 81996; Circulation-strike, San Francisco, 81997; Circulation-strike, West Point, 81701; Proof Clad Deep Cameo, 82026; Proof Silver Deep Cameo, 82027

Specifics of the Reverse Design

Description: The reverse depicts a young woman in traditional dress at the Court of Honor and Flag Circle, honoring the sacrifice of those who died in the Marianas Campaign of World War II. The design features the American flag and the Flag of the Commonwealth of the Northern Mariana Islands.

Designer: Donna Weaver. *Mint sculptor-engraver who made the model:* Joseph Menna. *Designer's initials and location:* DW near the base of the flagpole. *Engraver's initials and location:* JFM in the ground area.

Story and Background of the Design

American Memorial Park, established in 1978, serves as a living memorial to those who lost their lives during the Marianas Campaign of World War II. The 133-acre park includes a memorial court, flag circle, bell tower, and historical markers. Located on Saipan, the site marks one of the Pacific War's most decisive battles, which proved crucial to Allied victory.

The design selection process involved military historians, cultural representatives from the Northern Mariana Islands, and memorial preservation specialists. The final design bridges cultural traditions while honoring sacrifice, featuring both American and

Marianas symbols. The inclusion of traditional dress represents the enduring cultural heritage of the Marianas people and their resilience through wartime hardships, while the flags symbolize unity between the United States and the Northern Mariana Islands.

Numismatic Commentary

Released as the second issue of 2019 and the 47th coin in the series, the launch ceremony was held on April 30, 2019, at the American Memorial Park in Saipan. The event featured traditional Chamorro and Carolinian cultural performances, military honor guards, and presentations about the Marianas Campaign's significance. World War II veterans and their families participated, providing personal connections to the commemorated history. Collectors particularly appreciated the design's symbolic elements, with proof versions effectively capturing the subtle details of the traditional dress and dimensional quality of the flags.

2019-P, American Memorial Park (NMI)

MS-64	MS-65	MS-66	MS-67	MS-68
$0.50	$0.80	$2.65	$16	$61

2019-D, American Memorial Park (NMI)

MS-64	MS-65	MS-66	MS-67	MS-68
$0.50	$0.80	$2.65	$16	—

2019-S, American Memorial Park (NMI), Circulation Strike

MS-64	MS-65	MS-66	MS-67	MS-68
$0.80	$1.10	$2.65	$16	—

2019-W, American Memorial Park (NMI)

MS-63	MS-64	MS-65	MS-66	MS-67	MS-68
$47	$68	$108	$156	$403	$1,250

2019-S, American Memorial Park (NMI), Proof, Clad

PF-67DC	PF-68DC	PF-69DC
$1.50	$4.05	$9.50

2019-S, American Memorial Park (NMI), Proof, Silver

PF-67DC	PF-68DC	PF-69DC
$7.20	$8.50	$11

2019, War in the Pacific National Historical Park (Guam)

Circulation-Strike Mintage, Philadelphia: *116,600,000*

Circulation-Strike Mintage, Denver: *114,400,000*

Circulation-Strike Mintage, San Francisco: *945,719*

Circulation-Strike Mintage, West Point: *2,000,000*

Proof Mintage, San Francisco, Clad: *712,768*

Proof Mintage, San Francisco, Silver: *539,510*

GSID: Circulation-strike, Philadelphia, 81998; Circulation-strike, Denver, 81999; Circulation-strike, San Francisco, 82000; Circulation-strike, West Point, 81702; Proof Clad Deep Cameo, 82028; Proof Silver Deep Cameo, 82029

Specifics of the Reverse Design

Description: The reverse depicts American forces coming ashore at Asan Bay, commemorating the bravery and sacrifice of those who participated in the Pacific Theater campaigns during World War II. The design features soldiers advancing toward the beach and LSTs (Landing Ship, Tanks) in the background.

Designer: Joel Iskowitz. *Mint sculptor-engraver who made the model:* Michael Gaudioso. *Designer's initials and location:* JI near the water's edge. *Engraver's initials and location:* MG in the beach area.

Story and Background of the Design

War in the Pacific National Historical Park, established in 1978, preserves sites associated with the Pacific Theater of World War II. The park encompasses seven units throughout Guam, including battlefields, gun emplacements, trenches, and historic structures. These sites tell the story of both the American liberation of Guam and the experience of the Chamorro people under occupation.

The design selection process involved military historians, Chamorro cultural representatives, and World War II veterans' organizations. The final design was chosen for its representation of crucial amphibious operations in the Pacific. The inclusion of LSTs holds particular significance, as these vessels were essential for transporting heavy equipment to remote island battlefields. The depiction of soldiers advancing through the surf captures both the vulnerability and determination of American forces during these operations.

Numismatic Commentary

Released as the third issue of 2019 and the 48th coin in the series, the launch ceremony was held on May 3, 2019, at the park's Asan Beach Unit. The event included military honor guards, traditional Chamorro blessing ceremonies, and presentations about the battle for Guam. World War II artifacts provided historical context for the events depicted. Military numismatists praised the historical accuracy of the equipment and vessels, with proof versions particularly successful in capturing the sense of movement in the water.

2019-P, War in the Pacific National Historical Park (Guam)

MS-64	MS-65	MS-66	MS-67	MS-68
$0.50	$0.80	$2.65	$16	$108

2019-D, War in the Pacific National Historical Park (Guam)

MS-64	MS-65	MS-66	MS-67	MS-68
$0.50	$0.80	$2.65	$16	—

2019-S, War in the Pacific National Historical Park (Guam), Circulation Strike

MS-64	MS-65	MS-66	MS-67	MS-68
$0.80	$1.10	$2.65	$16	—

2019-W, War in the Pacific National Historical Park (Guam)

MS-63	MS-64	MS-65	MS-66	MS-67	MS-68
$47	$68	$108	$156	$403	$1,250

2019-S, War in the Pacific National Historical Park (Guam), Proof, Clad

PF-67DC	PF-68DC	PF-69DC
$1.50	$4.05	$9.50

2019-S, War in the Pacific National Historical Park (Guam), Proof, Silver

PF-67DC	PF-68DC	PF-69DC
$7.20	$8.50	$11

2019, San Antonio Missions National Historical Park (TX)

Circulation-Strike Mintage, Philadelphia: *142,800,000*
Circulation-Strike Mintage, Denver: *129,400,000*
Circulation-Strike Mintage, San Francisco: *947,001*
Circulation-Strike Mintage, West Point: *2,000,000*
Proof Mintage, San Francisco, Clad: *712,743*
Proof Mintage, San Francisco, Silver: *539,510*

GSID: Circulation-strike, Philadelphia, 82001; Circulation-strike, Denver, 82002; Circulation-strike, San Francisco, 82003; Circulation-strike, West Point, 81703; Proof Clad Deep Cameo, 82030; Proof Silver Deep Cameo, 82031

Specifics of the Reverse Design

Description: The reverse depicts elements of the Spanish Colonial Real coin to pay tribute to the missions. Within the quadrants are symbols of the missions: wheat symbolizes farming, the arches and bell symbolize community, a lion represents Spanish cultural heritage, and a symbol of the San Antonio River represents irrigation methods and life-sustaining resources.

Designer: Chris Costello. *Mint sculptor-engraver who made the model:* Joseph Menna. *Designer's initials and location:* CTC in the lower right quadrant. *Engraver's initials and location:* JFM in the lower left quadrant.

Story and Background of the Design

San Antonio Missions National Historical Park, established in 1978, preserves four Spanish colonial mission complexes and their cultural landscape. These missions—Concepción, San José, San Juan, and Espada—represent North America's largest concentration of Spanish colonial missions and achieved UNESCO World Heritage status in 2015. They tell a complex story of cultural interaction between Spanish missionaries, indigenous peoples, and frontier settlers.

The design selection process involved architectural historians, cultural anthropologists, and religious scholars. The final design innovatively references Spanish colonial coinage, creating a symbolic connection between the missions' economic and spiritual roles. The quadrant design holds significance by referencing both Spanish colonial monetary design and traditional mission architecture, with carefully chosen symbols representing agricultural innovation, community building, cultural heritage, and water management.

Numismatic Commentary

Released as the fourth issue of 2019 and the 49th coin in the series, the launch ceremony was held on September 5, 2019, at San Francisco de la Espada Mission. The event drew an international audience and featured Spanish colonial music, Native American blessing ceremonies, and traditional mission craft demonstrations. Numismatists particularly appreciated the design's reference to Spanish colonial coinage, creating a coin-within-a-coin effect. Proof versions were praised for capturing the intricate details of the symbolic elements.

2019-P, San Antonio Missions National Historical Park (TX)

MS-64	MS-65	MS-66	MS-67	MS-68
$0.50	$0.80	$2.65	$16	—

2019-D, San Antonio Missions National Historical Park (TX)

MS-64	MS-65	MS-66	MS-67	MS-68
$0.50	$0.80	$2.65	$16	—

2019-S, San Antonio Missions National Historical Park (TX), Circulation Strike

MS-64	MS-65	MS-66	MS-67	MS-68
$0.80	$1.10	$2.65	$16	—

2019-W, San Antonio Missions National Historical Park (TX)

MS-63	MS-64	MS-65	MS-66	MS-67	MS-68
$47	$68	$108	$156	$403	$1,250

2019-S, San Antonio Missions National Historical Park (TX), Proof, Clad

PF-67DC	PF-68DC	PF-69DC
$1.50	$4.05	$9.50

2019-S, San Antonio Missions National Historical Park (TX), Proof, Silver

PF-67DC	PF-68DC	PF-69DC
$7.20	$8.50	$11

2019, Frank Church River of No Return Wilderness (ID)

Circulation-Strike Mintage, Philadelphia: 223,400,000
Circulation-Strike Mintage, Denver: 251,600,000
Circulation-Strike Mintage, San Francisco: 946,859
Circulation-Strike Mintage, West Point: 2,000,000
Proof Mintage, San Francisco, Clad: 730,874
Proof Mintage, San Francisco, Silver: 539,510

GSID: Circulation-strike, Philadelphia, 82004; Circulation-strike, Denver, 82005; Circulation-strike, San Francisco, 82006; Circulation-strike, West Point, 81704; Proof Clad Deep Cameo, 82032; Proof Silver Deep Cameo, 82033

Specifics of the Reverse Design

Description: The reverse depicts a piloted drift boat on the rushing river encompassed by the steep walls of the Salmon River canyon. The design captures the wild and undeveloped nature of the wilderness area.

Designer: Emily Damstra. *Mint sculptor-engraver who made the model:* Renata Gordon. *Designer's initials and location:* ED near the canyon wall. *Engraver's initials and location:* RG near the water's edge.

Story and Background of the Design

The Frank Church River of No Return Wilderness, designated in 1980 and named for Idaho Senator Frank Church, is the largest contiguous wilderness area in the lower 48 states. Encompassing 2.366 million acres, it includes the main Salmon River (the "River of No Return") and its Middle Fork, which together form one of America's premier wilderness river systems. The landscape remains largely as it appeared to Lewis and Clark during their expedition.

The design selection process involved consultation with wilderness advocates, river guides, and conservation historians. The design candidates featured various aspects of the wilderness, including wildlife, mountain landscapes, and river scenes. The final selection was a dynamic representation of human interaction with wilderness, showing recreational use amid the overwhelming scale and power of the natural landscape.

The inclusion of a drift boat holds particular significance, as these vessels represent both historical river-running traditions and modern wilderness recreation. The steep canyon walls demonstrate how the Salmon River earned its nickname—historically, boats could travel downstream but could not return upstream through the rapids, requiring them to be dismantled and packed out.

Numismatic Commentary

This quarter was the fifth and final release of 2019 and the 50th coin in the series. The launch ceremony was held on November 6, 2019, at the Salmon-Challis National Forest Supervisor's Office in Salmon, Idaho.

2019-P, Frank Church River of No Return Wilderness (ID)

MS-64	MS-65	MS-66	MS-67	MS-68
$0.50	$0.80	$2.65	$16.00	$40.50

2019-D, Frank Church River of No Return Wilderness (ID)

MS-64	MS-65	MS-66	MS-67	MS-68
$0.50	$0.80	$2.65	$16	$54

2019-S, Frank Church River of No Return Wilderness (ID), Circulation Strike

MS-64	MS-65	MS-66	MS-67	MS-68
$0.80	$1.10	$2.65	$16	—

2019-W, Frank Church River of No Return Wilderness (ID)

MS-63	MS-64	MS-65	MS-66	MS-67	MS-68
$47	$68	$108	$156	$403	$1,250

2019-S, Frank Church River of No Return Wilderness (ID), Proof, Clad

PF-67DC	PF-68DC	PF-69DC
$1.50	$4.05	$9.50

2019-S, Frank Church River of No Return Wilderness (ID), Proof, Silver

PF-67DC	PF-68DC	PF-69DC
$7.20	$8.50	$11

2020, National Park of American Samoa (AS)

Circulation-Strike Mintage, Philadelphia: 286,000,000
Circulation-Strike Mintage, Denver: 212,200,000
Circulation-Strike Mintage, San Francisco: 955,145
Circulation-Strike Privy Mark Mintage, West Point: 2,000,000
Proof-Strike Mintage, San Francisco, Clad: 574,037
Proof-Strike Mintage, San Francisco, Silver: 427,191

GSID: Circulation-strike, Philadelphia, 82007; Circulation-strike, Denver, 82008; Circulation-strike, San Francisco, 82009; Circulation-strike, Privy Mark, West Point, 82010; Proof Clad Deep Cameo, 82034; Proof Silver Deep Cameo, 82035

Specifics of the Reverse Design

Description: The reverse design depicts a Samoan fruit bat hanging upside down in a tree with her pup, indicating the endless care and devotion this creature provides to her offspring. The National Park of American Samoa is the only US park that is home to this highly threatened species.

Designer: Richard A. Masters. *Mint sculptor-engraver who made the model:* Phebe Hemphill. *Designer's initials and location:* RaM to the viewer's left of the mother bat's head. *Engraver's initials and location:* PH hidden to the viewer's right of the mother bat's head.

Privy Mark on the Obverse Design

On the obverse of the West Point–minted coins, which have a W mintmark, is a "V75" within a decorative motif that is called a privy mark. This privy mark was added to certain coins dated 2020 to honor the 75th Anniversary of the End of World War II.

Story and Background of the Design

Established in 1988, the National Park of American Samoa is one of the most remote in the National Park system. Located about halfway between Hawaii and New Zealand, it comprises three volcanic islands; most of the land area is tropical rainforest. The lush foliage is home to a host of wildlife, including the fruit bats, whose population has been decimated by hurricanes, over-hunting, and habitat loss. An array of fish and other sea creatures make their homes in the areas—almost a third of the park's 13,500 acres—that are underwater. In addition to providing a sanctuary for these natural wonders, the park's lease agreement includes a pledge to honor and preserve Samoan culture and traditions.

Ten outstanding reverse designs were offered to represent the park. The striking image of the two fruit bats was supported by 22 out of 24 officials.

Numismatic Commentary

At the ANA World's Fair of Money, in Rosemont, IL, the final design for the National Park of American Samoa was announced on August 13, 2019. The design was well received by the attendees of that convention. Later, due to the Covid-19 pandemic, no public launch was planned, but the coins were available on the Mint's website after their release.

2020-P, National Park of American Samoa (AS)

MS-64	MS-65	MS-66	MS-67	MS-68
$0.50	$0.80	$2.65	$19	$94

2020-D, National Park of American Samoa (AS)

MS-64	MS-65	MS-66	MS-67	MS-68
$0.50	$0.80	$2.65	$19	$94

2020-S, National Park of American Samoa (AS), Circulation Strike

MS-64	MS-65	MS-66	MS-67	MS-68
$0.50	$0.80	$2.65	$16	—

2020-W, National Park of American Samoa (AS), V75 Privy Mark

MS-63	MS-64	MS-65	MS-66	MS-67	MS-68
$11.00	$12.00	$13.50	$32.50	$195	—

2020-S, National Park of American Samoa (AS), Proof, Clad

PF-67DC	PF-68DC	PF-69DC
$1.50	$4.05	$9.50

2020-S, National Park of American Samoa (AS), Proof, Silver

PF-67DC	PF-68DC	PF-69DC
$7.20	$8.50	$11

2020, Weir Farm National Historic Site (CT)

Circulation-Strike Mintage, Philadelphia: *125,600,000*
Circulation-Strike Mintage, Denver: *155,000,000*
Circulation-Strike Mintage, San Francisco: *961,229*
Circulation-Strike Privy Mark Mintage, West Point: *2,000,000*
Proof-Strike Mintage, San Francisco, Clad: *544,660*
Proof-Strike Mintage, San Francisco, Silver: *427,191*
GSID: Circulation-strike, Philadelphia, 82014; Circulation-strike, Denver, 82015; Circulation-strike, San Francisco, 82016; Circulation-strike, Privy Mark, West Point, 82017; Proof Clad Deep Cameo, 82038; Proof Silver Deep Cameo, 82039

Specifics of the Reverse Design

Description: This reverse design depicts an artist, wearing an artist's smock and holding a palette and a brush, painting on a canvas held in an easel. He is outside of Julian Alden Weir's studio at Weir Farm in Wilton, Connecticut. It is inspired by various images of the studio and by Weir's paintings created on the property, as well as descriptions of Weir and his fellow artists' creative inspiration from the rural environment.

Designer: Juston Kunz. *Mint sculptor-engraver who made the model:* Phebe Hemphill. *Designer's initials and location:* JK hidden in the tall grass to the viewer's left of the artist. *Engraver's initials and location:* PH hidden in the tall grass to the viewer's right of the artist.

Privy Mark on the Obverse Design

On the obverse of the West Point–minted coins, which have a W mintmark, is a "V75" within a decorative motif that is called a privy mark. This privy mark was added to certain coins dated 2020 to honor the 75th Anniversary of the End of World War II.

Story and Background of the Design

Weir Farm National Historic Site, established in 1990, celebrates the legacy of J. Alden Weir, recognized as the Father of American Impressionism. Located between Wilton and Ridgefield, Connecticut, this 68-acre cultural landscape encompasses 15 structures, including houses, barns, artists' studios, and outbuildings. Weir acquired the property in 1882, and today it remains the only national park dedicated to American painting.

The site features expertly preserved gardens, terraces, orchards, fields, and miles of original New England rock walls. From fifteen submitted designs, the final selection incorporated suggestions from the Commission of Fine Arts. As Superintendent Linda Cook noted, the design "perfectly captures the feel of the cultural landscape of the state, and how Weir Farm is connected to it through art, creativity and nature."

Numismatic Commentary

The chosen design, created by Justin Kunz, was announced at the American Numismatic Association's World's Fair of Money in Rosemont, Illinois, on August 13, 2019. This quarter represents the second release of 2020 and the 52nd coin in the series honoring national parks and historic sites across America's states and territories. Though Covid-19 restrictions prevented a public launch ceremony, the coins were made available through the Mint's website, with rolls and bags released later.

2020-P, Weir Farm National Historic Site (CT)

MS-64	MS-65	MS-66	MS-67	MS-68
$0.50	$0.80	$2.65	$17.50	$54

2020-D, Weir Farm National Historic Site (CT)

MS-64	MS-65	MS-66	MS-67	MS-68
$0.50	$0.80	$2.65	$16	—

2020-S, Weir Farm National Historic Site (CT), Circulation Strike

MS-64	MS-65	MS-66	MS-67	MS-68
$0.50	$0.80	$2.65	$16	—

2020-W, Weir Farm National Historic Site (CT), V75 Privy Mark

MS-63	MS-64	MS-65	MS-66	MS-67	MS-68
$11.00	$12.00	$13.50	$47	$208	—

2020-S, Weir Farm National Historic Site (CT), Proof, Clad

PF-67DC	PF-68DC	PF-69DC
$1.50	$4.05	$9.50

2020-S, Weir Farm National Historic Site (CT), Proof, Silver

PF-67DC	PF-68DC	PF-69DC
$7.20	$8.50	$11

2020, Salt River Bay National Historical Park and Ecological Preserve (USVI)

Circulation-Strike Mintage, Philadelphia: *580,200,000*
Circulation-Strike Mintage, Denver: *515,000,000*
Circulation-Strike Mintage, San Francisco: *949,947*
Circulation-Strike Privy Mark Mintage, West Point: *2,000,000*
Proof-Strike Mintage, San Francisco, Clad: *544,515*
Proof-Strike Mintage, San Francisco, Silver: *427,191*
GSID: Circulation-strike, Philadelphia, 82018; Circulation-strike, Denver, 82019; Circulation-strike, San Francisco, 82020; Circulation-strike, Privy Mark, West Point, 85050; Proof Clad Deep Cameo, 82040; Proof Silver Deep Cameo, 82041

Specifics of the Reverse Design

Description: The reverse of the coin depicts one of nature's many wonders. It illustrates a red mangrove tree in its earliest stages of life. The red mangrove begins as a very small plant and can grow to be 30 feet or more in height. This special species reproduces and grows in salt water. The design brings the story of the park's endangered mangrove forest to the attention of all.

Designer: Richard A. Masters. *Mint sculptor-engraver who made the model:* Joseph F. Menna. *Designer's initials and location:* RaM near the plant's roots on the viewer's left side. *Engraver's initials and location:* JFM near the plant's roots on the viewer's right side.

Privy Mark on the Obverse Design

On the obverse of the West Point–minted coins, which have a W mintmark, is a "V75" within a decorative motif that is called a privy mark. This privy mark was added to certain coins dated 2020 to honor the 75th Anniversary of the End of World War II.

Story and Background of the Design

Salt River Bay National Historical Park and Ecological Preserve, located on the northern coast of St. Croix in the U.S. Virgin Islands, represents both ecological significance and historical importance. The site contains endangered mangrove forests that support delicate ecosystems and marks the location of the first recorded conflict between Native Americans and European explorers, which occurred during Christopher Columbus's second voyage on November 14, 1493.

Six design proposals emphasized the bay's complex ecological balance, featuring turtles, fish, shells, and mangrove trees. After consultation between the Citizens Coinage Advisory Committee, Commission of Fine Arts, and park representatives, AIP artist Richard Masters' design was selected. The chosen design depicts a red mangrove tree in its early growth stages, highlighting the endangered forests' vulnerability. The reverse includes inscriptions of the site name, location, year of issue, and E PLURIBUS UNUM.

Numismatic Commentary

The design was unveiled on August 13, 2019, at the ANA World's Fair of Money in Rosemont, Illinois. This quarter represents the 53rd issue in the 56-coin America the Beautiful series. Though the Covid-19 pandemic prevented a launch ceremony, the coins were made available through the Mint's website.

2020-P, Salt River Bay National Historical Park and Ecological Preserve (USVI)

MS-64	MS-65	MS-66	MS-67	MS-68
$0.50	$0.80	$2.65	$16	—

2020-D, Salt River Bay National Historical Park and Ecological Preserve (USVI)

MS-64	MS-65	MS-66	MS-67	MS-68
$0.50	$0.80	$2.65	$16	—

2020-S, Salt River Bay National Historical Park and Ecological Preserve (USVI), Circulation Strike

MS-64	MS-65	MS-66	MS-67	MS-68
$0.50	$0.80	$2.65	$29.50	$338

2020-W, Salt River Bay National Historical Park and Ecological Preserve (USVI), V75 Privy Mark

MS-63	MS-64	MS-65	MS-66	MS-67	MS-68
$11	$12	$20	$54	$390	$8,120

2020-S, Salt River Bay National Historical Park and Ecological Preserve (USVI), Proof, Clad

PF-67DC	PF-68DC	PF-69DC
$1.50	$4.05	$9.50

2020-S, Salt River Bay National Historical Park and Ecological Preserve (USVI), Proof, Silver

PF-67DC	PF-68DC	PF-69DC
$7.20	$8.50	$11

2020, Marsh-Billings-Rockefeller National Historical Park (VT)

Circulation-Strike Mintage, Philadelphia: *304,600,000*
Circulation-Strike Mintage, Denver: *345,800,000*
Circulation-Strike Mintage, San Francisco: *945,449*
Circulation-Strike Privy Mark Mintage, West Point: *2,000,000*
Proof-Strike Mintage, San Francisco, Clad: *544,589*
Proof-Strike Mintage, San Francisco, Silver: *427,191*

GSID: Circulation-strike, Philadelphia, 82021; Circulation-strike, Denver, 82022; Circulation-strike, San Francisco, 82023; Circulation-strike, Privy Mark, West Point, 85051; Proof Clad Deep Cameo, 82042; Proof Silver Deep Cameo, 82043

Specifics of the Reverse Design

Description: The reverse of the coin depicts a young girl planting a seedling Norway spruce next to a grown tree. The scene represents the hopeful efforts of conservationists and the symbiotic relationship between mankind and nature.

Designer: Donna Weaver. *Mint sculptor-engraver who made the model:* Michael Gaudioso. *Designer's initials and location:* DW inside the center of the design to the viewer's left. *Engraver's initials and location:* MG below the young girl's knee.

Privy Mark on the Obverse Design

On the obverse of the West Point–minted coins, which have a W mintmark, is a "V75" within a decorative motif that is called a privy mark. This privy mark was added to certain coins dated 2020 to honor the 75th Anniversary of the End of World War II.

Story and Background of the Design

In 2018, the Mint's in-house and AIP artists submitted 11 candidate designs to represent the Marsh-Billings-Rockefeller National Historical Park in Woodstock, Vermont. By August 13, 2019, the CCAC and the CFA had jointly selected AIP artist Donna Weaver's design, which was truly in accordance with the theme of land conservation (the words are even included as a prominent inscription). The coin was the fourth release in 2020 and the 54th coin in the series.

Due to the Covid-19 pandemic, no launch ceremony was conducted, but the coins were available on the Mint's website. They were also available at branches of the People's United Bank in Woodstock and White River Junction, Vermont.

Numismatic Commentary

The park honored on the coin is located in Woodstock, Vermont; its farm and woodlands became a national park in 1998. It is named for three generations of landowners and their legacy of land stewardship.

George Perkins Marsh grew up on the farm in the early 1800s, and saw firsthand the effects of deforestation. Author of the treatise *Man and Nature*, he is considered the father of the modern American conservation movement.

The next owner, Frederick Billings, created several land-stewardship programs to preserve the land. He was followed by owners Laurance and Mary French Rockefeller, who opened the property to the public in the spirit of education and conservation. They donated the property to the National Park Service in 1992, and in June of that year it was opened as a national park.

2020-P, Marsh-Billings-Rockefeller National Historical Park (VT)

MS-64	MS-65	MS-66	MS-67	MS-68
$0.50	$0.80	$2.65	$16	$34

2020-D, Marsh-Billings-Rockefeller National Historical Park (VT)

MS-64	MS-65	MS-66	MS-67	MS-68
$0.50	$0.80	$2.65	$16	—

2020-S, Marsh-Billings-Rockefeller National Historical Park (VT), Circulation Strike

MS-64	MS-65	MS-66	MS-67	MS-68
$0.50	$0.80	$2.65	$16	—

2020-W, Marsh-Billings-Rockefeller National Historical Park (VT), V75 Privy Mark

MS-63	MS-64	MS-65	MS-66	MS-67	MS-68
$27.00	$40.50	$54	$130	$550	—

2020-S, Marsh-Billings-Rockefeller National Historical Park (VT), Proof, Clad

PF-67DC	PF-68DC	PF-69DC
$1.50	$4.05	$9.50

2020-S, Marsh-Billings-Rockefeller National Historical Park (VT), Proof, Silver

PF-67DC	PF-68DC	PF-69DC
$7.20	$8.50	$11

2020, Tallgrass Prairie National Preserve (KS)

Circulation-Strike Mintage, Philadelphia: *101,200,000*
Circulation-Strike Mintage, Denver: *142,400,000*
Circulation-Strike Mintage, San Francisco: *951,612*
Circulation-Strike Privy Mark Mintage, West Point: *2,000,000*
Proof-Strike Mintage, San Francisco, Clad: *561,452*
Proof-Strike Mintage, San Francisco, Silver: *427,191*

GSID: Circulation-strike, Philadelphia, 82011; Circulation-strike, Denver, 82012; Circulation-strike, San Francisco, 82013; Circulation-strike, Privy Mark, West Point, 85049; Proof Clad Deep Cameo, 82036; Proof Silver Deep Cameo, 82037

Specifics of the Reverse Design

Description: The reverse design features the majestic regal fritillary butterfly, in flight, above a background of both Indian and big bluestem wild grasses. The preserve contains 10,894 acres and is the largest remaining tallgrass prairie in all of North America. The inscriptions read TALLGRASS PRAIRIE, KANSAS, 2020, and E PLURIBUS UNUM.

Designer: Emily Damstra. *Mint sculptor-engraver who made the model:* Renata Gordon. *Designer's initials and location:* ESD above and to the left of the date. *Engraver's initials and location:* RG above and to the right of the date.

Privy Mark on the Obverse Design

On the obverse of the West Point–minted coins, which have a W mintmark, is a "V75" within a decorative motif that is called a privy mark. This privy mark was added to certain coins dated 2020 to honor the 75th Anniversary of the End of World War II.

Story and Background of the Design

The Tallgrass Prairie National Preserve serves as a reminder of America's pioneering history and vast prairie landscapes. Though its nearly 11,000 acres seem extensive, they represent only about 4% of the tallgrass areas that once dominated the American landscape. The preserve features more than 300 varieties of flowers and plants among the undulating grasses that inspired the "amber waves of grain" in "America the Beautiful."

From ten candidate designs reviewed in June 2018, Emily Damstra's creation, sculpted by Renata Gordon, was selected. The Citizens Coinage Advisory Committee chose the design featuring a regal fritillary butterfly, while the Commission of Fine Arts deliberated between this and an alternative showing a prairie chicken with a butterfly. Both designs incorporated the preserve's characteristic tallgrasses.

Numismatic Commentary

As the 55th issue in the America the Beautiful series, this quarter became available on November 16, 2020, through the Lyon County State Bank in Emporia, Kansas, and the Mint's website. Though the public launch ceremony was canceled due to the Covid-19 pandemic, the coin successfully captures the preserve's essence. The site not only preserves the natural prairie but also helps protect wildlife, including American bison, which have grown from just 541 specimens in 1889 to approximately 31,000 in the wild today.

2020-P, Tallgrass Prairie National Preserve (KS)

MS-64	MS-65	MS-66	MS-67	MS-68
$0.50	$0.80	$2.65	$17.50	$68

2020-W, Tallgrass Prairie National Preserve (KS), V75 Privy Mark

MS-63	MS-64	MS-65	MS-66	MS-67	MS-68
$11.00	$13.50	$21.50	$156	$403	—

2020-S, Tallgrass Prairie National Preserve (KS), Circulation Strike

MS-64	MS-65	MS-66	MS-67	MS-68
$0.50	$0.80	$2.65	$16	—

2020-S, Tallgrass Prairie National Preserve (KS), Proof, Clad

PF-67DC	PF-68DC	PF-69DC
$1.50	$4.05	$9.50

2020-D, Tallgrass Prairie National Preserve (KS)

MS-64	MS-65	MS-66	MS-67	MS-68
$0.50	$0.80	$2.65	$16	—

2020-S, Tallgrass Prairie National Preserve (KS), Proof, Silver

PF-67DC	PF-68DC	PF-69DC
$7.20	$8.50	$11

2021, Tuskegee Airmen National Historic Site (AL)

Circulation-Strike Mintage, Philadelphia: 160,400,000

Circulation-Strike Mintage, Denver: 304,000,000

Circulation-Strike Mintage, San Francisco: 858,572

Proof Mintage, San Francisco, Clad: 528,201

Proof Mintage, San Francisco, Silver: 350,323

GSID: Circulation-strike, Philadelphia, 85129; Circulation-strike, Denver, 85130; Circulation-strike, San Francisco, 85131; Proof Clad Deep Cameo, 85135; Proof Silver Deep Cameo, 85136

Specifics of the Reverse Design

Description: The reverse design depicts a Tuskegee Airmen pilot adjusting his headgear as two P-51 Mustang airplanes fly overhead. In the background is the control tower at Moton Field, the only primary flight facility for African-American pilot candidates in the U.S. Army Air Corps (Army Air Forces) during World War II. The inscription THEY FOUGHT TWO WARS arcs across the top as a reference to the dual battles the Tuskegee Airmen fought—fascism abroad and racial discrimination at home.

Designer: Chris Costello. *Mint sculptor-engraver who made the model:* Phebe Hemphill. *Designer's initials and location:* CTC under the airman's right arm. *Engraver's initials and location:* PH under the airman's parachute buckle.

Story and Background of the Design

The Tuskegee Airmen National Historic Site, established on November 6, 1998, commemorates a groundbreaking chapter in American military and civil rights history. The site honors more than 15,000 men and women of all nationalities who served there, including over 900 African-American pilots, of whom more than 350 saw active duty as fighter pilots. The program also trained navigators, bombardiers, mechanics, and support personnel.

During World War II, these pilots flew more than 15,000 sorties, primarily protecting Allied bombers. Despite facing racism and, for women at the site, sexism, they remained devoted to their service. The Tuskegee Airmen overcame significant obstacles both on and off the battlefield, often being denied access to facilities and opportunities available to their white colleagues, yet maintaining their commitment to excellence and duty.

Numismatic Commentary

Released on January 4, 2021, this quarter holds the distinction of being the 56th and final coin in the America the Beautiful Quarters Program, which began in 2010. As Mint Director David J. Ryder noted, "It is fitting that such a significant historic site will complete this successful coin program. The Mint is proud to honor the men and women who overcame segregation and prejudice to become one of the most highly respected fighter groups of World War II."

Following the outstanding success of the State Quarters Program, the followed with yet another highly successful multi-coin series: America the Beautiful (ATB) quarter dollars. The program began in 2010, and in each year released five different coin designs that highlight national parks, national historic sites, wildlife preserves, or some other natural beauty. Each state was represented, as was the District of Columbia and four U.S. territories. The 56th coin, issued as the final coin in the series, honored the Tuskegee Airmen.

2021-P, Tuskegee Airmen National Historic Site (AL)

MS-64	MS-65	MS-66	MS-67	MS-68
$0.50	$0.80	$2.65	$21.50	$122

2021-D, Tuskegee Airmen National Historic Site (AL)

MS-64	MS-65	MS-66	MS-67	MS-68
$0.50	$0.80	$2.65	$16	—

2021-S, Tuskegee Airmen National Historic Site (AL), Circulation Strike

MS-64	MS-65	MS-66	MS-67	MS-68
$0.50	$0.80	$2.65	$34	—

2021-S, Tuskegee Airmen National Historic Site (AL), Proof, Clad

PF-67DC	PF-68DC	PF-69DC
$1.50	$4.05	$9.50

2021-S, Tuskegee Airmen National Historic Site (AL), Proof, Silver

PF-67DC	PF-68DC	PF-69DC
$7.20	$8.50	$11

An Orderly Transition

The legislation that authorized the ATB quarters, the America's Beautiful National Parks Quarter Dollar Coin Act of 2008 (PL 110-456), specified that, after completion of the ATB program, a new, one-year-only quarter design would be struck to commemorate the 245th anniversary of what is commonly known as "Washington Crossing the Delaware"—a scene immortalized in a painting by Emmanuel Leutze in 1851. Although historically inaccurate, it was reproduced by American media for American history school texts. It now hangs in the Metropolitan Museum of Art in New York City.

2021, Crossing the Delaware

Circulation-Strike Mintage, Philadelphia: *998,800,000*
Circulation-Strike Mintage, Denver: *1,169,400,000*
Proof Mintage, San Francisco, Clad: *512,729*
Proof Mintage, San Francisco, Silver: *350,323*
GSID: Circulation-strike, Philadelphia, 85132; Circulation-strike, Denver, 85133; Proof Clad Deep Cameo, 85134; Proof Silver Deep Cameo, 198054

Specifics of the Reverse Design

Description: General Washington, wearing a Revolutionary officer's uniform, cloak, and tricorn hat, is placed at the left side of the coin. He faces to the right, pointing toward the opposite shore with his raised sword as he leads his men across the ice-choked Delaware River. Below the line of the sword is another boat, filled with American soldiers and keeping pace with Washington as the army head toward the Battle of Trenton.

Designer: Benjamin Sowards. *Mint sculptor-engraver who made the model:* Michael Gaudioso. *Designer's initials and location:* BS at lower left, on Washington's cloak. *Engraver's initials and location:* MG at far right, on the ice just below the tip of Washington's sword.

Story and Background of the Design

The authorizing legislation required the obverse of the one-year coin to revert to John Flanagan's portrait of George Washington that had appeared on the quarter dollar since its inception in 1932 until 1998. The reverse would depict General Washington, sword in hand, commanding his troops as they are displayed in a boat crossing the icy river. It portrays Washington's leadership in a new way, rather than simply copying the famous painting.

The design was unveiled on December 25, 2020, the 244th anniversary of the actual crossing. The new coin was released by the Federal Reserve on April 5, 2021.

2021-P, Crossing the Delaware

MS-65	MS-66	MS-67	MS-68
$0.80	$2.65	$16	—

2021-D, Crossing the Delaware

MS-65	MS-66	MS-67	MS-68
$0.80	$2.65	$16	—

2021-S, Crossing the Delaware, Proof, Clad

PF-67DC	PF-68DC	PF-69DC
$3.40	$4.05	$11

2021-S, Crossing the Delaware, Proof, Silver

PF-67DC	PF-68DC	PF-69DC
$7.20	$8.50	$11

11

American Women Quarters, 2022–2025: Analysis by Date and Mintmark

AMERICAN WOMEN QUARTERS

After the completion of the America the Beautiful (ATB) Quarters Program (2010–2021) and the one-year Crossing the Delaware issue (2021 only), a new program commenced: the American Women Quarters Program.

The authorizing legislation was the Circulating Collectible Coin Redesign Act of 2020, sponsored by Rep. Barbara Lee (D-CA) and Rep. Anthony Gonzalez (R-OH). As originally envisioned, it resembled the ATB series: 56 coins, with one for each state, the District of Columbia, and each of the U.S. territories. But that idea was modified to become five coins issued per year between 2022 and 2025, for a total of 20 coins. The reason for amending this series was because in 2026, the United States of America will celebrate the 250th Anniversary of its Independence—the Semiquincentennial.

In December of 2020, Congress passed the legislation authorizing the amended bill and it was signed into law on January 13, 2021. The new legislation was Public Law 116-330, and it required the U.S. Mint to consult with experts on the contributions of American women from the Smithsonian Institution American Women's History Initiative, the National Women's History Museum, and the Bipartisan Women's Caucus.

The objective for the Mint and for these groups of experts was to identify and to select prominent American women who could be honored by being placed in a series of quarter dollar coins over the next four years.

The More Complicated Design Selection Process

The Secretary of the Treasury was tasked with selecting the honorees after consultation with the experts identified and with public suggestions for potential honorees that were submitted to the National Women's History Museum, through a special web-portal created for these nominations. Unlike other programs where the Mint simply followed prior practices, there was a six-step process to coordinate and share information from these outside experts.

First, the Mint required the Smithsonian Institution's American Women's History Initiative and the National Women's History Museum to appoint Mint liaisons specifically for this program.

The next step in the process was to engage these liaisons and receive recommendations from them as to whether there were any other federal institutions that must be consulted. These liaisons recommended that the National Archives and Records Administration, the National Academy of Sciences, and the National Gallery of Art should develop a pool of accomplishments created by women that aided the development and history of America. The desire was also to incorporate these concepts from the general public and the Bipartisan Women's Caucus. These concepts had to include a wide variety of accomplishments and topics like suffrage, civil rights, science, and the arts, and they should honor women from different ethnic and geographic backgrounds.

The third step was to consult with the experts in the subject matters and with members of the Citizens Coinage Advisory Committee (CCAC), and after these consultations, develop formal concepts. The Director of the Mint would submit the formalized concepts to the Secretary of the Treasury.

Step four in the process was for the Mint to produce the original designs. They would be responsible for making them aesthetically pleasing and historically accurate, and ensuring that these formalized concepts could be struck properly given the designs.

The next step is a familiar one. The candidate designs would be given to the CCAC and to the Commission of Fine Arts (CFA) for review and comment. This is the step where the design modifications would likely take place, if any were required.

The final step was also expected to be the final selection phase, where the Mint would present final designs to all stakeholders and to the Secretary of the Treasury for approval.

An Appropriate Common Obverse

In appropriate recognition of the accomplishments of women, the obverse design to be used on all of these American Women quarters would be one from numismatic history. It was designed by one of the preeminent women designers of the day, Laura Gardin Fraser.

Fraser was one of the most prolific women coin designers and sculptors of her day. She was the first woman to design a commemorative coin. She designed the 1921 Alabama Centennial Half Dollar, the 1922 Grant Centennial Half Dollar and One Dollar gold coins, the 1925 Fort Vancouver Centennial, and the 1926 Oregon Trail Memorial Half Dollar.

Fraser designed a bust of Washington that she submitted as a candidate for the 1932 quarter dollar. Her design was recommended by many of the experts of the day, as well as the CFA. But the then-Secretary of the Treasury, Andrew Mellon, preferred the John Flanagan design that was actually used for the 1932 and subsequent quarters.

While some numismatists believe that Mellon had misogynistic motives for not picking Fraser's design, it might simply have been because he preferred the Flanagan design. While no one knows for certain which story is true, it is a fitting tribute to Laura Gardin Fraser that her beautiful rendition of Washington from 1932 adorns all American Women quarter dollars.

2022, Maya Angelou

Circulation-Strike Mintage, Philadelphia: 237,600,000
Circulation-Strike Mintage, Denver: 258,200,000
Circulation-Strike Mintage, San Francisco: 303,520
Proof Mintage, San Francisco, Clad: 699,097
Proof Mintage, San Francisco, Silver: 356,823
GSID: Circulation-strike, Philadelphia, 193257; Circulation-strike, Denver, 193258; Circulation-strike, San Francisco, 198055; Proof Clad Deep Cameo, 193259; Proof Silver Deep Cameo, 198060

Specifics of the Reverse Design

Description: The coin depicts Maya Angelou standing with her arms spread wide and raised, superimposed over the silhouette of a bird in flight and the rays of a rising sun, visuals referencing her literary career, particularly *Caged Bird*, and capturing the spirit of her activism. Her name appears to the left of the figure, below her arm and the bird's wing.

Designer: Emily Damstra. *Mint sculptor-engraver who made the model:* Craig A. Campbell. *Designer's initials and location:* ESD to left, below bird's tail feathers. *Engraver's initials and location:* CAC at right, below outstretched wing.

Story and Background of the Design

For the honorees of the American Women quarter series, all proposed designs were reviewed by representatives from the Smithsonian Institution and the National Women's History Museum, as well as representatives of the honorees' families. As a whole, family members preferred designs that specifically incorporated an image of the subject rather than just symbolizing each woman's contributions to society.

Guy Johnson, Angelou's son, and other representatives of her estate spoke in the discussions of the reverse designs with the CCAC and the Mint. Johnson specifically commented on how strong his mother's stage presence was; he felt that the design showing Angelou with her arms outstretched was the best representation of her bold, larger-than-life personality and skill as a dancer, in addition to her writing talents. CCAC members also commented on the energy and optimism of the image. This design was also the preference for the CFA and the Smithsonian. Several other suggested designs featured birds, both in and out of birdcages, to represent Angelou's most famous work, *I Know Why the Caged Bird Sings*.

Biography

The first coin of the American Women quarter series featured celebrated African-American writer, performer, and activist Maya Angelou (1928–2014). She came to national prominence with the 1969 publication of her first memoir, *I Know Why the Caged Bird Sings*, which recounted her difficult childhood in Arkansas. The award-winning story stayed on the *New York Times* bestseller list for two years and has remained in print ever since, despite frequent challenges and attempts to ban it over its frank discussions of racism, rape, teen pregnancy, and violence.

Though loved and supported by the grandmother who raised her, Angelou was open about her difficult life experiences, including being raped as a child by her mother's boyfriend. When she told what had happened, the rapist was briefly jailed; after his release he was found beaten to death, probably by her uncles. The already traumatized child believed her words had killed him, and for the next five years she only spoke to her brother, although she read every book she could get her hands on. She later credited this love of literature and the encouragement of a special teacher with helping her speak again.

Before becoming a writer, Angelou shared her talents as a performer, studying modern dance as a teen and singing and dancing in nightclubs to support herself and her son. She continued to make an impact on stage and in film throughout her career—dancing in a world tour of the opera *Porgy and Bess;* recording her first album, *Miss Calypso,* in 1957; appearing in the television miniseries *Roots;* and later composing music for musician Roberta Flack and directing a feature film. She shared her words in seven autobiographies, nearly 20 volumes of poetry, five essay collections, children's books, plays, and screenplays. She was asked to share her poem "On the Pulse of Morning" at President Bill Clinton's first inauguration in 1993, only the second poet and first African-American and first woman to do so. Among other recognitions, she received more than 30 honorary degrees, was nominated for a Pulitzer Prize and a Tony Award, won three Grammys for her spoken-word albums, and was awarded the Presidential Medal of Freedom by President Barack Obama in 2010.

2022-P, Maya Angelou

MS-63	MS-64	MS-65	MS-66	MS-67
$0.40	$0.40	$0.60	$5.40	$27

2022-D, Maya Angelou

MS-63	MS-64	MS-65	MS-66	MS-67
$0.40	$0.40	$0.60	$5.40	$27

2022-S, Maya Angelou, Circulation Strike

MS-63	MS-64	MS-65	MS-66	MS-67
$0.40	$0.40	$0.60	$5.40	$27

2022-S, Maya Angelou, Proof, Clad

PF-67DC	PF-68DC	PF-69DC
$4.05	$5.40	$11

2022-S, Maya Angelou, Proof, Silver

PF-67DC	PF-68DC	PF-69DC
$9.90	$12.50	$13.50

2022, Dr. Sally Ride

Circulation-Strike Mintage, Philadelphia: *275,200,000*
Circulation-Strike Mintage, Denver: *278,000,000*
Circulation-Strike Mintage, San Francisco: *304,120*
Proof Mintage, San Francisco, Clad: *699,097*
Proof Mintage, San Francisco, Silver: *356,823*
GSID: Circulation-strike, Philadelphia, 193260; Circulation-strike, Denver, 193261; Circulation-strike, San Francisco, 198056; Proof Clad Deep Cameo, 193268; Proof Silver Deep Cameo, 198061

Specifics of the Reverse Design

Description: Ride is depicted from the waist up, wearing an astronaut's coveralls with her name tag and a NASA emblem. To the right, a round shuttle port frames a view of Earth that Ride admired on breaks between her duties as an astronaut. The design is inspired by her quote, "But when I wasn't working, I was usually at a window looking down at Earth." Her name is included with the encircling inscriptions as DR. SALLY RIDE at lower right.

Designer: Elana Hagler. *Mint sculptor-engraver who made the model:* Phebe Hemphill. *Designer's initials and location:* EH at left, above shoulder. *Engraver's initials and location:* PH at right, above SALLY.

Story and Background of the Design

Of the five designs suggested to the various stakeholders, the image of Dr. Ride at the window of the space shuttle was by far the favorite. Dr. Tam O'Shaughnessy, Ride's partner, hoped it would be possible to include some additional text such as "physicist" and "educator," indicating more of Ride's work than just that she was the first American woman in space, but given the size of the image and the limited room on a quarter-sized planchet, adding more inscriptions would have muddled the design.

There was a great deal of debate on whether to include the title "Dr." in the inscription with Ride's name, as the individuals honored on the American Women quarters would feature a diverse range of accomplishments, and there was some confusion over which titles should be included for future coins. Ultimately it was determined this was a conversation for the Mint to have with honorees' family members and representatives, to see what they would like included. In this case, the Mint went forward with including Ride's earned degree, seeing it as both an important part of her life story and an opportunity to encourage young women in pursuing education and careers in STEM fields.

Biography

Dr. Sally Ride (1951–2012), the second woman honored in the American Women quarters series, is best known as the first American woman (and, it was later revealed, first LGBT person) in space in 1983. Her influence extended far beyond that historic flight.

A nationally ranked junior tennis player in her youth, Ride ultimately chose to pursue physics instead of a professional sports career. In 1977, while working on her PhD—the only woman in her program—she applied to become an astronaut for the Space Shuttle Program. She was one of just 35 people, including six women, selected from over 8,000 applicants.

In another first, Ride served as the first female capsule communicator during the second and third Columbia missions. During her time at NASA, she helped develop the shuttles' robot arms, "Canadarm." Her experience with the arm and CAPCOM led to her selection for STS-7, where she deployed and retrieved satellites. During a 2008 interview with CNN, Ride recalled how her first trip to space gave her a new perspective: "You can't get it just standing on the ground, with your feet firmly planted on Earth. You can only get it from space, and it's just remarkable how beautiful our planet is and how fragile it looks."

Ride returned to space the following year for STS-41-G and was training for a third mission when the Challenger disaster occurred in 1986. She was appointed to the presidential commission investigating the tragedy, and (it was revealed posthumously) she identified the O-ring failure that caused the disaster. She later served on the 2003 Columbia Accident Investigation Board, the only person to work on both panels.

After leaving NASA in 1987, she dedicated herself to educating the next generation of scientists, teaching at Stanford and UC–San Diego. With her partner Dr. Tam O'Shaughnessy and others, she founded Sally Ride Science to inspire young people—especially girls—in science, technology, engineering, and math (STEM). She was inducted into the National Aviation Hall of Fame in 2007 and was posthumously awarded the Presidential Medal of Freedom in 2013.

2022-P, Dr. Sally Ride

MS-63	MS-64	MS-65	MS-66	MS-67
$0.40	$0.40	$0.60	$5.40	$27

2022-D, Dr. Sally Ride

MS-63	MS-64	MS-65	MS-66	MS-67
$0.40	$0.40	$0.60	$5.40	$27

2022-S, Dr. Sally Ride, Circulation Strike

MS-63	MS-64	MS-65	MS-66	MS-67
$0.40	$0.40	$0.60	$5.40	$27

2022-S, Dr. Sally Ride, Proof, Clad

PF-67DC	PF-68DC	PF-69DC
$4.05	$5.40	$11

2022-S, Dr. Sally Ride, Proof, Silver

PF-67DC	PF-68DC	PF-69DC
$9.90	$12.50	$13.50

2022, Wilma Mankiller

Circulation-Strike Mintage, Philadelphia: *310,000,000*
Circulation-Strike Mintage, Denver: *296,800,000*
Circulation-Strike Mintage, San Francisco: *304,640*
Proof Mintage, San Francisco, Clad: *699,097*
Proof Mintage, San Francisco, Silver: *356,823*
GSID: Circulation-strike, Philadelphia, 193262; Circulation-strike, Denver, 193263; Circulation-strike, San Francisco, 198057; Proof Clad Deep Cameo, 193269; Proof Silver Deep Cameo, 198062

Specifics of the Reverse Design

Description: Mankiller is depicted from the waist up against a plain field gazing firmly to the viewer's right. The wind at her back blows her hair and lifts the edges of her traditional Cherokee shawl. In the field to the right is the seven-pointed star of the Cherokee Nation. WILMA MANKILLER runs edge to edge across the center of the coin, with PRINCIPAL CHIEF below and, below that, "Cherokee Nation" written in Cherokee syllabary.

Designer: Ben Sowards. *Mint sculptor-engraver who made the model:* Phebe Hemphill. *Designer's initials and location:* BS at lower left on shawl. *Engraver's initials and location:* PH at lower right between shawl's fringe.

Story and Background of the Design

The vote from the CCAC was unanimous in favor of the design (see description) ultimately chosen to represent Wilma Mankiller on the quarter. Members of the CCAC greatly appreciated small elements, like the wind blowing her hair and shawl, that added a sense of motion and purpose to the portrait, rather than just showing a static image.

Representatives of Mankiller's family appreciated the nods to various Cherokee symbols, like the diamond pattern on the shawl and the beaded necklace Mankiller wears in the design. Members of the Cherokee nation also weighed in on the design; they were the ones who suggested using Cherokee syllabary for the words "Cherokee Nation."

Biography

Wilma Mankiller (1945–2010) made history as the first woman elected Principal Chief of the Cherokee Nation in 1985. Her dedication to her culture and people shaped her life's work as an activist, social worker, and leader.

Born in Oklahoma and raised in San Francisco, Mankiller maintained strong connections to her Native culture through the urban Indian community. Her activism began when she supported the American Indian Movement's occupation of Alcatraz prison protesting the government's treatment of Native peoples. This experience inspired her career in social welfare, where she developed Native American youth centers and helped craft legislation that became the Indian Child Welfare Act protecting Native children in foster care.

Returning to Oklahoma, she focused on building her community and encouraging greater tribal self-governance, including projects to bring water infrastructure to under-developed areas. Her evident dedication led chief Ross Swimmer to choose her as his deputy chief in 1983, though they were political opposites. When he resigned in 1985 to join the Bureau of Indian Affairs, she stepped in as Principal Chief. She won two more terms—the second in a landslide—and oversaw a landmark 1990 self-determination agreement between the Cherokee Nation and the U.S. government that enabled the tribe to manage programs previously controlled by the BIA. During her tenure, annual tribal revenue doubled and Cherokee Nation enrollment more than doubled.

Health challenges led Mankiller to step down in 1995, but she remained active in advocating for women's rights, tribal sovereignty, and healthcare. Throughout her struggles, she emphasized what she called "a Cherokee approach to life," which she defined as "being able to continually move forward with kind of a good mind and not focus on the negative things in your life and the negative things you see around you, but focus on the positive things and try to look at the larger picture and keep moving forward."

Her legacy lives on through the many initiatives she championed that strengthened Cherokee self-governance and preserved cultural traditions while adapting to modern challenges.

2022-P, Wilma Mankiller

MS-63	MS-64	MS-65	MS-66	MS-67
$0.40	$0.40	$0.60	$5.40	$27

2022-D, Wilma Mankiller

MS-63	MS-64	MS-65	MS-66	MS-67
$0.40	$0.40	$0.60	$5.40	$27

2022-S, Wilma Mankiller, Circulation Strike

MS-63	MS-64	MS-65	MS-66	MS-67
$0.40	$0.40	$0.60	$5.40	$27

2022-S, Wilma Mankiller, Proof, Clad

PF-67DC	PF-68DC	PF-69DC
$4.05	$5.40	$11

2022-S, Wilma Mankiller, Proof, Silver

PF-67DC	PF-68DC	PF-69DC
$9.90	$12.50	$13.50

2022, Nina Otero-Warren

Circulation-Strike Mintage, Philadelphia: *225,000,000*
Circulation-Strike Mintage, Denver: *219,200,000*
Circulation-Strike Mintage, San Francisco: *305,560*
Proof Mintage, San Francisco, Clad: *699,097*
Proof Mintage, San Francisco, Silver: *356,823*
GSID: Circulation-strike, Philadelphia, 193264; Circulation-strike, Denver, 193265; Circulation-strike, San Francisco, 198058; Proof Clad Deep Cameo, 193270; Proof Silver Deep Cameo, 198063

Specifics of the Reverse Design

Description: Nina Otero-Warren sits at the left with hands clasped on the desk before her and a cluster of three yucca blossoms, New Mexico's state flower, at her elbow. At upper right is the legend "Voto Para la Mujer" (Votes for Women), in three lines, with NINA OTERO-WARREN in smaller letters below.

Designer: Chris Costello. *Mint sculptor-engraver who made the model:* Craig A. Campbell. *Designer's initials and location:* CTC at bottom center, below hands. *Engraver's initials and location:* CAC at center-right, above flowers.

Story and Background of the Design

Members of the CCAC appreciated the "quiet strength" shown in Otero-Warren's pose for the design chosen for the coin, seated and looking directly at the viewer, feeling that it best represented the qualities she had in her fights for suffrage, literacy, and education reform. The original designs presented used Otero-Warren's given name, Adelina; it was the family's request that the Mint include her preferred name, "Nina," on the coin. After determining that there wasn't space for both names, the family pointed out that even in her biography didn't include "Adelina" in the title and agreed that "Nina" was more appropriate if they could only use one name.

Biography

Nina Otero-Warren (1881–1965), the first Hispanic American to be featured on U.S. currency, was a pioneering advocate for education and women's suffrage, particularly emphasizing the importance of bilingual and bicultural outreach in New Mexico.

Beginning in 1914, she became a leading voice in New Mexico's suffrage movement. Recognizing that Hispanic community support would be crucial for New Mexico to ratify the Nineteenth Amendment, she insisted that all suffrage literature be published in both Spanish and English. Her effectiveness caught the attention of suffragist Alice Paul, leading to Otero-Warren's election as vice-chair of what would become the National Woman's Party (NWP), making her the organization's first Mexican-American leader. Her political connections—her cousin had been a territorial governor—helped her successfully lobby state congressmen for their support.

In 1922, she ran for New Mexico's seat in the House of Representatives, hoping to advocate for the Hispanic community, particularly regarding education. Though she lost the election—largely due to controversy over a previously private divorce—she continued working to expand educational opportunities as Santa Fe Superintendent of Instruction from 1917 to 1929. In this role, she championed bilingual and bicultural education at a time when many schools punished students for speaking Spanish or practicing Native cultures.

Otero-Warren's dedication to education continued through the 1930s when she served as Director of Literacy Education for the Civilian Conservation Corps and later worked with the Works Progress Administration on adult education. Throughout her career, she worked to bridge cultural divides between Anglo-American and Hispanic communities while celebrating the unique elements of Hispanic and Native culture, art, and language. Her legacy demonstrates how one person's dedication to cultural understanding and education can help build a more inclusive society.

2022-P, Nina Otero-Warren

MS-63	MS-64	MS-65	MS-66	MS-67
$0.40	$0.40	$0.60	$5.40	$27

2022-D, Nina Otero-Warren

MS-63	MS-64	MS-65	MS-66	MS-67
$0.40	$0.40	$0.60	$5.40	$27

2022-S, Nina Otero-Warren, Circulation Strike

MS-63	MS-64	MS-65	MS-66	MS-67
$0.40	$0.40	$0.60	$5.40	$27

2022-S, Nina Otero-Warren, Proof, Clad

PF-67DC	PF-68DC	PF-69DC
$4.05	$5.40	$11

2022-S, Nina Otero-Warren, Proof, Silver

PF-67DC	PF-68DC	PF-69DC
$9.90	$12.50	$13.50

2022, Anna May Wong

Circulation-Strike Mintage, Philadelphia: *226,800,000*

Circulation-Strike Mintage, Denver: *240,800,000*

Circulation-Strike Mintage, San Francisco: *304,680*

Proof Mintage, San Francisco, Clad: *699,097*

Proof Mintage, San Francisco, Silver: *356,823*

GSID: Circulation-strike, Philadelphia, 193266; Circulation-strike, Denver, 193267; Circulation-strike, San Francisco, 198059; Proof Clad Deep Cameo, 193271; Proof Silver Deep Cameo, 198064

Specifics of the Reverse Design

Description: Wong is depicted as if in a photo from a movie magazine, facing the viewer with her chin on her hand and surrounded by the bright lights of a movie marquee. She wears the straight bangs that defined her look as an international fashion icon and one of the first Flappers. ANNA MAY WONG appears to the left in an Art Deco typeface.

Designer: Emily Damstra. *Mint sculptor-engraver who made the model:* John P. McGraw. *Designer's initials and location:* ESD in field left of hand. *Engraver's initials and location:* JPM at lower right on hand.

Story and Background of the Design

CCAC members were torn over the design suggestions for Anna May Wong's coin, with too many great designs to pick from. For them, it ultimately came down to two options: the marquee design that ended up being minted or an image mimicking movie posters from the early film era, with Wong posing dramatically. For the latter design, committee members particularly liked the clever wording connecting the required inscriptions, "UNITED STATES OF AMERICA presents ANNA MAY WONG in QUARTER DOLLAR," and the overly dramatic pose reminiscent of the silent film era, when Wong began her career. The CFA and Wong's family preferred the marquee design, finding the close-up of her face to be particularly compelling.

Designer Emily Damstra said of her inspiration, "Many prominent actors from the 1920s and 1930s saw their name framed by lightbulbs on movie theater marquees, so I thought it made sense to feature Anna May Wong in this way. Along with the hard work, determination, and skill Anna May Wong brought to the profession of acting, I think it was her face and expressive gestures that really captivated movie audiences, so I included these elements next to her name."

Biography

Anna May Wong (1905–1961) was a pioneering Asian-American film star who helped normalize the image of Chinese Americans during an era of intense discrimination. Though acclaimed for her acting talent, she fought throughout her career against discriminatory casting practices.

Born Wong Liu Tsong, she chose her stage name "Anna May" by age eleven. Her first role—an uncredited extra in *The Red Lantern*—came at fourteen. After dropping out of high school to pursue acting, she landed her first leading role at seventeen in *The Toll of the Sea*, a silent film based on *Madame Butterfly*.

Despite critical praise, Wong found herself consistently relegated to supporting roles as either the "butterfly" (a doomed love interest) or the "dragon lady" (an exotic seductress). As curator David Schwartz noted, "She built up a level of stardom in Hollywood, but Hollywood didn't know what to do with her." Anti-miscegenation laws prevented her—as a person of Chinese descent—from kissing actors of other races onscreen. Leading roles routinely went to white actors, even in yellowface. This reached a crisis point in 1935 when MGM refused to consider Wong for the lead in *The Good Earth*, instead offering her the sole unsympathetic role. She declined and instead took a film crew to China, documenting her family's homeland throughout 1936.

Wong continued acting through the 1930s and '40s, often donating her earnings to United China Relief and advocating for China during its conflict with Japan. She performed occasionally in film and television through the 1950s, including starring in *The Gallery of Madame Liu-Tsong*, a series written specifically for her. She received a star on the Hollywood Walk of Fame in 1960, a year before her death. Her perseverance in the face of systemic racism continues to inspire Asian American performers who still challenge an entertainment industry that often "others" non-Anglo artists. The quarter honoring her marked the first time an Asian-American appeared on U.S. currency.

2022-P, Anna May Wong

MS-63	MS-64	MS-65	MS-66	MS-67
$0.40	$0.40	$0.60	$5.40	$27

2022-D, Anna May Wong

MS-63	MS-64	MS-65	MS-66	MS-67
$0.40	$0.40	$0.60	$5.40	$27

2022-S, Anna May Wong, Circulation Strike

MS-63	MS-64	MS-65	MS-66	MS-67
$0.40	$0.40	$0.60	$5.40	$27

2022-S, Anna May Wong, Proof, Clad

PF-67DC	PF-68DC	PF-69DC
$4.05	$5.40	$11

2022-S, Anna May Wong, Proof, Silver

PF-67DC	PF-68DC	PF-69DC
$9.90	$12.50	$13.50

2023, Bessie Coleman

Circulation-Strike Mintage, Philadelphia: 302,000,000
Circulation-Strike Mintage, Denver: 317,200,000
Circulation-Strike Mintage, San Francisco: 500,360
Proof Mintage, San Francisco, Clad: 593,245
Proof Mintage, San Francisco, Silver: 269,709
GSID: Circulation-strike, Philadelphia, 199021; Circulation-strike, Denver, 199022; Circulation-strike, San Francisco, 199023; Proof Clad Deep Cameo, 199036; Proof Silver Deep Cameo, 199037

Specifics of the Reverse Design

Description: The coin depicts a closeup of Bessie Coleman adjusting her goggles as she suits up in preparation for flight, her expression reflective of her determination to take to the skies, "the only place free from prejudice." Clouds rise up behind her, and in the field above, a biplane soars to the right. Her name is incused in the lower part of the border, and the date she obtained her pilot's license, 6.15.1921, is below.

Designer: Chris Costello. *Mint sculptor-engraver who made the model:* Eric David Custer. *Designer's initials and location:* CTC at lower left of COLEMAN. *Engraver's initials and location:* EC at lower right of COLEMAN.

Story and Background of the Design

When reviewing designs for Bessie Coleman, family members selected two that they would be happy using. One depicted Coleman standing with arms crossed, gazing seriously at the viewer while her plane flew behind her across a cloudy sky. This design was favored by the CFA, who appreciated the resolve indicated in her pose. The other preferred design showed a closeup of Coleman staring resolutely ahead as she adjusts her goggles with her plane flying behind her and included wing-like stripes to either side of her name and the date she received her pilot's license. This design was the favorite of the CCAC, who appreciated the importance of the date and thought the closer view of her face would help make the design more recognizable. The Mint elected to use the latter design.

Biography

Elizabeth "Bessie" Coleman (1892–1926) broke barriers as the first Black woman and first Native American to earn a pilot's license, achieving this milestone on June 15, 1921, despite the formidable obstacles of racism and segregation.

After leaving university due to financial constraints, Coleman moved to Chicago in 1915, where she worked as a manicurist. Inspired by pilots' stories from World War I, she determined to become an aviator herself. When American flight schools refused to admit her because she was both Black and female, she learned French and traveled to Paris to earn her wings from the Fédération Aéronautique Internationale. She remained in Europe for additional training in stunt flying, knowing that racial and gender discrimination would limit her employment options in commercial aviation back home.

As a professional aviator, Coleman became known for her skilled and daring performances. More importantly, she took a principled stand against prejudice, refusing to perform for segregated audiences and speaking nationwide about the importance of African-Americans pursuing aviation. "The air is the only place free from prejudice," she famously declared.

Coleman dreamed of establishing a flight school for African-Americans but never saw this realized. In 1926, while preparing for a show in Florida, she was thrown from a plane during a test flight when a wrench jammed the controls. The crash killed both Coleman and the mechanic who was piloting. More than 10,000 mourners attended her funeral in Chicago.

Her legacy lived on through William J. Powell's establishment of the Bessie Coleman Aero Club, which promoted aviation in the Black community and helped train some of the future Tuskegee Airmen of World War II. "Because of Bessie Coleman," wrote Powell, "we have overcome that which was worse than racial barriers. We have overcome the barriers within ourselves and dared to dream."

2023-P, Bessie Coleman

MS-63	MS-64	MS-65	MS-66	MS-67
$0.40	$0.40	$0.60	$5.40	$27

2023-D, Bessie Coleman

MS-63	MS-64	MS-65	MS-66	MS-67
$0.40	$0.40	$0.60	$5.40	$27

2023-S, Bessie Coleman, Circulation Strike

MS-63	MS-64	MS-65	MS-66	MS-67
$0.40	$0.40	$0.60	$5.40	$27

2023-S, Bessie Coleman, Proof, Clad

PF-67DC	PF-68DC	PF-69DC
$4.05	$5.40	$11

2023-S, Bessie Coleman, Proof, Silver

PF-67DC	PF-68DC	PF-69DC
$9.90	$12.50	$13.50

2023, Edith Kanakaʻole

Circulation-Strike Mintage, Philadelphia: *372,800,000*

Circulation-Strike Mintage, Denver: *368,600,000*

Circulation-Strike Mintage, San Francisco: *503,400*

Proof Mintage, San Francisco, Clad: *593,245*

Proof Mintage, San Francisco, Silver: *269,709*

GSID: Circulation-strike, Philadelphia, 199024; Circulation-strike, Denver, 199025; Circulation-strike, San Francisco, 199026; Proof Clad Deep Cameo, 199038; Proof Silver Deep Cameo, 199039

Specifics of the Reverse Design

Description: The coin depicts the face of Edith Kanakaʻole gazing out at the viewer, with her flowing hair and lei poʻo (head lei) merging into the elements of a Hawaiian landscape. EDITH KANAKAʻOLE is incused at the center. In the border below is the inscription "E hō mai ka ʻike" ("Grant us wisdom") is from one of her poems.

Designer: Emily Damstra. *Mint sculptor-engraver who made the model:* Renata Gordon. *Designer's initials and location:* ESD at lower left, below hair. *Engraver's initials and location:* RG at lower right between strands of hair.

Story and Background of the Design

All the designs suggested for Edith Kanakaʻole included elements of the native Hawaiian landscape to represent her efforts to preserve Hawaiian cultural practices and language. Several designs also showed her hula dancing or carrying a traditional drum used during her performances. But the strong preference of all the stakeholders was for the design chosen by the Mint. Members of the CCAC felt that the way Kanakaʻole's blowing hair morphs into the island landscape told a story of how intimately connected she was to her land. Members also appreciated the negative space added by the inclusion of the river; many of the other designs were heavily detailed, which would have been difficult to coin on something as small as a quarter.

There was much debate over the denomination: the inscription QUARTER DOLLAR (traditional since 1892) was favored by the CFA, but the CCAC felt "25¢" was bold and novel, as well as more visually balanced. The latter style appears on the coin.

Biography

Edith Kanakaʻole (1913–1979) was a renowned authority on and advocate for traditional Hawaiian language and culture. Following the devastating impact of Western contact on Native Hawaiian population and cultural practices since 1778, Kanakaʻole emerged as a leader in the movement to revitalize Hawaiian cultural identity.

Trained as a dancer by her mother, she passed this tradition to her children and community when she opened a hālau (school) after her mother's death. She began composing oli (traditional Hawaiian chants) and songs in the 1940s, choreographing hula to accompany many of them. Her hula group toured North America and Asia in the 1950s, spreading appreciation for the art form. Her recorded works twice won awards for "Best Traditional Album."

Despite having only a middle-school education, Kanaka'ole dedicated herself to sharing cultural knowledge broadly. She helped develop the first Hawaiian language program for public schools and taught at Hawai'i Community College and the University of Hawai'i–Hilo, where she helped establish a Bachelor of Arts degree in Hawaiian Studies. Her courses covered a comprehensive range of cultural subjects, including ethnobotany, Hawaiian oral arts, land use, Polynesian history, genealogy, ohana (extended Hawaiian family), and Hawaiian mythology.

Kanaka'ole received recognition as "Hawaiian of the Year" in 1977 and earned awards for her cultural leadership, including designation as "A Living Treasure of Hawai'i." According to the Mint, "her mo'olelo, or stories, served to rescue aspects of Hawaiian history, customs, and traditions that were disappearing due to the cultural bigotry of the time." With her inclusion in the American Women quarters program, Kanaka'ole became the first Native Hawaiian woman to be featured on U.S. currency.

2023-P, Edith Kanaka'ole

MS-63	MS-64	MS-65	MS-66	MS-67
$0.40	$0.40	$0.60	$5.40	$27

2023-D, Edith Kanaka'ole

MS-63	MS-64	MS-65	MS-66	MS-67
$0.40	$0.40	$0.60	$5.40	$27

2023-S, Edith Kanaka'ole, Circulation Strike

MS-63	MS-64	MS-65	MS-66	MS-67
$0.40	$0.40	$0.60	$5.40	$27

2023-S, Edith Kanaka'ole, Proof, Clad

PF-67DC	PF-68DC	PF-69DC
$4.05	$5.40	$11

2023-S, Edith Kanaka'ole, Proof, Silver

PF-67DC	PF-68DC	PF-69DC
$9.90	$12.50	$13.50

2023, Eleanor Roosevelt

Circulation-Strike Mintage, Philadelphia: *284,000,000*
Circulation-Strike Mintage, Denver: *271,800,000*
Circulation-Strike Mintage, San Francisco: *507,120*
Proof Mintage, San Francisco, Clad: *593,245*
Proof Mintage, San Francisco, Silver: *269,709*
GSID: Circulation-strike, Philadelphia, 199027; Circulation-strike, Denver, 199028; Circulation-strike, San Francisco, 199029; Proof Clad Deep Cameo, 199040; Proof Silver Deep Cameo, 199041

Specifics of the Reverse Design

Description: Roosevelt is shown with the scales of justice against a backdrop representing the globe, symbolic of her impactful work with the Universal Declaration of Human Rights. In the field below the main devices are the words UNIVERSAL DECLARATION OF HUMAN RIGHTS.

Designer: Don Everhart. *Mint sculptor-engraver who made the model:* Craig A. Campbell. *Designer's initials and location:* DE at left, below scale. *Engraver's initials and location:* CAC lower right field above PLURIBUS.

Story and Background of the Design

Of the designs suggested to the CCAC, family members, and other stakeholders, everyone agreed that the design selected did the best job at emphasizing Eleanor Roosevelt's international influence with the latitude and longitude lines of the globe in the background. While Roosevelt was an active participant in U.S. politics before and during her husband's presidency, her work with the United Nations following his death promoted humanitarian efforts worldwide. She was instrumental in mustering support for the adoption of the Universal Declaration of Human Rights, both in the U.S. and around the world, due to her ability to work with different and often opposing political blocs. The family also felt that this was the most accurate physical portrait of the designs proffered.

Biography

Anna Eleanor Roosevelt (1884–1962) transformed herself from a shy, self-conscious child into one of the most influential First Ladies in American history and a powerful advocate for civil and humanitarian causes. The niece of one president and wife to another—Theodore walked her down the aisle for her marriage to Franklin—she was educated to value independent thinking and social responsibility, working throughout her life on behalf of the underprivileged, including women, children, African Americans, and labor unions.

Following Franklin's paralytic illness in 1921, which she devotedly nursed him through, Roosevelt became his "eyes, ears, and legs," making public appearances on his behalf. As First Lady, she redefined the role, holding 348 press conferences over her husband's 12-year presidency. She supported working women by banning male reporters from these conferences, effectively forcing newspapers to keep female reporters on staff. She hosted a weekly radio show, wrote a daily syndicated newspaper column, and became the first First Lady to speak at a national party convention.

Roosevelt often took more progressive positions than her husband, particularly on civil rights. She frequently hosted Black guests at the White House and worked behind the scenes promoting legislation supporting African Americans. When the DAR refused to allow Black opera singer Marian Anderson to perform in Constitution Hall, Roosevelt resigned from the organization and arranged for Anderson to perform at the Lincoln Memorial. During World War II, she successfully advocated for women to be employed in defense industries, though she regretted not pushing harder for acceptance of more Jewish refugees.

After FDR's death in 1945, Roosevelt helped build support for the United Nations and served on its Commission of Human Rights (1946–1953), playing a major role in developing the Universal Declaration of Human Rights. President Kennedy appointed her to the Presidential Commission on the Status of Women in 1961 and as a U.N. delegate (1961–1962). She was made an honorary member of Alpha Kappa Alpha, awarded Sweden's Prince Carl Medal in 1950, and posthumously received one of the first U.N. Human Rights Prizes in 1968. Historians consistently rank her as the most influential American First Lady.

2023-P, Eleanor Roosevelt

MS-63	MS-64	MS-65	MS-66	MS-67
$0.40	$0.40	$0.60	$5.40	$27

2023-D, Eleanor Roosevelt

MS-63	MS-64	MS-65	MS-66	MS-67
$0.40	$0.40	$0.60	$5.40	$27

2023-S, Eleanor Roosevelt, Circulation Strike

MS-63	MS-64	MS-65	MS-66	MS-67
$0.40	$0.40	$0.60	$5.40	$27

2023-S, Eleanor Roosevelt, Proof, Clad

PF-67DC	PF-68DC	PF-69DC
$4.05	$5.40	$11

2023-S, Eleanor Roosevelt, Proof, Silver

PF-67DC	PF-68DC	PF-69DC
$9.90	$12.50	$13.50

2023, Jovita Idar

Circulation-Strike Mintage, Philadelphia: *190,600,000*

Circulation-Strike Mintage, Denver: *188,000,000*

Circulation-Strike Mintage, San Francisco: *503,840*

Proof Mintage, San Francisco, Clad: *593,245*

Proof Mintage, San Francisco, Silver: *269,709*

GSID: Circulation-strike, Philadelphia, 199030; Circulation-strike, Denver, 199031; Circulation-strike, San Francisco, 199032; Proof Clad Deep Cameo, 199042; Proof Silver Deep Cameo, 199043

Specifics of the Reverse Design

Description: Against a plain background, Idár stands with her hands clasped. The surface of her high-necked dress is filled with inscriptions referencing her life and accomplishments: MEXICAN AMERICAN RIGHTS; TEACHER, NURSE, and JOURNALIST; ASTREA (one of her pen names); the newspapers EVOLUCIÓN, EL HERALDO CRISTIANO, EL PROGRESO, and LA CRÓNICA; the organizations LA CRUZ BLANCA and LA LIGA FEMINIL MEXICANISTA; and her name, JOVITA IDAR.

Designer: John P. McGraw. *Mint sculptor-engraver who made the model:* John P. McGraw. *Designer/Engraver's initials and location:* JPM within body, to the left of clasped hands.

Story and Background of the Design

Breaking with the family preferences this time, members of the CCAC and Mint artists were overwhelmingly enthusiastic about the design chosen—the symbolism of a woman whose life was dedicated to words being made up of those words, the use of negative space, the stylistic similarities to Gustav Klimt all combined to make a striking coin. The CFA concurred with the CCAC, commenting on the power and beauty of the design. The image of Jovita Idar used in the design was based on her most famous portrait, which had been used in Texas history books for 30 years. The designs preferred by the family and Smithsonian representatives were also based on the same portrait but were more straight-forward, traditional depictions of Idar.

"It was a great honor designing and sculpting the Jovita Idar quarter," said coin designer and engraver John McGraw. "After talking with her family members, I was immediately inspired by her life. Curiosity and education were the driving force in my design, much like Jovita Idar's life work. I imagine the text, which makes up her body in the design, will inspire curiosity and teach the viewer how amazing Jovita Idar was."

Biography

Jovita Idar (1885–1946), journalist and activist, was born to a newspaper editor in Laredo, Texas, along the U.S.-Mexico border. Though initially trained as a teacher, her experience with severely underfunded Chicano schools—lacking even basic supplies like desks and textbooks—convinced her she could make a greater impact through journalism. She returned home to write for her father's paper, *La Crónica*.

The paper openly criticized anti-Mexican-American racism, social and economic inequities, and the Catholic Church's treatment of women. Idar focused her writing on education and women's rights, using various pseudonyms, including "Astrea," the Greek goddess of justice. After the lynching of a 14-year-old Mexican boy in 1911, the Idar family helped form El Primer Congreso Mexicanista (First Mexican Congress) to address such injustices. While still working at the paper, Idar served as the first president of the Liga Femenil Mexicanista (League of Mexican Women), one of the first known Latina feminist organizations. The league promoted bilingual education, provided financial assistance to the poor, and encouraged women's education and financial independence. "Educate a woman," she famously said, "and you educate a family."

When the Mexican Revolution reached the border in 1913, Idar volunteered as a nurse with La Cruz Blanca. She later wrote for *El Progreso*, but when the paper criticized President Wilson's involvement in the Mexican Revolution, Texas Rangers were sent to shut it down. Idar physically blocked their entrance to the paper's offices. Though they backed down initially, they returned later to destroy the printing presses.

After her father's death in 1914, Idar became editor of *La Crónica* and founded a weekly newspaper, *Evolución*, in 1916. She continued advocating for women and education throughout her life, starting a free kindergarten in San Antonio and volunteering as a Spanish interpreter at a local hospital. As an early feminist, she challenged societal boundaries while working for the betterment of women, men, and families alike.

2023-P, Jovita Idar

MS-63	MS-64	MS-65	MS-66	MS-67
$0.40	$0.40	$0.60	$5.40	$27

2023-D, Jovita Idar

MS-63	MS-64	MS-65	MS-66	MS-67
$0.40	$0.40	$0.60	$5.40	$27

2023-S, Jovita Idar, Circulation Strike

MS-63	MS-64	MS-65	MS-66	MS-67
$0.40	$0.40	$0.60	$5.40	$27

2023-S, Jovita Idar, Proof, Clad

PF-67DC	PF-68DC	PF-69DC
$4.05	$5.40	$11

2023-S, Jovita Idar, Proof, Silver

PF-67DC	PF-68DC	PF-69DC
$9.90	$12.50	$13.50

2023, Maria Tallchief

Circulation-Strike Mintage, Philadelphia: *185,800,000*
Circulation-Strike Mintage, Denver: *184,800,000*
Circulation-Strike Mintage, San Francisco: *502,200*
Proof Mintage, San Francisco, Clad: *593,245*
Proof Mintage, San Francisco, Silver: *269,709*
GSID: Circulation-strike, Philadelphia, 199033; Circulation-strike, Denver, 199034; Circulation-strike, San Francisco, 199035; Proof Clad Deep Cameo, 199044; Proof Silver Deep Cameo, 199045

Specifics of the Reverse Design

Description: Tallchief, in her ballerina costume from *Firebird*, is backlit in mid-leap. Below her are the words MARIA TALLCHIEF, with "Woman of Two Standards" inscribed below in Osage orthography.

Designer: Ben Sowards. *Mint sculptor-engraver who made the model:* Joseph Menna. *Designer's initials and location:* BS at left, below leg. *Engraver's initials and location:* JFM at right, below leg.

Story and Background of the Design

All the designs presented featured some form of balletic pose, but the design preferred by all the stakeholders was the only one featuring action and motion, with Maria Tallchief leaping across the coin. Committee members appreciated the power and strength shown in the movement, as opposed to the more static, "posed" look of many of the other designs. This and one other preferred design were the only two that showed Tallchief's whole body, and Mint artists were concerned from a design perspective of cutting off a dancer's legs.

The design chosen originally also included the inscription "America's Prima Ballerina," the subtitle of Tallchief's autobiography, but the CFA recommended that be removed in order to give more import to the inclusion of her Osage name, Wa-Xthe-Thonba or "Woman of Two Standards," for her dual identities as a proud Native American and an accomplished professional dancer.

Ben Sowards, the designer for the quarter, also designed the 2023 Native American dollar featuring Maria Tallchief.

Biography

Maria Tallchief, born Elizabeth Marie Tall Chief (1925–2013), was America's first prima ballerina and, with choreographer George Balanchine, helped revolutionize American ballet. From childhood, she and her sister Marjorie studied piano and ballet at their mother's urging. When she was 8, the family moved from Oklahoma to Los Angeles to pursue opportunities in dance and film. Despite facing discrimination that led her to change her surname's spelling to one word, she trained with renowned choreographers who inspired her dedication to ballet.

After graduating, Tallchief moved to New York and joined the Ballet Russe. Though encouraged to change her name to sound more Russian—a common practice for ballet dancers—she agreed only to use "Maria" instead of "Betty Marie," refusing to change "Tallchief" to "Tallchieva." Her pride in her heritage remained steadfast.

While with Ballet Russe, she caught the attention of choreographer George Balanchine. After their 1946 marriage, they spent a year in Paris, where she became the first American to dance with the Paris Opera Ballet. Returning to the U.S., they founded America's first professional ballet company, the New York City Ballet, where Tallchief became America's first prima ballerina. Though their marriage ended in 1952, they continued collaborating, with Balanchine creating 32 ballets for her, including her famous roles as the Firebird and the Sugar Plum Fairy in *The Nutcracker*—helping establish that work as an annual Christmas tradition.

Known for "dazzling audiences with her speed, energy and fire," Tallchief retired from performing at 41 but remained dedicated to ballet, co-founding the Chicago City Ballet with her sister in 1981 and teaching Balanchine technique at the Lyric Opera ballet school. Her Osage tribe honored her as "Princess Wa-Txthe-Thonba" ("Woman of Two Standards") in 1963, recognizing her achievements in both classical ballet and tribal roles.

2023-P, Maria Tallchief

MS-63	MS-64	MS-65	MS-66	MS-67
$0.40	$0.40	$0.60	$5.40	$27

2023-D, Maria Tallchief

MS-63	MS-64	MS-65	MS-66	MS-67
$0.40	$0.40	$0.60	$5.40	$27

2023-S, Maria Tallchief, Circulation Strike

MS-63	MS-64	MS-65	MS-66	MS-67
$0.40	$0.40	$0.60	$5.40	$27

2023-S, Maria Tallchief, Proof, Clad

PF-67DC	PF-68DC	PF-69DC
$4.05	$5.40	$11

2023-S, Maria Tallchief, Proof, Silver

PF-67DC	PF-68DC	PF-69DC
$9.90	$12.50	$13.50

2024, Reverend Dr. Pauli Murray

Mintage details not available at press time.

GSID: Circulation-strike, Philadelphia, 346868; Circulation-strike, Denver, 346869; Circulation-strike, San Francisco, 346870; Proof Clad Deep Cameo, 346871; Proof Silver Deep Cameo, 346872

Specifics of the Reverse Design

Description: The reverse design of the 2023 quarter in her honor depicts a bust of Murray in a realistic style, wearing eyeglasses and her priest's collar. The theme of the design is taken from her poem "Dark Testament, Verse 8": "Hope is a song in a weary throat." The word HOPE spans the field in a bold font, and Murray's face appears within the first two letters. A SONG IN A WEARY THROAT is inscribed vertically within the last two letters, and the denomination, 25¢, is placed vertically in the field between them. THE REVEREND DR. PAULI MURRAY appears in two lines below the main design.

Designer: Emily Damstra. *Mint sculptor-engraver who made the model:* Joseph Menna. *Designer's initials and location:* ESD at lower left, below H. *Engraver's initials and location:* JFM at lower right, below E.

Story and Background of the Design

Representatives from Murray's family and the various stakeholder organizations were immediately drawn to designs incorporating "Hope is a song in a weary throat," a line from her poem "Dark Testament." The CCAC members particularly appreciated how the chosen design integrated both Murray's face and the quote into the bold letters forming HOPE, feeling it represented both her literary achievements and her lifelong work fighting for justice and equality.

There was considerable discussion about including her religious title. Some felt it might detract from her other achievements as a lawyer, activist, and writer. However, her role as the first African-American woman ordained as an Episcopal priest was a significant milestone, and family representatives noted that her faith informed all aspects of her work for social justice. The decision to include THE REVEREND DR. aligned with previous decisions about titles, such as "Dr." for Sally Ride.

Biography

Rev. Dr. Pauli Murray (1910–1985) was a groundbreaking civil rights activist, lawyer, feminist, poet, and Episcopal priest whose work shaped both the civil rights and women's movements. Born in Baltimore, Murray faced early tragedy with her mother's death when she was three and her father's death in a state mental hospital—killed by a white guard—when she was twelve.

A precocious child who taught herself to read by five, Murray challenged Jim Crow laws even as a teenager, refusing to sit in segregated bus sections. After graduating high school at the top of her class, she attended Hunter College in New York City, working through the Depression to fund her education. There she joined a circle of Black intellectuals including Langston Hughes and W.E.B. DuBois, while developing her own voice as a writer and poet. During this period, she adopted the gender-neutral name "Pauli."

Murray's legal career began after working with the NAACP, where she impressed Thurgood Marshall and befriended Eleanor Roosevelt. At Howard University Law School, she faced gender discrimination as the only woman student, coining the term "Jane Crow." Though she graduated first in her class, Harvard rejected her because of her gender. She completed her advanced law degree at UC Berkeley instead, later becoming the first African-American to earn a JSD from Yale.

Her legal scholarship proved influential—her Howard thesis arguing against segregation influenced the NAACP's arguments in *Brown v. Board of Education*, and her law review article on gender equality later informed Ruth Bader Ginsburg's Supreme Court arguments. She co-founded the National Organization for Women in 1966 but withdrew over its neglect of working-class and Black women's issues.

In 1977, Murray made history again as the first Black woman ordained as an Episcopal priest, seeing this role as a new way to pursue justice. She was later canonized by the Episcopal Church. Throughout her career, Murray challenged intersecting forms of discrimination and advocated for comprehensive civil rights, earning recognition as a pioneering voice for social justice.

2024-P, Reverend Dr. Pauli Murray

MS-63	MS-64	MS-65	MS-66	MS-67
$0.40	$0.40	$0.60	$5.40	$27

2024-D, Reverend Dr. Pauli Murray

MS-63	MS-64	MS-65	MS-66	MS-67
$0.40	$0.40	$0.60	$5.40	$27

2024-S, Reverend Dr. Pauli Murray, Circulation Strike

MS-63	MS-64	MS-65	MS-66	MS-67
$0.40	$0.40	$0.60	$5.40	$27

2024-S, Reverend Dr. Pauli Murray, Proof, Clad

PF-67DC	PF-68DC	PF-69DC
$4.05	$5.40	$11

2024-S, Reverend Dr. Pauli Murray, Proof, Silver

PF-67DC	PF-68DC	PF-69DC
$9.90	$12.50	$13.50

2024, Hon. Patsy Takemoto Mink

Mintage details not available at press time.

GSID: Circulation-strike, Philadelphia, 374280; Circulation-strike, Denver, 374281; Circulation-strike, San Francisco, 374282; Proof Clad Deep Cameo, 346873; Proof Silver Deep Cameo, 346874

Specifics of the Reverse Design

Description: Patsy Takemoto Mink is depicted from the waist up, in three-quarter profile to the right. She smiles broadly, with both hands raised in a dynamic gesture. In her left is a sheaf of papers inscribed with TITLE IX; in her right, a pen is held as if she is about to sign. A lei around her neck recalls her native state of Hawaii. The U.S. Capitol is in the background; her name, in a typeface suggesting the 1950s or 60s, appears above it in three lines. The devices are surrounded by the required inscriptions E PLURIBUS UNUM and UNITED STATES OF AMERICA and the denomination, 25 CENTS. Below the portrait, the phrase EQUAL OPPORTUNITY IN EDUCATION highlights the importance of the Title IX legislation.

Designer: Beth Zaiken. *Mint sculptor-engraver who made the model:* John P. McGraw. *Designer's initials and location:* BZ at lower left, by elbow. *Engraver's initials and location:* JPM in field at lower right.

Story and Background of the Design

The CCAC and CFA were presented with several designs featuring Mink, but the one chosen stood out for its dynamic portrayal of her most significant legislative achievement. Family members particularly appreciated how the design captured Mink in a moment of legislative action, holding TITLE IX documentation in one hand and a pen in the other, suggesting the historic moment when this landmark legislation became law.

The inclusion of the U.S. Capitol building behind her emphasizes her role as the first woman of color elected to Congress, while the lei around her neck acknowledges her Hawaiian heritage. Some committee members initially questioned whether including both the Capitol and EQUAL OPPORTUNITY IN EDUCATION might make the design too busy, but the final arrangement proved both balanced and meaningful. The Mint's artists noted that positioning Mink's name in three lines helped create visual harmony with the architectural elements.

Biography

Patsy Takemoto Mink (1927–2002) was a pioneering legislator whose legacy includes co-authoring Title IX, landmark legislation that mandated equal opportunities for women in education. Born in Paia, Hawaii Territory, she grew up in a culture where Native Hawaiians and immigrants like her parents faced discrimination from wealthy white landowners. Though her family lived comfortably due to her father's career as a civil engineer, the Pearl Harbor attack heightened racial tensions, leading to her father's temporary detention and the family's destruction of their Japanese possessions.

At the University of Hawaii, Mink successfully protested against segregated student housing. After graduation, she faced rejection from medical schools because of her gender, leading her to pursue law instead. Even with her law degree from the University of Chicago, she encountered multiple barriers: law firms refused to hire her because she was a woman, had a child, and was in an interracial marriage. Undaunted, she opened her own practice, becoming Hawaii's first Japanese-American woman lawyer.

Mink's political career began in the Hawaii Territorial Legislature (1956–1958). In 1962, she made history as the first woman of color elected to Congress, where she championed civil rights legislation throughout the 1960s. Her most significant achievement came in 1972 as co-author of Title IX, which prohibited gender-based discrimination in federally funded educational institutions and programs, dramatically expanding opportunities for women in academics and athletics.

Throughout her twelve terms in Congress, Mink remained a steadfast advocate for social justice, education, and civil rights. She helped shape crucial legislation affecting education, childcare, and environmental protection. Her work on Title IX was so significant that after her death in 2002, the law was renamed the Patsy T. Mink Equal Opportunity in Education Act. She demonstrated how legislative action could create lasting social change, particularly in advancing women's rights and educational equity.

2024-P, Hon. Patsy Takemoto Mink

MS-63	MS-64	MS-65	MS-66	MS-67
$0.40	$0.40	$0.60	$5.40	$27

2024-D, Hon. Patsy Takemoto Mink

MS-63	MS-64	MS-65	MS-66	MS-67
$0.40	$0.40	$0.60	$5.40	$27

2024-S, Hon. Patsy Takemoto Mink, Circulation Strike

MS-63	MS-64	MS-65	MS-66	MS-67
$0.40	$0.40	$0.60	$5.40	$27

2024-S, Hon. Patsy Takemoto Mink, Proof, Clad

PF-67DC	PF-68DC	PF-69DC
$4.05	$5.40	$11

2024-S, Hon. Patsy Takemoto Mink, Proof, Silver

PF-67DC	PF-68DC	PF-69DC
$9.90	$12.50	$13.50

2024, Dr. Mary Edwards Walker

Mintage details not available at press time.

GSID: Circulation-strike, Philadelphia, 374283; Circulation-strike, Denver, 374284; Circulation-strike, San Francisco, 374285; Proof Clad Deep Cameo, 346875; Proof Silver Deep Cameo, 346876

Specifics of the Reverse Design

Description: The Dr. Mary Edwards Walker quarter presents her from the waist up in three-quarter profile to the left, as in photos from the war. She wears a simple, buttoned jacket with a plain brooch at the neck and the Medal of Honor on the left side of her chest, and her hair is in the curled style she often wore on the field. In her right hand, just visible, is her pocket surgical kit. Her medal of honor is enlarged in the field at left, with her name, DR. MARY EDWARDS WALKER, below in four lines. An off-center banner at the bottom reads MEDAL OF HONOR 1865.

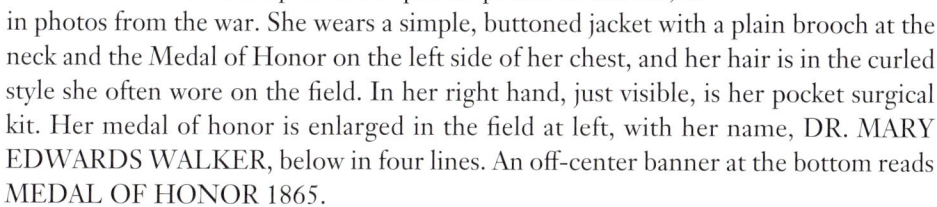

Designer: Phebe Hemphill. *Mint sculptor-engraver who made the model:* Phebe Hemphill. Designer/*Engraver's initials and location:* PH at right, at end of banner.

Story and Background of the Design

The design process for Dr. Walker's quarter focused on how best to represent both her groundbreaking medical career and her status as the only woman to receive the Medal of Honor. The chosen design depicts her in the modified military uniform she preferred, which itself represented her lifelong advocacy for dress reform. Family representatives and committee members alike appreciated that the design included her surgical kit, noting that it represented both her medical profession and her service during the Civil War.

There was considerable discussion about the size and placement of the Medal of Honor in the design. Some felt it should be more prominent, given its historic significance, while others worried that enlarging it might overwhelm Walker's portrait. The final design struck a balance by showing the medal both as she wore it and in an enlarged detail, allowing for better visibility of this important symbol on the small surface of a quarter.

Biography

Dr. Mary Edwards Walker (1832–1919) remains the only woman ever awarded the Medal of Honor. Born in Oswego, N.Y., she grew up in a progressive household where her parents treated their son and daughters equally, encouraging education and practical dress over restrictive fashion.

After graduating with honors from Syracuse Medical College in 1855—the only woman in her class—she married fellow doctor Albert Miller. Their unconventional wedding reflected her principles: she wore trousers under a short dress, omitted "to obey" from her vows, and kept her name. The marriage ended after a few years due to Miller's infidelity.

When the Civil War began in 1861, Walker attempted to join the Union Army as a surgeon but was rejected because of her gender. She served instead as a civilian nurse while continuing to perform surgical duties. In 1863, she finally received an appointment as "Contract Acting Assistant Surgeon (civilian)"—the first woman to hold this position.

Walker's wartime service was distinguished by her courage. She frequently worked near the front lines, including at Bull Run and Fredericksburg. According to Generals Thomas and Sherman, she often crossed enemy lines to treat the wounded and gathered valuable intelligence. In 1864, Confederate forces captured and imprisoned her for four months as a suspected spy, an experience that permanently affected her health.

Throughout her life, Walker challenged convention by wearing "reform dress"—typically a knee-length skirt over trousers, eventually adopting full male attire. She faced criticism and even arrest for her clothing choices, maintaining that she wore her own clothes, not men's. In recognition of her wartime service, President Johnson awarded her the Medal of Honor. When the award was rescinded in 1917 under new eligibility criteria, she refused to return it. Her medal was posthumously reinstated in 1977, making her one of only eight civilians to receive this distinction.

Beyond her medical practice, Walker wrote and lectured extensively on women's rights, dress reform, and marriage equality. She died just months before the ratification of the 19th Amendment, which granted women the right to vote.

2024-P, Dr. Mary Edwards Walker

MS-63	MS-64	MS-65	MS-66	MS-67
$0.40	$0.40	$0.60	$5.40	$27

2024-D, Dr. Mary Edwards Walker

MS-63	MS-64	MS-65	MS-66	MS-67
$0.40	$0.40	$0.60	$5.40	$27

2024-S, Dr. Mary Edwards Walker, Circulation Strike

MS-63	MS-64	MS-65	MS-66	MS-67
$0.40	$0.40	$0.60	$5.40	$27

2024-S, Dr. Mary Edwards Walker, Proof, Clad

PF-67DC	PF-68DC	PF-69DC
$4.05	$5.40	$11

2024-S, Dr. Mary Edwards Walker, Proof, Silver

PF-67DC	PF-68DC	PF-69DC
$9.90	$12.50	$13.50

2024, Celia Cruz

Mintage details not available at press time.

GSID: Circulation-strike, Philadelphia, 374286; Circulation-strike, Denver, 374287; Circulation-strike, San Francisco, 374288; Proof Clad Deep Cameo, 346877; Proof Silver Deep Cameo, 346878

Specifics of the Reverse Design

Description: Cruz is shown on the reverse of the American Women quarter from the waist up, wearing a rumba dress with lace trim and her hair piled high. Her pose is dynamic: although she stands to the left facing slightly away, her head is turned back toward the center. She holds a microphone in her right hand and reaches across the field and toward the viewer with her left, her partly open hand beckoning in a swirl of lace cuff. Her famous ¡AZUCAR! is inscribed to the right. Her name is placed at the bottom edge, with CELIA incused and CRUZ in relief.

Designer: Phebe Hemphill. *Mint sculptor-engraver who made the model:* Phebe Hemphill. Designer/*Engraver's initials and location:* PH at right, in field beyond sleeve.

Story and Background of the Design

The CCAC members were particularly enthusiastic about capturing Cruz in a moment of performance, noting how the design conveyed both her dynamic stage presence and her joy in performing. Family representatives appreciated the inclusion of her signature exclamation ¡AZUCAR! which became her trademark catchphrase and a celebration of her Cuban heritage.

The decision to render her name with CELIA incused and CRUZ in relief created a subtle but effective way to reference how she was known to her fans, often simply as "Celia." The design team worked carefully to ensure that her distinctive performance style would be recognizable even within the constraints of the quarter-sized canvas, paying particular attention to details like her elaborate hairstyle and the flow of her dress.

Biography

Celia Cruz (1925–2003), known as the Queen of Salsa, transformed Latin music and became one of its most influential performers. Born in Havana's working-class Santos Suárez neighborhood, she grew up immersed in diverse musical traditions including tango, bolero, guaracha, rumba, and Santería religious music. Despite her father's disapproval, she pursued singing, winning competitions on radio programs like "La hora del té." Though she briefly studied to become a teacher to please him, she followed her mother's encouragement and enrolled in the National Conservatory of Music.

Her breakthrough came in 1950 when she joined La Sonora Matancera as their first Black frontwoman. Her powerful voice, magnetic stage presence, and signature cry of ¡Azucar! ("Sugar!")—which began as an anecdote about ordering coffee—won audiences' hearts. After Fidel Castro's 1959 takeover of Cuba, she fled to the United States, settling in New Jersey. Her criticism of Castro's regime led to her being barred from returning to Cuba, even for her parents' funerals.

In 1965, Cruz embarked on a solo career, collaborating with Tito Puente and later joining Fania Records, where she became the undisputed Queen of Salsa—though she and her contemporaries considered it simply Cuban music. Her performances at venues like the Hollywood Bowl and international festivals helped spread Afro-Cuban music globally. She recorded 23 gold albums and won multiple Grammy and Latin Grammy Awards.

Cruz's impact extended beyond music to become a cultural icon, particularly for the Afro-Latino community. Her dynamic performances, elaborate costumes, and proud celebration of her Cuban and African heritage inspired generations. She continued performing into her later years, earning numerous honors including the National Medal of Arts and induction into multiple halls of fame. After her death in 2003, she was buried with a small container of Cuban soil she had saved from her homeland, symbolizing her enduring connection to her roots. Her posthumous honors included a 2016 Grammy Lifetime Achievement Award.

2024-P, Celia Cruz

MS-63	MS-64	MS-65	MS-66	MS-67
$0.40	$0.40	$0.60	$5.40	$27

2024-D, Celia Cruz

MS-63	MS-64	MS-65	MS-66	MS-67
$0.40	$0.40	$0.60	$5.40	$27

2024-S, Celia Cruz, Circulation Strike

MS-63	MS-64	MS-65	MS-66	MS-67
$0.40	$0.40	$0.60	$5.40	$27

2024-S, Celia Cruz, Proof, Clad

PF-67DC	PF-68DC	PF-69DC
$4.05	$5.40	$11

2024-S, Celia Cruz, Proof, Silver

PF-67DC	PF-68DC	PF-69DC
$9.90	$12.50	$13.50

2024, Zitkala-Ša

Mintage details not available at press time.

GSID: Circulation-strike, Philadelphia, 374289; Circulation-strike, Denver, 374290; Circulation-strike, San Francisco, 374291; Proof Clad Deep Cameo, 346879; Proof Silver Deep Cameo, 346880

Specifics of the Reverse Design

Description: The reverse of the quarter in her honor depicts her from the waist up, dressed in the traditional attire she often wore when lecturing. Her hair is in two braids down the front, and in her left hand she holds a book, representing her role as a writer. Behind her is a stylized horizon of diamond shapes with the sun rising above it; flying in front of its rays is a cardinal, representing her name, "Red Bird." In the field at left are the words AUTHOR / ACTIVIST / COMPOSER, with the denomination, 25 CENTS, below, and UNITED STATES OF AMERICA and E PLURIBUS UNUM surrounding. Her name, ZITKALA-ŠA, is at the bottom.

Designer: Don Everhart. *Mint sculptor-engraver who made the model:* Renata Gordon. *Designer's initials and location:* DE at lower left, below "CENTS." *Engraver's initials and location:* RG at lower right, below arm.

Story and Background of the Design

Representatives from the Yankton Sioux Tribe played a crucial role in the design selection process, particularly in ensuring the accurate representation of traditional attire and cultural elements. The inclusion of the cardinal, representing her name's meaning ("Red Bird"), was a detail specifically requested by tribal representatives to connect her English name to her Native heritage.

The CCAC members were particularly drawn to how the design balanced different aspects of Zitkala-Ša's life and work. The open book represents both her career as an author and her commitment to education, while her traditional dress acknowledges her dedication to preserving Native American culture. The rising sun behind her was seen as symbolic of her role in bringing Native American rights and culture into greater public awareness. Some committee members initially questioned whether including AUTHOR / ACTIVIST / COMPOSER might crowd the design, but the final arrangement proved both legible and meaningful.

Biography

Zitkala-Ša (1876–1938), born Gertrude Simmons, was a writer, musician, and activist who became one of the most important Native rights advocates of the early 20th century. Born on South Dakota's Yankton Indian Reservation to a Yankton Sioux mother and white father, she lived in her mother's teepee until age eight, when missionaries recruited her for their Indiana boarding school.

The boarding school experience proved traumatic. Students' traditional clothing was replaced with Western dress, their long hair was cut off—often forcibly—and their Native languages and cultural practices were forbidden. Despite the harsh conditions, Zitkala-Ša (meaning "Red Bird") excelled in writing and music, particularly violin. She later attended Earlham College and studied music in Boston, though she never felt fully accepted in white society.

As a teacher in reservation schools, she witnessed the Bureau of Indian Affairs' corrupt practices and the devastating impact of forced assimilation policies. Her 1900 series of autobiographical articles, including "Impressions of an Indian Childhood" (later collected in *American Indian Stories*), brought these issues to public attention. She also preserved Native American oral histories in *Old Indian Legends* and collaborated with William F. Hanson on *The Sun Dance Opera*, the first opera to incorporate Native American themes and music.

Though she initially rejected Christianity in favor of Native spirituality, she later embraced Catholicism while continuing to advocate for tribal traditions. She worked extensively with the Society of American Indians, advocating for full citizenship for Native Americans while preserving tribal sovereignty. After citizenship was granted in 1924, she co-founded the National Council of Native Americans to advance Native voting rights.

Throughout her career, Zitkala-Ša straddled two worlds, using her understanding of both cultures to advocate for Native rights. She challenged the government's assimilation policies while working within the system to achieve reform, particularly in education and cultural preservation. Her writings continue to influence discussions of Native American identity and rights.

2024-P, Zitkala-Ša

MS-63	MS-64	MS-65	MS-66	MS-67
$0.40	$0.40	$0.60	$5.40	$27

2024-D, Zitkala-Ša

MS-63	MS-64	MS-65	MS-66	MS-67
$0.40	$0.40	$0.60	$5.40	$27

2024-S, Zitkala-Ša, Circulation Strike

MS-63	MS-64	MS-65	MS-66	MS-67
$0.40	$0.40	$0.60	$5.40	$27

2024-S, Zitkala-Ša, Proof, Clad

PF-67DC	PF-68DC	PF-69DC
$4.05	$5.40	$11

2024-S, Zitkala-Ša, Proof, Silver

PF-67DC	PF-68DC	PF-69DC
$9.90	$12.50	$13.50

2025

At the time of the printing, images were not yet available of the last five honorees in the American Women Quarters Program. They are (in order of release):

Ida B. Wells (1862–1931) was an investigative journalist, civil rights leader, and anti-lynching activist. Born into slavery in Mississippi, she became a teacher and later co-owned the *Memphis Free Speech* newspaper. After three of her friends were lynched in 1892, she began documenting and exposing lynching through detailed investigative reporting. Her work faced fierce opposition, forcing her to relocate to Chicago, where she continued her activism. Wells co-founded the NAACP and advocated for women's suffrage, particularly highlighting the experiences of Black women.

Juliette Gordon Low (1860–1927) founded the Girl Scouts of America in 1912. Born in Savannah, Georgia, she envisioned an organization that would prepare girls for leadership and active citizenship. Starting with just 18 girls in Savannah, she developed a program that combined practical skills with outdoor activities and civic engagement. Despite becoming deaf in adulthood, Low dedicated her life to growing the Girl Scouts, which has since shaped the lives of millions of American girls.

Dr. Vera Rubin (1928–2016) was a pioneering astronomer who provided the first evidence for dark matter in galaxies. Her groundbreaking observations of galaxy rotation rates in the 1970s revealed that galaxies contain far more mass than can be seen. Despite facing significant gender discrimination early in her career, Rubin became one of the most influential astronomers of the 20th century. Her work fundamentally changed our understanding of the universe's composition.

Stacey Park Milbern (1987–2020) was a disability justice activist and community organizer. Born with muscular dystrophy, she became an advocate for disability rights as a teenager. Milbern co-founded the Disability Justice Culture Club in the Bay Area and worked to ensure disabled people, particularly those of color and LGBTQ+ individuals, had access to healthcare and emergency services. During the COVID-19 pandemic, she organized mutual aid networks before her untimely death on her 33rd birthday.

Althea Gibson (1927–2003) was the first Black athlete to break the color barrier in international tennis. She won multiple Grand Slam titles, including Wimbledon and the U.S. Open in both 1957 and 1958. Rising from humble beginnings in South Carolina, Gibson faced and overcame racial segregation in tennis. After her tennis career, she became the first Black woman to join the LPGA tour. Her achievements paved the way for future generations of Black athletes in tennis and other sports.

Notes

Chapter 1
1. My own mother, née Ruth Eleanor Garrett, married while she was a schoolteacher in Honesdale, Pennsylvania, in the mid-1930s, but had to keep the matter a secret, or she would have been fired. She resigned at the end of the term.
2. William Manchester, *The Glory and the Dream: A Narrative History of America, 1932–1972* (Boston: Little, Brown, 1974), p. 23.
3. Ibid. (p. 16). Seemingly, the Manchester account was either lightly researched or omitted the full story—in particular, the admitted Communist involvement and agitation. For further reading see Douglas MacArthur's Reminiscences (New York: McGraw-Hill, 1964), which seems to depict almost a different event!
4. Letter from White to M.F. Amrine, February 4, 1931, reprinted in *Selected Letters of William Allen White, 1899–1943* (New York: Henry Holt, 1947), p. 311.
5. This album later passed to John J. Ford Jr. At the sale of the Ford collection (Stack's) in 2004, it was purchased by a leading Southern currency specialist. A similar album, made by Clark for himself, went to a New England buyer.
6. John W. Adams, *United States Numismatic Literature, Volume II*, Twentieth Century Auction Catalogs (Crestline, California: Kolbe, 1990), passim.

Chapter 2
1. Quotation provided by Roger W. Burdette, from research in the National Archives for the forthcoming book *Renaissance of American Coinage, 1909–1913*.

Chapter 3
1. Old style for February 11, 1731/32. In 1752, the calendar was adjusted by 11 days, making the date February 22; the beginning of the calendar year changed from March 25 to January 1.
2. Washington tolerated slavery and took no action to abolish it. His will specified that his slaves be freed after his wife's death.
3. The medal commemorated Washington's siege that forced the British to evacuate Boston by sea in 1776, preventing their troops from endangering New England.
4. Jared Sparks (1789–1866) served as president of Harvard University from 1849 to 1853.
5. *The Journals and Letters of Samuel Curwen*, as quoted in "Samuel Curwen as a Numismatist," *American Journal of Numismatics* (September 1869).

Chapter 4
1. Biographies of Mellon abound in print and on the Internet. As is true for many other "captains of industry," the facts are hard to find, especially regarding some of the immense legal and tax problems he had (which seemingly diminished with his donation of the National Gallery of Art to the citizens of America).
2. This letter and others (not published here) make it evident that the commission was generally unaware of the traditions of American coinage, and that in an earlier era it was standard practice to use the same designs across many different denominations—as with Liberty Cap, Draped Bust, Capped Bust, Liberty Seated, and other motifs.
3. The Commission of Fine Arts was often casually referred to as the Fine Arts Commission in much correspondence within and outside the Treasury Department.
4. In 2005 the website for the North Dakota state quarter gave a detailed overview of the Flanagan-Flannagan confusion, which by that time had spread to hundreds of other Internet mentions and even a standard numismatic reference book on Washington quarters. Additional errors in print and on the Internet have resulted from numismatists' confusing the year 1932 with 1933. Franklin D. Roosevelt was elected president in November 1932 and was inaugurated on March 4, 1933, by which time the Washington quarter had been created and placed into circulation. Accordingly, the Roosevelt administration had nothing to do with selecting the design.
5. Cornelius Vermeule, *Numismatic Art in America* (Cambridge, Massachusetts: Belknap), p. 177.
6. David T. Alexander, "The Circle of Friends of the Medallion: An Appreciation in American Medallic History." *American Numismatic Association Centennial Anthology* (1991).
7. Roger W. Burdette, communication to the author, December 10, 2005; information from National Archives data.
8. The three medals mentioned in this paragraph are critiqued by Cornelius Vermeule in *Numismatic Art in America*, pp. 124 and 125.
9. One of the great controversies in scientific circles in the early 20th century was the Smithsonian's strong endorsement of Langley as the inventor of powered flight, said to have preceded the accomplishments of the Wright brothers. This stance was finally dropped.
10. Curiously, the Flanagan hairstyle is identical to that on another 1785 bust by Houdon, that of Marie-Sébastien-Charles-François Fontaine de Biré, newly appointed treasurer-general under Louis XVI!
11. Jean Bradfield, "The Detroit Story," *The Numismatist*, November 1962.
12. Eva Adams, "These Changing Dimes," transcript of talk, *The Numismatist*, December 1964.
13. Convention report in *The Numismatist*, October 1965.
14. From a February 8, 1966, commentary by Director Adams to Congress, reported in *The Numismatist*, June 1966.
14. Years later, in 1975, quarters dated 1776–1976 (or, more literally, "1776 • 1976"—with a bullet) were prestruck at the Philadelphia, Denver, and San Francisco mints.
16. Details from *The Numismatist*, October 1977.

Chapter 5
1. *The Numismatist*, February 1986.
2. Communication with the author, December 19, 2005.
3. Herbert P. Hicks, "The Washington Quarter Reverse: A Die-Variety Bonanza," pp. 249, 251. Walter Breen's description that now two leaves touch the tops of AR in DOLLAR *(Encyclopedia of U.S. and Colonial Proof Coins, 1722–1977)* is wrong; they do not.
4. Hicks, "Washington Quarter Reverse," p. 248.
5. Paul Gilkes, "The 'Mule' Train: Five Years Since Errors Struck," *Coin World*, May 2, 2005. Other sources were also consulted. I was involved in the sale of the Wallis specimen.

Chapter 7
1. *Abe Kosoff Remembers* (New York: Sanford J. Durst, 1981) chapter 203 (originally printed April 12, 1967).
2. During the 1970s, governors Virgil Hancock and John J. Pittman were in the forefront of persuading the association to adopt standards. As the manager of ANACS a few years later, Thomas K. DeLorey lent his wisdom and influence to many ANA grading policies.
3. I hasten to add that the standards mentioned previously are those codified by the ANA, not by me. For my money, I would not want to grade Bicentennial and statehood coins without looking at their reverses.

Chapter 8
1. Comments to the author, December 19, 2005.
2. Communication to the author, December 14, 2005.
3. David W. Lange, USA Coin Album, *Numismatist*, July 2002.
4. *Coin World*, November 14, 2005.
5. David W. Lange, USA Coin Album, *Numismatist*, November 2002.
6. Ibid.
7. For detailed information on coin-market price cycles see Bowers, *The Expert's Guide to Investing In and Collecting Rare Coins* (Atlanta, Georgia: Whitman, 2005). Few if any of these investment peaks and valleys surprised long-time numismatists.

Chapter 9
1. Complete details can be found in *United States Mint 2000 Annual Report*.
2. As an example, no announcement of the California quarter launching in 2005 was sent out in time to be included in the national weekly numismatic newspapers and monthly magazines or in coin club bulletins within California.
3. *Numismatic News*, June 13, 2000.
4. Paul Gilkes, "Sales of Silver Quarter Proof Set End . . . ," *Coin World*, July 5, 2004.
5. Barbara J. Gregory, "In the Wake of Lewis and Clark," *Numismatist*, August 2003.
6. Michele Orzano, "The State Quarters: Define Your State's Spirit," *Coin World*, April 19, 2004.
7. Article by Michele Orzano published in *Coin World*, May 14, 2001.
8. As one of many examples, certain 1783-dated Washington tokens are signed T.W.I. and also E.S. on the reverse. Thomas Wells Ingram was the die engraver who used a design by artist Edward Savage.
9. Article by Michele Orzano published in *Coin World*, May 14, 2001.
10. Selected information is from the U.S. Mint website.
11. Certain information is from "Pennsylvania Unveils 'Commonwealth' Quarter," U.S. Mint website.
12. Certain information is from "Georgia's Governor Barnes Unveils Peach," U.S. Mint website.
13. Certain information is from "U.S. Mint Rounds Out 1999 with New Quarter Honoring Connecticut," October 7, 1999, U.S. Mint website.
14. "A New Piece Added to Maryland's History," March 13, 2000, U.S. Mint website.
15. Lori Montgomery, "Two-Bit Identity Crisis; Imprint Befuddles the Free—Make That 'Old Line'—State," *Washington Post*, March 14, 2000.
16. First identified and researched by John Kraljevich and featured in the Eliasberg Collection of World Gold Coins sale by American Numismatic Rarities, March 2005.
17. Not included in this figure are these novel coins: At the Denver Mint a die "bearing a South Carolina quarter dollar reverse that was intentionally paired with a 2001-D Sacagawea dollar obverse to strike a mule on a manganese-brass clad dollar planchet," a caper that was detected. However, "it is not known whether specimens . . . escaped the mint facilities. None have been reported in the coin market" (Paul Gilkes, "Mint Made, Caught Additional Mules, Treasury Reports Reveal Three Double-Denomination Coins," *Coin World*, November 3, 2003).
18. U.S. Mint website, June 2004. Certain other information is from "U.S. Mint Celebrates Summer With the Launch of New South Carolina Quarter," U.S. Mint website May 26, 2000.
19. These tokens were retired in 2005 and replaced by E-ZPass.
20. Paul M. Green, *Numismatic News*, November 9, 2004.
21. "Inconsistency Dogs Designer Credit: Not All 'Designers' of State Quarters Gain Recognition," *Coin World*, May 14, 2001.
22. Communication to the author, September 14, 2004.
23. Michele Orzano, "Kentucky Will Not Recognize Artist as Designer of 2001 State Quarter," *Coin World*, September 17, 2001.
24. Certain information is from "North Carolina Quarter Takes Flight," U.S. Mint website, March 12, 2001.
25. Certain information is from "Anchors Aweigh for Rhode Island's New Quarter," U.S. Mint website, May 21, 2001.
26. From August 6 to August 9, 2001, the Mint had a special 72-hour sale event offering rolls, 100-coin bags, and 1,000-coin bags, resulting in the sale of 10,423,200 coins to collectors and souvenir hunters.
27. Pat Healy, "Quarreling Over Quarters," *Columbia Missourian*, November 17, 2002, p. 1A.
28. Paul Gilkes, "2001-D Kentucky Quarter Circulates: Coin Not Due Until Fall Joins Vermont Coin in Circulation," *Coin World*, June 11, 2001.
29. Certain information is from "Celebrate the Launch of the Kentucky Quarter" and other releases on the U.S. Mint website.
30. U.S. Mint website, June 2004.

31. Gwenda Bond, "Quarter Design Finalists Named," office of the governor of Ohio, July 15, 1999.
32. Mike Pulfer, "Quarter Designs Rolling In," Cincinnati Enquirer, May 15, 2000, quoting Gwenda Bond, a spokesperson for the governor.
33. Healy, "Quarreling Over Quarters."
34. Orzano, "Kentucky Will Not Recognize Artist."
35. "Spiked Head" variety—Certain clad Proof examples of the 2002-S Tennessee quarters have a die break running from the top of Washington's head to the border. Similar cracks are known for Iowa, Florida, Texas (the Texas crack is in a different location), and Minnesota quarters. Such pieces have an additional value (Ken Potter, "2005-S 'Spiked Head' Proof Seen," *Numismatic News*, May 17, 2005— Potter, who has a special interest in such varieties, reports on them as they are discovered).
36. U.S. Mint website, June 2004. Additional information from "U.S. Hits Right Note With Tennessee Quarter," U.S. Mint website, January 14, 2002.
37. This is the lowest quantity for any circulation-strike variety of any statehood quarter, from any mint, to this time. The Philadelphia Mint was closed for nearly six of the normal 10 weeks in the standard production period, to remedy violations pointed out by the Occupational Safety and Health Administration (Paul Gilkes, "Florida Quarter Dollar Mintages Reverse Recent Downward Trend,"*Coin World*, June 7, 2004).
38. Ken Potter, "2005-S 'Spiked Head' Proof Seen," *Numismatic News*, May 17, 2005.
39. Michele Orzano, "Mint Changes Legend on Ohio 25¢," *Coin World*, July 30, 2001. Fine Arts Commission information from a transcript of the commission meeting regarding the Ohio quarter; also a letter from J. Carter Brown, chairman of the Commission of Fine Arts, to Associate Mint Director Pickens, June 13, 2001: "In regard to the Ohio coin . . . the inscription 'Birthplace of Aviation' still presents a problem because most people will think of the event that took place in North Carolina. As the state of Ohio is honoring Ohioans in aviation rather than events, why not say 'Birthplace of Aviation Pioneers'? There is room for it on the coin as designed, and I would think it would solve the problem to everyone's satisfaction."
40. Certain information is from "The United States Mint Launches Louisiana State Quarter," U.S. Mint website.
41. Michele Orzano, "Mint Drops State's Original Choice, Uses Another," *Coin World*, September 3, 2001.
42. Michele Orzano, "Designs that Work," state quarters column, *Coin World*, August 25, 2003.
43. R.W. Julian, communications to the author, December 24 and 27, 2005.
44. William H. Dillistin, *Bank Note Reporters and Counterfeit Detectors, 1826–1866* (New York: American Numismatic Society, 1949), p. 70.
45. U.S. Mint website, June 2004.
46. Paul Jackson, letter to author, August 10, 2004. Jackson, designer of the Missouri quarter dollar, has kept in contact with other artists involved.
47. Certain information is from "United States Mint Unveils Illinois Quarter," U.S. Mint website.
48. Paul Gilkes, "2003 State Quarter Designs Under Final Review," *Coin World*, April 8, 2002.
49. The combined mintage of 448,800,000 circulation strikes from these two mints represents the lowest in the statehood series to date, in contrast to 1,594,616,000 circulation strikes for the 2000 Virginia quarters, the high-level record holder to date.
50. Summer Douglass, "Maine Artist Complains About Design," *Coin World*, August 19, 2002.
51. Ibid.
52. Summer Douglass, "Maine Residents Select Design for 2003 State Quarter Dollar," *Coin World*, September 2, 2002.
53. Paul Gilkes, "Fine Arts Panel Pans Design, Rejects Showing Gateway Arch, Lewis and Clark," *Coin World*, July 8, 2002.
54. Michele Orzano, "U.S. Mint Officials May Meet Missouri Quarter Dollar Artist," *Coin World*, September 16, 2002.
55. Conversation with the author, July 28, 2004.
56. Ed Reiter in *COINage*, February 2005: "The machine, manufactured by Kusters Engineering of the Netherlands, contains two rollers which impart corrugated surfaces to coins or planchets by squeezing them at very high pressure. When defective coins are defaced in this manner, portions of the original design may still be visible—but not enough, in the Mint's estimation, to give them any value as minting errors. . . . The U.S. Mint purchased two of the machines—one for the main Mint in Philadelphia and one for the Denver branch. Their rollers squeeze coins and planchets with a force of 26 tons and can process pieces of metal at a rate of 1,000 kilograms per hour. The machines went into regular operation in mid-2003 and waffled examples are known of all six 2003-dated coin denominations from the Lincoln cent through the Sacagawea dollar."
57. Certain information is from "United States Mint Declares New Arkansas Quarter a Natural Beauty From the Natural State," U.S. Mint website, October 28, 2003.
58. U.S. Mint website, June 2004.
59. This is the lowest Denver Mint production to this time for a statehood quarter. Many show lightly struck details.
60. Steven M. Bieda, a state representative from Michigan, designed the reverse of the 1992 Olympic commemorative half dollar (U.S. Mint website, June 2004).
61. Michele Orzano, "Cheers and Jeers: Michigan's 2004 State Quarter Design Brings Happiness to Some, Groans to Others," *Coin World*, February 16, 2004.
62. Communication to the author, May 6, 2004.

63. Of the combined production from these two mints, more than 11,000,000 were sold at a premium in the form of rolls, 100-coin mini-bags, and 1,000-coin bags.
64. "Spiked Head" variety—Certain clad Proof examples of the 2004-S Florida quarters have a die break running from the top of Washington's head to the border. Similar cracks are known for Tennessee, Iowa, Texas (with the crack in a different position), and Minnesota quarters. Such pieces have an additional value (Ken Potter, "2005-S 'Spiked Head' Proof Seen," *Numismatic News*, May 17, 2005).
65. Certain information is from "Florida Quarter Launches," by Jim LaFemina, Public Affairs Office, U.S. Mint website.
66. Illustrating a Spanish galleon along with other motifs, the 2004 Florida quarter is one of the few to include a distinctly numismatic scene, in this case indirectly. Centuries ago, the Spanish treasure fleet, typically consisting of a dozen or more vessels, returned from possessions in the New World, bearing gold and silver coins and ingots for the royal coffers. The typical homeward route called for a rendezvous at Havana, then passage northward along the east coast of Florida, then into the broad Atlantic. During the time of the equinoctial storms (now known as the hurricane season), certain of these ships—including virtually the entire fleets of 1715 and 1733—perished on the shoals and beaches of Florida. Many coins have been recovered from the remains of these vessels, to the delight of the collecting community.
67. G.C. Carnes, letter to the author, August 10, 2004.
68. Certain information is from "The Eyes of Texas and the Nation Are on Austin as the United States Mint Launches the New Texas Quarter," U.S. Mint website.
69. A striking-ceremony for the 2000-D quarters was held at the Denver Mint on July 12, 2004 (*Numismatic News*, July 27, 2004).
70. To this point this was the record-low mintage figure among state quarters, displacing the 2000-P Ohio (217,200,000), the previous record holder.
71. "Spiked Head" variety—Certain clad Proof examples of the 2004-S Iowa quarters have a die break running from the top of Washington's head to the border. Similar cracks are known for Tennessee, Florida, Texas (the Texas crack is in a different location), and Minnesota quarters. Such pieces have an additional value (Ken Potter, "2005-S 'Spiked Head' Proof Seen," *Numismatic News*, May 17, 2005).
72. Issue of August 2004.
73. This figure includes an unknown number of the Extra Leaf High and Extra Leaf Low varieties. Of the Extra Leaf High coins, an estimated 2,000 or are so known. The U.S. Mint estimates that just 35,000 to 50,000 of this variety were made. Using the higher (50,000) figure would suggest that this variety is more than 4,500 times more rare than the regular quarters without an extra leaf. Of the Extra Leaf Low coins, an estimated 3,000 or so are known. The Mint made no estimate of the mintage for this variety, but it was probably slightly higher than for the Extra Leaf High. The estimated populations for both of these varieties are subject to change.
74. Selected information is from "Wisconsin Quarter Launch," J.D. Harrington, external relations, U.S. Mint website.
75. Among the submissions was this one—art, not a concept—as described by Leon A. Saryan, from the studio of Daniel Carr (designer of the Maine and Rhode Island quarters and important in the New York scenario): "One of the best submissions in this genre was the Old Abe eagle drawn by a talented out-of-state artist who had already submitted winning designs for other states. The drawing was submitted via a state resident who was a friend of the artist. It was a very professional presentation, a stunningly beautiful numismatic eagle that outclassed almost every other eagle in two centuries of United States coinage.... This Old Abe eagle was special. I was immediately attracted to the design, but was a little put off by the fact that it originated from outside the state, since this was against the spirit (if not the ground rules) of the process.... I am still haunted by that rendition of Old Abe." Based upon Saryan's description, I can only hope that this majestic depiction of the national bird is used on some other coin in the future!
76. Saryan's article, "Designing the Washington Quarter," *Centinel*, Winter 2004–05, vol. 53 no. 4, was among the information sources used here.
77. *Coin World*, February 6, 2006
78. Michele Orzano, "Patience Is a Virtue," *Coin World*, February 9, 2004.
79. Paul Gilkes, "California Launches Quarter," *Coin World*, February 21, 2005.
80. November 15, 2004.
81. "Spiked Head" variety—Certain clad Proof examples of 2005-S Minnesota quarters have a die break running from the top of Washington's head to the border. Similar cracks are known for Tennessee, Florida, Texas (the Texas crack is in a different location), and Iowa quarters. Such pieces have an additional value (Ken Potter, "2005-S 'Spiked Head' Proof Seen," *Numismatic News*, May 17, 2005).
82. "Thousands Celebrate 'Land of 10,000 Lakes' Quarter," U.S. Mint website. Also, *Numismatist*, March 2005.
83. "Minnesota," U.S. Mint website.
84. *Numismatist*, March 2005.
85. "Minnesota," U.S. Mint website.
86. *Numismatic News*, June 1, 2004.
87. Don Hamilton, "Flip a Coin: Heads—or Salmon? Or Beavers?" *Portland (Oregon) Tribune*, August 19, 2003.
88. "Crater Lake Edges Mount Hood," *Numismatic News*, May 25, 2004.
89. "Oregon Selects Crater Lake for 2005 State Quarter Dollar," *Coin World*, June 14, 2003.
90. Paul Gilkes, "Oregon Quarter Mintage Highest Since Louisiana," *Coin World*, August 29, 2005.
91. Certain information is from "Kansas," U.S. Mint website, and from "Nation Gets First Buffalo Quarter," U.S. Mint website, September 9, 2005.
92. "Kansas to See Quarter September 9," *Coin World*, July 18, 2005.
93. Don Carbaugh, *Numismatist*, August 2004, p. 29.
94. "Mint Green-Lights Alterations Requested for Kansas Design," *Numismatic News*, June 1, 2004.

95. Certain information is from "West Virginia" and "West Virginia Quarter Celebrates Engineering Triumph," U.S. Mint website.
96. Gary Waddell, "Design for Nevada Quarter Begins," www.klastv.com, June 23, 2004.
97. Michele Orzano, "States Select 2006 25¢ Designs," *Coin World*, June 20, 2005.
98. The Citizens Coin Advisory Committee also favored the bighorn sheep design (Bill Fivaz, committee member, communication with the author, December 23, 2005).
99. Paul Gilkes, "Panels Agree on Nevada," *Coin World*, February 14, 2005.
100. Posted on the Internet. The State of Nebraska website and the U.S. Mint website also furnished much information.
101. "Nebraska Sends Four to Mint," *Numismatic News*, October 12, 2004.
102. "Nebraska," *Coin World*, January 31, 2005.
103. Gilkes, "Panels Agree."
104. Much information is from news releases from the governor's office posted on the Internet.
105. Gayle Perez, "First Lady Frances Owens Seeks Nominations for Colorado's Commemorative 25-Cent Piece," Pueblo Chieftain website.
106. Michele Orzano, "Colorado Ponders Designs," *Coin World*, March 28, 2005.
107. Tom Noe resigned as chairman in 2005.
108. As Bill Fivaz correctly stated, there is no typical "peak" on Pikes Peak, in the form of a prominent, well-defined top. The mountain is amorphous, and viewed from a dozen different angles, it has a dozen different shapes. Those not familiar with the actual peak are often surprised when they view it in person. The diecutter for the 1860 Clark, Gruber & Co. "Pikes Peak" $10 and $20 gold coins, who is believed to have lived in the East, depicted it as a conical mountain with a pointed top.
109. In reality, Mesa Verde is set in a large opening, low in the face of a vertical cliff.
110. Bill McAllister, "CCAC Makes Quarter Choice," *Coin World*, April 4, 2005.
111. Paul Gilkes, "Review Panel Approves Colorado Coin Designs," *Coin World*, April 4, 2005.
112. *Numismatic News*, July 27, 2004.
113. Michele Orzano, "States Select 2006 25¢ Designs," *Coin World*, June 20, 2005. Certain information also taken from the U.S. Mint website.
114. Certain information from the U.S. Mint website.
115. Paul Gilkes, "CFA Recommends Another Bison," *Coin World*, October 11, 2004.
116. "CCAC Endorses Pheasant for SD," *Numismatic News*, October 12, 2004.
117. "South Dakota Prepares for Quarter Selection," *Numismatic News*, November 9, 2004.
118. *Numismatic News* website, November 12, 2005.
119. News release from Governor Kempthorne's office, July 27, 2005.
120. *Numismatic News* website, November 12, 2005.
121. Michele Orzano, "Utah Forms Quarter Panel," *Coin World*, October 11, 2004.
122. "Doubled die reverse on D.C. quarter," *Coin World*, May 25, 2009.

Chapter 10

1. Such information for later America the Beautiful quarters sometimes varied; check the Internet for details.
2. *Coin World*, July 12, 2010.
3. During a visit by the author and his family in 1988, clouds of smoke were seen from a forest fire in the distance. It later spread and consumed about one third of the park, including many lodging facilities.
4. Issue of October 25, 2010.
5. Sources include Paul Gilkes, *Coin World*, October 11, 2010.
6. Sources include Paul Gilkes, *Coin World*, December 6, 2010.
7. Bill McAllister, "CCAC Splits on Gettysburg quarter designs," *Coin World*, February 15, 2010.
8. Paul Gilkes, *Coin World*, February 14, 2011, was the source of certain information.
9. Sources include Paul Gilkes, *Coin World*, April 11 and May 9, 2011.
10. Sources include Rhonda Kay, CoinNews.net, June 17, 2011.
11. Author's personal visits and experience.
12. Sources include Paul Gilkes, *Coin World*, December 2011, and other news articles.
13. When this coin was released the author was not familiar with the site commemorative. By this time numismatic interest in the America the Beautiful series was mild at best. In discussions with a Mint official I suggested that if the name of the state would be put at the top border of the reverse, they would be easier to recognize at sight. "Great idea," I was told. "I wish you had said this two years ago."
14. Information from Paul Gilkes, *Coin World*, July 16, 2012.
15. Information from Paul Gilkes, *Coin World*, February 2, 2010, and other sources.
16. Information from Paul Gilkes, *Coin World*, March 31, 2014.
17. Information from Paul Gilkes, *Coin World*, May 2016 issue.

Credits and Acknowledgments

Creative Director, Matt Jeffirs
Editorial Director, Diana Plattner
Graphic Designer, Matt Heller
Pricing Editors, John Feigenbaum and Patrick Ian Perez

American Numismatic Rarities provided many illustrations (by Douglas Plasencia), helped with research, and assisted in other ways.

Casey Baeslack of ANACS made text suggestions and grading comments. **Becky Bailey** of the U.S. Mint helped with information and background on the state quarters. **Steven M. Bieda** discussed the creation of the Michigan state quarter and furnished an illustration. **Wynn Bowers** reviewed the text and made suggestions. **Roger W. Burdette** conducted research in the National Archives and furnished legislative, Treasury, Commission of Fine Arts, and other documents and correspondence relating to the background of the design, 1930 to 1932. **Garrett Burke,** designer of the 2005 California quarter dollar, wrote the foreword and also helped with copyediting the manuscript. **Greg Burns** helped with information on the California quarter.

Terry Campbell commented on the design selection process for the New York quarter. **G.C. Carnes** sent information concerning the Texas quarter dollar. **Daniel Carr,** artist for three of the state quarters, helped in several ways. The **Commission of Fine Arts,** Washington, D.C., provided certain documents. **José Cortez** provided photos.

Beth Deisher, editor of *Coin World,* provided extensive information.

Gloria Eskridge of the U.S. Mint answered inquiries and helped in other ways.

Howard Feltham corresponded concerning state quarters. **C. John Ferreri** provided an illustration. **Bill Fivaz** gave recollections concerning the creation of the Georgia quarter design and made suggestions concerning die varieties. He also provided photographs and price information for certain issues. **Roberta A. French** worked on extensive research assignments and the transcription of comments and documents.

David L. Ganz reviewed portions of the book and made suggestions. He also supplied legislative information. **Jeff Garrett** provided major assistance and advice with the compilation of price data and also supplied coins for photography. **David Gladfelter** suggested a source for information.

Steve Hayden supplied classic Washingtoniana items. Former Mint director **Henrietta Holsman Fore** facilitated inquiries and helped in other ways. The **estate of Bernard Heller** provided postcard imagery of expositions. **Charles R. Hosch** shared notes he kept on state quarters.

Paul Jackson sent information concerning state-reverse quarters in general and his work on the Missouri design in particular. **Katherine Jaeger** reviewed the text and made suggestions. Former Mint director **Jay Johnson** gave reminiscences and comments concerning coinage. **R.W. Julian** provided historical and numismatic information on George Washington, the early years of the Washington quarter, and the Indiana state quarter.

Cathy LaPerle, of the U.S. Mint, answered inquiries and provided many images for selection. **Robert Leonard** reviewed the manuscript and made suggestions. **Brett Lothrop** discussed the weakly struck details of many 2001-D Michigan quarters.

Dwight N. Manley supplied an in-person report on the California quarter launch ceremony and an illustration of a rare early Washington medal. **Cynthia Meals** of the U.S. Mint helped with information and research. **John Mercanti,** sculptor-engraver at the U.S. Mint, helped in several ways. **Scott Miller** provided a portrait of John Flanagan. **Tom Mulvaney** took the majority of photographs of individual quarters in chapter 8 and elsewhere. **Michele Orzano** shared information and research gathered during the course of her writing for *Coin World* on the subject of state quarters. **Kathleen J. Oviatt** of ANACS made text suggestions and provided grading comments.

Listings in chapter 11, *American Women Quarters, 2022–2025,* are adaptations of articles that ran in *The Numismatist* as the coins were released, and are used here by permission of the publication.

Jesse Patrick provided information about 1932 design proposals and reviewed the manuscript. **Bob Paul** sent information concerning "waffle coins." **Spencer Peck** shared information concerning the New Jersey quarter dollar design process. **Ken Potter** provided illustrations.

Alex Shagin corresponded about various state quarter designs. **Mark Smith** corresponded about the 2004-D Wisconsin quarter varieties. **Rick Snow** told the story of the 2004-D quarters with extra leaves. **Thomas Snyder** furnished a large file of clippings and news items relating to design and distribution of the 2004 Wisconsin coins. **J.T. Stanton** furnished manuscript pages of the new fourth edition, volume II, of the *Cherrypickers' Guide to Rare Die Varieties* (Bill Fivaz, co-author), enabling the revised Fivaz-Stanton numbering system to be included here together with related rarity information (on the Universal Rarity Scale). He also provided photographs. **Don K. Stout**

corresponded about state quarters. **David M. Sundman** made suggestions. **Donald Sundman,** Mystic Stamp Company, provided illustrations.

Steve Tanenbaum supplied classic Washingtonia items. **Gar Travis** suggested several information sources for the Maine quarter and the history of the lighthouse depicted on it.

The U.S. Mint provided photographs of state-reverse quarters and launch ceremonies and helped in other ways.

Frank Van Valen did copyediting and made valuable suggestions. **Eric von Klinger** corresponded concerning aspects of state quarters.

Fred Weinberg provided information on Mint error coins. **Ben Weinstein** provided details about the first identification of "extra leaf" 2004-D Wisconsin quarters. **Stephanie Westover,** Littleton Coin Co., provided certain coin illustrations. **Frank Wight** discussed die characteristics of quarters.

In addition, news articles, letters, and other reports published in *Coin World, COINage, Coins* magazine, *Numismatic News,* and *Numismatist* were of great help.

Certain staff members of *Coin World*, particularly **Michele Orzano, Beth Deisher,** and **Paul Gilkes,** assisted with information on the state-reverse quarter dollars from 1999 to date; documents pertaining to the 2002 Ohio quarter were particularly important. Certain uncredited historical illustrations are from Q. David Bowers LLC.

In this age of the **Internet,** many obscure facts and points were checked on various websites, generally credited in the notes.

ABOUT THE AUTHOR

Q. David Bowers has been in the rare-coin business since he was a teenager, starting in 1953. He is a founder of Stack's Bowers Galleries and is numismatic director of Whitman Publishing. He is a recipient of the Pennsylvania State University College of Business Administration's Alumni Achievement Award (1976); he has served as president of the American Numismatic Association (1983–1985) and president of the Professional Numismatists Guild (1977–1979); he is a recipient of the highest honor bestowed by the ANA (the Farran Zerbe Award); he was the first ANA member to be named Numismatist of the Year (1995); and he has been inducted into the ANA Numismatic Hall of Fame maintained at ANA headquarters. He has also won the highest honors given by the Professional Numismatists Guild. In July 1999, in a poll published in *COINage,* "Numismatists of the Century," Dave was recognized as one of six living people in this list of just 18 names. He is the author of more than 50 books, hundreds of auction and other catalogs, and several thousand articles, including columns in *Coin World* (now the longest-running by any author in numismatic history), *The Numismatist,* and other publications. His books have earned more "Book of the Year Award" honors bestowed by the Numismatic Literary Guild than have those of any other author. He and his firms have presented the majority of the most valuable coin collections ever sold at auction. Dave is a trustee of the New Hampshire Historical Society and a fellow of the American Antiquarian Society, the American Numismatic Society, and the Massachusetts Historical Society. He has been a consultant for the Smithsonian Institution, the Treasury Department, and the U.S. Mint, and is research editor of *A Guide Book of United States Coins.* For many years he was a guest lecturer at Harvard University. This is a short list of his honors and accomplishments. In Wolfeboro, New Hampshire, he is on the Board of Selectmen and is the town historian.

INDEX
State, D.C., Territories, America the Beautiful, and Crossing the Delaware Quarter Designs

Alabama
America the Beautiful, 344–345
State, 181–182

Alaska
America the Beautiful, 285–286
State, 244–246

American Samoa
America the Beautiful, 337–338
D.C. and Territories, 256–258

Arizona
America the Beautiful, 269–270
State, 242–244

Arkansas
America the Beautiful, 264–265
State, 187–188

California
America the Beautiful, 267–269
State, 198–200

Colorado
America the Beautiful, 298–300
State, 217–222

Connecticut
America the Beautiful, 339–340
State, 149–150

Crossing the Delaware, 346

Delaware
America the Beautiful, 305–307
State, 143–144

District of Columbia
America the Beautiful, 318–320
D.C. and Territories, 252–253

Florida
America the Beautiful, 300–301
State, 190–191

Georgia
America the Beautiful, 328–329
State, 148–149

Guam
America the Beautiful, 333–334
D.C. and Territories, 255–256

Hawaii
America the Beautiful, 284–285
State, 246–247

Idaho
America the Beautiful, 336–337
State, 230–232

Illinois
America the Beautiful, 309–310
State, 180–181

Indiana
America the Beautiful, 323–324
State, 176–178

Iowa
America the Beautiful, 317–318
State, 193–195

Kansas
America the Beautiful, 343–344
State, 205–206

Kentucky
America the Beautiful, 310–311
State, 168–169

Louisiana
America the Beautiful, 303–304
State, 174–175

Maine
America the Beautiful, 282–284
State, 183–184

Maryland
America the Beautiful, 292–293
State, 153–154

Massachusetts
America the Beautiful, 331–332
State, 151–152

Michigan
America the Beautiful, 324–325
State, 188–190

Minnesota
America the Beautiful, 327–328
State, 201–202

Mississippi
America the Beautiful, 276–277
State, 178–179

Missouri
America the Beautiful, 320–321
State, 185–187

Montana
America the Beautiful, 273–275
State, 227–228

Nebraska
America the Beautiful, 301–302
State, 211–217

Nevada
America the Beautiful, 290–291
State, 208–211

New Hampshire
America the Beautiful, 287–289
State, 156–157

New Jersey
America the Beautiful, 321–322
State, 146–148

New Mexico
America the Beautiful, 281–282
State, 240–242

New York
America the Beautiful, 307–308
State, 160–163

North Carolina
America the Beautiful, 304–305
State, 163–164

North Dakota
America the Beautiful, 313–314
State, 223–224

Northern Mariana Islands
America the Beautiful, 332–333
D.C. and Territories, 260–261

Ohio
America the Beautiful, 289–290
State, 172–173

Oklahoma
America the Beautiful, 278–279
State, 237–240

Oregon
America the Beautiful, 271–272
State, 203–204

Pennsylvania
America the Beautiful, 272–273
State, 144–146

Puerto Rico, Commonwealth of
America the Beautiful, 279–280
D.C. and Territories, 253–255

Rhode Island
America the Beautiful, 329–330
State, 165–166

South Carolina
America the Beautiful, 315–316
State, 154–155

South Dakota
America the Beautiful, 293–294
State, 225–227

Tennessee
America the Beautiful, 294–295
State, 170–171

Texas
America the Beautiful, 335–336
State, 192–193

U.S. Virgin Islands
America the Beautiful, 340–341
D.C. and Territories, 258–259

Utah
America the Beautiful, 297–298
State, 234–237

Vermont
America the Beautiful, 341–342
State, 166–168

Virginia
America the Beautiful, 296–297
State, 158–160

Washington
America the Beautiful, 275–276
State, 228–230

West Virginia
America the Beautiful, 311–313
State, 206–207

Wisconsin
America the Beautiful, 325–326
State, 195–198

Wyoming
America the Beautiful, 265–267
State, 232–234

American Women Quarter Designs

Angelou, Maya, 349–350
Coleman, Bessie, 357–358
Cruz, Celia, 370–372
Gibson, Althea, 374
Idar, Jovita, 362–363
Kanaka'ole, Edith, 359–360
Low, Juliette Gordon, 374

Mankiller, Wilma, 352–353
Milbern, Stacey Park, 374
Mink, Hon. Patsy Takemoto, 367–368
Murray, Rev. Dr. Pauli, 365–367
Otero-Warren, Nina, 354–355
Ride, Dr. Sally, 350–352

Roosevelt, Eleanor, 360–362
Rubin, Dr. Vera, 374
Tallchief, Maria, 364–365
Walker, Dr. Mary Edwards, 369–370
Wells, Ida B., 374
Wong, Anna May, 355–357

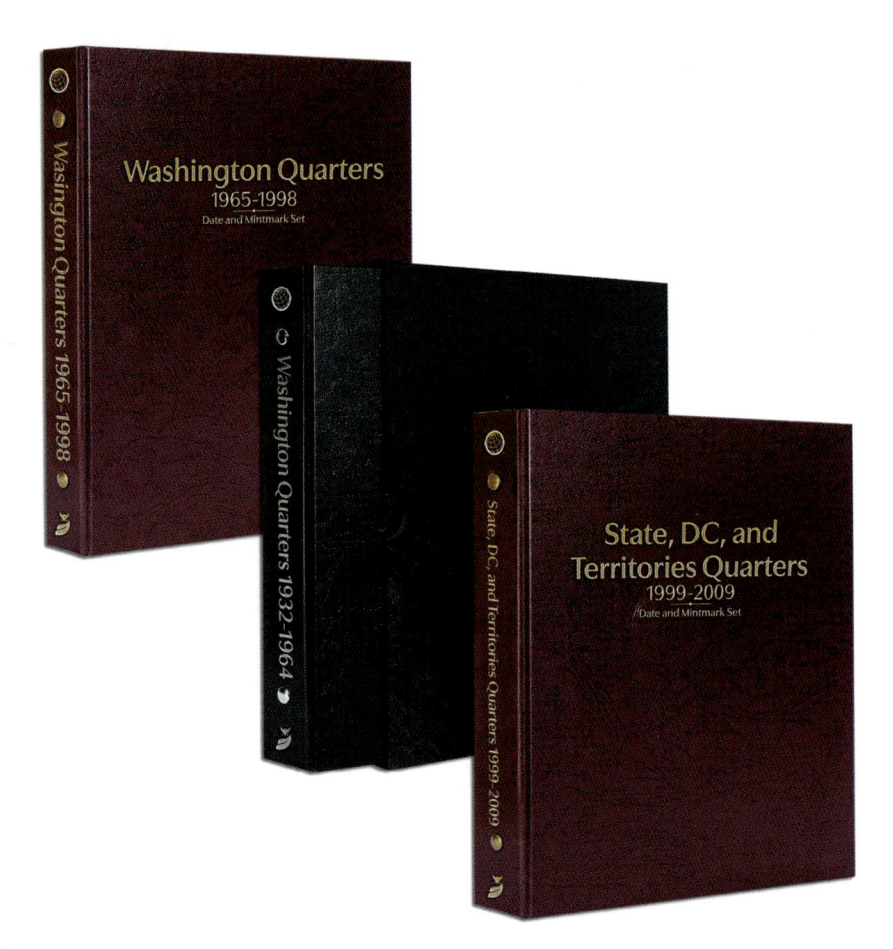

Collect with confidence, collect with prestige.

Introducing Whitman Prestige™ albums—where sophistication meets function. Featuring an expanded size, enhanced construction, and soil-resistant grained leatherette available in burgundy or black. Complete with a protective slipcover, this premium album is perfect for showcasing your coins. Order Today!

Whitman
800·546·2995